PSYCHOSOCIAL CARING THROUGHOUT THE LIFE SPAN

PSYCHOSOCIAL CARING THROUGHOUT THE LIFE SPAN

Editors

IRENE MORTENSON BURNSIDE, R.N., M.S.
PRISCILLA EBERSOLE, R.N., M.S.
HELEN ELENA MONEA, R.N., M.S.

McGRAW-HILL BOOK COMPANY

New York   St. Louis   San Francisco   Auckland   Bogotá   Düsseldorf
Johannesburg   London   Madrid   Mexico   Montreal   New Delhi
Panama   Paris   São Paulo   Singapore   Sydney   Tokyo   Toronto

NOTICE

Medicine is an ever-changing science. As new research and clinical experience broaden our knowledge, changes in treatment and drug therapy are required. The editors and the publisher of this work have made every effort to ensure that the drug dosage schedules herein are accurate and in accord with the standards accepted at the time of publication. Readers are advised, however, to check the product information sheet included in the package of each drug they plan to administer to be certain that changes have not been made in the recommended dose or in the contraindications for administration. This recommendation is of particular importance in regard to new or infrequently used drugs.

1234567890   DODO   7832109

This book was set in Times Roman by Monotype Composition Company, Inc. The editors were Mary Ann Richter, David P. Carroll, and Henry C. De Leo; the designer was Rafael Hernandez; the production supervisor was Milton J. Heiberg. The drawings were done by J & R Services, Inc.
R. R. Donnelley & Sons Company was printer and binder.

Library of Congress Cataloging in Publication Data
Main entry under title:

Psychosocial caring throughout the life span.

Bibliography: p.
Includes index.
1. Developmental psychology. 2. Helping behavior.
3. Nurse and patient. I. Burnside, Irene Mortenson,
date   II. Ebersole, Priscilla. III. Monea,
Helen Elena. [DNLM: 1. Psychology, Social—Nursing
texts. 2. Nurse-patient relations—Essays. 3. Human
development—Nursing texts. WY87 P973 (P)]
BF713.P79   155   78-16372
ISBN 0-07-009213-3

ACKNOWLEDGMENTS

Bronte, Emily Jane   Selected lines from the poem "To Imagination" by Emily Jane Bronte. Copyright 1941, *The Complete Poems of Emily Jane Bronte* by C. W. Hatfield. Reprinted by permission of Columbia University Press, New York.

Capote, Truman   Selected lines from *The Grass Harp* by Truman Capote. Copyright 1951. Published by Random House, Inc., New York. Reprinted with permission.

Eliot, T. S.   Selected lines from the poem "The Wasteland" by T. S. Eliot. Copyright 1934. *The Wasteland and Other Poems.* Published by Harcourt, Brace, and Company, New York. Reprinted with permission.

Jacobsen, Josephine   Selected lines from the poem "Let Each Man Remember" in *The Shade Seller* by Josephine Jacobsen. Copyright 1974. Published by Doubleday & Company, Inc., New York. Reprinted with permission.

McClelland, Ross Allen   Selected lines from the poem "Fantasy" from *The Errant Dawn* by Ross Allen McClelland. Copyright 1969. Published by Olivant Press, Homestead, Florida. Reprinted with permission.

St. Vincent Millay, Edna   Selected lines from *Collected Poems,* Harper & Row. Copyright 1939, 1967 by Edna St. Vincent Millay and Norma Millay (Ellis). Reprinted with permission.

Moustakas, Clark E.   Selected lines from *Portraits of Loneliness and Love* by Clark E. Moustakas. Copyright 1974 by Clark E. Moustakas. Published by Prentice-Hall, Inc., Englewood Cliffs, New Jersey. Reprinted with permission.

Rilke, Rainer Maria   "Sonnet #19" in *Sonnets to Orpheus* by Rainer Maria Rilke translated by C. F. MacIntyre. Copyright 1960 by C. F. MacIntyre. Reprinted by permission of University of California Press edition 1971, Berkeley, California.

Sarton, May   "Letters to a Psychiatrist—Letter 5" from *Collected Poems, 1930-1973* by May Sarton. Copyright 1974 by May Sarton. Published by W. W. Norton & Company, Inc., New York. Reprinted with permission.

... to my grandfather, who taught me much about the aging process.
Irene Mortenson Burnside

... to Raymond, my caring partner, who continually cultivated that counterpart of self I did not know.
Priscilla Ebersole

... to the children and adolescents, from whom I gained pleasure and pain in nurturing...to the one I lost.
Helen Elena Monea

CONTENTS

LIST OF CONTRIBUTORS

Irene Mortenson Burnside, R.N., M.S.
Author and Lecturer,
Monte Sereno, California

Priscilla Ebersole, R.N., M.S.
Assistant Professor of Psychiatry in
Nursing, California State University,
San Francisco, California

Ann McCue, R.N., M.S.
Clinical Specialist, Ackerly Child Psychiatric Service; Assistant Professor of
Psychiatry in Nursing, University of
Louisville School of Medicine,
Department of Psychiatry.
Louisville, Kentucky

Helen Elena Monea, R.N., M.S.
Clinical Specialist, County of Marin,
Community Mental Health Services,
San Rafael, California

Lynn Noonan, R.N., M.S.
Clinical Nurse Specialist,
Outpatient Mental Health
Clinic, Veterans Administration
Hospital,
San Diego, California

Mary Joy Ostrovski, R.N., M.A.
Director, Geriatric Day Treatment Center, Community Mental Health District V,
San Francisco, California

Joseph H. Pierre, M.A.
Gerontology Consultant,
Salem, Oregon

G. Michelle Reilley, Ph.D.
Former Doctoral Student, Psychological
Services Center, University of Nevada,
Reno, Nevada

Judith Tiktinsky, M.S.W.
Lecturer, Health
Sciences Department,
University of California,
Berkeley, California

PREFACE

In recent years there has been a tremendous increase in the amount of literature on developmental aspects throughout the life span. The purpose of this textbook is to selectively organize, evaluate, and interpret some of the data, concepts, theories, and issues about developmental aspects of all ages. The delineation of pragmatic interventions in aspects of caring is an integral part of this book. The life span approach was selected as a framework for this text to help caregivers better understand the continuity of emerging tasks of individuals as they age. The book is designed so caregivers may better anticipate some of the growth needs of persons of all ages, including the very, very old. Books regarding the developmental approach usually minimally describe the last stage of life; this textbook places emphasis on the last part of life because the aging process is complex, and the care of the aged person must necessarily involve other disciplines.

This book is intended for a variety of disciplines. Because psychosocial caring transcends any one discipline, a variety of professionals and para-professionals may identify portions of the book related to their various roles. For example, this book may be of value to activity coordinators, instructors (full-time, in-service, and continuing education), nurses, occupational therapists, physical therapists, physicians, psychologists, recreational therapists, social workers, theologians, and others. The content is for all levels of baccalaureate students, but graduate students may also find the book useful as a reference for psychosocial development.

The text is divided into three parts. Part 1 includes selective topics that affect the lives of children, adolescents, and their caregivers. The focus is on healthy — not pathological — growth and development. The issues, topics, and trends in child mental health are voluminous, hence the selected topics. Part 2 examines the transition to young adulthood and middle age. Part 3 explores the last stage of life, including young-old age and old-old age.

The need for caring is a theme of the entire book. In Chapter 1 Monea discusses the development of caregiving and meaningful relationships. The dynamics and development of the caring quality are also discussed so that the reader may better understand caring.

In Chapter 14 Ebersole describes the caring that evolves after about age 35 and emphasizes that caring embraces more than self, family, and friends. She makes the point that there are many who need caring—so many, in fact, that the capacity for caring in some persons may short-circuit from overload.

In Chapter 27, Burnside continues the theme of caregiving in the later years of life and elaborates on the special quality and nurturing abilities of the old and the very old. She builds on Ebersole's discussion of the special quality of being able to care about and be concerned about so many persons and the entire world.

As you read this text, we hope you will absorb and synthesize a basic philosophical attitude in psychosocial care—an open attitude toward new as well as conventional approaches to health care—and that you will *always care in a humanistic way.*

We wish to acknowledge the following persons for their caring and encouragement in our work on this book: Chaplain Walter Johnson for his counsel and collaboration, Patricia Ryan for her photographic artistry. Others who shared and cared in a variety of ways were: Mary Boldi, Maria and Phyllis Eggert, Patricia Gamaleri, Dwain Johnson and family, John Karaagac, Lorraine, Jason and Laura Kester, Pat and Laura Song, Kerry and Mary Thomas and Sammy Woog.

We are especially grateful to our friends, colleagues, relatives, clients, and patients who generously shared their personal experiences or their photographs with us, or who simply helped us to better understand development across the life span.

A very special note of appreciation is due Diane Miller for unflagging editorial assistance, and to Evelyn Butorac and Pearl Bladek for the bulk of the typing.

As this book goes to press, we have been saddened by the sudden death of our young editor, Mary Ann Richter, who worked with us during the production of this book.

Irene Mortenson Burnside
Priscilla Ebersole
Helen Elena Monea

PSYCHOSOCIAL CARING THROUGHOUT THE LIFE SPAN

PART
123

Infancy
through
Adolescence

It is not only wisdom
  to be wise
And on the inward vision
  close the eyes
But it is wisdom to believe
  the heart

Santayana

Introduction
to
Part 1

This portion of the book discusses the humanism necessary to help people grow and take care of themselves. As you read, you may encounter some new ideas and some that are not so new. Most of the important issues in the care of infants, children, and adolescents are touched upon. The task of selecting and then wading through the literature, clinical reports, and research material and of selecting examples from my own experience was a monumental one. There is a vast amount of literature on child and adolescent development. If an issue is not covered here, the omission is due to limitations of space, not a lack of caring.

Chapter 1 discusses how we, as care givers, evolve into our roles, and it stresses the importance of developing our own caring philosophy.

Chapter 2 focuses on alternative ways of giving birth and on the influence of these methods on parents and child.

The world of the preschooler and the care of children in settings other than the home are discussed in Chapter 3. Family patterns in the United States are changing drastically, and the effect of this on children is discussed in Chapter 4, which also discusses single parents.

Chapters 5, 6, and 7 deal with separation. Chapter 5 presents some of the theory and research concerning helping children and parents deal with loss. Chapter 6 is about separation as a result of divorce. As an aside, I suggest that you read Chapter 7 when you do not feel vulnerable to powerful statements about dying children.

How do we help children learn about caring? Chapter 8 describes a research study in which adolescents were trained to develop one-to-one caring relationships with institutionalized elderly persons. I especially wanted to include a discussion of a research project for those readers who are interested and/or involved in doing research. Reilley presents the theory behind this research and the actual implementation of the project.

Chapter 9 begins with a discussion of caring for children from racial and cultural groups different from one's own. The remainder of the chapter focuses on studies of sexuality and ethnicity. The seldom-talked-about experience of a child who views parental intercourse and the taboo topic of incest are discussed. The last two topics were included not only because those who work with families are having to deal increasingly with these problems but also because so little has been written on how to help children and families handle these traumatic experiences.

Chapter 10 presents innovative approaches by people working in the real world: a teacher training children to increase their intuitive powers, a child psychiatrist helping children with catastrophic illnesses through peer and self healing, an art therapist using methods that can be adapted to the classroom, and many more.

In these pages you will meet people who "walk among the stars" as they take innovative approaches to holistic health (Juster, p. 108).

Welcome to the world of caring.

Chapter 1

THE DEVELOPMENT OF CARING AND CARE-GIVING ROLES

Helen Elena Monea

> To care, to love one in the winter
> of despair; a crocus
> Sprouts through—
> Not alone in the garden.
>
> *Helen Elena Monea*

Caring is the primary concept of this book. It is essential to successful care giving and meaningful relationships. Since caring is the major characteristic of the helping professions, care givers must understand the dynamics and development of the caring quality. It is hoped that this chapter will stir your interest in your development as a care giver. How did you evolve in the caring role? What keeps you in the nurturing role? Is your work a satisfying growth experience? In what direction are you going? You can expand your horizons by examining your philosophy, attitudes, and feelings concerning your involvement in taking care of other human beings.

I recall that my own care-giving role began on my first day of kindergarten, and I believe that the quality of caring can be traced back to individual experience.

THE QUALITY OF CARING

Sobbing could be heard among the many sounds of children playing on their first day of kindergarten. A little girl was standing in a corner looking forlorn; tears streamed down her cheeks as her mother left her to face a new experience in the outside world. I quickly approached the little girl and said, "Don't cry, Harriet,

I'll take care of you." This is my earliest memory of assuming the caring and care-giving role. A cry for help had moved me into action. My own nurturing role developed early.

The desire to assume caring roles can stem from having been nurtured by another human being and from identifying with that person during one's life. The opposite can also happen: Inappropriate nurturing or the lack of a nurturing person can lead to a subsequent need to work through, or compensate for, the missing nurturing in one's life. Some individuals move into caring roles because of a desire to acquire status, reap financial gain, or fulfill parental expectations. Whatever the motivation, the ability and skill of each care giver vary. Some people care without causing the other human being to feel dependent, guilty, or resentful; some care through their listening ability, self-awareness, and respect for the other person's social, public, and personal space. Some individuals are astute observers of behavior but are less adept at direct dialogue and interventions. Others have the gift of disseminating knowledge and developing theories and have less interest in the affective domain.

No one individual is endowed with all the components of caring. My own concern for the quality of care stems from having observed people who were inappropriately placed in the health care system; for example, some people who work directly with patients would be more effective as indirect care givers—in administrative positions, for instance. Others do not belong in or enjoy any caring role.

The concept of caring is the basis of some disciplines. Recently, nursing educators who were aware of the diminishing quality of care or of a lack of care designed courses to teach empathy, which is one aspect of caring. (See Leininger's list of the aspects of caring in Chapter 27.) If a person has not experienced caring in his or her lifetime, empathy is difficult to learn. One way to improve the quality of caring would be to examine the motivations and caring abilities of prospective students.

School systems may fail in the caring quality. Crowded classrooms, archaic educational curricula, and the energy that must be expended on discipline can drain the average teacher. Some leave the profession, while others stay and become increasingly apathetic and/or frustrated. Lepman cites the experience of Marcus, a 6-year-old Australian boy:

> "On the first day of school our teacher asked us where we lived. Street and father's name. I stood up and said, 'In Heaven.' 'What number?' asked the teacher, not even looking at me. Then I became angry and I said, 'My father is dead, and in Heaven there are no numbers.' Then everybody laughed! It is terrible when your father is in Heaven . . ." (p. 72).

How can we create more caring situations? Although this is a complex problem, providing positive nurturing experiences during infancy and childhood through appropriate parenting would result in more of the caring that is needed in a technical society. Assisting care givers in coming to terms with their own philosophy of life would also be of help.

A PHILOSOPHY OF CARING

Having a philosophy of life gives meaning to one's existence and one's work. I have found that certain aspects of existential philosophy fit my own concept of caring and care giving. However, discussing existentialism is like making taffy: The more you stretch it, the more there is to work with, and the stickier it becomes. It is not my intent to explain the intricate dynamics of the existential philosophy; rather, I want to delineate briefly three elements of that theoretical framework which I find to be congruent with a caring philosophy: (1) commitment, (2) responsibility, and (3) the I-thou concept.

Commitment

Commitment is a basic theme in existential thinking; to make one's life as meaningful as possible and to live as fully as one can, require accepting rather than detaching oneself from joy and sorrow (Clemence). Hammarskjöld viewed commitment as something worthwhile: "How far both from muscular heroism and from soulfully tragic spirit of unselfishness which unctuously adds its little offering to the spongecake at a *Kaffeeklatsch,* is the plain simple fact that a man has given himself completely to something he finds worth living for" (p. 67).

Commitment involves both finding something worth living for and being open to changing ideas, values, and attitudes. All too often, professionals trained in one school of thought commit themselves to a single approach. For example, Freudian-trained professionals are criticized for adhering to theories and approaches that in many instances do not fit the needs of contemporary society. Some professionals—Gaylin, Bowlby, Rush, and Fromm, for example—reject certain aspects of Freud's theoretical structure.

Bühler quotes Freud, who was deeply committed to his theories but who had the courage to give up some aspects of his anxiety theory when he was 70, at which time they were no longer useful: "We must be patient and await fresh methods and occasions of research. We must be ready, too, to abandon a path that we have followed for a time, if it seems to be leading to no good end" (pp. 193–194).

The Experiential Approach

Holistic care, a recent trend in health care, has great potential. An increasing number of workshops focus on holistic care. The educational system also has the potential to institute changes that will improve learning. As a teacher, I have found the experiential approach, which integrates the affective and the cognitive domains, to be successful. My commitment to experiential teaching came out of the recognition that learning at any age needs to focus on inquiry, motivation, and relevance. The experiential model incorporates the learner's body, mind, and feelings, leading to a more holistic experience. Students usually gain a deeper understanding of themselves and the topic under discussion, and they can identify and solidify their own commitment to caring (Monea).

I continually modify learning experiences to include new concepts that are relevant, and I change the format of the learning experiences to adapt to students' needs as much as possible. Such flexibility increases my knowledge of each student and of my own abilities or limitations, and I attempt to show students that I care about them. They identify with the caring, and often a class cohesiveness develops which increases both sharing and learning. It is a most difficult way to teach because of the emotional involvement. The instructor must always be alert to group process. It is also time-consuming because of the need to collate materials and arrange the environment for the various exercises. This teaching approach requires a commitment and openness to change. See *Instructor's Manual t/a Nursing and the Aged* (Monea) for specific information on, and exercises in, experiential teaching.

Responsibility

Commitment means responsibility for living fully and meaningfully (Clemence). Individuals who live existentially encounter suffering and adversity, and therefore they need courage to accept full responsibility for their actions. If one teaches experientially or works creatively as a therapist, one must anticipate criticism and/or sabotage from those who do not understand the methods used or who are bound to traditional ways of teaching and working.

In caring, if one is to effectively help another person grow in the relationship, one needs to take responsibility for knowing oneself and also the other person. Mayeroff stated: "To care for someone, I must KNOW many things. I must know, for example, who the other is, what his powers and limitations are, what his needs are, and what is conducive to his growth; I must know how to respond to his needs, and what my own powers and limitations are" (p. 13).

Knowing oneself is important when working with children, for they often perceive the adult's feelings and attitudes before the adult does. The authors of Chapters 6 and 7 tell how they combined their self-knowledge and their knowledge of children in clinical situations involving separation and death. McCue used art to help a youngster express his feelings and to work through the pains of separation caused by divorce. The therapist was aware of her own strengths and limitations during the final phase of the relationship, when the youngster became angry with her because she was leaving. Noonan and Tiktinsky give a sensitive description of children who are facing death and who test out their limitations and strengths in the dying process. A variety of modalities were implemented: art, play, visits, and parent involvement. *Working with dying children requires much responsibility, courage, and sensitivity.*

I-Thou Relationships

Existential encounters are based on an I-thou level of relationship instead of an I-it level (Clemence). Human beings do not want to be treated as though they were nonexistent or as if they were objects. Relating to people on the humanistic level instead of the object level improves the quality of the relationship. The person being cared for feels accepted and respected, and trust in the care giver increases. For instance, Marcus, the Australian boy mentioned earlier, was being treated as an object, and the teacher ignored his pain. Moustakas helps teachers develop an I-thou level of caring with students by increasing sensitivity and authentic communication. *Such experiences need to be part of teacher-training requirements if we are to have a humanistic society.* Often children identify with teachers and, as a result, learn attitudes and values that influence their future lives. Opportunities to experience and grow in the caring process are important for young people, who will be the future care givers.

The work of Boldi, a nutrition teacher in Alta Loma, California, is an interesting example. She and her students planned a Hawaiian luncheon for a local senior citizens' club. They spent several weeks studying the nutritional needs of the elderly, and they eliminated from their menu inappropriate items such as nuts or foods containing seeds, which can aggravate denture or abdominal problems. They considered all aspects of their guests' needs, including psychosocial, sensory, and environmental factors. They used flowers and colorful table settings, and they made sure that there was sufficient light. To establish personal contact and rapport, each student greeted his or her own guest with a lei, a kiss, and an "Aloha." Background music was kept at a low-enough level to give a festive air without making it difficult to hear. A door prize of a fresh pineapple was given to each guest so that no one would feel left out.

Adolescents can also develop care-giving roles with youngsters. Some schools have programs under which older students act as tutors, mental health aides,

Figure 1-1 Adolescents can learn to care for younger children; this helps them gain parenting skills. *(Courtesy of Dwain Johnson.)*

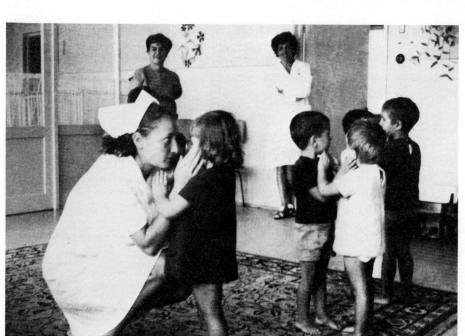

Figure 1-2   Romanian preschoolers are taught by staff members to care by looking at, touching, and hugging one another. (*Courtesy of Helen Monea.*)

teachers' aides, or big brothers or sisters. See Figure 1-1. Troubled adolescents who themselves have been acting out or who have learning difficulties often gain self-confidence and increased self-esteem by helping a younger child.

I have observed adolescents helping young children in the educational system in Romania. The first day of school in this socialist country is a joyous occasion; the children are welcomed with music and flowers. On the first day, each first grader is assigned a high school student who will act as his or her big brother or sister for the rest of the year. The older students' interest and excitement are reflected in the manner in which they assume the role of care givers to the younger pupils.

In the preschool Romanian programs, children are taught to learn the caring process through movement and music. Children and staff members work in pairs and, with background music, are encouraged to gaze into each other's eyes and to touch and hug each other. See Figure 1-2. Touching is part of caring in some cultures but is forbidden in others. See Chapters 9 and 29.

Some high schools in the United States offer courses in which students act as care givers of preschoolers in a nursery school located in the high school itself. Students learn practical and theoretical applications of child care. These courses are often offered in conjunction with the study of family life. Students can discuss, plan, and role-play a marriage ceremony. Resource people, such as marriage counselors and family planning professionals, discuss aspects of marriage and family life. Learning about the responsibilities of adult life and about caring for someone else can help students improve their future parenting ability and the quality of their relationships.

THE ESSENCE OF CARING

What is the essence of caring? To care for another person is to help that person grow and actualize. Caring is a process of relating to someone, and it involves the development of mutual trust and the deepening of the relationship. This can occur as a parent cares for a child, as a teacher cares for a pupil, or as a psychotherapist cares for a client (Mayeroff).

Gaylin includes love in caring. In order to be loving, we must feel lovable. "The degree to which we are nurtured and cared for will inevitably determine the degree to which we will be capable of nurturing and caring" (Gaylin, p. 45). Gaylin and Mayeroff have identified the following components of caring:

- *Ability to love*. Caring is a form of loving. The ability to care evolves from the experience of being nurtured and cared for. One must feel lovable to be a loving person. Caring about oneself and being able to love oneself are a prerequisite to caring for others.
- *Knowledge*. To care for someone, we must know the other person's strengths, limitations, and needs; who that person is; and how to respond to that person's needs. We also need to know our own powers and limitations.
- *Patience*. Patience consists in giving space and time and in allowing for floundering, confusion, and play.
- *Honesty*. Seeing others as they really are and not as we would like them to be requires being honest with ourselves and those we care for. Our motives for caring need to be examined. As teachers, we need to see students and their needs as they really are, not as stereotypes; we must also avoid using the student-teacher relationships as a means of self-aggrandizement. As writers, we need to be honest enough to examine and develop the ideas of others instead of trying to prove that our own ideas are correct.
- *Trust*. Being honest develops trust. Students trust the teacher if they know the teacher will not try to dominate them, force them into a mold, or overprotect them. Care givers must trust their own ability; teachers must trust their own ability to provide a learning climate; philosophical writers must trust their feelings for relevant ideas that ring true; and parents must trust their judgment concerning when to be firm. If we do not trust ourselves, we will doubt our actions, focus our attention on ourselves, and become indifferent to the needs of others.
- *Humility*. Continually learning about the other person is part of caring; we must never cease learning about others. We must take pride in our own strengths but not glorify them. We must appreciate our own limitations and not resent them.

- *Hope*. We must have hope that the other person will grow as a result of our caring. We must not indulge in wishful thinking or have unrealistic expectations.
- *Courage*. With hope comes the courage to stand by the other person in trying circumstances. Hope and courage are intertwined.
- *Caring for oneself.* All the components of caring for others also apply to caring for oneself. To care for oneself is to be responsive to one's own needs to grow; it is not an egocentric manner. If we cannot care for ourselves, we cannot care for another person.

THE DEVELOPMENT OF CARING

Gaylin traces the development of caring and loving through developmental processes that are ignored or incompletely developed by theorists such as Freud and Erikson, and he sees *dependency as the gateway leading to the development of the caring ability, with nurturance, attachment, separation, and identification as the developing processes of caring*. The helplessness of the child initiates the protective response of the adult. Being helpless is not the danger; being helpless and *unloved* is. Responding to babies with appropriate physical and psychological nurturance is one way of helping them develop their humanness.

The following are some suggestions for developing a caring role:

- Examine your own philosophy of care giving in light of commitment, responsibility, and I-thou relationships.
- Assist students in examining their own philosophies and their motivations for accepting caring roles.
- Focus on the positive aspects of the person you are caring for—his or her capacity to be human. This does not mean that you should ignore the person's limitations.
- Be a role model for children and adolescents as you encourage and engage them in care-giving roles.
- Take care of yourself. Be aware of your level of energy and of your strengths and limitations. Balance work with play. Overloading yourself by giving too much reduces the quality of the care you can provide.

Attachment: A Basis of Caring

Attachment is the basis of caring and loving. Klaus and Kennell define attachment as "a unique relationship between two people that is specific and endures through time" (p. 2). In studying mother-infant bonding, they found that behaviors such as fondling, cuddling, kissing, and prolonged gazing indicated attachment and served to transmit affection and sustain contact. Attachment may continue in the adult life of the child even without geographic closeness or physical contact, as evidenced by parents who respond to a cry for help from their sons and daughters after 40 years (Klaus and Kennell).

The origin of attachment is elusive; although we can see and feel attachment, we cannot prove that it is innate or learned. Gaylin believes that a combination of nature and nurturing capacities in a stable, supportive environment aids in the process of bonding two individuals. (The word "bonding" is often used interchangeably with "attachment.") The mystery of the bonding lies not in gratification through food but in human gratification, i.e., the quality and intensity of caring. The quality of caring and the transmission of caring are influenced by how the child interprets the mother's readiness to give comfort, how the mother responds to the child, and how the mother is influenced by the child's behavior (Klaus and Kennell).

Separation at Birth
Studies indicate that the amount of separation time at birth influences the quality of maternal attachment and care-giving skills. In 1936 at the Chicago World's Fair, mothers whose premature infants were exhibited were not permitted to take care of them. Cooney, the promoter, had great difficulty convincing the mothers to accept their infants after they had reached a weight of 5 lb. Mothers whose infants had to be away from them for a few days or a week so that they could be given special treatment had difficulty developing the appropriate care-giving skills. Some mothers felt threatened by the fact that their infants would not survive, and some began mourning early (Klaus and Kennell). The mothers' anxiety and fears concerning the infants probably evoked patterns of awkward touching, inappropriate holding, and limited eye contact, which influenced the attachment of the mothers to their infants.

In the past 15 years, intensive-care staff members have observed that premature infants are sometimes brought to hospital emergency rooms in a battered condition. There is evidence of more battering and more failure to thrive without organic cause among newborn, hospitalized, and premature infants than among infants not separated from their mothers (Klaus and Kennell).

Klaus and Kennell described studies of Barnett and his coworkers concerning the maternal side of interactional deprivation at birth. They found that only mothers whose babies were delivered at home experienced *no* interactional deprivation due to separation. This finding has implications for present-day management of most normal births in the United States. Mothers are separated from their infants except in those few hospital programs offering natural childbirth and home-type methods of delivery. Chapter 2 describes methods of childbirth. Fathers as care givers are also being increasingly studied. The stereotype of the American father as being passively involved is disproved. Studies of triadic interactions of mother, father, and infant have shown the father to be more active and dominant than the mother in touching, holding, and verbalizing (Parke).

The Importance of Attachment to the Parents
It seems critical for the infant to become attached to the parents during the first few minutes and hours of life (Klaus and Kennell). What happens to children who are orphaned because the mother dies in childbirth or who are immediately

separated from their parents at birth for other reasons? The quality of the care giver who replaces the parents greatly influences the ability of the child to attach and identify. Children do tend to be resilient; they survive some of the most troubled times. The experience of coping develops strength and an appreciation of caring in some children. Many creative leaders, successful business people, and great artists survived troubled childhoods (Goertzel and Goertzel). Arnstein writes that children from troubled homes often have unsatisfactory love relationships and develop poor parenting skills in later life. Inadequate parenting may produce tough children. Children who suffer from lack of care giving can become strong or tough; however, the tough person has low self-esteem, is on the defensive, and exploits people to gratify a need for power (Arnstein). The same author states: "We need fewer tough people in this world and more quietly strong and loving ones who do not need to declare their strength but who can go about making the world a better one through their compassionate concern for others less fortunate. These are the people whose strength and capacity to love have been cultivated since the days of their infancy" (Arnstein, p. 218).

Professionals can interfere with the attachment process by lowering the morale of mothers and minimizing their responsibility. Klaus and Kennell focus on Brazelton's remarks concerning three reasons why mother and infant are separated in institutions: (1) Physicians and nurses like to have people depend upon them, and the less choices or autonomy a patient has, the greater the care giver's rewards; (2) childbirth is treated as if it were a pathological condition; and (3) physicians and nurses devalue the role of parents in order to be the primary care givers of the newborn.

Institutions Reward Conformity

Institutions' insistence on conformity to rules is a factor in inappropriate care giving. Ground rules include (1) limited visiting hours, (2) specific feeding times, and (3) regimes exercised in the name of efficiency and economy. All these directly hinder the development of attachment in the infant-parent relationship. How can the situation be improved without depriving staff members of feeling rewarded? It may be necessary to educate professionals concerning their own needs that may interfere with the attachment process and the needs of patients. It may be important to redirect the caring process toward more family involvement. The professional also will need to be empathic and tend to both the mother's and the infant's needs. One way to do this might be to help the mother preserve her psychic and physical energy so that she can deal with her inner experience and her feelings about motherhood and have the opportunity to bond together with her infant—to do things *for* the mother to free her so that she has the energy to care for her child.

Separation

Attachment and separation are closely related. Separation is necessary for growth as the infant is weaned from breast to bottle, from diaper to toilet, and from home to school. Children who experience the security of caring parents develop ego strength and a sense of self, and they separate naturally from their parents because of an eager curiosity about their environment. Those who do not grow up in a caring environment suffer stress and carry the burden of insecurity throughout their adult years.

Separation brings anxiety; "separation anxiety" is a typical reaction of the infant and should not be taken as an indication of pathology or as an "index of attachment." *A total absence of anxiety would be more evident of atypical development in attachment and separation* (Gaylin). Separation is a step toward independence, and independence is a step toward caring; however, independence does not assure the ability to care unless the person has a sense of adequacy and a sense of self (Gaylin). Chapters 5, 6, and 7, which describe clinical experiences of care givers with children, discuss separation anxiety more fully.

Identification

Identification is a complex and normal part of the process of becoming mature; it gives us the capacity to love. Caring does not proceed in an orderly sequence through stages of attachment, separation, and identification, but rather as alternating experiences in all phases of the process. Identification theory has never been studied in a more positive relationship of loving. Freud used it inconsistently, modifying the term as needed. Erikson limited his theory of identity to the individual and the environment and did not deal with the relationship of one individual to another; the emotions he describes are shame and pride, not love (Gaylin).

The rudiments of identification have been considered to be the stretch motions in utero, which gradually expand into a more sophisticated sense of self as the person gains experience in the outside world. The initial major identification occurs with parents and then with significant others through the processes of (1) approval, (2) imitation, and (3) mirroring on a conscious and an unconscious level. If we cannot satisfy our needs, we unconsciously choose people who may effectively meet them. First attachments to parents have the most lasting impression. Children identify with parents, on whom they depend for survival, and they gain parental approval by exhibiting the behavior that the parent likes (Gaylin). Some parents reinforce "cuteness" for girls and aggressiveness for boys.

Young children also commonly identify with firemen, policemen, teachers, and nurses, for example—all care givers. On the other hand, adolescents often identify with status figures, depending upon the generation trend—prominent television or movie idols, rock performers, and athletes. As children and adolescents continue to grow and emerge into mature beings, other identifications influence them and shape them into the persons they would like to be.

What happens to children who are raised in multiple-family units, for example, communes? Weisberg found that children in communes have the advantage of many adults who are more available to talk, visit, and plan house rules with them. Consequently, their opportunities for identification can be enhanced. On the other hand, it can be confusing for the child to have many authority figures who give directions, particularly if they are inconsistent in discipline. Youngsters in such situations could become authoritarian themselves or have difficulty coping with authority in the future (Fogg). Children can become manipulative by arousing competition between the real parent and the surrogate parent, for example, between parent and teacher, between parent and relative, and between divorced parents. If adults know and recognize the developmental process and needs of the child, if they are secure in their own identification, and if they are able to recognize their own vulnerability in the caring process, the need for competition and/or manipulation can be reduced.

There is no guarantee of the capacity to love. For instance, a child who identifies with a sadistic or neglectful parent learns cruelty (Gaylin). Yet at the same time, attachment of the child to the deficient parent can be strong. A recent television news report in San Francisco showed a mother being physically restrained from rescuing her child from authorities who were removing her children from the home because of her severe neglect and abuse. There was a tragic scene of wailing and crying. The youngest child kept screaming, "I want my mama."

Developing a conscience is related to approval and identification. Acceptable behavior is developed through fear of punishment and through our ego ideal, i.e., what we would like to be or ought to be. *The rebellion of young people has been due not to the lack of ability to identify with authority figures but rather to a hunger for identification and a lack of role models.* Young adults have been attracted to many movements; this reflects their need to search for appropriate models, which have not been present in their immediate environment. The brutality and violence in our country have developed not from economic deficiencies but from multiple factors, and punishment is often used as a solution. A better approach would be to strive for a more caring community (Gaylin).

Reflections on the Growth of Identification

My own experience with identification brings back memories of significant people other than my parents who shaped my life. Some examples are an unforgettable family friend who nurtured my creativity and sense of curiosity through his delightful storytelling and the walks we took together to pick flowers, an elementary school music teacher who stirred my love for music, and a geography teacher who sparked my interest in travel to foreign countries. The high school nurse who praised me for handling an emergency while she was unavailable initiated my identification with the nursing profession. These people are still with me as I look at flowers, listen to music, and assume a care-giving role in my daily life personally and professionally. Gaylin indicates that we identify with some attributes of a person and ignore others. I often wonder what selection process I used *not* to identify with some people. Several adults with whom I could not identify caused me to feel inadequate and foolish—a cross handicraft teacher who physically punished me, a gruff storekeeper who scolded children if they talked loudly, and an aloof neighbor who seldom spoke to anyone.

Since the process of identification is complex and has not been fully studied in terms of caring, the future may bring new ideas. For instance, what is the selection process that goes on in negative identification? Is that part of the person we do not choose to identify with related to a similar trait in ourselves? Could rejecting identification with an individual be related to a certain weakness? Until these ideas are explored, it is obvious that you and I and the world are in need of caring.

REFERENCES

Arnstein, Helen S.: *The Roots of Love,* Bantam, New York, 1977.

Barnett, Clifford R., P. Herbert Leiderman, Rose Grobstein, and **Marshall Klaus:** "Neonatal Separation: The Maternal Side of Interactional Deprivation," *Pediatrics,* **45**(2):197–205, 1970.

Bowlby, John: *Separation: Anxiety and Anger,* vol. II, *Attachment and Loss,* Basic Books, New York, 1973.

Bühler, Charlotte: *Values in Psychotherapy,* Free Press, New York, 1962.

Clemence, Sister M.: "Existentialism: A Philosophy of Commitment," *American Journal of Nursing,* **66**(3):500–505, 1966.

Fogg, Susan: "Growing Up in Communes," *San Francisco Sunday Examiner & Chronicle, Scene,* Apr. 24, 1977, p. 9.

Fromm, Eric: *The Art of Loving,* Harper & Row, New York, 1974.

Gaylin, Willard: *Caring,* Knopf, New York, 1976.

Goertzel, Victor, and **Mildred G. Goertzel:** *Cradles of Eminence,* Little, Brown, Boston, 1962.

Hammarskjöld, Dag: *Markings,* Knopf, New York, 1969.

Juster, Norton: *The Phantom Tollbooth,* Random House, New York, 1972.

Klaus, Marshall H., and **John H. Kennell:** *Maternal-Infant Bonding: The Impact of Early Separation or Loss on Family Development,* Mosby, St. Louis, 1976.

Lepman, Jella (ed.): *How Children See Our World,* Avon, New York, 1971.

Mayeroff, Milton: *On Caring,* Harper & Row, New York, 1971.

Monea, Helen E.: *Instructor's Manual* t/a *Nursing and the Aged,* McGraw-Hill, New York, 1976.

Moustakas, Clark: *The Authentic Teacher,* Doyle, Cambridge, Mass., 1969.

Parke, R.: "Father-Infant Interaction," in M. H. Klaus, T. Leger, and M. A. Trause (eds.), *Maternal Attachment and Mothering Disorders: A Round Table,* Johnson and Johnson, Sausalito, Calif., 1974.

Rush, A. K.: "What Is Feminist Therapy?" in A. V. Mander and A. K. Rush (eds.), *Feminism as Therapy,* Random House, New York, and The Bookworks, Berkeley, Calif., 1974.

OTHER RESOURCES

FILMS

Cria: Spanish film with subtitles. A sensitive portrayal of growing up in an adult world. Carlos Saura.

Small Change: French film with subtitles. A loosely structured comedy dealing with the resiliency of children aged 2 to 14. François Truffaut.

The Gift: 11 min/16 mm/color. A film about loving and giving centering on a child's gift to her mother. Distributor: Barr Films, P.O. Box 5667, Pasadena, Calif. 91107.

Chapter 2

HELLO, WORLD!
DIMENSIONS OF BIRTH

Helen Elena Monea

YOU

That first sudden look of you,
blue eyes, wild with wonder and pain.
That first hungry cry of you,
and the heavens, the heavens, have been rearranged.

Patricia Gamaleri

A 93-year-old widower reminisced to me about how he had helped his wife deliver their third baby in their cabin in Kansas because the doctor was delayed. When I asked how he had known what to do, he replied, "I jest watched that doctor the last couple of times and did the same." When their fourth baby was born, however, he was relieved not to have the responsibility. "The sack on the baby's head was a fiber sack. The doctor nipped it off very easy." See Figure 2-1.

The trend today toward welcoming a child into the world via the natural mode is reminiscent of centuries-old customs. The difference is that the mother is prepared, the father is involved but is not responsible for the delivery, and a minimal amount of drugs is used. Expectant parents are increasingly insisting on their right to have choices concerning the type of delivery and the amount of family involvement. This movement is viewed with skepticism by some professionals, while others are moving ahead with home deliveries and alternative birth centers. The mode of delivery established by the medical profession is being challenged. Women object to being treated as if they were ill; for example, they are prepared as if for surgery, and there is minimal communication with

Figure 2-1   A baby is born. *(Courtesy of Sammy Woog, aged 5½.)*

care givers, who wear masks and often disappear at the very moment the woman in labor needs support. Such complaints are increasing, and the number of natural childbirths is doubling every 2 years in the United States (Tanzer). Advocacy groups are forming, and changes are bound to occur. Arms (cited in Fager) predicts that it will be another 10 years before conflicting professional groups reach complementary decisions.

METHODS OF CHILDBIRTH

The women's liberation movement supports the natural approach to childbirth because it is another way of freeing women from the oppression of being treated like subordinate human beings. The approach fits in with the two primary goals of the liberation movement: to give women control over their own bodies and to help them achieve greater self-realization and awareness of their full potential as human beings (Tanzer). Several approaches to natural delivery have been used.

The Dick-Read Method

The oldest method of natural childbirth was developed by an obstetrician, Grantly Dick-Read. During an 8-week course, the woman is taught to do abdominal breathing and to concentrate on what is happening inside her body. The course covers nutrition, exercise, overall labor training, and awareness of anxiety. Choices of medication are also covered (Mindel).

The Lamaze Method

The Lamaze method is based on breathing techniques and on the couple's working together. It is not described as a natural childbirth method because the woman may choose to have medication if she desires. The Lamaze method is rooted in methods developed by European scientists in the 1880s, such as obstetrical hypnosis, which was replaced by a psychoprophylactic method based on Pavlovian principles. Lamaze, a French obstetrician, visited the Soviet Union to observe the approach and introduced the method successfully in 1951. An American woman who gave birth with Dr. Lamaze as her obstetrician felt so strongly about it that she wrote a book in the hope that American women would try the method. Initially there was reluctance and minimal acceptance, but the approach is steadily growing in popularity (Tanzer).

The Leboyer Method

A recent innovation developed by a French obstetrician, Leboyer, focuses on the child. A more humanistic approach than that of holding the newborn upside down and slapping it is used. The transition from the womb to the outer world is made more gentle; the environment is peaceful, and there is soft lighting. The baby is placed on the mother's body until breathing begins, allowing for touch by the mother before the umbilical cord is severed; then the baby is placed in a water bath. Thus the child is protected from overstimulation caused by too many lights, from having the oxygen supply cut off too soon, and from inappropriate touching, all of which occur in traditional medical settings (Leboyer).

What influence would this type of delivery have on the future development of an infant? A French researcher, Daniele Rapoport, studied 120 Leboyer babies at 1, 2, and 3 years of age. They were found to have better coordination and to walk earlier than average babies their age. More than 80 percent had no sleeping disorders or digestive problems. There was no difficulty in toilet training or self-feeding. The mothers found the babies alert, inventive, and able to use both hands well ("Evidence of Gentler Babies"). The question that might be posed would concern the possibility that these babies could have developed in the same way if they had had selective parents who were competent in nurturing them.

ADVANTAGES OF NATURAL CHILDBIRTH

Another reason to search for alternative methods of childbirth, besides improving the care of the mother and the infant, concerns the mortality rate. Our richly endowed and sophisticated nation has the highest infant mortality rate of any Western industrialized society. Holland is the leader in natural childbirth and has one of the lowest infant mortality rates in the world. Half of the births occur at home and are attended by midwives. In Holland, the midwife is a respected and accepted colleague in the health care system (Arms, 1975). In the United States, legal technicalities interfere with home deliveries, and there is medical opposition to lay midwives in certain states. Legislative efforts to license lay midwives are under way due to surveys and recommendations being made by committees on childbirth practices, professional standards of education for midwives being established, and the public being made more aware of the issues surrounding childbirth (Fager). Not all physicians are opposed to home deliveries. In Chicago, a group of physicians have organized to support families and doctors interested in home births. Other home birth societies are evolving in Boston, Seattle, and Toronto (Maynard).

Ironically, the reverse was true in the past. During the Renaissance, midwives were protecting their practice from intrusion by scientists and physicians. By the twentieth century, after the introduction of anesthesia and forceps, physicians and hospitals had gradually taken over the practice of delivering babies (Tanzer). An advantage of midwife delivery in nineteenth century Vienna was the low incidence of illness. Epidemics swept through maternity hospitals. One out of ten women delivered by medical students died of childbed fever, while those delivered by midwives had a low incidence of illness. After medical students were taught to scrub their hands with disinfectants before delivering a baby, the epidemic was reduced (Tanzer). A study conducted by Mehl (cited by Ellis) in northern California shows fewer complications during childbirth and a lower infant morbidity and mortality rate for home deliveries by either physician or midwife than for hospital deliveries throughout the whole state of California. Only 5 percent of mothers attended by midwives suffered from vaginal lacerations, compared with 40 percent of those delivered by physicians. The physicians were less experienced than the midwives, who prided themselves on deliveries without tears and on the use of perineal massage and gentle head delivery (Ellis).

Home Delivery

The advantages of a home delivery include a more relaxed environment where the expectant mother can arrange for her own comfort. She is also free to carry out routine activities which aid in making contractions stronger and less frequent because of the distraction. She can be given light nourishment to keep up her strength; in the hospital nothing is given by mouth because of the possibility that a general anesthetic may have to be administered. The woman is not disturbed by other mothers in labor, and she can choose her own position for delivery; the traditional stirrup is not used, and she is not strapped to a narrow bed-table

(Maynard). The main disadvantage is the risk of complications. If problems arise for the mother or the infant in the process of labor or delivery, only emergency equipment is immediately available, and the ride to the hospital can decrease the chances for survival. Some communities provide emergency transport links between home and hospital for high-risk women (Arms, 1977). On the other hand, there are risks associated with hospital delivery, such as from anesthesia and forceps.

Alternative Birth Centers

A compromise combining the advantages of home delivery and the safety features of the hospital environment is becoming more popular as hospitals are implementing alternative birth centers. High-risk women—those with a health problem—are usually not accepted in this type of program and are delivered using the traditional medical approach. Although their needs for safety are greater, they would profit from the intimate and caring atmosphere just as much as low-risk mothers.

Expectant parents are asking for minimal interference with the natural process of birth (no forceps) and for the right to keep the baby in their presence from the moment of birth (Maynard). The latter was described in the preceding chapter as being vital for bonding between infant and parents. In one case a woman and her husband struggled through a difficult labor, determined to resist a cesarean section. They succeeded only because of much perseverance and support from the midwives and because of the husband's strong opposition to hospital medical intervention (Fager).

DRUGS USED BEFORE AND DURING BIRTH

Drugs used before and during labor can have serious implications for mother and infant. Thalidomide, for instance, has been shown to cause deformities in newborn babies. Excessive bleeding in newborn infants can be attributed to barbiturates and aspirin; antidepressants and several antihistamines have also been suspected of producing abnormalities. Tanzer found that anesthesia caused 5 percent of deaths and was a contributing factor in another 5 percent.

A nationwide campaign by federal agencies and the University of Southern California is alerting expectant mothers of the danger to the fetus due to consumption of alcohol during pregnancy. Two drinks daily of hard liquor can cause fetal damage. The National Council on Alcoholism projected in 1977 that out of the 250,000 abnormal infants born, 6000 would suffer from the alcohol syndrome, including retardation of growth, heart defects, congenital eye and ear problems, extra digits, and disturbed sleep patterns ("Two Alcoholic Drinks a Day Can Cause Fetal Abnormalities, Institute Reveals"). Adolescents often overindulge in alcohol, and 1 teenager in 20 has a drinking problem (Keniston and The Carnegie Council on Children). Since pregnancy is increasing in the teenage population and since teenagers are at high risk, care givers will need to be aware of preventive measures that their young clients should take. Tobacco, another widely used drug, constitutes a hazard. Williams reports statistics showing that, in both this country and England, babies whose mothers smoke are smaller than babies whose mothers do not smoke. Low-birth-weight babies run a higher risk in terms of complications and are weaker than babies of normal weight.

PSYCHOLOGICAL IMPACT ON PARENTS

Significant findings have demonstrated the advantages of natural childbirth from a psychological point of view (Tanzer). Tanzer studied two groups of women for 5 years; one group chose to deliver by conventional methods, and the other group by natural childbirth.

One issue explored was the type of woman who chooses natural childbirth. Tanzer cites critics who have charged that women who choose natural childbirth need to prove their femininity and hunger for authority and domination. Critics also say that a woman who wants her husband present at delivery is sadistically forcing him to view the suffering he has caused her, thereby proving that women are the superior sex. Tanzer's study demonstrated that these charges are not true (1972). Both groups of women studied were psychologically healthy in terms of anxiety levels, feelings of security, and self-concept. This is a prime example of how male attitudes demean women and activate liberation movements.

Tanzer found great differences in attitudes and responses to labor between the natural childbirth mothers and the conventional childbirth mothers. The mothers who delivered through conventional means experienced pain, screamed, and felt helpless, in contrast to the natural childbirth mothers, who were happy, confident, and calm. Obviously, the difference is due to being ". . . taught exactly what to expect and do at the onset of labor" (Tanzer, p. 97). The natural childbirth mothers were wide awake throughout the birth process; they observed and were aware of more and reported on the experience more fully than the conventional childbirth mothers. After the birth, the natural childbirth mothers felt euphoric and physically well, while the conventional childbirth mothers had little to report because of the effects of the anesthesia.

How did the mothers in both groups feel about themselves? The natural childbirth mothers experienced increased self-esteem, supporting the widely held view that natural childbirth improves a woman's self-image. The reason for the improved sense of self was related to the process of natural childbirth itself, not to the feeling of rapture, the presence or absence of pain, or the presence or absence of the husband.

The amount of pain experienced was related to menstrual history and amount of drugs administered. Women who had poor menstrual histories experienced more pain than those with better histories. The natural childbirth mothers reported less pain, although they had more opportunity to experience it than the conventional childbirth mothers. The mothers delivering the natural way used fewer analgesics than the conventional childbirth mothers. Those who were heavily sedated either did not remember all the pain they suffered or else they gave a distorted description of the experience.

Participation by the Father

Where is the best place for a father to be—inside or outside the labor and delivery setting? Traditional methods exclude the father from the experience, while natural childbirth advocates strongly recommend that the father be present throughout labor and delivery. Tanzer's study revealed that fathers should be present during birth:

1. Women who experienced feelings of rapture had their husbands at their sides. The rapturous feelings gave them a healthier perception of the world and of themselves.
2. The natural childbirth women viewed their husbands as positive figures; this sharing of an intensely personal experience added a richer dimension to their marriages and increased their sense of family. The conventional childbirth women viewed their husbands as negative or neutral figures, and there was no intense emotional sharing.

Tanzer points out that men may have more of a need to play a role in birth than we realize. She found that husbands expressed positive feelings about having participated in the childbirth experience. This finding has a major implication for the basic attitude in our culture that there are psychological differences between men and women. Evidence of male identification with childbirth, such as the couvade (in which the new father imitates the behavior of his wife during delivery and the postpartum period), has been documented in primitive cultures and exists in our own society (Tanzer). See Figure 2-2.

Participating in the childbirth experience did not interfere with the men's masculinity, as it has often been thought to do. Rather, they emerged strong, competent, and supportive, all attributes of maleness. In contrast, the husbands of the conventional childbirth women appeared weak, childlike, and in need of care. Consequently, conventional childbirth women can become dominant and controlling and may be viewed as castrating their husbands, charges frequently made against natural childbirth women. Conventional childbirth may be responsible for further alienation of the sexes (Tanzer).

The Sobering Experience

Becoming parents can be viewed as a developmental crisis. The relationship between two people changes with the addition of another human being who needs care and attention. A new father aptly described the event as a "sobering experience." He was a young adult in therapy and was coping with drug dependence through aggressive, demanding, and manipulative behavior. He changed overnight after witnessing the birth of his child. The next day he looked tired and meek and had a distant look in his eye. I have heard other fathers,

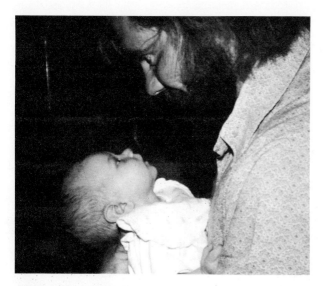

Figure 2-2   A father and baby. *(Courtesy of Priscilla Ebersole.)*

married and not married, say that they had a similar feeling of instantly maturing when they became parents.

Other reactions of fathers include a sense of rivalry with the baby. They are used to getting all their wives' attention, and they resent suddenly having to share it; this can trigger memories of sibling rivalry during childhood. Some fathers shy away from holding or caring for the infant, feeling that this would be unmasculine (Dodson). In less than 5 percent of prospective fathers, acute reactions to the pregnancy and/or birth have led to extreme behaviors. In an article in *Behavior Today* ("The Trauma of Fatherhood"), a psychiatrist and a psychologist note stresses suffered by fathers as a result of increased responsibility, feelings of rivalry with the baby, or the fear that the infant will act as a binding force in an unhappy marriage.

Involving the father in the birth not only seems to have potential for improving the mental health of the parents but also gives the newborn a better chance of being accepted and loved when he or she finally goes home.

PSYCHOLOGICAL IMPACT ON CHILDREN

Who is present to greet the newborn infant other than care givers? Fathers are often excluded in traditional medical deliveries, except in progressive hospitals. Including children in labor and delivery is a natural and culturally approved activity for some families. In middle-class America, it is a new phenomenon that is growing with the natural childbirth movement. See Figure 2-3.

Some children are introduced to the birth process through indirect methods. A young mother brought her preschool daughter to see several films on different

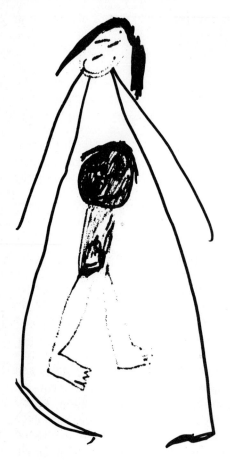

Figure 2-3 Mom is going to have a baby. *(Courtesy of Sammy Woog, aged 5½.)*

techniques of childbirth at a San Francisco educational birth center. The child's questions centered on what was "hurting the mommy" during the scenes showing labor and delivery. The mother interpreted the questions as curiosity and was oblivious to her daughter's anxiety. My concern for the child, who was sitting next to me, mounted as the next film revealed scenes of a midwife attending a mother in a home delivery. Two siblings were present and were seated on the bed next to the mother. The children were in great distress, crying throughout the procedure. There was no support for the children, verbal or nonverbal. Memories of my student nursing days came back as I recalled my reaction when a nursing instructor quickly escorted me and some fellow students into a delivery room without preparing us for what we were about to see. We were filled with awe and shock since it was the first time we had witnessed a delivery. If young adults can have strong reactions to birth, I wondered what impact it would have on this child, particularly since she was viewing the scene with her own mother.

Children in the San Francisco area are now being allowed to be present at deliveries. Some professionals are making observations on their reactions. When research is implemented in this area, some of the questions posed will have to focus on the child's understanding of the event; the fantasies, fears, and/or guilt that can be aroused; and the impact of the experience on the relationship with the new sibling. A longitudinal study will also have to be made concerning later influences on the youngster's identity and appropriate ways of preparing the child. Anthropological studies have dealt with children's reactions to birth. For instance, the Jarara Indians of South America give birth with anyone present who wishes to attend, including the mother's small children. In contrast, children of the Cuna Indians of Panama do not learn about sexual intercourse until the marriage ceremony (Mead and Newton).

CHILDBIRTH IN OTHER CULTURES

A variety of attitudes toward, and customs concerning, childbirth exist throughout the world; some resemble our own, and others are quite different. Tanzer cites historical and anthropological studies of methods of childbirth and attitudes toward it. The Cuna Indians treat pregnancy as an illness. The pregnant woman is under the constant surveillance of a medicine man, who keeps her under medication throughout labor (Mead and Newton).

Childbearing was viewed as a defiling event in ancient cultures. The woman was considered unclean and was isolated for 40 days after delivery. The ancient Hebrews, although they developed the first vaginal speculum and performed the earliest cesarean sections, were not as progressive in their attitude toward childbirth. They, too, considered birth defiling and the woman unclean, subjecting her to a purification period ranging from 30 days if she bore a son, to 60 days if she delivered a daugher (Cianfrini). Vestiges of these attitudes exist today. As an adolescent and a member of a Romanian Greek Orthodox church, I was discouraged from attending services during my menses, and I remember that new mothers were not allowed to leave home or attend church for a short period of time after delivery. Such customs could be interpreted dynamically as reflecting the desire of men to control women and keep them in a second-class position. Evidence of this can be traced to the ancient Greeks, who considered the male to be dominant. Greek writings describe the pregnant woman as having a good color if the fetus was a male and a bad color if it was a female (Cianfrini). Other demeaning attitudes toward sex can be found in Bulgarian villages, where the people, although concerned with the pregnant woman's welfare, think of pregnancy as being somewhat immoral because of its sexual implications.

Customs also differ concerning sexual intercourse during pregnancy. Among the Yahgan of Tierra del Fuego in South America, relations are ceased as pregnancy advances. Sexual intercourse is encouraged up to the first 5 months among the Chagga of Tanzania in Africa, and a Siriono woman who was experiencing intermittent labor pains had intercourse with her husband to stimulate uterine contractions (Mead and Newton).

A World Health Organization report described the custom of sewing the vaginas of preadolescent girls in a Somalian rural village to protect them from rape and assure their virginity when they entered the marriage market. Rural Somalian girls are sold like livestock, and a virgin's price can be as high as 100 camels if the husband is rich. Money from the United Nations Children's Fund (UNICEF) was used to implement new approaches to women's liberation by improving literacy among midwives and educating them in better prenatal care and methods of delivery. One of several positive results is that some of the midwives now refuse to perform circumcisions on girls and uphold their belief by not allowing their own daughters to be circumcised (Hancock).

Brazilian women have cesarean sections if they can afford them because they fear the pain of normal delivery and because they mistakenly believe that normal deliveries can cause permanent vaginal and uterine deformities. Six out of ten deliveries in Brazilian private clinics are by cesarean section. Although the cesarean approach is considered unethical and illegal unless it is used for a medical reason, a majority of Brazilian obstetricians who perform cesarean sections believe that this is the best method because it causes no harm to the figure, can be done quickly, and is more profitable ($500 for a normal delivery, compared with $1200 for a cesarean delivery). Dr. Joǎo Junes, a Health Ministry official, is combating the private medical systems that have fostered a public relations campaign in favor of cesarean deliveries ("For Those Who Can Afford Them, Brazilian Women Prefer Caesarean Birth").

Political and economic influences have an impact on mothers and infants. In socialist countries such as Yugoslavia the attitude is that all citizens should be productive, including new mothers (Klerman and Jekel). In consulting with people working in the health care system in Romania, another socialist country, I learned that new mothers have little choice but to return to work and place their babies in nurseries. The Romanian preventive health care system includes punitive action. While she is receiving prenatal care, the woman is fined if she does not keep her clinic appointments. The government has encouraged an abundance of babies to make a "strong country." Although the Romanian preventive health care program is rigidly enforced, there is a superior network of coordinated agencies, and children are top priority, the opposite of the situation in the United States.

Since we are a nation of many races, cultures, and creeds, we have many different customs concerning childbirth and attitudes toward it. The goal, however, regardless of philosophy, is the best possible care of the mother, the father, and the infant.

The following is an overview of important issues in childbirth:

- The trend toward natural childbirth is increasing. Methods include those of Dick-Read, Lamaze, and Leboyer. There is also a trend toward home deliveries and alternative birth centers.
- Tanzer offers data indicating that natural childbirth has advantages over conventional methods:

The woman tolerates pain better, is more confident, has increased self-esteem, and is happier.

The husband's participation in natural childbirth adds a rich dimension to the marriage and fosters a sense of family as a result of having shared an intensely personal experience.

Husbands are more interested in, and have more positive feelings about, participating in the experience than has been thought.

The father's participation does not interfere with his masculinity; rather, he emerges as a strong, competent, and supportive figure.

- Allowing children to view the birth of a sibling is common in some cultures and is the subject of increasing interest in the United States. Longitudinal research will need to be done on the psychological impact of this.
- It has been predicted that a baby boom will begin in 1980 and that the average woman will have more than three children by 1990 (Wolfe).

BABY BOOMS

With the exception of the increased teenage birthrate, fewer babies are being born today. We are in a baby bust. During World War II, the average number of babies born per woman was 3.5. In 1972 the number dropped to 2.08, dipping to 1.8 in 1977 (Wolfe). Changing sexual values, the women's movement, the Pill, and abortion have had their impact. A prolonged reduction in the number of births has economic, sociological, and cultural implications. Obstetricians, hospitals, teachers, publishers of children's books, and baby-food manufacturers are feeling the economic pinch (Wolfe).

Easterlin, a professor of economics at the University of Pennsylvania, is considered the father of the accepted baby-boom theory (Wolfe). He postulates that people decide to have babies on the basis of their subjective feelings about how well off they are and that these feelings depend upon the number of people in their cohort group. Lee, an economist and demographer at the University of Michigan, expands on Easterlin's theory. He emphasizes the differences between one's childhood expectations and one's economic status as an adult. For instance, children who were raised during the Depression expected the worst when they grew up but found themselves better off than they had thought they would be; consequently, they had more babies. Conversely, their children grew up in an affluent age and expected the best, only to be faced with limited work opportunities. As a result, they had few babies. Their children, though expecting hard times, are finding that things are not so bad because their generation is small in number (Wolfe).

Sociologist Etizioni of Columbia University has raised the question of the implications for our society of fewer children and a proportionately large number of old people. This will mean fewer people who are able to work and more people who need services, and the working population will have to bear the burden of financial support of the older, nonworking population. Wolfe also mentions the possibility that our nation will become very conservative and lacking in innovation; she bases this on the rationale that only a young society can be creative. This is a narrow view, however, since Wolfe does not take into account the fact that we stifle creativity in aging persons because we believe they have limited abilities to contribute.

Demographers predict that there will be a shift toward increased childbearing in about 1980, with individual women having more than three children by 1990 (Wolfe). The National Center for Health Statistics has reported a 6 percent rise in births from September 1976 to April 1977. Reports indicate that the marriage rate was up in 1977, with no increase in the divorce rate ("Birth Rate Is Moving up from Its 1976 Low-Point"). The present rise in the birthrate may be due to the large number of World War II babies who are now in their prime reproductive years.

A shift in the birthrate activates a shift in attitudes. The lowered birthrate today coincides with the attitude that motherhood is not a highly respectable or desirable occupation. In the 1960s this shift in attitude required an acceptance of birth control, careers for women, and abortion. Demographers Sklar of the University of California at Berkeley and Berkovof of the California State Department of Health also predict an increase in childbearing, although they do not believe that women will revert to the attitude that motherhood is the only satisfactory occupation or aspiration for a woman (Wolfe).

Teenage Pregnancy: The Babies Are Coming

There is a baby boom among today's teenage population. *International Family Planning Digest* reports that teenage pregnancy is becoming "epidemic" worldwide; 10 percent of American teenage girls become pregnant yearly, and two-thirds of these pregnancies are unintended ("Teenage Pregnancy"). A *Behavior Today* news release ("And Teenage Pregnancy") cites that Planned Parenthood records show a steady increase of pregnancies among girls 15 to 19 years old. However, illegitimate births for girls 15 to 19 years old had declined in 1976 for the first time since 1962. This was mainly due to a 4 percent decrease in the rate for black teenage girls, while the rate for white teenage girls increased 2 percent (Monthly Vital Statistics Report). Lieberman, family planning project director of the American Public Health Association, believes that white adolescents are becoming more sexually active, while black adolescents are beginning to use family planning ("Illegitimate Births Rise for White Adolescents").

The reasons why unmarried school-aged girls become pregnant have changed over the years. Before 1930 bad companions, immorality, and mental deficiency were blamed. During the 1930s environmental causes such as poverty and broken homes were thought to be contributing factors. During the late 1930s and the 1940s, the culture or way of life of certain groups was considered an important cause. Since then, illegitimacy has been viewed as a result of psychological determinants, i.e., as a result of emotional problems or as a way of satisfying

Figure 2-4 Arrival of the baby. (*Courtesy of Sammy Woog, aged 5½.*)

unmet emotional needs (Vincent). Although these factors contribute, none can be held primarily accountable for the problem (Herzog). Liben notes that intrapsychic approaches have been used to study sexual activity and pregnancy among white middle-class women, while sociological and epidemiological approaches have been used in the study of lower-class nonwhite women. Presently, the following multiple causes are considered important:

1.   The age of fertility, or ability to conceive, is lower. In 1940, the mean age of fertility was 13.5 years of age, as compared to the 1960s, when the mean age was 12.5 years (Zackarias, Wuntman, and Schatzoff). A study conducted in 1965 found that girls who begin to menstruate earlier than average conceive sooner and are more likely to have sexual relations than those who begin later (Cutright).

2.   Adolescents start to have premarital sexual experiences earlier today than they did in the past. They seek affectional and sexual satisfaction, rejecting society's standards (Tighe). The influence of the feminist movement upon the double standard is evidenced in their relationships. According to Kappelman, the teenage boy, instead of wondering "Will she or won't she?" now asks himself, "How do I say no?" ("Teenage Sexuality Today").

3. Society's attitudes toward adolescent sexuality hinder teenagers from learning about and accepting their sexuality. Consequently, they have difficulty handling situations involving sex ("Birth Rate Is Moving up from Its 1976 Low-Point").
4. Young adolescents' capacity for impulse control is poorly developed. Older adolescents are better able to guard against the risk of pregnancy in sexual activity than younger adolescents (Tighe).
5. Contraception sabotage is one way of dealing with independence from parental ties. Boys may encourage girls not to use contraceptives in order to preserve their masculinity (Tighe).
6. Girls are subjected to peer-group pressure to please boys and be attractive to them. This makes a girl vulnerable to a boy's attempt to seduce her to prove his masculinity (Tighe).
7. All the media expose teenagers to sexual stimulation (Stepto et al.).
8. Illegitimacy can also be caused by mobility from rural to urban areas, where there are fewer social inhibitions concerning sexuality. The movement of rural Negroes has been shown to be a contributing factor to high nonwhite illegitimacy rates (Cutright).

Hazards of Teenage Pregnancy

The infant in an adolescent pregnancy is at high risk because of the pregnant teenager's underdevelopment physically, psychologically, and socially. Most American teenagers attain their full height and gynecologic maturity by 17 years of age (Stepto et al.). However, the average age of teenage mothers in the United States is 16 years (Jovanovic). When the teenage mother's body is not fully developed, complications occur, such as premature labor, low birth weight, neonatal mortality, toxemia, and anemia. A criterion for the readiness of the adolescent body to properly nurture a growing fetus is pelvic adequacy. Ballard and Gold indicate that determination of pelvic adequacy can be made between the ages of 14 and 15.

The mother's racial background and socioeconomic situation are also important factors. It is well known that the poor, for a variety of reasons, suffer more health disabilities than the nonpoor. Mortality rates for infants and mothers have disproportionately improved among the white population and socioeconomically favored individuals, in contrast to blacks and individuals on a lower socioeconomic level (Stepto et al.).

The female adolescent has not yet matured in terms of sexual identity. Consequently, some young mothers treat their infants as toys or rival siblings. The emotional immaturity of adolescent parents is a contributing factor in the battered infant syndrome (Harris). Pregnant teenage girls may also commit suicide (Stepto et al.). As the number of complications increases, the incidence of suicide rises among teenage pregnant girls (Gabrielson et al.). In the Middle East, unwed teenage mothers sometimes commit suicide or are murdered by their families because of sexual taboos ("Teenage Pregnancy").

The following is an overview of important issues in teenage pregnancy:

- There is a baby boom among today's teenage population; some causes are:
  Relaxation of the double standard
  Lower age of fertility
  Media exposure to sexual stimulation ("And Teenage Pregnancy"; Tighe).
- The teenager is at high risk because of physical, psychological, and social underdevelopment (Stepto et al.).
- Negative attitudes toward teenage sexuality and toward pregnancy among teenage girls are delaying the provision of educational, medical, and social service benefits to pregnant adolescents (Klerman and Jekel).
- The incidence of suicide rises among teenage pregnant girls (Gabrielson et al.). The emotional immaturity of adolescent parents is a contributing factor in the battered infant syndrome (Harris).

Nutrition is an important factor for an expectant mother of any age, but it is crucial for the pregnant adolescent. During adolescence, increased nutrition is needed because of the growth spurt. The dietary habits of adolescents are often the opposite of what they should be. Teenagers consume a large quantity of food sporadically, snacking on nonnutritious food and skipping meals. Their eating habits seem to correlate with what is happening to them developmentally. They are often in a state of turmoil as a result of the physical and psychological changes they are undergoing. They are neither children nor adults, and yet they are expected to be mature. For the teenage mother, it is doubly difficult to cope with the adolescent desire to be slim and the increase in appetite due to increased energy requirements (King and Jacobson).

The importance of nutrition to the pregnant woman is being increasingly recognized. Malnutrition among pregnant women can be related to limits placed on the amount of weight gain. Limited weight gain is no longer viewed as healthy for the expectant mother (Williams). A study by the National Institutes of Health has revealed that certain complications of pregnancy can be diminished as a result of a maternal weight gain of 30 to 34 lb or more. A Montreal nutrition education program involving poor and minimally educated pregnant women produced astounding results. The women gained more weight without complications and had bigger babies, and the health records of the infants were better than average (Williams). A megavitamin program, initially designed to alleviate symptoms of mental illness, could well be modified to benefit the adolescent expectant mother who is at high risk because of her immature and rapidly growing body and her poor eating habits.

Prevention

Preventive health care is necessary to counter the problems of teenage pregnancies. Cultural attitudes influence the type and quality of the services provided. In the United States, there is a stigma attached to early motherhood, and punitive action may be taken by schools and the family. Often the young woman must leave school; sometimes she is forced into marriage or is encouraged to have an abortion or give up her baby for adoption. When attitudes are not punitive, the system can benefit the adolescent. Sweden's social welfare orientation deemphasizes the stigma of illegitimacy, and appropriate provisions are made for the child. In Denmark, programs focus on total family needs; counseling, financial support, vocational training, and day-care facilities are provided. The Dutch have a network of centers for unwed mothers (Klerman and Jekel). Some Americans equate services for school-aged pregnant girls with an approbation of sexual activity and out-of-wedlock pregnancies among teenagers. However, the Dutch have the lowest rate of out-of-wedlock pregnancies in the world (Furstenburg).

Attitudes in the United States are slowly changing. In the 1960s special programs were designed for school-aged pregnant girls that enabled them to continue their education while receiving medical and social service benefits. The programs grew in number from 35 in 1968 to over 200 in 1972. Programs can be considered successful if the young women graduate from high school and if the intervals to their next pregnancies are lengthened. Assessment of these programs has been hindered by a lack of time, staff, and funds. The comprehensive programs serve a vital need, but they may not be effective unless they provide for continuing contact with the young mother after the baby is born (Klerman and Jekel).

Educational approaches must include interpersonal relationships and focus on providing information about the maturing adolescent body, family life, and methods of contraception. This information should be presented by sensitive and understanding professionals and lay people. Such approaches are crucial if the adolescent is to make intelligent choices instead of being guided by misinformation, myths, and street talk. We must also eradicate the belief that giving teenagers information about birth control will lead to an increase in their sexual activity. Hacker found that adolescents are less likely to use birth control methods if they are uninformed or feel uneasy about sex ("Birth Rate Is Moving up from Its 1976 Low-Point"). Furstenburg found that providing contraceptives to school-aged girls who had had one child did not increase their sexual activity. Legal implications and parental attitudes also delay the implementation of vital programs and services. However, laws are increasingly freeing the adolescent to obtain medical aid and contraceptive information without parental approval. Abortion is another factor that must be considered open-mindedly in relation to adolescent expectant mothers as well as expectant mothers of any age.

Birthrates are higher in lower socioeconomic areas. Economic deprivation can make the future seem bleak, and sexual activity can be an escape from the depressing aspects of the present (Klerman and Jekel). Reducing poverty is vital not only for the health of teenage mothers but also for the well-being of all people in all age groups and at all socioeconomic levels.

There is growing evidence that prenatal and birth experiences have an impact on the adult personality. *Behavior Today* ("Giant Steps toward a Prenatal

Psychology'') cites European reports demonstrating that the fetus is sensitive to sound, taste, and the daily rhythm of the mother and that it continues the mother's waking and sleeping patterns after birth. Studies done on animals have shown that a biochemical substance that is excreted as a result of stress has deleterious effects upon the fetus; human babies may well be affected in the same way. There is also evidence that we may have traces of memories of prenatal psychic life.

In New York, a natal therapy is being developed on the basis of the idea that the circumstances of one's birth are related to one's basic personality patterns. For example, people who were born prematurely could be predisposed to feelings of dependency and rejection. The therapy focuses on reexperiencing the birth process (''Natal Therapy Developed as Psychotherapeutic Adjunct''). Although this is not primary prevention work, it indicates the growing emphasis on prenatal and birth experiences as cogent factors in human development.

REFLECTIONS

The subject of childbirth is an enormous one and has not been discussed completely in this chapter. Many issues remain to be explored concerning the successful entrée of the infant into the world and its proper care afterward. I hope that the reader either was introduced to new concepts or had the opportunity to review previous knowledge concerning issues faced by care givers and families.

The following is a list of suggestions for care givers:

- Examine your attitude toward natural childbirth and avoid imposing your own values on prospective parents who are deciding on a method of childbirth.
- If appropriate, encourage fathers to be involved in the process, including delivery and care of the infant after birth.
- Make sure that the expectant mother knows exactly what to expect and do at the onset of labor (Tanzer).
- Work on any negative attitudes you may have concerning adolescent pregnancy and sexuality.
- Work to establish special programs for school-aged pregnant girls so that they can receive educational, medical, and social service benefits.
    The programs should last long enough so that there is continued contact with the young mother after the birth of her child (Klerman and Jekel). Educational approaches must include interpersonal relationships and information about the maturing adolescent body, family life, and contraception.

REFERENCES

"And Teenage Pregnancy: The Problems Are Not Mechanical," *Behavior Today,* 8(30):3, 1977.

Arms, Susanne: *Immaculate Deception: A New Look at Women and Childbirth in America,* Houghton Mifflin, Boston, 1975.

———: "Birth by the Book: Prenatal Primers," *The San Francisco Bay Guardian,* Aug. 25–Sept. 2, 1977, pp. 15–16.

Ballard, Walter M., and Edwin M. Gold: "Medical and Health Aspects of Reproduction in the Adolescent," *Clinical Obstetrics and Gynecology,* 14(2):338–366, 1971.

"Birth Rate Is Moving up from Its 1976 Low-Point," *Behavior Today,* 8(30):1–3, 1977.

Cianfrini, Theodore: *A Short History of Obstetrics and Gynecology,* Charles C Thomas, Springfield, Ill., 1960.

Cutright, Phillips: "The Rise of Teenage Illegitimacy in the United States: 1940–1971," in Jack Zackler and Wayne Brandstadt (eds.), *The Teenage Pregnant Girl,* Charles C Thomas, Springfield, Ill., 1975.

Dick-Read, Grantly: *Childbirth without Fear: The Original Approach to Natural Childbirth,* 4th ed. by Helen Wessel and Harlan F. Ellis (eds.), Harper & Row, New York, 1972.

Dodson, Fitzhugh: *How to Father,* New American Library, New York, 1975.

Ellis, Junius: "The Big Push toward Home Childbirth," *Moneysworth,* Oct. 11, 1976, pp. 16–17.

"Evidence of Gentler Babies," *The New York Times,* Jan. 30, 1977, p. 7:3.

Fager, Chuck: "The New Birth Movement: A Revolution That Starts at Home," *The San Francisco Bay Guardian,* Aug. 25–Sept. 2, 1977, pp. 11–13.

"For Those Who Can Afford Them, Brazilian Women Prefer Caesarean Birth," *The New York Times,* Jan. 4, 1971, p. 18: 1.

Furstenburg, Frank F., Jr.: "Preventing Unwanted Pregnancies among Adolescents," *Journal of Health and Social Behavior,* 12(4):340–347, 1971.

Gabrielson, Ira W., Lorraine V. Klerman, John B. Curie, Natalie C. Tyler, and James F. Jekel: "Suicide Attempts in a Population Pregnant as Teenagers," *American Journal of Public Health,* 60(12):2289–2301, 1970.

"Giant Steps toward a Prenatal Psychology," *Behavior Today,* 3(28)1–3, 1977.

Hancock, Graham: "Setting Out on the Road to Liberation," *San Francisco Sunday Examiner & Chronicle, Sunday Punch,* Sept. 11, 1977, p. 7.

Harris, Herbert X.: "The Range of Psychosomatic Disorders in Adolescence," in John G. Howells (ed.), *Modern Perspectives in Adolescent Psychiatry,* Brunner/Mazel, New York, 1971, pp. 237–253.

Herzog, Elizabeth: "Unmarried Mothers: The Service Gap Revisited," *Children,* 14(3):105–110, 1964.

"Illegitimate Births Rise for White Adolescents," *Behavior Today,* 7(11):3, 1975.

Jovanovic, D.: "Pathology of Pregnancy and Labor in Adolescent Patients," *Journal of Reproductive Medicine,* 9(61): 64–68, 1972.

Karmel, Marjorie: *Thank You, Dr. Lamaze: A Mother's Experiences in Painless*

Childbirth, Lippincott, Philadelphia, 1959; Dolphin Books, Garden City, N.Y., 1965.

Keniston, Kenneth, and The Carnegie Council on Children: *All Our Children: The American Family under Pressure,* Harcourt, Brace Jovanovich, New York, 1977.

King, Janet C., and Howard N. Jacobson: "Nutrition and Pregnancy in Adolescence," in Jack Zackler and Wayne Brandstadt (eds.), *The Teenage Pregnant Girl,* Charles C Thomas, Springfield, Ill., 1975.

Klerman, Lorraine V., and James F. Jekel: *School-Age Mothers: Problems, Programs and Policy,* Linnet Books, imprint of Shoe String Press, Hamden, Conn., 1973.

Leboyer, Frederick: *Birth without Violence,* Knopf, New York, 1975.

Liben, Florence: "Minority Group Clinic Patients Pregnant out of Wedlock," *American Journal of Public Health,* 59(10):1868–1881, 1969.

Maynard, Fredelle: "Home Births vs. Hospital Births," *Woman's Day,* June 28, 1977, pp. 10–12, 162–164.

Mead, Margaret, and Niles Newton: "Cultural Patterning of Perinatal Behavior," in Stephen A. Richardson and Alan F. Guttmacher (eds.), *Childbearing: Its Social and Psychological Aspects,* Williams & Wilkins, Baltimore, 1967.

Mindel, Valerie: "How to Do It—and Where?" *The San Francisco Bay Guardian,* Aug. 25–Sept. 2, 1977, pp. 13–15.

Monthly Vital Statistics Report, Advance Report, Final Natality Statistics, 1976, 26(12):4, March 29, 1978.

"Natal Therapy Developed as Psychotherapeutic Adjunct," *Behavior Today,* 7(40):3, 1976.

National Institute of Health: *Women and Their Pregnancies: A Collaborative Per-*inatal *Study of the National Institute of Neurological Disease and Stroke,* Superintendent of Documents, Washington, D.C., 1972.

Stepto, Robert C., Louis Keith, and Donald Keith: "Obstetrical and Medical Problems of Teenage Pregnancy," in Jack Zackler and Wayne Brandstadt (eds.), *The Teenage Pregnant Girl,* Charles C Thomas, Springfield, Ill., 1975.

Tanzer, Deborah, with Jean Libman Block: *Why Natural Childbirth? A Psychologist's Report on the Benefits to Mothers, Fathers and Babies,* Schocken Books, New York, 1972.

"Teenage Pregnancy," *San Francisco Sunday Examiner & Chronicle, This World,* Aug. 21, 1977, p. 23.

"Teenage Sexuality Today: How Does a Boy Say 'No'?" *Behavior Today,* 8(23): 5–6, 1977.

Tighe, Patti: "A Social Psychiatry View of Female Adolescent Contraception," in Lorraine V. Klerman and James F. Jekel (eds.), *School-Age Mothers: Problems, Programs and Policy,* Linnet Books, imprint of Shoe String Press, Hamden, Conn., 1973.

"The Trauma of Fatherhood: Bizarre Behavior Cited," *Behavior Today,* 7(36):4, 1976.

"Two Alcoholic Drinks a Day Can Cause Fetal Abnormalities, Institute Reveals," *Behavior Today,* 8(24):1, 1977.

Vincent, Clark E.: *Unmarried Mothers,* Free Press, New York, 1961.

Williams, Phyllis: *Nourishing Your Unborn Child,* Avon, New York, 1974.

Wolfe, Linda: "The Coming Baby Boom," *New York,* Jan. 10, 1977, pp. 38–42.

Zackarias, Leona, Richard J. Wurtman, and Martin Schatzoff: "Sexual Maturation in Contemporary American Girls," *American Journal of Obstetrics and Gynecology,* 108(5):833–846, 1970.

OTHER RESOURCES

FILMS

All My Babies: 55 min/1953. An award-winning documentary filmed in Georgia. It shows a licensed midwife giving prenatal care to two clients, delivering their babies, and accompanying them to a well-baby clinic. Restricted to professional use only. University of California, Extension Media Center, Berkeley, Calif. 94720.

Natural Childbirth: 30 min. A husband and wife are shown sharing the birth experience, with special emphasis on the father's role. Produced by Dr. Robert Bradley. Jay Hathaway Production Services, 4846 Katherine Avenue, Sherman Oaks, Calif. 91423.

The Story of Eric: 35 min/color/1971. Describes the rationale behind, and the technique of, Lamaze training for childbirth. A couple are followed through the wife's pregnancy and the delivery. Produced by the American Society of Psychoprophylaxis in Obstetrics, Los Angeles chapter.

Birth without Violence: 30 min/1974. Shows the Leboyer method of childbirth, which includes soothing background music. Produced by Frederick Leboyer (in France), New Yorker Films, 43 West 61st Street, New York, N.Y. 10023.

Loving Hands: 23 min/color. Shows a young mother practicing the traditional Indian art of infant massage. Directed by Frederick Leboyer, New Yorker Films, 43 West 61st Street, New York, N.Y. 10023.

Young, Single, and Pregnant: 18 min/color/1973. Depicts the advantages and disadvantages of solutions chosen by four teenage women to the problem of an unwanted pregnancy. One married the father and kept the baby, one opted for single parenthood, one put her baby up for adoption, and one had an abortion. University of California, Extension Media Center, Berkeley, Calif. 94720.

CHILDBIRTH INSTITUTES

Holistic Childbirth Institute
1627 Tenth Avenue
San Francisco, Calif. 94122
An association of independent professionals (childbirth educators, labor attendants, midwives, nurses, and physicians) and lay people that focuses on improving the quality of childbirth practices in the community. A certificate program for training holistic childbirth educators is offered, and a call-in resource file of doctors, midwives, and educators is available. The institute also sponsors workshops and symposia in communities and major cities for the purpose of discussing critical issues in childbirth.

Center for Family Growth
555 Highland Avenue
Cotati, Calif. 94928
A nonprofit educational corporation offering public education in the process of childbirth through yoga, natural childbirth training, parents' workshops, and family counseling.

Chapter 3

ME, MYSELF, AND I

Helen Elena Monea

I have a messy desk
I have milk money that rolls,
I have a lazy pencil,
a book that won't open,
a mouth that whispers,
I have a zipper that doesn't want to,
homework that won't work,
and a hand that throws crayons,
I have a shirt that's out,
shoelaces that won't tie.
And sometimes I wet my pants—
but never on purpose.

*Albert Cullum**

The poem above lists some of the concerns of preschool children, more and more of whom are now involved in educational experiences in a variety of settings: nursery schools, kindergartens, day-care centers, and Head Start programs. Instead of focusing on the growth and development of preschoolers, which are widely discussed in the literature, this chapter will touch on some of the history of preschool education and the implications of this type of experience for mothers and children. Because of limitations of space, children below preschool age are not discussed in this chapter. For discussions of children in this age group, the reader is referred to the work of Fraiberg (1959) and Thorp (1975).

* Albert Cullum, The Geranium on the Window Sill Just Died but Teacher You Went Right On, Dial, New York, 1971. Copyright by Harlinquist 1971.

Preschoolers have left the "magic" world of the baby and the toddler. Very young children have ceased believing that they can magically cause the appearance of the bottle or breast on demand or obtain sweets by saying "cookie" or "Mama." Growth and development are taking place rapidly. The "omnipotent magician" in the high chair soon finds that the audience—parents and educators—no longer believe in his or her magical powers. See Figure 3-1. Parents and educators of preschoolers bring reality, truth, and reason into their lives (Fraiberg).

NURSERY SCHOOLS

Nursery schools originated in England. The MacMillan sisters established the first such schools there at the beginning of World War I because many mothers were drawn into the war effort. The MacMillan sisters believed that the early years were crucial to later development, and in their schools they provided educational experiences and physical care. Montessori began her work in Italy, where she provided fine educational experiences for children living in the slums of Rome. American educators studied the early schools in England and Italy and then established similar ones in the United States (Taylor).

Cooperative Nursery Schools

The first cooperative nursery school in the United States was begun in 1916 by a group of faculty wives at the University of Chicago who wanted to obtain social education for their children and parent education for themselves and who also wanted some free time to do Red Cross work. The university provided them with professional guidance, and the school was conducted cooperatively with

Figure 3-1 The "American magician." *(Courtesy of Phyllis Eggert.)*

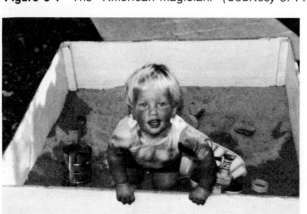

a trained teacher. Parent cooperatives followed in the 1920s on the East and West Coasts and then spread to Seattle, British Columbia, and the Midwest (Taylor).

"I just didn't know how interesting my daughter was until I watched her here. At home I'm so busy taking care of her and a thousand other things I've never really seen her before as the fascinating *person* she is" (Taylor, p. 27). This mother was describing her experience in a cooperative nursery school. Many mothers have only limited time in which to really get to know their own children. The cooperative nursery school offers mothers the opportunity to gain an understanding of their children, and this understanding gradually begins to replace judgmental attitudes. Instead of thinking how badly a child is behaving, the mother comes to understand why he or she is behaving in that particular way and how to help the child. Another mother describes this kind of understanding: "Jason went out to paint—I followed him—so different from last year when he followed me! . . . Jason gives me a great big smile as he runs past me. I think he is enjoying his new found independence as much as I am" (Kester).

In the cooperative nursery school, the teacher and the parents *together* are responsible for the entire educational program. The teacher is often an employee of the parents' group and may also supervise the parents' work, consult with them about the children's growth and development, and guide the children into various activities. In the case of parents who cannot set up such preschool groups—for example, culturally deprived parents in low-income brackets—some adult education departments pay the teacher and provide office space. Taylor met with low-income groups once weekly and noticed remarkable improvements in the children's socialization and creativity as well as in parental insight. At the end of the term, the parents were asked to write about or discuss their experience. They were told not to worry about spelling and grammar. One mother, responding to an inquiry about how her parenting skill had been affected, said, "You don't need to hit the children to make 'em mind. They understand talk" (Taylor, p. 168).

Parent-teacher relationships are usually warm and cooperative, although a few disagreements are normal. Sometimes the teacher's past experience with his or her own parents interferes in the relationship. A teacher may be more comfortable relating to children than to parents. On the other side, the *mothers may feel threatened by the teacher, whom they consider a specialist in child development*. A very young teacher who has never had children can feel threatened by the mothers' broader experience.

Clarification of roles reduces anxieties and friction. One way to do this is to have the parents write simple lists of the things they expect from the teacher and to have the teacher enumerate the things he or she expects from the parents. Exchanging these expectations can increase mutual trust and enhance the children's learning experience. One teacher, who was very sensitive to mothers, fondly said: "I'm only one, and there are twenty of you. You can see more things than I about what we should do here. If you think of something special it would be good to do on your day, phone me about it and we'll plan together" (Taylor, p. 280). Developing this sense of "we" and using the mothers' skills and knowledge make the learning experience richer for the children, the mothers, and the teacher.

Day Care and Other Realities

Day care was developed a century ago. It gained in popularity after World War I because of a variety of needs and attitudes: fatherless families, deprived mothers who were suffering from economic or emotional difficulties, and children who needed better care and extra educational assistance. The attitude that society should accept new responsibilities for the development and care of children, using the best available resources to equip them to live in a rapidly changing society, contributed to changes in family structure and freed women to seek fulfillment outside the home (Steinfels and Steinfels).

Day-care facilities face the problem of a lack of qualified staff members, and this results in custodial-type care and/or inappropriate care. Even teachers who are highly creative and give warmly to children must spread their attention among many children. This is a typical problem faced by public school teachers as well. Untrained staff members who are not knowledgeable concerning children's growth and developmental needs may fear children. Another problem is that the difference between discipline at home and discipline at school can confuse children and cause frustration or withdrawal. For example, one teacher told a class that it was dangerous to put candles in jack-o'-lanterns. Later at home, one of the youngsters was distressed when the family put candles in some jack-o'-lanterns. The teacher had been trying to tell the children not to *carry* or *play with* jack-o'-lanterns containing candles. The youngster, however, could not reconcile what the teacher had said with what the family was doing (Ebersole).

Sometimes a child spends 12 h a day (6 A.M. to 6 P.M.) or longer in a day-care center while a parent works. The child usually has a quick supper and must go to bed before he or she can share the day's experiences. When both child and parent have had such a day, neither has the energy to nurture their relationship.

I have observed some professionals in preschool settings who are overzealous in their views and who impose their philosophies on parents, who resent the assistance. For instance, a psychologist who was highly skilled in behavior modification wanted to help a black woman who had the responsibility of raising a granddaughter. The psychologist suggested that the child attend a Head Start program, which the child strongly resisted. The grandmother was bewildered by the direction of the help and viewed it as further "spoiling" the child. The child was grieving for her natural mother. Possibly a play therapy situation, in which she could have worked out her separation anger, would have been more constructive.

Head Start Programs

Head Start programs were originated in an attempt to prepare children for kindergarten who otherwise would not be ready in terms of socialization and cognitive skills. The programs began as a summer project for 3- to 5-year-olds.

The Office of Economic Opportunity created them as part of President Lyndon Johnson's "war on poverty." Later, the programs were conducted on a year-round basis under the direction of the U.S. Department of Health, Education, and Welfare. Over 6 million children have completed the program at a cost of approximately $3½ billion. Programs are also conducted on Indian reservations; these are run by tribal councils. There are also special programs for migrant workers that provide care for children as young as 2 years of age. The annual operating cost of Head Start programs has increased to $475 million for 1977; this averages out to $1505 per child in the year-round programs and $175 per child in the summer sessions ("Operation Head Start: Still Going Strong").

The main goal of such programs is to enrich the lives of children from poor families who are deprived by lack of motivation, ill health, and/or their parents' ignorance about educational opportunities. Most Head Start programs involve the parents in varying degrees; for example, they may serve as teachers' aides or work on committees. The programs have been reported to be successful; studies of youngsters who were involved in the initial session in 1965 and who are now prospective high school graduates indicate that they are ahead of their peers who did not participate in the program ("Operation Head Start: Still Going Strong").

One innovation in some Head Start programs has been to include physically handicapped children. However, teachers who lack experience with the handicapped are often unable to deal with such children. Some youngsters in the classroom may shy away from a handicapped child, while others may touch the child or stare curiously. Physically disabled children may have to be excluded from Head Start programs because staff members are not trained to work with them.

GRAND CARE GIVERS

Senior citizens are becoming involved in the necessary task of helping care for preschoolers through a variety of programs: the Foster Grandparent program, retired senior citizens' volunteer programs, and local community volunteer organizations. The older adult has the delightful experience of being a "grand care giver," enjoying the responsibility and the nurturing relationship, while the child gains from the caring older adult. Each helps the other through caring and sharing, and the older adult contributes wisdom and experience. Generally, such relationships are fruitful and beneficial for staff members, the child, and the older adult. However, like any other relationship, these can go awry. Senior volunteers and staff members occasionally find the experience trying. See Figure 3-2.

One older adult shared his frustration with me. He was not able to establish a relationship with some of the children. He was too rigid, and his energy was quickly depleted. He was not in step with the philosophy of the school, where the children were expected to discover things for themselves. The adults in the school were there to assist the children in their discoveries, not to direct or instruct them. The children perceived this man's help as interference and reacted

Figure 3-2. Not all youngsters have preschool experience. Some play in the community, where relationships with older people in the neighborhood may evolve naturally. *(Courtesy of Harvey Finkle.)*

to it strongly. I suspect that the experience was more difficult for the man than for the youngsters, since he needed and wanted to be with children. Their rejection added to his low self-esteem. In such situations, alternatives may be considered: (1) change the grand care giver's expectations through training, (2) give closer support and supervision, and (3) assign him or her to children who can handle more direct guidance. Too often, staff members do not have time to work through such difficulties, and the grand care giver leaves. Teachers are also becoming more skilled at selecting grand care givers, and they choose older adults who will fit into their programs, thus preventing conflict. See Figure 3-3.

In matching older adults with younger children, one must also consider the attitudes of the children toward aging. In a recent study conducted by graduate researchers at the University of Maryland, children between the ages of 3 and 11 were interviewed; the children tended to view the elderly as "sick, sad, tired, dirty and ugly," feeling that they would never be old themselves ("How Children View the Elderly," p. 4). Previous experience with older adults may influence a child's attitude toward the elderly. See Figure 3-4.

CHILD CARE: A SOCIALIST APPROACH

The socialist approach to raising young children is to encourage participation in day-care centers. The differences between child-rearing practices in the United

States and those in socialist countries are a function of societal goals. Americans place the primary responsibility for raising children on the family, while in the Soviet Union the responsibility is thought to rest with persons or groups outside the family, such as in communal or collective settings (Bronfenbrenner). Nearly 80 percent of Russian women are employed, which has caused the responsibility of child rearing to shift from the family to public institutions. This reinforces the Soviet ideology of favoring communal child rearing, which encourages conformity and collectivist ideals (Jacoby).

Although the communal day-care system is favored, there is a gap between theory and practice. Despite expanding preschool facilities, only 10 percent of Soviet children under age 2, and 20 percent of those between the ages of 3 and 7, are enrolled in nurseries or kindergartens (Jacoby). A contributing factor is parental ambivalence about placing a child in an institutional setting. The *babushka* (grandmother) takes care of the children at home, which is the preferred arrangement. Babushkas and other aging relatives play an important role in

Figure 3-3 The older adult must be carefully screened for volunteer work. This woman, because of her hearing aid, may have difficulty doing such work. *(Courtesy of Patricia A. Gibson.)*

Figure 3-4 Some children are fortunate to have a warm relationship with a grandparent, which can foster a child's sense of identity and self-worth. The grandparent is rewarded by the satisfaction of being instrumental in the child's development. *(Courtesy of Pat Song.)*

Russian children's lives. Three-generation households are common, and Russian families are less mobile in terms of geographic location than families in the United States. However, as the Soviet government responds to young married couples' growing demand for housing suited to the nuclear family rather than the three-generation family, child-rearing practices will undergo change. Middle-aged Soviet women have more education and work experience, and this has influenced their attitudes. Some say that when they become grandparents, they do not want to stay home and take care of their grandchildren.

I heard similar views expressed when, as a member of a United States and Romanian health-team exchange visit, I visited agencies and homes in Romania. In one town only 10 percent of the children were enrolled in *crèches* (nurseries). I learned that all children aged 3 and up would be required to attend *gradenitas* (preschools) by 1980. See Figure 3-5. Although the educators stressed that the purpose of the ruling was to prepare preschoolers for kindergarten, there were more powerful influences. Through confidential communication with other professionals, I learned that the government's goal is to build Romania into a strong industrial country by having all the people work and to reinforce the ideology of the socialist government, i.e., that the group, not the individual, is important. What better way than to begin with the very young (Monea, Boldi, Coopersmith, Jampolsky, and Tilden)?

THE ISSUE OF RESPONSIBILITY

Child-care issues in the socialist countries and the United States are similar. Responsibility for children is an issue in the United States (Payne), and the Soviets ask whether institutional care adequately replaces family care during the early years of a child's life and how well institutions meet the needs of children (Jacoby). To find answers to these questions, we need to look at a deeper issue, *our own philosophy of parenting care* (Payne). As discussed in Chapter 1, developing our own philosophy provides a basis for giving therapeutic care. Helping a parent to decide whether a child should be cared for at home or in another setting requires a sensitivity to that parent's attitudes, culture, and beliefs as well as sufficient knowledge concerning the implications of the type

Figure 3-5 Romanian preschoolers scramble to the school gate as American visitors arrive. *(Courtesy of Helen Monea.)*

of care selected for the growth and development of the child. If we are strongly biased in favor of a particular approach, naturally we cannot be sufficiently objective to help a parent make such decisions.

Lief, a psychiatrist, offers an unconventional alternative to the current policy of supporting day-care centers ("The Alternative to Day Care: Motherhood"). If the government would consider subsidizing mothers so that they could stay at home with their children, those who preferred to be with their children would be able to. Lief also recommends more flexible schedules for mothers of young children.

The following list provides an overview of issues in child care:

- A variety of programs have been developed to care for the preschooler; these evolved from the educational or economic needs of families. Those which are based on educational philosophies, such as Montessori programs and Head Start programs, may prepare children for kindergarten more adequately in terms of socialization and cognitive skills.
- The culture and the political ideology of a country influence who takes responsibility for developing and implementing programs:
   Socialist ideology holds that the group is important, not the individual. The state assumes the responsibility for providing group day-care facilities and strongly advocates that parents leave youngsters in these settings. American ideology is based on individualism; parents are expected to take the major responsibility for deciding whether a preschooler stays at home or attends a day-care facility.
- Staff members need special knowledge and training in child development in order to give optimum care in any type of child-care program.
- Sensitivity to, and understanding of, parents' attitudes, cultural background, and beliefs are crucial to successful teaching and child care. In order to prevent conflict in the child, there must be consistency between the values, discipline, and directions he or she is exposed to in the home and at school.
- In a cooperative nursery school, parents gain a deeper understanding of their children by observing them and writing down their observations.
- In cooperative nursery schools, a mother may feel threatened by a teacher, who represents expertise in child development; conversely, the teacher can feel threatened by her own inexperience and view the mother as an expert in child care.
- Older adults are increasingly being involved as grand care givers with preschoolers. Careful screening and appropriate matching ensure a successful experience for both the child and the older person. The young child's attitude toward aging is crucial in the match.

Day care, whether educational or custodial, is here to stay. The traditional attitude that children belong at home with their mothers until they are ready for kindergarten is rapidly changing. As will be discussed in Chapter 4, more women are becoming dissatisfied with the role of full-time housekeeper and mother;

many are finding jobs and placing their children in day-care centers. Middle-class mothers who are concerned with enriching their children's development select a preschool program not because it provides care but because it will enhance the child's emotional and physical well-being.

The direction in which early childhood care and education evolve will have many implications for the growth and development of preschool children. The care given a preschool child can increase or decrease the child's anxiety about "a mouth that whispers" or "milk money that rolls."

REFERENCES

"The Alternative to Day Care: Motherhood," *Behavior Today,* **7**(43):3, 1976.

Bronfenbrenner, Urie: *Two Worlds of Childhood: U.S. and U.S.S.R.,* Simon and Schuster, New York, 1972.

Cullum, Albert: *The Geranium on the Window Sill Just Died but Teacher You Went Right On,* Dial, New York, 1971.

Ebersole, Priscilla: Personal communication, November 1977.

Fraiberg, Selma H.: *The Magic Years: Understanding and Handling the Problems of Early Childhood,* Scribner, New York, 1959.

"How Children View the Elderly," *Input,* **5**(3):4, 1977.

Jacoby, Susan: "Who Raises Russia's Children?" *Saturday Review,* Aug. 21, 1971, pp. 40–43.

Kester, Lorraine: Personal communication, November 1977.

Monea, Helen E., Mary Boldi, Stanley Coopersmith, Gerald Jampolsky, and **Steve Tilden:** "The Education–Mental Health Team Exchange Visit to Roumania," manuscript prepared for the U.S. Department of Health, Education, and Welfare, East-West Exchange Program, Office of International Health, Rockville, Md., 1974.

"Operation Head Start: Still Going Strong," *U.S. News and World Report,* **83**(5):67, 1977.

Payne, Patricia A.: Day Care and Its Impact on Parenting," *Nursing Clinics of North America,* **12**(3):525–533, 1977.

Steinfels, Peggy, and **Peter Steinfels:** "Day Care: Patchwork Realization, or Utopia?" in Arlene Skolnick and Jerome H. Skolnick (eds.), *Intimacy, Family and Society,* Little, Brown, Boston, 1974, pp. 415–432.

Taylor, Katharine Whiteside: *Parents and Children Learn Together,* Teachers College, New York, 1967.

Thorp, Isobel H.: "The Toddler: 1–3 Years," in Gladys M. Scipien, Marilyn A. Chard, Jeanne Howe, Martha Underwood Bernard, and Patricia J. Phillips (eds.), *Comprehensive Pediatric Nursing,* McGraw-Hill, New York, 1975.

OTHER RESOURCES

FILMS

Day Care Today: 30 min/color/1973. Shows three community-oriented day-care centers for children of factory employees and university-related training centers. Includes comments by child-care workers and parents. Distributor: University of California, Extension Media Center, Berkeley, Calif. 94720.

Nursery School Child–Mother Interaction: Three Head Start Children and Their Mothers: 41 min/1969. Focuses on the mother's role in the child's alertness to the environment and in the child's social adjustment. Three black mothers and their 4-year-old boys are shown. Produced and narrated by Dr. Marianne Marschak of New York University. Distributor: University of California, Extension Media Center, Berkeley, Calif. 94720.

The Education–Mental Health Team Exchange Visit to Roumania: 10 min/color/ slide-tape. Focuses on the education, health, and welfare of Romanian children. A segment on nursery schools and kindergartens is included, and the professionals are shown visiting various government agencies. Produced and narrated by Steve Tilden for the U.S. Department of Health, Education, and Welfare.

PERIODICALS AND PUBLICATIONS

Children: Published by the Children's Bureau, U.S. Government Printing Office, Division of Public Documents, Washington, D.C. 20402.

The Parent Cooperative: Newsletter of Parent Cooperative Pre-schools International (quarterly), P.O. Box 40123, Indianapolis, Ind. 46240.

ORGANIZATIONS

Child Study Association of America
9 East 89th Street
New York, N.Y. 10028

Association for Childhood Education International
3615 Wisconsin Avenue, N.W.
Washington, D.C. 20016

National Education Association (NEA)
1201 Sixteenth Street, N.W.
Washington, D.C. 20036

Chapter 4

EMERGING FAMILIES: EFFECTS ON CHILDREN

Helen Elena Monea

A family to me is sharing with each other about our thoughts and dreams and our wonders. Families should be proud to all have the same last name. That's what a family should be.

Junior high school student

A family is people who share hardship together. My family's motto is "One for all and all for one."

Junior high school student

A family is a group—two or more people or sometimes a person and a pet. They may or may not reside together, but they do provide some emotional input and interaction. They are bound together by some common goals. Sexual satisfaction and protection of the young may be some shared expectations.

Young adult

A family is a unit composed of two or more interacting members. Needless to say, types of families differ greatly depending on cultural values, social and economic status, and forces from within and from without. There are expanding families, one-parent families, older families, extended families, etc. Each has individual needs. One associates families with two or more people, but one of the most neglected families is that of the senior citizen, who is left alone to survive in our communities.

Young adult

The quotations above and in Figure 4-1 reveal that the word "family" can have many meanings, depending upon one's orientation and personal experiences. Traditionally, a family consists of adults and children who live together either in an extended situation, which includes grandparents, or in a nuclear situation, which includes only two parents and their children. Changes in society, such as the single-parent family and communal living, are modifying the meaning of "family." As another alternative, many couples are now choosing to remain childless.

HISTORICAL PERSPECTIVE

Historically, families have been established to meet particular needs. During the Middle Ages, marriages were planned for the purpose of transferring property between two families. The industrial revolution witnessed the breakdown of the self-sufficient extended family into smaller units, with a subsequent transference of duties such as education of children to the schools and with mass-produced goods replacing those made by family members. Today's family is also meeting

Figure 4-1 What is a family? *(Courtesy of a young boy.)*

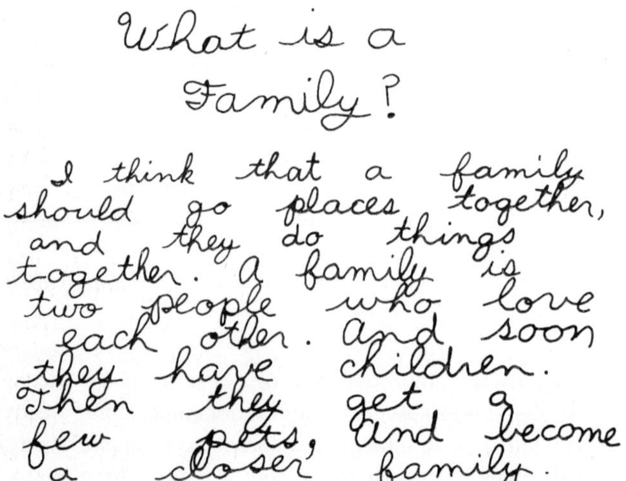

> What is a
> Family?
>
> I think that a family
> should go places together,
> and they do things
> together. A family is
> two people who love
> each other. And soon
> they have children.
> Then they get a
> few pets, and become
> a closer family.

Figure 4-2 In the past, families were photographed with the father seated and the mother standing; the photographer encouraged them to look serious. Were these the good old days? After reading this chapter, look at this photograph again and think about the ways in which families have changed since it was taken. *(Courtesy of Helen Monea.)*

different needs. In the past, marriage was based primarily on economic need. Now, the concept of marriage includes fulfillment of emotional, physical, and economic needs, and there is a mixture of attitudes about how these needs should be met. These expanded expectations of the family are affecting family patterns and, consequently, children (McCary). See Figure 4-2.

The emerging family pattern is based on mutual affection, equality, and autonomy (Burgess, Locke, and Thomes). Elder cites studies tracing the origin of this companionship system to the generation of children born during World War I, who reached marrying age in the early 1930s. Important changes that occurred included (1) greater equality and sharing in marriage; (2) less punitive, more supportive relations with children; and (3) greater flexibility in allowing children to make their own decisions. The more ready availability of higher education has been cited as a factor in the egalitarianism of young couples in the 1930s.

Farber interprets changes in family patterns as being due to the Depression, which encouraged breaks with the past by heightening discontent with traditional life-styles. Elder makes the opposite interpretation: The hardships endured by families during the Depression resulted in a loss of affection and feelings of companionship among family members. Although some families were brought into closer harmony by a common hardship, others were strained to the breaking point. Evidence suggests that socioeconomic security favored the emergence of companionship in family relationships, particularly in middle-class families.

Changes in children from deprived families were consistently in a conservative direction, toward traditional values and relationships. *A high priority of family life for men and women from deprived backgrounds is having children, rather than establishing marital understanding or companionship.* These value orientations among Depression children cannot be traced to educational or occupational status (Elder).

THE DILEMMA OF MODERN MARRIAGE

One dilemma of modern marriage concerns the expectation that both the emotional and the economic needs of the husband and wife should be met. This changing expectation of marriage causes dysfunction in working-class families, where there is the least incentive for change (Rubin). The woman in the working-class family assumes the role of housewife and mother, while the husband assumes the controlling and authoritative role. The women who participated in Rubin's study came from working-class families and were aware that they were unhappy. Some attempted to improve communication with their husbands, but without success. The men were aware of their wives' discontent but did not know what to do about it. Because of financial pressures and boring, unsatisfying jobs, many of the men turned to drinking, engaged in violent behavior, or withdrew in silent despair (Rubin). The children suffered in many ways. They were exposed to values of a larger society which demeaned their parents' accomplishments and way of life and therefore made the parents less acceptable as role models. The parents had less respite from their responsibilities because they would trust only grandparents or relatives as baby-sitters. For those who did use unrelated baby-sitters, economic considerations limited the amount of diversion they could afford. Rubin found their world to be full of pain.

COMMUNE FAMILIES

The commune family combines characteristics of both the extended family and the companionship system. The "hip" (middle-class) communes are a reaction against middle-class American values. Freedom of expression is given high priority. Living together as brothers and sisters, without a hierarchical system of power, is a goal; however, such families do have recognized leaders. Many communal homes are decorated colorfully and imaginatively. Casual pillows for seating, candlelight, incense, and mandalas (an Eastern symbol of the universe—

see Chapter 10) provide a relaxed, peaceful, and mystical atmosphere. Naturalness is highly valued in food, clothing, and architecture. Spontaneity is upheld, often at the expense of a member's privacy. Conflicts do arise, however, over privacy, communal sharing, work, and money (Berger, Hackett, and Millar).

Communal ideology has serious consequences for children. Children are considered autonomous human beings who are equal to adults. Most important, parents are not held responsible for their children's behavior, as in most middle-class American families. Although the philosophy is to treat children as equals, there are different patterns of care for different children. Mothers have the primary responsibility for infants and "knee babies," and an infant may be placed at any breast, not only its mother's (Berger et al.). Although the commune may consider this a radical idea, the "wet-nurse" role has existed for centuries. Children are fed, bathed, and toileted in groups. The 2- to 4-year-olds, who are less dependent on continuous supervision, are cared for by a group of mothers. Fathers are not required to be attentive; however, some do participate in feeding, cuddling, and playing with children. See Figure 4-3. Children over 5 years of age are expected to behave like other members of the family, including participating in marijuana "hits" in the family circle (Berger et al.).

Children in communal families are affected by the attitudes toward them and the interpersonal relationships between them and the adults. Children are considered worthy of love and respect but not necessarily attention. Some commune mothers are not completely devoted to their own children. They view their own lives as unsettled and their futures as uncertain, and they are unwilling to sacrifice their need for personal growth and identity to full-time child rearing. Hip relationships are fragile; when tension arises, *there are few cultural or structural constraints to sustain the relationship.* Consequently, a child's natural parents are not always available. Because of limited space and the attitude that normal functions need not be hidden from public view, children are regularly exposed to sexual activities. The sexist creed does not prevail in any hip commune, but

Figure 4-3   Commune child and father. *(Courtesy of Priscilla Ebersole.)*

women do tend to do the traditional work of cleaning, cooking, and child care. There are exceptions, and some women assume leadership roles, but on the whole they are less expressive and forceful than men about ideological issues (Berger et al.).

The above description is of one mode of communal living; many others are evolving. For example, a group of "straight" couples may share one house, or groups of single people and married couples with children may live together. There are also rural settlements in which couples live in single dwellings on the same property and share in the communal work. The trend toward group living may continue for several reasons: (1) It is a way of combating dehumanizing aspects of our society, (2) it meets the need for caring and being cared for, and (3) it is a way of collectively coping with rising prices and a growing scarcity of space. Table 4-1 lists the implications for family life of conventional and countercultural family patterns. In terms of the issues of child rearing, labor, sex, care of the aged, and religion, the "conventional family appears to place second best to the counterculture potential," although neither shows great promise (Whitehurst, p. 399).

CHILDREN AND THEIR NEEDS

Family circumstances are critical in determining a child's development, since 98 percent of all children are raised in families (Keniston and The Carnegie Council on Children). Considering the needs of children and parents is crucial in helping families with children. We must keep in mind all aspects of growth and development and be open to new theories; for instance, Maslow's concept of the hierarchy of needs (that the basic needs for food, shelter, and clothing must be satisfied before higher-level needs can arise) may not be completely true. As another example, the theory that nourishment is a primary source of attachment to the mother by the infant is no longer well supported. "Now it is held that all human needs are inter-related and inter-dependent in a subtle, complex and continuous way. For example, an unhappy baby may reject food and, even if he takes it, he may fail to thrive; or a child may fight sleep for fear that his mother or father may leave home" (Pringle, p. 33).

Gross and Macewan have identified the following important abilities that children will learn if their needs are met:

1. The ability to feel deeply and be sensitive toward other people
2. The ability to trust themselves and use their initiative
3. The ability to solve problems in a creative and collective way

The following needs have been identified as important in children's lives (Pringle):

1. *The need for love.* Children need a stable, continuous, dependable, and unconditional loving relationship with their parents or other significant persons. This forms a basis for later relationships and for the development of self-approval, self-acceptance, and a positive self-identity.

Table 4-1. Evaluation of Conventional and Counterculture Families

Problem or Issue	Conventional	Counterculture
Child-rearing	Inhibited, control-oriented, achievement, competition, conditional love, insecurity in isolation	Child as "treasure," relative freedom, cooperation, security in multiple adults
Labor, economics, leisure	Private economic struggle, materialism as an end, sex-role stereotypes, cash- and things-oriented leisure	Economic sharing, utility orientation toward things, attempt to break stereotypes, simple leisure and productive recreation
Conflicts	Inhibited, circumscribed conflict by "rules" and games, little growth and change, stable tensions unresolved	Growth- and change-oriented, open tension toward either resolution or breakup, more options for change
Family solidarity	Externally derived, often contrived and artificially supported, ingenuine at times but secure	Internally derived, at times primarily a response to external pressures, normative struggle to create rules, order
Privacy	At times may be too much, (children?) but in general implies isolation of the family unit	Mostly too little currently due to norms of sharing and economic privations, making housing a problem, need for better information
Sex	Inhibiting, but with "approved" adaptations, essentially nonproductive of growth—rather encourages duplicity and gaming (e.g. sexuality) cocktail party	Sensual hedonism, respect for variations, openness, but with problems of working in normative vacuum (or within old cultural framework hanging over)
The aged	Little place, little promise	Little place, some promise—based on idea of return to older forms utilizing aged
Religion	Social control oriented, externally supported, ritualized for control purposes, guilt-directed	Meditative, self-unity oriented, noninstitutionalized, at times community directed, personal-natural, integrative, positive, accepting

Source: Whitehurst, p. 400, © 1972, by the National Council on Family Relations. Reprinted with permission.

2. *The need for security.* Children need the security of a stable family relationship in which expectations, attitudes, and behavior are consistent and dependable. The security of a familiar environment and established routines gives children a base line for meeting the responsibilities associated with maturing and for coping with the outside world.

3. *The need for new experiences.* In order to achieve optimal mental growth, children need to be exposed to new experiences and to master increasingly difficult age-appropriate tasks. Play allows for integration between children's inner feelings and the outside world; during play, children learn to handle their emotions and gain control over their bodies. Using language develops children's reasoning ability, increases their understanding of the world around them, and facilitates their communication in interpersonal relationships.

4. *The need for praise and recognition.* Children need loving adults to give them an incentive to overcome the difficulties of emotional, social, and intellectual learning. Adults should offer praise and recognition of a child's accomplishments and should gear their expectations to the child's capabilities.

5. *The need for responsibility.* Children need to practice being independent under adult guidance; this increases their confidence in decision making and their awareness and understanding of their feelings and emotions.

PARENTS AND THEIR NEEDS

Our society tends to blame parents, making them feel guilty for their children's mental and/or physical dysfunction; they are seldom viewed with compassion, as human beings capable of making mistakes. When we blame parents for their children's deficiencies, we overlook many facts about the dynamics of human development and the effect of the larger environment. The development of the child's personality does not depend on parenting alone; biological and environmental aspects are also contributing factors. We must understand all aspects of total family needs and plan effective programs in light of this understanding (Joint Commission on Mental Health of Children).

If we are to help children, we must first help parents. Parents have the following important needs:

1. Parents need a respite from family responsibilities; work, hobbies, and other activities of interest provide this.

2. Parents need emotional support as they face the realities of parenthood (McBride).

3. Parents need to understand themselves, changes in their marriage, and their own expectations of their children.

4. Parents need to find new ways of relating to, and caring for, their children. Time should be set aside for child-parent contact, and an informal neighborhood support system for child care should be established (Bronfenbrenner, 1977).

5. Parents need to understand their children's growth and developmental needs (Dodson).
6. Because of our increasingly complex social, economic, and health systems, parents need to learn to function as coordinators and advocates for their children (Keniston and The Carnegie Council on Children).
7. Parents need to be able to provide a sufficient income for their families; this enhances their own self-concept and the self-concepts of their children (Keniston and The Carnegie Council on Children).

Parental Roles

Changing family functions and definitions affect the role of parents. The father, for instance, has usually been considered the breadwinner, spending less time in the home and taking less responsibility for child care. This imposed role has weakened relationships between fathers and children and has caused discontent among mothers, who are usually burdened by child-care responsibilities, household duties, and sometimes jobs outside the home. Women are becoming increasingly dissatisfied with their roles and are suffering from feelings of isolation, boredom, and loss of identity. Their role in marriage is not conducive to mental or physical health. According to one study, the healthiest women are single. The least healthy men are single, and the healthiest men are married. Married women show the most signs of physical and mental strain (Bernard). As they become increasingly dissatisfied with their roles, women are searching for work and/or interests outside the home, and there is a consequent trend toward involving husbands in an extended role of child guardian and housekeeper. The core problem is that men have too few roles in family life, which restricts their personalities, while women have a multiplicity of roles, which exhausts their energy (Green). A wider range of possibilities for both is needed.

The father's role in the family is in danger of becoming extinct unless it is re-created or redefined (Green). The masculine role needs to include caring for children, and men must have opportunities to gain an understanding of child development and child care so that they will feel at ease with their children (Green). Society's attitudes toward the man's role in child care will change slowly, however, since the man has usually been the provider. Mead (1953) has found that many societies assign different tasks to males and females but that, inevitably, the males' tasks are more prestigious. Fathers are viewed as less vital in parenting, and therefore less value is attached to their role as parents. However, children need fathers as well as mothers. The advantages for children of dual parenting are difficult to achieve outside marriage (Green). Since dual parenting is important, fathers and mothers must plan opportunities to spend time with their children. In some countries—Spain, for example—such planning is easier because all activity stops for several hours during the afternoon; businesses close, and families can have late lunches together.

Guidelines to assure that marriages will allow for children's well-being may evolve. Mead (1970) suggests two models: (1) a marriage in which there are to be no children and in which an option for divorce is made easy; and (2) a marriage in which the couple's primary satisfaction would be the raising of children and from which divorce would be made very difficult. Both kinds of marriage could be possible with the same partner. As a third alternative, we might reduce divorce rates by creating more socially acceptable ways in which married people could satisfy their emotional needs outside the marriage (Green). Underlying all the options would be the major guideline that people who choose to become parents should genuinely want to love and care for a child and, above all, should have the ability to be responsible parents. See Figure 4-4.

SINGLE-PARENT FAMILIES

More and more people are becoming single parents as a result of death of a spouse, divorce, or separation. Some single people are also adopting children.

Figure 4-4 The family and baby. *(Courtesy of Sammy Woog, aged 5½.)*

From 1970 to 1977, the percentage of children living with a female parent increased from 11 to 16 percent. The largest percentages of increase were among children living with a divorced or never-married mother. The percentage of children living with a father or with neither father nor mother increased only marginally (U.S. Bureau of the Census). Horowitz and Perdue describe the problems of a one-parent family living in a two-parent-oriented society. The single parent may be overloaded, both emotionally and in terms of work and responsibilities. The single parent may also feel guilty about a child who does not have a parent of the same sex with whom to identify. Although some research has indicated that the absence of one parent does not necessarily endanger the child's gender identity (Heilbrun), the attitude still prevails that two parents are better than one. Another problem that single parents face is unlimited opportunities to express their sexuality.

Multiple demands, limited resources, and loneliness often cause depression in single parents, which affects their functioning and may make their children feel insecure, guilty, and fearful. Professionals often have negative and biased attitudes toward single-parent families. Horowitz and Perdue believe that a support system should be established to help single parents develop better social skills and self-assessment skills so that they can better cope with their problems.

Single Men as Parents

An increasing number of divorced fathers are becoming heads of single-parent families. There is some prejudice against fathers' gaining custody of their children after a divorce because men are viewed as lacking nurturing capabilities. This attitude may result in a child's being put in the custody of the mother even when he or she would be happier and better off with the father. Historically, women have been viewed as better able to care for children, and the courts still adhere to this idea. We need to consider which is the most competent parent. Victor and Winkler interviewed single divorced fathers and found that those who had full custody of their children either had taken prime responsibility for child care and the home during the marriage or were more interested in challenge than in security and had good coping abilities. McFadden found that single fathers were flexible in every area of their lives; they wondered whether this characteristic was acquired as a result of the experience of single fatherhood or whether the male who takes the responsibility of parenting is a flexible individual to begin with. See Figure 4-5.

Becoming a single father usually means learning about the daily care of children. Some fathers adapt readily. One father commented that the home and the children were easier to manage since his wife left. He said that he and the children could make decisions without having to consider another adult's opinion.

Studies on single men as parents are being conducted in major universities, and a National Center for Child Custody Information is being planned that will address itself to the extensive problems of custody, including the acceptability of fathers as single parents (Victor and Winkler). The courts will need to develop better criteria for deciding which parent should be awarded custody.

Figure 4-5 Single parenting. *(Courtesy of Pat Ryan.)*

In contrast to the situation in our culture, Korean children always remain with the father when a divorce occurs. The mother is usually restricted from seeing them until they are older. Divorced fathers usually remarry, and then problems may arise because of the new mother. Widowers tend not to remarry but to raise the children themselves (Song).

Chapter 2 discussed the father's role and men's nurturing abilities. Parke and Sawin studied middle-class fathers whose wives had had their babies using the Lamaze method; they found that these fathers were as much involved with their babies as their wives were. The researchers questioned whether the involvement was due to the fact that they were in the same room with the mother, who would encourage interaction; whether the fathers were more interested because they had attended classes in the Lamaze method; or whether being well educated and of the middle class enhanced their caring abilities. Parke and Sawin also studied lower-class fathers who had not participated in Lamaze classes or been present during delivery. When they were alone with their infants, the lower-class fathers were just as nurturant to their babies as the mothers. They held them and smiled at them more often than the mothers did (Parke and Sawin). Although these researchers found that mothers and fathers were equally involved with their newborn babies, there were differences in the interactions. For instance, while the fathers talked to their babies more and were more playful with them, they were less apt to take part in activities such as feeding, diapering, and wiping the child's face. Other studies have shown that fathers continue to interact with their children through touching and playing, while mothers tend to interact with them verbally.

On the basis of their studies, Parke and Sawin define parental competence as follows: ''Parental competence is a question of how sensitively parents interpret, and react to, infant cues and signals. Success in caretaking and playing depends largely on reading the subtle changes in the infant's behavior correctly and reacting properly'' (p. 111). This definition, then, *does not exclude fathers as competent parents.*

The father's interaction has a strong effect on the child's development, especially in the case of boys. How well and how much fathers interact with their infants influences the child's socialization. Children cope better and are more at ease in social situations when fathers take care of them and play with them (Parke and Sawin). The father contributes to the infant's cognitive development through play, while the mother more often contributes through verbalization. Parke and Sawin agree with PTA groups that advocate parenthood training in the high school curriculum. Chapter 1 discusses such training.

Single men who have never been fathers are now adopting children to satisfy a basic need to nurture a child and thus fulfill their lives. Such men are usually in their mid-thirties and have gained satisfaction from working with other people's children in the role of teacher, therapist, or community worker (Levine). Usually, they do not want to marry, but they do have a strong desire to care for a child. However, these men may face discrimination from biased adoption agency personnel, who often assume that they are homosexuals (Klein; Levine) or that they are compensating for their inability to find a woman to love (Levine).

Consciousness-raising groups for men can be of assistance to single fathers. Such groups are being established to help men find a new focus for living. Their goals are to help men relate on a feeling level, explore their aggressive competitiveness, and deal with their fears about homosexuality (Klein). Our society must be educated to accept fathering as a valid role for a man.

Single Women as Parents

Single women also want to be parents. Some are motivated by a need to assert their independence by assuming total responsibility for a child (Klein), and some women have a genuine desire to nurture a child. Whatever the motivation, the single woman who chooses the parental role needs ego strength and financial security. Occasionally a woman with limited ability to give affection sees the parental role as a way of gaining affectional gratification. Such a situation endangers the child's development. The parent who needs the child for self-gratification will stand in the way of the child's efforts to establish other relationships and move into adulthood.

NATURAL PARENTS AS CARE GIVERS

The natural parent is not always the best care giver. The assumptions, both theoretical and moral, that the natural parents provide the best care must be reconsidered. Cohen cites a British study by Tizard of adopted children that refutes the maternal-deprivation hypothesis so often used by adoption agencies. Children were studied who were separated from their natural families and found that they "learned to love by being loved and cared for, even though love didn't start until the age of four, five, or, in the case of one child, seven" (p. 134). Role reversal was expected. The adoptive parents felt that the child was their own, while the real parents viewed the child as not theirs. Tizard commented that social workers are adamant about returning children to their natural mothers even when the mothers are ambivalent about caring for them or are not prepared to do so. Such social workers have fostered guilt in a natural mother, driving her to reclaim her child (Cohen). I have seen this happen in the United States, where agency staff members dogmatically believe that a natural mother can give the best care.

Cohen cites the limitations of the British research but at the same time finds that it provides a ray of hope concerning children who have not experienced love and attention in their early years.

LESBIAN MOTHERS

Lesbian mothers are becoming more visible and assertive in demanding their rights to raise their children. In a recent court case, a lesbian mother who was divorcing her husband so that she could live with her lover faced prejudice because of her sexuality. She consequently lost custody of her children to the father. The children were unexpectedly removed from the home by the police and the husband while the mother was away, causing them much stress and unhappiness (Jullion).

Whatever the situation of the single parent, the well-being of the children must be the primary consideration when deciding on arrangements for their care.

CHILDLESSNESS

Although this chapter focuses on families with children, the growing number of couples who choose to remain childless should be mentioned. In the past, a couple without children were often considered deviant by family, friends, and others in the community. The pressure to comply with society's belief that married couples should have children produced guilt and anger. Sometimes couples had children simply to conform to society's expectations.

An increasing number of couples today are planning not to have children or to have them at a later time, when they feel they will be better prepared for parenthood emotionally and economically. Those who choose not to be parents are still looked at askance. Even developmental theories discriminate against women without children. Erikson, for instance, stated in his theory of development that the adult who has created a family and thus helped others grow has achieved a certain integrity and ego maturity that cannot be gained through other accomplishments; however, a study of 590 professional women showed the opposite. Welds found that women without children experienced the same sense of fulfillment and maturity ("Childless Women"). Welds questions Erikson's emphasis on parenthood as a necessary experience for continued development. As indicated in Chapter 1, we must be open-minded concerning changing theories. Negative attitudes toward childlessness can have a detrimental influence on child care. A therapist who agrees with Erikson may give inappropriate counseling to clients who are trying to set goals in their lives. People who work with children must be sensitive to, and accepting of, those whose lives do not include children.

BIRTH ORDER

A child's personality is influenced by his or her birth order in the family. Forer, a psychotherapist, finds that birth-order information helps her gain a deeper understanding of her clients. However, *she cautions care givers not to make general assumptions or use birth-order information automatically.* Only after evidence in other areas has been gathered is it suggested to the client that his or her birth order may be an influence in personal relationships. Consideration of *all* factors influencing a person's life seems to be Forer's stance. No one birth-order position is the best; each has its advantages and disadvantages. Forer gives suggestions for helping children overcome the disadvantages associated with each birth-order position. The book is recommended to the reader as a reference because it is informative, interesting, and well written.

Firstborn Children

Hoffman and Hoffman[1] cite studies conducted between 1933 and 1965 on the influences of birth order on children's personalities. Although the findings are inconclusive, there seem to be certain predictable effects of birth order on firstborn children:

1. They are more likely to be role models for younger siblings and to help in the care of younger siblings.
2. They learn to conceal aggression, while later-born children more readily express aggression.
3. They feel that their siblings are favored by the parents.
4. They are more likely to be physically punished than younger siblings.
5. They tend to perform better in school than later-born children. This is due to a combination of parental aspirations and personality attributes, not necessarily superior intelligence.
6. They are more apt to be timid and ill at ease in social situations.
7. They are likely to be favored by grandparents and other relatives.

[1] Adapted from "Family Structure, Socialization, and Personality," by John A. Clausen in *Review of Child Development and Research*, Vol. II, (eds.) Lois Wladis Hoffman and Martin L. Hoffman, © Russell Sage Foundation, New York, 1966.

8. Female firstborn children are more responsible, aggressive, and competitive than later-born female children. The reverse is true for males.
9. Fathers exercise greater authority in relation to firstborn children in large families, while mothers are more involved with the youngest siblings.
10. Asthma is more frequent among firstborn children, and duodenal ulcer among youngest children.

More recent studies continue to show the effects of birth order on development. The social, affectionate, and care-giving behaviors of mothers in relation to firstborn and second-born children have been studied. They paid less attention to the second-born child unless it was a male or of the opposite sex from the firstborn. For instance, male second-born children with older sisters received the same amount of maternal attention. Female second-born children with firstborn sisters received the least amount of maternal attention. The following factors may account for the differences: less time required to take care of one child than two; less excitement about a second birth; the novelty associated with taking care of a boy infant; competition from older siblings for time and attention; and an improvement in mothering abilities with the second child, with the result that less time is required to carry out care-giving tasks (Jacobs and Moss).

The effects of the birth of a sibling on the personality of a firstborn child were studied in a northern Italian community. *Firstborn children under age 3 who had had an exclusive and therefore intensive relationship with their mothers experienced the most frustration because of the arrival of a sibling.* By 3 years of age, a child is better able to share the mother's attention and to face difficulties without her help and protection (Cornoldi and Fattori). Because of cultural influences on child-rearing practices, however, a similar American study might show that firstborn children have different reactions.

Middle Children: The Second Child

Being the second child of three often is the most difficult position. These children are wedged between a powerful older sibling, with whom they compete, and the youngest sibling, who receives the most parental attention. Very likely they have more social problems with teachers and peers. They are more excitable, demanding, and attention-seeking than their older or younger siblings.

Girls are more affected by the second position than boys; for instance, a middle boy of three brothers tends to be less anxious than his siblings, while a middle girl of three sisters may be more serious, more depressed, or more anxious than her sisters. In adulthood, the same girl may continue to have needs for attention, since she was the least favorite child (Forer).

Later Middle Children

Later-born boys with more sisters than brothers tend to have high self-esteem. The self-esteem is much greater if the boy happens to be the *only* male child. First girls born after several boys also tend to develop high self-esteem. Adults who were born in the late middle position tend to be self-reliant and responsible and to relate well to others. They can cope well in threatening situations because, as children, they had experience defending themselves in peer-group situations without parental assistance. They are less moralistic, they resist social pressures, and they show less anger in common situations (Forer).

The Baby

I was the youngest of four children; I recall that my mother referred to me (even when I was middle-aged) as "my baby." Families tend to view the youngest child as a baby throughout his or her life (Forer). The last-born is often a "spoiled child." Parents may accord special privileges to the youngest, on whom they lavish their attention. Siblings, however, may delegate unpleasant chores to the youngest or subject this child to teasing and ridicule.

The last-born child may also be deprived in some ways, such as wearing clothes handed down from siblings and being given their old toys to play with. I remember resenting wearing my sister's hand-me-down clothing, and these childhood memories have affected me in my adult life.

The last-born usually is more cheerful, more playful, and more popular than his or her siblings, which can also raise self-esteem. However, self-esteem is lowered if parents and siblings suppress the last child, and dependency can also be a problem if the older siblings become too protective (Forer).

The Only Child

Forer bases her therapeutic work on birth-order research and theory. She indicates that the major characteristics of an only child, especially a boy, are increased self-confidence, dominance, verbal ability, and perfectionism. Only children are not jealous because they have never had to compete with siblings, but they do occasionally suffer from loneliness. They learn to do things alone, solve problems alone, and keep busy with solitary projects. They are also eager to please authority figures.

Forer cites three psychological hazards that impede the child's growing into adulthood: (1) Only children do not have the opportunity to interact with siblings in a way that can provide a well-rounded sense of identity, or of the "adult within." Girls especially are affected by this lack since parents protect girls more than boys. Forer's female clients who were only children often remark that they still *feel* like children. (2) Many only children grow into adulthood with a limited sense of competence and skill since there were no brothers or sisters with whom they had to compete; girls are more affected in this way than boys. (3) The only child feels almost *too* secure. The child learns how to control and dominate a parent and does not feel that he or she will lose the parent's love, as children with brothers and sisters sometimes feel.

I have always viewed only-children sympathetically because their world is inhabited mainly by adults. However, this is a stereotyped view according to Falbo, a psychologist. She studied four personality traits in only children—

selfishness, loneliness, personal adjustment, and independence—and found that, compared with children with siblings, only children were more trusting, were not necessarily more lonely or friendless, were not more neurotic or introverted, preferred to be leaders rather than joiners, and had greater verbal ability. Falbo assures parents that only children do not need a brother or sister to attain healthy individual growth.

Only children often cannot tolerate the frustrations of long-term, committed relationships, and therefore they can move in and out of love relationships quickly. Forer advises parents raising an only child to provide ample social experiences, beginning in the early years, to counteract this tendency.

INTELLECTUAL ABILITY

A theory explaining why later-born children, especially those from large families, tend to have lower intellectual abilities than firstborns has been posed by Zajonc, a psychologist, and Markus, a political scientist (Tavris). The theory is based on the hypothesis that mental ability is influenced by the total family constellation. As I understand it, the more adults in the family, the greater potential for intellectual development. Firstborns have the greatest advantage if they are raised in extended families in which there are two grandparents and two parents. Each succeeding child after the firstborn has a lesser chance of developing optimal mental ability. Spacing the birth of children can be helpful in this regard. According to Zajonc and Markus's theory, children raised by a single parent are at a certain disadvantage; twins are also at a disadvantage because of close spacing; and children whose parent or parents are away for extended periods, such as for business reasons, suffer most.

This theory, if it proves true, can overcome some of the cultural bias of intelligence tests. For example, according to this theory, blacks do not have deficient genes; rather, the circumstances of their lives are those which hinder growth of mental ability. Black families have more children than white families, there is closer spacing of the children, and there are more one-parent households. Jews score well on intelligence tests since many come from smaller two-parent families. Other contributing factors are economic level, cultural background, and educational opportunities. On the basis of this theory, Zajonc predicts that Scholastic Aptitude Test scores, which have declined in the last dozen years, will rise in about 1980. Students taking the tests will be children born in the 1960s, which means that there will be more firstborn students from smaller families. These students are now in junior high school, and their test scores are rising. A clearer understanding of the theory can be obtained by reading Tavris's article, which includes graphic charts.

The implications for educators and parents are obvious. Not all the responsibility will be placed on the curriculum. Prospective parents need to be counseled regarding the advantages of spacing children to give them optimal opportunity for growth.

ECONOMICS

A recent study has shown that the incidence of mental illness doubles in families with incomes below $4000. The researchers stated that obtaining adequate income through employment is more beneficial than community action or psychotherapy ("Poverty Is Depressing"). Work is necessary not only for survival but also for self-esteem. Children are affected by parents' unemployment, low pay, or inability to get a job because of discrimination. Young children are aware of how the work world values or devalues a parent. The parent need not say a word to communicate feelings of powerlessness, worthlessness, and helplessness. Children absorb these feelings and grow up to think of themselves as their parents do, feeling inadequate and having low self-esteem (Keniston and The Carnegie Council on Children). Keniston and The Carnegie Council on Children make the following recommendations for overcoming this problem: (1) All parents should be given the opportunity to work for decent wages, (2) work hours should be flexible to allow for the demands of family life, (3) there should be an appropriate system of income support, and (4) parents with full-time responsibilities should be given part-time work.

Working mothers are faced with the difficulties of locating work and finding someone to take care of the children; they must also deal with society's attitude that mothers belong at home with their children. The importance of not separating the mother and infant at birth because of the possibility of interfering with the attachment process has been documented by recent research (see Chapter 1). However, Pringle warns us that we may be teaching mothers that infants require their undivided attention for the first 2 or 3 years, thus confining the woman physically and socially to her family unit. Mead (1954) reports anthropological evidence showing that the mother-child tie is not as important as we have been led to believe. She thinks that the concept is a subtle form of antifeminism in which men, under the guise of elevating motherhood, tie women more tightly to their children than is necessary.

Working Mothers

Working mothers may experience discrimination by employers, legislators, and educators who refuse to provide adequate free child-care services (Yudkin and Holme). Consequently, many mothers must find their own solutions to child-care problems. In the family where both parents work, the mother usually has the responsibility for the children as well as her career responsibilities. Career and family problems are also experienced in the eastern European socialist countries (Rapoport and Rapoport). I interviewed working mothers in Romania who left their children in nurseries and day-care centers. As a guest in their homes, I witnessed them taking the responsibility for entertaining guests, caring for the children, and carrying out household duties, with no help from their husbands. The women complained that their families could not survive financially unless both they and their husbands worked; some felt guilty about letting someone else take care of their children, and yet none expected their husbands to share the burden.

Effects of the Great Depression

A longitudinal study done in Oakland, California, followed preadolescent Depression children into middle age, and revealed how economic deprivation influenced their relationships, careers, life-styles, and personalities (Elder). Economic responsibilities shifted to the wives and children; the mother became the decision maker. The children's accomplishment of developmental tasks was influenced. Some young people were unable to enjoy being protected and dependent during adolescence, which is a common experience in more stable and/ or affluent times. Being responsible for helping their families speeded their accomplishment of the developmental tasks of gaining independence from the family and of establishing self-direction, while domestic tasks drew some children more closely into the family. Domestic chores were appropriate for girls at that time, and boys more often found jobs outside the home (Elder).

Economic Deprivation

Economic deprivation and loss of status have a major psychological effect on children. According to reports of mothers in economically deprived families, their children became acutely sensitive to others and emotionally vulnerable. The children erroneously felt that they were held in low esteem by their age-mates. Emotional reactions were easily brought on by disappointments and frustrations, and they responded with anger, anxiety, or crying, particularly girls. Early marriages among the daughters of middle-class families that lost status and financial security were linked with their emotional states and the deprivation.

The overall impact of economic deprivation was more negative among the adults from the working class who experienced economic loss and more positive among the middle-class individuals who were deprived financially. The latter were evaluated as having more ego strength and capacity for growth. The children of the middle-class deprived families received greater support in problem solving than the children from working-class homes, and they were brighter and more ambitious. Those who experienced economic deprivation, as compared with those who did not, viewed their life between childhood and middle age as more of a growth process because of the difficult times experienced in childhood. They found life to be more satisfying. The implications of this are that children can achieve personal growth by being involved in hardships if the involvement is not exploitative or excessive and if they are given a sense of belonging and of commitment to the welfare of others. Although some may feel that the experience made their lives purposeful, a theory prevails that people raised during the Depression want to prevent their children from experiencing similar hardships (Elder).

The hard times experienced during the Depression years have been cited as a reason for these individuals' extraordinary work commitment, desire for security, and difficulty participating in pleasurable activities without feeling guilty. The ability to play as well as work is a vital aspect of a well-balanced individual. Children who are not provided with appropriate socialization opportunities and smooth transitions from childhood into adolescence often can never experience a comfortable balance of love, work, and play. The lack of a quiescent stage in adolescence among Depression children may remain a factor throughout their lives. A Harvard study bears out the theory that childhood experiences have an influence on whether an adult can live a balanced life. Men with poor social adjustments "did not know how to play," could not be on intimate terms with their parents or their children, and relied heavily on drugs and alcohol. An explanation for these findings could be that the capacity to love is an objective measure of mental health ("Men with Successful Careers Likely to Have Happy Marriages").

MENTAL HEALTH FOR THE POOR

What happens when a child and/or a family needs mental health services? The very poor have the least access to such services, while the rich can afford costly private facilities. This discrepancy is due not only to lack of available funds but also to the belief among some psychiatrists that low-income mentally ill or emotionally disturbed children and youth are untreatable. Children from lower-class families are often assigned to inexperienced therapists, are less likely to be given intensive psychiatric treatment, and are more often diagnosed as psychotic or borderline psychotic (Joint Commission on Mental Health of Children).

The dropout rate from treatment is higher among lower-class than among middle- or upper-class persons (Joint Commission on Mental Health of Children). One reason for this may be that the therapeutic process does not meet the needs of the poor. When I was being trained as a family therapist (which I discuss more fully in Chapter 10), I recognized that the methods I was taught did not meet the needs of poor families. The approach was more appropriate for middle- and upper-class families, where verbalization and creative approaches are used to generate communication, problem solving, and insight. Poor families have different needs and viewpoints. Better rapport is obtained if the therapist uses clear, concrete problem-solving approaches. I have found that poor families expect the therapist to "do something" immediately to bring about changes; when changes do not occur, they may not return for therapy. Language is another barrier. Unfamiliar words cause them to feel uneasy. I try to use words that I believe are in their vocabulary and to avoid a condescending tone.

MENTAL HEALTH FOR THE UPPER CLASSES

Reverse discrimination occurs among upper-class persons and rich persons. The attitude prevails that upper-class people have fewer mental health needs than those in the middle or lower classes. Affluence has its own problems. As a school counselor in an affluent community, I found that children from wealthy families needed mental health services as much as those in any other socioeconomic group. Family pressure to sustain and improve their status in life affected the lives of these children. Many had little contact with their parents. The mothers were busy with tennis, sailing, entertaining, or community affairs, while the fathers held prestigious positions that kept them from spending time with their families. Fifty percent of the parents had been divorced. In counseling groups, common topics were experiences with a mother's boyfriends or a father's girlfriends and difficulties in deciding which parent to live with after a separation and divorce. The children were well traveled, sophisticated, and not wanting for material things. Parental expectations of high achievement brought many into the guidance office. Drug use, underachievement, and discipline problems were some of the ways in which the students manifested their alienation and their need for attention. Middle-class children suffer from similar pressures to achieve, and those who cannot meet parental expectations may become anxious and fearful (Joint Commission on Mental Health of Children).

THE CHILDREN OF AFFLUENCE

At the extreme end of the socioeconomic scale are the children of millionaires. Grinker, a psychiatrist who works with very rich children, finds that they often feel empty and are bored and chronically depressed. The grandparents of his wealthy clients were European immigrants who had worked hard and amassed fortunes. The parents had continued to work hard but were away a great deal of the time, leaving the child care to servants. The children had inherited the value that money is power and can protect one from the evils of the world. Rich children and poor children are deprived in similar ways. Both groups suffer from parental absence because of work and from a lack of strong, constructive role models. The difference between the two groups is that the unhappiness of the poor may lead them to commit crime and thus gain public disapproval, while the rich often cope with their unhappiness by indulging in activities that arouse public envy. The rich child who is raised by various parent substitutes feels unloved and undervalued and does not have a stable sense of self.

Grinker stresses the need for a nonjudgmental attitude on the part of therapists who work with wealthy clients. He also notes that staff members have been intimidated by such clients' status and have granted requests to lift suicide precautions; as a result, clients have killed themselves. It cannot be overemphasized that unless we understand, accept, and are at ease with clients who are different from us—whether they are poor, wealthy, or from a different culture—optimum assessment and treatment cannot occur.

Although there are differences in the mental health needs of the various socioeconomic groups, a major problem is *parental alienation*. It is time to bring parenting back into families, for children are children wherever and whoever they are, and they need a parent's love and care.

TELEVISION: INFLUENCE ON CHILDREN AND FAMILIES

Television has become extremely important as a child-care arrangement. The average preschooler spends 33 h per week watching television, or one-third of his or her waking hours, while the average sixth grader watches for 31 h (Rubenstein, Comstock, and Murray). Too often, parents use television as a baby-sitter when they cannot provide supervision and companionship for their children. Consequently, children abuse television by watching it too much. McCue cites studies indicating escalating hazards of this for children. Episodes showing violence and aggression are becoming increasingly common, particularly on Saturday mornings. Children may imitate the aggressive behavior they see either immediately or later in a trying situation, causing problems for the family and the community. Excessive viewing of violent and aggressive programs can instill patterns of aggressive behavior in an immature audience. Children see that even the "good guy" is rewarded for such behavior (McCue). Reports indicate that physicians are seeing symptoms of television-related heightened aggression in children as well as injuries sustained when children were imitating incidents seen on television. Epileptic seizures and nightmares have also been linked to television watching ("TV Violence Causing Medical Problems").

Efforts by various pressure groups have not influenced television programming; the aggressive and violent scenes continue. Some ways of dealing with the problem are being recommended. Corder-Bolz's study revealed that children learn and retain more if an adult explains or interprets the events portrayed. He recommends that parents join their children in viewing so that they can clarify what is presented, instead of leaving them unattended in front of the set ("Parental Interpretation of TV Can Be Educational for Children"). Bronfenbrenner (1972), a child development specialist, recommends a new kind of programming that would involve active family viewing and joint creative activities. NBC has begun a parent-child viewing participation program entitled "Special Treats" that is designed to stimulate simple communication between child and adult. Kaye has designed a guide for parents, including a children's workbook, to assist them in monitoring programs. These are middle-class approaches to parental guidance. It is not known whether they will appeal to parents from lower socioeconomic groups, where there is more television watching.

The main danger of television lies more in the behavior it prevents than in the behavior it produces; i.e., it prevents interaction between family members that promotes children's learning—talking, playing games, and having discussions—and it interferes with the process of helping children grow into mature human beings (Bronfenbrenner, 1972).

Appropriate programming can be beneficial; for instance, Liebert found that specially designed programs can alleviate children's fear of dogs and visits to the dentist. Television can promote growth in children if there is appropriate program design and parental supervision.

Five families who watched television on the average of 25 to 70 h per week were studied by the *Detroit Free Press* to see how they would cope with giving up television for 1 month. The families had varied withdrawal symptoms, including nervousness, difficulty in sleeping, and inability to relate to a spouse. The children missed television the most, but some discovered that listening to the radio could be an adventure in imagination. Some families enjoyed reading, listening to music, and increased socialization. When the television sets were turned on again, the reactions ranged from having a viewing orgy to permanently reducing the number of hours watched (Hanauer).

ABUSE IN THE FAMILY: THE CHILDREN

Undoubtedly, there is increasing evidence that child abuse is epidemic in the United States. Child abuse has been attributed to learned patterns of behavior from parents and to the personality of the parent; in addition, a child who is born prematurely or who is mentally retarded or physically handicapped has an increased risk of abuse. Such a child carries the double burden of being different and of arousing the parent's anger. Early identification and intervention may break the cycle (Friedrich and Boriskin).

Richard J. Gelles and his colleagues have found that violence directed at children, spouses, and siblings is common in undisadvantaged, undisturbed, and thoroughly average American homes ("Violence Begins at [the Average American] Home"). Their findings will be described in their forthcoming book entitled *Violence in the American Family.* These researchers have defined abuse as an act by a parent that could be considered assault if perpetrated on a stranger or another adult. Using this definition, Gelles and his colleagues found the following: (1) There was at least one violent episode in 63 percent of the families they studied with children living at home aged 3 to 17; (2) one violent act was reported by 68 percent of the mothers and 58 percent of the fathers during the year of the study (1975); and (3) 76 percent of the mothers and 71 percent of the fathers reported one violent episode during the years of rearing their child.

The frequent argument that mothers are more prone to violent episodes because they spend more time with their children is challenged by these researchers. They hypothesize that there is more to the dynamics of abuse than simply the time factor. Male children were more likely to be treated violently by parents than female children. The true level of the violence may be higher than reported because the mode of data collection was self-reporting and respondents may have concealed information about dangerous acts such as using or threatening to use a knife or a gun ("Violence Begins at [the Average American] Home"). Methods of discipline may change if similar studies continue to show that spanking constitutes abuse.

Holidays are times when people can become depressed rather than happy, which is society's expectation. A Florida protective service agency has reported an increase in child abuse during the holidays. Stress and financial problems contribute to the aggression ("Child Abuse Increases during Yule Season"). People working with children and families in any setting need to be alert to the possible dangers of holiday stress so that they can help prevent abusive episodes.

Therapists work toward preparing their clients for the holidays, when happy memories from the past increase conflict and cause depression. I found that temporary preventive strategies worked for a family in which the husband battered the wife and occasionally the children. Two weeks before the Christmas holidays, we planned for the family members to be apart from one another for certain specified periods of time. We also planned to reduce holiday activities and entertaining, and we reviewed what each member of the family did to provoke the father's anger. These were only temporary strategies; the underlying problem would need working through on a long-term basis.

Until preventive measures can be implemented, protective services are being established in communities; these range from "hot lines" for parents and children to child-abuse therapy teams in community mental health centers. A unique facility for battered children is being established in Los Angeles, California. Children's Village, U.S.A., is a special school with living quarters, a church, and an animal farm; there are also living quarters for parents, and staff-monitored family visits are allowed ("New Facility for Battered Children to Emphasize Family Unit").

In California, care givers are required by law to report evidence of child abuse. Educators and those in the helping professions use caution and sometimes desist from reporting abuse in order to prevent being sued, particularly if the evidence is minimal. Proof is difficult to obtain, and often the children defend their parents. On the other hand, parents who do not abuse their children may meet with hostility from a suspicious hospital staff when a child is treated for injuries resulting from an accident. It is hoped that with the increasing development of preventive and protective services, there will soon be a reduction in child abuse.

THE FUTURE

What is the future of the family? The need to belong to a family will continue, regardless of the form the family takes. People need people. Family ties will continue to meet the human needs for stability, continuity, and unconditional affection (Bane). How these needs are met in the future will depend upon all aspects of our lives—economic, psychosocial, and societal.

Forer cites studies indicating a trend toward smaller families. A characteristic of the smaller family will be that children will be the center of family attention and activity. However, some theorists predict that the child will *not* be the center of attention if the trend toward both parents' working continues. Being the center of family attention is not helpful to the child, the parents, or society (Forer). The child becomes too preoccupied with his or her own needs and does not learn to consider those of others. In order to live comfortably, individuals need to think of others as well as themselves. The trend toward looking out for oneself was fostered by the "togetherness" movement of child-oriented families after World War II. Children in such families were the center of attention and developed the consequent need for immediate gratification (Forer).

And how about the far future? There is increasing evidence that space colonies will be a reality within some of our lifetimes (Fairlie; Tracy). The nuclear family, as we know it, could cease to exist, and there could be other drastic changes. For instance, upon returning from a trip through space, you might find that you were younger than your children! Whatever happens, people will still need people, regardless of the dimensions of change.

REFERENCES

Bane, Mary Jo: *Here to Stay: American Families in the Twentieth Century,* Basic Books, New York, 1976.

Berger, Bennett M., Bruce M. Hackett, and **R. Mervyn Millar:** "Child-Rearing Practices in the Communal Family," in Arlene Skolnick and Jerome H. Skolnick (eds.), *Intimacy, Family and Society,* Little, Brown, Boston, 1974, pp. 441–463.

Bernard, Jessie: *The Future of Marriage,* World, Tarrytown-on-Hudson, N.Y., 1972.

Brandwein, Ruth A.: "Women and Children Last: Divorced Mothers and Their Families," *Nursing Digest,* **4**:39–41, 1976.

Bronfenbrenner, Urie: "Who Cares for America's Children?" in Louise Kapp Howe (ed.), *The Future of the Family,* Simon and Schuster, New York, 1972, pp. 139–158.

—— and **Susan Byrnn:** "Nobody Home: The Erosion of the American Family (a conversation with Urie Bronfenbrenner)," *Psychology Today,* **10**(12):41–47, 1977.

Burgess, Ernest W., Harvey J. Locke, and **Mary Margaret Thomes:** *The Family: From Traditional to Companionship,* 4th ed., Van Nostrand, Princeton, N.J., 1971.

"Child Abuse Increases during Yule Season," *Behavior Today,* **7**(2):4, 1976.

"Childless Women," *San Francisco Sun-day Examiner & Chronicle, This World,* Nov. 6, 1977, p. 34.

Clausen, John A.: "Family Structure, Socialization and Personality," in Lois Wladis Hoffman and Martin L. Hoffman (eds.), *Review of Child Development Research,* vol. 2, Russell Sage, New York, 1966.

Cohen, David: "Adoption," *Psychology Today,* **11**(6):128–134, 1977.

Cornoldi, Cesare, and **Lucia Cornoldi Fattori:** "Age Spacing in First Borns and Symbiotic Dependence," *Journal of Personality and Social Psychology,* **33**(4): 431–434, 1976.

Dodson, Fitzhugh: *How to Father,* New American Library, New York, 1974.

Elder, Glen H., Jr.: *Children of the Great Depression: Social Change in Life Experience,* University of Chicago Press, Chicago, 1974.

Erikson, Erik H.: *Childhood and Society,* Norton, New York, 1963.

Fairlie, Henry: "Space Travel: You Could Return Younger," *San Francisco Sunday Examiner & Chronicle, This World,* Oct. 16, 1977, p. 29.

Falbo, Toni: "Does the Only Child Grow Up Miserable?" *Psychology Today,* **9**(12):60–65, 1976.

Farber, Bernard: *Guardians of Virtue: Salem Families in 1800,* Basic Books, New York, 1972.

Forer, Lucille K., with **Henry Still:** *The*

Birth Order Factor, Pocket Books, New York, 1977.

Friedrich, **William,** and **Jerry Boriskin:** "The Role of the Child in Abuse: A Review of the Literature," *American Journal of Orthopsychiatry,* **46**(4):580–590, 1976.

Green, **Maureen:** *Fathering: A New Look at the Creative Art of Being a Father,* McGraw-Hill, New York, 1976.

Grinker, **Roy R., Jr.:** "The poor rich," *Psychology Today,* **11**(5):74–81, 1977.

Gross, **L.,** and **P. Macewan:** "On day care," *Women: A Journal of Liberation,* **1**(2): 26–29, 1970.

Hanauer, **Joan:** "Tube Unplugged: 5 Families Describe Painful Ordeal," *San Francisco Sunday Examiner & Chronicle, Datebook,* Jan. 8, 1978, p. 21.

Heilbrun, **A. B.:** "An Empirical Test of the Modeling Theory of Sex-Role Learning," in I. Reiss (ed.), *Readings on the Family Systems,* Holt, New York, 1972.

Horowitz, **June Andrews,** and **Bobbie Jean Perdue:** "Single-Parent Families," *Nursing Clinics of North America,* **12**(3): 503–511, 1977.

Jacobs, **Blanche S.,** and **Howard A. Moss:** "Birth Order and Sex of Sibling as Determinants of Mother-Infant Interaction," *Child Development,* **47**(2): 315–322, 1976.

Joint Commission on Mental Health of Children: *Crisis in Child Mental Health: Challenge for the 1970's,* Harper & Row, New York, 1970.

Jullion, **Jeanne:** "It Was Sufficient That I Was a Dyke," *Common Sense,* **4**(10):6–7, 1977.

Kaye, **Evelyn:** *The Family Guide to Children's Television: What to Watch, What to Miss, What to Change and How to Do It,* Pantheon, New York, 1974.

Keniston, **Kenneth,** and **The Carnegie Council on Children:** *All Our Children:*

The American Family under Pressure, Harcourt, Brace Jovanovich, New York, 1977.

Klein, **Carole:** *The Single Parent Experience,* Walker, New York, 1973.

Levine, **James L.:** *Who Will Raise the Children? New Options for Fathers (and Mothers),* Lippincott, Philadelphia, 1976.

Liebert, **Robert N.:** "Television and Children's Aggressive Behavior: Another Look," *American Journal of Psychoanalysis,* **34**(2):99–107, 1974.

McBride, **Angela Barron:** *The Growth and Development of Mothers,* Harper & Row, New York, 1973.

McCary, **James Leslie:** *Freedom and Growth in Marriage,* Hamilton, Santa Barbara, Calif., 1975.

McCue, **Ann:** "Television, Violence and Childhood Aggression," unpublished paper presented at the meeting of the American Association of Psychiatric Services for Children, Louisville, Ky., May 12–13, 1977.

McFadden, **Michael:** *Bachelor Fatherhood: How to Raise and Enjoy Your Children as a Single Parent,* Walker, New York, 1974.

Maslow, **Abraham:** *Toward a Psychology of Being,* Van Nostrand Reinhold, New York, 1968.

Mead, **Margaret:** *Male and Female,* Morrow, New York, 1953.

———: "Some Theoretical Considerations on the Problem of Mother-Child Separation," *American Journal of Orthopsychiatry,* **24**:471–483, 1954.

———: "Marriage in Two Steps," in H. A. Otto (ed.), *The Family in Search of a Future,* Appleton-Century, New York, 1970.

"Men with Successful Careers Likely to Have Happy Marriages," *Behavior Today,* **7**(21):3–4, 1976.

"New Facility for Battered Children to Emphasize Family Unit," *Behavior Today,* 7(38):4–5, 1976.

"Parental Interpretation of TV Can Be Educational for Children," *Behavior Today,* 7(32):5, 1976.

Parke, Ross D., and **Douglas B. Sawin:** "Fathering: It's a Major Role," *Psychology Today,* 11(6):109–112, 1977.

"Poverty Is Depressing," *San Francisco Examiner & Chronicle,* May 8, 1977, sec. B, p. 5.

Pringle, Mia Kellmer: *The Needs of Children,* Schocken Books, New York, 1975.

Rapoport, R., and **R. N. Rapoport:** "The Dual Career Family: A Variant Pattern and Social Change," *Human Relations,* 22(1):3–30, 1969.

Rubenstein, Eli A., George Comstock, and **John P. Murray (eds.):** *Television and Social Behavior,* report to the Surgeon General's Scientific Advisory Committee on Television and Social Behavior, U.S. Department of Health, Education, and Welfare, 1972.

Rubin, Lillian Breslow: *Worlds of Pain: Life in the Working-Class Family,* Basic Books, New York, 1976.

Song, Pat: Personal communication, Oct. 25, 1977.

Tavris, Carol: "The End of the I.Q. Slump," *Psychology Today,* 9(11):69–74, 1976.

Tracy, Phil: "Space: The Ultimate Suburb," *New West,* 2(23):30–32, 1977.

"TV Violence Causing Medical Problems," *National Enquirer,* October 1977, p. 9.

U.S. Bureau of the Census: *Current Population Reports,* ser. P-20, 323, "Marital Status and Living Arrangements, March 1977," U.S. Government Printing Office, Washington, D.C., 1978, p. 5.

Victor, Ira, and **Win Ann Winkler:** *Fathers and Custody,* Hawthorn, New York, 1976.

"Violence Begins at (the Average American) Home," *Behavior Today,* 8(13):3–4, 1977.

Whitehurst, Robert N.: "Some Comparisons of Conventional and Counterculture Families," *The Family Coordinator,* 21(4):395–401, 1972.

Yudkin, S., and **A. Holme:** *Working Mothers and Their Children,* Sphere Books, London, 1969.

OTHER RESOURCES

FILMS

A Family Upside Down: 2 h. The story of an older married couple who are forced to separate. The film deals with the effects of this upon the couple, their children, and their teenage grandson. Original screenplay by Gerald Di Pego. Ross Hunter Productions.

Cipher in the Snow: 23 min/16 mm/color/ 1973. A dramatization of a true story of a boy who was psychologically abused. The story on which the film was based won first prize in an NEA teachers' writing contest. Produced by Brigham Young University, Media Marketing W-STAD, Provo, Utah 84602.

Family: Lifestyles of the Future: 22 min/ color/1972. Margaret Mead discusses the stresses on the contemporary isolated nuclear family and the growth of alternative communal living groups. The film shows a rural commune with 50 members, a small urban commune consisting of two married couples and their children, and a three-person family made up of a man and two women. Distributor: University of California, Extension Media Center, Berkeley, Calif. 94720.

Fragile—Handle with Care: 26 min/16 mm/ color/1975. A documentary, narrated by Bill Cosby, on mental and physical abuse of children. The film deals with the reasons for abuse and its effect on children. Prevention of child abuse and legal considerations are also covered. KTAR-TV Productions and Independent Order of Foresters. Contact: James Martin, High Court of Southern California, 100 Border Avenue, Solana Beach, Calif. 92075.

Chapter 5

SEPARATION IN LIVING AND DYING: AN OVERVIEW

Helen Elena Monea

> It is important to learn that one can sustain a loss and
> endure. Able to move apart as well as come together,
> individuals need to free themselves from a crippling object
> hunger which makes them hang on too cruelly here, avoid
> becoming reinvolved there.
>
> *Michael Glenn*

This chapter is intended to set the stage for the discussion in later chapters of children's responses to separation caused by divorce and death. A brief review of theories and research on separation is presented.

COPING WITH SEPARATION

How an individual child copes with separation and loss depends upon his or her life-style, developmental capability, environment, cultural background, and psychosocial characteristics. When we cope, we are attempting to deal with a threatening, challenging, or gratifying situation (Murphy and Moriarty). The origin of coping capacity is not simple. Murphy and Moriarty, after making a longitudinal study of coping in children and adolescents, reported that the resiliency of children still remained puzzling to them. Coping involves a drive within the child, the child's needs, the freedom to deal with challenges, and support from those in the child's environment (Murphy and Moriarty). Vulnerability, the susceptibility to impaired functioning during stress, influences how the youngster will cope (Murphy and Moriarty). Children have varying degrees of vulnerability.

Effects of Separation

Children at age 2 or 3 exhibit a pattern of coping with separation from their mothers. Initially there is a *protest* of tears or anger. Then there is a quiet response, *despair,* intermingled with the hope that the parent will return. Finally the child enters a *detachment* phase, in which he or she remains uninterested in the mother or does not recognize her. These three phases coincide with psychoanalytic theory: The protest is separation anxiety, the despair is mourning, and the detachment is defense (Bowlby). The length of the detachment phase is influenced by the length of the separation. Ambivalent feelings emerge; in children below the age of 2 or 3, the detachment can be permanent if the separation continues for longer than 6 months (Bowlby).

Contrary to reports in the literature that brief separation causes acute stress and despair, London researchers have found that with optimal substitute care, anxiety can be kept to a minimum and development can continue without interruption. The 1½-year-olds in the research were able to transfer completely to the new care giver, while the 2½-year-olds were more ambivalent. The institutionalized child showed evidence of trauma and cumulative stress after 6 years of age (Robertson and Robertson).

Children who experience a lack of caring during a separation are more apt to have emotional reactions to separation experiences later in life and to use defensive maneuvers to protect themselves against stress (Hansburg). Early adolescents who have been abandoned commonly cope through self-destructive behavior; however, living with an emotionally insensitive or unresponsive parent can be more devastating to the inner security of the child than the experience of separation (Hansberg).

Effects of Divorce

What are some of the effects of divorce? Divorce counseling studies indicate that the parent's functioning in the postseparation period is crucial to the child's development. A role reversal of care giving usually occurs. Parents often seek support from older children and adolescents, who are not as dependent upon the parent for psychosocial functioning, and they may involve the youngsters in conflict with the divorced spouse. The realities of the separation must be lived through for several years before equilibrium can be regained (Wallerstein and Kelly).

The crisis of divorce reduces competitiveness among children in some instances. Siblings mobilize themselves and help one another. Some children, however, complain of physical ailments, become preoccupied with the home, or engage in acting-out behavior. There is less anxiety after a divorce when the parents' relationship made a child's life unbearable.

The child whose parents are divorced must bear the burden of prejudice, even on the part of mental health professionals (Gettleman and Markowitz). The trend toward greater social acceptability of divorce is a healthy one (Gardner).

It is important that children be protected from the detrimental effects of separation and divorce. Gardner believes that a child needs both a mother and a father for healthy psychological development and that single parents cannot fulfill both roles. As an alternative to marriage, living together has advantages and disadvantages. On the positive side, it prevents people from entering into another poor marriage. Living together need not cause psychological difficulties unless (1) there is a series of such relationships and (2) the parent has ambivalent feelings about the relationship. A parent who is living with a member of the opposite sex must face the fact that his or her children may be subjected to criticism from peers. If the parent makes excuses about the relationship or tries to cover it up, the children can feel alienated. Children in such a situation need to understand that they can have friends regardless of their parents' marital status if they are friendly and considerate and if others enjoy being with them (Gardner).

Bringing a new parent into the home can be difficult. Children who are not prepared for a new parent can view the person as an intruder, and they may try to scare the new parent away or test the new parent's feelings about them. They may assume a Cinderella role to gain sympathy from peers and family friends to protect them against the ''wicked adult.'' When children from two different marriages are brought together under one roof, the stage is set for conflict concerning territoriality, competition, and discipline problems.

We must study the effects of divorce if we are to know when we should intervene to prevent detrimental effects.

Hetherington acknowledges that for the past 20 years studies of a father's absence have focused on boys. Paternal absence during World War II initiated research which revealed that a sense of estrangement developed between fathers and sons who were separated and that boys raised without fathers tended to be more feminine, less aggressive, and more dependent. The feminine behaviors decreased with cultural pressures to exhibit appropriate masculine behaviors. Some boys compensated by developing extreme masculine behaviors; however, their basic feminine identification was frequently retained. These studies supported the theory that young boys model their personalities after the personality of a father figure (Hetherington).

The father plays an equally important role in the development of a girl's sexual identity. Hetherington explored the effects of paternal absence and loss on girls aged 13 to 17 who attended a community recreation center. Her findings suggest that the effect of paternal absence on daughters manifests itself during adolescence as an inability to interact appropriately or comfortably with males. The adolescent girls in her study whose parents were divorced had developed critical attitudes toward males, while those whose fathers had died had positive images of their fathers and felt that no other men could compare with them. The girls whose parents were divorced dated earlier and more frequently and were more apt to engage in sexual intercourse; the girls whose fathers had died tended to date later and to be sexually inhibited and shy. Early separation from a father was shown to have more pronounced effects on adolescent behavior than separation after the age of 5.

Future studies would need to focus on families in which there are boys and on families in which the mother has remarried. Hetherington suggests that since the effects of a father's absence on a girl are not manifested until adolescence, important evidence may be gained by studying mature women. Attitude studies can also prove fruitful. As graduate students, a colleague and I compared the attitudes of children from broken homes toward their parents with the attitudes of children from intact family units. We asked 10-year-old children to take a story-completion test concerning a trip to the moon made with their families. The children from intact homes referred to their parents in the third person more frequently than the children from broken homes. On the other hand, the children from broken homes referred to their parents as "mother" or "father" more frequently than the children from intact families. We interpreted this finding to mean that the children from broken homes were more aware of their parents than the children from intact homes and that this accounted for the form and the frequency of the children's references to their parents (Paukstelis and Pazdur).

A limitation of research studies is that care givers cannot apply the findings in practical situations. For several years, I worked with a troubled adolescent girl who exhibited the characteristics described in the Hetherington study. Her father had left the home when she was 5 years old. As a preschooler, she had been molested by a family friend. Her behavior with men was seductive, coy, and sometimes aggressive. She experienced sexual intercourse as a preadolescent and was in conflict with her mother, who constantly accused her of sexual misconduct. Both she and her mother would have been helped greatly by early intervention at the time of initial inappropriate sexual experience. This girl will probably work through her sexual identity and the effects of her experience throughout her adult life. Cure takes longer than prevention.

LIVING WITH DYING

Giving care in the face of death is one of the most crucial aspects of helping people. The more we know about death and about our own thoughts, feelings, and fears concerning death, the better we will be able to help people who are dying and their survivors. It is essential for care givers to be able to deal with the topic of death. For example, I remember choosing to attend school the day my father died rather than participating in the funeral preparations. I wanted to be given support and sympathy and to keep busy with other things. Instead of understanding, the teacher sent me home. Part of me wanted to gain some relief from the pain by keeping busy, while another part yearned to be cared for. I have since learned that this is a common response to the death of a loved one. The reaction is not one of denial; rather, it is related to the ego's protective device of furnishing strategies for coping according to the individual's capability to handle stress. In light of this, care givers should realize that it is important for them to be available, but not hovering, in such situations.

As a young adult, I experienced the sudden death of a patient whom I was bathing. I was shocked, and again I felt the need to be given support and to keep busy. The nursing instructor felt unable to handle the situation and sent me to the nurses' dormitory, where no one was available to give me the support I needed. There was no discussion of the dead patient in the dormitory, in the classroom, or on the ward. Death was a forbidden topic. Not even when we were taught to prepare a body for the morgue were we free to talk about the mystery of death. Things are not much different today, as Chapter 7, on the death of a child, discloses.

While working as a nurse in an industrial setting, I was faced with many crises. During a blizzard, the chemistry building exploded, injuring and killing employees. I accompanied patients to the hospital in the ambulance. One patient moaned loudly above the blare of the siren, "I'm going to die," and asked that his wife not be told because she was pregnant. I attempted to comfort him by reassuring him that he would be all right. He died the next day. I cringe now at this utterly nontherapeutic statement. I was more helpful when dealing with survivors, and I recognized that relating to a dying person is more stressful than relating to someone who is recovering from an illness or an injury. The preparation of care givers for their first experience with death needs to include making them aware of their own vulnerability so that they will not expect too much of themselves. With increasing sophistication and knowledge on the part of the public and professionals, death undoubtedly will become a more acceptable topic of discussion, as sex has, and our understanding of, and communication with, those facing death and loss will improve.

The greatest asset we have as care givers in situations involving death is the ability to respond sensitively to the survivor's or the dying person's needs or wants at any given moment. Some people are born with this ability, while others develop it through learning. Combining knowledge and sensitivity results in a great advantage. While I was consulting with baccalaureate nursing students, they shared with me their feelings of insecurity about intervening with dying patients and their families. They could accurately assess a person's attitude toward impending death by determining which stage of dying that person was in—anger, depression, bargaining, or acceptance—but they were unable to perform the important task of relating to the person. An adolescent girl with a terminal brain tumor was not told her prognosis; however, she indicated that she was concerned about death by such statements as "My flowers are dying" or "The egg yolks look dead this morning." The students missed the opportunity to relate to this dying adolescent because of their own anxiety, which kept them from recognizing the true meaning of her words.

Certain patterns of reactions to death in the dying person and in survivors have been identified by clinicians and researchers, beginning with the classical study of Lindemann, who studied survivors of the Coconut Grove holocaust, and the latest studies of Kübler-Ross. Some clinicians and researchers are finding data that contradict or are incompatible with theories related to (1) stages of dying and (2) the development of the concept of death in children. Noonan and Tiktinsky (see Chapter 7) found a different process of mourning from that postulated by Kübler-Ross, which progresses from denial to acceptance of death. Their patients experienced all the elements of anger, depression, bargaining, and acceptance simultaneously, in varying degrees.

Roberson studied the various stages of the development of the concept of death in children. Since there is no complete agreement as to the characteristics or the age ranges of each stage, Roberson used the three most commonly cited stages. During the preschool years (stage 1) the child does not recognize that death is final. During early childhood (stage 2) there is a *beginning* realization that death is irreversible. In preadolescence (stage 3) death is finally viewed as inevitable and irreversible (Alexander and Alderstein; Nagy; Safier). On the basis of his research, Roberson suggests that future researchers recognize that *children today may not conceive of death the way children 25 years ago conceived of it* and that *children mature sooner today than they did when the older studies were made*. Another problem for researchers is that of determining at what age the concepts of life and death are fully mature. He found that children have mature concepts of life and death before age 11 or 12, which is in disagreement with past research. Kastenbaum and Aisenberg suggest that we free ourselves from contemporary "establishment" orientations to this subject and be ready to consider other potentially useful approaches to understanding human development.

The Survivors: Siblings

Parents sometimes transfer their love of a lost child to surviving siblings, with disastrous results. For example, the younger brother of a school-aged girl died suddenly. The brother had been the mother's favorite, and the mother began bestowing an abundance of affection upon the girl. The girl became more silent and less spontaneous and developed a haunted look. She felt guilty, insecure, and unable to handle the attention that had always been showered on her brother.

Schiff states that one of the most difficult tasks a parent who has lost a child must face is that of continuing to parent the remaining siblings. As in divorce, there can be role reversals in care giving and comforting. Other problems of remaining siblings include guilt that they may have caused the death of the brother or sister, being compared with the dead child, and reluctance to visit the dead child's grave. Schiff interviewed teenagers and adult men and women who had experienced the death of a sibling in childhood. None remembered positive interactions with their parents during the grieving period.

Parents and care givers who counsel parents may find helpful the following suggestions offered by Schiff:

1. Take time to comfort and talk separately with each child and help reveal any feelings of guilt that may be harbored.
2. Continue calm discipline as before the death, because this gives security to the remaining children.
3. Allow children to laugh and play during the early stages of bereavement.

4. Give choices about visiting the cemetery.
5. Do not avoid talking about the dead child, but do not aggrandize. Living children can react in opposite behavior to gain attention.

Jackson offers these suggestions:

1. Know when to talk about death, i.e., when the child wants to.
2. Be honest.
3. Share feelings on the child's level of understanding.
4. Understand that children's grief is acted out in anger, in overt cruelty, or in playing dead.
5. Acknowledge that other loved ones will not die or leave.
6. Help children understand that adults cry too as a way of expressing feelings.
7. Be cautious about making disparaging remarks about the hospital and doctors in order that children do not attach fear and apprehension to people and places.

Death of a Parent

When a parent dies, a child faces a unique situation because of the special nature of the tie. An adult has meaningful relationships with many people—spouse, parents, children, friends, and colleagues—whereas a child has all his or her love invested in the parents. Knowing when to tell a child that a parent is dying is difficult. If the dying parent is aware of the approaching death, the children sense this and may ask, "Is Daddy going to die?" (Furman). It is helpful to respond in a way that acknowledges concern and to mention the physician's role, for example, "I can well understand that you worry that Dad will die. I have thought about it too. Right now the doctor can make him feel better" (Furman, p. 19). When the parent is near death and the child can no longer visit, the youngster can be informed that the doctors have no other way of helping the parent but will make sure that the parent is comfortable until death occurs. In the case of sudden death, it is recommended that the remaining parent acknowledge the fact and not try to cover it up in an attempt to make the reality more palatable. A barrier can be set up if the parent is not honest and leaves the child to struggle alone with confusing and frightening thoughts (Furman).

Identification with the dead parent is manifested by the youngster's wearing articles of the deceased's clothing, such as shoes or a tie. The opposite happens when identification is avoided for fear of the same fate. The end of mourning is also trying, as the child seeks a new love object. The surviving parent is aware of the child's need and sometimes reproaches the youngster for wanting a new parent. Problems can also arise if a new parent is provided before the youngster is ready.

In working with children who were already in therapy when their parents died, Furman found that there were favorable and unfavorable effects on their personalities. Some children showed improvement in areas such as reality testing, toleration, and verbalization of affect. The experience of loss and appropriate mourning did not necessarily strengthen the child's personality, but he or she did stand a better chance of handling later stressful experiences. The stress of loss is greater for the younger child, who has a limited ability to test reality and to overcome anxiety and dependence on the adult; this can result in behavior difficulties later and interfere with the ability to mourn (Furman).

Pets can be of help in two ways:

1. A very young child has usually an unconscious wish that a critically ill parent will die because he or she feels neglected. When the parent dies, the youngster feels guilty, depressed, and/or terrified of suffering the same fate. When the child turns to the surviving parent, who is unable to offer comfort because of his or her own grief, the youngster's feelings of guilt, depression, and fear deepen. At this point, a pet's silent, nondemanding acceptance helps the child survive the trauma.

2. A pet's death provides a child with an emotional experience that will make it easier to cope with future losses (Levinson).

Surviving: The Marriage

The death of a child can affect a marriage. Each parent may feel unable to cope with the other's grief. For instance, a mother became uninterested in sex because of the association with the conception of the dead child. Her husband, however, had a need for intimacy, which he was forced to satisfy outside the marriage. This couple solved their problem successfully, but not all husbands and wives are so fortunate. Sometimes husbands stay away from home in order to avoid painful memories. In contrast, one husband preferred to stay near his wife, shying away from work until she began accompanying him to his job. Financial burdens also cause stress; one man who could not cope with both the loss of the child and the barrage of medical bills left the family (Schiff).

Many bereaved couples who cannot withstand the many pressures decide to get a divorce. Sometimes a couple are in a better situation to help each other after the marriage is over. Schiff does not indicate whether she interviewed parents who were divorced or unmarried couples living together. Would the dynamics among such couples be different? Groups of bereaved parents have been established; they can offer support and understanding and can make referrals, if necessary, to other agencies for marital counseling (Schiff).

The following is an overview of issues in divorce and death:

- It is important that children be protected from possible detrimental effects of separation and divorce. A divorced or separated parent's relationships with members of the opposite sex need not create psychological difficulties for the children if:

   There is not a series of such relationships.

   The parent does not try to cover up the relationship.

   The children understand that they will have friends regardless of the parent's marital status if they are friendly, courteous, and considerate of others and if others enjoy being with them (Gardner).

- How well the parent functions in the postseparation period is crucial to the development of the child (Wallerstein and Kelly).
- Children may experience guilt, thinking that they caused the divorce.
- It is important for children to be cared for by adults of both sexes. A father's absence can cause a boy to adopt feminine behavior, while a girl without a father will have difficulty relating to males during adolescence and perhaps adulthood (Hetherington).
- Role reversal can occur after a divorce; the parent may depend upon the child for comfort and support.
- Children's concepts of death vary with the age of the child. Children arrive at a mature concept of death earlier today than in the past (Kastenbaum and Aisenberg).
- In the case of the death of a child, siblings may experience guilt, thinking that they were the cause.
- A difficult task of the parents of a deceased child is that of continuing to parent the surviving siblings. In one study, teenagers and adults who experienced the death of a sibling in childhood could not remember positive interactions with their parents during the grief period (Schiff).
- Role reversal may occur; the bereaved parent may turn to the surviving siblings for support.
- The effects of death can be buffered by a pet, who can give the child nondemanding acceptance. The death of a pet can also help a child adjust to future losses (Levinson).
- When parents die, children experience the loss more intensely than adolescents or adults (Furman).
- Loss and appropriate mourning do not necessarily strengthen the child's personality; however, the experience may help the child cope better with future loss and separation (Furman).
- The death of a child affects a marriage. Sexual activity may remind the parents of the child, they may be unable to sustain their relationship because of their grief, and financial pressures can add to their burden (Schiff).

The Dying Child

Whether to tell a child about his or her impending death is a controversial, highly emotional issue. Often children who are not told the truth know they are facing death because of clues they pick up from staff members or their families. They then try to protect their families and care givers from the burden of disclosure. Families and care givers may not tell a child the truth in an effort to spare the child from the tragic experience of facing death. Increasingly, professionals are adopting the philosophy that dying children have a right to know about their situation and that care givers should be trained how and when to be honest with dying children. Handling this task with a sensitive consideration of the child's personality, coping ability, and cultural and family background can alleviate much suffering on the part of both the child and the survivors. You may arrive at your own conclusions concerning this crucial aspect of caring for dying children after reading Chapter 7.

REFERENCES

Alexander, Irving, and **Arthur M. Alderstein:** "Affective Responses to the Concept of Death in a Population of Children and Adolescents," *Journal of Genetic Psychology,* **93:**167–177, 1958.

Bowlby, John: *Separation: Anxiety and Anger, vol. II, Attachment and Loss,* Basic Books, New York, 1973.

Furman, Erna: *A Child's Parent Dies: Studies in Childhood Bereavement,* Yale, New Haven, Conn., 1974.

Gardner, Richard A.: *Psychotherapy with Children of Divorce,* Aronson, New York, 1976.

Gettleman, Susan, and **Janet Markowitz:** *The Courage to Divorce,* Simon and Schuster, New York, 1974.

Hansburg, Henry G.: "The Use of the Separation Anxiety Test in the Detection of Self-destructive Tendencies in Early Adolescence," in D. V. Siva Sankar (ed.), *Mental Health in Children,* vol. III, PJD Publications, Westbury, N.Y., 1976.

Hetherington, Mavis E.: "Girls without Fathers," *Psychology Today,* **6**(9)47–52, 1973.

Jackson, Edgar N.: *Telling a Child about Death,* Hawthorn, New York, 1965.

Kastenbaum, Robert, and **Ruth Aisenberg:** "Death as a Thought," in Edward S. Shneidman (ed.), *Death: Current Perspectives,* Mayfield, Palo Alto, 1976.

Kübler-Ross, Elisabeth: *On Death and Dying,* Macmillan, New York, 1969.

Levinson, Boris: "The Pet and the Child's Bereavement," *Mental Hygiene,* **51**(2): 197–200, 1967.

Lindemann, Erich: "Symptomatology and Management of Acute Grief," *American Journal of Psychiatry,* **101:**141–148, 1944.

Murphy, Lois Barclay, and **Alice E. Moriarty:** *Vulnerability, Coping and Growth: From Infancy to Adolescence,* Yale, New Haven, Conn., 1976.

Nagy, Maria: "The Child's View of Death," in Herman Feifel (ed.), *The Meaning of Death,* McGraw-Hill, New York, 1959, pp. 79–98.

Paukstelis, Aldona, and **Helen (Monea) Pazdur:** "A Comparative Study of Children's Attitudes towards Parents: The Broken Home vs. the Whole Family," unpublished graduate study, University of California, San Francisco, 1966.

Roberson, Whitney Wherrett: "The Concepts of Life and Death in the School Age Child," M. A. thesis, San Francisco State College, 1972.

Robertson, James, and **Joyce Robertson:** "Young Children in Brief Separation," *Research Relating to Children,* Bulletin 36, September 1975–February 1976, p. 139.

Safier, G.: "A Study in the Relationships between the Life and Death Concepts in Children," *Journal of Genetic Psychology,* **105:**283–294, 1964.

Schiff, Harriet Sarnoff: *The Bereaved Parent,* Crown, New York, 1977.

Wallerstein, Judith S., and **Joan B. Kelly:** "Divorce Counseling: A Community Service for Families in the Midst of Divorce," paper presented at the annual meeting of the American Orthopsychiatric Association, Atlanta, 1976.

OTHER RESOURCES

ORGANIZATION

The Shanti Project
1137 Colusa Avenue
Berkeley, Calif. 94707

A nonprofit organization providing free counseling for patients and families facing life-threatening illness or death. The following books on topics of importance to parents and children were recommended in the organization's newsletter, *Eclipse,* 1(2), 1977–1978:

The Death of a Pet or Wild Animal

Carrick, Carol: *The Accident,* Seabury, New York, 1976. Recommended for ages 2 to 10.

Viorst, Judith: *The Tenth Good Thing about Barney,* Atheneum, New York, 1971. Recommended for ages 2 to 7.

A Child's Reaction to the Illness or Death of a Grandparent

Coutant, Helen: *First Snow,* Knopf, New York, 1974. Recommended for ages 8 to 10.

Miles, Miska: *Annie and the Old One,* Little, Brown, Boston, 1971. Recommended for ages 8 to 10.

The Loss of a Parent

LeShan, Eda J.: *Learning to Say Goodbye,* Macmillan, New York, 1976. Recommended for ages 8 and over.

Illness and Death in Children

Lee, Virginia: *The Magic Moth,* Seabury, New York, 1972. Recommended for ages 11 and up.

Shuman, Ron: *Day by Day,* Scrimshaw, Oakland, Calif., 1977. Recommended for ages 8 and up.

Chapter 6

SEPARATION ANXIETY IN A NURSE-PATIENT RELATIONSHIP

Anne McCue

> I wouldn't have [emotional] problems if we hadn't got
> divorced. I think I will get divorced seven times.
>
> *Paul (10 years old)*

Paul made the above statement during therapy in a nurse-patient relationship.
It expresses the conflict that divorce and subsequent separation anxiety produce.
The concept of separation anxiety is operant in any nurse-patient relationship
because when the goals of treatment have been reached, the relationship
ends. Utilizing the relationship, including its termination, as a growing experience
requires an understanding of the concept of separation anxiety. This chapter will
define separation anxiety and briefly discuss related theory. Separation anxiety
will be discussed in the framework of a play therapy experience with a 10-year-
old boy. Clinical vignettes from that experience will be presented to illustrate
the manifestation and handling of separation anxiety within a year-long nurse-
patient encounter.

I was the therapist for 10-year-old Paul, whom I saw three times weekly in
play therapy. Paul was 5 when he and his two brothers were initially separated
from their father, then returned to their father, and finally permanently separated
from their mother by divorce. The father was eager for the children to grow up
so that they could take care of themselves. Paul and his brothers spent 2 years
with a series of baby-sitters as mother substitutes until their father remarried.
During those 2 years they did not have the comfort and security that preschoolers
and school-aged children need. When he was 8, Paul was admitted to a children's

psychiatric hospital because of aggressive and antisocial behavior at school and at home. His father had remarried when Paul was 7. That marriage ended in divorce when Paul was 10, at which time he was in therapy.

I have chosen to consider the concept of separation anxiety for several reasons. First, it was a frequent and recurrent theme in Paul's life; he experienced the related fears in other important relationships. Second, I too experienced separation anxiety as termination with Paul approached. Third, in child psychiatric nursing, one is always involved in helping children cope with the normal process of growth, which includes progressively being separated from parents, family, and home, moving into the wider world of school, teachers, and friends. Anticipating and experiencing these separations lead to anxiety. Learning to handle separation in childhood will prepare a person to handle separation anxiety in relationships that are formed and terminated later in life. "It is important to learn that one can sustain a loss and endure. Able to move apart as well as come together, individuals need to free themselves from a crippling object hunger which makes them hang on too cruelly here, avoid being reinvolved there. Getting and losing are part of the same process: one its beginning, the other its end. But they follow one another in circular, not linear, fashion" (Glenn, p. 445).

SEPARATION ANXIETY: NORMAL VERSUS PATHOLOGICAL

In psychoanalytic terms, separation anxiety is defined as "a fear of desertion by or the loss of an important person . . . [separation anxiety] has its roots in the pre-Oedipal periods when the child's dependency is in the ascendance" (Nemiah, p. 143). I am using this definition of separation anxiety because it acknowledges the impact of the early years of childhood development on a person's approach to an expected loss and because it does not define separation anxiety as a pathological process. Bowlby describes separation anxiety as "the inescapable corollary of attachment behavior—the other side of the coin; therefore it is normal to be prone to separation anxiety. . . . It is exhibited in the everyday life of all of us" (1960, pp. 102, 110). Adults may experience separation anxiety as the recurrence of childhood separations or in the reality of a current situation such as a forthcoming move to a new city or the loss of a loved one.

Bowlby (1960) has developed a theory of separation anxiety that is based on his analytical background combined with his observations of relatively healthy children admitted to hospitals. He found that a child who has had a normal relationship with his or her mother and who has not been previously separated from her will exhibit a predictable sequence of behavior. There are three phases in this sequence: protest, despair, and detachment. Monea discusses these behaviors in more detail in Chapter 5. Separation anxiety is seen as an outgrowth of the protest phase, when the child cries loudly, expects the mother to return, and rejects alternative mother figures. The separation anxiety is "a reaction to the danger of losing the object" of love (i.e., the mother) (Bowlby, 1960, p. 92).

Bowlby (1961) stresses the time element of separation anxiety; it is a response to the threat of loss, occurring *before* the loss actually takes place. He further differentiates separation anxiety from grief and mourning, which evolve as responses to the lost object after the loss has actually been experienced. Later in life, anxiety—including separation anxiety—can function as a warning signal of impending danger.

How might separation anxiety exceed normal levels and assume pathological proportions? Bowlby looks at some early childhood separation experiences which have the potential of developing pathological intensity. First, this could happen if a child is separated from the mother and there is no acceptable substitute for her and nobody to provide comfort and security. Hostility in the separation situation, e.g., from a rejecting mother, can also lay the foundation for pathological separation anxiety. "An excess of separation anxiety may be due either to an experience of actual separation or to threats of separation, rejection, or loss of love" (Bowlby, 1960, p. 106). It is possible that, prior to the divorces, Paul felt that both mothers rejected him or stopped loving him. His stepmother openly said that she could not handle Paul and his siblings along with her own child from a previous marriage.

The development of separation anxiety as a result of separation from the mother has been documented in research by Bowlby and others. Robertson validated it in research with hospitalized children. Spitz has looked at the hatred and hostility which can emerge as a result of separation from the mother. Winnicott has also found that anxiety will result from "failure in the technique of infant care, as for instance failure to give the continuous love support that belongs to mothering" (Winnicott, p. 98).

SEPARATION ANXIETY AS A RESULT OF DIVORCE

There is a dearth of literature and research on separation anxiety resulting from divorce. Although Bowlby's theory is based on hospitalized children, separation anxiety can certainly be seen in children who experience other kinds of separation. One could speculate that the impact of separation due to divorce would have more long-range effects than separation due to hospitalization. The separation of divorce is permanent, and there is inevitably family tension in the process leading up to divorce. Paul was very much involved in the process of divorce in his family. He spoke of it in the first person: "We are going to get a divorce." "We got a divorce." "I wouldn't have [emotional] problems if we hadn't got divorced." "I think I will get divorced seven times."

One might interpret Paul's last statement as a reflection of his understanding of marriage or as a prediction concerning his own life, instead of as a reflection of his anxiety concerning his father's marriages. Paul was surprised to learn from other children on the ward that not all parents get divorced. One research study with over 500 subjects found that "divorce, separation and desertion by parents more than doubles the probability that the children will also become divorced or separated" (Langer and Stanley, p. 164).

SEPARATION ANXIETY: A THERAPEUTIC APPROACH

In order to illustrate the manifestation of separation in this nurse-client relationship, I will cite several situations which elicited separation anxiety in Paul, including one in which I, too, experienced separation anxiety.

The first situation in which Paul experienced separation anxiety in therapy was related to his stepmother. Four months after therapy began, Paul wrote his stepmother a letter inviting her to come and see a movie at the hospital and telling her that she was very nice. He drew a picture of himself as a very tiny figure saying the words ''Love, Paul.'' He also drew a much larger picture of his mother walking their dog and cat. See Figure 6-1.

At the time, I did not think much about the letter, despite the fact that it was very unusual for Paul to write to anyone. It was a couple of weeks after this letter was written that Paul's stepmother announced her intention of getting a divorce. When he wrote the letter, Paul was probably feeling the effects of what

Figure 6-1 Dear Mom.

Despert describes as the emotional divorce which always precedes a legal divorce. One can speculate that writing the letter, an unusual thing for Paul to do, was a way of handling his fears that his stepmother was pulling away from the family. He was expressing separation anxiety, although I did not recognize it as such. He may have been hoping that his stepmother would accept his invitation (and love) and that this would prevent his losing her.

Paul's stepmother left shortly before Thanksgiving. Paul was anticipating Thanksgiving without a mother. He chose drawing as the medium for expressing his anxiety. The day before he went home for Thanksgiving, Paul drew a picture of himself as a dot stranded alone on an island with two pieces of bread. At the same time, he talked a lot about food.

This time I realized that Paul was about to face his first extended home visit without a mother. He was about to experience being in a motherless family again. I chose to intervene by telling Paul part of my assessment of his situation, encouraging him to verbalize his feelings, and then acknowledging the reality of the situation. I did this by saying that Thanksgiving was coming and that people often think about food in relation to Thanksgiving. I wondered aloud whether he was thinking about Thanksgiving at his house. He was able to verbalize his fears that there would be no Thanksgiving dinner because his stepmother would not be there to fix it. Also, he said that if he had no mother to feed him, he might starve. Then we looked at the reality of his home situation. His father had money to buy food and always kept enough food in the house. His father cooked, and his grandmother helped out occasionally. However, it was true that his stepmother would not be there, and we acknowledged that it is scary for a 10-year-old boy to lose his second mother.

Loss of a Second Mother

The impact of losing a second mother overshadowed a lot of Paul's activities during the year. His behavior regressed to earlier levels; he plugged toilets to flood them, and he fought a great deal with peers. A few months after his stepmother's departure, Paul drew a picture of himself walking through a 10,000-mile-long cave in search of his home, which was in the ocean at the end of the cave. See Figure 6-2. He began the journey as a little dot. At one point he said he died on the way because there was not enough fruit to eat. Using Bowlby's (1960) sequence of separation behavior, one could interpret the drawing as despair over the loss of a mother and all that she stands for in the home.

McDermott, a clinician and researcher, has found that children are often made to feel small, weak, and incredibly vulnerable by the whole divorce experience. This was frequently noted on psychological testing: "Children felt unable to fend for themselves, and in dire danger of being injured, crushed or stepped on by external forces" (McDermott, p. 424). In therapy Paul often expressed these feelings of smallness and vulnerability. In the cave drawing (Figure 6-2) and others, one can see the representation of smallness and aloneness. Paul expressed the feelings that McDermott describes in other ways besides drawing. He invented many games in which he was devoured by a monster or a giant. He was

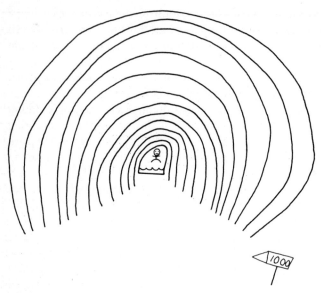

Figure 6-2 Boy in a cave. A little boy (shown as a dot above) started walking in a cave that was 10,000 miles long. In one version of the story, the boy died on the way because there was no fruit for him to eat. In a later version he had to find his home, which was in the ocean at the end of the cave.

often seriously wounded by the enemy and came close to death in his army games. The army battles, which he had played repeatedly for a couple of years with his previous therapist, were still full of blood, killing, torture, suffering, and anguish.

   Paul displayed what McDermott and others describe as "the extraordinary readiness of the child to interpret the experience of separation as an expression of hostility on the part of the parent, and to assume that this action was justified by the child's wrongdoing, the child then identifying with the hostile, rejecting parent, accepting the fantasy of a crime that deserves punishment, and assuming the guilt that such an act requires" (McDermott, p. 424). Paul was puzzling over the departure of his stepmother and was attempting to alleviate his guilt feelings when he explained, "We were being good when she left." In one of his doll-playing games, a family was ravaged by tragedy; when it was over, there were three boys and one man left behind, the same number of people that his mother and stepmother had left behind. At such times, I would intervene by starting an exchange about the hurt and anger people feel when someone important leaves them.

Terminating with Staff Members

In the hospital, Paul experienced the loss of a number of people with whom he had developed a close relationship. As expected, separation anxiety appeared each time. Because of my knowledge of separation anxiety and because I knew when the separations were going to occur, I was able to help Paul prepare for them. Although the separation anxiety was painful, it was not overwhelming. Whenever a staff member who was close to Paul announced that he or she was leaving, I would treat the departure in terms of the end of a meaningful relationship. For example, when Vicki, a staff member, left, I pointed out that Paul had had a lot of good times and some bad times with her and that he had gained many things from having known her—things he would always be able to use in the future. I told Paul that Vicki was leaving for personal reasons and that she would miss Paul and knew that he would miss her. I acknowledged the reality of the pain and the difficulty of the loss. Paul could not accept my approach entirely. "They do it on purpose; they know they're doing it" (leaving and hurting him). On the day Vicki left, just prior to therapy, he gave her a picture he had drawn for her. In therapy he built a castle from blocks and toppled it with a grand crash. From the debris of the castle he built a small jail. Paul said that the artist who had made the castle was an evil man. He was building a jail for some children. The children were pleading not to be separated from their mothers. "We don't want to go; we didn't do anything." The mothers were pleading for their children. Paul finally caught the mean artist and put him in jail because of all the terrible things he had done.

My understanding of the concept of separation anxiety shaped my intervention in this situation. Knowing Paul's history and knowing that he had just drawn a picture for Vicki led me to think that her leaving was stirring up feelings of separation anxiety from past separations, especially the separations from his two mothers. The mean artist who was doing horrible things, including jailing children, could represent Paul's feelings of guilt that he was the reason Vicki was leaving. I decided to offer Paul the opportunity to express any guilt feelings, if indeed he was feeling guilty of doing "terrible mean things." Therefore, I asked whether the artist who made the castle was the same artist who made the picture for Vicki. "Yes, he is," Paul replied. I handled that by considering the possibility that he was feeling responsible for some of the rough times he had had with Vicki and was now feeling sad about losing someone he liked so much. He went on to talk about how he had felt when other people he liked had gone away, including his real mother and his stepmother.

Loss of Hospital Friends

In the hospital Paul also had to deal with the loss of patients who had become his friends. This was a realistic preparation for the future loss of school friends and neighbors who would one day move away. In therapy Paul talked about an older boy named John who was going to be discharged soon. Paul had idolized John and would miss him very much. To help Paul handle this separation anxiety, I suggested that he draw a picture of John and that we talk about all the things he enjoyed doing with John. He drew a picture of John and listed the things he liked about him. Again we discussed the fact that people gain from having known someone they like, even though it is difficult when that person goes away. Later, Paul wrote John a letter wishing him well in school and asking him to write. Writing letters is one way in which many people handle separation anxiety and reassure themselves that they will not completely lose contact with the person from whom they are separated. After John was gone, Paul still idolized his lost friend and missed him, but he handled the loss well.

Short-Term Separation from the Therapist

A few times, Paul also had to face being separated from me when I took vacations. As my vacations approached, he sometimes used fantasy to protect himself symbolically. Prior to one vacation, he talked about sleeping for 2 weeks. He had me read "Snow White" aloud to him, and he chanted the names of two of the dwarfs: "Happy, Sleepy, Happy, Sleepy, Happy, Sleepy." My knowledge of separation anxiety and of Paul made me wonder whether he was shielding himself from his anxiety by wishing for 2 weeks of sleep. I intervened by wondering aloud whether he was thinking it would be nice to sleep for 2 weeks while I was away. "How did you know?" was his response; if he could sleep through my vacation, it would be just as if I had not gone away. I explained that most people worry about what it will be like when someone leaves them and that they wish the person would stay. Paul seemed relieved that I now knew how he felt; he then started playing some of the games he had been playing recently in therapy, as though he were now free to move on to other things.

Another time, to prepare for the anticipated loss of therapist and to deal with separation anxiety before one of my vacations, he put some toy soldiers into a drawer during the last therapy hour before my departure. He said that they were going into the deep freeze for a week. When I returned, he went immediately to the drawer and told the soldiers that they could thaw out now. I chose not to intervene in this handling of separation anxiety because Paul was doing such a fine job himself.

Termination

Knowing that those vacation separations were not permanent made them tolerable for Paul, and he experienced minimal separation anxiety. Things were different when I told him I would be leaving permanently—for me as well as for him. I had spent a year as Paul's therapist and was feeling guilty and apprehensive about imposing another separation on him during the same year in which the second divorce in his family had occurred. I was also feeling sad because I liked Paul and would miss working with him. At the same time, I was excited about moving and was looking forward to the new experiences ahead of me. I knew that part of my own growth involved accepting the fact that I had to leave behind some things that would be hard to part with. I knew that the process of leaving Paul would be a difficult one, and I dreaded his reaction to my leaving. In some ways I wanted to deny the fact myself, and I managed to "forget" to tell Paul for several days after I had intended to break the news. My guilt feelings were compounded by the fact that my coworkers wondered how my leaving would affect Paul. In addition, I knew that I would really miss him.

It was true that Paul's treatment was not complete and would be interrupted by my leaving. Sometimes at work and sometimes at home, as I made preparations to leave and said good-bye to friends, I wondered whether I was doing the right thing. It was difficult to leave so much behind when I was not sure what the move would bring. Yet I knew I needed to take the risk involved in moving toward my own personal goals, despite the difficulties involved. In such a situation, one "task for the therapist is 'working through' the leave-taking experience with his patient and using it as an occasion for growth instead of avoidance or collapse" (Glenn, p. 439). Realizing that I was experiencing separation anxiety made it possible for me to carry through with my plans to leave and to help Paul deal with his many feelings of anger, sadness, and rejection as he anticipated the loss.

Paul's Responses to Termination of Our Relationship

In therapy, Paul's responses to my leaving covered a wide range of feelings. Initially, he cheered. Then he said he would visit me. The route I would travel became a means for expressing his feelings. At first he drew road maps with stop signs; later he left them out. See Figure 6-3. He drew dangerous animals, spiders, and earthquakes which would get me. In his stories he was the one who saved me from those perils of the road, so how could I manage without him? Eventually, we explored his concerns about having another therapist.

Paul also responded by playing some dramatic games filled with double crosses and tricks. In one army game he was the victim of many wrongs, including treachery and being shot in the neck and arm. Danger and death were more prominent themes than usual in his play. Once he said about a soldier, "You know how he can stand it?" "How?" I asked. "A long, long time ago he was forced to do something. Guard himself." Paul proceeded to build a jail or cage around himself. "There was a spell cast from which he would die." I said, "There must be a way to save him." A doctor and a nurse appeared. I asked whether they were going to help him out. "Yes, *he* is," Paul said, implying that the nurse would not. Then he constructed an operating room, where his wounds were treated. Although he was afraid he would die, he was saved and went back to fighting in the army.

Another time he drew a picture of himself floating in space, a small figure separated from his spaceship with his lifeline severed. He expressed many such feelings of vulnerability and of fear of death. In one game the soldiers all froze and died. He screamed with anguish for them as they fell, spiraling down to their death.

Paul Expresses Anger

Along with his wish that he could prevent my leaving, Paul was able to express the anger he felt toward me and toward others who had left him, including his

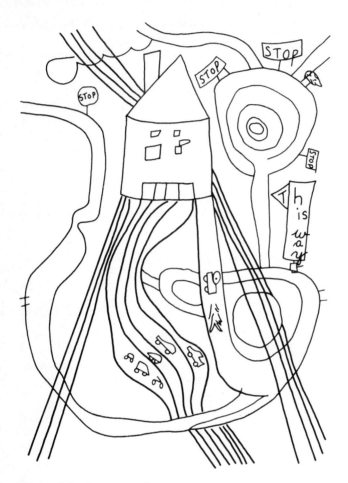

Figure 6-3 Apartment house.

two mothers. I had told him that I knew he would have some reactions to my leaving and that this was all right. Paul manifested the angry, hostile reactions which Bowlby (1960) and McDermott describe; he swore at me, both verbally and in his newly learned cursive writing; he told me how terrible I was; and he engaged in episodes of throwing things, hitting me, and kicking me, to the point where I had to restrain him. As the relationship came to a close, amidst the protests we looked at what we had gained from it and at how we had grown, acknowledging that we would miss each other and that it was a difficult separation for both of us.

During the course of therapy, Paul had experienced a number of separations. He was learning to deal with the normal terminations in the life of a 10-year-old. However, he was still coping with the effects of losing two mothers and, at the end, anticipating the loss of his therapist. As the ending of our relationship approached, I was able to utilize my understanding of separation anxiety and my past experience to provide support through supervision. All these factors enabled me to identify and cope with my own manifestations of separation anxiety and to help Paul do the same. I feel that the experience helped me grow as an individual and increased my ability to handle future separations in my personal and professional life and to help patients work through separation anxiety.

SUGGESTIONS FOR ENHANCING COMMUNICATION WITH CHILDREN

McCue's interventions for separation anxiety can be modified to work with children in other settings such as clinics, hospitals, schools, and homes. The following suggestions can be used as a baseline to facilitate and enhance communication with children. These suggestions (developed by Helen Monea) are not intended to prepare staff to be therapists but to use principles of the therapeutic approach to help children communicate with care givers.

- The world of children is play; the use of art media, games, and story telling facilitates expression of feelings and thoughts that accompany separation anxiety, such as sadness, guilt, and anger.
- Prepare children for staff absences by:
    Giving them ample time to know about the absence and whether it is temporary, such as a vacation, or permanent
    Helping them express their own feelings and thoughts about the absence
    Avoiding the interpretation of their drawings and games, and encouraging them to express their own interpretations
    Sending a picture postcard during your vacation absence or writing letters during a permanent absence. (If you are close to a particular child, these actions may help reduce the feeling of rejection or help alleviate the fear that she or he made you disappear. If you believe you will not be able to write, it is best not to promise. For some children, consider that continuing contact after termination may not be helpful.)
    Sharing your feelings about your departure in a way that is both honest and understandable to the child. (Confidentiality and honesty can strengthen the child's trust in you.)
    Being prepared to receive cheers, anger, or withdrawal as termination approaches. (See Chapter 10.)
- Prepare yourself for termination. Be aware of your own feelings and thoughts about termination.
    Acquire support from an appropriate person such as another staff member, supervisor, or confidante
- Since you are working with children, analyze how comfortable you are in their world.

IMPLICATIONS FOR THE FUTURE

As one of the outcomes of this experience, I have become concerned about (1) the long-range effects of divorce, including the relationship between parental loss and separation anxiety, and (2) the way in which families are helped to cope with the crisis of divorce. Paul's family had no professional intervention during the first divorce. During the second divorce, Paul was in therapy because of many problems, and this divorce was dealt with. For part of this time, Paul's father and one brother were in therapy briefly. During both divorces an approach such as family therapy might have enabled the family to cope with their many and mixed reactions before and after the actual divorce. Children of divorce, like Paul, may need help in overcoming separation anxiety, including fears of death, starvation, and abandonment whenever an important separation occurs. How a divorce is experienced may have serious implications for future interpersonal relationships and the ability to deal with future separations and losses. For theory and guidelines see Chapter 5.

Divorce is becoming increasingly common in our culture. It is a time of crisis for those involved. If nurses and other health workers are going to intervene to assist and support families through a divorce, they need to base their interventions on an understanding of the impact of divorce and the needs of those involved. For this to happen, it is imperative that rigorous research be continued on the immediate and long-term effects of divorce on the individual, the family unit, and the larger social systems.

REFERENCES

Bowlby, John: "Separation Anxiety," *The International Journal of Psychoanalysis,* **41:**89–113, 1960.

———: "Separation Anxiety: A Critical Review of the Literature," *Journal of Child Psychology and Psychiatry,* **1:** 251–269, 1961.

Despert, J. L.: *Children of Divorce,* Doubleday, Garden City, N.Y., 1953.

Glenn, Michael: "Separation Anxiety: When the Therapist Leaves the Patient," *American Journal of Psychotherapy,* **25**(3):437–446, 1971.

Langer, Thomas, and Michael Stanley:

"Childhood Broken Homes," in *Life Stress and Mental Health,* Free Press, New York, 1963.

McDermott, John F.: "Divorce and Its Psychiatric Sequelae in Children," *Archives of General Psychiatry,* **25**(5):421–427, 1970.

Nemiah, John C.: *Foundations of Psychopathology,* Oxford, New York, 1961.

Robertson, J.: *A Two-Year Old Goes to Hospital:* Tavistock Child Development Research Unit, London, 1953.

Spitz, R.: "Aggression: Its Role in the Establishment of Object Relations," in R.

Loewenstein (ed.), *Drive Affects Behaviour,* International Universities Press, New York, 1953.

Winnicott, D. W.: "Anxiety Associated with Insecurity," *Collected Papers: Through Paediatrics to Psychoanalysis,* Basic Books, New York, 1958.

OTHER RESOURCES

BOOKS

Richards, Arlene K., and Irene Willis: *How to Get It Together When Your Parents Are Coming Apart,* David McKay, New York, 1976.

Salk, Lee: *What Every Child Would Like Parents to Know about Divorce,* Harper & Row, New York, 1978.

Chapter 7

APPROACHING A CHILD'S DEATH AND THE PARENTS' LOSS

Lynn Noonan and Judith Tiktinsky

> I have often felt when a child dies that the world should stop, at least for a moment. I am somehow surprised or angry when the sun still shines or people continue about their business as usual.
>
> *Judith Tiktinsky*

This chapter describes the experiences of two mothers whose adolescent sons had leukemia. The caring took place in a hospital pediatric service, and the mothers were involved in the care of their children. We shall discuss our clinical work with the mothers and then the care given the children; we shall also illustrate some of the intricacies of the psychological responses in the context of the parent-child relationship. This chapter does not attempt to examine certain issues which vary with the age of the leukemic child or to deal with the reactions of the siblings or the father to the child's approaching death.

Kübler-Ross has described a series of discrete stages of dying, beginning with denial and proceeding toward an acceptance of death. Our experience suggests a different process, in which elements of denial, anger, bargaining, depression, and acceptance exist together in varying degrees in any one person at any time. The balance of these elements changes in a dying individual over time, depending to a large extent on changing realities. *The mourning process embodies both defensive and coping aspects.* Individual parental response depends on previous life experience, present adaptations, and the nature of the child's illness.

TASKS OF PARENTS

The most uniquely difficult aspect of long-term terminal illness rests in the uncertainty of the timing and manner of the child's death. Anticipatory mourning begins at the time the parents know of the child's diagnosis. The diagnosis is often perceived as an actual loss, and parents tend to respond as if the child will be lost that very day.

After a relatively brief period of time, the parents may be able to take their child home from the hospital. The parents must then live with the constant threat of the anticipated loss, while still maintaining a relationship with the child. This process seems to involve a delicate balance between denial and acceptance of the fact that the child is actually dying; the denial wards off the parents' grief and allows the relationship to continue. At the same time, the parents need to be able to accept the child's death when it becomes imminent, although they cannot be certain when that will occur.

In the midst of the immediate crisis around the diagnosis, parents are faced with a great number of tasks. Consciously or unconsciously, they must decide how to maintain or modify their usual parental functioning and how to adjust the family to the new reality. The manner of handling these tasks and coping with these events varies with families and individuals and even in the same individual over time. There are very different orientations when a child is in remission, for example, as opposed to when he or she suffers a relapse. With the suspension of the imminent threat of death, future orientations can be remobilized, and the focus returns to life and to maintenance activity.

When a child goes into relapse, the family members again change their orientation. The child's illness takes precedence over other family concerns, and thoughts of the future are suspended. Grief increases as the death becomes more imminent. Frequently, the needs of siblings are minimized or neglected completely. Even when a child is treated as an outpatient, the frequent visits for medical treatments, combined with the child's response to chemotherapy and radiation therapy, serve as a constant reminder to the parents of the approaching loss.

In our work with families, we must consider all these issues. We must retain flexibility and be alert to the changes which families undergo. Both the parents and the child need a friend. Somehow we must maintain enough objectivity so that we can bring a different perspective into the situation; we have to help the parents separate their perceptions and needs from those of their sick child, and yet we must be ready to evaluate the needs of others in the family. *The parents need to be sure that we are concerned and involved.* If they perceive us as just doing our job, they cannot be receptive to our efforts. We show that we care by maintaining contact with them in the interim between hospitalizations, by responding to crises, and by simply sitting and talking with them when there is no crisis. As we hear the parents expressing guilt, anger, and grief and as we listen to them bargaining for their child's life, we try to move softly with them in the direction they must go. By involving ourselves with the grief, easing the guilt, and providing an outlet for the rage, we can help the parents be strong enough to remain available to the child and yet able to let go.

During our first meetings with a family on the ward, we know little about them. We cannot yet know what their concerns are or what is most important to them. Rarely do we have a full picture of what their experience with the illness has been. Initially, we engage in a sorting-out process with the family. Both the child and the parents begin to express their preferences for, and confidence in, certain staff people. Since different people prefer different staff members, all personnel should be willing to become involved with terminally ill children and their families. Once a family has chosen one or two primary people, the rest of us function as auxiliary staff. We continue our involvement with the child or the parents, but we coordinate our efforts so that the primary person becomes the main source of support and has the major responsibility for exploring important issues and family concerns.

WORKING WITH THE MOTHER

The following sections will discuss some aspects of the process that the mother undergoes when a child dies; we will also describe ways in which ward staff members can be helpful in these situations.

Tom's Mother

Tom, an 11-year-old white boy, and his mother, Pat, came to our unit in December 1972. Tom died of leukemia in March 1974. I remember my first interactions with Pat vividly. I asked how Tom was doing that day. Pat stood wringing her hands; she began to respond to my question, but then she started talking about one of the doctors. Finally she stopped speaking altogether and began to cry. She could not tolerate the idea that Tom was close to death or that he might know of his prognosis. However, she was sufficiently convinced of the reality of the situation to have a priest baptize him and administer the last rites. Pat rarely left the hospital room. She interposed herself between Tom and the staff members when they attempted to care for him. It was difficult for us to separate her concerns from Tom's.

Experience with other families at the point of initial diagnosis made me realize that these responses were not unusual for a mother who learns that her child, who was healthy in September, is now dying in December. In addition, Tom and his mother were new to the city and unfamiliar with the hospital. Because Pat would not come out of Tom's room, I went in. I intruded into what seemed to me to be a funeral atmosphere and found myself making conversation with a woman who had no particular interest in talking with me. Pat was grieving, and it took most of her energy to deal with her grief and the many medical staff members who continually entered and left Tom's room. At first, we talked mainly about concrete things: how Tom was doing, what medicine he was taking, when the next bone-marrow transplant was scheduled, etc. Gradually, I began to talk about how Pat must be feeling and how difficult it was for her. As we grew to know each other, she began to leave Tom's room to have a cup of coffee with me, but she did this only when our play worker went in to be with Tom. Eventually, she was able to leave Tom alone so that he could have some privacy.

After a while, Pat began to tell me about her husband and the seven other children at home, who ranged in age from 7 to 18. She was torn between her concerns for her family at home and her need to stay with Tom.

The clinical nurse specialist (Lynn Noonan) and I both spent time with Pat daily. She would frequently call one of us by the other's name. I do not believe this really reflected a confusion about who we were; rather I think that she perceived our function as being the same. We both became people she could talk to about her most intimate concerns, doubts, and fears. Pat was terrified that if she were gone, even briefly, Tom would die. When we talked to her about the needs of her other children, she was able to verbalize her fantasy that if she left Tom, she would literally be abandoning him to die. Once these feelings were out in the open and respectfully acknowledged, Pat became more flexible in balancing Tom's needs and those of the rest of her family. She returned home to care for the other children, and on one occasion she took a vacation with her husband.

We discussed many things. One time Pat revealed a feeling of terrible guilt. She had tried to abort herself when she was pregnant with Tom. She reasoned that his illness was retribution for this act. During another period, when Pat felt particularly discouraged about Tom's illness, she described a recurrent dream from which she always woke crying and was unable to get back to sleep. In her dream she was at a funeral; she could see the coffin but could not see who was in it. At this point, she woke up crying.

The dream contained many elements, but we focused on discussing her concern about whether to select a funeral plot for Tom. She said that she was not ready for Tom's death and thought that perhaps the dream reflected this. She suggested that it might be her brother in the coffin, since he had had a severe heart attack. Pat also felt that her dream was a prophecy, since other dreams of hers had come true. I suggested that sometimes parents quite naturally wish that their child would no longer be in pain and that the ordeal would be over. She rejected this possibility and talked about the memory of her mother's death and Tom's reaction to visiting his grandmother in a hospital. Whatever this dream meant to Pat, she ceased having it after we talked about it.

As time went by, Pat became very well informed about leukemia, the various drug protocols, how to monitor intravenous feedings, the most effective needle size, and the location of the best veins. She was gradually acquiring knowledge, absorbing the fact of death, and learning how to help her child bear the misery with maximum comfort. She had enormous strength and was able to act as Tom's advocate with the medical staff. She learned to assess what was medically required and what Tom could tolerate, since he responded better when he knew exactly what to expect. *If someone attempted to carry out a procedure that had not previously been explained to Tom, he would refuse to cooperate until his private physician had been contacted.*

Pat's attitude vacillated between acceptance of the fact that Tom would die and the hope that he would be saved. When Tom felt better, her hopes surged; when he felt worse, she experienced enormous disappointment, anger, and fear of losing him and talked of the agony of waiting and not knowing what would happen. She feared becoming hopeful because the renewed hope made the pain of disappointment that followed more unbearable.

In the beginning Pat wanted to protect Tom from what he already knew—that he was dying. No one told Tom directly, but gradually Pat became aware that he knew. She was able to see this as she became more accepting of the reality. Her concerns shifted to what his death would be like: Would he be in pain? Would he hemorrhage? Using the time left in the most satisfying way possible became uppermost in her mind. She allowed Tom to engage in activities that had been forbidden earlier, such as swimming, bike riding, and going to the movies. She was able to limit some more dangerous activities, such as fighting with other children. She worried about bruises and the constant danger, but she found the strength to let him live as normally as possible when he was at home.

Tom and Pat had been with us for over a year when they decided to make one last desperate effort to save Tom's life by arranging for a bone-marrow transplant in another city. Although Pat was certain that the procedure would be futile, at least Tom would have one last chance. When Tom returned to our unit with Pat and his stepfather, they understood that he would die with us. Tom had made the decision to return. It was a reunion. They were glad to see us, and they talked about the transplant and their decision to return. They were calm, sad, exhausted, and perhaps relieved. They had done all that could be done, and now they seemed ready to accept what was to come.

People came and went throughout the weekend, visiting quietly. However, Tom's condition steadily declined, and by Monday evening he was close to death. Shortly after I entered the room, Tom asked his mother to get his clothes out of his suitcase. She asked him gently where he was going and explained that he was probably dreaming. I noticed that on the dresser was a note that read, "Pedi Staff: Remember me, Tom." Pat spent the rest of her time with Tom sitting close by him and occasionally holding him and cooing softly. Tom died quietly, surrounded by his parents and the people who cared about him. Shortly afterward, Pat turned to me and said, "He knew. That's why he asked for his clothes."

John's Mother

From the beginning, John's mother, Lynette, exhibited feelings that shifted rapidly from denial to acceptance. Lynette, a black woman, was losing not only her child but also a companion, a protector, and a person on whom she had depended. At first it was difficult for her to visit John in the hospital because she could not tolerate seeing him so sick. She sat mournfully, watching him carefully, as if she expected him to die at any moment. When she did not come to visit him, she called repeatedly to inquire about him. She often called to find out what he had been able to eat at meals. The nurses watched with difficulty while John struggled, in spite of painful mouth ulcers, to drink a container of milk to calm his mother. Lynette equated John's failure to eat with his giving up. Her urging him to eat was an attempt to magically ward off his death. When she was frantically pushing John to eat and be strong, she was certain he would not die.

She resented any suggestions from others that John would not recover. Although I sensed that she wanted me to leave her alone, she beckoned me to stay whenever I started to leave or to bring our conversation to a close.

It was at about this time that a black public health nurse on our service also began working with Lynette and gradually assumed greater responsibilities as the primary worker for this mother. In her continuing contacts with Lynette, the public health nurse helped her understand John's behavior, as well as the effect of her behavior on him. Although Lynette indicated that she did not understand the disease, her questions to the private physician reflected a good comprehension. There was a frantic, desperate quality about her. She wanted to know how to save her son; if that could not be done, she wanted to know how long he had to live. Her resistance to us seemed to reflect her feeling that we were there because John was dying. To accept us would be to precipitate John's death.

Tom's death heightened Lynette's concern about John's condition. She was visibly upset and seemed to resent us for suggesting that John might also die. She denied strongly that this would happen, and she thanked us for being available and assured us that she had nothing to discuss. Tom's death was the first of a series of events which resulted in Lynette's acceptance of John's illness. After Tom died, Lynette sat in the parents' lounge and asked about his death. She was shocked that he had died. With Tom's death, her last vestige of hope crumbled. Lynette talked about her terror of losing John, and yet she verbalized for the first time her acceptance of the reality. A second significant event occurred one afternoon after John returned from the x-ray department. He was given medication and soon fell asleep. He began talking out loud in his sleep. Lynette became very upset, thinking that John was dying and that these were his last words. A nurse tried to assure her that John was given morphine for pain and that his talking was due to the drug. Lynette became agitated. In her mind, morphine was given only when someone was dying. To her this was a clear statement that John was near death. When she realized that John was not currently receiving chemotherapy, she reasoned that it had been terminated because it was futile. This incident culminated in Lynette's being able to acknowledge and respond to the reality of John's approaching death. She began to stay overnight in the hospital and was with him when he died.

The public health nurse kept in touch with Lynette after John's death. Lynette recalled the content of conversations we had had prior to her son's death. She commented that she had heard what we said and that it helped now, although at that time she had not been able to respond to us.

GOALS IN WORKING WITH PARENTS

Much of what we have described in our work with parents is focused on our ability to help them with the process of dying, of losing a child who needs a "lifetime" of their attention *now*. We worked toward the goal of helping parents be free to live, free to mourn their loss, and then free to establish other relationships. They will relive their experience with their dying child many times.

We feel that our efforts help parents accept their loss and marshall their strength to go on with their lives.

WORKING WITH THE DYING CHILD

Our main goal in working with children and their families is to help the parents realize their own needs and those of the other family members while still meeting the needs of their sick child. We recognize that the family is made up of individuals with different, sometimes conflicting needs, and *we initiate a relationship with each family member.* We focus on the quality of life by making each day as normal and as full as it possibly can be in the hospital. We try to help dying children share their feelings about death and reach a level of acceptance that will allow them to die peacefully, with dignity, and with people they love nearby.

Working directly with a child involves careful interpretation of the child's verbal and nonverbal messages. Equally important are the responses from the staff, including talking, action-oriented play, and nurturing physical contact. After the diagnosis is given, each child experiences a vast range of reactions according to his or her individual frame of reference and in his or her own unique style. Being confronted with a life-threatening illness arouses certain needs and concerns in children. Some of the most common ones are discussed below.

While the parents of a child who has recently been diagnosed as having a life-threatening illness are struggling with feelings of denial, the child becomes aware that something is terribly wrong. Some parents decide that they do not want the child to be told anything, and some wonder what to tell the child and how to do it. A child who observes his or her parents' fears and anxieties, but who is told nothing, uses fantasies and immature perceptions to explain the events. These may be more frightening than the reality. Open discussion of the diagnosis and a willingness to hear the child's concerns and fantasies allow the child to begin to cope.

Tom

Tom (whose mother's reactions were described earlier) was an 11-year-old white boy. Four weeks after he was diagnosed as having leukemia in his hometown hospital, he was transferred to our unit. His mother, Pat, let us know that the hometown nurses had cared about him and had cried when he left, which seemed to be her way of asking us to care about him also. Pat decided that he could be told he had leukemia, but not that it was life-threatening. For days Tom withdrew by rolling himself up in his blankets with his face turned to the wall, and telling staff members to stay away. Although Tom's behavior was interpreted by some staff members as reflecting a wish for isolation, this was not at all what he wanted. Tom displayed ineffective denial, he withdrew, and he regressed to a dependent state.

We experienced a great deal of anxiety. Was this the right time to challenge his withdrawal? Was Tom's behavior related to his mother's denial? Tom seemed near death several times, and we considered his withdrawal natural in these circumstances. We constantly assessed and discussed clinical judgments with staff persons. Finally, we decided that when withdrawal is not due to physical pain or to imminent death, but rather is the reaction of a terrified child who does not know where to turn, we should intervene.

The social worker (Judith Tiktinsky) gently challenged Tom's withdrawal; however, he continued to lie still and to remain silent. When she said that she knew how frightened and unhappy he was and that she would like to stay with him, he responded with eye contact. As the social worker's relationship with him progressed, he allowed her to playfully tickle him and pull him out of bed. In several days he was able to run around the room, play aggressively, and shoot dart guns.

Tom often showed that he needed to be considered special by the staff members. During his year of almost continuous hospitalization, he developed a special relationship with nearly everyone. As most children do, Tom rejected a totally professional attitude. He usually responded to action rather than verbalization. He related best with "Gimme five handslaps," Indian wrestling, and mischievous pranks. He knew he was special when he was taken on outings to the park or the beach and when he held popcorn parties in his room. Tom needed to give to us, and he did this by serving the whole staff spaghetti he cooked on a hot plate in his room; he relished watching seven or eight doctors and nurses slurping spaghetti through isolation masks!

Sick children choose certain persons for specific roles: Some are to play with and to give comfort, and some are to be the target of anger and frustration. Often the target of anger is the float nurse or the new doctor on call, who "can't do it like the other doctors." At times the roles are interchangeable. Some of Tom's closest friends were interns and residents toward whom he directed much anger during a medical procedure but who were seen as friends soon after.

Children may initially view death as a catastrophe over which they have no control. This elicits a great deal of fear as well as rage. They experience these powerful feelings as they focus on coping with daily problems related to the disease. Soon after they become ill, leukemic children face overwhelming tasks involving the mechanics of their illness: repeated painful blood tests, chemotherapy, and bone-marrow transplants.

In the beginning, Tom was terrified of having intravenous procedures started. He protested by yelling and refusing to cooperate, and once he hit a doctor. Although we did not understand what an intravenous procedure meant to him, we decided to let him have as much control as possible over each procedure to help him cope with his fear. It worked. Tom developed an elaborate ritual which necessitated his agreement as to the exact chemotherapy being used. He told the doctors what size needle to use, where to rub when it hurt, and what veins were thrombosed, and he argued about which veins were usable. He was usually right! When new doctors came, they were amazed that we supported the ritual. It was frustrating for them and required much patience, but most of them willingly accepted the situation. Tom was able to move from passive withdrawal to active choice in coping with his illness.

Months later, Pat told us that when Tom was young, he had visited his hospitalized grandmother, who had had an intravenous needle in her arm. The grandmother had died soon after that visit, and Tom had associated an intravenous needle with death. It was only by working closely with both Tom and his mother that we were able to understand this fear. In spite of our initial lack of understanding, we were finally able to help him deal with his fear by allowing him to have some control over the medical procedures.

Most leukemic children have specific fears related to dying: Will I hurt? Will I bleed? Will I be alone? Tom was able to express his concerns in response to the death of a 4-year-old leukemic friend. He initiated questions about whether she hurt or bled; and during the weeks following her death he was able to relate these questions to his own fears of dying.

Leukemic children's anger is focused especially on medical procedures, but it can be directed toward anyone or anything. Their anger is directed toward parents, who allow medical staff members to hurt them, as well as toward the staff members who are doing the hurting. Some children scream, yell, and cry. We can help others discharge their anger through aggressive play, such as shooting dart guns, punching balls, or wrestling. Tom sometimes attacked the staff with water-filled syringes, and he was often squirted back. However, there are also times when it is very painful for a staff member to be the focus of anger. *It is difficult to see a child suffering from an illness that we cannot cure. When we have to perform a painful procedure on a child who is already hurting, and in addition be the target of the child's anger, the situation can feel intolerable.*

Some children view their illness as a punishment for doing something or wishing for something that was wrong. They feel guilty and attempt to protect their parents from suffering. Tom shared his mother's fantasy that if she left him, he would die. One afternoon, Pat was at home with another sick son. Tom awakened from a dream, screaming and thrashing about in bed. A nurse tried to put her arms around him to comfort him. He continued thrashing and screamed that he wanted to jump out the window and die so that people would not have to suffer on his account and worry about him and so that he would not be sick anymore. He was able to tell the nurse that he had had a frightening dream in which he was falling from a cliff but never landed. He just kept falling and falling. He insisted that the nurse stay and hold him until his mother returned. At other times, Tom told us of dreams about being on a plane that crashed and a ship that sank and about the devil coming to get him. He talked about fantasies of giving his body away to someone else or giving his illness away.

Before he left for his bone-marrow transplant in a city several hundred miles away, Tom teased the nurses about how they would cry when he left; he wanted to be sure that we would miss him. The bone-marrow transplant was extremely painful for Tom, since it necessitated 2 months of isolation from family and friends. He begged us to visit him and call him. He told his mother, "If I can't be with my friends, I might as well die."

Some children who experience support in dealing with their illness and who can communicate their feelings are amazing in their ability to accept their own death. Months before he had the bone-marrow transplant, Tom chose his brothers and their friends as pallbearers. *When the family was told that the bone-marrow transplant had not worked, Tom demonstrated acceptance of his death by deciding how he wanted to live his last few days.* He insisted on going to Disneyland in a wheelchair. He then wanted to go home and see his brothers and sisters. (See Chapter 30 for similar termination strategies used by the aged.) Tom invited neighborhood children in and told his father to bring home hamburgers for everyone. He chose the clothes he wanted to be buried in from the Sears, Roebuck catalog. The next day he returned to our unit. It was painful for us to see Tom so weak and near death. During the 3 days before he died, Tom saw each person he had been close to and had missed while he was away. He then withdrew and found it too painful to talk or be touched, and yet asked for his friends to be with him. He let go and died peacefully on March 21, 1974.

John

John dealt with similar issues, though very differently from the way Tom did. John was a very mature 12-year-old black boy who acted as man of the house and was the primary support for his mother. His mother needed him to be strong so that he could protect her from the reality of his illness; thus John needed strength for her as well as for his own pride. Because we knew John, his mother, and his four brothers and sisters for only 3 months, time was a crucial factor. He arrived the week after Tom left for his bone-marrow transplant.

Our approach was to initiate a relationship with John so that he could talk if he chose to. During the first month, he remained withdrawn and depressed, frequently banging his head on the bed or pounding his fist. His mother was able to tolerate only a short visit with him each day. We continued to tell him that we would like to sit with him if he would agree to this. He indicated that he wanted us there, but he talked only about going home, never about his illness. Rather than expressing his concerns sporadically, as Tom did, John chose to deal with many issues during one intense hour of conversation. He had been told that he needed to remain in the hospital for more treatments, and yet he was feeling better than he had during the past month.

He was sitting up in bed painting when I told him that I wanted to be with him for a while. He kept his eyes on his painting and commented, "When I came here, I was just dizzy. I've felt much sicker since I've been here." Since he had been told the medical facts of his illness, I felt that he had another concern, and so I reflected the statement back to him. He looked at me and said, "Why me? Why did I get this disease?" I asked him what he thought. He wondered whether he had caused it by playing too hard. He told me that his mother kept saying, "Why, John?" I assured him that he had done nothing to cause the illness and that there was no way in which he could have prevented it. He slowly nodded his head, which seemed to mean that he had needed to hear that. I asked him whether he knew anyone else who had leukemia. He said, "A few weeks ago I saw a television program, and a few kids had leukemia. One girl got better and went home." He quickly added, "And I know I'll get better." I softly said, "John, maybe sometimes you wonder." He stopped painting, looked directly at me, and sighed, "Yes, sometimes I don't think I'll ever get better." He paused and then told me that he could take a day or a week in the hospital, but not a month. I commented, "John, you've been here a month." He looked at me again and said, "Yeah, sometimes I don't think I can take it here anymore." We talked about how he felt and about what frightened him. He wanted to be strong, and yet he needed to cry to feel better. He named the nurses with whom he had been able to cry.

I asked him what worried him. He said that he was worried about his mother. She cried a little bit at the hospital, but he knew that she cried a lot at home. She cried because she was sad about his illness. He wanted just an hour out of the hospital—to be with his family, go fishing, have a meal, and go for a drive. Quietly, I said that it sounded as if he wanted a lot more than an hour. Then he changed his mind and said that he wanted an hour for a meal with his family. "I know I'll have to come back here, and I will." It seemed that he had come to grips with his illness and the prognosis in his own way. He wanted to spend more time with his family, as he had before he became sick.

John lived 2 months longer. During that time, he spent several weeks at home. When he was hospitalized, he enjoyed evening parties with his whole family, where there was home-cooked food, music, and dancing. He became close to several nurses and doctors and was able to share more of his pain and anger. When he was able to ask for back rubs to relieve his discomfort, his head banging decreased. John had mouth ulcers, which made it painful for him to talk. Although he could not communicate verbally, he wanted someone with him constantly. During the hours I rubbed his back, I sometimes verbalized for him the frustration, fear, or anger he might be feeling. If my impressions were correct, he let me know by patting me on the back and nodding his head.

There were days when John was so weak and angry that he asked for medication to relieve the pain and yelled at the nurse before she left the room for not having it there immediately. Sometimes he called the nurses "shitheads" and ordered them out of the room, which was painful for them since they wanted to do anything to help him be more comfortable. *We realized that he could scream and cry only with staff members; he needed to appear strong with his mother.*

Three days before he died, John was in a talkative, teasing mood. He warmly thanked all the nurses and doctors who were his friends. I sensed that this was his way of saying good-bye. He asked me for the necklace I was wearing. I told him that it was very special to me and that he could wear it. Later he asked me, "Why did you let me wear this?" I said, "Why do you think?" He grinned and said, "Because I'm special to you, and I know I'm your friend."

Two days before he died, John's mother came to stay with him. She could not, however, acknowledge to John that she knew he was dying. One minute she expressed concern that he would become addicted to morphine, and the next minute she asked me for help with the funeral plans; she was unable to deal with the fact that John was dying.

That evening it was obvious that the staff's work with Lynette had been helpful. John asked his mother to read the Twenty-third Psalm. She did, and then she quietly related to his two greatest concerns. She said, "John, when you die, you'll go to Heaven." He protested, "But I'm 12" (old enough to be accountable for his sins). His mother assured him that he had been good and had done nothing wrong. And then she said, "John, when you die, I'm going to be all right, and the other children will be all right too." At that point I left so that they could be alone.

The next day Lynette and John were able to talk, and so we gave them support and let them have some privacy. When I went in to say good-night, John seemed to be asleep, and his mother was at his side. I whispered to his mother that I was leaving but would return in the morning. John opened his eyes and said, very slowly, "I'm ready to go to God now. I'm ready to die—I'm ready—and it won't be long now." He asked his mother to kiss him. She did, and she cried.

He looked at me and said, "Lynn, thank you for being my friend. I'm glad I got to know you."

I was unable to say anything.

He said again, "I'm glad you're my friend. Thanks for talking with me. I'm going home now." He continued to look at me, awaiting a response.

All I could say was, "John, you really are special to me." I reached out my hand, and he kissed it. My way of saying good-bye was to ask him whether I could kiss him. He said yes.

Early that morning, just before he died, he expressed acceptance of his death, and possibly a wish to protect his mother, by pulling the sheet over his head.

REACTIONS OF THE STAFF

When we started our jobs, we did not really expect that children on the pediatric ward would die. The first child who died after our arrival was a 7-year-old boy with leukemia; the child's parents had been indifferent to our support before he died and were indifferent to the support we offered them that night. They quickly left the hospital.

We were confronted with our own denial. The child looked as if he were asleep, but when we touched him, his hands felt cold. Judy felt immobilized and sat at the desk watching through the door; she had never seen a dead body and had never been to a funeral. I had been to too many funerals, and yet I had never known a child who had died. I felt that I had to be responsible and active in supporting the pediatric nurse. There was no alternative but to prepare the body for the morgue. Because I was the only support available for the pediatric nurse, I felt compelled to assist.

There was a feeling of unreality. This was a child we had known as a person, and we had feelings for him. There seemed to be a great lack of dignity in the process of placing his body in a plastic bag and name-tagging his feet. In fact, this activity was almost unbearable for me because 2 years ago that night my mother had died.

We were not sure what anybody needed, especially ourselves. We were not sure how to support each other. Afterward, we sat and talked and held an infant; we needed a symbol of the beginning of life. We do not remember whether another child with leukemia was on the ward at the time, and we did not talk with any parents or children there about the death.

We felt furious and abandoned. No one was on duty except one pediatric nurse and a float nurse. The doctor left after we arrived, and the nursing supervisor would not come to the pediatrics unit. She remained unavailable the rest of the night. In working out my own feelings about the lack of support, I arranged to do three things. First, I told the residents and interns how difficult that night had been and asked for support in the future. They agreed to give support either by talking with the children and their families or by being available to talk with staff members afterward. Then I spoke with the nursing supervisors, who agreed to prepare the body and be available for support. Because of the close emotional bond many nurses have with these children, we felt it was necessary for individual nurses to have an option *not* to prepare the body. Finally, since I recognized that staff nurses were the only people who could not leave the unit when a child died and that they needed other options and support, I asked them how they handled their feelings when a child died. They said that they cried alone and sometimes talked with another nurse.

This child's death raised several questions: Can we share our grief with the family? Is it all right if we cry with them? Will the doctors be available for support? Can we break the unspoken rule that a child's death cannot be openly talked about? Would it be possible for staff members to have weekly meetings so that they could openly discuss their feelings and support one another? During the past year, we found that the answer to all these questions was "yes." Judy describes these events in her presentation of the following case material.

The morning John died, the night nurse notified the public health nurse and me at 5 A.M. John's mother had not yet been told. We went into the room together. Lynette awoke. She seemed to realize immediately what had happened, and she went to John's body. She began crying inconsolably and implored John to wake up. At first, the public health nurse and I stayed with her. Then, because the public health nurse had a good relationship with Lynette, she stayed to provide support for her while I checked on other children and families.

The night nurse told me that the mother of a leukemic child needed me immediately. The nurse was aware that John was the second child with leukemia who had died while this mother and her child had been on the floor. As I went into the room, the mother was looking out the window, crying softly. She turned to me and said, "Why me? Why is this happening to me?" We spent a good deal of time talking about her feelings. She said that each time a child with leukemia died, she felt as if death were standing on the other side of the door, just waiting to take her child. We talked about the pain that she experienced and the difficulty of waiting and not knowing when her child would be gone. Gradually we started talking about other issues.

There was a good deal of activity on the floor by this time. There were audible sounds of Lynette's mourning in John's room. Many of the parents were standing out in the hallway looking somewhat bewildered and frightened. I felt some conflict between this mother's needs and the needs of the rest of the families. I explained my dilemma to her, and she said, "No, I know you have to go. Don't worry about me." Although I knew that she was really pleading with me to stay, I left her and proceeded to seek out other patients and parents on the floor who were greatly affected by John's death.

Prior to John's death, I had been aware that most parents of hospitalized children consciously or unconsciously fear that their child may die as a result of a hospital procedure, no matter how minor. Yet in spite of this, I was surprised that John's death evoked such strong fears among the other parents. I spent a brief amount of time with one mother whose child had just been taken to surgery for a tonsillectomy. She knew that John had died, and she expressed the fear that her daughter might die in surgery because she knew of another child who died during a tonsillectomy.

Each parent and child on the floor responded somewhat differently to the situation. One 15-year-old girl, who had been close to John, immediately got on the phone seeking support from her friends and her mother. Other families sat quietly, while others required explanations of what had happened, how John had died, and what the problem had been. Another child, whose arm had been amputated, and her mother were visibly upset but did not want to talk about it and did not want much information.

The second leukemic child on the floor was a 13-year-old girl, Carla, whose parents had been extremely reluctant to let her know much about leukemia and the probable prognosis. When Carla asked me what was going on, I explained that John had died of leukemia. Carla and her mother both began to cry. I stayed with Carla for a while; I told her a little bit about John and said that he had died quietly and that he had had a different kind of leukemia from hers. I asked her whether perhaps she was upset because John's illness and her illness had the same name. She replied, "Yes." I said that I knew she was concerned, but that if she did not feel like talking about it, that was fine. She was crying, but said that she did not feel like talking now. I told her that I would be available anytime she wanted to talk.

After speaking with all the parents and the children, I learned that the rest of the staff had been busy checking in with the families on the floor. Members of the nursing staff were equally sensitive to one another's needs and would frequently ask, "How're you doing?" It seemed that the staff members had learned what can be done to provide support and comfort to the parents of a child who has died, to other children and their families, and to one another.

SUMMARIZING STATEMENTS

Issues with Parents

- Elements of denial, anger, bargaining, depression, and acceptance can exist together in varying degrees in any parent at any one time.

- Because they cannot be certain when death will occur, parents need to balance mourning for the child and maintaining a close relationship with the child.
- Parents' concerns shift over time as the illness progresses. Sometimes they attempt to protect the child, and they often feel guilty, angry, and fearful of the loss. Later, their concerns shift to the importance of the quality of life and then to questions of what the death will be like.

Issues with Children

- In response to the diagnosis and the parents' denial, dying children fearfully withdraw into fantasies. We must then intervene to develop a relationship.
- Children need to feel that staff members consider them special, and they choose the people they want to be close to.
- Medical procedures elicit enormous amounts of fear and rage. Children need to have some control over these procedures to cope with their fear.
- Children express a great awareness of death in their play, their conversation, and their dreams.
- Children feel ashamed and guilty about being ill, and they want to protect their parents from suffering.
- Children have an ability to accept their own death.

Issues with Staff

- Staff members should work as a team.
- Flexibility is a key to effective care.
- A preventive mental health orientation is important.
- Support for staff members after a child dies should include:
    Sharing grief with the family
    Crying with the family
    Talking openly about death
    Weekly group meetings to discuss feelings
    Support of one another
    Support from doctors

CONCLUSION

We have enormous respect for the families of the children we have worked with, and in this chapter we have tried to present some of what we have learned about their hopes and sorrows and their fears and concerns. We have also tried to show how we helped them and how they, in turn, helped us.

REFERENCE

Kübler-Ross, Elisabeth: *On Death and Dying,* Macmillan, New York, 1969.

OTHER RESOURCES

FILMS

Coping: 16 mm/22 min/color/1972. Focuses on a young boy, fatally ill with leukemia, and the way in which his family supports him and helps him cope with his fear of dying. Distributor: University of California, Extension Media Center, Berkeley, Calif. 94720.

You See, I've Had a Life: 16 mm/32 min/b and w/1974. Documents the final months of a 13-year-old boy dying of leukemia and the ability of his family and professionals to help him live a normal life as long as he can. A student from Temple University made this award-winning film, which may dispel the notion that a child must never be informed about his or her impending death. Distributor: University of California, Extension Media Center, Berkeley, Calif. 94720.

Chapter 8

PSYCHOSOCIAL CARING OF ADOLESCENTS FOR THE ELDERLY

G. Michelle Reilley

> The thirst for companionship, which drives us so often into error and adventure, indicates the intense loneliness from which we suffer.
>
> *Abraham Joshua Heschel*

As age segregation increases in our society, less consideration is given to possible benefits of age integration. This chapter describes a study in which high school students were given the opportunity to function as psychosocial care givers in one-to-one relationships with elderly persons. I believe that the development of relationships between adolescents and elderly adults is of prime importance in exploring the benefits of age integration. Increasing young people's awareness of various aspects of aging is also important.

This chapter describes a doctoral study that integrated two values: the importance of using adolescents as care givers for the elderly and the resulting increase in the young people's awareness of aging. This study was completed through the University of Nevada in 1976. Another study with the same values was begun in 1978 by the Department of Adult and Community College Education at North Carolina State University. This study was entitled "An Analysis of a Lesson Series in Changing Adolescents' Attitudes toward the Aged."

First I shall discuss the background and rationale of the project and then briefly explain the plan. Then the students' training and some of their experiences will be described in detail. The chapter ends with a discussion of results and conclusions, implementation problems, and future research topics.

RATIONALE: ADOLESCENT–ELDERLY ADULT RELATIONSHIPS

Interaction between generations can lead to better understanding and acceptance, besides being a valuable learning experience for all involved (Mumford; Robbins). I believe that interaction between high school students and elderly adults can be especially fruitful. The anthropological literature suggests that cross-generational friendships are often the warmest of interpersonal relationships because the problems of authority, rivalry, guilt, and ambivalence are reduced (Bohannan; Radcliffe-Brown). Weemer, using a free-association task, found separate psychological concerns for different age groups, particularly for nonadjacent age groups. Presumably, in an adolescent–elderly adult friendship, the two people are quite different from each other, which should facilitate discovery on both their parts. I believe that this difference in viewpoints is not so extreme, however, as to hinder interaction.

The similarities between the two groups provide additional support for the idea of fruitful relationships between them. Adolescents and elderly persons share several unique characteristics, the most important of which is an uncertain status in today's society (Frankel; Matteson). Adolescents are caught between childhood and adulthood; they are no longer children, but they are not accorded true adult status. The aged also, particularly those in institutions, are not accorded true adult status. Institutionalized elderly persons have another thing in common with high school students: Much of their activity is regulated by others. For the aged, the regulators are the staff of the institution, and often it is the elderly person's family, not the elderly person, who decides whether, when, where, and for how long the institutionalization will take place. Similarly, high school students' activities are usually regulated by their families (parents in particular) and by the staff of another institution, the school. High school students and elderly persons, then, seem to be in a unique and advantageous position for interaction. Another similarity exists in that each group member has or will experience membership in the other group: the aged were adolescents once; adolescents will someday be aged.

Adolescence is typically described as a period of extreme change, conflict, and instability, during which psychological problems are rife (Feldman; Matteson; Shore and Massimo). Old age, too, is a time of psychological problems. In 1971, the American Psychological Association estimated that at least 3 million elderly persons were in need of mental health services (Butler and Lewis). Elderly people and adolescents face three important psychological problems: lowered self-esteem, difficulty with warm interpersonal relationships, and loneliness. These problems will be discussed separately in relation to each age group.

Psychological Problems of Adolescence
Lowered self-esteem. Rosenberg describes low self-esteem as follows: "Low self-esteem . . . implies self-rejection, self-dissatisfaction, self-contempt. The individual lacks respect for the self he observes. The self-picture is disagreeable

and he wishes it were otherwise'' (p. 31). According to Collier, the high school years are a time of tremendous self-doubt. Teenagers usually feel less acceptable than they actually are, and often they consider themselves quite unlikable. Some high school students experience low self-esteem almost constantly; many are plagued intermittently. Collier stresses that these self-esteem crises are normal.

There are several reasons for preoccupation with self-esteem in adolescence (Rosenberg). Major life decisions are often made during these years, and some of the questions adolescents struggle with include: What are my life goals? What will I make my lifework? What kind of life partner will I choose? Rapid physical and psychological changes are also occurring, and these changes affect adolescents' opinions of themselves and tend to heighten their interest in these opinions. Adolescence is also a time of uncertain sex roles. It is a traumatic period between childhood and adulthood during which one's status seems to be constantly changing. Such continual change often has a detrimental effect on self-esteem (Katz and Zigler).

Rosenberg points out the strong relationship between self-esteem and skill in interpersonal relationships. Persons with low self-esteem often experience difficulty maintaining warm interpersonal relationships (Gold and Douvan).

Difficulty with warm interpersonal relationships. As adolescents explore their opinions of themselves, they are also exploring their estimations of others. Adolescence is a period of intensified learning about relationships (Matteson). Adolescents become highly interested in others and develop a need for affection (Muuss).

Warm interpersonal relationships in adolescence also facilitate several developmental tasks (Sullivan). Friendship involves trust, which implies a responsibility toward the trusting individual. Being responsible toward another aids in the developmental task of growing from dependence to independence (Monea). An independent person, in contrast to one who is dependent, is expected to meet responsibilities. Not only do adolescents learn about friendship, but they also learn about themselves. They often discover and share various concerns, resentments, and doubts of which they otherwise might not become aware. This process of exploring unfamiliar, perhaps unknown, feelings may lead to a greater sense of self-worth (Jersild).

Exploring unfamiliar feelings with a friend of the same sex is particularly important. There is a strong need for personal friendships and associations with members of one's own sex in adolescence (Muuss). Same-sex peers could be especially helpful in the struggle to develop sexual identity, but adolescents learn to distrust these peers because they are competitors for the attention of members of the opposite sex.

In addition to distrust of peers, Muuss refers to the crisis of self-cognition, during which independence from parents and teachers is sought. Thus young persons are often somewhat alienated from peers, parents, and teachers. Havighurst and Taba note that a young person's "ideal self" is usually highly influenced by adults outside the family. Such adults are sometimes the best candidates for warm interpersonal relationships, and they may help relieve a third psychological problem of adolescence, loneliness.

Loneliness. The literature suggests that the great majority of young people, even those who seem completely adjusted, suffer from varying degrees of loneliness (Deutsche). Many adolescents live in solitary isolation, unable to share their worries and fears with others. Often they must be content with imagined, rather than real, companions (Jersild).

One need not be physically alone to be lonely. Young people have an ability to seem quite alone even when surrounded by others, a phenomenon that has been noted among institutionalized elderly people. Adolescents' air of detachment and loneliness while dancing is often obvious. Loneliness can be most painful in the context of the enforced sociability of a crowd. It is in such settings that the contrast between superficial contact and warm interpersonal relationships may be most striking (Jersild).

Psychological Problems of Old Age

Lowered self-esteem. Research indicates that the aged often experience lowered self-esteem. Schwartz and Kleemeier report diminishing self-esteem as one ages. According to Zinberg and Kaufman, self-image, which is established early in life, is closely related to the concept of the body. As one grows older, a shift in "body image" becomes necessary. This shift may be difficult to accept and integrate psychologically and may result in decreased self-esteem.

Difficulty with warm interpersonal relationships. Several authors have found that maintenance of warm interpersonal relationships becomes harder as one grows older (Birren; Cavan, Burgess, Havighurst, and Goldhammer). Poor health often results in less energy and less mental and physical agility; these conditions seem to contribute to disruption of interpersonal relationships. Poor health may also result in less time available for interaction with others. Aged persons, especially those in institutions, often cannot travel because of physical impairments and thus cannot return friends' visits. Disruption of interpersonal relationships appears to be a factor in poor adjustment. Livson compared the characteristics of well-adjusted and poorly adjusted elderly men and found that those who had adjusted well to aging were more active socially. Visiting friends was a major recreational activity for 81 percent of the well-adjusted men but for only 47 percent of those who were poorly adjusted. The highest suicide rates tend to occur in areas in which there are few family and neighborhood ties (Bromley). Bromley believes that the high rate of minor neurosis and physical illness among elderly women may be due partly to a reduction in family and social interaction. Having few warm interpersonal relationships can easily lead to the third psychological problem, loneliness.

Loneliness. According to Sullivan, when the basic human need for interaction with others is not met, the result is loneliness and lowered self-esteem. Loneliness in the aged is often compounded by geographic separation from friends and family, poor health, language and cultural barriers, loss of important others (often through death), and realization of one's own impending death (Burnside). Fromm-Reichmann describes loneliness as a state of mind in which one basically forgets that one had friends in the past and loses hope of forming close relationships in the future.

Residents of hospitals and extended care facilities seem especially vulnerable to feelings of loneliness. They must cope with the loss of their former residences and the freedom they enjoyed there and with their failure to live up to the cultural ideal of independence and self-reliance. Persons in nursing homes are often in poor health and desire human contact but are too weak to initiate interaction with others. In addition, a severe loss—for instance, the death of a care giver (usually the spouse)—may be involved in an elderly person's relocation to a hospital or similar facility. It is not surprising, then, that although they are surrounded by others, institutionalized elderly persons frequently complain of loneliness.

Attempts to Relieve Problems

Psychotherapy. Adolescents and institutionalized elderly people experience similar problems of lowered self-esteem, difficulty with warm interpersonal relationships, and loneliness. Psychologists have traditionally attempted to deal with these problems through individual and family psychotherapy. Unfortunately, therapy is not readily available to older persons (Bahn; Butler and Sulliman). One obstacle to treatment is the high cost of therapy (Butler and Lewis). Another obstacle is the pessimism of mental health professionals concerning the treatability of elderly persons (Gibson). This attitude often either becomes a self-fulfilling prophecy or results in therapists' failure to provide any treatment at all (Gallagher, Sharaf, and Levinson). Therapy can also be difficult for adolescents to obtain because of the expense and because it is sometimes necessary for all the family members to become involved, which they may not want to do. In addition, even if therapy is begun, adolescents often lack the necessary insight into their problems (Lorand). Finally, even if these obstacles are overcome, the efficacy of psychotherapy is questionable. Some researchers believe that the recovery rate for persons in psychotherapy is no higher than the spontaneous recovery rate for persons not in treatment (Eysenck).

Community programs. In recent years, as a result of the growth of community psychology, other solutions to the problems of adolescent and elderly persons have been sought. Community mental health centers have not proved successful, mainly because they have not been sufficiently funded, housed, or staffed (Butler and Lewis). Various advice centers and telephone counseling services for young people are becoming popular; such agencies seem to be effective (Lambert, Rothschild, Altland, and Green). Unfortunately, they are expensive to staff; if they are staffed by volunteers, training becomes necessary. Money and time limitations create a shortage of agencies. Community psychologists are now faced with the problem of deciding which programs most effectively and economically benefit young persons and the aged.

Recently, a few community programs have brought various age groups together through visitation. In most of the programs, at least one age group is institutionalized. In a study by Russo, juvenile-delinquent boys visited psychiatric patients for 12 to 18 h per week for 4 months. Changes occurred in both the delinquent boys and the patients. The boys showed improvement in self-concept and in acceptance of authority, and the patients improved in terms of cleanliness, independence, sociability, and cooperation. Another program involved institutionalized children and noninstitutionalized elderly adults. Rybak, Sadnavitch, and Mason designed a foster-grandparent program involving mentally retarded children. Results indicate that the program improved psychosocial adjustment in the aged participants. A solution to the problems of institutional isolation and role-deprivation was attempted by bringing old and young persons together (Solon, Amthor, Rabb, and Shelley). Elderly adults and young mentally retarded people, residents of two separate institutions, formed one-to-one relationships and participated in joint activities. Although program evaluation was purposely not included, the researchers believe that the participants benefited from "self-help while helping the other" (Solon et al., p. 3). College students worked with elderly adults during a year-long geriatrics course at the University of California (Safier). Each student was assigned one elderly patient, who was either institutionalized or living in the community. The importance of this experience in training was emphasized, but no program evaluation was attempted. Hallauer and Gordon included program evaluation in their investigation of the separate and combined effects on attitudes toward the elderly of visiting with aged persons and of taking a course in aging. Members of different age groups—elderly persons and college students—were again brought together. It was found that the course alone significantly improved the students' attitudes on the positive scale items; the combination of course and visiting was found to be even more effective. Significant changes did not occur as a result of visiting alone.

Another method of promoting age integration is through the use of volunteers in institutions for the elderly. Usually, volunteers provide two types of services: interaction with residents and group activities. Unfortunately, there is a lack of volunteer support in institutions for the elderly. Zepelin and Stutzman found a ratio of approximately 1 volunteer to every 10 residents in their study of 75 facilities. This ratio is quite low, and because it is based only on those facilities which chose to return the questionnaires, the true figure is probably even lower.

RATIONALE FOR THE STUDY

Research indicates that lowered self-esteem, difficulty maintaining warm interpersonal relationships, and loneliness are the three main psychological problems that adolescent and elderly persons face today. Although research suggests that these problems decrease as social interaction increases, a review of the literature reveals no attempt to test these specific ideas empirically in a field setting.

In the study reviewed here, seven high school volunteers participated in a 6-week visitation program with institutionalized elderly adults. An experiential approach was used in training. A second group of seven students participated only in the visitation program; a control group of equal number was not trained and did not visit. Seven elderly adults were visited by trained students; another seven were visited by untrained students. A control group of elderly persons was not visited.

The high school students and the elderly adults were encouraged to develop and maintain one-to-one relationships in an attempt to modify the problems of lowered self-esteem, loneliness, and difficulty with warm interpersonal relationships. Because social interaction seems to be an important factor in the self-esteem of elderly persons, it was thought that visiting might increase their self-esteem. Additionally, it was thought that acceptance by someone other than peers, family, and teachers might contribute to the high school students' self-esteem. This seemed especially likely in view of the fact that adolescents often feel distrustful of these three groups. The literature suggests that self-esteem and warm interpersonal relationships are positively related, although causality is debatable. The students were able to practice developing such relationships; this is an art which is needed throughout life, and it is thus important that it be learned in the earlier years. In addition, this study included the training variable, with the expectation that training would increase the students' awareness of various aspects of aging, which in turn would improve the effectiveness of their visits. It was expected that the efficacy of the visits would increase, but not significantly, at least with regard to self-esteem.

All the participants were assessed before the study was begun and near the end of the study so that their experiences could be evaluated. Statistical evaluation focused on changes in self-esteem in the elderly persons and the students. Clinical evaluation focused on the development of mutually beneficial one-to-one relationships and on changes in the students' awareness of aging. Journals kept by the student visitors and follow-up interviews with the elderly adults were used as aids in clinical evaluation. The journals and the interviews were also useful in examining changes in difficulty with warm interpersonal relationships and in loneliness.

The following hypotheses were explored:

1. After 5 weeks, the elderly participants in the trained and untrained groups would experience greater increases in self-esteem scores than participants in the control group.
2. After 5 weeks, the adolescent participants in the trained and untrained groups would experience greater increases in self-esteem scores than participants in the control group.

Two additional hypotheses were explored informally on the basis of clinical evaluation:

1. The development of one-to-one relationships between the students and the elderly persons in this program would be mutually beneficial.
2. The program would be an effective method for increasing the young people's awareness of various aspects of aging.
   a. Training would be likely to increase the effectiveness of the program.

METHOD

This chapter focuses on the participants' experiences during the study, rather than on the formal statistical results. Therefore, the research methodology will not be presented in detail.

Participants

The students were volunteers from a local high school; there were 2 boys and 19 girls. Their ages ranged from 14 to 18, and their grades in school ranged from the ninth to the twelfth. The elderly volunteers were obtained through two local convalescent hospitals and met the following criteria: They had to expect to be in the hospital for at least 6 weeks, they had to be able to talk and to think clearly enough to maintain a relationship over time, and they could not be terminally ill. The elderly participants included 16 women and 5 men, ranging in age from 54 to 91. Five participants resided in one hospital, and 16 in the other.

Procedure

Administration of pretests. All members of the classes from which the adolescent participants were obtained were given the Rosenberg Self-Esteem Inventory (RSEI). Teachers gave the tests to the students as a group, in the classroom. Three days later I visited the classrooms, briefly outlined the program, and asked for volunteers. The program was discussed individually with each potential elderly volunteer. Each person who chose to participate was given the RSEI. The marital status of each participant was ascertained. Tests were administered individually and were read aloud. The administrators were fellow graduate students.

Assignment of groups and pairs. The elderly participants were randomly assigned to the trained, untrained, or control group. Because of problems concerning students' schedules and transportation to the training sessions, it was decided that the sessions would be held during class time and that the trained group would be made up of health students. Child development students made up the untrained group. Health students were chosen for training because a room in which to hold the sessions was available during their class period, whereas no room was available during the class period of the child development students. The control group was composed of students from both classes. There were no significant differences between the three groups on the RSEI.

Groups were matched as closely as possible on (1) hospital residence of the elderly person, (2) sex of the elderly person, and (3) sex of the student. Each student visitor was randomly assigned an elderly partner of the same sex.

Training. Training and visitation began the same week. It was expected that training would increase the efficacy of the visits and also provide the students with support and with the opportunity to discuss ideas and reactions.

Visitation. The students and the elderly persons worked out visitation times among themselves. All students who visited were asked to commit themselves to 1 h of visitation per week for 6 weeks. They were asked to adhere to the 1-h time commitment as closely as possible. Visitation by trained students began shortly after the first training session; visitation by untrained students began the same week.

Administration of posttests. After 5 weeks, the participants took the RSEI again. It was decided to administer the posttests after 5 weeks rather than after 6 weeks in order that the participants could be retested while the visitation program was ongoing, rather than while it was ending. As before, graduate students administered the scales individually. After 5 weeks, teachers again administered the RSEI in the classroom.

THE TRAINING SESSIONS

Experiential training sessions, each 1 h in length, were held in a small study room in the high school. Two sessions were held during the first week of visitation, and one session was held during each of the following weeks. The sessions will be discussed individually.

Session 1

Each person introduced himself or herself and answered one or more of the following questions: "What do you expect to gain from taking part in this program?" "What do you hope to learn?" "Would you like to share with us any experiences you have had with elderly people?"

Several students were interested in the program because they had had enjoyable relationships with grandparents who had since died. Others planned careers in health-related fields and wanted exposure to health care settings. Some students said they had no particular reason for participating in the program; they just thought that talking with an older person would be fun.

Various aspects of convalescent home environments were discussed, with help from those students familiar with similar settings.

Suggestions were given regarding the first visit. The students were told that because many of the elderly persons were partly deaf and could not see well, it might be necessary to sit close to them. It was also suggested that they limit the first visit to ½ h or less and that they set up regular visitation times, which would make things easier for both persons. I stressed the importance of letting the aged persons know, from the beginning, that the program would last only 6 weeks. The students were also told to check with the elderly person regarding a convenient time for each visit.

The journals were explained, and transportation was arranged. I gave each student the name and room number of his or her partner. The students were enthusiastic and excited about visiting and wanted to start as soon as possible.

Session 2

During the second session, we discussed the initial visits: what they had been like, what problems had occurred, and in what ways they had differed from or matched expectations. One girl told the group that she had not realized the elderly people would be as old and ill as they were, and she said she had been upset at first. However, she said that as she talked with her elderly partner, her uncomfortable feelings had diminished. Another student related a similar experience. One boy found that his elderly partner was more outgoing and talkative than he had expected.

The students then chose partners within the group and participated in an experiential aging exercise designed to emphasize the idea that people of all ages have much in common. The students sat in pairs, facing each other. In brief, each student imagined his or her partner at age 6, at age 25, at age 50, and at age 75. Most important, the students were told to imagine the hopes, wishes, and fears of each age which tie together past, present, and future. After imagining the partner at age 75, each student was asked to imagine himself or herself at that age.

The students were given the opportunity to share their feelings about this exercise, first with their partners and then with the group. Several students felt that the exercise increased their understanding of the aging process. Others had difficulty imagining themselves at age 25 or older. Age 75 was the most difficult; one student said, "I'm used to looking ahead, not behind, and at 75 it's mostly behind."

Session 3

Most of session 3 was devoted to communication exercises. Visiting experiences were related to the exercises, which focused on the effects of I-messages, of various body distances and positions, and of the presence or absence of eye contact.

I explained I-messages and you-messages, with the help of a student who was familiar with their use (Gordon). The principles underlying the two types of messages were discussed, and examples were given. The students chose partners and practiced using I-messages. Each student's reactions to this exercise were then shared with the other members of the group.

The students again chose partners for the remaining exercises (Satir). Each pair of students sat back to back, about 18 in apart, and carried on a conversation. Then they sat and talked with their backs touching.

Next, one partner stood, and the other sat on the floor. After 30 s, the positions were reversed. The partners were instructed to maintain eye contact throughout this exercise and to discuss their reactions to the back-to-back exercises.

For the last exercise, both partners sat on the floor facing each other. One partner, partner A, was to avoid all eye contact with the other partner, partner B. Partner B was to attempt to maintain constant eye contact with partner A. After a few moments, the roles were switched. The dialogue was based on their reactions to the previous standing-sitting exercises.

During the remaining time, the students shared their reactions to each exercise with the group. They were surprised at the impact that distance and position had on their feelings toward their partners. They applied these new realizations to their communication with the elderly adults.

Session 4

During this session, the students discussed their visits and the problems they had encountered. Group cohesiveness was becoming apparent by this time. The students offered one another suggestions concerning each of the issues that arose. One elderly woman had told Jane, her student (all names are fictitious), that she no longer wished to be visited. Jane was understandably upset. The group members were supportive, but at the same time they pointed out other ways of viewing the incident. Urging Jane to try again, they suggested various approaches that she might use during the next visit. In short, the group helped Jane find the courage to visit the woman again. (When she did, the woman told her that she was sorry for what she had said and was glad Jane had come again.)

Another student, Jonah, brought up the topic of reminiscence. The value of reminiscing became apparent when Jonah told the group that, during their first visit, he and his elderly friend had spent over an hour looking through the latter's old photographs.

During the remainder of the session, the students shared their thoughts, feelings, and expectations concerning the first 2 weeks of the program. In general, they were enthusiastic about visiting, although several students had found the first visit somewhat frightening and difficult. Subsequent visits, however, had been more relaxed. Several students were surprised by the older adults' poor health, even though this had been discussed during the first session. Expectations about convalescent hospitals were confirmed for many group members. These students were distressed by what they considered the callousness and lack of caring on the part of staff members and by the residents' curtailed freedom. Both topics were discussed at length.

Session 5

During the fifth session, each student imagined being an elderly participant in the program. The students thought and talked about this idea for several minutes; then they formed pairs and role-played visits. Role playing continued until each student had had a chance to play an elderly person.

The ensuing discussion touched on various topics: the possible difficulty involved in the entry of a randomly chosen stranger into one's room, and subsequently into one's life; the relationship as a two-way process—the need to give and an equally strong need to receive; and the value of reminiscence.

The group members shared their visiting experiences. Questions, comments, and problems were managed basically by the group, *rather than by me*.

Session 6

The sixth session focused on special characteristics of elderly persons. The following characteristics, listed by Butler and Lewis (pp. 23–26), were used to aid the discussion:

1. A desire to leave a legacy
2. Assumption of the "elder" function

3. Attachment to familiar objects
4. A change in the sense of time
5. A sense of the life cycle
6. Creativity, curiosity, and surprise
7. A sense of consummation or fulfillment in life

Several students talked about new ways of viewing life and the world which they had acquired from being with their elderly friends. A student who had frequently moved from state to state drew a parallel between her attachment to familiar objects and her elderly friend's attachment. Termination of visits and sessions was discussed briefly; most students planned to continue visiting.

Session 7

By this time, the topic of death had arisen several times during the students' visits. I provided information about the stages of dying (Kübler-Ross, 1969, 1974). Little factual information was given because the students were more concerned with exploring their personal reactions. They were keenly interested in their elderly friends' attitudes toward death, and they used these as aids in sorting out their own feelings. For example, one boy said he had always been afraid to die. His elderly friend, however, talked about death in a nonfearful way, and so the student began to reevaluate his attitudes and to feel somewhat calmer about it himself. Suicide in old age, the right to die, and the advantages and disadvantages of prolonging human life were discussed.

Termination of the visits and the sessions was again an issue. The students wanted both the visits and the sessions to continue.

Session 8

The final session was unstructured; there was music, and refreshments were served. This session simply provided time to talk over the program and say good-bye. Several students did not want the sessions to end and asked whether both training and visitation could continue. Most students planned to continue visiting; their elderly friends had become both important and rewarding to them.

THE RELATIONSHIPS

As the relationships developed, it became apparent that the visiting process was evoking a wide variety of reactions in both the students and the elderly adults. These reactions ranged from joyful tears to feelings of rejection.

One elderly woman, Ms. Hutton, surprised and deeply touched her visitor by giving her a bar of soap. It was the woman's last bar of her favorite scent. The gift brought tears to Sally's eyes because she realized that Ms. Hutton considered her an important person in her life.

Another student, Jane, felt rejected when she was told not to visit again. Jane's experience was discussed in a previous section.

The students helped their elderly friends with daily exercises. Catrin's partner had recently injured her hip and needed to use her legs. During their visits, she and Catrin walked together around the hospital. Patricia's elderly friend, Miss Wall, suffered from arthritis, and so Patricia, after consulting with the nurses and physical therapists, helped Miss Wall perform the appropriate exercises to relieve the pain.

As previously mentioned, Jonah's partner shared with him his collection of old photographs. This pair of friends thoroughly enjoyed their visits. Jonah's face invariably glowed after a talk with Mr. Malden.

Especially strong feelings of reciprocal caring were obvious in five relationships:

Cristin and Ms. Boston. Cristin was an independent, mature student who hoped to become a physical therapist; Ms. Boston was also quite independent. During her interview, Ms. Boston said, "I have a strong feeling for anyone who's trying to make something of themselves." This relationship was characterized by a particularly high degree of mutual respect and caring.

Sasha and Mrs. Murphy. During the interview, Mrs. Murphy discussed her belief in the importance of spending time with persons of various ages. She said that the different generations had not been so isolated in the past and had grown apart only recently. Mrs. Murphy felt that the visits had helped Sasha, but she did not specify in what way. From Sasha's journal it was obvious that she felt she was helping Mrs. Murphy. Sasha was experiencing problems with her family and with school, which, according to her journal, she and Mrs. Murphy discussed during the visits. These two people were able to both give and receive in their relationship.

Kim and Miss Donaldson. This, too, seemed to be a two-way relationship. Kim enjoyed "doing something" for Miss Donaldson, who enjoyed teaching Kim. The following is a quotation from this student's journal: "Miss D. says she doesn't understand why she had to go to the home because she says that the younger generation has to learn from the older folks and she says they can't learn if the older folks are in rest homes."

Molly and Ms. Brady. Ms. Brady felt that her young visitor had eased her loneliness. The elderly woman also believed that she, in return, had helped Molly become more outgoing. It is likely that regular visits from Molly helped orient Ms. Brady, who was sometimes confused.

Terese and Mrs. Hamilton. Mrs. Hamilton was often confused, and Terese probably gave her continuity in an individual way, in addition to keeping her better aware of time and her surroundings. Terese's journal notes that Mrs. Hamilton's confusion gradually decreased over the weeks.

As the friendships grew, both the students and the elderly adults found themselves anticipating the visits. Caring for one's partner seemed to increase in both the young and the old participants. See Figure 8-1.

RESULTS

Statistical evaluation indicated that the effects of the intergenerational relationships on the participants' self-esteem were minimal. A Kruskall-Wallis analysis

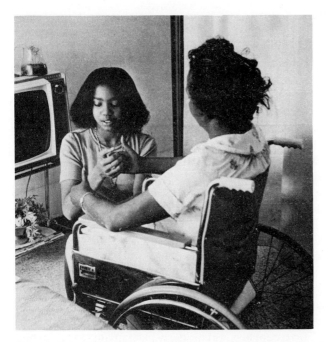

Figure 8-1 Two of the participants of the study developed a close relationship. *(Courtesy of Helen Monea.)*

of variance indicated no significant differences between student groups: $H(2) = 0.429$. Similarly, no significant differences were found for the elderly participants: $H(2) = 0.517$. As expected, training did not prove to be a discriminating factor.

Clinical evaluation indicated that the relationships were mutually beneficial and that the young persons' awareness of aging increased. No formal statistics were computed.

This discussion will focus first on the statistical results, or the effects of the relationships on the participants' self-esteem. Next, in the context of clinical impressions, the discussion will explore the development of mutually beneficial relationships between the young and the old persons as well as increases in the students' awareness of aging.

Statistical Evaluation

It was expected that the students in the trained and untrained groups would experience greater increases in self-esteem than the students in the control group. This hypothesis was not supported. One decrease was found in the untrained group, and no increases were found in any group. Deirdre, the student whose self-esteem decreased, did not differ from the other students in terms of sex, age, grade, desired occupation, or amount of contact with the researcher.

However, she did differ regarding health—she was ill for 10 days. Perhaps her poor health contributed to the lowered score.

When the elderly participants' self-esteem increased, their visitors did not experience corresponding increases. The explanation for this lack of change may be that the students were busier than the elderly participants, and thus the program was not as important to their self-esteem. Attending school, interacting with friends and family members, engaging in sports and other extracurricular activities, and doing schoolwork all took up the students' time and may have affected their self-esteem; in contrast, many of the elderly participants reported they did little and seldom went anywhere. Perhaps the other activities in which the students were involved had a sufficient influence on their self-esteem so that visitation was not important in this regard.

The literature suggests that the elderly participants in the trained and untrained groups would have been likely to have experienced greater increases in self-esteem than those in the control group. This hypothesis was not supported in any group, although several individual increases occurred.

Some elderly persons in the sample experienced increases in self-esteem, and some experienced decreases, resulting in a lack of significant differences for the entire sample. A 30 percent change was considered large enough to be not attributable solely to error. Therefore, *increase* is defined as a 30 percent gain, and *decrease* is defined as a 30 percent loss. Five elderly participants experienced increases; two of these were visited by trained students, and three were visited by untrained students. The participant who experienced a decrease was discussed previously.

The possibility that certain combinations of styles of relating might produce changes and that certain other combinations might have no effect was explored. The interviews with the elderly adults, the students' journals, and the results of observing the visits were examined to gain information about individual styles of relating within each student-adult pair. The relationships of the five participants whose scores increased were previously discussed; these were the relationships in which reciprocal caring was especially apparent. Certain combinations of relating styles did in fact bring about changes; certain other combinations did not. The characteristics of the effective combinations were (1) reciprocal feelings of helping each other; (2) discussion of families during visits; (3) two-way, give-and-take processes of relating; (4) comfortable feelings on the part of students during the visits; and (5) students' recording of internal, subjective feelings in their journals.

Several methodological problems affected the results for both the elderly participants and the students. These problems included the small number of participants and the length and intensity of the study. A ceiling or floor effect may have been operating. The elderly persons' self-esteem may have been affected by uncontrollable factors: marital status, amount of involvement in hospital activities, age of visitor, site differences, sex of participant, and extraneous circumstances. (Similar factors could have affected the students.) A closer examination, however, reveals that none of these factors was significant.

To summarize, the examination of the effects of the intergenerational relationships on the participants' self-esteem yields several possible explanations for the nonsignificant results.

Clinical Evaluation

The development of mutually beneficial one-to-one relationships between the old and young persons and the increase in the students' awareness of various aspects of aging will be examined clinically. The investigator's clinical impressions of the study in general will also be presented.

Mutually beneficial relationships. The interviews and the students' journals indicated that the participants benefited from the relationships. All but two of the elderly adults reported that the visits helped them in some way. Typical comments included: "Lifts my spirits." "I like to talk—I'm lonely." "Good to have someone from the outside to talk to." "Reminds me about taking my medicine, does my hair, and talks with me." "Don't get as lonesome—at my age I need visitors. She brings things that help me in my mind. It's boring to sit." The journals also revealed the elderly persons' feelings: "She's lonesome. She kept saying she wanted me to come back."

The students wrote about the ways in which they benefited too. The following are quotations from the journals: "It was really fulfilling, and I think I may keep visiting her after the 6 weeks are up." "I got a lot out of it and enjoyed it." "I felt just great." "I like visiting her because it makes me happy." "I just felt neat." "This project that I was working on for you is a very good idea. It has helped me out a lot. Thank you." Another indication that the relationships were at least rewarding, if not beneficial, is the fact that most of the students continued visiting after the program ended.

Students' awareness of aging. The students' awareness of various aspects of aging seemed to increase. Their verbal comments suggested that they became more knowledgeable about institutions, problems with staff members, and curtailments of freedom. One student wrote in her journal: "I realize how people can be lonely and yet have so many people around." Another student expressed surprise that her elderly friend could be "so old and so young, too." Many students' feelings shifted over the 6 weeks. At first the students seemed to enjoy visiting because they were helping the elderly participants; later they enjoyed the visits because the elderly adults had become their friends.

The value of training sessions became obvious when awareness of various aspects of aging was considered. In addition to the gains mentioned above, the trained students reported that the communication exercises made their visits more comfortable. They said that they had not previously realized the impact that eye contact, body position, and distance had on their conversations with the elderly individuals. The trained students seemed to develop a greater appreciation and enjoyment of reminiscence and a better understanding of what death meant to their elderly friends. Finally, the students who participated in training became conscious of, and often were able to change, their own stereotypes about the aged. It is believed that the study accomplished the purpose of increasing the students' awareness of various aspects of aging.

General impressions. Even though self-esteem and positive attitudes toward old people did not significantly increase, my impression is that changes occurred. If measures of loneliness or general happiness had been taken, perhaps the results would have been significant. The present study may have focused on the wrong variables.

I also suspect that, for the students, certain effects will become obvious only in later years. These effects are difficult to predict and discuss adequately because they are not described by any single variable. Perhaps the best way to discuss them is in terms of their effects on the students' philosophies of life. For example, in the final training sessions, the students tended to raise issues concerning the meaning of life and what they wanted from their own lives. The relationships with the elderly persons appeared to have been highly thought-provoking. One student seemed to be striving to grasp her elderly friend's philosophy of life when she wrote: "I really care a lot for her because she is a very loving person. She doesn't say anything against people. She is a very happy person, even though she has been through a lot. I hope I'll be that way." Another student wrote: "I, myself, can identify with his philosophy of life."

Conclusions

The following conclusions were drawn:

1. The visitation program did not result in significant changes in the elderly adults' or the students' self-esteem.
2. The development of one-to-one relationships between the students and the elderly persons was mutually beneficial.
3. The visitation program seems to have been effective in increasing the young persons' awareness of various aspects of aging. The training sessions increased this effectiveness.

DIFFICULTIES IN IMPLEMENTATION

A number of problems occurred during the implementation of the program. Transportation was a major difficulty. Initially, I had planned to use a convalescent hospital 8 mi from the high school. Several students did not have transportation, and many of them lived in outlying communities. Therefore, another hospital, 5 min by car from the high school, was selected. The switch caused a week's delay.

Another difficulty was subject selection. A larger number of students than elderly persons volunteered. Many of the elderly individuals who agreed to fill out the self-esteem questionnaires did not want visitors. Several persons who originally wanted visitors later changed their minds. Because there were fewer elderly volunteers than I had expected, I had to use two convalescent hospitals.

Administering the questionnaires to the elderly took longer than was anticipated. The questionnaires were administered to the elderly volunteers individually, either by me or by a fellow graduate student. We had expected the older persons to respond rather slowly, but we did not expect that the depth of our own emotional reactions would increase the length of time. We were saddened by the obvious depression and loneliness of many of the elderly people, and we needed to meet several times during the questionnaire administration to talk over our feelings and provide support for one another.

One student volunteer, Katie, presented another type of problem. She kept postponing her visits during the first week of the study. Although she was not visiting, she insisted that she wanted to participate in the program. She seemed to be afraid of any close contact with another person, while at the same time genuinely craving such contact. On one occasion, Katie arrived at the convalescent hospital and, before reaching the door, literally ran off with some friends who happened to pass by. At the end of the first week, Karen, one of Katie's friends and also a volunteer, informed me that Katie was 4 months pregnant. Karen was the only person Katie had yet told. The three of us met and discussed what Katie planned to do, with respect to both her pregnancy and the program. Shortly thereafter, Katie told her mother and was promptly sent away to a home for pregnant teen-agers.

One week a bad snowstorm left students in the outlying areas snowbound and unable to visit. Flu caused further disruptions of our plans. Several times students arranged to visit on a particular day, only to find that their friends were ill. In spite of this, the enthusiasm of the students and the elderly adults did not wane.

This chapter has discussed a study in which adolescents were given the opportunity to function as psychosocial care givers for elderly persons. The emphasis was on the students' personal experiences in training for visitation and in developing the intergenerational relationships. The students reported that they found their experiences both rewarding and fulfilling. In the process of caring for the elderly persons, the students realized that their aged friends were reciprocating by also caring for them.

FUTURE RESEARCH TOPICS

This study draws attention to the following research issues.

Although the variables explored in this study did not change, it is likely that other variables did. What are these variables? How do one-to-one relationships with elderly individuals influence students' philosophies of life? Is visiting several different persons or visiting a new person every time as beneficial as one-to-one relationships?

The length and timing of visits, as well as the nature of visits, may influence program results. What is the minimal length of time necessary for effective visitation? Is a plateau effect created by infrequent visits? If so, what is an optimal frequency of visits? Does greater or lesser structure of visits increase the effectiveness of visitation programs?

Personality factors such as the age and maturity of students may be highly important. What is the relative efficacy of visitation by high school students and visitation by college students? Do independent, insightful students develop these traits through training? How can training sessions be improved? Are trained or untrained students more likely to continue visitation after the program is completed?

SUGGESTIONS FOR IMPLEMENTATION OF A SIMILAR PROGRAM

Rationale

- Both elderly persons and adolescents can benefit from intergenerational relationships. Both age groups need someone special who will listen to them and offer understanding and support.
- Elderly people and adolescents are subject to similar psychological stresses:
    Lowered self-esteem
    Loneliness
    Concerns about independence
    Difficulty with warm interpersonal relationships

Training Programs

- Some high schools have established integrated community service programs as a way of helping young people learn to care about others in the community.
- Community agencies such as churches and Scout groups involve young people in visiting the elderly in their homes, at institutions, and at day-care centers.

Training

- Training based on experiential methods such as those described in this chapter has great potential for:
    Helping adolescents appreciate and understand the needs of the elderly
    Helping adolescents develop self-awareness
    Helping adolescents use their learning constructively
- In implementing such a program, the adolescents and the elderly persons must be carefully matched according to needs, personality, and maturity of the adolescent.
- *Not all adolescents and elderly people are interested in or appreciate each other.*

Guidelines

- Gain written permission from parents and be available as a liaison to prevent misunderstandings.
- Be available at the visiting site, if possible, or nearby to give consultation and support and to handle any issues and conflicts that may arise.
- Be prepared for the students' reactions to certain aspects of institutionali-

zation, such as a depressing atmosphere or an uncaring attitude on the part of staff members. Adolescents' reactions to the depression and loneliness of institutionalized elderly persons can trigger their own conflicts.

- Tell the students that planned visits may be interrupted or canceled without notice because of medical treatments or fluctuations in the health and mood of the elderly persons.
- Discourage the students from taking notes during their visits, which may be interpreted by staff members as a breach of confidentiality.
- Be prepared for students to miss scheduled visits because of after-school commitments, absences from school, or forgetfulness. If possible, involve parents in transportation.

REFERENCES

Bahn, A.: *Outpatient Population of Psychiatric Clinics: Maryland, 1958–59,* Public Health Monograph no. 65, 1959, U.S. Department of Health, Education, and Welfare.

Birren, J.: *Psychology of Aging,* Prentice-Hall, Englewood Cliffs, N.J., 1964.

Bohannan, P.: *Social Anthropology,* Holt, New York, 1963.

Bromley, D.: *The Psychology of Human Aging,* Penguin, Baltimore, 1966.

Burnside, I.: "Loneliness in Old Age," *Mental Hygiene,* **55**(3):391–397, 1971.

Butler, R., and M. Lewis: *Aging and Mental Health: Positive Psychosocial Approaches,* Mosby, St. Louis, 1973.

Butler, R., and L. Sulliman: "Psychiatric Contact with the Community-Resident, Emotionally-Disturbed Elderly," *Journal of Nervous and Mental Disease,* **137**(2):180–186, 1963.

Cavan, R., E. Burgess, P. Havighurst, and H. Goldhammer; *Personal Adjustment in Old Age,* Science Research, Chicago, 1949.

Collier, J.: *The Hard Life of the Teenager,* Four Winds, New York, 1972.

Deutsche, H.: *Selected Problems of Adolescence,* International Universities Press, New York, 1967.

Eysenck, H.: *The Effects of Psychotherapy,* International Science Press, New York, 1966.

Feldman, R.: "Normative Integration, Alienation, and Conformity in Adolescent Groups," *Adolescence,* **7**(27):327–339, 1972.

Frankel, G.: "The Multipurpose Senior Citizens' Center: A New Comprehensive Agency," *Gerontologist,* **6**(1):23–27, 1966.

Fromm-Reichmann, Frieda: "On Loneliness," in H. M. Bullock (ed.), *Psychoanalysis and Psychotherapy,* University of Chicago Press, Chicago, 1959.

Gallagher, E., M. Sharaf, and D. Levinson: "The Influence of Patient and Therapist in Determining the Use of Psychotherapy in a Hospital Setting," *Psychiatry,* **28**(4):297–310, 1965.

Gibson, R.: "Medicare and the Psychiatric Patient," *Psychiatric Opinion,* **7**:17–22, 1970.

Gold, M., and E. Douvan: *Adolescent De-*

velopment, Allyn and Bacon, Boston, 1969.

Gordon, T.: *Parent Effectiveness Training,* Wyden, New York, 1974.

Hallauer, D., and **S. Gordon:** "Impact of a Friendly Visiting Program on Attitudes of College Students toward the Aged," paper presented at the twenty-eighth annual meeting of the Gerontological Society, Louisville, Ky., October 1975.

Havighurst, R., and **H. Taba:** *Adolescent Character and Personality,* Wiley, New York, 1949.

Jersild, A.: *The Psychology of Adolescence,* Macmillan, New York, 1963.

Katz, P., and **E. Zigler:** "Self-Image Disparity: A Developmental Approach," *Journal of Personality and Social Psychology,* **5**(2):186–195, 1967.

Kübler-Ross, E.: *On Death and Dying,* Macmillan, New York, 1969.

———: *Questions and Answers on Death and Dying,* Macmillan, New York, 1974.

Lambert, B., B. Rothschild, R. Altland, and **L. Green:** *Adolescence: Transition from Childhood to Maturity,* Brooks/Cole, Monterey, Calif., 1972.

Livson, F.: "Adjustment to Aging," in S. Reichard, F. Livson, and P. G. Peterson (eds.), *Aging and Personality,* Wiley, New York, 1962, pp. 93–108.

Lorand, S.: "Treatment of Adolescents," in A. Winder and D. Angus (eds.), *Adolescence: Contemporary Studies,* American Book, New York, 1968, pp. 24–33.

Matteson, D.: *Adolescence Today: Sex Roles and the Search for Identity,* Dorsey, Homewood, Ill., 1975

Monea, H.: "Developmental Reactions in Adolescence," in M. E. Kalkman and A. J. Davis (eds.), *New Dimensions in Mental Health: Psychiatric Nursing,* 4th ed., McGraw-Hill, 1974.

Mumford, L.: "For Older People—Not

Segregation, but Integration," *Architectural Record,* **119**(5):191–194, 1956.

Muuss, R.: *Theories of Adolescence,* Random House, New York, 1969.

Radcliffe-Brown, A.: "Introduction," in A. Radcliffe-Brown and D. Forde (eds.), *African Systems of Kinship and Marriage,* Oxford, New York, 1960.

Robbins, I.: "Housing for the Aging," in *Charter for the Aging,* New York State Joint Legislative Committee on Problems of the Aging, New York, 1955, pp. 300–332.

Rosenberg, M.: *Society and the Adolescent Self-Image,* Princeton, Princeton, N.J., 1965.

Russo, R.: "Mutually Therapeutic Interaction between Mental Patients and Delinquents," *Hospital and Community Psychiatry,* **25**(8):531–533, 1974.

Rybak, W., J. Sadnavitch, and **B. Mason:** "Psycho-Social Changes in Personality during Foster Grandparents Program," *Journal of the American Geriatrics Society,* **16**(8):956–959, 1968.

Safier, G.: "Undergraduate Nursing Students and Their Experience in Gerontology," *The Gerontologist,* **15**(2): 165–169, 1975.

Satir, V.: *Peoplemaking,* Science and Behavior Books, Palo Alto, Calif., 1972.

Schwartz, A., and **R. Kleemeier:** "The Effects of Illness and Age upon Some Aspects of Personality," *Journal of Gerontology,* **20**(1):85–91, 1965.

Shore, M, and **J. Massimo:** "The Chronic Delinquent during Adolescence: A New Opportunity for Intervention," in G. Caplan, and S. Lebovici (eds.), *Adolescence: Psychosocial Perspectives,* Basic Books, New York, 1969, pp. 335–342.

Solon, J., R. Amthor, M. Rabb, and **J. Shelley:** "Linking Young and Old Institutionalized People," paper presented at the twenty-eighth annual meeting of the

Gerontological Society, Louisville, Ky., October 1975.

Sullivan, H.: *Interpersonal Theory of Psychiatry,* Norton, New York, 1953.

Weemer, A.: "Shifts in Concerns from Adolescence to Late Maturity," *Dissertation Abstracts International,* **32**(5-B): 2992, 1971.

Zepelin, H., and **J. Stutzman:** "Volunteer Support for the Institutionalized Elderly," paper presented at the twenty-eighth annual meeting of the Gerontological Society, Louisville, Ky., October 1975.

Zinberg, N., and **I. Kaufman:** *Normal Psychology of the Aging Process,* International Universities Press, New York, 1963.

OTHER RESOURCES

FILMS

Miles to Go before I Sleep: 16 mm/78 min/color. The story of an old man and a 14-year-old girl dealing with the mistrust that exists between the old and the young. The two are brought together by an interested social worker, and a bond of trust is finally formed between them. Distributor: Learning Corporation of America, 1350 Avenue of the Americas, New York, N.Y. 10019. *The Shopping Bag Lady:* 16 mm/21 min/color. A teenage girl matures after an encounter with a homeless old lady. She develops compassion when she recognizes her own fears of aging. Distributor: Mass Media Associates, 2116 North Charles Street, Baltimore, Md. 21218.

YOUTH PARTICIPATION IN COMMUNITY DEVELOPMENT

The Switching Yard
1022 Sir Francis Drake Boulevard
San Anselmo, Calif. 94960

Chapter 9

ETHNICITY AND SEXUALITY: THEIR IMPACT ON CARING

Helen Elena Monea

> Mommy, Mommy, the kids at school made fun of my
> eyes. They can't see them. They said they're like
> almonds.
>
> *Laura, a 6-year-old Korean child*

Laura's mother sympathized with her hurt child and responded, "What do they think they have, walnut eyes?" (Song). Such teasing is a common experience for children who look different from their peers. See Figure 9-1. People in all age groups whose features or skin color is different or who wear different clothing are prime targets for teasing. During a high school graduation speech, a valedictorian reviewed the 4 years he spent in an integrated class of black and white peers. He acknowledged the variety of ways in which the school had attempted to implement desegregation and change attitudes: busing, seating black and white students next to each other in the classroom, and holding special dance classes taught by black students and attended by white students. His message was that it is harder to "put down" someone you know. The valedictorian touched on the root of the problem: the big "put-down" ("As We See It"). See Figure 9-2.

THE BIG PUT-DOWN

From where does the need to "put down" another person arise? This is a profound question with many conceptual answers, depending on the theory you draw from: psychoanalytic theory, ego psychology, or sociology. This chapter will discuss various concepts of prejudice. According to Bettelheim and Janowitz,

Figure 9-1 Eastern children who have different facial features may be teased or discriminated against by their peers. Teachers need to examine their own attitudes toward prejudice if they are to provide a democratic classroom environment that allows for the free pursuit of learning and growing. *(Courtesy of Pat Song.)*

"Prejudice reduces anxiety because it suggests to the person that he is better than others, hence does not need to feel so anxious" (pp. 54–55). The greater the person's anxiety, the more he or she will use prejudice as a means of gaining control. Another useful concept is that of the relationship between identity, ethnic hostility, and prejudice. The search for identity includes finding ego strength and personal control. Those who fail to find an effective personal identity may temporarily or permanently use prejudice as a detour. Adolescents, for example, may use prejudice in their search to discover who they are (Bettelheim and Janowitz).

IDENTITY DIFFUSION

Erikson has discussed intolerance as a defense against the "identity diffusion" experienced by adolescents (Bettelheim and Janowitz). The adolescent experiences identity diffusion when he or she is unable to synthesize an identity or "take hold" of life. Identity diffusion, coupled with strong self-doubt about one's ethnic, social, personal, or sexual identity, can evolve into prejudice—for example, boy against girl, Jew against Gentile, and "hip" against "square." The fear experienced in identity diffusion is very important because it contributes to intolerance.

Figure 9-2 Photography appeals to students. In this racially mixed classroom, students working together learn how to develop film. These students are using a light-tight bag that enables them to handle film outside a darkroom. *(Courtesy of Dwain Johnson.)*

A temporary overidentity can occur when one belongs to a clique or a crowd that excludes those who are "different" in terms of skin color, cultural background, or personal tastes. Erikson stresses the importance of understanding prejudice, which does not necessarily mean condoning or imitating the prejudiced behavior or actions of others. Such actions of intolerance are necessary for "defense against a sense of identity diffusion" (Erikson, p. 92). Such a defense is not restricted to adolescents. It is also used by people who experience anxiety, self-doubt, and confusion about who they are. Feeling like a "nobody," they silence their anxiety by telling themselves, "At least I am not a Negro, or a Jew; and this makes me at least something more than a nobody" (Bettelheim and Janowitz, p. 58).

DEVELOPMENTAL VALUE FORMATION

Konopka has developed a meaningful and practical theory based on developmental value formation. In her view, values arise from the ethical relationships between human beings that develop out of the process of interaction with one another and with the system in which they live. The values change as the individual changes and is changed. Konopka evolved this theory from her reading and from her experiences as a Jew in Berlin. Jews were considered inferior by the Nazis, and she and her family were the victims of extreme prejudice. Throughout her youth, she learned (and was hurt) by asserting two basic absolutes in which she believed: (1) the dignity of the individual and (2) the responsibility of all people for one another.

The development of values is both an intellectual and an emotional process that peaks in adolescence. Konopka traced the development of value formation from early childhood through adolescence. See Tables 9-1 to 9-3. The development of value formation does not stop at adolescence, however; a rethinking of life goals continues into middle age, as described in the chapters in Part 2. Elderly people have settled on their values and can review their lives in terms of these values. (See the discussion of reminiscence in Chapter 28.)

Konopka's life experiences shaped her value formation, and I believe that my experiences have shaped mine. From early childhood, I was part of an ethnic group whose members were considered second-class citizens. My parents immigrated from Romania in 1917 and settled in a racially mixed section of an industrial town near a metropolitan area. I lived in close contact with other minority groups. There was much intolerance and prejudice and also a "pecking order" of respect, with the Jewish families at the top and the Mexican and black families at the bottom. I now realize how much I learned as a child about establishing rapport with people whose racial background is different from my own. This learning was particularly helpful during the school riots of the 1960s, when I was a university faculty member.

In private practice, I was once asked to help a group of Korean parents understand their children, who were rebelling against the Korean customs. One aspect we focused on was values and identification. As a first-generation American, I understood the double bind of children who were born in one country but whose parents identified with another. I shared one fantasy that children may experience in this double identity. A teenage Eurasian girl believed that she would

Table 9-1.   Value Formation: Preschoolers

Behavior	Values
Do not question, but frequently resist.	Values related to acceptance or rejection of other human beings are significant and unconsciously formed.
Will resist openly or pretend adjustment to a person not liked.	
Example of value behavior: Caucasian nursery school child touching and being touched by black classmates. Differences were found, but children of both races perceived hair as soft and pretty.	Value learned by children in the example: incorporation of variety and beauty.
	A value or prejudice is reinforced by parents or other adults who have the same value or prejudice.

Table 9-2. Value Formation: School-aged Children

Behavior	Values
Raises questions, but mostly accepts or follows the preferences of adults.	Formation of values is more conscious than during the preschool years.
Preferences of the adult world are still accepted or followed.	Values are beginning to be emotionally reordered internally.
	At this age gaining more strength in adolescence.

have to choose either her American or her Oriental values by her sixteenth birthday. No one had told her that she would be expected to do this. As we explored the difficulties faced by their Korean children, the parents began to realize the stresses to which they were being subjected. See Figure 9-3.

DISCONTINUITIES IN DEVELOPING VALUES

First-generation children experience discontinuities in value and identity development. Children of certain minority groups, such as Negroes, Indians, and Mexicans, enjoy a more sensual early childhood than American children (Erikson). The crisis occurs when (1) the parents and teachers use corrective measures to Americanize the children, which creates discontinuities, and (2) the children begin to disavow their sensual and overprotective mothers and perceive them as hindering their formation of a more American personality (Erikson).

CAN WE REDUCE PREJUDICE?

How can we reduce prejudice? A review of studies on prejudice indicates that intimate contact with someone from another racial or ethnic group does not necessarily change attitudes. In a boys' interracial camp, boys whose feelings of prejudice increased had a great need to defy authority, while boys whose feelings of prejudice decreased had few aggressive tendencies and had favorable attitudes toward their parents and others. In another study, efforts were made to change patterns of hostility and to increase personal control. The children in this study, also at an interracial camp, experienced a significant reduction in their feelings of prejudice and asked to extend their stay at camp (Bettelheim and Janowitz).

In the mid-1960s, thousands of white families adopted children from other racial and cultural backgrounds because few white infants were available for adoption and because these families were committed to racial equality (Scarr-Salapatek and Weinberg). The adoptive parents were generally warm, comfortable, and relaxed with their children and ran democratic households in which the children and the adults shared responsibilities and participated in activities together. The children's natural parents had relatively little education and below-

Table 9-3. Value Formation: Adolescents

Behavior	Values
Have strong capacity for thinking and feeling.	Participation in decision making.
	Honesty.
Reevaluate values—a universal major characteristic.	Equality and variety.
Will not compromise their egalitarian values.	Spiritual values with rejection of competition and worldly goods.
May become cynical.	Some groups value the contemplative life, while other groups value hard work, poverty, and discipline.
The most significant age of value formation.	
	Feelings are highly valued, with rejection of rational thinking.

Figure 9-3 Parents and teachers need to understand the dual identity crisis that first-generation children face. Integrating the value systems and cultural customs of both countries can be an enriching experience for a child. The Korean youngster below is wearing the national Korean dress, *chogori chima*. The feathered fans originated in the early years of Korean royalty. *(Courtesy of Pat Song.)*

average IQs. These children's IQs improved, showing the influence of environmental factors. Black action groups, however, are pressuring adoption agencies not to allow interracial adoption.

Thompson used a film model to modify ethnic attitudes in 6- and 7-year-old Caucasian children. She recommends that researchers consider the obvious models in the child's environment, such as parents, teachers, and peers, as transmitters of societal attitudes and that they determine the variables of these models' influences before beginning to modify racial attitudes. Thompson reviews previous studies on factors affecting formation of racial attitudes such as age, intellectual ability, socioeconomic status, and sex. Very young Caucasian children have not yet learned their culture's negative stereotypes and do not seem to develop them with their first interracial experience.

One influence on the racial prejudice of white preschool children was found to be the use of the labels "black" and "white," which contributed to the already present tendency of the children to evaluate black persons negatively and white persons positively. The study found that the terms "Negro" and "Caucasian" did not contribute to a prejudiced attitude (Katayama).

ETHNICITY AND SEXUALITY

A study of third graders' attitudes toward one another found that sex had a greater influence on prejudice than race. Asher and Singleton (cited in Greenberg), of the University of Illinois, studied white and black third graders who had been in integrated classrooms since kindergarten. Their studies indicated that children who start out in integrated schools develop better racial attitudes and better relationships with classmates than those who start out in segregated classes. The children were asked to rate their classmates on a 5-point scale. Their ratings of members of the opposite sex were lower than their ratings of same-sex classmates. The same children will be retested in the sixth grade. Note Table 9-4, which indicates that 38.9 percent of the black population in the United States is under the age of 18.

Reiss explored why some groups are more sexually permissive than others. Twelve hundred high school and college students aged 16 to 22 were included in the study. One of Reiss's findings was that the less sexually permissive a group is traditionally, the greater the possibility that new social forces will influence group members to become more sexually permissive. Black men, traditionally considered to be highly sexually permissive, were found to be least likely to have their sexual standards changed by social forces. Groups traditionally considered to be sexually unpermissive, such as white females, showed the greatest sensitivity to social forces. People in the lower social classes with traditions of greater sexual permissiveness were found to be less sensitive to social forces.

Regarding parental attitudes toward sexual activities of sons as opposed to daughters, Reiss found that the more daughters a white father has, the more strongly he feels about his own sexual standards; the more sons he has, the less

Table 9-4. Analysis of Black Population Projections by Major Age Groups, 1975 and 2000.

Item and Age	1975	2000 for Series I	II	III
Numbers (000)				
All ages	24,517	36,379	33,325	30,963
Under 18	9,547	12,522	9,982	8,110
18–64	13,165	20,915	20,401	19,911
65+	1,805	2,942	2,942	2,942
55+	3,254	5,334	5,334	5,334
60+	2,616	4,011	4,011	4,011
Median age	23.5	27.8	30.9	33.3
% distribution				
All ages	100.0	100.0	100.0	100.0
Under 18	38.9	34.3	30.0	26.2
18–64	53.7	57.5	61.2	64.3
65+	7.4	8.1	8.8	9.5
55+	13.3	14.7	16.0	17.2
60+	10.7	11.0	12.0	13.0

Source: U.S. Bureau of the Census, 1975.

strongly he feels about his beliefs. The reverse was found in the case of white mothers. Reiss suggested that this might be due to white parents' unfamiliarity with the special sexual problems of a child of the opposite sex. The differences between the sexual attitudes of blacks and those of whites may well be due to the discrimination blacks have suffered over the centuries and their resultant low status. Economic pressures may cause the breakup of black families and weaken blacks' commitment to marital values, with a consequent increase in sexual permissiveness.

HOMOSEXUALITY

Homosexuality may be one of the greatest sources of the "put-down." Junior high school students in sex education groups have explored many of their concerns with me: "How am I different from girls?" "How am I different from boys?" "What happens when you have intercourse?" "What is it like?" (Pazdur). Children's tendency to make demeaning remarks about male instructors who have feminine traits may be due to an underlying anxiety about their own sexuality.

Parents fear that their children may identify with homosexual teachers. However, the etiology of homosexuality has been shown to be complex, and research has failed to verify genetic, environmental, or hormonal factors as direct causes (Monea).

THE PRIMAL SCENE

Adults often either underestimate a child's awareness of sexuality or prefer to ignore it. Parents frequently have difficulty finding the time and privacy necessary for sexual intimacy. Some couples plan special nights in a motel, send the children to the movies, or wait until the children's bedtime, hoping for the best. If the worst happens and a child intrudes on a scene of sexual intimacy, the parents' embarrassment often prevents them from handling the situation in a way that is helpful to the child.

In some countries, such an occurrence is treated in a natural, nonchalant way. A young man from South America told me how his parents handled his intrusion upon their lovemaking. They greeted him fondly, and his father issued an invitation for him to "come back later."

In some countries, parents and children share the same bedroom, and this does not seem to interfere with the children's sexual growth and development. In Korea, traditionally children sleep in the same room with their parents until they are 5 years old. When they enter kindergarten, they are expected to be more independent, and they no longer share the parental bedroom. Korean adults do not have memories of parental intimacy (Song).

Most children begin to have thoughts related to parental intercourse at about 7 or 8 years of age (Frankel and Harrison). In the case of Korean children, this provides an interesting paradox since the Korean people treat intimacy with discretion, no off-color jokes are allowed, and there are no open displays of affection. It is considered ill-mannered for parents to show affection in the presence of others or to hug, kiss, or scold children in the presence of grandparents (Song). The Westernized Korean has modified these attitudes. Similarly, in the Japanese culture, touching is not always necessary for showing affection; a loving look from the parent can make the child feel warm and loved (Takamura).

Viewing parents' intercourse can result in distorted views of sexuality or in sexual inhibitions in later life; however, psychiatrists Frankel and Harrison assure us that pathology is not the inevitable outcome. They have outlined the following suggestions for interventions:

1 When parents ask for help after a child has viewed them during intercourse, the professional should attempt to alleviate their guilt and anxiety and encourage them to engage in appropriate verbal communication with the child in relation to their concerns and beliefs.
2 When parents report that they suspect their child has viewed them during intercourse, the professional should assess whether the parents can communicate effectively with the child. When assessment is difficult, consultation with mental health professionals could be useful.
3 In some cases the child's behavior, such as a preoccupation with sex,

excessive curiosity about sex, or sleep disturbances, indicates that he or she may have viewed the parents during intercourse, even though the parents themselves have not expressed any concern in this regard. In such situations the professional should assess whether the family habits and lifestyle are conducive to sexual exposure. If they are, it should be determined whether this is the result of naïveté or pathological motivation. An educational approach is appropriate when the former is the case; the latter situation would require collaboration with a mental health specialist (Frankel and Harrison).

A preschooler had viewed her divorced father being intimate with his girlfriend. She was a quiet but friendly child at school, but at home she pretended the primal scene with the boys in the neighborhood, which was upsetting to her parents and to the boys' parents. She was at a stage when she liked to imitate adults, and she was deriving great satisfaction from the attention she received when she "played bedtime." One home visit was made with the mother and her boyfriend. They were given information about children's normal sexual curiosity and felt relief as they gained understanding about their embarrassment and how to help the child and themselves.

The effect of viewing sexual intercourse depends upon the child's level of maturity. During the first year of life, there may be no effect because of limited perceptual abilities. Children aged 3 to 4, however, may be significantly affected. They may interpret intercourse as an aggressive or perhaps a sadistic act. Children at this age are especially interested in their parents' bedroom since they feel excluded from this area (Frankel and Harrison).

SEXUAL ABUSE: THE FAMILY AND OTHERS

The subject of sexual abuse of children elicits strong feelings of revulsion and disbelief. Parents often alert their children not to talk with strangers or to take candy or go for a ride with them. A growing problem, however, is sexual abuse within the family. As discussed in Chapter 1, a person known to the child and the family may abuse the child. Studies indicate that the father, a male relative, or a boyfriend of the mother is most often the abuser. The mother may be aware of the situation but fails to do anything about it for conscious or unconscious reasons. Sometimes the mother has overstimulated the male child; this can happen particularly if the father is absent. Adults of the same sex as the child can also behave in a sexually inappropriate way with the child (Brant and Tisza).

INCEST

Incest, the ultimate taboo, is not uncommon and occurs in families on every economic level and from every racial group. The definition of incest and the punishment for it differ from state to state. In Santa Clara County, California, it is considered that any person who functions as a parent or guardian, though not necessarily a blood relative, can be guilty of incest (Ramsey). The most frequently reported type is father-daughter incest, followed by brother-sister incest, which is less traumatic. During the past 5 years, more than 400 families, mainly white and of the middle class, have been helped by the Santa Clara County Sexual Abuse Treatment Program. It is estimated that 40,000 to 60,000 children are sexually abused by their parents or care givers each year (Ramsey). Many cases go unreported and untreated because the parents fear social humiliation, because the child is afraid to tell the parents, or because there is a pathological bond between the abuser and abused. While most cases of incest among lower socioeconomic groups are called to the attention of the police and child welfare agencies and then are handled by the courts, cases of incest among upper-class families are more frequently handled by private therapists (Ramsey).

Child psychiatrists Brant and Tisza, who work as consultants to emergency room staff members, suggest the following guidelines for those who are involved in the treatment of sexually abused children:

Support system. Use an interdisciplinary team approach to provide mutual support and encourage the sharing of responsibility.

Child and family focus. Try to understand family factors contributing to the child's vulnerable position. Determine the roles, rules, and boundaries within the family; usually these are indistinct in families in which children are abused.

Safety and controls. Assess the parents' superego strength and their capacity for impulse control and reality testing. Help the family members feel safe in working out their problems with a therapeutic team. If the child seems in danger, use the court as a monitor and protector.

Solutions can be problems. Temporary placement of the child into a foster home may expose the child to a similar abuse situation. Court hearings can be traumatic for both the child and the family. Provide support and minimize the trauma as much as possible.

EXPLOITATION OF CHILDREN

Pornography using children as subjects has been a big business. Just recently the Senate passed a bill to stop the sale, distribution, and production of pornographic material using children as subjects. Such exploitation of children obviously feeds on the mental aberrations of buyers, viewers, and producers. The blame seems to rest with parents who allow their children to be exploited in this way. Other forms of exploitation by some parents are much more subtle and less traumatic; the "backstage mother" who lives through her daughter is a familiar example.

SUGGESTIONS FOR ETHNIC AND RACIAL CARING

- Children and young people need to be encouraged to discover a variety of value systems and to question their own values and those of others (Konopka).

- Young people must be helped to work through value questions and not accept values on a purely emotional basis.
- Assertion training for children is helpful in teaching them to take responsibility for their own rights and those of others (Konopka).
- Children should be exposed to the customs and traditions of cultures other than their own (Monea).
- Parents must be helped to understand and cope with the first-generation child's difficulty in establishing an identity (Monea).
- Care givers should search their own value systems on both an emotional and an intellectual basis (Monea).
- The education of young children can be improved so that fewer of them will become intolerant adults (Bettelheim and Janowitz).
- Teacher training should be upgraded to include early and continuous contact with children and adults in disadvantaged areas in a variety of educational and noneducational activities (Strom).
- College curricula must be modified to develop the techniques and skills essential to teaching in depressed areas (Strom).
- Teachers should become involved with nonschool agencies responsible for overcoming poverty and extending civil rights so that they can gain insights into the problems and life-styles of inner-city families (Strom).

CONCLUSION

Ethnicity and sexuality are complex, complicated fields of study, especially in relation to children. This chapter has touched on only a few of the problems that children's care givers may expect to face in these areas.

REFERENCES

As We See It: 1976. A series of 26 videotapes about racial integration in high schools written and researched by high school students. WTTW Educational Station, 5400 N. St. Louis Avenue, Chicago, Ill. 60625.

Bettelheim, Bruno, and Morris Janowitz: *Social Change and Prejudice: Including Dynamics of Prejudice*, Free Press, New York, 1964.

Brant, Renee S. T., and Veronica B. Tisza: "The Sexually Misused Child," *American Journal of Orthopsychiatry*, **47**(1): 80–90, 1977.

Erikson, Erik H.: "Identity and the Life Cycle," *Psychological Issues*, **1**(1), Monogr. 1, International Universities Press, New York, 1959.

Frankel, Steven, and Saul I. Harrison: "Children's Exposure to Parental Intercourse," *Medical Aspects of Human Sexuality*, **10**(9):115–119, 1976.

Greenberg, Joel: "Early Integration May Cut Prejudice," *San Francisco Sunday Examiner, The World*, Oct. 23, 1977, p. 32.

Katayama, David Taro: "Evaluative Connotations of Racial Labels Black and

White as a Contributing Factor in the Development of Racial Attitudes in Preschool Children," M. A. thesis, San Francisco State University, San Francisco, 1975.

Konopka, Gisela: "Formation of Values in the Developing Person," *American Journal of Orthopsychiatry,* **43**(1):86–96, 1973.

Monea, Helen: "Developmental Reactions in Adolescence," in M. E. Kalkman and A. J. Davis (eds.), *New Dimensions in Mental Health: Psychiatric Nursing,* 4th ed., McGraw-Hill, New York, 1974.

Pazdur, Helen C.: "Innovation: The School Nurse as a Mental Health Specialist," *The Journal of School Health,* **39**(7): 449–457, 1969.

Ramsey, Judith: "My Husband Broke the Ultimate Taboo" (report from the Santa Clara County Child Sexual Abuse Treatment Program), *Family Circle,* **90**(3): 42+, Mar. 8, 1977.

Reiss, Ira L.: "How and Why American's Sex Standards Are Changing," in Helen Z. Lopata (ed.), *Marriages and Families,* Van Nostrand, Princeton, N.J., 1973, pp. 163–168.

Scarr-Salapatek, Sandra, and Richard A. Weinberg: "When Black Children Grow Up in White Homes," *Psychology Today,* **9**(12):80–82, 1975.

Song, Pat: Personal communication, September 1977.

Takamura, Jeanette: Personal communication, June 1977.

Thompson, Susan Lynn: "Modification of Ethnic Attitudes in Six and Seven-Year-Old Caucasian Children Using a Filmed Model," M. A. thesis, California State University, San Francisco, 1973.

U.S. Bureau of the Census, 1975.

OTHER RESOURCES

FILMS

Can We Immunize against Prejudice? 7 min/16 mm/1954. Depicts three couples attempting to rear their children free from prejudice, each in a different way. The three ways are: setting a good example, inducing the right attitude through knowledge, and relying on law and order. In spite of their efforts, each child develops the symptoms of prejudice. The film does not present solutions but is a catalyst for audience discussion. Distributor: University of California, Extension Media Center, Berkeley, Calif. 94720.

Incest: The Victim Nobody Believes: 21 min/16 mm/color/1976. A documentary about the problem of sexual assault on children. Three victims of incest tell their stories of fear, confusion, isolation, and guilt. Distributor: Mitchell Gebhardt Film Co., 1380 Bush Street, San Francisco, Calif. 94109.

Chapter 10

PSYCHOSOCIAL DEVELOPMENT OF CHILDREN: HOLISTIC CARE-GIVING APPROACHES

Helen Elena Monea

> Now and then, though, someone does begin to grow
> differently. But we do our best to discourage awkward
> things like that. . . . Oddly enough, they often grow ten
> times the size of everyone else . . . and I've heard that
> they walk among the stars.
>
> *Norton Juster*

This chapter discusses some innovative approaches designed to help children learn and grow. A variety of disciplines have been involved in finding creative ways of working with children.

In recent years there has been a trend away from the "rat race" of Western society toward a simpler life-style. Gregg (cited in Elgin and Mitchell) has described the movement as being directed toward "voluntary simplicity" or a life-style that is balanced between inner and outer growth. It does not consist in going "back to nature" or living in poverty, but rather in simplifying one's life so that one is less dependent on complex institutions. This trend counterbalances the emphasis on material goods. The quality of human relationships will be based on exploring inner potentials for a rich life, and one of the values of the new society will be intuition (Elgin and Mitchell).

INTUITIVE TRAINING

Intuitive training is geared toward using energy that transcends conventional verbal and nonverbal communication. Messages can be sent between two people whose eyes are closed and who are sitting at some distance from each other. The exciting thing is that every person has the capability of intuitive transmission, though some more than others. Not all attempts to transmit messages or pictures are successful. With practice, individuals can increase their ability to send and receive messages using this special energy. No one is sure what mechanism is responsible for this unconventional mode of communication. Indications are that an electromagnetic field around our bodies radiates outwardly and functions as a transmitter. Developing the intuitive part of ourselves involves (1) relaxing the body, (2) paying attention to dreams, (3) concentrating on geometric forms, and (4) learning crafts (Ornstein).

June Milich, of the Wholistic Health and Nutrition Institute in California, is a pioneer in the field of training children to develop and heighten their intuitiveness. She describes her work as follows:

Intuitive knowledge is gained through perceiving from the senses information that is not physical or tangible. *Intuitiveness as explored in my classes does not concern just the psychic ability of the child; rather, I work with all the senses to heighten the capacity of every sense.* Intuitive capacities are inherent in all the physical sensations of touch, smell, vision, hearing, and taste. I use exercises and approaches based on my experiences in personal growth. To work in this fashion, one must be willing to experience the processes and to grow through increased self-awareness. Usually children can make contact with their intuitive nature and express their sensory awareness with more ease than adults. What is accomplished in the classes varies with the abilities of the children. Those who remember their dreams become stronger in dreaming or more vocal about their dreaming, while those who work well with groups seem to be more stimulated in their relationships. The focus is on helping them accept and trust the intuitive nature of learning through various modes of communication: dream discussions, feeling their energy or aura (light around the body), and other phenomena. Such explorations do not lead to confusion if the teacher moves slowly and carefully, keeping the best interests of the children in mind. Children can accept what adults call "unusual experiences" surprisingly well.

The children are not working from a "head space" or point of reference that requires understanding of an occurrence or situation that needs to be proved or repeatable to be real. However, some children are not at ease with this intuitive knowledge in themselves; this may be due to their own mistrust or to a family environment that does not confirm the importance of feelings, dreaming, and decision-making based on "a sense of the situation." A "sense of the situation" is what is perceived outside the usual modes of perception. For example, one can sense certain qualities of a situation or a person without having a physical or tangible basis for doing so. Subsequent events often validate such perceptions. A lack of validation sometimes comes through the spoken comments of others, but more often it is the unspoken doubts that children perceive.

Children who do have intense intuitive experiences often adapt to skeptical responses from others by not sharing the information gleaned intuitively. This failure to acknowledge children's ability can be confusing to them. Children presume that their own intuitive experiences are a reality for everyone. When families and school environments do not support the process, this part of the child's nature is denied by those who are in a position of guidance. I feel that the lack of validation creates self-doubt and mistrust of a process that is natural.

When children experience the exercises described below for the first time, they are apt to be restless, or they may giggle as a reaction to what seems unusual. Once the first session is over, however, they begin to experience themselves in a wonderful new way and are eager to do more. If a child does not wish to participate, I suggest that he or she sit, watch, or rest. The child is apt to join in later. It is important that a child not be "punished" for not joining in the exercises.

Along the Yellow Brick Road

I developed the title of my workshops from the book *The Wizard of Oz* because it is symbolic of growth (Baum). Dorothy starts on the spiraling yellow brick road to find her way back home. This path guides her and her companions to Oz, where, through various adventures, they realize that they have within themselves the sources of growth and personal power. The workshops as outlined are held on a weekly basis; each session lasts 1½ h.

The following are the specific exercises I use during the second and fourth weeks of the course:

Exercise 1: Grounding. Relaxing and developing a feeling of connection with the earth and the present.

Exercise 2: Palming. Using a physical exercise to stimulate physical and perceptual vision. See Figure 10-1.

Exercise 3: Communication magic. Using extrasensory perception exercises as a way of exercising sensory communication other than through eyes.

Exercise 4: Life space. Reexperiencing one's total life from birth to the present, on the basis of feelings.

Exercise 5: Mandala, or making a god's eye. The mandala is another way of relaxing and grounding. Making a god's eye is a physical interpretation of a sensory stimulation.

Exercise 6: Dreams (fourth week). Supporting the insights and significance of vision through dream activities in relation to the waking world.

Experiences are accomplished in three ways: (1) individually, (2) with a partner, and (3) as a group. Classes emphasize the whole body, especially the senses. The goal is to connect the intuitive process and power with children's needs. *The younger the children, the more they need to act out a concept.* Therefore, each session is mainly a series of exercises and activities meant to stimulate and confirm the children's ability to be intuitive. Many of the techniques I use have their origin in spiritual systems; I am sensitive to the children's spiritual beliefs and those of their families, and I carefully plan exercises that will not infringe upon those beliefs.

Figure 10-1 Children rest their eyes using the Chinese method of palming, which relaxes them and prepares them for intuitive training. *(Courtesy of Helen Monea.)*

I encourage the children by telling them to trust what feels right for them. A thought that feels right is like clothes that fit so well that one hardly notices them. The children begin to understand that developing their intuitive nature is a process involving trust and experience. Trust lets the experience happen, and experience confirms or questions one's original insight.

I developed the exercises gradually using experiences from my own childhood and late teenage years as major resources; I included dreaming, conscious explorations of my intuitiveness, learning hatha yoga, meditation, personology, and the I Ching and T'ai Chi. I first taught the exercises in second- and third-grade classrooms; later I held after-school workshops.

After the final exercise, the children and I always have a treat consisting of tea, nuts, or fruit. After much concentration on the intuitive nature, the treats help to reconnect body and mind. See Figure 10-2.

Exercise 3: Communication Magic

Seeing through Other Parts of the Body
We can "see" through touch. The following short exercise helps children recognize that "sight" occurs in other parts of the body besides the eyes:
Directions. Have the children work in pairs, taking turns. Describe what they can expect; for example, their eyes will be closed, and you will place a piece of paper or material in front of them to touch. While they are touching, they are to visualize the color of the object. Their partner serves as a reality source. See Figure 10-3.
Responses. Children correctly guess the colors of objects with their eyes closed a majority of the time. *When they try too hard to guess, they often miss.* Apparently, there is a relationship between trying to do something by creating

or predicting an image instead of letting the sensory communication create the image.

Practice in Inner Vision

This experience involves extrasensory perception or practice in inner vision. This not only demonstrates communication via our sixth sense but also teaches children that responsibility lies in the effective sending and receiving of messages.

Directions. Divide the class into two groups. Tell group 1 that they are receivers. With their eyes closed, they are to try to visualize the picture being shown to group 2 by the leader. Group 2 is told to look at the picture intently for 3 to 4 min. They close their eyes and concentrate on sending a visualization of the picture to group 1. Group 1 is told to concentrate on receiving with their eyes closed. When they are ready, have them share images describing what they saw. See Figure 10-4.

Responses. Some tangential things occur. The scene is received, or the receivers see a picture that has not yet been shown. On one occasion, a piece of blue paper with no writing was interpreted by the sender as an ocean, and by the receiver as a beach. The color blue took on different manifestations for the sender and for the receiver. Our thought processes can have a snowball effect, one thought leading to another, which influences the transmission process.

Guidelines

Although the exercises may seem simple, certain precautions should be taken; these are powerful experiences and must be taken seriously:

1. Keep the process simple and encourage everyone to be gentle with one another and respectful of the others' mind and body space.

Figure 10-2 Children enjoying treats and clowning after exercises. *(Courtesy of Helen Monea.)*

Figure 10-3   This child is concentrating on identifying the color of the paper through touch, that is, "seeing without sight." *(Courtesy of Helen Monea.)*

2. Do only exercises that you, as a teacher or leader, have tried out and experienced positively. Your feelings can influence the group response.
3. *Emphasize the experiencing, not so much the talking or explaining or rationalizing.*
4. There is essentially no right or wrong way to do the exercises. Each child is exploring his or her own personal reality. Play down competition.
5. Point out that all people have talents in certain areas; some are good at baseball, and others are good at swimming. Similarly, some people may also be better at learning to enhance their intuitive abilities than others.

HOLISTIC HEALING AND GROWING

The new frontier in holistic health care has its own terminology; for example, the word "healing" refers to wholeness, or restoring the integrity of the person's mind and body. The medical model uses terms such as "cure" and "remedy," which imply treating only the body. Increasingly, research is showing that what affects the body also affects the mind, and vice versa.

Chapter 1 discussed a philosophy of caring based on wholeness—both body and mind—and also pointed up the need to explore new ways of increasing health potential. Some care givers are tucked into safe niches and do not explore new spheres of psychological care. Others have enriched their caring through holistic health approaches. Gerald Jampolsky, a child and adult psychiatrist in California, creatively uses his talents for helping children (and their families) who suffer from learning disabilities and/or catastrophic illnesses. He states: "I have never really been satisfied with the traditional medical model or psychiatric model where people do things to people on a vertical basis. I do not believe in the traditional categories that the psychiatric profession uses. I really feel that we are all equally insane'' (p. 8).

Children and Catastrophic Illness

''Am I going to die?'' ''What is it like?'' ''Will it hurt?'' These are questions asked by children facing a life-threatening illness. (See Chapters 5 and 7.) Adults are reluctant to answer such questions because they are afraid of saying the wrong thing, because they fear the pain they themselves will feel, or because they are frightened about their own death (Jampolsky). Jampolsky recognizes that children with a serious illness need a friend they can talk with who is nonjudgmental, loving, and unafraid of discussing death. He worked with such children and staff members at The Center for Attitudinal Healing in Tiburon, California. The goal was to help children with a catastrophic illness heal one another and themselves. The premise was that children can help one another in the healing process far more effectively than adults can.

In traditional medicine, the patient is the *passive recipient of treatment*. The healing model designed by Jampolsky, the staff members, and the children

Figure 10-4 A group ''sends'' and ''receives'' mental pictures. The senders (with their backs to the camera) are attempting to convey the picture of the house to the receivers opposite them. *(Courtesy of Helen Monea.)*

allowed active self-healing and healing of peers. The model consisted simply of "getting rid of fear and bringing about inner peace" (Jampolsky, p. 13). They worked with two emotions: love and fear. Love was considered real, while fear was considered false because our minds manufacture it. Children with a life-threatening illness frequently experience fear. Therefore, Jampolsky reasoned that eliminating fear would bring inner peace. A loving environment was created where children were given complete acceptance and where adults felt safe in saying anything and yet learned to be sensitive, nonjudgmental, and accepting of others, i.e., more loving.

Before the staff members began their work with the children, Jampolsky developed a number of processes using the imagination to help them become *emotionally detached* from the past and the future and concentrate on the present. The processes helped reduce the staff members' need to control and predict; this need is ingrained in the medical model but is not appropriate for the holistic healing model. An effort was made to become detached from words that reinforce patterns of control, such as "impossible," "can't," "but," and "should." Pretending to have a mental blackboard, the staff members would erase the words each time they realized they were using them. Another exercise, "The Yellow Balloon," was used first to help the staff members and later to help the children. This was an active imagination exercise about fears and was carried out as follows (Jampolsky):

1. Close your eyes and think of a container.
2. Into the container, put all the things you can think of that you feel guilty or fearful about. Also put in anything that has been a painful experience for you.
3. Now imagine that a large yellow balloon filled with helium gas is being attached to your container.
4. Even though part of you wants to hang on to the container, you let go of it, and the container rises into the air. The yellow balloon becomes smaller and smaller and finally disappears completely.
5. Notice how much lighter you feel.
6. You can open your eyes now.

When the staff members felt they were ready, they invited a number of children to help plan and be involved in a group experience. Nine children, aged 7 to 17, participated. At the first group meeting they established a common bond and talked about the things they were most fearful about. Gradually, they became less fearful and were able to discuss death. At the following meetings, they talked about fears of dying, imagined what it would be like to die, and drew pictures about death.

A strong mutual respect developed rapidly as a result of the honest communication. The children learned from one another, regardless of age difference. When a 7-year-old boy's hair began to fall out, he became fearful about returning to school. The older children who had already experienced hair loss shared their reactions with him and gave him advice. In another instance, peers were helpful when an 11-year-old girl was referred to the agency after she refused to return to school. She had had the devastating experience of having her wig fall off while she was playing volleyball at school.

The group also used mental imagery, which has helped some cancer patients come to terms with death (Simonton). One child developed a mental picture of two gremlins in his blood vessels that allowed the good cells to go by but dissolved the bad cells.

When a child was too ill to attend meetings, the other group members formed a circle and joined hands for a group meditative experience; they visualized a white healing beam of light being sent to the child who was absent. The group met with parents a few times, and the parents were supportive of the program because of the positive responses of their children.

The children in this group have written a book, *There Is a Rainbow behind Every Dark Cloud* (Taylor and Jampolsky), that answers children's questions about their own illness; it will eventually be placed in doctors' offices, schools, and hospitals. Plans are also being considered to develop teams consisting of one volunteer and one child; the teams would visit other children facing a life-threatening illness.

HELPING CHILDREN GROW THROUGH ART

Reading, writing, and arithmetic have always been considered the major subject matter areas in the curriculum, while the arts have often been thought of as the icing on the cake. A countermovement is now under way to give support to an art curriculum. New evidence indicates that the arts are beneficial to children; drawing and painting help children establish their identity as well as improve abilities in subjects such as math, science, and reading (Williams).

There is a trend in holistic care giving toward developing the part of the brain that is responsible for creativity and visual-spatial abilities. Traditionally, education has focused on developing verbal and analytical abilities. This can hinder children in perceiving and learning about the world. Although it is not clear how the arts help children learn, it is known that by the time a child is 6 years old, countless associations based on sensory perceptions of sight, touch, and sound have been stored in the brain as learning via an unknown process. These associations are critical in the ability to remember events from the past. If such associations are prevented from forming during the early years, the development of the brain can be stunted (Williams).

In one innovative program, students write and perform in their own plays, illustrate their own texts, and use the media of dance to learn math (Williams).

For many years art therapists have used art to develop self-awareness and communication skills. Lillian Rhinehart, a registered art therapist in California, uses the scribble to help individuals learn about themselves and the world. She describes her work below:

I trust the authenticity of the encounter with the creative process. I trust the graphic statements which come out of that encounter. I acknowledge, too, that graphic and visual statements (I am using these terms interchangeably) can be masked, covered over, or not allowed to emerge. The degree to which we are aware of the way we prevent creative visual statements from emerging and the degree to which we are willing to risk trusting the encounter and to work at becoming less rigid—to that degree our graphic statements are authentic. Even with the tightest controls, we are not as totally in control as we would like to believe.

When it comes to trusting authentic visual statements, I would say, for instance, that I trust the statements of my left hand more than I trust those of my right hand. I am right-handed, and therefore the statements of my right hand are controlled, molded, formed, and practiced. I would further say that, in exploring an aspect of myself, I am more trusting of the graphic statements I make with my eyes closed—as in working with clay—or while doing a series of scribbles. It takes a lot of fast scribbling with the dominant hand to get into discovery scribbles.

A scribble is simply that—a series of random lines placed on paper. The object is not to draw something but to stay with nondrawing. This is a developmental process which all persons experience in early childhood. According to Di Leo, children between the ages of 13 months and 3 years scribble. Kellogg has studied thousands of drawings of preschool children, and she considers the scribble to be the first developmental step in learning to draw pictorial forms. Di Leo states that the vast literature devoted to children's drawings supports the developmental theory. All researchers agree that the scribble is the first development step. Objects, shapes, and forms begin to emerge and eventually develop into recognized pictorial forms.

Naumburg uses the scribble as a nonthreatening technique which can evoke, out of the unconscious realm, emerging forms that are relative to the psychological states of being. In educational settings, the value of discovery of forms in this process is very exciting and positive, especially for those who consider themselves lacking in artistic skill. I use this technique in all the classes I teach, as well as with private clients. A series of physical exercises using the arms, hands, and upper body releases tension and loosens muscular control. The individual continues to loosen up while exploring vertical and horizontal patterns in the air, further relaxing conscious processes and allowing unconscious patterns to emerge for placement on paper.

Another way of working with the scribble is to do a series of quick scribbles on large paper, working sometimes with the eyes closed and sometimes with the nondominant hand. This is a projective technique and is most commonly used by art therapists in beginning individual and group sessions. It is essential that plenty of paper be available, especially if the dominant hand will be used. Several sheets of scribbles are necessary to loosen up. Large newsprint, 18 by 24 in, works very well and is inexpensive. After the scribble or a series of scribbles have been rendered, the scribbler must find and develop with color the forms that he or she sees. There are many variations on the use and development of the scribble technique. Sometimes, so that the forms will be more easily visible, the scribble is done with a black oil pastel or felt-tip pen. See Figure 10-5.

Color tends to draw attention, and therefore it often detracts from the form rendered. Color can be used to develop the scribble—to accentuate and give clarity to the projected form. A full range of colors may be used, or the scribbler can be limited to one color. In working with the integration of opposites, the directions can be: "Select from a series of scribbles the most liked and the least liked." Next the scribbler is directed to use the least-liked scribble and the most-liked color and then to work with the most-liked scribble and the least-liked color. Following this, a final integration can be made by developing a composite of most- and least-liked scribbles with most- and least-liked colors; good-quality paper and a more fluid medium are used at this point.

Because the scribble approach is nonthreatening for those who feel artistically inept, it can be used in most educational as well as therapeutic settings. Variations and modifications can be adopted according to the psychological makeup of the participants.

All that has been said thus far concerning the scribble technique and variations is applicable to the classroom setting. In a high school setting, while application would be the same, the approach would have to be altered. Younger children

Figure 10-5 A group practices self-expression through scribbling. Note the multiple swirls and the feeling of movement in the emerging designs as the participants express themselves. *(Courtesy of Lillian Rhinehart.)*

are still closely connected to the play aspect of the scribble and readily enjoy the process of discovering forms in the scribble. Adolescents are in the process of growing to adulthood and have begun consciously to model toward maturity and away from childhood. Developmentally, the scribble is the first form the child works with. Out of it comes recognized basic shapes which develop into people, houses, trees, animals, suns, and so on. As stated earlier, children have gained control over the shapes, forms, and representations that they wish to paint or draw. In this process, they move toward and develop the finer eye-hand coordination necessary for writing development. Now, when you ask adolescents to do a scribble or a series of scribbles, you place them in a position of calling to mind their infancy and their awkward childhood. You are suggesting regression. The persona of the adolescent and those of his or her peers are nearer to that of the adult. To scribble is to become once again the child, who was lacking in control. *For this reason it is imperative to give adolescents some rationale for working with the scribble technique.* They will be interested in a discussion of creativity and of ways in which the creative process can be activated, including the scribble technique. They can appreciate that the technique is nonthreatening for those who feel they have no artistic talent.

Another important point is that the students should work with the medium nonverbally with one another and share the same paper; this is a progressive step from the scribbles each has done alone. Discussion and feedback time should follow each activity. Finally, after the progression is completed, the teacher or facilitator can make a general statement about the rapport that they have just established.

As the groups become larger, one of the quicker ways of allowing the experience to be shared is to have the students describe in writing what the experience meant to them and then read these descriptions aloud to the group. If there is time, a general feedback session can follow.

This activity can be used to establish natural groupings for committee work in specific areas of the curriculum, as well as for building rapport.

This is one of several nonthreatening ways of working with art media. Most art therapy approaches are applicable for use with all age levels, which is one of the many reasons I believe the field of art therapy has much to offer educationally as well as therapeutically.

Art Media with Disturbed Children

Art can be used effectively in working with children and adolescents in a therapeutic situation. Edith Kramer, an art therapist, works with underprivileged, disturbed children in New York City. In her book, *Art Therapy with Children,* she points out that, when planning an appropriate art experience, one needs to consider the child's background and level of development in order to select the most appropriate media. She raises some of the issues described in Chapter 4, such as the similarities between poor children and rich children and the impact of television on them. Both suffer from a lack of human relationships. They distrust adults, and they have an insatiable hunger for material goods along with a need to waste and/or destroy the goods as soon as they obtain them. Television seems to escalate their distrust of adults. A pseudorelationship develops between the television entertainer and the child, who turns to the television set to relieve feelings of loneliness, anxiety, and isolation. Because of sponsors' demands, the entertainer uses ingratiation and seduction to influence the audience to buy certain products. However, since children are perceptive, they soon learn to distrust the entertainer, recognizing the exaggeration and the lies. The children are then in a bind; they are dependent upon people whom they cannot trust. This situation results in diminished ability to seek out healthy relationships, lack of strength of inner resources, and development of a dependent personality (Kramer).

Disturbed adolescents today are both deprived and spoiled; they attempt to gain what they want through destruction and violence, feeling that they can get something for nothing (Kramer). Our culture impinges upon the growth of children. The Victorian age demanded excessive control of children and tolerance of hypocrisy. Today's children suffer from society's tolerance of violence. For the child who has been inhibited and controlled but who is well integrated, the playful artistic experience of making scribbles and splashes can be liberating; however, children and adolescents who have insufficient ego strength and who suffer from loss of identity will not benefit greatly from the scribble experience. Because their world is chaotic and cluttered with meaningless stimuli, they cannot see themselves in the scribbles or blots of paint. Asking them to represent themselves on a piece of paper makes them aware of a frightening loss of identity. Although they are free of feelings of guilt, they are overwhelmed by their defenselessness against the loss of identity and against their impulses of rage and desire. The experience with art may alleviate their feelings of emptiness simply because they have created something; however, what they have created is not a valid representation, and the beneficial effects do not endure (Kramer).

Clay as a Medium in Group Therapy

I used clay as a medium to help a group of socioeconomically privileged pre-adolescents terminate our relationship after we had met together for a year on a weekly basis. They were a volatile group, and a few members kept up an uproar as a way of distancing and testing me. They were able to show they cared only by resisting me and provoking interaction. For instance, when I began to talk about terminating our meetings, they clapped and shouted "Hooray!" and said they did not like the meetings. It was a trying year. I felt nervous before the last session, expecting either that no one would attend or that I would meet with greater hostility than usual.

I decided to use clay to break through this barrier and allow warm feelings to be expressed; clay is a powerful medium because it allows for unconscious expression. The children in this group suffered from problems with human relationships as described by Kramer, but they had ego strength and negative self-identities. I felt that they could benefit from the experience of using a lump of clay to express themselves. As I had anticipated, they initially reacted to the clay by saying, "That's kindergarten stuff." When I explained that using the clay would help them express something difficult—saying good-bye—they immediately began working with the clay. The process is described below:

> I announced the date of termination early in the spring quarter and continually reminded the students at subsequent sessions. I opened our final session by announcing that this was the last time we would meet. There was a shout of "Hooray!" After this exclamation, I was very surprised and pleased that they were immediately able to face a discussion about leaving.
>
> I decided to use art material as a medium to help them express themselves at termination. Introducing clay modeling into groups is reported to permit direct expression of inner experiences and to speed the therapeutic process (Ulman as cited in Pazdur). I asked each member to shape the clay into the way she saw herself in the group. The resultant figures were symbolic and meaningful.
>
> It was significant that the girl who was the blocker in the group molded the clay into a large ball surrounded by a circle of small balls. She identified the large ball as all the problems she couldn't talk about; the circle of balls represented her specific problems, such as relatives, food, and boyfriend. When I told her I saw her as the blocker in the group, she admitted that she didn't want to talk about her problems.
>
> The "expediter" produced a figure of a man representing death (her grandfather had recently died). To help her express herself more satisfactorily, I encouraged her to write her feelings. This brought out more scared feelings about people leaving her (her friends moving away). This was then related to my leaving and the termination of the group meetings.
>
> The most unexpected reaction came from the girl who was the "rough as nails" tomboy and difficult to handle in the classroom—she did and said what she pleased. Her clay model was a large teardrop, which she held to her eye as she cried, "I don't want the meetings to end!" We talked about how she had tried to contribute to the group but that the girls had not helped her. This related to the time she sat with her head hidden in her arms. I had commented on her nonverbal behavior and was immediately resisted by the blocker who said, "Quit bugging her!" We were now able to discuss why they had continually blocked our meetings. . . .
>
> Although termination was sad for the girls and me, I felt a sense of accomplishment when, for the first time, there was a real closeness in their attitudes, actions, and words. They expressed their sorrow through tears and verbalized a regret that there would not be more meetings. One member wisely put it, "We've done more work today than we ever have" (Pazdur, pp. 285–286).

HELPING CHILDREN GROW THROUGH MOVEMENT

Children learn through movement as well as through art. The holistic movement supports harmony between body and mind. Yoga and T'ai Chi Ch'uan are Eastern philosophies based on the mind-body concept. Exercising the body through harmonic movements lets the mind feel free. Adherents of Eastern philosophies frequently speak of the relaxing and exhilarating experience of paying attention to their entire being.

According to some theories, children learn first through sensorimotor experiences; these are considered building blocks. Learning then progresses sequentially to a higher level, cognition. Other theories are more multifaceted and are not based on a hierarchy of sensorimotor development. Regardless of theory, movement has been accepted as a way of improving children's grades and helping them develop positive self-identities.

Some high schools provide special training in movement to help adolescents become more comfortable with, and aware of, their bodies. One of the greatest concerns of adolescents is how to handle the changes that are taking place in their bodies. Sensitive movement teachers working in high schools can help adolescents accept and be comfortable with their bodies and improve their self-image. I have seen adolescent girls walking with more confidence, straighter backs, and less embarrassment after a semester of a movement class. The girls learned to be more agile and more accepting of their growing bodies as they exchanged joking comments about blossoming breasts and hips, occasional pimples, or being too short or too tall. Younger children often are less self-conscious about their bodies and about participating in movement classes.

In some schools, male professional dancers are involved in trying to help boys take advantage of movement. The stereotype of male dancers as being homosexual may be a problem at first, but after several sessions the boys' attitudes change, and they become more comfortable and enjoy the experience.

Movement and Discrimination

Movement classes in an integrated school in Alabama helped prevent the development of racial prejudice. The community did not wholeheartedly welcome integration, but the movement classes helped the children play and learn together creatively. Black and white hands intermingled, with seemingly no sense of race (Terry). As discussed in Chapter 9, bringing children together in a common activity helps break down barriers.

Mixing races and cultures can enrich children's learning experience. Learning a new language increases one's sensitivity to, and understanding of, people different from oneself. Multicultural education can be a way of resolving interracial tensions in the future and of developing more equal opportunities so that the talents of the culturally divergent population can be tapped (Guertin). A unique way of combining movement and learning a new language has been developed in Japan and is currently being used successfully in Hawaii. Ruth D. Miho, of Honolulu, is an expert on this special method of learning a new language. Below she describes the work of the Labo International Exchange Foundation:

> The Labo International Exchange Foundation features experiential activities focusing on cross-cultural and international aspects; people from different

countries listen to stories in two languages for the purpose of learning a target language. The stories are presented through good-quality tape recordings and colorful books. The primary springboards for learning are activities such as body movement, pantomime, creative dramatization, and arts and crafts.

Labo parties are held weekly. The children meet with a Labo tutor, whose main attribute is a willingness to learn along with the children. The learning involves not only the target language but also increased self-knowledge and knowledge of others. The Labo party members and their tutor share the strange and the familiar as the stories unfold sentence by sentence in both the target language and the native language, with appropriate musical backgrounds. A warmup period, involving movement, songs, or games, brings closeness to the group. The story is played twice. On the second playing, the group members interact spontaneously with one another, moving together, pantomiming, and/or speaking story parts.

The goal is for activities to unfold naturally, joyfully, and at a comfortable pace for each person in a group. The spontaneity and closeness depend upon how well the group members are acquainted and on their willingness to relate freely to one another. Group members may continue to use their native language until they are ready to move on. Many times both languages are used. Parents and tutors who are unskilled in the target language may try out new sounds along with the children. *Thus barriers between the young and old are broken down as they join together in the learning experience.*

One of the traditional Asian stories is "Tanuki," which is about a badger-dog trickster who can change his appearance, personality, and voice. He can be a perfect gentleman and have tea with the Queen of England, or he can become a rascal with a stomachache because he ate too many of the priest's green persimmons.

Western offerings include *Romeo and Juliet,* with full orchestral background. This play offers opportunities for dramatizing, from sword fights to love scenes. Another favorite is one of Aesop's fables in which there is an exciting fight between red ants and black ants; while listening to the story the children pretend to be grasshoppers, flowers, the sun, or a stream. See Figure 10-6.

Sometimes these activities are enjoyed at home; the parents and the children use headsets to listen to the Labo machines.

Holistic Learning

Elsewhere I have written about theories, guidelines, and lesson plans that I use in experiential teaching with adults; these techniques can easily be adapted for working with children or for training staff people who will be caring for children (Monea, 1976).

Fantasy training has been used with a group of disadvantaged racially mixed preschool children in Detroit. The researchers, Saltz and Johnson, found that fantasy training can improve symbolic and causal thinking and thus facilitate later learning ("Fantasy Training: A Key to Development"). Fairy tales are

Figure 10-6   Children are playing the part of a grasshopper jumping over a flower. After listening to a story in Japanese and English, they choose their roles to play the story. *(Courtesy of Helen Monea.)*

acted out in small groups; the method is similar to the Labo method, described above. A difficult fairy tale is simplified by highlighting the essentials of the story.

The action-oriented learning parallels what Milich states earlier in this chapter: the younger the children, the greater the need for action.

Bettelheim finds that children benefit from fairy tales. Children need to understand what is going on in their conscious minds in order to be able to cope with what is going on in their unconscious. Spinning out daydreams that allow for rumination, rearranging, and fantasizing helps children cope with growing up. The fairy tale offers new dimensions to the child's experience that he or she would not be able to discover alone. Middle-class parents may deprive their children of the fairy-tale experience because they believe that since fairy tales do not give true impressions of life, they are unhealthy. They fail to understand that normal children do not believe that fairy tales describe the world realistically (Bettelheim). Fairy tales and fantasy can be developmental tools for helping children grow.

Movement in Family Therapy

Movement can be used to facilitate family communication. I have used action-oriented techniques (movement) based on Satir's conjoint family therapy. As indicated in Chapter 4, the approach is not suitable for every family. As is true when one uses art therapy, the family's life-style must be considered when planning the appropriate techniques. I have found action-oriented techniques and art therapy to be effective in working with families who are familiar with, or knowledgeable about, therapeutic and innovative approaches. Other families will not risk looking at themselves in a new way. When this happens, I modify, move more slowly, or shorten the time of sessions, depending on the family members' development, defenses, and needs. With some families, I do not use the techniques at all. Young children often are enthusiastic about doing something they perceive as fun, and this may influence their parents to try something different. Children seem to be able to express themselves better through action and art than through the discussion that takes place during the family session.

The family described below had problems in communication, especially the mother and the father. The mother was verbal and aggressive, while the father was nonverbal and passive. Because of their parents' inability to communicate, the children received double messages from them; as a result, a pattern evolved in which the father was the "good guy" and the mother was the "bad guy." Two of the four children, Kurt and Denny, are mentioned. Kurt, the oldest, was the identified problem in the family because of severe drug abuse, causing hospitalization. I used a "sculpting" technique, which required all family members to move instead of sitting and talking:

> The method that appeared to be the most helpful both to the family and to me was "sculpting." Sculpting involves having each family member take a turn at physically moving the other members of the family into positions in relation to each other, in two sequences: (1) in the way he saw them in "reality," and (2) as he would like to see them. The technique is used to help family members visualize the interrelations in the family and to communicate their feelings about their various roles. Once the family members are placed in the positions suggested to the "sculptor" by his perception of their roles and relationships, he is instructed to approach each person and ask him how he feels about being placed in that particular position. After a discussion (conducted on a feeling level), the sculptor repositions the family members according to their wishes and the ways he would like to see them. The discussion is then repeated.
>
> With this family, in each sculpt, Kurt was always positioned farthest away from the other members, while the parents were always placed close to each other. I had expected the parents to appear further apart in the sculpture than they were portrayed because of their dysfunctional communication. However, they both expressed positive feelings toward each other and over the fact that their children portrayed them in such close proximity. But they still asked for more understanding from each other. Denny portrayed himself as being in touch with everyone, but positioned himself facing away from the two older children since he felt that they received more parental attention than he did. Usually a quiet child, Denny was unusually verbal and forthright in his sculpting role, and everyone encouraged this expression of his feelings and agreed with his interpretations. In the re-sculpting of the family into the patterns indicated by

the various members' wishes, Kurt was always moved into a position closer to the rest of the family.

The sculpting sessions were highly successful because they gave each member equal opportunity to express feelings and to interact with other family members. Sculpting, however, must be used at the appropriate time in the family therapy sequence. It is most effective at the point where members are having difficulty in relating to each other and in acknowledging their feelings (Monea, 1974, p. 170).

USING YOGA WITH CHILDREN

Some teachers use yoga to reduce restlessness and tension in the classroom (Diskin). Yoga was developed in India centuries ago; the word "yoga" means "joining things together," specifically joining the body and mind together by stretching the body, breathing correctly, and putting the mind to rest. Diskin describes the exercises and includes photographs and sketches to help teachers learn how to use yoga approaches in the classroom. If you are interested in using yoga, be sure that you have experienced the concept before implementing it. You must also protect the children from injury by telling them to stop an exercise if they feel any painful sensations. Adults must take similar precautions since ligament and muscle damage can occur as a result of stretching parts of their bodies that are unused to exercise.

CHILDREN AND MEDITATION

Transcendental meditation (TM), which has been used for thousands of years in Tibet and India to quiet the mind and body, is becoming increasingly popular in the United States. The contemplative experience has been shown to accelerate healing and reduce blood pressure. Norvell has studied the effects of meditation on children's learning and behavior. He found that children who practiced TM developed higher IQ levels and had a better ability to memorize than children of the same age who did not practice TM. Children who meditated daily were more tranquil, responded more obediently to parental requests, and tended to be less rebellious.

Parents trained in TM were found to be more controlled and less tense. Norvell's book focuses on parents' teaching TM to their children. Although this is a fine idea if the parents themselves have had experience with TM, most TM teachers, including my own, do not believe that anyone should attempt to teach TM without formal training. This position has been challenged by critics who say that the teachers are profit-oriented. However, I believe that those who undertake any exercise that influences the mind must be competent and experienced in the process; there is much that we still do not know about the human mind.

The meditation exercises that Norvell suggests are aimed at developing intuitive and extrasensory perception in children. Care givers may wish to read the book and compare Norvell's approach with that of Milich, described earlier in this chapter.

CONCLUSION

This chapter has dealt with the commitment philosophy and with alternative ways of caring for people, as discussed in Chapter 1. Not all the newer trends could be included because of space limitations; however, it is hoped that this chapter has provided some insight into newer care-giving approaches and has encouraged readers who are not already involved in these approaches to try something new. If you are already involved in holistic approaches, the chapter offers validation by others who "walk among the stars" (Juster, p. 108).

Because of new and different growth experiences, children today may be able to progress through the stages of psychosocial development with less difficulty than children in past generations. They may have an improved sense of identity and a greater ability for intimacy as they move into adulthood. The psychosocial development of young adults is the focus of Chapters 11 and 12.

REFERENCES

Baum, Frank L.: *The Annotated Wizard of Oz: The Wonderful Wizard of Oz,* Introduction, Notes, and Bibliography by Michael Patrick Hern, Potter, New York, 1973.

Bettelheim, Bruno: *The Uses of Enchantment,* Random House, New York, 1977.

Di Leo, Joseph: *Young Children and Their Drawings,* Brunner/Mazel, New York, 1970.

Diskin, Eve: *Yoga for Children,* Warner Books, New York, 1976.

Elgin, Duane S., and **Arnold Mitchell:** "Voluntary Simplicity: Life-Style of the Future?" *The Futurist,* 11(4):200–203, 1977.

"Fantasy Training: A Key to Development," *Behavior Today,* 6(2):356, 1975.

Guertin, Jeanne M.: "Introduction: Mul-ticultural Education," *Educational Horizon,* 55(4):167, 1977.

Huxley, Aldous: *The Art of Seeing,* Montana Books, Seattle, 1975.

Jampolsky, Gerald: "Peer and Self Healing in Children with Catastrophic Illnesses," paper presented at Tomorrow Belongs to the Children, Symposium, Stanford University Hospital and Children's Hospital, Palo Alto, Calif., Mar. 23, 1977, and New Dimensions in Health Care: The Total Approach, Houston, June 11–12, 1977.

Juster, Norton: *The Phantom Tollbooth,* Random House, New York, 1972.

Kellogg, Rhoda: *Analyzing Children's Art,* National Press Books, Palo Alto, Calif., 1969.

Kramer, Edith, with introduction by **Muriel**

M. Gardiner: *Art Therapy with Children,* Schocken Books, New York, 1975.

Monea, Helen Pazdur: "A Family in Trouble: A Case Study of a Family in Conjoint Family Therapy," *Perspectives in Psychiatric Care,* 12(4):165–170, 1974.

————: *Instructor's Manual to Accompany Nursing and the Aged,* McGraw-Hill, New York, 1976.

Naumburg, M.: *Dynamically Oriented Art Therapy: Its Principles and Practice,* Grune & Stratton, New York, 1966.

Norvell, Anthony: *Teach Your Child Transcendental Meditation,* Drake, New York, 1976.

Ornstein, Robert E.: *The Psychology of Consciousness,* W. H. Freeman, San Francisco, 1972.

Pazdur, Helen (Monea): "Group Work with Children: A Child Psychiatric Nurse's Experience," *American Nurses' Association Clinical Conferences,* Appleton-Century-Crofts, New York, 1970.

Satir, Virginia: *Conjoint Family Therapy,* Science and Behavior Books, Palo Alto, Calif., 1964.

Simonton, Carl O.: "Management of the Emotional Aspects of Malignancy," paper presented at New Dimensions of Habilitation for the Handicapped, Symposium, University of Florida, Gainesville, June 14–15, 1977.

Taylor, Pat, and **Gerald Jampolsky:** *There Is a Rainbow behind Every Dark Cloud,* Center for Attitudinal Healing, Tiburon, Calif., 1978.

Terry, Walter: "World of Dance," *Saturday Review,* Feb. 5, 1972, pp. 20–22.

Williams, Roger M.: "Why Children Should Draw: The Surprising Link between Art and Learning," *Saturday Review,* Sept. 3, 1977, pp. 10–17.

OTHER RESOURCES

FILMS

Children Who Draw: 16 mm/44 min/b and w with color drawings/1956. An award-winning film showing how a classroom of 6-year-old Japanese children express their feelings through drawings and other work and how their home and school experiences influence their drawings. Distributor: University of California, Extension Media Center, Berkeley, Calif. 94720.

Hello, Up There!: 16 mm/8 min/color. An award-winning film dealing with the distance between adults and children. Children's drawings, paintings, and comments provide insight into the way youngsters see and feel about the adult world. Distributor: Learning Corporation of America, 1350 Avenue of the Americas, New York, N.Y. 10019.

The House That Jack Built: 16 mm/8 min/color. A satire on modern conformity. This award-winning animated film laughs at the way we cope with the present-day "rat race" but takes seriously our quest for ways to improve the quality of life. Distributor: Learning Corporation of America, 1350 Avenue of the Americas, New York, N.Y. 10019.

RECORDS

Creative Listening, vol. 1, Music and Imagination Experiences for Children. Helen Bonny. Distributor: Institute for Consciousness and Music, Baltimore, Md. 21218.

Yoga for Children of All Ages: Marilyn Zwaig Rossner, 3949 St. Antoine Street, Montreal, Quebec, Canada.

ORGANIZATIONS

The Center for Attitudinal Healing
19 Main Street
Tiburon, Calif. 94920

East West Academy of Healing Arts
33 Ora Way
San Francisco, Calif. 94131

The Holistic Life University
Holistic Media Service
1627 Tenth Avenue
San Francisco, Calif. 94122

Metaphysical Center and Bookshop
420 Sutter Street
San Francisco, Calif. 94108

Wholistic Health and Nutrition Institute
150 Shoreline Highway
Mill Valley, Calif. 94941

The traffic of adulthood. *(Courtesy of Pat Ryan.)*

PART 123

Young Adulthood, Middle Age, and Preretirement

Dialogue

I wrapped the years about
me as they came,
Inside this cloak of days I
am the same.
Yet, each sunrise of leaden
or rosy hue
Whispers gently. "Alive
and new."

Anonymous

The moment of life
Held, transformed, renewed
Never captured

Priscilla Ebersole

Introduction
to
Part 2

This segment deals with the journey from young adulthood to old age: the opposing forces, the unity, the struggle against the status quo, the polarity of the sexes, and the vitality of the process.

The contributors to this part were selected by virtue of their subject expertise and proximity to the age about which they write. Generally accepted theories are elaborated, and some recent theoretical speculations are included; all are embellished by personal anecdotes and the writers' intimate awareness of age-related issues. Ms. Ostrovski clearly delineates the search for identity, relevant adult models, peer supports, and intimacy. Ms. Ebersole focuses on the middle-aged adult, yet the same issues are present throughout the adult years. Widowhood has been presented from both theoretical and personal perspectives, which add to our understanding of this major disruption in life-style. Mr. Pierre demonstrates the reflective activity and search for order and meaning that become paramount as one recognizes that the major portion of life has been experienced. The philosophy throughout emphasizes the caring and sharing of life experience.

In an attempt to view development holistically it becomes problematic to assess the impact of constantly shifting socialization processes and to separate human nature from nurture, external pressures from internal motivation, and genetics from opportunity. In an effort to avoid artificial separation of developmental influences, it seems most tenable to carefully examine the masculine and the feminine experience. This is done most extensively in Chapters 17 to 20.

Childhood and adolescent educational institutions are essentially sexless, but adult men and women encounter fundamental differences in social expectations. Young adults are now breaking away from sex-role stereotypes and are taking advantage of the many available options, but the present middle-aged population is strongly endowed with certain sex-typed characteristics. Middle age is experienced much differently by a man than by a woman. Since widowhood is a major threat to middle-aged women and retirement is a major threat to middle-aged men, each of these crises is examined accordingly. Admittedly, this is changing.

Many transitions and crises seem to be related to sex roles. Indeed, it appears that men and women are vulnerable in chronologically reciprocal patterns.

While I certainly do not espouse inequality of opportunity, I do subscribe to the notion that men and women are very different and say with the French, *vive la difference*.

Chapter 11

TRANSITION TO ADULTHOOD
Mary Joy Ostrovski

> There's so much to do and so little time.
>
> *John, aged 21*

> When I was in my twenties, I was concerned with
> exploring, experimenting, and trying to find out who and
> what I was, separate from my parents. Time seemed
> endless. At around 27 or 28, I started to feel panicky and
> scared. I didn't have a profession, I had just broken up
> with my lover, and I knew I had to do something.
> Nothing was the same then. All the old guidelines
> seemed to have vanished.
>
> *Pamela, aged 32*

Until recently, concepts of human development applied only to children and adolescents. It was thought that once a person had reached age 21, he or she had attained full adulthood. The individual was then expected simply to "carry on with living." Major research has recently revealed what was only suspected before: There are developmental tasks and goals of adulthood that relate both to external events and to inner psychological and emotional urges. Further, people seem to experience certain transitions and crises throughout the life-span.

In the past, adults had to rely mainly on clichés and folk sayings to give them clues about the meaning of their innermost feelings. For example, restlessness in marriage has been described as the "seven-year itch." In fact, "the median duration of marriage before divorce has been about seven years for the last half century" (Glick and Norton, p. 4). Research findings are indicating that subtle shifts in adult personality structure may indeed occur with regularity and consistency in both sequence and timing over the years.

Slogans have also served as indexes of developmental stages. In the turbulent late 1960s, young people were exhorted by their leaders, "Don't trust anyone over 30." In fact, there is much in developmental theory and research to indicate a shift in the late twenties and early thirties away from concerns with the environment and toward those of the inner life (Sheehy, p. 28). This kind of shift would make for less political interest, solidarity, and action; therefore, the individual over 30 could be viewed as abandoning peers and breaking trust. See Figure 11-1.

Currently, there is no one, single well-defined body of knowledge concerning human development. In particular, information regarding adults is sketchy and incomplete. While the emerging developmental model, which employs transitions and stage theory, gives promise of a more complete theoretical framework, there continues to be wide disparity of thought. There is no agreement as to exactly when adulthood begins, nor is there agreement regarding the chronological ages of young adulthood. Generally, however, young adulthood is thought to span the years between age 18 and age 40 (LeVeck). Probably there is a fading of adolescence into adulthood, with diverse factors causing a variance in timing. Thus we may encounter a 35-year-old man who has an adult concept of respon-

Figure 11-1 The big apple.

sibility and a clear sense of his own identity. Socially, however, he may be only 18 (he suffers from extreme self-consciousness and is still living at home), and biologically he may be 65 (he has heart trouble or arthritis) (Kimmel). And so, in some senses, chronological age can be a poor indicator of adulthood. However, it may be a useful and objective index for measuring change with time and for studying progressive and sequential changes during the life cycle (Kimmel).

DEVELOPMENTAL MODEL

To the end of elucidating more clearly adult development in the form of tasks, goals, stages, and transitions, a new behavioral science is emerging. Several universities in the United States are now offering graduate programs in human development that encompass the entire life-span and view human life as a process. While each program has its special interests and emphases, all the programs combine features that have major implications for researchers, theorists, and clinicians. Two major concepts are fundamental: the holistic approach and stage and transition theory.

The Holistic Developmental Mode

The study of development is becoming more holistic; that is, it is becoming increasingly concerned with understanding all the factors that affect human beings as they pass through the life cycle. Accordingly, this approach draws from many disciplines: anthropology, psychology, psychoanalytic thought, sociology, biology, and physiology (Waechter). Such issues as physical appearance, the stimulation level of the immediate milieu, and current cultural conflicts are of interest. There is concern for the process and not merely the product, with its partially understood causations and incomplete content. In these respects, the field seems strikingly humanistic. All variables have merit, and the complexity of the human state is given full credence.

Stage Theory

Stage theory is an integral part of developmental thought. Generally, stage theory sees development as one-directional; that is, each stage builds on the previous one. Tasks not completed in a previous stage will retard the individual's full development and impede his or her general flow toward maturity. Various theorists view each stage as involving particular goals and tasks.

Crucial to stage theory is the concern with transitions between the stages. It is assumed that there are normative developmental crises or stresses which constitute transition points between stages. These may be preceded by an external event and/or an inner urge. The onset of a transition is probably preceded by a state of readiness or "willingness," and the crisis comes to an end when new behavior is organized (Waechter). Certainly, there are some crises for which preparation is impossible, such as the sudden, unexpected death of a spouse. While current thinking about transitions tends to view them as situations calling for some definitive personality restructuring, it is acknowledged that subtle shifts are taking place at all times. Transition theory focuses on identifying precedents to the transition, the process of the transition itself, and the resolution.

The Role of Culture

There is concern as to the role of culture in helping or hindering the individual as he or she copes with these seemingly more stressful times in the life cycle. Relatively little work has been done on refusal to go through stages, nor is there acknowledgment that individuals may be aware that it is time to enter a new stage and yet, for unknown reasons, decide not to make the transition into that stage. Such a failure may constitute what is commonly known as psychopathology. For example, in one study, older adults who refused to do a life review, a process thought by some theorists to be a task of old age, demonstrated more depression than those who used their reminiscences to review their lives (Ostrovski).

Waechter states:

> Personality dysfunction, as defined by the norms of a particular society, can then be seen as an understandable, if not inevitable result of the individual's inability to master tasks or life experiences by virtue of inadequacies in his environment, because of other concurrent life stress, or because of emotional, social, or intellectual immaturity at the stage in which these experiences occurred. Personality distortions can be viewed primarily as variations of "normal" functioning and can be understood in the light of the normal processes of growth and development (p. 31).

Waechter's view of dysfunction may be of benefit to traditional psychotherapy. In this model, holistic and "here-and-now" approaches suggest the efficacy of short-term treatment based on difficulties with stages and transitions (Rosenberg). Anxiety would be viewed as a force to be used for change and growth rather than as a result of past psychic conflict necessitating long, expensive, and—for most people—geographically unavailable treatment. Psychiatric diagnoses, which tend to fixate personality with negative and non-growth-enhancing outlooks, would become less important. As a result, there would be more possibilities for growth and for passage through normative crises. *The role of the therapist would change from that of a parental substitute, which involves deep dependency issues that take a great deal of time to resolve, to that of educator and facilitator at more of a peer level.* Time in treatment would thus be decreased, and the individual would not have to feel that he or she was struggling alone with problems that no one had ever faced before.

The study of human development may provide clues to normality and thereby offer relief to those progressing through transitions. There may be comfort in knowing that there are some guidelines for the journey through previously uncharted territory. This perception in turn may increase tolerance of anxiety when "going through changes" in one's life as well as increase tolerance of others who seem troubled. It may be helpful to know that these difficult times are temporary and that there are measures one can take that can be of enormous help. Simply listening and "being there" may be the most positive caring thing that one person can do for another. The theme of listening and "being there" is touched on throughout this book in relation to a variety of age groups in varying situations.

An awareness of the enormous complexities of the human being and of impinging forces brings more appreciation for our nature, and an awareness of multiple causality may serve to alleviate the effects of the puritan ethic, which is probably responsible for much distress in the form of low self-esteem, a judgmental tendency, and an inability to enjoy life and to give pleasure to ourselves in even the simplest ways.

Interventions and aids to facilitating stages could prove helpful. Knowing the stages could help care givers tolerate anxiety (in themselves and others) and support individuals in the most helpful ways. It might be useful to assist people in identifying possible directions and forces in their lives as they try to handle confusing situations. Helping people get in touch with their strengths, vulnerabilities, and needs may provide clarification and give them a "handle" that will enable them to marshal their personal resources in solving their problems.

DEVELOPMENTAL THEORIES OF YOUNG ADULTHOOD

Shakespeare was one of the first to mention particular tasks associated with certain periods in the life-span. In *As You Like It* (Act II, scene 7), he delineated "seven ages" in a somewhat cynical fashion. While Shakespeare mentions only the roles of men in these lines, in general the stages he describes have parallels in present theory and research describing the cycle of human development. Shakespeare's stages of the lover and the soldier most clearly relate to young adulthood, and they also remind us of Freud, who believed that in order to be normal, a person should be able to love and to work (*lieben und arbeiten*). Shakespeare's lover is certainly engaged in loving, and the soldier may well be at least tentatively occupationally involved. Soldiers are still a concern in our society; the veterans of the Vietnam and the Korean wars still suffer from the impact of their experiences.

Freud, however, was not speaking of sequential development for adults when he articulated his injunction. Rather, he meant that *genital* loving and work productiveness are paramount to adults and should enhance each other (Erikson).

Many centuries before Shakespeare, the Hindu scriptures of India described four distinct life stages, each calling for a certain response. The individual passed through the stages of (1) student, (2) householder, (3) retired person, and (4) pilgrim, which marked the beginning of the true education of adulthood. A person in the final stage of *sannyasin* was defined as "one who neither hates nor loves anything" (Smith, pp. 51–66). Theoretical models that have emerged during the twentieth century include those of Bühler, Jung, Erikson, and, more recently,

Levinson et al., and Sheehy. In the 1930s, Charlotte Bühler and her associates studied 400 biographies and autobiographies collected in Vienna. They established five biological phases and placed emphasis on parallels between the biological processes of growth, stability, and decline and the psychosocial processes of expansion, culmination, and curtailment of activities and accomplishments. The second phase (ages 15 to 25) and the third phase (ages 25 to 45) have particular relevance for the young adult. One of Bühler's students describes these phases:

> The young person just passed through childhood—the first phase of life—makes the first plans about his life and his first decisions in adolescence or shortly afterwards. Here begins the second phase of experience. It is characterized first through the fact that the young person wishes to acquire contact with reality. He experiments with people and professions. An "expansion" of his person takes place. Also characteristic for him is the temporary nature of his attitudes as to what his life calling will be. . . . At the end of the second phase . . . the individuals have become clear as to their definite attitude toward life. . . . During the third phase, vitality is still at its high point, while direction and specification are now present, so that very often this time is found to be the culmination period for subjective experience (Frenkel-Brunswick, pp. 1–34).

In summary, it can be said that this view of adult development suggests that the life cycle may be seen in terms of two general tendencies: (1) growth and expansion and (2) contraction (Kimmel).

Stage Theories

While Jung's thinking had to do mainly with people past the age of 35, he offered some formulations from his clinical practice and his particular psychological theories that have relevance for the young adult. For Jung, the period of youth involves giving up dreams of childhood, dealing with the sexual instinct and feelings of inferiority, and generally widening the horizon of life. *Jung believed that a person exhibits neurosis during a particular stage of life only if the work of the earlier stage has not been completed.*

Like those of Jung, Erikson's formulations involve stage concepts and were derived from clinical impressions and a particular view of psychology—a Freudian view. Erikson has theorized eight stages of life, each involving a crisis or turning point for the individual. Like Jung, and similar to Bühler, Erikson sees each stage building on the one preceding it. These stages stretch from birth to death. While Erikson emphasized the crises of childhood more than those of adulthood, he described the following conflicts that young adults must resolve: identity versus role confusion, intimacy versus isolation, and generativity versus stagnation. Much of his work remains to be tested empirically, but nevertheless it provides useful, descriptive insights into the study of the life cycle (Kimmel). Criticisms of the Eriksonian model can be found in Chapter 21.

Identity versus Role Confusion

The crisis of this stage, which begins with the onset of puberty, involves gathering together learning from the past in the form of roles and skills and applying this learning to adult tasks. These tasks include developing and seeking appropriate occupational outlets, dealing with idols and ideals, and maintaining a sense of continuity in the face of great psychological upheavals. The danger, then, is confusion, which can lead to paralysis; this would preclude mastery of the developmental tasks of this stage and prevent movement to the next stage. Erikson notes that although episodes of delinquency and outright psychotic behavior are common at this age, the outlook is more hopeful for a young person who experiences such episodes than it is for persons in other age groups who do so. Also, among young people there is much overidentification with creeds, groups, members of the opposite sex ("falling in love"), and charismatic leaders. This can be viewed as a device whereby ego-diffused young persons can escape focusing on themselves by becoming engrossed in something or someone else; this device can also help them understand themselves better as they see themselves in relation to the idea or the person identified with. Clannishness may be a feature of some of the groups that the young person is a part of; this may further serve to defend against diffusion and permit an identification that is helpful until a more individualized self-concept can be formed. A "psychological moratorium" occurs in adolescence between morality learned by the child and ethics to be developed by the adult (Erikson).

Intimacy versus Isolation

In this stage, the young adult, who now has a newly won identity, is ready to fuse this identity with the identities of others. This involves intimacy, that is, the capacity to commit oneself to affiliations and partnerships, even though this may call for considerable sacrifice and compromise. The person must be able to face and master fears of ego loss in situations calling for self-abandonment—friendships, close affiliations, inspirations, intuitions from the inner self, and sexual union and orgasm. Erikson states: "The danger is isolation, that is, the avoidance of contacts which commit to intimacy" (p. 266). Gradually, as a resolution of these two opposing forces, the competitive encounter and the sexual embrace are differentiated and become subject to what Erikson calls "that ethical sense which is the mark of the adult" (p. 264).

Generativity versus Stagnation

This is the crisis of the seventh stage of life, which is probably the longest; it begins with early adulthood and extends late into life. This crisis involves that which will outlive the individual and thus is centered on productivity and creativity. There is concern as to the establishment and nurturance of the next generation, either one's own offspring or those of others. In this particular kind of relationship, the young receive guidance, and the mature are needed. See Figure 11-2.

Figure 11-2   Footsteps. *(Courtesy of Patricia Keen.)*

When generativity does not take place, stagnation in the form of pseudointimacy or early invalidism—physical or psychological—takes place.

While Erikson does not expand on the tasks of human development for these stages, he does give descriptions and general outlines and attempts to focus on the main issues of the developing individual. Much of his work lays the foundation for that of later theoreticians and researchers. See Table 11-1.

Like Jung and Erikson, Levinson and his associates assume that there is something that can be called "adult development." In a report dated May 1972, they articulated a theory developed during the third year of a projected 4-year study in which interviews and TAT material on a sample of 40 men, all of whom were then aged 35 to 45, were reviewed. The focus of this study was on developing a theory of adult male development between the ages of about 20 and 45. Unfortunately, Levinson et al. did not directly study men between the ages of 20 and 30. Transitions, periods, and stages are an integral part of this theory.

Table 11-1. Theories and Tasks of Young Adulthood

Theorists	Theories and Tasks
Bühler	*Second phase*
	Making first plans about life
	Contacting reality
	Experimenting with people and professions
	"Expanding" the personality
	Third phase
	Direction and specification present
	Culmination of subjective experiences
	Vitality at a high point
	Clear, definite attitude toward life
Jung	Giving up dreams of childhood
	Dealing with the sexual instinct
	Dealing with feelings of inferiority
	Widening horizons of life
Erikson	*Identity vs. confusion*
	Beginning adult tasks
	Developing occupational outlets
	Dealing with idols and ideals
	Maintaining sense of continuity in the face of psychological upheavals
	Taking a moratorium period, if possible
	Intimacy vs. isolation
	Committing oneself to concrete affiliations and partnerships
	Admitting psychic entrance of intuition
	Developing sexual unions and experiencing orgasm
	Generativity vs. stagnation
	Establishing something of the self that will endure beyond personal death
	Nurturing the next generation
Levinson et al.	*Leaving the family (ages 16 to 24)*
	Increasing self-parent differentiation
	Creating emotional and financial distance from family
	Moving from family home
	Getting into the adult world (ages 20 to 27 or 29)
	Establishing new home base
	Forming an adult life of one's own
	Forming friendships
	Developing sexual bonding
	Fashioning initial life structure
	Age-30 transition
	Reexamining, reaffirming, and discarding commitments

Settling down (ages 28 to 32)
Making deeper commitments to individuals, pursuits, and work
"Making it" occupationally

Sheehy   *Pulling up roots (ages 18 to 22)*
Locating oneself in a peer group and assuming a sex role
Deciding on an occupation
Forming an ideology or world view
Physically leaving home; emotionally beginning to leave home
Deidealizing the parents
Trying twenties (ages 22 to 28)
Taking hold of the world and more clearly defining what one feels one
    should be doing
Finding a mentor if possible
Building a test structure for life—occupational and possibly in terms
    of relationships
Age 30
Coping with feelings of restlessness and a desire to "break out"
Reexamining life; coming into a new awareness
Changing occupation or renewing commitments
Reassessing relationships
Clearing time of beginnings and endings
Searching for identity; turning inward
Beginning to "hear" parental injunctions
Dealing with a sense of time compression
Dealing with an awareness of mortality, brought on by beginning signs
    of biological aging
Rooting and extending (early and middle thirties)
Settling down
Making commitments and investments of all sorts

Diekelmann   Establishing independence from parents—physical, financial, and
    emotional
Beginning to stop "living for" parents
Developing a sense of one's own values
Challenging of parents and society in order to clarify oneself
Examining belief systems
Developing a sense of personal identity
Discovering individual uniquenesses
Deciding on an occupation
Forming intimate relationships outside the family

Gould   *Ages 18 to 22*
Substitute friends for family
Unique psychology and subculture
Are more open to new ideas about the world; are less repressed

Table 11-1.   Theories and Tasks of Young Adulthood (*continued*)

Theorists	Theories and Tasks
	Ages 22 to 28
	Feel they are part of the "now generation"
	Concentrate on becoming competent in the real world and developing self-reliance
	Make less use of friends as substitutes for family
	Ages 29 to 34
	Assurance of what to do wavers
	Question motives
	Are more self-reflective; reawake strivings buried in the twenties
	Focus on family, especially children
	Marriage may be stressful and deidealized
	Active social life less important
	Want to make more money

Sources: Bühler; Diekelmann; Erikson; Gould; Jung; Levinson, et al.; Sheehy.

Transitions

Leaving the Family

The first transition is "leaving the family"; it occurs somewhere between adolescence and adulthood. This transition requires 3 to 5 years, starting at ages 16 to 18 and ending at ages 20 to 24. This stage corresponds roughly to Erikson's stage during which the crisis is that of identity versus role diffusion. Internally, there is an increase in self-parent differentiation and in psychological distance from the family; this process is ongoing, of course, during the life-span but is initially crucial to this period of life. Externally, this transition is characterized by changes such as moving out of the family home and becoming less financially dependent. New roles and living arrangements make for more autonomy and responsibility.

There may be affiliation with an institution, such as the military or college. Thus a "home base" is provided, and there is some degree of structure, control, support, and maintenance. Some amount of autonomy is possible, and there are opportunities to form relationships with other young adults.

Levinson notes, as other authors do, that young adults from the working class or those who live in ghettos may not experience such transitions or "psychological moratoriums." Rather, they may have to assume the adult roles of work and marriage as soon as they finish high school or before (Diekelmann; Kimmel).

Getting into the Adult World

The transition ends when the balance shifts and the young person begins to enter the adult world. Now the center of gravity of the person's life shifts from the family (or an equivalent social matrix) to a new home-base situation, and there is an effort to form an adult life of one's own. Probably this period begins in the early twenties and ends at around age 27 or 29. Levinson sees it as a time of exploration and provisional commitments to roles, alliances, relationships, and interests. See Figure 11-3.

According to Levinson, there are wide variations in the course, duration, and outcome of this period. This period involves Erikson's crisis of intimacy versus isolation. Thus, issues of friendship and sexual relationships are paramount. There is also concern regarding choice of an occupation and an emphasis on fashioning a life structure "that provides a viable link between the valued self and the wider adult world" (Levinson et al., p. 250).

Settling Down

The next transitional period occurs between ages 28 and 32 and is the time between the stages of getting into the adult world and settling down. Levinson et al. have termed this period the "age-30 transition." For some, this transition is characterized by confusion and internal chaos; others engage in a more quiet reevaluation and life review and alter their behaviors so that they can better pursue newly discovered goals.

The settling-down period extends from the early thirties to the mid-thirties. It involves deeper commitments to individuals and to work and other pursuits.

Figure 11-3   Several people building a stage set. *(Courtesy of Pat Ryan.)*

Long-range plans are made, and the person feels a need to bring order into his or her life and to operate within patterns. There is also a need to "make it" occupationally and a sense that the time in which to advance is running out.

The man in this period may regard himself as autonomous; he feels free of parental and societal influences. According to Levinson et al., this is illusionary and lays the foundation for accomplishment of the task of the next stage: the reduction or removal of these illusions without a concomitant development of cynicism.

Sheehy's theories resemble those of Levinson et al. with respect to stages and transitions in adult development; she does, however, introduce much more detail and delineation. Her data are the result of 115 in-depth interviews and an extensive literature search. *Unlike other theorists, she deals with both men and women and then goes on to discuss adult development and couples.*

Pulling up Roots

Sheehy sees ages 18 to 22 as a time of pulling up roots and physically leaving the family. There may be some departures and returns, as for college, the military, short-term travel, and brief "trial" marriages. Rebounds are not uncommon at this age; the person may return to live with the family for a while before again setting out into the world. The tasks of this period, according to Sheehy, are "to locate ourselves in a peer group role, a sex role, an anticipated occupation, an ideology or world view. As a result, we gather the impetus to leave home physically and the identity to begin leaving home emotionally" (p. 27).

Another painful but liberating task of this period is that of deidealizing the parent (or parent substitute) so that one can learn to have confidence in one's own judgment. Diekelmann notes that this process may be extraordinarily painful for both parents and children and that it may not be possible for them to discuss it together. It is a time for another redefinition of that most primary of relationships; this redefinition is perhaps more radical in view of the actual physical leave-taking of the child.

This period is characterized by the testing of capacities and the seeking of individual truths. There may be a great deal of exploring, of going from one extreme to another, of experimenting, and possibly of depending excessively on others for definition.

There is a feeling that "real life is out there waiting to happen to me" and that everything in the world is brand new and is to be experienced for the first time (Sheehy, p. 40). The person also feels great loneliness, possibly for the first time (Sheehy). There is confusion as the person tries to find what Sheehy defines as a consistent way of feeling and behaving that makes sense both to the person and to those who are most important in his or her life.

The issue of Erikson's moratorium is raised by Sheehy, who sees it as a positive and perhaps badly needed time in which to take time out from the tasks of young adulthood and sort out childhood and adolescence. It consists of a gathering together, while still functioning, in some fashion, in the outside world.

This period typically lasts a year or two; the person may drop out of college or drift in and out of occupations (Sheehy). It is probable that there are other moratoriums in the life cycle, but these have yet to be clearly defined.

The Trying Twenties

According to Sheehy, during the twenties there is an attempt to take hold of the world and to master what it is one feels one is supposed to be doing. Sheehy delineates clear tasks of this period, which are seen as enormous and exhilarating. A major endeavor is "to shape a dream, that vision of one's own possibilities in the world that will generate energy, aliveness, and hope" (Sheehy, p. 85). A second task is that of preparing for one's lifework and finding a mentor. Other energy goes toward forming the capability of intimacy without sacrificing identity, which has been purchased at a high price. The first test structure around which the person's life will revolve is erected and provisionally chosen. Underneath this powerful and seemingly optimistic exterior, there is a fear of formlessness and a realization that even though not everything is known, one must still act. Introspection is avoided at this stage since it would divert the person from the tasks at hand. See Figure 11-4.

Becoming One's Inner Custodian

Sheehy advances the concept of the "inner custodian" to articulate the role of parental messages within the young adult (p. 37). These messages may function to a fair extent during the twenties, but they gradually lose their power as individuality forms and as the person makes choices that are clearly his or her own. The inner custodian is developed as the person observes what happens internally and externally when injunctions are not adhered to, learns from experiences, and tests his or her own limits. The inner custodian provides an illusory comfort during trying times, but eventually, probably in mid-life, it ceases to hold sway. It is then discarded in favor of inner self-direction (Sheehy).

According to Sheehy, the next transition occurs at age 30. There are feelings of dissatisfaction with the choices made during the twenties as well as feelings of restlessness and a desire to "break out" (Sheehy, p. 138). This transition occurs between ages 28 and 32 and is marked by the turning of the search for identity from outward directions to inner dimensions (Sheehy). It is a time of coming into new awarenesses; occupational choices are discarded, renewed, or deliberately set aside until later. Relationships are reassessed, contracts are altered, families are begun, and divorces are initiated. There is a switch from what one "should" do to what one wants and desires. There is a beginning willingness to "hear" the inner custodian and acknowledge its presence and influence (Sheehy, p. 139). *There is a dawning realization that life is much more complicated and hurtful than had been thought during the twenties* (Sheehy). Signs of aging may start to become apparent at this time, leading to a realization of one's own mortality and a sense that one's time is limited. Turning 30 in itself may be an occasion for a life review and reassessment.

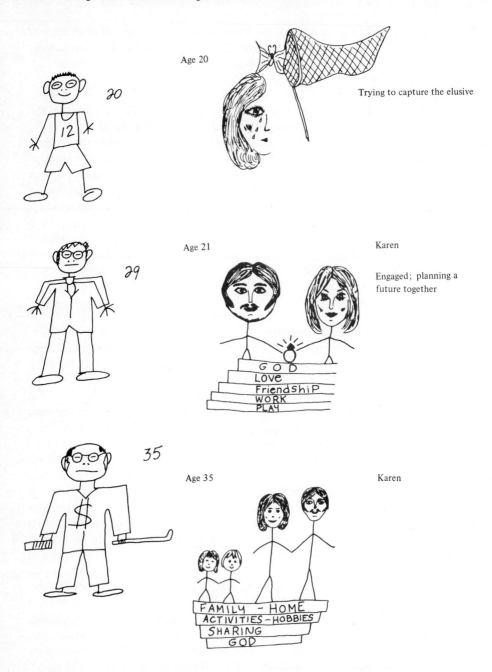

Age 20

Trying to capture the elusive

Age 21

Karen

Engaged; planning a future together

G O D
Love
Friendship
WORK
PLAY

Age 35

Karen

FAMILY - HOME
ACTIVITIES - HOBBIES
SHARING
GOD

Figure 11-4 People between the ages of 20 and 35 were asked to draw "something" that would typify themselves at age 20, as they are now, and as they see themselves at 35.

Rooting and Extending

Sheehy describes the early thirties as a period of "rooting and extending." A settling down takes place, and investments and commitments of all sorts are made (Sheehy, p. 148). Although Sheehy does not elaborate a great deal on this stage, it can be speculated that other processes are occurring. Many experience a feeling of calm during their early and middle thirties; there is a rest from the turbulent transition that occurs at age 30 and a respite from the frantic and often unformed twenties. The world starts to make a bit more sense, and some order is perceived. The person gradually stops thinking in terms of polarities, and a flow develops. There is less blaming of society, parents, and authority figures for the problems of the world, and the young adult begins to take more responsibility for his or her own thoughts and behaviors. There still may be some "acting out" in regard to power issues with available authority figures, but this is more a process of working out these feelings than of rigidly accusing others. The person may try to become a peer to parents; he or she is now aware of the similarities between the generations and of the role of heritage. Learning to relax and have fun is a major task for some in this age group. One young adult sums up her mid-thirties as follows:

> In my twenties I wanted to explore, to do everything differently from the way my parents had done them, to be radically unique. I didn't want anything that was conventional, and I chose to marry a man who I knew, somewhere in my being, would be unacceptable to my parents. He was deliciously dangerous. The funny thing is that I did get married and have a child even in the midst of all the rebelling against middle-class values. Now that I'm 33, I find myself wanting a position of respect in the community, one that involves responsibility and commitment. I find that I'm more comfortable with middle-class things such as a car, a permanent address, and a mate who doesn't see other women or push me around. I guess I just got tired of being uncomfortable physically and of always trying to change my inner life. Maybe I'm ready to be an adult.

SUMMARIZING

Statements Based on the Literature
- It is not known exactly when adulthood begins. Chronological age may be a useful, objective index for measuring change with time over the life cycle (Kimmel).
- The developmental model is holistic and draws from many disciplines (Waechter).
- Stage theory views development as one-directional; each transition is probably preceded by a readiness state (Waechter).
- Two general tendencies described by Bühler as cited in Kimmel are (1) growth and expansion and (2) contraction.
- Jung states that neurosis appears only if the work of the earlier stage has not been completed.

- A transition described by Levinson et al. occurs when the person leaves his or her family. This transition begins at about 16 to 18 years of age and ends at about 20 to 24 years of age; it lasts 3 to 5 years.
- A painful task of ages 18 to 22 is that of moving away from the parents and developing confidence in one's own judgments (Sheehy).
- Working-class people and people living in ghettos may not experience a moratorium during adolescence; they may assume the adult role of work or marriage before or right after finishing high school (Diekelmann; Kimmel).
- Between the early and late twenties, one is getting into the adult world; this is a time of exploring and of making provisional commitments (Levinson et al.).
- Some people experience confusion and internal chaos between the ages of approximately 28 and 32; others do a quiet reevaluation (Levinson et al.).
- Self-parent differentiation and psychological distance from the family are especially important from about age 16 to about age 24 (Sheehy).
- The settling-down period, which begins in the early thirties and lasts until approximately age 40, is characterized by deeper commitments, long-range planning, and a need for order (Levinson et al.).
- Rooting and extending are characteristics of the early thirties (Sheehy).
- Short-term treatment is effective when based on difficulties with stages and transitions (Rosenberg).
- Persons who refused to do a life review were found to be more depressed than those who were able to reminisce (Ostrovski).

GUIDELINES FOR INTERVENTION

- Be knowledgeable concerning the various stages of growth and development.
- Assist persons who are experiencing periods of confusion to identify possible directions and forces in their lives.
- Help people recognize their strengths as well as their vulnerabilities. This may provide a temporary source of strength until they can muster up the personal resources to work out their problems.
- Two general tendencies in the life cycle are (1) growth and expansion and (2) contraction. Help people determine in which direction they are moving and what some of the reasons for this might be.
- An awareness of the transitions that may occur between developmental stages is crucial to intervention. Be alert for external events and inner urges at the onset of a transition.
- Consider whether a person seems to be ready to make a transition, that is, whether he or she is willing to move on.
- Although there may be value restructuring, subtle shifts in personality are constantly taking place.
- List the available supports in the milieu if there is a crisis to be resolved.
- Use here-and-now approaches and short-term treatment approaches when there are difficulties with various stages and transitions.

- As a therapist, move from the role of parental substitute to that of educator and facilitator and maintain more of a peer relationship.
- Do not underestimate attentive listening and "being there" as powerful forms of positive caring in the therapeutic situation.

CONCLUSION

Developmental theory is a relatively new and emerging body of knowledge. It is in the process of forming and therefore is idealistic, partial, and subject to error. The work of Bühler, while receiving less attention currently than that of Erikson, lays much of the framework for adult developmental theory, particularly with regard to the use of in-depth interviews as a way of gathering data. Erikson's work, which is more recent, provides a background for the more detailed stage, transition, and task theories of Levinson et al. and Sheehy. While a great deal of theory has been forthcoming in more recent years, much actual testing of assumptions and validating of concepts will have to be done.

REFERENCES

Bühler, Charlotte: "The Developmental Structure of Goal Setting in Group and Individual Studies," in Charlotte Bühler and Fred Massarik (eds.), *The Course of Human Life,* Springer, New York, 1968.

Diekelmann, Nancy: *Primary Health Care of the Well Adult,* McGraw-Hill, New York, 1977.

Erikson, Erik H.: "The Eight Ages of Man," in *Childhood and Society,* 2d ed., Norton, New York, 1963.

Frenkel-Brunswick, Else: "Studies in Biographical Psychology," *Character and Personality,* **5**(9):1–34, 1936.

Glick, Paul, and **Arthur Norton:** "Perspectives on the Recent Upturn in Divorce and Remarriage," U.S. Bureau of the Census, 1972, p. 4.

Gould, Roger: "Growth toward Self-Tolerance," *Psychology Today,* **8**(9):74–78, 1975.

Jung, Carl G.: "The Stages of Life," tr. by R. F. C. Hull, in J. Campbell (ed.), *The Portable Jung,* Viking, New York, 1971.

Kimmel, Douglas C.: *Adulthood and Aging,* Wiley, New York, 1974.

LeVeck, Paula J.: "Developmental Reactions in Young Adulthood," in M. E. Kalkman and A. J. Davis (eds.), *New Dimensions in Mental Health: Psychiatric Nursing,* 4th ed. McGraw-Hill, New York, 1974.

Levinson, Daniel F., Charlotte M. Darrow, Edward B. Klein, Maria H. Levinson, and **Braxton McKee:** "The Psychosocial Development of Men in Early Adulthood and the Mid-Life Transition," in D. F. Ricks, A. Thomas, and M. Roff (eds.), *Life History Research in Psychopathology,* University of Minnesota Press, Minneapolis, 1974.

Ostrovski, Mary Joy: "Life Review and

Depression in Late Life," unpublished master's thesis, Lone Mountain College, San Francisco, 1977.

Rosenberg, Blanca N.: "Planned Short-Term Treatment in Developmental Crises," *Social Casework,* **56**(4): 195–204, 1975.

Sheehy, Gail: *Passages: Predictable Crises of Adult Life,* Dutton, New York, 1976.

Smith, Houston: *The Religions of Man,* Harper & Row, New York, 1958.

Waechter, Eugenia: "The Developmental Model," in M. E. Kalkman and A. J. Davis (eds.), *New Dimensions in Mental Health: Psychiatric Nursing,* 4th ed., McGraw-Hill, New York, 1974.

OTHER RESOURCES

FILMS

Sometimes I Wonder Who I Am: 16 mm/b and w/5 min. A poignant film by Liane Brandon of a young woman's search for self-identity as she contemplates the career she could have had while she is performing the daily tasks of being a housewife and mother. Distributor: New Day Films, P.O. Box 315, Franklin Lakes, N.J. 07417.

Men's Lives: 16 mm/color/43 min. A documentary by Josh Hanig and Will Roberts about masculinity in America. Filmed interviews of men and boys, and some women, reveal a microcosm of masculine attitudes. Distributor: New Day Films, P.O. Box 315, Franklin Lakes, N.J. 07417.

Chapter 12

YOUNG ADULTHOOD
Mary Joy Ostrovski

> My parents and I are not close like we used to be.
>
> *Susan, aged 25*

> It takes a long time to become conscious, to realize that
> emotional pain is part and parcel of everyday living.
>
> *Ward, aged 34*

Young adults coming into their early twenties face different inner realities than their parents faced at the same age. In all probability, developmental areas slighted by one generation (because of historical and cultural pressures) may be dramatically emphasized by the next generation. For this reason, Haan's report on the longitudinal Oakland Growth and Guidance Studies, which deal with people born between 1921 and 1928, is important. Those in this cohort are the parents of today's young adults. Haan found that, over the years, men in this group had developed greater social control and self-confidence. Concurrently, several more tender, merely reactive characteristics were lost. For women, the socially appropriate female characteristics associated with becoming a wife and mother (protectiveness and sympathy) were attained with losses in self-assertiveness and confidence, sexual enjoyment, and expressiveness. These findings, so clear and precise, appear to be tied to cultural content and would probably not be replicated in other studies with subjects of different ages (Haan). Obviously, this is another cultural backdrop for the young adult and in all probability has given rise to such phenomena as the abandonment of the work ethic in favor of "experiencing life," the rise in the number of working women, and sex-linked movements such as gay liberation and feminism.

Because of the rapidity of cultural change and the inherent complexities, families are unable to prepare their children adequately for future roles (Kimmel). Mead, in her book entitled *Culture and Commitment: A Study of the Generation Gap,* writes of a phenomenon she calls "cofigurative cultures" (1970b). In this model, the young must "develop appropriate styles of behavior for which there are no parental models" (Mead, 1970b, p. 46). One could speculate that this is burdensome and confusing for young people. Coupled with Americans' tendency to romanticize reliance on individuality, it seems that this sort of culture would foster depression among adults. *Educational institutions cannot fully prepare and support the young either; young adults must rely even more on peer groups and their own resources.* Probably, with time, Mead notes, our culture will become a "prefigurative culture" in which the young will lead the old into the unknown (1970b). It follows that the young will be the culture bearers and that older people will look to them for clues as to appropriate behaviors. Certainly, this is apparent in present-day American society, where the fashions and life-styles originated by young people are often adopted by older adults; the wide-spread popularity of denim clothing is a case in point.

POSITIONS OF IDENTITY AND INTIMACY

According to Marcia, there are four "normal" positions in which people are likely to find themselves during the identity-formation period. Marcia's work draws on that of Erikson and is an important addition to his theory concerning the crisis of the fifth stage of the life cycle: identity versus role confusion.

Probably, true intimacy, which Erikson describes as occurring during the stage marked by the crisis of intimacy versus isolation, is developed in the later years of young adulthood. It is hoped that by then the turmoil of establishing identity has passed. Nevertheless, intimacy does occur earlier in various forms and at various levels. It is likely that there is a blending of identity and intimacy rather than a rigid succession of stages. Therefore, intimacy will also be discussed in relation to each identity position.

The Moratorium Position

The first position is the *moratorium* position. Young adults in this group are actively struggling to find the right commitments while not making any investments in other people or in occupations. They are in crises yet to be resolved (Marcia).

Relationships such as peer friendships and sexual involvements are transient, serial, and often experimental. There is much exploration of situations and people seen by parents as unacceptable. While some of these associations may have a rebellious component, they may also assist in the search for identity as well as providing relatedness at some level. Certainly brief marriages fulfill this function.

Pseudointimacy is common in this position and may be seen as a preliminary exploration into intimacy and/or a temporary need satisfaction. True intimacy, with its enduring commitments and compromises, is not common in the moratorium period, although relationships begun at this time may at a later date become truly intimate.

There is a searching for values that can be claimed and integrated as one's own. Accordingly, there is wide exploration of, and experimentation with, one's own limits as well as those of society. The overall feeling tone may be one of elation and buoyancy; time seems endless, and youth is forever. Some young adults may feel the pressure of being on an uncharted course; this is, of course, a prelude to the feeling that many older adults have about their lives, but experiencing it for the first time is uniquely difficult. Parents may be overconcerned about the "undecided" young adult and urge him or her to "settle down." If the sense of anxiety about the lack of structure is great enough, this will distract the young adult from relating to others or to his or her environment except at a superficial level (McCary). There may be real frustration at "not finding anything I like." The process of seeking may be very painful and seemingly without end. For those in long-term educational programs, certain tasks of this stage may have to be delayed. One girl said, "I can't think about being romantically involved with a man right now. I'm only 21, and it'll be a long time before I'm finished with dental school and will have the energy for a relationship."

Child-parent alienation may be a feature of the moratorium period for some families. Periods of complete estrangement and total lack of communication are not uncommon. Reconciliation occurs as the young adult's identity stabilizes and as the parents come to accept that they and their child have honest and heartfelt differences.

Young people in this position may find themselves in a variety of circumstances. Certainly, many of the activists in the late 1960s were in a period of moratorium. Kimmel notes that some young adults may be more troubled than others by the problem of linking their individual identity to the social order. The activists of the late 1960s have now turned 30, the age they least trusted, and for the most part they are responsible family people. According to Vaillant, who studied a nonpatient population of males, those who were more in favor of civil rights in 1964 and more opposed to escalation of the Vietnam war in 1967 tended to be more emotionally healthy than those who were not politically involved.

Traditionally, women have not been part of this group. It was assumed that their identity was rooted in being wives and mothers. They were not encouraged to search and explore; indeed, they were prohibited from doing so by various social injunctions. It may be true that interpersonal relationships are most able to facilitate identity formation, as McCary notes. To ask a person to choose between a social-biological role and any other type of pursuit prevents development of solid identity.

Other styles used by young adults in the moratorium period are (1) vagabonding;

(2) starting and dropping out of college; (3) experimenting with different living arrangements, for example, communes; and (4) having scattered job experiences. Temporary commitments to causes and philosophies such as the alleviation of world hunger, the ecology, and Eastern religions are common today. These commitments will, with time, become integrated into the personality structure of the young adult, but they will not have the importance they did during the moratorium period.

The Identity-Foreclosed Position

The second position in which people are likely to find themselves during identity formation is the *identity-foreclosed* position. Young adults in this group are very sure of what they want to do and seem to make commitments without a crisis and without a strenuous search (Marcia). The absence of a crisis may or may not mean eruption of an identity crisis in later life (Sheehy). Those in this group may have chosen to adjust to a situation rather than to seek out and test. Traditional life-styles, sex roles, and approaches to intimacy are more often seen in this position. For some, marriage may be a means of obtaining both identity and intimacy. Probably this is a very difficult way of accomplishing these two tasks simultaneously. Carl Rogers alludes to this in his book, *Becoming Partners,* when he details the stormy, ever-changing, and rewarding marriage of Eric and Denise. See Figure 12-1.

It is possible that, for some, the struggle to adjust to a situation may turn into a decision not to struggle but rather to alter the situation itself. By that time, emotional growth may be blocked, and there may be a loss of the capacity to enjoy life and pleasurable activities (McCary). It may be necessary to leave the situation entirely in order to make contact with oneself again. Understandably, divorce is often the route taken in an attempt to grasp identity. During the initial separation many people experience a feeling of release and a very real resurgence of adolescent feelings of rebellion, shyness, low self-esteem, and faltering self-confidence with members of the opposite sex. Identity issues are at the fore, and a kind of moratorium period may ensue.

Kimmel notes that while the number of divorces has been increasing since the 1960s, the rate is lower than it was following World War II. Interestingly, however, divorced people are not remarrying as rapidly as they did in the 1950s, and therefore the "pool" of single adults is increasing. Data regarding single life-styles are not available, but it is safe to say that issues concerning identity and intimacy are being resolved in nontraditional ways. Undoubtedly, relaxation of sexual mores facilitates more intimacy than was previously sanctioned for single young adults.

Those in the identity-foreclosed group have passively accepted the identity that their parents and their culture set out for them and have proceeded to live their lives according to "shoulds." Predictably, this group is more authoritarian than any other group (Marcia). Until recently, in our culture, this was the slot into which most young women were expected to fit. Sometimes they did this on

Figure 12-1 A traditional wedding. *(Courtesy of Patricia Keen.)*

the rebound from a flirtation with the moratorium position: there was too much anxiety involved in the search. More likely, they felt the pull of traditional messages and exhortations. One could speculate, as Sheehy does, that Patty Hearst was "handed" a moratorium period and thus avoided a foreclosed identity (p. 60).

Feeling tones of this state may be of confidence, of sureness, of "being in tune," and of "doing what I'm supposed to be doing." Time sense is based on external events such as marriage, the birth of children, and the purchase of a house. There may be underlying feelings of unsureness, but this is due to inexperience, not to identity confusion. Observers of this age group, including their peers, may feel they are boring, insensitive, or lucky. See Figure 12-2.

Factors influencing the possibility of a foreclosed identity are geographic location and the openness of the original family to strangers and new ideas. Probably those who go straight into adult roles after high school, with no intervening period, "work out their occupational and marital identity 'on the job' " (Kimmel, p. 78). There is no possibility of a moratorium for them.

For some young adults, joining a group such as the "Moonies" or turning to Eastern religions may be a way of avoiding a struggle for an identity or of providing themselves with a moratorium period. There is relief from confusion in finding an entire framework that has a body of theory, offers discipline, and

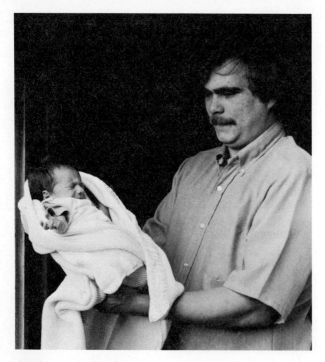

Figure 12-2 A young father with his baby—"two beginnings." *(Courtesy of Patricia Keen.)*

dictates attitudes and behavior. Thus the young adult may not effectively attain his or her own identity, but rather escapes the struggle by replacing parent with cult.

The Identity-Diffused Position

Marcia's third identity-formation position is that of the *identity-diffused*. Identity diffusion is also discussed in Chapter 9. Young adults in this group have shrunk from the task of defining what it is they want and how they feel. Parents, teachers, and friends seem to expect something from them that they cannot give. They are not able to rebel; it is as if they are in a state of limbo. This also makes the necessary struggle for identity impossible. They remain, even though employed and/or married, uncommitted to anything or anyone. They seem to perform well enough in school and in social roles, but they always feel like misfits. Often when they make early attempts to define themselves, they become immobilized by their feelings of inferiority or alienation. Unlike those in the moratorium position, they do not seem driven to do much about their situation; they are not in a state of crisis (Marcia). Their time sense is diffuse and vague; on some occasions time passes rapidly, and on others it drags. There seems to be no continuity of time or sense of its importance.

Women who have just graduated from college are frequently in this group. Constantinople examined 952 undergraduates using Erikson's measure of personality development. She found that although the women seemed more mature when entering college, it was the men who moved consistently over the 4 years toward a resolution of their identities. The academic environment supported and encouraged the male students in making their career choices and gaining confidence. For many women, the same pressures and opportunities led to a prolonged sense of identity diffusion. Again, there was the feeling that the women had to choose between pursuing a career and being a parent, a choice no young man is asked to make. Thus the women, as long as they could not make this decision or put it off, were unable to resolve their identities (Constantinople). See Figure 12-3.

The Identity-Achieved Position

The fourth position is that of the *identity-achieved*. This group have been in a crisis and have come through it. Young adults in this position have developed a sustained personal stance with regard to their sense of purpose and their view of the world. They are also likely to be a good deal older (Marcia). Those who began their identity crisis with a rigid philosophy may now find that a new and stable philosophy has formed. They are more ready for intimacy than young adults in the other positions, and they are freer to care about other persons and about others' ideas (McCary). Regardless of the life-style that an individual in this group adopts, intimacy can now become full-blown. It may be expressed in a variety of ways—in a communal setting with many others; in one-to-one relationships, either heterosexual or homosexual; and in deepening friendships

Figure 12-3 Pride and expectancy. *(Courtesy of Patricia Keen.)*

and occupational ties. There is less anxiety in their relationships and less defensiveness; it is easier to throw off reactions that are inappropriate. Rules are more understandable, and there is more warmth and respect for others (McCary).

Identity-achieved young adults are found in a variety of circumstances; often they have reverted to their parents' modes, but with new and rearranged inner lives. They are different from those in the identity-foreclosed position. For instance, many young adults who now attend college come from families in which the head of the household does not have a college education. After college, many of these young adults will take on blue-collar jobs or jobs requiring manual labor, similar to the jobs of their parents. Previous to college, this would have been unthinkable to both parent and child. Now it seems comfortable to both.

Other identity-achieved young adults live in rural areas, having gone there directly after the urban upheavals. In many ways, they are adopting the life-styles of their grandparents. They till the soil, raise animals, go to community meetings, and do handicrafts. For most, it is a way of being in control that was not possible in the cities and a way of being responsible for themselves and their families. See Figure 12-4.

Although young adults in the identity-achieved group also undergo periods of stress, they tend to be able to survive crises, transitions, and life changes

Figure 12-4   Identity-achieved young adults live in the country and may follow the life-styles of their grandparents. Note the additional family member peeking out between the two adults. *(Courtesy of Gary Stewart.)*

because of a sense of humor, a joyful outlook, flexibility, and a workable philosophy.

In sum, here are four "normal" identity positions in which people are likely to find themselves during the identity-formation period (Marcia). These identity styles also reflect intimacy styles as young adults move through this period. There is a possibility that an individual might adopt one of the positions as a permanent life-style and way of perceiving the world. It is also possible that a person might progress partway through a position, return, move on, and then eventually come back for total resolution. All four positions may concurrently exist in the same person, depending on the circumstances which activate a position.

HEALTH AND STRESS

Most young adults have healthy bodies that are fully functioning and at peak effectiveness. Physical maturation occurs early in young adulthood, and the body's capacity to mend itself through cell multiplication and tissue repair is intact. Motor functioning is at an optimum level. The cardiovascular system may begin to show signs of aging before the other systems; hypertension and related cardiac problems, including silent heart disease, are being found with increasing frequency among young adults. An EKG at this time would detect disease as well as provide a base line for future monitoring (Diekelmann).

Despite this highly developed and fully functioning system, young adults are prone to much physical and emotional illness. Young adults are more prone to colds, allergies, asthma, and skin problems. They may suffer from migraine headaches up to age 30, but usually not after that (Troll). Depression is common among young adults, a fact that is often unacknowledged and unrecognized. Depression is characterized by feelings of helplessness and hopelessness about one's ability to cope, by flat emotional tones, and often by an inability to focus and identify the feelings of sadness. Typically in this society, which pays undue homage to youth and vigor, young adults are not thought to suffer depression, either by themselves or by others. It may be due to unexpressed anger which has been turned inward, or it may be a reaction to a loss—leaving college, failing to get a job, or the death of a friend. An inability to express anger may result from a fear of retaliation or from a concern about seeming impolite, unreasonable, childish, or irresponsible. Certainly, in this culture, many see any expression of anger as an immediate prelude to physical violence. Depression can also be a response to certain environmental conditions or situations, such as the "experience of lacking power and control over one's own life, that is, helplessness" and the "experience of not receiving sufficient reward or satisfaction from one's surroundings, that is, low positive reinforcement and nonrecognition" (Butler, 1976b, p. 28).

Should the depression increase in intensity or become a chronic condition, suicidal ideation is likely to occur. Suicide is the third leading cause of death among young adults (Bahra). In the last decade there has been a 90 percent increase in suicide among males aged 15 to 24 and a 50 percent increase in suicide among females of the same age. Accidents, often thought to be subliminal suicide, are the leading cause of death among males up to age 35 (*Metropolitan Life Statistical Bulletin*). The person most likely to attempt suicide in this age group is a male graduate student who is alone much of the time, who comes from a middle-class family, and who is not satisfied with his present achievements, despite having average to above-average grades (Seiden). Precipitating events include serious interpersonal conflicts, unemployment, and disappointment in work. While young people make more suicide attempts than older people, their attempts are less successful and may be seen as primarily a way of asking for help.

Common signs that a person may be contemplating suicide include:

Self-neglect
Decreased muscle tone
Slumped shoulders
Slowed gait and speech
Lack of interest in work
Hypermobility
Impairment of reality testing
Expression of high degree of helplessness and hopelessness
Impairment of judgment and object relationships
Decreased cooperativeness
Anorexia and weight loss
Increased pain threshold
Sleep disturbances
Feelings of depression, anger, bitterness, fear, or panic (in a few instances, feelings of happiness or peacefulness)

Precipitating events include:

Serious interpersonal conflict
Marital discord or family discord
Loss of personal resources
Unemployment or disappointment in work
Heavy drinking before the attempt

A person is more likely to attempt suicide if he or she has made previous attempts. Those who try to commit suicide often have a history of hostile relationships, a poor work history, or a history of antisocial behavior.

Care givers should observe the following guidelines when intervening in cases of potential suicide:

Elicit the suicidal ideation and fantasies.
Ask the person directly and openly about his or her thoughts.
Do not dare or challenge the person. Young adults are impulsive and may feel the need to prove that they can accept challenges and take risks.

Reassure the person that such thoughts are common in young adulthood.
Activate a sincere and readily available support system.
Assist with psychiatric hospitalization if an attempt seems imminent or likely.

This high morbidity rate among younger adults is due to the many stresses
and changes that characterize this period of life. Rachel Cox has studied the
typical concerns of young adults. She selected 63 college undergraduates who
were student council members and who were defined as "normal" by this study:
that is, they had the capacity to function at least passably well in all roles on a
daily basis, they were reality-oriented, they were not hospitalized, and they
contributed appropriately to their families and the community.

Six specific areas were investigated: (1) relationships with parents, (2) work,
(3) attitudes toward further education, (4) attitudes toward parenthood, (5)
attitudes toward marriage, and (6) financial management. The subjects were
interviewed while they were attending college and then again 10 years later. At
the time of the follow-up interviews, their ages ranged from 30 to 36; 95
percent were economically self-supporting, 93.5 percent were married, and all
were functioning in self-selected roles. While the subjects continued to be
"normal," the years of passage had not always been smooth: "At least ten had
gone through periods of profound disheartenment; in four of these cases the
discouragement probably verged on a mild depression. One subject experienced
an anxiety state. One had attempted suicide. Two others had briefly considered
it. Serious problems in their marriages had distressed thirteen" (R. Cox, p. 45).
See Table 12-1.

Those who had not experienced a difficult transition said that they wondered
how well they would cope with unhappiness. In general, the stresses that were
reported related directly to the tasks and transitions associated with beginning

Table 12-1. Most Frequently Reported Stresses between College and the 10-Year Follow-Up Interview (N = 63)

	Frequency
Shattered love affair	25
Career development slow or disappointing	24
Parents' marriage broken by divorce or marked by conflict	24
Harassed by indecision about whether vocational choice is good	23
Long-continued financial dependence on parents after college	22
Relation to mother too close emotionally, too dominated by her, or too distant from her	22
Neuroticism in parent	19
Relation to father too close emotionally, too dominated by him, or too distant from him	19
Financial pressures (regardless of income level)	19
Financial problems or insecurity in parents' home	16

Source: From R. D. Cox, p. 73.

young adulthood. It is significant that despite their difficulties, the majority of the subjects were able to complete the tasks of young adulthood (R. Cox). The role of support (environmental or human) was not investigated in this study.

Common sense dictates that those who must cope with a great deal of stress and with heavy burdens are likely to become ill. According to Holmes and Masuda, stress can trigger illness because the effort required to cope with the stress may weaken the individual's resistance to disease. Therefore, illness may be the predictable result of a major life crisis. A scale devised by Holmes and Rahe rates life events according to a stress-point hierarchy. Correlation is then made with illness. When the point values of life-event changes that have occurred within a year's time add up to more than 300, illness may lie ahead—pathological depression, heart attack, or other serious physical ailments. The significance of this scale is that even "positive change" can bring stress and possible illness (Holmes and Masuda). As Toffler states, "alterations of life styles which require a great deal of adjustment and coping correlate with illness—whether or not these changes are under the individual's own direct control and whether or not he sees them as undesirable" (p. 293). Although Holmes and Rahe did not investigate various factors with regard to the occurrence of stress, *it is probable that what is stressful changes from culture to culture, from time to time, and with varying geographic locations.* See Table 12-2.

INTERVENTIONS

The Care Giver

In working with young adults, it is necessary to consider several factors in order to be of real assistance. The young adult in distress is also struggling with self-definition, and interventions must be geared to this. Giving advice, making judgments as to what is right and wrong, and initiating confrontations may turn the individual away. It is more helpful if the care giver assumes an attitude of listening, having time, "being there," and caring enough to really try to understand the situation. If the care giver does not try to suggest immediate solutions to stated problems, this may further enable the person to grasp the emotional climate of the circumstances.

Another factor to be considered is *the role of the care giver, which will vary from situation to situation.* There may be a need for assistance with problem solving, with discovering alternatives, with sorting out appropriate aids in the environment, or with learning how to maintain and nourish a changing relationship with parents. Accordingly, *the care giver may be a facilitator, a mentor, a resource informant, or a one-time helper with a problem or a crisis.* Care givers for middle-aged persons are discussed in Chapter 14; Chapter 27 discusses care givers for the elderly.

When a young adult asks for assistance with problem solving, it is crucial first to identify the problem, with all its facets, and to locate exactly where the difficulty and distress are focused. Listening with an understanding and empathic

Table 12-2. The Social Readjustment Rating Scale

Life Event	Value
1. Death of spouse	100
2. Divorce	73
3. Marital separation	65
4. Jail term	63
5. Death of close family member	63
6. Personal injury or illness	53
7. Marriage	50
8. Fired at work	47
9. Marital reconciliation	45
10. Retirement	45
11. Change in health of family member	44
12. Pregnancy	40
13. Sex difficulties	39
14. Gain of new family	39
15. Business adjustment	39
16. Change in financial state	38
17. Death of close friend	37
18. Change to different line of work	36
19. Change in number of arguments with spouse	35
20. Mortgage over $10,000	31
21. Foreclosure of mortgage or loan	30
22. Change in responsibilities at work	29
23. Son or daughter leaving home	29
24. Trouble with in-laws	29
25. Outstanding personal achievement	28
26. Wife begins or stops work	26
27. Begin or end school	26
28. Change in living conditions	25
29. Revision of personal habits	24
30. Trouble with boss	23
31. Change in work hours or conditions	20
32. Change in residence	20
33. Change in schools	20
34. Change in recreation	19
35. Change in church activities	19
36. Change in social activities	18
37. Mortgage or loan less than $10,000	17
38. Change in sleeping habits	16
39. Change in number of family get-togethers	15
40. Change in eating habits	15
41. Vacation	13
42. Christmas	12
43. Minor violations of the law	11

Source: Holmes and Rahe, p. 213. Reproduced with permission.

ear is often helpful, and reflecting statements provide a "sounding board" which can make it possible to further pinpoint feelings and concerns. Acknowledgment of the difficulty of the struggle is often a crucial step in releasing energy for discovering solutions. It may also be helpful to share similar experiences of one's own. Of course, this type of sharing is brief; it is not a device whereby the care giver settles unfinished business or vents frustration. It may prove helpful to the young adult to verify the lack of cultural supports in his or her struggles, using comments such as, "Things are changing rapidly, and there are few guidelines because problems, dilemmas, and solutions are different from what they were 10 years ago."

Once the problem is well identified, the possibility of solutions arises. It may be that a breathing space is needed before various alternatives can be brought up for consideration. Deep emotional investments may make it impossible to look at solutions at particular points in time. In some instances, the resolution may occur spontaneously at a later date.

Should the decision be made to proceed with the solution stage of problem solving, it is important to consider any and all alternatives, including those which might seem drastic or even silly. Once that is done, it is possible to move to the evaluation of various options. Role playing may be helpful where a specific situation must be dealt with, such as a job interview, ending a relationship, or trying to set limits with parents. The young adult and the care giver assume, in turn, both roles in the situation. The actual situation may turn out somewhat differently, but the role playing can help prepare the person and also uncover new ideas and unspoken expectations. Once a solution or course of action has been decided on, the young adult can move to implementation, which is followed at some later point by evaluation. After a particular event has occurred, it is helpful to discuss it, to point out and give support for positive and growth-enhancing behavior, to diffuse leftover feeling, to delineate areas that might be troublesome in the future, and to sum up what took place.

An especially difficult area for young adults to deal with is parental intrusiveness. They may feel guilty when it becomes necessary for them to set limits on parental intrusiveness so that they can proceed with the tasks of young adulthood. It may be helpful to point out that the intrusiveness once had a lifesaving function, i.e., that parents must know where their small children are at all times for the children's own safety. However, being intrusive with young adults is not appropriate; this is a leftover behavior from earlier times that needs changing.

It may also be helpful for the young adult to know that the parents are probably also struggling with the new relationship and that they may be confused and unsure of how to handle their feelings. There may be much irritation between the generations as each searches for new identities within the relationship. *Another way of helping young adults with regard to their parents is to let them know that it is natural for them to feel dependent on their parents at times and that often this triggers the parents' feeling that they must be more involved in their child's life.* Again, validation of feelings is crucial.

Parental intrusion may take the form of exhortations which were appropriate in the past but which are now experienced by the young adult as pressuring and may be barriers to future growth: "Hurry up" or "Be successful." Identifying these messages, softening them, and building in self-support statements may lessen their often paralyzing effect. The person's energy is then freed for making his or her own judgments about people and situations.

Other supports, besides the care giver's direct assistance, may be available: groups, courses, and self-help books; friends; holistic health maintenance regimens; mentors; and psychotherapy.

Groups, Courses, and Books

In many areas of the country, it is now possible to enroll in classes or join groups that give support and facilitate growth. Books on self-development are readily available. It is important to stress that while some of these may be of benefit, none contains the "eternal truth" or is the last word on individual development. Some have causes to promote; others insist that theirs is the only way and that a complete change of life-style is necessary for fulfillment. The young adult must be discriminating and integrate into his or her life only the information and advice that seem exactly right.

In many urban areas there are women's groups. These groups, which can aid in clearing away the identity diffusion that so many women feel, are sponsored by various women's organizations, mental health centers, and other social agencies. They may be based on the National Organization for Women's format for consciousness raising and address such issues as anger, motherhood, friends, and sex. Other groups exist solely to offer support. Although men's groups have not been as common as women's groups, some are now in existence and deal with "macho" problems interfering with work and interpersonal relationships.

Those who are inexperienced with groups may feel the need for a facilitator or a format, while those with more group experience may be comfortable being leaderless; in some groups a natural leader emerges. Care givers might encourage young adults to form their own self-help groups or serve as organizers and facilitators of such groups.

Courses are now being offered that view distress as a transition with which some individuals may need assistance. Some of these courses are offered in extension units or at universities, and others in adult education programs. These courses are concerned with the effects of life-style changes, with decision-making, and with facilitating coping skills, flexibility, and crisis survival. Assertiveness training, which has emerged from the field of behavior therapy, offers assistance in developing "the capacity to express oneself freely—to express positive and negative feelings without embarrassment, to stand up for ourselves and prevent others from taking advantage. Self assertion is different from aggression where one person intrudes upon another" (Butler, 1976a, p. 5).

Currently, the market is flooded with self-help books that promise total self-knowledge and the ultimate in relationships; generally they are concerned with awareness and with helping people become what they "truly are." Young adults may find that some of these offer concrete help and support, but that others are in fact punitive and coercive. Here, as in other areas, a critical eye may prevent disillusionment.

Support from Friends

Many people find that friends are an invaluable support in times of crisis. Young adults, however, who may be unsure of their identity and who are thus probably incapable of true intimacy, may not find friends as helpful as other sources. It is possible, though, for young adults to get feedback and information from each other on specific situations and relationships. They can also suggest other resources to each other. Simply learning that another human being is struggling with the same issues can be a relief and can help in arriving at solutions. It is important to be alert to feelings of dependency when dealing with friends; while good relationships always have elements of dependency, young adults are in the process of becoming independent and are vulnerable to extreme dependency on friends. *Friends may not always have the emotional energy to be of help, even though they would like to.*

Holistic Health Maintenance Regimens

In recent years, responsibility for preventive health regimens has become an individual matter. Jogging and running, both of which reduce stress, enhance self-mastery, and exercise vital muscles (including the heart), have become mainstay exercises for many young adults. Tennis, which offers release for aggressive and competitive energies as well as providing an arena for socialization, has also become popular.

A recent health movement—holistic health—began in California; it seeks to help individuals learn to accept responsibility for their own health or illness. To that end, the philosophy is basically educational and informative. Eastern thought and medicine and American Indian medicine both combine with Western medicine to address the whole individual: body, mind, and spirit. The truly holistic approach embraces several different programs and combines the judicious use of each: biofeedback, yoga, energy therapy, nutrition, acupuncture, faith healing, iridology, massage, hypnosis, and herbal medicine. For those trained only in Western medicine, some concepts of holistic health may require the suspension of usual belief systems before the intent and approach of the movement can be appreciated. See Figure 12-5.

Mentors

The concept of the mentor as having crucial importance in the young adult's development first appears in the work of Levinson. He notes that the absence of mentors may be associated with various developmental impairments. The mentor is an adviser, a guide to the adult world, and a helper in deciphering

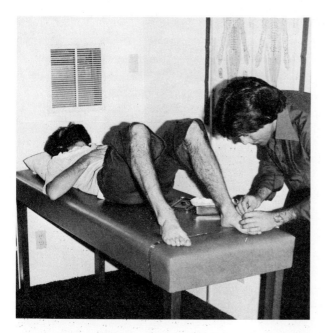

Figure 12-5 A person receiving an acupuncture treatment. *(Courtesy of Pat Ryan.)*

messages from occupational settings. He or she understands the dreams and aspirations of the young person and supports and furthers them. The mentor is often 8 to 15 years older than the young person and can be a teacher, a supervisor, an experienced coworker, a coach, or a psychotherapist. The mentor is clearly an individual in Erikson's generativity stage, teaching and nurturing the next generation. Monea describes the effect of teachers in her youth in Chapter 1.

The number of relationships with a mentor in an individual's life varies, but few people have more than three or four before becoming mentors themselves. The relationship may endure for as long as 10 to 12 years but generally lasts only 3 to 4 years (Levinson et al.). It is usually terminated by the young person following disillusionment, a fight, or simply the realization that a peer status has developed: "I just outgrew him" (Levinson et al., p. 250).

Women have more difficulty finding a mentor than men. At present, there are very few female mentors available because of the absence of women in senior positions. This situation is, of course, changing.

A woman with a male mentor must be aware of the inherent problems of sexism and eroticism. The man may not, however much he may wish to do so, take the woman's career aspirations as seriously as he would another male's. Feelings of sexual interest are inevitable for both parties. Having a liaison with a mentor involves the risk of channeling all energies into one person with whom one has, of necessity, a temporary relationship. For some women, this is not a problem.

Psychotherapy

For some young adults, psychotherapy may be an aid in removing barriers to emotional growth. A therapist may serve as a guide, a mentor, a minor guru, or the sole support person during a deep depression. It may be difficult to choose a therapist and/or a form of therapy because the feelings leading to the decision to seek such help are often vague and confusing and may consist of generalities such as "I just feel lifeless" or "I am not happy and haven't been for some time, although I can't put my finger on it." Some young adults go into psychotherapy because of a crisis such as a suicide attempt; others are prompted by impending decisions, such as those concerning job transfers or marriage.

It may be helpful to view therapy as either problem-oriented or growth-oriented. Problem-oriented therapies focus on specific problems and include such approaches as behavior modification and hypnotherapy. Alcoholics Anonymous and Weight Watchers are problem-oriented, as is most sex therapy.

Growth-oriented therapies, such as gestalt therapy, primal therapy, and psychoanalytically oriented psychotherapy, tend to be lengthy and more costly but probably produce longer-lasting and broader results (Manfield).

Rosenberg describes a form of psychotherapy called Planned Short-Term Treatment (PSTT); it is based on Erikson's epigenetic model and views crises as developmental and as having potential for growth. Initially, the therapist and the client agree on specific goals to be worked toward within a certain amount of time. Treatment is focused on the present, and is highly segmental, and communication is direct and open. There is the assumption that treatment of the presenting problem will serve as a lever to other growth. Termination includes summation of progress and discussion regarding future work following therapy.

Selecting a therapist may include interviewing several therapists while looking for a "fit" and someone with whom to build trust and closeness. It is crucial to follow instincts and individual judgment in this most intimate matter. Specific questions to ask a potential therapist are:

"What are your therapeutic orientations and biases?"
"What is your academic background?"
"What are your fees?"

In the therapy process itself, it is critical to feel good as self-knowledge comes. Feeling mostly shame or pain may be a reason to change therapists. A therapist should be someone who enjoys watching and participating in growth. See Figure 12-6.

The client decides when to end the therapy; therapists do not give out diplomas. Therefore, it is imperative to leave when the instinct dictates. Before leaving, however, it is important to discuss the decision with the therapist during several sessions in order to feel "clean and clear" about it (Manfield, p. 21).

"*I think I've finally pinpointed your problem — too much awareness!*"

© 1977 by NEA Inc.

Figure 12-6 *(Reprinted by permission of Newspaper Enterprise Association.)*

SUMMARIZING STATEMENTS BASED ON THE LITERATURE

- Present-day young adults had fathers who in their own development achieved social control and self-confidence (Haan).
- The characteristics associated with being a wife and mother—protectiveness and empathy—are attained at the expense of losses in (1) self-assertiveness, (2) confidence, (3) sexual enjoyment, and (4) expressiveness. These findings appear to be tied to cultural content (Haan).
- Because of the rapidity of cultural change and the resulting complexities, parents are unable to prepare their children adequately for their future roles (Kimmel).
- The young must develop styles of behavior which are appropriate but for which there are no parental models (Mead, 1970b).
- Marcia describes four normal positions in which young persons find them-

selves during the period of identity formation: (1) the moratorium position, (2) the identity-foreclosed position, (3) the identity-diffused position, and (4) the identity-achieved position.
- The cardiovascular system may show signs of aging early (Diekelmann).
- Suicide is the third leading cause of death among young adults (Bahra).
- The young person most likely to commit suicide is a middle-class male graduate student who is alone much of the time and who is dissatisfied with his grades (Seiden).
- In the last decade, there has been a 90 percent increase in suicide among males aged 15 to 24 and a 50 percent increase in suicide among females of the same age (*Metropolitan Life Statistical Bulletin*).
- Mentors may be of crucial importance in the development of young adults (Levinson et al.).

GUIDELINES FOR INTERVENTION

- Listen carefully for suicide ideation in depressed young adults.
- In counseling young adults, do not give advice or pass judgment about what is right or wrong; use confrontation with discretion.
- Listen in an understanding, empathic way; use reflecting statements to further pinpoint feelings and concerns.
- After a problem has been well defined, allow the young adult some time to consider alternatives.
- Parental intrusiveness is difficult for young adults to handle. Point out to them that such behavior had a lifesaving function when they were youngsters, even though it is no longer appropriate.
- Tell young adults that their parents may also be struggling with the new relationship.
- Assure them that feelings of dependency on parents are natural.
- Suggest helpful classes, books, etc. Women may find that groups are helpful in problems with identity diffusion.
- Mentors may be of crucial importance in young adults' development. Be sure that a woman with a male mentor is aware of the potential problems.
- When a young adult is trying to select a therapist, be sure that he or she knows the right questions to ask in order to make the best choice.

CONCLUSION

This chapter has considered the cultural and historical background of today's young adult and the effects of this on the developmental tasks of young adulthood, as outlined in Chapter 11. It is apparent that stresses not known to previous generations are now exerted on today's young adult, and support must now be engendered at a peer level. Some of these supports include (1) assistance with problem solving, (2) help from friends, (3) books, (4) groups and educational programs, (5) health regimens, (6) mentors, and (7) psychotherapy.

REFERENCES

Bahra, Robert J.: "The Potential for Suicide," *American Journal of Nursing,* **75**(10):1782–1788, 1975.

Butler, Pamela E.: "Programs in Behavior Therapy," Behavior Therapy Institute, Mill Valley, Calif., 1976(a). (Pamphlet.)

———: *Self Assertion for Women: A Guide to Becoming Androgynous,* Canfield, San Francisco, 1976(b).

Constantinople, Anne: "An Eriksonian Measure of Personality Development in College Students," *Journal of Developmental Psychology,* **1**(4):357–372, 1969.

Cox, Harvey: "Why Young Americans Turn to Eastern Religions," *Psychology Today,* **11**(2):36–42, 1977.

Cox, Rachel Dunaway: *Youth into Maturity: A Study of Men and Women in the First Ten Years after College,* Mental Health Materials Center, New York, 1970.

Diekelmann, Nancy: *Primary Health Care of the Well Adult,* McGraw-Hill, New York, 1977.

Haan, Norma: "Personality Development from Adolescence to Adulthood in the Oakland Growth and Guidance Studies," *Seminars in Psychiatry,* **4**(4):339–414, 1972.

Holmes, T. H., and **Minoru Masuda:** "Psychosomatic Syndrome," *Psychology Today,* **5**(11):71–72, 106–108, 1972.

Holmes, T. H., and **R. H. Rahe:** "The Social Readjustment Rating Scale," *Journal of Psychosomatic Research,* **11**(2):213–218, 1967.

Kimmel, Douglas C.: *Adulthood and Aging,* Wiley, New York, 1974.

Levinson, Daniel F., Charlotte M. Darrow, Edward B. Klein, Maria H. Levinson, and **Braxton McKee:** "The Psychosocial Development of Men in Early Adulthood and the Mid-Life Transition," in D. F. Ricks, A. Thomas, and M. Roff (eds.), *Life History Research in Psychopathology,* University of Minnesota Press, Minneapolis, 1974.

McCary, James Leslie: *Freedom and Growth in Marriage,* Hamilton, Santa Barbara, Calif., 1975.

Manfield, Phillip: "How to Choose a Therapist," unpublished master's thesis, Lone Mountain College, San Francisco, 1975.

Marcia, J. E.: "Development and Validation of Ego Identity Status," *Journal of Personality and Social Psychology,* **3**(5):551–559, 1966.

Mead, Margaret: "A Conversation with Margaret Mead and T. George Harris on the Anthropological Age," *Psychology Today,* **4**(2):59–64, 74–76, 1970(a).

———: *Culture and Commitment: A Study of the Generation Gap,* Doubleday, Garden City, N.Y., 1970(b).

Metropolitan Life Statistical Bulletin, **57**: 5–6, May, 1976.

Rogers, Carl R.: *Becoming Partners: Marriage and Its Alternatives,* Dell, New York, 1972.

Rosenberg, Blanca N.: "Planned Short-Term Treatment in Developmental Crises," *Social Casework,* **4**(4):195–204, 1975.

Seiden, Richard: "The Problem of Suicide on College Campuses," *Journal of School Health,* **41**(5):243–248, 1971.

Sheehy, Gail: *Passages: Predictable Crises of Adult Life,* Dutton, New York, 1976.

Toffler, A.: *Future Shock,* Random House, New York, 1970.

Troll, Lillian: *Early and Middle Adulthood,* Brooks/Cole, Monterey, Calif., 1975.

U.S. Bureau of the Census: *Current Population Reports: Characteristics of American Youth: 1972,* ser. P-23, no. 44, 1973.

Vaillant, George E.: "Natural History of Male Psychological Health," *Archives of General Psychiatry,* **32**(4):420–426, 1975.

OTHER RESOURCES

FILMS

Not So Young Now As Then: 16 mm/color/ 18 min. This film by Liane Brandon observes a fifteenth high school reunion focusing on areas of human relations, sex roles, identity, aging, etc. Distributor: New Day Films, P.O. Box 315, Franklin Lakes, N.J. 07417.

Joyce at 34: 16 mm/color/28 min. An award-winning documentary by Joyce Chopra and Claudia Weill that portrays the conflicting demands of family life, a career outside the home for a new mother, and the need for cooperation in order to achieve equality without guilt. Distributor: New Day Films, P.O. Box 315, Franklin Lakes, N.J. 07417.

Chapter 13

A HOLISTIC VIEW OF MIDDLE AGE
Priscilla Ebersole

> In middle age we starve
> For ascension,
> Look back to childhood teachers
> But have outgrown them.
> Mature love needs new channels,
> How long has it been—
> What starving years—
> Since I was permitted
> To cherish wisdom?
> I bend tenderly
> Toward the young
> With open heart and hands.
> I share in a great love.
>
> *May Sarton*

How does one *become* middle-aged, and what does it mean? Poets and philosophers have extolled youth and old age, but "in over two thousand years very few people have ever written about middle age by way of either praise or condemnation, for in our culture it has not been seen as a separate and special time of life. There was only youth and, when that was gone, old age" (Hunt and Hunt, p. 19).

Someone has said that middle age is the time between foolishness and wisdom. The middle-aged have experience with life, but often they do not have enough time to reflect on the meaning of their experience. They have a massive accumulation of social, emotional, and intellectual skills, and their problems may be commensurate with, or sometimes go beyond, their abilities to solve them.

The following are expectations of the middle-aged:

Commitment
Responsibility
Individuality
Power
Territorial acquisition
Accumulation of material goods
Stability
Wisdom
Provision of guidance to the young
Awareness of mortality
Expansion of interests
Acceptance of visible bodily changes

Why have the middle-aged been so little studied? First, they are not captive subjects if they are healthy and functioning in society. Second, an extended middle age is a relatively new phenomenon in the United States. In 1776 half the people in the nation were under 16, and three-quarters were under 25 (Hunt and Hunt). Third, they generally maintain low visibility while carrying the social, cultural, and economic burdens of society. Fourth, the American adult male has been reluctant to discuss his innermost feelings with anyone (Chew, 1976). Fifth, serious attention is usually reserved for people who somehow present a problem, at which point federal funding becomes available for research—witness the accumulation of data about old age within the last decade.

Another problem in studying the middle-aged is defining who they are. This is somewhat akin to the problem of studying the aged. People between 35 and 65 (the accepted parameters of middle age) are no more alike than people between 65 and 95. The complexity increases as we recognize that chronological age is, at best, an artificial delineator. To further complicate the matter, developmental stages in adulthood are not necessarily synchronous: for instance, an adult may be physically very mature, socially advanced, emotionally youthful, and psychologically immature (Huyck). Of course, some congruence is inevitable, since one would probably not be socially advanced without having some emotional control and psychological understanding.

Is middle age less interesting, provocative, or problematic than other stages of life? Is the generally accepted view that these are the ''stable years'' true, or is it that we really know so little about these years? This chapter will introduce the reader to what is known about the majority of middle-aged American citizens living today. Most have lost their immigrant heritage, if they had one; many are aware of this and are actively trying to retrieve some of the breadth and depth of their background.

Perhaps one of the changes in the mid-life course is a shift from goal orientation to process orientation. In young adulthood one still expects to ''arrive,'' but by middle age one is usually more aware of the continuous evolution of life processes.

A young adult writes:

> When I reach middle age, the main thing I hope to feel is stable. By then I think I should know more about myself and what is really important. I should be able to tell where my priorities lie and whether my dreams have a chance of coming true. If I find I can't succeed with my plan, I imagine it would be very disappointing and difficult to accept.
>
> One thing I will miss greatly will be my young children. Letting them go must be an impossible yet necessary task. I enjoy very much being needed. It will be very hard not to be such a necessary part of their lives, and yet there must be some relief in not being solely responsible for their well-being. I look forward to a lot less confusion in all areas of my life.
>
> At 28 I feel little different from the way I felt at 18; it's hard to imagine feeling any different at 38 or 48. I can't see myself any older than I am now. I feel as if I will always be 28. I suppose in middle age you must accept the fact that you are aging.

Attempts to understand adulthood must take into account generational changes, cohort differences as the impact of national and world events is perceived, and relationships between the generations. All these factors are intertwined to increase the complexity of defining intrinsic developmental processes during adulthood.

There are pronounced variations in both timing and pattern of development according to sex, social class, and ethnic or cultural group, as well as according to age cohort and generation. On almost any dimension—cognitive, personality, family, career—women will show differences from men, working-class people from middle-class people, black people from white people, Italians from Jews, and those who grew up in one point of history from those who came of age in another (Troll).

There are also certain tasks appropriate to middle age. Kaluger and Kaluger (pp. 264–283) list the following:

Renewal of couple relationships
Rediscovering dormant creativity
Taking on civic responsibility
Developing a wholesome relationship with parents
Learning to parent one's adult children
Coping with in-laws gained through the marriage of children
Coping with menopause
Preparing for retirement
Grandparenting
Acknowledging plateaus in most areas of life
Maintaining or establishing healthful living patterns

IMPORTANCE OF HISTORY

Erikson (1975) has attested to the importance of viewing the psychogenic development of an individual through the lens of historic development. Many identity crises in mid-life may be precipitated by major social changes.

What, then, are some of the important historic facts that have had an impact on those who are now middle-aged?

Cohort of 1910–1920

Those born between 1910 and 1920 have witnessed more radical changes in terms of the economy, world thought, and opportunities than any cohorts born after them (Troll). They felt the impact of the great migration from Europe that took place between 1901 and 1910. The Great Depression and World War I had less impact on them since they were not yet assuming adult responsibilities. They did carry the greatest responsibility during World War II, though the cohorts born after them were more evident on the battle line. Many of this group prospered in wartime industry and achieved an affluence they had never dreamed of. They seemed to emphasize the hurried accumulation of material goods, perhaps a reaction to their memories of the meager days of the Depression. (See Chapter 4.) Although most did not have highly specialized training, there was a broad range of job opportunities. These people now have a full view of the effects of educational opportunity; wars; major changes in technology, travel, and scientific thought; and the development of immunology, among other things. People in this group are preparing for, or are in, the period of adjustment to retirement. *Because of the complexity of their life experience and the extreme variations they have witnessed, they may require and expect a vital retirement.*

Cohort of 1920–1930

A 51-year-old man said, "I dreamed I was standing by the most beautiful stream and I didn't have a fishing license."

People born between 1920 and 1930 have known war and affluence throughout most of their life-span, and they have experienced increasing governmental control of all aspects of life. Their freedom and options have been limited by rules and regulations. They have had more security and homogeneous early education than any previous generation. Their children are grown, and some have grandchildren. They were strongly influenced by their parents in the direction of diligent work and dependability. Most males, and some females, were in the armed services and emerged with veterans' benefits, disabilities, and educational opportunities. Many retired from the service in their forties and began a second career. Some of them suffered lasting physical and psychological damage. (See Chapter 19.)

The days of individualism and of the "jack-of-all-trades" had vanished by the time they reached adulthood, and most became conformists. Most women assumed traditional roles, and family togetherness was highly prized, although the suburban life-style, long commutes, or heavy job demands often kept husbands from participating in family life to the desired degree. Prosperity and the wartime psychology led these people to produce a great crop of babies. (See Chapter 2.)

This is now the group in power; they are heavily represented in organizations and institutions. They have also experienced the effects of inflation, and they are familiar with the technological advances that have made it both necessary and easier for wives to manage a job and a home. People in this group, who are now in their fifties, are the ones expressing so much nostalgia about the pre- and post-World War II years; to them, that was the time of urgency, uncertainty, youth, and excitement.

One major change experienced by the 1920–1930 cohort was an exposure to varied life-styles. A great population migration occurred as the armed services dispersed the young around the country and around the world. Young people and their families migrated en masse to industrial centers, where good wages were available to all. People were brought alongside regional and ethnic groups whom they had rarely encountered before. The result for many was a new awareness of prejudices and the self-awareness that accompanies such exposure (Simm). (See Chapter 9 for a discussion of the nature of prejudice.)

Some middle-aged women in this cohort resumed their college studies, which had been interrupted in their youth. They were the "trailblazers" for the cohort to follow.

Cohort of 1930–1940

People in this group have an increasing number of options and are asking many questions. They are the ones experiencing mid-life crises now. (See Chapter 17.) They have lived through the era of quantum physics and nuclear fission, with all its awesome potential. Most have had some college training and have known affluence and abundance; many have opted for less traditional life-styles. Their children have been raised in an atmosphere of free expression. Their crisis may be related partly to a growing awareness of human potential. Their representatives stepped foot on the moon. Many of them have taken advantage of adult education opportunities available through community colleges, veterans' benefits, and government loans and stipends.

Cohort of 1940–1950

Those who were born between 1940 and 1950 (now in their early thirties) have been influenced, to an extent not fully recognized, by watching television during their impressionable years. (See Chapters 4 and 10.) We have become an increasingly visually oriented society, and the impact of this on values and expectations has been profound. Inflation and international police actions (war) have colored the entire lives of this group. They have small families, and few can afford a single dwelling unit.

PEOPLE WHO DO NOT FIT

One of the unfortunate results of such rapid change is that people of a particular temperament may not fit well into their historic time (Troll). A student talked with one such man, who was clearly an anachronism: "He was a retired bron-cobuster-cowboy who had traveled all over the Midwest during his life. He described the places he had seen and some of his experiences, and he told me how horses were just like women. He was an easygoing, mellow man, and as he reminisced I found I liked this cowboy and felt very close to him." This man seemed able to adapt to the present by thinking back on a time when he *fit* the best. Some have never known a time when they were in step with others. This may, in fact, be a boon to humanity as trailblazers and heroes emerge from each cohort group to renew hope for the common person seeking the most out of life.

As we begin to look at development during the middle years, it is well to remember that the differences we perceive over time are just as likely to be cohort differences as age changes.

Development in the Middle Years

Relatively few theorists have attempted to define specific developmental stages of middle age. The most basic theoretical foundations are derived from the work of Peck, Erikson (1963), Jung, Bühler, Kuhlen, and Neugarten (1968b). Much that marks development in adults takes place within a relatively stable biological system and is constrained or facilitated by historic, cultural, and social parameters (Kimmel). For many, certain milestones or significant events have made a marked impression and formed a fulcrum for a turning point in life (Kimmel). These milestones seem related to interpersonal events or insight experiences. Events that are anticipated do not seem to have the same personal impact as those which happen unexpectedly.

Sutterley and Donnelly have noted the following complexities of development:

Development is complex, and all aspects are closely interrelated.

Development is both quantitative and qualitative.

Different aspects of development occur at different rates.

The tempo of development is not even.

Patterns of development are continually modified by the historical context.

There are crises in development that emerge later with greater force when not satisfactorily resolved at the proper time.

There is an innate tendency for an organism to seek its optimum potential for development.

Individuals develop in their own manner and become more uniquely themselves with increasing age.

A study involving 200 interviews with persons between the ages of 40 and 50 found that people in this age group view that decade of life as containing the most potential for human growth, except for the first decade. By the age of 40, most people have experienced themselves as learners, lovers, and mourners, and they feel self-assured and confident in most situations. They rely on experience now, rather than instinct. Yet this is also seen as a crisis-ridden period, with the potential for a personal renaissance by age 50 (Davitz and Davitz). See Figure 13-1.

Stability and power are major themes of adult development. Sociologists have pointed out that in traditional agrarian societies the elders held power, while in modern industrial societies the power, wealth, and influence are concentrated among the middle-aged (Hunt and Hunt). They are the norm bearers and the decision makers, and though we live in a society oriented to youth, it is controlled by the middle-aged (Neugarten, 1968a). Much of the youth subculture is a direct response to this situation. Keeping one's sense of perspective in a youth-oriented society is certainly one of the vague but important tasks of middle age. If, indeed, the middle-aged are responsible for social norms, then the cultivation of youth orientation must be approved by the power group.

Kaluger and Kaluger make the point that in early life growth tends to be vertical, upward, and forward. This is the stance of our society as well, but we need roots to nourish the growth process. Personally and culturally, the mature years are the time of weaving an ever more intricate network of roots below the surface of our lives if we wish to sustain life and growth (Johnson).

Figure 13-1   Self-portrait of a middle-aged man.

Adult development can be viewed from a social systems perspective, in light of a mechanistic model, a perceptual-cognitive-motivational model, a behavioral model, or an ecological model. In the mechanistic model, the individual is a task-oriented, performing organism. According to the perceptual-cognitive-motivational model, it is that which goes on inside the head that counts. The behavioral model is concerned with overt behavior in natural environments and with the effects of negative and positive reinforcement. In the social systems approach, the environment and behavior are so intertwined as to be almost inseparable. Recent emphasis on ecological systems identifies the mutual, dual impact between the individual and the environment (Altman). None of the models, however, is sufficient to give a holistic view of the individual. This chapter and those which follow will present a view of development that considers an adult as transcending theoretical parameters and as potentially self-transcendent.

A man views his development as follows:

When I was a kid, I thought I would live forever. At 47, I feel my mortality keenly. The "mort" in mortality relates to death. I think about death frequently, and I accept the fact that it will happen to me in the subjective near future. I'm not fearful of the prospect.

When I was 16, which seems a significant age—more so than 21—I had plans, dreams, and visions. Now, I still have plans, but they are shorter-range and more "realistic," perhaps. Now I expect neither fame nor fortune. The chance of either, I realize, is remote. About the only aspect of my own youth that I am disappointed to be without is the trim, hard physique, which has given way to overweight and "out of shape" that will probably always be my lot from now on.

I notice with regret that I am not desirable to the pretty young girls, as I once was—and that's too bad because in most ways I'm a better man than I ever was.

I feel responsible for so many people's lives now; when I was younger, I'm sure I was selfish and had no one's welfare to worry about but my own. My children are grown, but all of them still seem to need me in some way—at least they need my approval.

My sex drive is still strong, but perhaps I'm less aggressive, and I'm often happy simply to go to sleep. And I'm less self-centered in that regard, too.

But mainly, I feel keenly that there is little *time* left. In another decade or so, I'll be 60—and *everyone* knows that 60 is too old to do youthful things. I want to sail around the world, and I regret that I'll be 60 when I'm able financially to do so.

Looking back at my accomplishments, I see nothing significant. *A lot of work, which, really, was of little consequence in the large scheme of things.* I'm well respected in my own small town, in my field, but there has really been no contribution of note to shout about—and, realistically, probably there never will be. And there is the big difference. When I was 16, I thought surely I'd make my mark someday.

Although I've always been a materialist, oddly, I've little material wealth to show: a small business, struggling along from day to day to meet its obligations, and a relatively meager net worth.

But I'm an optimist and a striver, and life has never been dull—and I expect it never will be. I feel prepared to meet any challenge that might present itself, and generally I expect to "come out on top."

I'm still dealing with tomorrow, rather than reminiscing about the past. Men my age are generally the dominant group. My contemporaries are the power figures in the community, although that seems to depend largely on the individual person's reliability and conservatism. Those who stayed put and plodded along generally have the greatest accumulation of power and/or wealth. Those who looked for greener pastures and took the chances generally are less well-heeled. Native intelligence and drive really seem to have less effect on the final result.

How do I feel about middle age? I accept it. I know that it is the inevitable successor of youth. I accept also the inevitability of old age, if I am fortunate enough to reach it. And I have a vision of my own old age: I see myself enjoying new people and foreign places, good food and wine, and the companionship of my old mate—reminiscing, perhaps, with pictures and shared anecdotes in a comfortable situation. Time is fleeting—I expect it soon. See Figure 13-2.

Figure 13-2   A couple walking down the street, arm in arm. (*Courtesy of Pat Ryan.*)

This man's account embodies the developmental issues that most frequently emerge during the middle years:

1. The need to do something significant in the world (Erikson's [1963] concept of generativity
2. An awareness of the gentle component of his nature (Jung—the emergence of the anima)
3. A cultivation of wisdom, relationships, and flexibility (Peck)
4. Growth and expansion (Kuhlen)
5. The subjective speed of time (Wallach and Green)
6. Introspection (Bühler)
7. The salient themes of work, love, time, changes in self-concept, and death (Neugarten, 1968b)

But there is more to this man: an undergirding *joie de vivre*.
What of his wife? Here is her account:

> When I was very young, my grandmother lived with us. She seemed very old, and I loved her very much. I believe this relationship removed most of my fear of growing old, but nothing prepared me for the fact it would happen so soon! It seems that each phase of my life has passed before I fully enjoyed it, and while I look back, I'm moved into another age group. I don't see signs of my maturity within myself, but rather through the people around me. Suddenly the children are *grand*children; my little sister is in her mid-forties.
>
> The telltale signs of an aging body I bitterly resent. It seemed amusing when my older sister had to remove her glasses for close work; it doesn't seem funny now. I didn't realize I could feel so heavy until I tried to show a child how to jump rope. I hear myself saying more often, "I used to . . ." because I can't now. My own mother's vigorous good health makes me feel young again when I'm with her, but it also gives me a kind of disorientation as to my present role.
>
> There are advantages to maturity. I am more self-confident and have more confidence in my mate. I wouldn't wish to be young again, but I wish I could hold back time a little now.

As Bardwick has observed, a woman's development is more closely tied to the ebb and flow of interpersonal relationships than a man's development is. Self-esteem is tied less to accomplishment and more to affiliation, especially among women who are strongly socialized to the stereotyped feminine role (Kimmel). For some women, the manner in which others perceive them is a strong motivating factor through their adult years (Bardwick). By and large, women deal with the same issues as men: shifting time orientation, body monitoring,[1] and appropriate age-role behavior. Neugarten (1968a) states that women are more inclined to define their age status by the timing of events within the family cycle and are more concerned with monitoring their husband's health than their own, since they are aware of the possibility of widowhood.

---

[1] This is an awareness of body nuances and is not necessarily hypochondria (Neugarten, 1968a).

Peck (1964, pp. 88–92) has identified the following characteristics as desirable in the middle-aged person:

Cathectic or emotional flexibility. "The capacity to shift emotional investments from one person to another and from one activity to another" (p. 89)

Mental flexibility. The capacity to use experience and prior mental sets as guides, rather than inflexible rules, in the solution of new problems

Ego differentiation. The capacity to pursue and to enjoy a varied set of major activities in life and not to rely entirely on one or two life roles

Body transcendence. The capacity to feel whole and happy because of one's social and mental powers and to avoid preoccupation with health, physique, and bodily comfort

Ego transcendence. The capacity to engage in a direct and gratifying manner with the people and events of daily life, with a strong concern for the well-being of others rather than for self-centered desires

Body satisfaction. Satisfaction with one's own body

Sexual integration. The capacity to mesh one's sexual desires with other aspects of life, such as affection for the sexual partner, and the ability to integrate sexual and other motivations in social relationships

Stability and flexibility. The capacity to adhere to one's values and still be open to new ideas

GENERATIVITY

One cannot look at middle age without examining the concept of generativity introduced by Erikson (1963). The conflict centers around the issue of ego-interest expansion versus increasing self-centeredness and stagnation (Peck). Generating ideas, values, policies, and products that transcend individual need provides the route to further development and satisfaction. Creativity flowers with the fertilizer of experience. When development is stalled by overwhelming life situations, transcendence may be sought through drugs, alcohol, frenetic activity, and sexual escapades. Ideally, people would recognize the ebb and flow of development and allow themselves times of retreat as well as times of productivity. All the tasks of the stages preceding the stage of generativity (maintaining trust, autonomy, initiative, industry, identity, and intimacy) continually reemerge for further refinement and understanding as one continues to develop. Our lives are not a house we are building but rather an orchestra we are conducting. Sometimes the music is full and resounding, and at other times we hear only the faint sound of a piccolo; it is the overall composition that provides joy and enrichment.

Stage theories, such as those of Erikson (1963), Peck, and Havighurst, all reflect our own culture and our time in history, and resolution is tied to successful socialization. If we are to identify any universal psychosocial developmental stages, we must do a great deal more cross-cultural research.

NEED SATISFACTION

Satisfaction of needs is a fundamental motivator toward development. Maslow's conceptual framework defines a hierarchy of needs that is useful in understanding an individual's focus of physical and psychic energy. See Figure 13-3. Generally, in mid-life one has provided for the basic needs and can focus on the areas of self-esteem and self-actualization. However, one never maintains a position on the pinnacle; there are always ups and downs. Kuhlen has outlined sources of frustration in meeting certain needs: (1) the status accorded to members of certain age groups in our society, (2) economic demands (these are particularly great during the thirties and early forties), (3) physical problems, (4) skill deficits brought about by rapid technological advances, and (5) commitments and life circumstances which make one feel boxed in or which limit one's freedom to move, thus instilling feelings of helplessness.

COMPONENTS OF THE SELF-VIEW

From Kimmel's viewpoint, individuals develop because of "I" perceptions that become incorporated into various "me's." The "me's" include roles, sexual identity, status, competencies, and personal views of the self incorporated from

Figure 13-3 Maslow's hierarchy of needs.

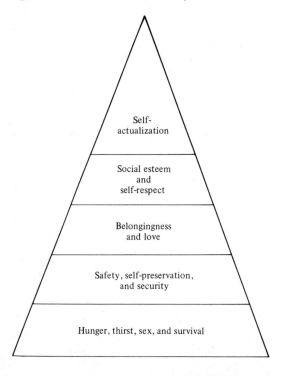

the numerous interactions with significant others through time. This is an inter-actionist view of development drawn from the theories of George Herbert Mead. Obviously, the more important people in one's life influence one's self-view the most. At this point, it may be interesting to see how young adults view their middle-aged parents.

The Self-View and Intergenerational Exchange

"My father is thinking of death and dying and is suffering from 'old soldier's syndrome'—he wants me to send him to an old soldier's home if he ever becomes debilitated and dependent." This young adult heard the ambivalence in her father's pleas and assured him that since he had taken care of her when she was dependent, she wanted to do the same for him if he became dependent.

One young adult was amazed at her parents' ability to expand their viewpoint and support her right to an interracial marriage. A high school student gained new understanding of her parents' coping capacity and love when they gave her the support she needed during an extramarital pregnancy, without overwhelming her with their attention.

A college student was instrumental in helping her mother define her educational goals and return to college.

Another young adult astutely perceived that her father's rages and insults were a cover for his fears concerning his children and for his inability to express his own tender feelings.

One mother attempted to have her oldest daughter act as a parent to younger siblings. When the daughter brought this to her attention, they arrived at a realistic resolution of the problem.

Intergenerational Support

According to data obtained from students in family nursing classes at San Francisco State University, many middle-aged women identify strongly with their adult daughters, to the neglect of their own identity as mature women. Mothers are most often sought for advice and wisdom, and fathers are frequently excluded from these intimate exchanges. If the couple's relationship is unsat-isfactory, the daughter may become the father's confidante.

The reciprocity of understanding between young adults and middle-aged parents was frequently mentioned by these students. In the case of young adults without parents, a parental surrogate was often identified, giving credence to the notion that young people need mentors and times of sharing with those in the middle years. See discussion of mentors in Chapter 12. When parents were able to share their concerns and worries, this seemed to have a significant impact on the young adults' awareness of middle age.

Comparison with Cohorts

Another aspect of the individual's self-view is the way in which he or she is perceived by contemporaries. Personality "fit" (age-appropriate behavior) at a given age is defined by social time clocks (Neugarten, Moore, and Lowe). However, age constraints seem to be more influential during young adulthood than later in life (Troll). Late parenthood is becoming increasingly common in this age of extended education. Following are the reflections of a friend who married and had her family in mid-life:

> Marrying late gives you ample time to "sow your wild oats." This is an important feature for the man as well as the woman. Both seem more willing to settle down and be faithful to one person, which is a good emotional foundation for a marriage. You don't suffer from the "Gee, I may have missed something" syndrome. Becoming parents late in life is an absolute blessing. I have had time to "do my thing," and I feel willing and delighted to spend time with my children. I don't feel cheated by having to take them with me or having to stay at home with them. We do not feel the financial stress that younger parents might. We can provide material advantages, as well as love and attention, that will allow our children to develop to their fullest potential. Finally, having children after 35 somehow keeps parents young longer. We go sledding, ice skating, and swimming, for example, which we would not do if we didn't have young children. We enjoy the association with the young parents of our children's school friends.

It appears from these observations that some "off-time" events do not detract from enjoyment but actually enhance satisfaction. Conversely, off-time events that align one with a group of people older than oneself may be harder to bear;

Figure 13-4 "Me" in the future—at 90?

Figure 13-5 "Me" when I'm old—75? "I have always wanted to be elegant but have never quite had the time. When I am old I will be elegant."

women who are widowed early and men who involuntarily retire early offer prime examples of this. (See Chapters 18 and 19.)

When my friend's second child started school, I was celebrating my twenty-fifth wedding anniversary. When one begins to mark the events of life by the quarter century, the impact of the passage of time is felt with great force. Some couples use this occasion to renew their marriage vows. One friend even wore her wedding dress, with some pride! Little has been written about the importance of anniversary celebrations except in terms of pathological reactions. Traditional time markers may provide occasions that stimulate reflection, introspection and evaluation of meaning rather than task accomplishment.

PREPARATION FOR OLD AGE

Many have concluded that development in the middle years is the presager of old age. It is as if living the middle years well ensures that one will have a gratifying old age. See Figures 13-4, 13-5, and 13-6. However, it appears quite likely that the funds to support our old age will have disappeared long before we need them, and we can anticipate a longer life and higher medical bills. We may be employed longer, because of either desire or necessity. There will be more opportunities for advanced education when we are old. The middle-aged and older adults are being courted, as the youths vacate the campuses (Reiner). Cain believes that we will demand more "things," since we have been materialistically "spoiled." More people will be alone, with more leisure time, and thus there is the potential for creative pursuits or overwhelming loneliness. Our political power bloc will start to crumble as the children of the "baby boom" (following World War II) move into middle age. They presently constitute 37 percent of the voting-age population in the United States ("The Voting Population and Presidential Elections"). Those between ages 45 and 64 at present constitute only 29 percent.

The environment will have a greater influence over our options than it has in the past. Our energy expenditure and our living space may be considerably limited by scarcity of resources (Moos). Different needs of people at various points in the life cycle may result in incongruous living situations because of natural, socioeconomic, political, and environmental design.

It seems that the key to a satisfactory old age lies in the maximum development

Figure 13-6 "Readin' and rockin.'"

of a wide variety of intrapersonal and interpersonal sources of satisfaction during the middle years. Successful adaptation now affects not only our own present and future but also the quality of life of those generations before and after us. Middle age is not a thing apart but a part of the whole.

Guidelines for Development during the Middle Years

Diekelmann has suggested the following guidelines for development during the middle years:

Free psychic and physical energy by maintaining some comfortable routines.
Limit responsibility for older and younger generations.
Take time out for introspection and self-renewal.
Develop some new friendships and interests.
Nurture physical well-being.
Develop an awareness of a network of resources to be used when needed.
Seek anticipatory guidance concerning the needs of aged parents.
Assess values and goals for relevance to the present situation.
Prepare for the future intellectually, emotionally, and economically.
Trust intuition as well as intellect.

REFERENCES

Altman, Irwin: *The Environment and Social Behavior,* Brooks/Cole, Monterey, Calif., 1975.

Bardwick, Judith: *Psychology of Women,* Harper & Row, New York, 1971.

Bühler, C.: "The Human Course of Life in Its Goal Aspects," *Journal of Humanistic Psychology,* **4**(1):1–18, 1964.

Cain, Leonard: "Creative Life Styles," paper presented at a meeting of the Western Gerontological Society, Denver, 1977.

Chew, Peter: *The Inner World of the Middle Aged Man,* Macmillan, New York, 1976.

Davitz, Joel, and **Lois Davitz:** *Making It from 40 to 50,* Random House, New York, 1976.

Diekelmann, Nancy: "Health Care in the Middle Years," paper presented at the Colorado Nurses' Convention, Vail, August 1976.

Erikson, Erik: *Childhood and Society,* 2d ed., Norton, New York, 1963.

——: *Life Historically and the Historical Moment,* Norton, New York, 1975.

Havighurst, Robert: *Developmental Tasks and Education,* McKay, New York, 1972.

Hunt, Bernice, and **Morton Hunt:** *Prime Time,* Stein and Day, New York, 1975.

Huyck, Margaret: *Growing Older,* Prentice-Hall, Englewood Cliffs, N.J., 1944.

Jacobi, Jolande: *The Psychology of C. G. Jung,* Yale, New Haven, Conn., 1973.

Johnson, Walter: Personal communication, August 1977.

Jung, Carl G.: "The Stages of Life," tr. by

R. F. C. Hull, in J. Campbell (ed.), *The Portable Jung,* Viking, New York, 1971.

Kaluger, George, and **Meriem Kaluger:** *Human Development: The Life Span,* Mosby, St. Louis, 1974.

Kimmel, Douglas: *Adulthood and Aging,* Wiley, New York, 1974.

Kuhlen, Raymond: "Developmental Changes in Motivation during the Adult Years," in Bernice Neugarten (ed.), *Middle Age and Aging,* University of Chicago Press, Chicago, 1968.

Maslow, Abraham: *Toward a Psychology of Being,* Van Nostrand, Princeton, N.J., 1962.

Mead, George Herbert: "Mind, Self and Society," in Anselm Strauss (ed.), *George Herbert Mead: On Social Psychology,* University of Chicago Press, Chicago, 1964.

Moos, Rudolf: *The Human Context: Environmental Determinants of Behavior,* Wiley, New York, 1976.

Neugarten, Bernice: *Personality in Middle and Late Life: Empirical Studies,* Atherton, New York, 1964.

———: "The Awareness of Middle Age," in B. Neugarten (ed.), *Middle Age and Aging,* University of Chicago Press, Chicago, 1968(a).

———: "Toward a Psychology of the Life Cycle," in B. Neugarten (ed.), *Middle*

Age and Aging, University of Chicago Press, Chicago, 1968(b).

Neugarten, Bernice, Joan Moore, and **John Lowe:** "Age Norms, Age Constraints, and Adult Socialization," in B. Neugarten (ed.), *Middle Age and Aging,* University of Chicago Press, Chicago, 1968.

Peck, Robert: "Psychological Developments in the Second Half of Life," in B. Neugarten (ed.), *Middle Age and Aging,* University of Chicago Press, Chicago, 1968.

Reiner, Steven: "Back to School at 35," *Mainliner,* **21**(10):57–59, 1977.

Sarton, May: "Letters to a Psychiatrist: Letter 5," in *Collected Poems,* Norton, New York, 1974.

Simm, Eleanor: Personal communication, 1977.

Sutterley, Doris, and **Gloria Donnelly:** *Perspectives in Human Development: Nursing throughout the Life Cycle,* Lippincott, Philadelphia, 1973.

Troll, Lillian: *Early and Middle Adulthood: The Best Is Yet to Be—Maybe,* Brooks/Cole, Monterey, Calif., 1975.

"The Voting Population and Presidential Elections," *Metropolitan Life Statistical Bulletin,* **57**:4, October 1976.

Wallach, Michael, and **Leonard Green:** "On Age and the Subjective Speed of Time," *Journal of Gerontology,* **16**(1):71–74, 1961.

OTHER RESOURCES

BOOK

Lanson, Lucienne: *From Woman to Woman,* Knopf, New York, 1975. A self-help book of questions and answers for lay people of all ages.

FILMS

A Brand New Life: 16 mm/74 min/color. A film about a middle-aged couple preparing for their first child. Rental, $60; lease, $600. Distributor: Learning Corporation of America, 1350 Avenue of the Americas, New York, N.Y. 10019.

Tell Me Where It Hurts: 16 mm/78 min/color. Focuses on a middle-aged housewife who is groping for recognition as a person. Distributor: Learning Corporation of America, 1350 Avenue of the Americas, New York, N.Y. 10019.

Chapter 14

CARE GIVING IN THE MIDDLE YEARS
Priscilla Ebersole

> I dreamed I was planting small plots of corn at two-week
> intervals throughout the year in order to provide a
> continuous supply of grain to consumers. I felt
> great satisfaction in being able to do this.
>
> *Dream of a 50-year-old man*

> Corn, among the ancient Indians, symbolized the life force
> and continuity of life.

> Among the Guatemalans, corn is viewed as the mythical
> father of life.

Sometime after the age of 35, one comes to the realization that the main function of the middle years is caring, in its broadest sense, and that this expanded concern includes more than family and friends. Ideally, one has the energy to care for one's neighbor, the community and its institutions, the nation, and the world. There are so many people and so many things to be cared for. How to expend one's loving energies appropriately becomes a serious dilemma. *The capacity for caring with which we are endowed may become short-circuited as a result of an overload.* Inequities and sham may severely shake our confidence in the institutionalized structures that are meant to assist in the caring functions. Many individuals have abandoned the cause and joined the cynics in repeating that caring in its ultimate sense is self-serving.

Caring probably is self-serving. Gaylin has made a convincing case concerning the inherent capacity and need for caring built into each human being. If one strives toward self-actualization, the need to care cannot be neglected. The very anxiety generated by our aggressive instincts suggests an inner core of compassion. The tendency to overemphasize the hostile, territorial, and aggressive aspects of human behavior implies uneasiness with them. These traits are also easier to identify, measure, and assess scientifically. Compassion, love, concern, commitment, and caring are often measured on an intuitive level, and the varied expressions of these components of human nature are learned through identification. The human being is very flexible and will develop the inherent capacities most cultivated in the society. Obviously, cultural models are incorporated. Fromm (1977) believes that the psychological premises of industrialism, which regard maximum individual happiness and selfish indulgence as basic human goals, are not sufficient for humanistic development.

According to Gaylin, we have rejected ourselves as a species, viewing the failure of our technology to produce the remedies for the human dilemmas of the world. We have a sense of impotent rage, abandonment of meaning, unworthiness, and failure. The inability to love ourselves as a species has profound effects on our capacity to care for one another. We are in an age of disillusionment. We have relinquished our individual care-giving capacity in deference to state controls, and we are disappointed with the results. Stripped of our faith in the individual's concern for others and of the opportunity to communicate through giving and taking on an individual basis, we feel diminished.

Identification with, and loyalty to, societal groups and institutions ensures public safety and group caring; however, as institutions grow, they begin to generate power, and the caring function is sometimes lost. What is the answer? Since cultural models and institutional structures are controlled largely by the middle-aged, this chapter will examine caring and commitment as they relate to family, work roles, and society in general.

CARING DURING THE MIDDLE YEARS

Troll (1975) questions whether there are systematic changes in the desires to be powerful, to get close to others, to achieve, to take care of others, and to be taken care of by others. In middle age the need to be helped is weak, and the need to help others is strong, according to Kimmel and Stein. Is "helping" caring? Mayerhoff says that there are two kinds of caring: the kind that allows something or someone to emerge independent of the care giver and the reciprocal caring that implies a continued exchange of care and commitment in a mutually supportive manner. The first kind of caring is given from a position of strength to assist a person or a thing toward maturity; the second kind is a sustaining, growing exchange between equals, each actualizing the other when possible.

Adults are usually in both positions: caring for those ideas and people in society which need nurturance and maintaining reciprocal relationships of commitment and mutual growth. In stressful circumstances adults may regress to needing more care than they are able to give. These are the times when sensitive institutional care givers are most needed.

Another viewpoint on caring is particularly pertinent to health professionals. In medicine there is a propensity toward "curing." However, if we substitute an "a" for the "u," "curing" becomes "caring"; the difference lies in doing as opposed to being (Johnson). Even if we cannot always cure, we can always care. May says: "Care is a state in which something does matter; care is the opposite of apathy. Life comes from physical survival; but the good life comes from what we care about" (p. 164).

Several goals of adulthood are achieved through the caring process: the goals of being worthy and loved, of being strong and superior, and of being good and loving (Gaylin).

Care giving has progressed through several phases historically; it has been ascetic, romantic, pragmatic, and holistic (Bevis). All these styles may be seen in various care givers at present.

1. The *ascetic,* who practices self-denial, may give excellent care but be unable or unwilling to care for himself or herself.
2. The *romantic* has a feeling of missionary zeal and an ebullient love of mankind. This diffuse caring may be difficult to translate into action on the individual level.
3. The *pragmatist* meets his or her own needs and the needs of others on a practical level.
4. The *holist* demonstrates the highest level of caring, which involves acceptance; nurturance; allowing others the freedom to find their own way and to make their own mistakes and resolutions; the sensitivity to provide support to those who need someone to lean on temporarily; and the wisdom to allow himself or herself to seek respite from the nurturance of others when this is needed.

We all have the need to care for others and to be cared for in reciprocity. The proportions and intensity are, doubtlessly, continually in flux. An energy-exchange model may be a useful construct if not carried to extremes. For example, the following trite statements may be a hindrance in providing care:

"You can't give love from an empty bucket."
"There isn't enough caring in the world to fill her needs—she's just like a sieve."

At this stage in human evolution we poorly understand the energy sources of the body, and we are even less knowledgeable concerning those of the psyche. Gaylin contends that a basic human energy source is the core of supreme love within our nature.

The previous discussion notwithstanding, most caring behavior comes back to the pragmatic—how to care and be cared for within the family, the work situation, and the community. Jung and Erikson (1959) suggest that our capacity for caring normally begins to expand from a small epicenter, becoming larger and ever more diffuse until our commitment to others becomes more universal than personal. In the natural course of events, people lose individuals with more frequency as they proceed through adult life, and therefore this tendency may be in the service of adaptation and ego function. Thus we have arrived back at the point where we can say that caring is self-serving in a most fundamental way.

The following are some final comments on caring:

1. Erikson (1969) analyzes the changes that Gandhi went through between age 35 and age 50 in caring for the adversary through nonviolent opposition and conflict (a good description of the interaction between many middle-aged couples!) and adds that Gandhi's was an advanced moral position, hard to arrive at before age 40 (Chew).
2. Intensity of interaction may indicate a high level of caring, just as passivity may indicate a degree of noncaring.
3. The capacity for caring varies among individuals and within each individual during the life-span.
4. The intensity of caring may diminish with distance—geographic and emotional—and with the passage of time.

Middle age is the time when care-giving demands are broadest. The young adult, the adolescent, the parent, and, with increasing frequency, the grandparent occupy the concern of the middle-aged. In addition to intimates, the mature adult cares for the community and its institutions. He or she is responsible for providing the largest portion of the social system's goods, services, and monetary and moral support. By and large, responsibility for the maintenance of any technological culture resides with the middle-aged. The replenishment necessary to carry out this responsibility comes from interaction with family, friends, social organizations, and vocational settings. This chapter will discuss all these areas of potential satisfaction and dissatisfaction.

FAMILY FUNCTION

The notion of the modern family as an isolated, vulnerable nuclear unit is not supported by the research (Bengtson and Black; Rose; Shanas, Townsend, Wedderburn, Friis, Milhøj, and Stethouwer). Affluence and mobility have resulted in separate dwellings for nuclear families, but the generations exchange support in many ways. See Figure 14-1. In fact, the nuclear family may not be the best living arrangement for the male, the female, or the children, although it is certainly the most manageable in a society bent on expediency (Prock). Several studies seem to demonstrate the need for contact with the older and younger generations, and some distinct patterns emerge. For instance, during the middle years married couples are less likely to live near their relatives than are single, widowed, or divorced people (Gibson). Parents tend to remain closer to daughters than to sons, and when they are old they are more likely to move in with daughters (Adams, 1971; Schorr; Troll, 1971). In general, working-class couples live closer to their relatives than middle-class couples. Adams (1968) points out that middle-class careers are more likely to require geographic mobility than the jobs of the working class.

Figure 14-1 The generations exchange support in many ways, as this photograph shows. Note the family pet observing. (*Courtesy of Pat Ryan.*)

Three-fourths of the young married adults in Hill's et al. three-generation study saw their parents weekly, and 40 percent of the middle-aged people in the study saw their parents weekly. The strongest supportive linkage between generations usually follows the female line (Adams, 1971; Leichter and Mitchell), and, in contrast to popular belief, urban families visit each other more than those in rural areas (Bultema). Even though there are many variables not identified in these studies, the important fact is that family members continue to demonstrate concern and care for one another even when they do not live together.

A middle-aged couple's family unit often consists of adolescents and/or young adults and the parenting couple. Educational expenses and the children's romances may be stressful to the couple, but problems with aging parents can be more distressing than those with children (Diekelmann). Bischof states that the greatest problems faced by the middle-aged couple are opposition to their children's marriages and provision of care for aged parents. The couple often feel caught between the needs of their children and the needs of their parents (LeShan).

MARITAL SATISFACTION

Because of internal and external pressures, mid-life seems to be a time of dissatisfaction with marriage. In one study, 21 percent of the women who had been married 20 years or longer were very dissatisfied with their marriages, and this was reflected in dissatisfaction with all other areas of their lives as well (Blood and Wolfe). The least satisfied middle-aged couples are those with teen-agers still in the home. After the children leave home, there tends to be more marital satisfaction, and for those who remain married it tends to increase (Deutscher). At ages 40 and 50, both men and women rank companionship and understanding as the most important aspects of marriage. Sexual relations and being a parent are ranked third and fourth, with men ranking sexual relations before parenting, and with women ranking them in the reverse order (Clausen).

It seems that middle-aged couples who remain together either experience a renewal of intimacy in a "second honeymoon" phase or develop a satisfactory relationship based on needs and expectations that are different from those of the earlier years (Blood and Wolfe; Feldman). Pineo found that after 20 years there is a "cooling off," or "unmatching" factor, resulting in decreases in compan-ionship, sexual relations, and demonstrations of affection. The interactions of the couples in Pineo's study were markedly different from what they had been in earlier years, and the couples talked more about objective things than about subjective things; they were also more sober and sedentary in their interactions (Feldman). All the findings cited must be viewed in terms of cohort and class differences and may not be applicable generally, especially in times of such rapid social change.

Older couples often live under conditions that younger people would not tolerate, but divorces in all age groups are increasing in the United States and will probably continue to do so as individuals see more options available to them. Bernard calls attention to the fact that the postparental stage of marriage is a brand-new phenomenon in human history. Few couples lived long enough in the past to spend many years together after the children were grown. We are just now beginning to recognize the importance of this wholly new form of marriage; its potentials for satisfaction have hardly been explored. Many people, from a religious or species-propagation perspective, view marriage as related primarily to reproduction rather than to pleasure. A new sexual, intellectual, and emotional companionship can develop when there is no longer the need for a child-focused family life. Gould found that people in their late forties and fifties increasingly seek affection and sympathy from their spouses as they experience shared personal losses and changes in status; deep sorrow can have as much meaning in their relationship as joy. Peer partnership develops for some couples as they engage in new vocational or creative pursuits. The Hunts and the O'Neills have written books together. Many couples share creative pursuits.

For some couples the transition to the postparental stage results in serious deterioration of the marriage. They may have grown so distinctively in different directions that there is little left to share. When the normal distractions of family life are reduced, they are faced with the vast chasm between them. Divorce can mean liberation; however, as one psychologist (Pike) put it, a couple who have raised a family together may get a divorce, but they are never truly separated.

Thurner found distinct differences in the way males and females view marriage in the middle years. In a comparison of young newlyweds, couples facing the departure of the last child, and couples facing retirement, it was found that the middle-aged women gave the least positive evaluations of marriage. Middle-aged men focused on their wives' performance as wives and mothers, while middle-aged women were likely to focus on their spouses' personal or behavioral idiosyncrasies; also, they invariably talked of their husbands' role as provider and parent. Most of those couples hoped there would be greater closeness after the children left home.

From the perspective of women, marital satisfaction tends to be lowest during the period preceding the launching of the children. The middle-aged partners may be out of phase in terms of their dominant careers: the man's is growing or reaching a plateau, while the woman's is abating or coming to an end. This incongruence seems to be more taxing to women than to men, as are the disagreement and friction that often accompany having teenage children in the home. Data indicate that middle-aged men's perceptions of spouse and children are closely intertwined; women are more likely to evaluate the two relationships independently. From this study it was concluded that the persons most likely to be dissatisfied with their spouses are women who have difficulty carrying out conventional feminine roles and men who feel that family responsibilities and pressures have hindered the pursuit of their personal goals (Thurner).

RELATIONSHIPS WITH CHILDREN

The young adult's struggle for identity and independence (Erikson, 1959) is hard on family life, but maturing children also provide much satisfaction. The Hunts have stated that it can be most gratifying to share one's experience and judgment with grown children. As noted in Chapter 12, however, the experience and judgment of the middle-aged may not be particularly relevant to the needs of today's young adults. Streib points out that parents of adult children place greater emphasis on their ties with the children than the children place on their ties with the parents.

Parents with a planned agenda for their children's vocational or educational pursuits usually face disappointment. The man who has invested his life in a family business with the hope of passing it on to his son may find that the son is prepared to go in an entirely different direction (Diekelmann).

As children grow up, the intensity of their identification with the parents decreases, but for parents it is quite the opposite. There is a continually growing sense of identification as the child becomes an adult and begins to parallel the parent's own experience. Same-sex identification is usually the strongest. The more the parent gives, sacrifices, or relates to the child, the greater the strength of the identification (Gaylin). For some, the adult child represents a second chance to accomplish what the parent has been denied.

The relationship with married children requires tact, judgment, and an appropriate distance. Mothers seem to have far more difficulty with this task than fathers, perhaps because of strong feelings of maternal devotion. It may be difficult for them to understand that young couples need to solve their own problems and establish their own identity as a couple (LeShan).

The task is much more complex for those middle-aged parents who may be called upon to adjust to their children's entering into homosexual relationships, interracial marriages, communal life-styles, and alliances sans marriage. Considerable flexibility and understanding are needed to accept the partners in these new life-styles, since the generational changes have been so rapid and young people may have their own unique set of values; however, many researchers have found more similarities in values and personality between young adults and their parents than among similar people of the same generation (Bengtson and Black; Kalish and Johnson; Troll, Neugarten, and Kraines). This may indicate that "changes over the adult years are masked by historic shifts that have led to similar value changes in all adults living at that same time" (Troll, 1975, p. 48). In spite of age and cohort shifts in values and attitudes, it seems that family effects are most pervasive.

GRANDPARENTING

Since the early 1900s most people have become grandparents at a younger age (Neugarten and Weinstein). Recent statistics (Troll, 1975) show some reversal of this trend (since Neugarten's studies) and indicate that couples are marrying later and deferring parenthood or rejecting it altogether. Presently, however, many middle-aged couples become grandparents at a time when they can fully enjoy the experience; their health is good, their energy level is high, and they are financially secure. See Figure 14-2. However, middle-aged women who are pursuing their own interests may be irritated by expectations that they will assist in the care of the grandchildren (Troll, 1975). The feeling level toward grandchildren seems to be influenced by sex linkage. Maternal grandmothers and paternal grandfathers are closer to grandchildren than maternal grandfathers and paternal grandmothers (Kahana and Kahana).

Grandparenting is one of the tasks of most middle-aged couples, and Neugarten and Weinstein have identified five specific coping styles: (1) formal, (2) fun seeker, (3) surrogate parent, (4) reservoir of family wisdom, and (5) distant figure.

1. *Formal.* The grandparents provide occasional services and special treats. Parental roles are not assumed.
2. *Fun seekers.* The grandparents indulge the grandchildren and enjoy pleasurable activities with them.
3. *Surrogate parent.* The grandparents assume the role of the parents, as when the mother works or the parents are ill.

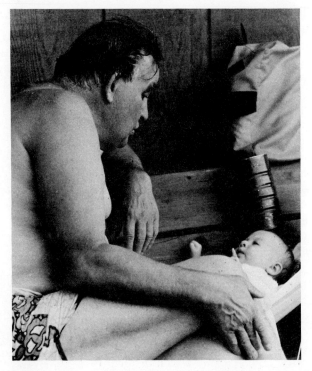

Figure 14-2 Grandparents in the present cohort of middle-aged couples may enjoy the grandparenting role because of good health, high energy level, and financial security. (*Courtesy of Pat Ryan.*)

4. *Reservoir of family wisdom.* The grandparents—particularly the grandfather—share experience and teach special skills.
5. *Distant figure.* The grandparents are seen infrequently on holidays or other ritual occasions; they assume a benevolent role.

Middle-aged grandparents characteristically adopt the fun-seeker style.

Grandparenting may fluctuate between trial and delight and often provides an opportunity to do what one was unable to do as a parent.

An important function of grandparenthood emerges as older family members die; then the middle generation assumes the responsibility for maintaining family traditions and history. This is an especially significant task in these times of rootlessness and rapid change. Duvall says that a family's emotional, intellectual, cultural, biological, material, and personal legacies continue through a generational spiral. This preservational task of the middle generation can easily be neglected in deference to more pragmatic concerns.

RELATIONSHIPS WITH AGING PARENTS

Attaining "filial maturity" is considered an ongoing task of middle age and is accomplished when one can see one's parents as individuals rather than in relation to one's own needs (Blenkner). Feelings toward aging parents have not been investigated to the extent that interactional level, residential and aid patterns have been researched. Some time ago Havighurst noted that the last developmental task of middle age is adjusting to aged parents and making life as satisfactory as possible for both generations.

Some patterns of parental care giving have been identified by Robinson and Thurner:

1. Parents-in-law are treated in a more ritualized manner than parents. More women than men bring in-laws into the home; the man's parents usually stay from 2 to 6 months, as compared to 3 to 5 years for the woman's parents.
2. There is some attenuation of filial bonds and obligations upon a parent's remarriage.
3. Assistance is usually in terms of providing services, giving financial aid, doing household chores, obtaining physical and psychological care, and including the parent in family rituals. The death of one parent generally increases the services provided to the remaining parent. Most often, women provide these helping services.
4. Parents who age successfully and happily continue to provide emotional sustenance for middle-aged children, particularly for those who are in precarious marriages or have been recently divorced.
5. There is "evidence of self-protective disengagement from a deteriorating parent, with the perception of the parent shifting from that of an individual to that of an object" (p. 18).
6. Personality changes in the aged bring about defensive behavior such as anger and rejection in the middle-aged; the stresses of care giving may blur or distort previously positive perceptions of the parent.
7. Projections of one's own life expectancy and late-life satisfaction seem to be strongly linked to the circumstances of the parents.
8. When care of a parent has extended over a period of years, there may be a sense of liberation when the parent dies and guilt related to this feeling.

While these findings were drawn from interviews with a select group of middle- and lower-middle-class white couples, the conclusions increase our awareness of the complexity of relationships between the middle-aged and their aged parents. In the vast majority of cases there is close contact between the generations even when they do not reside together (Riley and Foner; Shanas et al.).

The professional helping person can act as advocate for both generations by providing information about community resources that will relieve some of the burdensome aspects of the relationship and free more energy for satisfying interactions. At present, there are far too few community supports for the middle-aged as they attempt to meet the needs of several generations.

EXTENDED FAMILY RELATIONSHIPS

Siblings and other kin provide few consistent support structures for the middle-aged within our culture. Because of the small families that were characteristic of the twenties and thirties, people today between the ages of 40 and 55 probably have only one or two siblings. There have been few studies dealing with the impact of this, and we are left with far more questions than answers. For instance, which sibling is most likely to care for an aged parent? Robinson and Thurner found that birth order is not a factor in this; the data suggest that the least psychologically healthy child suffers the most over the care-giving aspects of providing for parents. Chapter 4 discusses characteristics associated with the various birth-order positions.

We know that birth order has a significant effect on personality and adaptation as one grows up, but sibling significance in adult relationships has been poorly explored (Adler; Toman). There are only vague impressions concerning the effects of siblings on development throughout life.

The impact of sibling death in the middle years is another area in which there are many questions still to be answered. Clinical experience indicates that men experience crisis on the anniversary of a male sibling's death; they may become panicked as they reach the same age or feel guilty if they have surpassed the dead sibling in age and/or accomplishment. These observations cannot be stated as a general trend, however. A care-giving oldest sister may experience each sibling death as a mother that loses a child. While these feelings are irrational, they do have an effect upon one's emotional equilibrium.

Relationships with siblings are rarely as close as those with parents (Young and Willmott). Accomplishment may be measured against that of one's siblings, or one may feel some vicarious sense of pride when a sibling becomes successful (Troll, 1975). In times of crisis or illness, siblings may draw together for support, both economic and emotional. Brothers tend to offer financial aid and to assist in practical arrangements (Lopata). In later life, widowed sisters may establish households together. Brothers often assume some surrogate fathering roles toward the children of divorced or widowed sisters, and in earlier times, when women's legal status was tenuous, they often took physical action against their sisters' abusive spouses (Frey).

Cousins and more distant kin usually appear on ritual occasions, but specific supportive patterns have not been found (Troll, 1975). Many adults have a favorite aunt or uncle, often an early childhood hero or heroine.

NONTRADITIONAL SUPPORT SYSTEMS

There are many life-styles besides that of the conventional family. Some of the following are becoming increasingly visible: the divorced male or female with grown children, the male or female living alone, the middle-aged couple with young children, the couple with children from previous marriages, the homosexual couple, the female "chum" relationship, "swinging" in mid-life, and communal living. Who do these people care for, and who cares for them? Obviously, the answers to these questions will be as varied as the life-styles themselves. When structural supports are less traditional, caring professionals may need to be more readily available. Supports may be less consistent; there may be fewer feelings of obligation and duty and greater feelings of freedom. Some of the more traditional middle-aged people may be envious or rejecting.

The myriad life-styles of young adults are being increasingly adopted by the middle-aged. Are there special problems in these situations unique to those in the middle years? We have heard about the importance of physical attractiveness in some homosexual relationships, which may become a larger concern as one ages. Energy levels may become important as one chooses a more taxing life-style—bringing up young children, coping with teenagers from two sets of parents, or launching young adults by oneself. The age norms and age constraints outlined by Neugarten, Moore, and Lowe may affect these groups adversely if they feel out of step with others of their cohort.

Men and Women Alone

Caring and clustering seem to be basic human needs and responses. What, then, happens to men and women who are alone during the middle years? Single people often experience various forms of discrimination, such as the following:

1. There may be social ostracism from couple functions; an unattached male or female seems to threaten married couples.
2. Sexual availability may be assumed.
3. Restaurant personnel seem loath to seat a single person in a "good" spot. Unescorted women may not be admitted.
4. Single middle-aged men may seek the company of younger women; middle-aged women who date younger men, however, are looked upon askance.
5. Unexpected changes in name or marital status can create consternation among friends and peers.
6. Single same-sexed individuals residing together may be assumed to be homosexual.
7. Family members may expect the single person to be more readily able to provide financial assistance or care for the aged parents because he or she "has fewer responsibilities."
8. "Liberated women" may face hostility from traditional men.
9. Credit policies, particularly for single women, may be more stringent.
10. Insurance rates are higher for single people, particularly life insurance and automobile insurance for men.
11. In rental housing, single middle-aged women are favored.
12. The tax structure penalizes the single person.

An in-depth study would undoubtedly turn up evidence of other types of discrimination, but, superficially, it seems that single people are in a position similar to that of left-handed people: society is not geared to their needs. A nurturing and caring posture toward them seems to be the exception rather than the rule. Being aware of the cultural stigma may give one a more understanding view of single people and their life patterns. Given a reluctant share of nurturance from many directions, how are their needs met?

Work as a Source of Nurturance for Singles

It would seem that single people might expect and give more in the work situation. However, this is not borne out by studies. Irelan and Bond found that married men opt for early retirement much less frequently than single men. This might suggest that single men are less needy, less attached to their work role, or not as healthy as married men. Women often derive little satisfaction from their jobs, since most work in lower-level positions. Their professional opportunities and simple economic need seem to be more important than work as emotional sustenance. The highest work participation rate among all nonmarried women occurs in those aged 45 to 54, and the numbers are increasing (Sheppard).

A new middle-aged woman is emerging, as are opportunities for more satisfying work. Many more women now have the opportunity for a stimulating career. Entine advises women facing unemployment or low job satisfaction to seek part-time employment and use their additional time for public service or recreational pursuits. Many are reentering educational programs and developing new careers. Interestingly, men are also showing an increasing tendency to drop out of the work force partially or fully during the middle years. Many have found that corporations and civil service provide no mechanism for self-actualization, even in the higher echelons (Entine). With the increasing economic burdens of middle age; inflation; and disillusionment with, and lack of trust in, industry, academia, and government, even more may temporarily drop out. Several single women I interviewed said that dissatisfied men have sought a relationship with them to sustain themselves financially and emotionally while they "found" themselves. The women looked on this with a jaundiced eye, saying that they had fought incredible odds to advance in their careers, had learned to live alone and like it, and at that point could do very well without a man in their lives. This is not necessarily a prevailing viewpoint.

Women alone for the first time, as a result of widowhood or divorce, lack the self-assurance that is gained from years of experience in the work world; however, they have experience with a broad range of life activities and a stability of purpose (Entine). Each woman makes the adjustment to a career in a highly individual way, and many succeed in spite of the odds. Women who are basically shy may have trouble "selling" themselves. Choice of a field is crucial, and career counseling may be of help in finding a field of interest with career potential. Women who have devoted the majority of their lives to home and family may find themselves devalued and their ability questioned.

Women who return to work after a long absence find many positions open to them that were previously open only to men; however, there is much "tokenism" in the job world today, and women need a strong self-concept to succeed in such positions.

What sustains men and women who are alone besides work-role commitment? The answers to this question are probably as varied as the individual men and women. Bachelors often value personal freedom and avoid intense involvement; statistics show that they do not thrive as well physically or emotionally as married men (Troll, 1975). The reasons for this are unclear; it may be that men who are the most adaptable, the healthiest, the most psychologically sound, or the least imaginative in terms of life-style are the ones who marry. For women, the reverse seems to be true. Women who have never been married are emotionally and physically stronger than married women, and they are happier (Prock)! They have years of experience with coping alone, and their self-esteem is not as dependent on others as the self-esteem of family-oriented women. Atchley takes a somewhat different position and states that single women may avoid marriage because of a desire to stay close to their families. For these women, the death of the parents may be particularly traumatic.

Single men may have a symbolic family, generally gained through their occupations, in which they serve as mentor (father) to many younger men and women (Levinson, Darrow, Klein, Levinson, and McKee). Some women who have become particularly successful in their fields are emerging as mentors. The caring energies of such men and women are then directed toward the professional advancement of younger people. (See Chapter 12 for discussion of mentors.)

Many single men and women hold a very important position in extended families; they act as role models for children when the parents are unable to do so adequately, they serve as somewhat impartial arbiters in tense family situations, and they often provide an example of a colorful life-style that the other family members can vicariously enjoy. It is not uncommon for them to assume heavy responsibilities for aging parents and, at times, for the families of siblings.

It has been commonly assumed that people who are alone are somehow deficient in their ability to establish and maintain relationships. There are labels for them: the "loner," the "isolate," the "hermit," the "swinger," etc. As long as perpetuation of the species is a strong subliminal goal, society will exert some negative pressure on people who live outside the traditional family, even if this is subtle and even tinged with envy. As our social priorities shift, we may laud the single life-style and denigrate the traditional family. Synanon labels couples who have children "breeders." All this shows only that the assessment of psychological health is more often bound to cultural needs than to individual satisfaction. Men and women who have opted for an "isolated" life-style are well practiced in autonomy and self-reliance by the time they reach their middle years. About 9 percent of older adults in the United States have never married, and while they have missed some of the "good" things of life, they have been spared the grief that comes with the illness or death of a spouse or children (Atchley, p. 299).

A close friend of mine has been alone for 75 years; she is now 104. She is by far the most competent, well-adapted, and caring person I have ever met. She is described in detail in a case study in Chapter 23. Though she has had few intimate relationships, her life has been filled with friendships. At the risk of being sticky, I must say that her home has been the world, and her family the family of man.

INVOLVEMENT OUTSIDE THE FAMILY

People exchange services and obtain and give support in many settings other than the family: in educational programs, vocational and avocational pursuits, and social activities. For some, such involvements provide their main sustenance. Below we shall explore the significance of these involvements and their effect on the quality of life and the exchange of caring.

Work

The world of work provides structure, opportunities for mastery, and a way to express caring. For most men and many women, most waking time in the middle years are spent at work. A frustrating job or depersonalized surroundings may, as Kimmel suggests, increase the importance of the family and leisure pursuits as sources of competence and satisfaction or may keep the person from feeling successful in any area of his or her life. Some jobs require too much personal investment and leave little time for the family; others involve continuous competition between family and job for the individual's emotional and physical energy. If the individual is in an occupation in which care giving is a major function, the family may receive short shrift.

Satisfaction in an occupation may have more to do with taking advantage of opportunities than with choosing the direction in which one's career will go. Opportunity, of course, is dependent upon sex, ethnic origin, intelligence, and economic supports. Wilenski found that one-third of financially secure middle-class persons had what is described as an orderly work history; that is, they had made a gradual vertical movement up the status ladder. Therefore, two-thirds of successful people seem to be moving along as opportunity dictates. Wilenski also suggests that the *pattern* of work history (orderly or disorderly) has a greater impact on social role than any *one* of the work positions. Individuals who make a sudden or major shift from an otherwise orderly work career are in another category and are viewed as having the ability to take risks and face insecurity (Kimmel). Such major job changes would be likely to occur at turning points in an individual's personal development and may contribute to self-actualization. Incongruence between one's expectations and the realistic possibility of attaining career goals often precipitates a crisis in men between 40 and 55 that results in a revision of goals.

Successful businessmen studied by Neugarten were found to have a sense of maximum capacity and ability to handle a highly complex environment and their individual idiosyncrasies. It seems evident that occupational success enhances one's view of the middle years. One middle-aged colleague said, after a particularly harrowing month of meeting multiple demands within her job and social setting, "I know now that I can handle anything; I have never felt so effective." Success in one area of life seems to beget success in other areas, though many middle-aged people measure their competence by job status.

In a study by Pfeiffer and Davis, about 75 percent of people between the ages of 46 and 71 said they derived more satisfaction from work than from leisure-time activities. Ninety percent of the men and eighty percent of the women said they would continue to work even if they did not need the money. The "work ethic" is still strong among people in this age group. Another factor may be important: One 50-year-old male said that, for him, there was an inverse correlation between sexual activity and work. He felt that as sexual activity diminished, work-related activity assumed greater importance. Quinn et al. deny the existence of the "blue-collar blues" in the majority of the working population and report that there is no evidence of widespread job dissatisfaction. Ninety percent of workers report job satisfaction (Troll, 1975).

Some age differences have been observed in job satisfaction. Men between 30 and 40 change jobs because of dissatisfaction, while those between 40 and 50 do so when there are opportunities for advancement. By age 50, aspirations for advancement have largely subsided, and most men have come to terms with the jobs they have (Clausen), even though they may dislike the long hours or the tensions associated with their work. Men seem able to cope with just about anything but downward mobility. Clausen found that downwardly mobile middle-class males were withdrawn and prone to self-defeating behavior, psychosomatic ailments, anxiety, and feelings of inadequacy. Interestingly, working-class people who have moved up to the middle class are more giving and sympathetic than those with middle-class origins. This ability to identify with the struggles they have known personally is discussed in Chapters 19 and 20.

Leisure

How is leisure related to the capacity for caring? Leisure provides the opportunity to care for oneself and to seek renewal and re-creation. The pursuit of leisure can be exhausting, but exhaustion can be refreshing. Some people play tennis for the sheer joy of swatting the ball, while others work hard at improving their game, to the point where it becomes more of a job than a leisure-time pursuit. Many middle-aged people are very task-oriented, and making the switch to leisure for its own sake will not be easy. When there is more leisure time each week than working time, some people will not know what to do with it and may feel vaguely uncomfortable about "wasting" time. See Figure 14-3.

Free time is expected to increase for each successive cohort group. Men born in 1960 will have 9 more years of nonworking time than men born in 1900 (Kreps). Shorter workweeks, longer vacations, periodic leaves of absence, and early retirement will force the middle-aged to give more thought to recreation and

Figure 14-3   Some people may feel vaguely uncomfortable about "wasting" time on leisure. Leisure time can be a time for reflection, as in the above photograph, and also a time to enjoy nature. (*Courtesy of Pat Ryan.*)

leisure. A study of intellectually elite persons showed that they viewed leisure as more "honest" than work and preferred more leisure time than other adults (Neulinger and Raps). It is reasonable to expect that such individuals might have more opportunity to make leisure a satisfying experience (Kimmel). For some, increased free time may mean that family members must bear the burden of providing satisfactions that were previously derived from working.

Leisure may become an increasingly important aspect of educational curricula. Those who say that the schools should cut the "frills" and spend more time on the "basics" may have lost sight of the realities of life. They are not mentally prepared for the student fortified with computer, tape recorder, and tennis racket whom we see trudging off to school today.

Kelly defined four types of leisure: (1) unconditional leisure, (2) coordinated activity, (3) complementary activity, and (4) preparation and recuperation:

1. *Unconditional leisure.* Leisure that is freely chosen and is undertaken for its own sake.
2. *Coordinated activity.* Leisure that is freely chosen but is in some way

related to the person's occupation. It may provide an antidote to, or a diversion from, work.

3. *Complementary activity.* Leisure that is neither freely chosen nor directly related to the individual's work. It includes activities that one is "expected" to participate in because of his or her position in a profession or in the community.
4. *Preparation and recuperation.* Activities that are directly related to, and determined by, one's occupation, e.g., entertaining clients (Kelly).

Other conceptualizations may be developed that will give us some guidelines toward self-renewal and the meaning of leisure.

People's leisure histories are remarkably consistent throughout their lives. Those who actively sought family togetherness, relaxation, and peace and quiet show a high degree of satisfaction (Oliver). People with little interest in their jobs may find their salvation in leisure-time activities (Hearn). In one study, most successful life-styles of men and women between 40 and 70 were shown to be characterized by integrated patterns of work and leisure (Havighurst and Feigenbaum). There are marked class and cohort differences in work and leisure patterns (Maddox).

As has been noted, leisure is becoming a more important aspect of our lives, and each person must satisfactorily define his or her needs and the methods of fulfillment. We know that stress is the greatest hazard in our society; a goal of caring professionals would be to counsel people in leisure, stress reduction, and joyous living.

SUSTAINING FRIENDSHIPS

There are many views of the nature and meaning of friendship during the middle years. Hunt and Hunt say that middle age is second only to adolescence as a period for forming new friendships. One can consciously and deliberately make room for new friendships while leaving some behind that are no longer appropriate. Age discrimination is least operative during the middle years, and it is not uncommon for a middle-aged person to have friends between 30 and 60 and to feel close to them all. Troll (1975) states that social contacts as one grows older tend more toward giving to others than toward getting from others; acquaintances decrease in importance, but personal friends do not. Keeping old friends seems to be one of the consolidation processes of later adulthood, just as making new friends is one of the expanding processes of youth. Sharing of childhood and adolescent experiences is an important part of friendship in late adulthood, particularly among women (Jones). Social and geographic mobility may decrease the incidence of lifelong friendships, and, as Toffler suggests, this may be adaptive in a rapidly changing society. According to Neugarten, Moore, and Lowe, social clocks and their dictation of appropriate age and role behavior may influence the choice of friends, though Troll and Schlossberg found greater age constraints for the friends of early life than for those of later life. There is probably more freedom to select friends as one develops a firmer sense of self and greater wisdom.

My own friendships formed during the "chum" stage (ages 10 to 12) of preadolescence have persisted through the years, in spite of differences in life-styles. See Figure 14-4. These early peer identifications and self-confirmations represent a constancy of self, when on infrequent occasions I meet these old friends and we remember things about ourselves that have become submerged. Old friends enrich my self-view, as I enrich theirs. I feel renewed. I would agree with Adams (1968) that during the young adult years family relationships take precedence over friendships; the expenditure of energy within the family is draining, and fewer friendships will be maintained. The friends of those years are close to the individual in age and role behavior. As the family departs, friendships again become increasingly important. Now, rather than confirming the self-image, friends provide new insights and demonstrations of caring.

WIDENING HORIZONS

Erikson (1975) has made the profound observation that a multiplication of energies results from the individual's interplay with a widening radius of individuals and institutions. This is the position of most people in middle age. There is a continual outpouring of energy in a widening radius through family, work, social, and organizational contacts; in many cases the infusion of energy from these sources results in a fairly stable exchange within an individual's support system. Perhaps this is the reason why so many middle-aged people function

Figure 14-4 Friendships formed during the "chum" stage in youth may continue for many years, even though the individuals' life-styles vary considerably. (*Courtesy of Pat Ryan.*)

exceedingly well in meeting demands from family, kin, and community. Organizations and industrial corporations provide an aspect of caring for members or employees; some are paternalistic or authoritarian but are nevertheless interested in the optimum function and satisfaction of participants within their system. Although the motivation may not necessarily be humanitarian, one can still derive feelings of security and comfort from "belonging." Loyalty to one's *place* is somewhat like loyalty to one's kin: insiders may grouse to their hearts' content, but outsiders had better not.

Because many regard their vocational setting, their professional organization, or their union as their chief support in a materialistic world, we can think of these as "care givers" for the middle-aged, knowing that the middle-aged are also, by and large, the administrators of these organizations. The caring is demonstrated in a practical manner. Thus people become very disgruntled if *their* corporation merges, if *their* union functions poorly in their interests, or if *their* professional organization has little clout. The middle-aged rely, to a large extent, on impersonal organizations and institutions to meet their needs. This may be a reason why the middle-aged are seen as the strongest protectors of the "establishment." We *are* the establishment and need not be apologetic.

In her eightieth year, Florida Scott-Maxwell expressed her gratitude to those people in society who had put the brakes on idealistic reform. She felt free at her age to try anything, just as young people feel ready to make rapid and revolutionary change. In spite of the obvious need for progress in humanizing the community at large, someone must slow the process enough so that we can observe the repercussions. That is the job of those in the middle years. Actual progress in caring begins with each of us and can take place at any age.

SUMMARIZING STATEMENTS BASED ON THE LITERATURE

- If one strives for self-actualization, the need to care cannot be neglected (Gaylin).
- In middle adulthood, the need to be helped is weak, and the need to help is strong (Kimmel and Stein).
- There are two kinds of caring: the kind that allows something or someone to emerge independent of the care giver and the reciprocal kind, which implies a mutual supportive exchange (Mayerhoff).
- Historically, care giving has passed through several phases: (1) the ascetic, (2) the romantic, (3) the pragmatic, and (4) the holistic (Bevis).
- The capacity for caring expands from a small epicenter and becomes larger until our commitment to others is more universal than personal (Erikson, 1959; Jung).
- The strongest supportive linkage between generations usually follows the female line (Adams, 1971; Leichter and Mitchell).
- Problems with aging parents can be more distressing than those with children (Diekelmann).

- Couples often feel caught between the needs of children and the needs of aging parents (LeShan).
- One study showed that after 20 years of marriage there is a cooling off, or "unmatching" factor, that results in decreased companionship, sexual relations, and displays of affection (Pineo).
- Males and females view marriage in the middle years differently (Thurner).
- For some parents, the adult child represents a chance to accomplish what the parent was denied (Gaylin).
- Relationships with married children require tact, judgment, and an appropriate distance (LeShan).
- Since the 1900s, people have become grandparents at an earlier age (Neugarten and Weinstein). Recent data, however, show a reversal of this trend (Troll, 1975).
- Five specific coping styles of grandparents include (1) formal, (2) fun seeker, (3) surrogate parent, (4) reservoir of family wisdom, and (5) distant figure (Neugarten and Weinstein).
- Attaining "filial maturity" is an ongoing task of the middle years and is accomplished when we see our parents as themselves rather than in relation to our needs (Blenkner).
- In the vast majority of cases, there is close contact between the generations, even when they do not reside together (Riley and Foner; Shanas et al.).
- The single person sometimes has special problems in obtaining adequate nurturance.
- Frustrating work or a depersonalized work milieu may increase the importance of the family (Kimmel).
- In one study, 25 percent of persons between 46 and 71 derived more satisfaction from work than from leisure-time activities (Pfeiffer and Davis).
- Middle-class downwardly mobile males have been shown to be withdrawn and prone to self-defeating behavior, psychosomatic ills, anxiety, and feelings of inadequacy (Clausen).
- Free time will increase for each successive cohort group (Kreps).
- There are four types of leisure: (1) unconditional leisure, (2) coordinated activity, (3) complementary activity, and (4) preparation and recuperation (Kelly).
- Middle age is second to adolescence as a time for forming new friendships (Hunt and Hunt).
- Social and geographic mobility may decrease the number of lifelong friendships (Toffler).

GUIDELINES FOR INTERVENTION

- Try to serve as an advocate for both generations by providing information.
- Be aware that the problem of aging parents may be very distressing and that middle-aged couples may need counseling and support in this area.

- Help middle-aged couples sort out the priorities in their own needs, their children's needs, and their parents' needs.
- Help eliminate myths such as the one that there is little or no contact between generations.
- Be aware of the ways in which the single person is discriminated against.
- In assessing middle-aged persons, be aware of the importance of their work to them and of the consequences (e.g., depression or feelings of low self-worth) which may result if work is withdrawn or reduced drastically.
- Discuss future leisure-time activities with the middle-aged person or couple since free time will increase in later years.
- Encourage the formation of new friendships in mid-life and also the renewal and/or sustenance of friendships formed during the "chum" stage.
- Encourage client to identify potential sources of support and caring.

REFERENCES

Adams, B. N.: *Kinship in an Urban Setting,* Markham, Chicago, 1968.

————: "Isolation, Function and Beyond: American Kinship in the 1960's," in C. B. Broderick (ed.), *A Decade of Family Research and Action,* National Council on Family Relations, Minneapolis, Minn., 1971, pp. 163–185.

Adler, Alfred: "Individual Psychology," in C. Murchison (ed.), *Psychologies of 1930,* Clark University Press, Worcester, Mass., 1930, pp. 395–405.

Atchley, Robert: *The Social Forces in Later Life: An Introduction to Social Gerontology,* Wadsworth, Belmont, Calif., 1972.

Bengtson, Vern, and **K. Dean Black:** "Intergenerational Relations and Continuities in Socialization," in P. Baltes and W. Schaie (eds.), *Personality and Socialization,* Academic, New York, 1973.

Bernard, J.: *The Future of Marriage,* World, Bantam Books, Tarrytown-on-Hudson, N.Y., 1973.

Bevis, Em: Nursing Curriculum Workshop, San Francisco State University, San Francisco, 1976.

Bischof, L. J.: *Adult Psychology,* Harper & Row, New York, 1969.

Blenkner, M.: "Social Work and Family Relationships with Some Thoughts on Filial Maturity," in E. Shanas and G. Streib (eds.), *Social Structure and the Family: Generational Relations,* Prentice-Hall, Englewood Cliffs, N.J., 1965.

Blood, R., and **D. M. Wolfe:** *Husbands and Wives: The Dynamics of Married Living,* Free Press, New York, 1960.

Bultena, G.: "Rural-Urban Differences in the Familial Interaction of the Aged," *Rural-Sociology,* 34(1):5–15, 1969.

Chew, Peter: *The Inner World of the Middle Aged Man,* Macmillan, New York, 1976.

Clausen, J. A.: "The Life Course of Individuals," in R. Atchley and M. Seltzer (eds.), *The Sociology of Aging: Selected Readings,* Wadsworth, Belmont, Calif., 1976, pp. 38–50.

Deutscher, Irwin: "The Quality of Post-parental Life: Definitions of the Situation," *Journal of Marriage and the Family,* **26**(1):52–59, 1964.

Diekelmann, Nancy: *Primary Health Care of the Well Adult,* McGraw-Hill, New York, 1977.

Duvall, E. M.,: *Family Development,* 4th ed., Lippincott, Philadelphia, 1971.

Entine, Alan (ed.): *Americans in Middle Years: Career Options and Educational Opportunities,* Ethel Percy Andrus Gerontology Center, Los Angeles, 1974.

Erikson, Erik: "Identity and the Life Cycle: Selected Papers," *Psychological Issues,* Monogr. no. 1, 1959.

————: *Gandhi's Truth: On the Origins of Militant Non-Violence,* Norton, New York, 1969.

————: *Life History and the Historical Moment,* Norton, New York, 1975.

Feldman, H.: "Parent and Marriage: Myths and Realities," address given at the Merrill-Palmer Institute Conference on the Family, Detroit, 1969.

Frey, Catherine: Personal communication, 1976.

Fromm, Erich: *To Have or To Be,* Harper & Row, New York, 1977.

Gaylin, Willard: *Caring,* Knopf, New York, 1976.

Gibson, G.: "Kin Family Network: Over-heralded Structure in Past Conceptualization of Family Functioning," *Journal of Marriage and the Family,* **34**(1): 13–23, 1972.

Gould, Roger: "The Phases of Adult Life: A Study of Developmental Psychology," *American Journal of Psychiatry,* **129**(5): 33–43, 1972.

Havighurst, R.: *Developmental Tasks and Education,* McKay, New York, 1952.

———— and **K. Feigenbaum:** "Leisure and Life Style," *American Journal of Sociology,* **64**(4):396–404, 1959.

Hearn, H. L.: "Career and Leisure Patterns of Middle-Aged Urban Blacks," *The Gerontologist,* **11**(2):21–26, 1971.

Hill, R., N. Foote, J. Aldous, R. Carlson, and **R. Macdonald:** *Family Development in Three Generations,* Schenkman, Cambridge, Mass., 1970.

Hunt, Bernice, and **Morton Hunt:** *Prime Time,* Stein and Day, New York, 1975.

Irelan, Lola M., and **Kathleen Bond:** "Retirees of the 70's," paper presented at the Southern Conference on Gerontology, Gainesville, Fla., March 1974.

Johnson, Walter: Personal communication, 1976.

Jones, D.: "Sex Differences in the Friendship Patterns of Young Adults," unpublished paper, 1974.

Jung, Carl: "The Stages of Life," tr. by R.F.C. Hull, in J. Campbell (ed.), *The Portable Jung,* Viking, New York, 1971.

Kahana, E., and **B. Kahana:** "Theoretical and Research Perspectives on Grand-parenthood," paper presented at the meeting of the American Psychological Association, Miami Beach, 1970.

Kalish, R., and **A. Johnson:** "Value Similarities and Differences in Three Generations of Women," *Journal of Marriage and the Family,* **34**(1):49–55, 1972.

Kelly, John: "Work and Leisure: A Simplified Paradigm," *Journal of Leisure Research,* **4**(1):50–62, 1972.

Kimmel, Douglas: *Adulthood and Aging,* Wiley, New York, 1974.

Kimmel D., and **M. Stein:** "Variations in Self-rated Personality Needs as a Function of Sex, Age, and Socioeconomic Status from Adolescence to Old Age," paper presented at the convention of the American Psychological Association, Montreal, 1973.

Kreps, Juanita: "The Allocation of Leisure to Retirement," in F. Carp (ed.), *The Retirement Process,* U. S. Department of Health, Education, and Welfare, 1966.

Leichter, H., and **W. E. Mitchell:** *Kinship and Casework,* Russell Sage, New York, 1967.

LeShan, Eda: *The Wonderful Crisis of Middle Age,* McKay, New York, 1973.

Levinson, Daniel, Charlotte Darrow, Edward Klein, Maria Levinson, and **Braxton McKee:** "The Psychosocial Development of Men in Early Adulthood and the Mid-Life Transition," in D. F. Ricks, A. Thomas, and M. Roff (eds.), *Life History Research in Psychopathology,* vol. 3, University of Minnesota Press, Minneapolis, 1974.

Lopata, H. Z.: *Widowhood in an American City,* Schenkman, Cambridge, Mass., 1973.

Maddox, G. L.: "Retirement as a Social Event in the United States," in J. C. McKinney and F. T. deVyver (eds.), *Aging and Social Policy,* Appleton-Century-Crofts, New York, 1966, pp. 119–135.

May, Rollo: *Love and Will,* Norton, New York, 1969.

Mayerhoff, Milton: *On Caring,* Harper & Row, New York, 1971.

McCammon, R. W.: *Human Growth and Development,* Charles C Thomas, Springfield, Ill., 1970.

Neugarten, Bernice (ed.): *Middle Age and Aging,* University of Chicago Press, Chicago, 1968.

———, **J. W. Moore,** and **J. C. Lowe:** "Age Norms, Age Constraints, and Adult Socialization," *American Journal of Sociology,* **70**(6):710–717, 1965.

——— and **K. Weinstein:** "The Changing American Grandparent," *Journal of Marriage and the Family,* **26**(2): 199–204, 1964.

Neulinger, John, and **Charles Raps:** "Leisure Attitudes of an Intellectual Elite," *Journal of Leisure Research,* **4**(3): 196–207, 1972.

Oliver, D. B.: "Career and Leisure Patterns: Middle-Aged Metropolitan Out-Migrants," *The Gerontologist,* **11**(2): 13–20, 1971.

O'Neill, Nena, and **George O'Neill:** *Open Marriage,* M. Evans, New York, 1972.

Pfeiffer, Eric, and **Glenn Davis:** "The Use of Leisure Time in Middle Life," part 1, *The Gerontologist,* **11**(3):187–195, 1971.

Pike, Catherine: "Psychological Implications of Being a Middle Aged or Older Woman," paper presented at symposium entitled Gynecological Problems of Older Women, Division of Continuing Education in Nursing, University of California, San Francisco, March 1976.

Pineo, P. C.: "Disenchantment in the Later Years of Marriage," *Marriage and Family Living,* **23**(1):3–11, 1961.

Prock, Valencia: "The Mid-Stage Woman," *American Journal of Nursing,* **75**(6):1019–1024, 1975.

Quinn, R., G. Staines, and **M. McCullough:** *Job Satisfaction: Is There a Trend?* U.S. Department of Labor, Manpower Research Monograph no. 30, 1974.

Riley, M. W., and **A. Foner:** *Aging and Society, vol. 1, An Inventory of Research Findings,* Russell Sage, New York, 1968.

Robinson, Betsy, and **Majda Thurner:** "Parental Care Taking: A Family Cycle Transition," paper presented at the twenty-ninth annual scientific meeting of the Gerontological Society, New York, October 1976.

Rose, A. M.: "Factors Associated with the Life Satisfaction of Middle-Class, Middle Aged Persons," *Marriage and Family Living,* **17**(1):15–19, 1955.

Schorr, A.: *Filial Responsibility in the Modern American Family,* U. S. Department of Health, Education, and Welfare, Social Security Administration, 1960.

Schwartz, Felice: in Alan Entine (ed.), *Americans in Middle Years: Career Op-*

tions and Educational Opportunities, Ethel Percy Andrus Gerontology Center, Los Angeles, 1974, p. 38.

Scott-Maxwell, Florida: *The Measure of My Days,* Knopf, New York, 1969.

Shanas, Ethel, P. Townsend, D. Wedderburn, H. Friis, P. Milhøj, and **J. Stethouwer:** *Older People in Three Industrial Societies,* Atherton, New York, 1968.

Sheppard, Harold: "Work and Retirement," in Robert Binstock and Ethel Shanas (eds.), *Handbook of Aging and the Social Sciences,* Van Nostrand Reinhold, New York, 1976, pp. 286–309.

Streib, Gordon F.: "Intergenerational Relations: Perspectives of the Two Generations on the Older Parent," *Journal of Marriage and the Family,* **52**(1):7–21, 1967.

Synanon Foundation Representatives: Presentation to family nursing class, San Francisco State University, 1977.

Thurner, Majda: "Midlife Marriage: Sex Differences in Evaluation and Perspectives," paper presented at the twenty-seventh annual meeting of the Gerontological Society, Portland, Oreg., 1974.

Toffler, Alvin: *Future Shock,* Random House, New York, 1970.

Toman, Walter: *Family Constellation; Its Effect on Personality and Social Behavior,* 2d ed., Springer, New York, 1969.

Troll, Lillian: "The Family of Later Life: A Decade Review," *Journal of Marriage and the Family,* **33**:263–290, 1971.

————: *Early and Middle Adulthood: The Best Is Yet to Be—Maybe,* Brooks/Cole, Monterey, Calif., 1975.

————, **Bernice Neugarten,** and **R. J. Kraines:** "Similarities in Values and Other Personality Characteristics in College Students and Their Parents," *Merrill-Palmer Quarterly,* **15**:323–337, 1969.

———— and **N. Schlossberg:** "How 'Age Biased' Are College Counselors?" *Industrial Gerontology,* **10**:14–20, 1971.

Wilenski, H. L.: "Orderly Careers and Social Participation: The Impact of Work History on Social Integration in the Middle Mass," *American Sociological Review,* **26**(4):521–539, 1961.

Young, M., and **P. Willmott:** *Family and Kinship in East London,* The Free Press of Macmillan, New York, 1957.

OTHER RESOURCES

FILM

Tell Me Where It Hurts: 78 min/color/1974. The story of a middle-aged housewife who questions her own existence and wonders about her future. After 20 years of marriage, she joins a women's discussion group, finds a job, and begins to seek her own identity. Distributor: University of Michigan, Audio-Visual Education Center, 416 Fourth Street, Ann Arbor, Mich. 48104.

Chapter 15

THAT VITAL VEHICLE: THE BODY

Priscilla Ebersole

> Each man, though he sees others dying all around him,
> never believes that he himself will die.
>
> *Bhagavad-Gita*

Although it has been said that we begin to die the moment we are born, it takes middle age to make us aware of our awesome dependence on the intricate mechanism of the body. The body serves to implement our goals and provide satisfaction throughout our lives; it is the vehicle of many pleasures and is also our early warning system. The body endures a remarkable amount of abuse and neglect with amazing resilience, adapting to unusual conditions over time.

A healthy body is usually valued the most in retrospect. Though frequently we ignore the vital vehicle which transports our psyche and soul, it may be the major factor in our gaining or failing to gain satisfaction, both intrapersonally and interpersonally. Our bodies bestow status or stigma depending on their structure, level of functioning, and integrity.

Holistically, the body is an energy source and a personal responsibility. The body is controlled by the mind and becomes increasingly a preoccupation of the mind when it functions with less precision. Sometimes the focus is entirely on this vehicle—the marvelous body.

Caring for one's body during the middle years consumes more time and thought than in youth, though people vary enormously in their bodily awareness. For most people, as long as the body functions well, it is given little thought; however, when it functions poorly, it becomes the focus of considerable attention. Our personal, social, and psychological development are inextricably intertwined with physiological function.

There is probably less individual variation in bodily development during midlife than in social, psychological, and intellectual growth, although a small percentage of people experience premature or delayed development. Bühler found that the "biographical curve" of life is correlated with the biological curve for those people who are most centered on their bodies. See also Chapters 11 and 21. People who value their strength or physical attributes will show psychological patterns of aging as they perceive the visible signs of aging. Those who value intellectual function and interpersonal skills tend to feel young for many years after their bodies show signs of age (Troll). Bodily function often correlates with feelings of worth, particularly in the case of men who value strength and women who are especially attractive.

Generalizations about physiological changes in the adult years must be made with caution as there are significant differences between certain groups and a wide range of individual variation.

FACTORS INVOLVED IN GROUP VARIATIONS

A progressive increase in weight and height has been observed for adults worldwide in the last century; our heads are becoming proportionately larger, and our feet are becoming longer (Donahue). The reasons for these changes are unclear but may include such things as improved environmental conditions, a reduction of infectious diseases, better nutrition, and evolutionary changes in genetic pools through cross-breeding of various human groups (Troll). Nutrition, climate, and exercise levels affect the aging process of whole groups of people, though none of these is as significant alone as when in combination with other factors.

INDIVIDUAL DIFFERENCES

It is clear that we have much individual responsibility for the manner in which our bodies function. By paying attention to diet, exercise, rest, environmental hazards, and stress exposure, we can do much to promote healthful living. Good habits in mid-life can delay aging and minimize its undesirable effects.

Nutrition

We probably have more control over our diet than over most other things in our lives, and yet we often exercise the least discretion in this area. We need less food in mid-life than we did in young adulthood, and we can afford more. Both the spread on the table and the body of the middle-aged person tend to expand. Social activities usually include an abundance of food and drink selected to titillate the palate more than to nourish the body. Processed foods requiring little or no preparation become an important adjunct to busy lives. In summary, we may consume more food and receive less nutrition—to say nothing of the enormous amount of additives and preservatives that we ingest.

The need for specific nutrients shifts somewhat in the middle years, and individuals have idiosyncratic needs.

Biorhythms: Sleep and Rest

Internal mechanisms that influence our need for rest and sleep are being seriously studied. It is becoming apparent that chronophysiology (biorhythms) influences how frequently and how well we rest as well as many other aspects of our lives. Biorhythms tend to desynchronize in situations affording inadequate environmental cues. Without clocks and day-night cues, subjects' inner time varies immensely. Fortunately, most middle-aged people follow a fairly consistent schedule, although many are experiencing the effects of jet lag and of jobs requiring odd hours; however, the body does adapt to such extrinsic pressures, given time. Goldberg states: "Each of us has a unique interior drummer that continually coordinates the rhythmic fluctuations of hormones, moods, sleep and waking; neither our well-being nor our sanity can easily march to a different beat" (pp. 71–72). All of us have certain periods of vulnerability during the day. Care givers can use an awareness of this to help themselves and their clients correct erratic living habits; if that is not possible, at least they can understand the reason for the resultant decreased ability to function.

Sleep

Since the average person will spend 15 years of his or her adult life asleep, it seems important to be cognizant of sleep patterns throughout adulthood. Most aspects of sleep remain stable through the middle decades, particularly the individually characteristic number of hours of sleep per 24 h and the amount of REM (dream) sleep (Troll). After 40, people tend to spend progressively less time in deep (stage 4) sleep and may feel less rested in the morning (Thompson and Marsh). Though there appear to be no studies on the relationship between amount of stage 4 sleep and the experience of aging, one must wonder whether it is significant. Webb says that during the forties changes in the substructure of sleep become most prominent, with diminished deep sleep and increased periods of awakening.

The sleep of women is more resistant to age changes; generally, a middle-aged woman will have the sleep patterns of a man 10 years younger than she is. There is little change in the amount of sleep until age 60, then there is a slight rise in the amount required over a 24-h period. Changes in life-style and physical ailments may affect these patterns (Webb). Individual differences in amount of sleep required increase with age, but REM and stage 2 sleep remain markedly consistent throughout the adult years.

Individual needs for sleep vary markedly; some people require only 3 to 4 h per night, while others need 10 to 12 h. Obviously, some people experience much more waking time than others.

In summary:

1. Patterns of sleep undergo natural changes associated with age.
2. There are wide individual differences in the timing and pace of these changes.

3. Problems occur more as a result of our expectations about sleep and our social needs than as a result of intrinsic sleep changes.

An item of interest to care givers is that people on regular sleep schedules experience increased sensory acuity between 5 and 7 P.M. At the end of the day, the senses of taste, smell, hearing, and sight are enhanced (Kreiger). The implications are that this would be a time for relaxation and enjoyment of one's sensory impressions.

Relaxation and Exercise

Relaxation and exercise seem so intertwined as to be dependent on each other. In middle age there is less tendency to go to extremes on either end of the continuum; nevertheless, overactivity and fatigue are antecedent to many chronic diseases of middle life. "It is not the absence of vitality which frequently handicaps man but an absence of knowledge as to how to use the energy that is inherent in his organism" (Sokoloff, p. 135). The study of biodynamics (energy preservation and renewal and the sources of vitality) is still poorly understood, 40 years after Sokoloff's study. The present generation of middle-aged people may have more problems with biodynamic balance than previous generations. Inactivity is increased by the affluence that enables them to buy labor-saving appliances, a car for every member of the family, and the services of domestics and gardeners, for example (Diekelmann). Walking is excellent exercise and can be revitalizing, but it is often neglected because of time pressures.

Loss of physical strength begins at about 30, with a 10 percent loss between then and age 60 (Timiras). Middle-aged people should be advised to participate in activities that involve coordination rather than speed, strength, or endurance (Diekelmann). Exercise can help maintain and sometimes restore strength to unused muscles, but periodic avid overexertion is not advisable. One can maximize strength in later adulthood by exercising consistently, generally living at a slower pace, and reserving top capacity for special occasions (Timiras).

Generally, in mid-life the back and leg muscles lose more strength than the arm muscles; however, exercise of the leg muscles seems effective in improving cardiac function and decreasing the tendency toward arteriosclerosis (Troll). Diekelmann has quoted White as saying that when one is walking, 30 percent of the circulation of the heart is carried on by the leg muscles; thus walking is a good way to give the heart a rest. Timiras has equated general body tone to the strength of the leg muscles and has said, "If you want to know how flabby your brain is, feel your leg muscles" (Troll, p. 18).

I am reminded of the vast differences between individuals as I think of an 80-year-old man who single-handedly erected a smokehouse in Montana from hand-hewn logs and shakes. I have a vivid mental picture of him running up and down the ladder, carrying bundles of shakes, and ferociously hammering on the roof. I believe he had been accustomed to that kind of activity most of his life.

Stress: Environmental and Personal

In spite of efforts to obtain adequate nutrition, rest, and exercise, many people develop ailments. Stress is our greatest adversary today. We have stereotyped stress as a component of success, particularly among high-powered executives. Chew found that this may be a myth. In two surveys, executives who were queried responded that they did not find their jobs too stressful, and this was borne out by physical examinations. Several surveys indicate that the lower one's position in a company is, the more he or she is apt to develop a stress-related disease.

This finding bears out the idea that stress is generally more acute in situations where one feels helpless, powerless, and lacking in autonomy (Colligan). An actual or a threatened loss of a source of gratification, with resultant feelings of hopelessness, can precipitate disease in vulnerable organs and can lead to death. Illness frequently emerges during periods of stress. Cobb and Kasl studied 100 men who had been laid off from a Detroit automobile plant. Over a 2-year period, he found many cases of severe depression, ulcers, arthritis, hypertension, and alcoholism, as well as a suicide rate 30 times the average. Family members also had an increased incidence of illness, leading to the conclusion that the whole family is affected by the loss of the husband's job and his feelings of hopelessness about finding another. This is a realistic fear for men over 50. Holmes and Rahe's stress scale (see Chapter 12) can alert care givers to the vulnerability of certain middle-aged clients to disease. Awareness of the helplessness factor could be a valuable predictive tool.

Some people undoubtedly have a higher stress tolerance than others. Those in our culture with the greatest capacity to cope with stress and change are likely to be the most successful psychologically and personally. Learning to cope is also a matter of practice; therefore, those who have been subjected to the least stress may be more vulnerable to physical disease when they are abruptly confronted with a major loss or change.

There is an increasing concern about environmental stresses on the organism. Crowding, noise, and inclement weather may all produce adverse effects. We are also beginning to ponder the effects of being bombarded with violence by the media. On the other hand, most middle-aged people have adapted to such stresses gradually and are unaware of their effects until they withdraw to a restful ambiance and again smell the grass and see the stars. "Getting away from it all" may involve more than pure psychological renewal—it may preserve life and health.

Interestingly, Luscher makes a strong case for the importance of color in the environment. He says that we have a somatic susceptibility to certain colors. Reds excite the nervous system, while blues are calming and can bring on an actual decrease in cardiac rate and breathing rate, as well as a fall in blood pressure. Industrial environmental planners have been aware of the effects of certain colors, but knowledgeable use of color can benefit our daily lives even more. Luscher says that if an organism requires psychic or physical regeneration and release from tension or stress, the instinctive response will be to choose darker colors; if the organism needs to dissipate energy by means of strenuous activity, the instinctive response will be toward brighter colors. The Luscher Color Test is used by physicians in Europe as a diagnostic aid. It enables them to detect high stress levels before physiological effects are evident. An inexpensive paperback book, *The Luscher Color Test,* includes lengthy interpretive tables; however, its most important contribution is that it points up the significance of an aspect of the environment that may be overlooked.

In summary, exercise, avoidance of noxious substances in the environment, improved dietary habits, adequate rest, and a reduction in stress all help middle-aged people cope with their changing bodies.

EXPECTABLE BODILY CHANGES IN THE MIDDLE YEARS

The most common indication of chronological aging is the graying of the hair (Fozard, Nuttal, and Waugh); it is probably also the easiest to remedy! Other normal changes include decreased visual and auditory acuity, decreased musculoskeletal integrity, decreased metabolic rate, and decreases in secretions and hormones. Chronic disorders such as arthritis, obesity, cancer, cardiovascular problems, diabetes, and reproductive disorders occur more frequently with aging (Diekelmann). The specifics and the implications of these changes will be explored in some depth. For additional information, the reader can consult Finch and Hayflick or Timiras.

To a large extent our world of action and reaction is governed by our sensory impressions. This becomes particularly important in mid-life, when sensual acuity begins to diminish noticeably, in effect reducing the richness of our impressions. We are not without compensation; years of past experience assist us. There is a general slowing of the nervous system, particularly after 50, often with pervasive behavioral effects. Troll suggests that if we read more slowly, move more slowly, and talk more slowly, we are literally "on another wave length." We know, however, that we have a good deal of company! Even by the time we are 33 years old, our skill and dexterity have declined measureably (Fozard et al.), although the actual quality of task performance does not seem to be affected by this (Birren). To repeat, experience is our ally.

The most common specific sensory changes among the middle-aged are visual and auditory. Hearing begins to decline after age 20, and thereafter there is a gradual loss of auditory perception, particularly for high-frequency sounds. Men, because of higher occupational noise levels, suffer hearing loss to a more noticeable degree than women (Timiras). In the future we might expect more women and younger people to experience greater deficits in hearing as they enter diverse occupational fields. The noise of jets is commonplace for the traveling public, and people of both sexes are bombarded with environmental noise from youth onward.

Problems with vision are particularly distressing in our visually oriented society. By age 50 most people use reading glasses since the lenses of the eyes lose their elasticity with age, leading to changes in accommodation and convergence. Farsightedness increases, and pupil size decreases. Lighting needs to be brighter, and night driving becomes more difficult, as one needs more time to recover from glare or adapt to darkness. Color vision holds up well through late middle age, though more light is needed to fully appreciate the variance of shades. Retinal changes are rare before 60, and visual acuity does not deteriorate markedly during the adult years (Timiras).

Other sensory changes may be less noticeable. Taste sensitivity remains acute until at least age 50; later the finer nuances of taste may be lost although sweet, sour, salty, and bitter tastes are still clearly distinguishable. Many middle-aged people, at a time when they least need this, begin to increase their intake of salt and sugar. This may reflect a decreasing number of functional taste buds. Enjoyment of taste is also strongly affected by psychological expectations and experience over the years. After age 40, sensitivity to odor decreases slightly, and this affects responsiveness to taste. Cigarette smoking decreases olfactory sensitivity and dulls taste. Olfaction has a strong refractory response; people become unaware of their own body odors and of the smell of ever-present pollutants in the atmosphere.

Sensitivity to touch increases up to about age 45 and then decreases sharply. Sensitivity to heat and cold remains high. Sensitivity to pain remains steady until about age 50 and then declines differentially for different parts of the body (Timiras). However, pain tolerance may decrease in the presence of chronic discomfort.

The sense of balance is at its best between ages 40 and 50, although I cannot remember hearing of anyone learning to walk a tightrope at that age!

Redistribution of fat and conversion of muscle tissue to fat and connective tissue may be the most distressing evidence of age in our culture, in which slimness is so much admired. The size of the bust and chest decreases, and the hips and abdomen spread. Bischof says that the middle-aged stop growing at both ends and expand in the middle.

The hair thins, recedes, and turns gray during the forties, more so for men than for women. Coarse hair appears in the nose, ears, and eyelashes of men and on the upper lip and chin of women (Troll). The skin loses its elasticity, and wrinkles become noticeable; the lower third of the face slips downward, bags form under the eyes, and the pockets of the plastic surgeon bulge. Much time and money are spent combating these physical changes of age, and when these assets are lacking, people tend to show their age more quickly. While many believe in accepting these changes gracefully, much depends on one's profession. For many, the appearance of youthfulness increases their opportunities and may in fact influence their own self-esteem to an appreciable degree. The search for the fountain of youth is not unique to our culture and will not disappear with it.

HEALTH PROBLEMS IN THE MIDDLE YEARS

General health in the adult is highly variable. Recuperative powers slow down, fatigue and illness increase, blood pressure rises, and dental problems are more frequent. McCammon, in a longitudinal study, found that throughout the adult years people tend to get fewer acute illnesses and to develop more chronic ailments.

Cardiovascular Problems

Cardiovascular problems increase throughout life. Lifetime activity levels seem to have a significant influence on this, and Stringer and Pittman found that workers in jobs requiring little physical exertion were more prone to coronary artery disease than those who expended more energy (Troll). The peak years for heart attacks are ages 55 to 59 (Owen). Middle-age coronary artery disease is responsible for a third of all deaths of men between the ages of 45 and 54. Sudden deaths from heart attack are far less common in women (Hunt and Hunt).

Cancer

Death rates from cancer have been decreasing in certain age groups since 1964, but there has been an abrupt rise of 8.5 percent for males aged 45 to 49 and a rise of 7.8 percent for females aged 55 to 59. The reasons for these changes are not clearly understood (Metropolitan Life Statistical Bulletin). Breast cancer is a concern of many women, since it is the number one killer of women in their forties (Grandstaff) and affects 1 out of every 15 women at some point in their lives (Chew).

The following factors have been found to contribute to the risk of breast cancer:

1. A family history of breast cancer. This is the most significant factor.
2. Age.
3. Long-term estrogen therapy. However, findings in this area are equivocal.
4. Nulliparity.
5. Not having nursed a baby. However, women who do not nurse their babies may not have a greater risk than those who do so for brief periods.
6. Mammary dysplasia.
7. Mammography in women under 50.
8. A long menstrual history, i.e., early menarche and late menopause.

Fortunately, monthly self-examination of the breasts enables women to obtain early treatment and avoid adding to these tragic statistics. Figure 15-1 shows the breast examination procedure.

Diabetes

Diabetes is a disease of the middle years. Fifty percent of the 3 million diabetics in the United States are between the ages of 45 and 64 (Hunt and Hunt).

Diseases of the Reproductive System

Health problems of the middle years often involve the reproductive organs. Forty percent of men over 60 have some prostate enlargement, often asymptomatic; this condition is rare before age 50 (Cant).

Arthritis

Arthritis pain may become an inhibiting factor in the pursuit of many activities. The wear and tear on joints obviously progresses over the years, and among those in certain occupations it becomes quite common. Interestingly, most of the health hazards of the middle years are stress-related diseases. We now know that arthritis, cancer, diabetes, and cardiovascular problems are definitely linked to stress.

MAINTAINING VITAL FUNCTION

Increased attention to consumerism has affected the way people view their bodies. It is encouraging to observe people seeking more information and taking

Figure 15-1 Self-examination of the breasts. (From *American Journal of Nursing*, **77**(9):1450–1451, 1977. Courtesy of American Cancer Society ©. Reprinted with permission of American Cancer Society and American Journal of Nursing Company.)

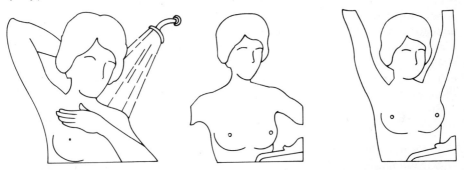

In the shower: Examine your breasts during bath or shower; hands glide easier over wet skin. Fingers flat, use right hand to examine left breast, left hand for right breast. Check for any lump, hard knot, or thickening.

Before a mirror: Inspect breasts with arms at sides. Next, raise arms high overhead. Look for changes in contour, a swelling, dimpling of skin, or changes in the nipple. Then, rest palms on hips; press down firmly to flex chest muscles. Left and right breast will not exactly match. Regular inspection shows what is normal for you.

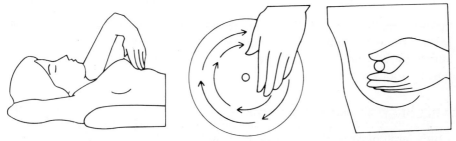

Lying down: To examine right breast, put a pillow or folded towel under right shoulder. Place right hand behind head. With left hand, fingers flat, press gently in small circular motions around an imaginary clock face starting at outermost top of right breast for 12 o'clock. A ridge of firm tissue in the lower curve

of each breast is normal. Move an inch at a time, toward the nipple. This requires at least three more circles. Now slowly repeat procedure on your left breast. Finally, squeeze the nipple of each breast gently; squeeze nipples between thumb and index finger. Report any discharge.

responsibility for adequate self-care. Innumerable workshops and symposia are being held all over the country, offering information and experiences that increase the participants' awareness of the potential for optimum health. A symposium presented by the Institute of Human Knowledge and the University of California in San Francisco is representative of such approaches. The subjects covered included (1) the determinants of health, (2) the "medicalizing" of America, (3) the dimensions of self-care, (4) the women's health movement and self-help groups, (5) what to do when no doctor is available, (6) what consumers should know about medical care, and (7) self-control. The lay public is much more informed concerning health matters today than in the past; we are less the passive receivers of care than the initiators of it. During this conference Thoresen claimed that self-control is not necessarily a stable personality trait but rather a learned ability that can be used to alter one's behavior and applied to problems such as sleep disorders, obesity, headaches, and smoking. Though we still look to the medical profession for health care, most of the important factors in good health operate outside the medical domain.

Chew discusses the value of having a predictive view of one's health. An organization called the Life Extension Institute (with offices in Manhattan, Los Angeles, San Francisco, and San Diego) is dedicated to motivating middle-aged men to take better care of their health. The institute provides annual health examinations for executives of more than 1500 companies. Individuals complete a 40-page "Health Hazard Appraisal," and the institute outlines steps that will enable them to increase their predicted life-span. The cost is no greater than that of an examination performed by a general practitioner.

Since health maintenance becomes a matter of conscious concern for many middle-aged people, the following issues should be brought to their attention:

1. When should they see a physician?
2. Whom should they see? In an age of specialization, this becomes a question of real concern and even implies some degree of self-diagnosis.
3. When are consultation and confirmation needed?
4. What are the risks of proposed treatment plans?
5. What nontraditional methods of care are suitable, and when?

Care givers need to be aware that individuals suffering from illness may need family or professional advocates during difficult periods. Client participation in terms of consent and decision making can never be neglected, however, as autonomy is vital to self-confidence and has direct effects on the person's potential for recovery.

WELLNESS IN THE MIDDLE YEARS

People are concerned not only about health but also about developing "high-level wellness":

High-level wellness for the individual is defined as an integrated method of functioning which is oriented toward maximizing the potential of which the individual is capable. It requires that the individual maintain a continuum of balance and purposeful direction within the environment in which he or she is functioning (Dunn, pp. 4–5).

We are becoming more aware of our potential for full healthful functioning and of our capacity for self-healing in all its dimensions. At a recent conference on the West Coast ("The Mind Can Do Anything"), varied approaches to wholeness were presented; the topics covered included healing powers, the effects of music, breathing exercises, and various aspects of extrasensory perception. There were more middle-aged than youthful persons in the large audience. Other methods currently being used to attain wellness include biofeedback, acupressure, acupuncture, meditation, iridology, Kirilian photography, visualization, yoga, and modified combinations of all these. The search seems clearly to be toward a level of functioning that we have not commonly experienced in the past. Involved is not just self-preservation but also an attempt to abolish some of the limitations our bodies impose on our symbolic selves (Hayakawa). Holistic health care does this by emphasizing healing, the maintenance of health, the consciousness of potential, and the prevention of illness rather than the treatment of disorders (Pelletier).

We are also beginning to understand that principles of folk medicine may contain some innate wisdom. Many of these methods were well established when Western civilization was in its infancy. Puerto Rican folk healers (*Espiritismos*), Indian medicine men, and others have brought our attention back to the concept of natural harmony, the Dionysian principle, and the power of suggestion. It seems a shame that during a few scientific centuries the wisdom of the ages has been rejected. Perhaps we are beginning to develop a more wholesome balance between science and magic. In Brown's view they both fit on a continuum of mechanisms for coping with the awesome aspects of nature, both personal and environmental. Surely the middle-aged, who are most victimized by the pressures of social structure and conformity, need an expanded view of the self to release their creative capacity for health and renewal.

SUMMARIZING STATEMENTS BASED ON THE LITERATURE

- People who value intellectual functions and interpersonal skills tend to feel young after their bodies show signs of age (Troll).
- Each person has a unique interior drummer that coordinates rhythmic fluctuations (Goldberg).
- During the forties, the substructure of sleep becomes more prominent; there is diminished deep sleep and increased awakening (Webb).
- There is an absence of knowledge concerning how to use the energy inherent in one's body (Sokoloff).
- Persons on regular sleep schedules experience increased sensory acuity between 5 and 7 P.M. (Kreiger).
- Loss of physical strength begins at about 30, with a 10 percent decrease between then and age 60 (Timiras).

- Affluence increases our inactivity (Diekelmann).
- Stress is generally most acute in situations where one feels helpless, powerless, or lacking in autonomy (Colligan).
- Specific sensory changes, especially hearing loss, become noticeable during middle age (Timiras).
- Sensitivity to pain remains steady until about age 50 and then declines differentially for different parts of the body (Timiras).
- General health in the adult years is highly variable. In the adult years, people tend to get fewer acute illnesses and to develop more chronic ailments (McCammon).
- Lifetime activity levels may influence proneness to coronary artery disease (Stringer and Pittman).
- Most of the health hazards of middle years are stress-related diseases.
- Breast cancer is the number one killer of women in their forties (Grandstaff).
- There is value in having a predictive view of one's health (Chew).
- Holistic health care emphasizes healing, the maintenance of health, the consciousness of potential, and the prevention of illness (Pelletier).
- Folk medicine should be respected (Brown).

GUIDELINES FOR INTERVENTION

- Advise middle-aged people to participate in activities which involve coordination rather than speed, strength, or endurance (Diekelmann).
- People have a somatic susceptibility to colors, and color is an important aspect of the environment. Consider the implications of this in working with the middle-aged (Luscher).
- Alert middle-aged clients to the importance of adequate exercise, a supportive environment, improved diet, adequate rest, and a reduction in stress.
- Alert the middle-aged person to the normal body changes of middle age, such as decreased visual and auditory acuity and decreased musculoskeletal integrity, and also to the higher incidence of arthritis, obesity, cardiovascular problems, and diabetes among the middle-aged (Diekelmann).
- Be available to help families cope with the stresses of illness and inform them of other resources and options (Owen).
- Encourage monthly self-examination of the breasts.
- Encourage client participation in terms of consent and decision making during illness.
- Consider the significance of folk medicine and cultural beliefs when working with middle-aged clients.

REFERENCES

Birren, James: *Relations of Development and Aging,* Charles C Thomas, Springfield, Ill., 1964.

Bischof, L. J.: *Adult Psychology,* Harper & Row, New York, 1969.

Brown, Marie: "Cultural Differences That Make a Difference in Nursing," *Chautauqua: Hawaii East,* Colorado Nurses' Convention, Aug. 7, 1977, Vail, Colo.

Bühler, C.: "The Course of Human Life as a Psychological Problem in Developmental Psychology," in W. R. Looft (ed.), *A Book of Readings,* Dryden, Hinsdale, Ill., 1972, pp. 68–84.

Cant, Gilbert: "Male Trouble," *The New York Times Magazine,* Feb. 16, 1975, p. 68.

Chew, Peter: *The Inner World of the Middle-Aged Man,* Macmillan, New York, 1976.

Cobb, S., and **S. Kasl:** "Some Medical Aspects of Unemployment," in G. M. Shatte (ed.), *Employment of the Middle-Aged,* Charles C Thomas, Springfield, Ill., 1972, pp. 87–98.

Colligan, Douglas: "That Helpless Feeling: The Dangers of Stress," *New York,* **8** (23):28–31, July 14, 1975.

Diekelmann, Nancy: *Primary Health Care of the Well Adult,* McGraw-Hill, New York, 1977.

Donahue, Phil: National Broadcasting Company telecast, Aug. 9, 1977.

Dunn, Halbert: *High-Level Wellness,* Beatty, Arlington, Va., 1973.

Finch, Caleb, and **Leonard Hayflick:** *Handbook of the Biology of Aging,* Van Nostrand Reinhold, New York, 1977.

Fozard, J. L., R. L. Nuttal, and **N. C. Waugh:** "Age-Related Differences in Mental Performance," *International Journal of Aging and Human Development,* **3**(1):19–43, 1972.

Goldberg, Vicki: "Do Body Rhythms Really Make You Tick?" *New York,* **10**(7):71–75, Feb. 14, 1977.

Grandstaff, Netta: "Workshop III: Informed Consent in Surgery—Options in Mastectomy," from *Health in the Middle Years: A Symposium about Women,* American Friends Service Committee, San Francisco, 1976.

Hayakawa, S. I.: *The Semantic Barrier: A Theory of Personality and Communication,* Walter V. Clark Associates, East Providence, R.I., 1954.

Hunt, Bernice, and **Morton Hunt:** *Prime Time,* Stein and Day, New York, 1975.

Institute of Human Knowledge and University of California: *Self-Care Symposium,* San Francisco, March 1977.

Kreiger, D. T.: "The Hypothalamus and Neuroendocrinology," *Hospital Practice,* **6**(9):87–89, 1971.

Luscher, Max: *The Luscher Color Test,* tr. and ed. by Ian Scott, Pocket Books, New York, 1971.

Metropolitan Life Statistical Bulletin, "Recent Trends in Mortality from Cancer," **57**:6, June 1976.

The Mind Can Do Anything, conference presented at Marin Civic Center, Marin, Calif., October 1976.

Owen, Bernice: "The Middle Years: Coping with Chronic Illness," *American Journal of Nursing,* **75**(6):1016–1018, 1975.

Pelletier, Kenneth: "Mind as Healer, Mind as Slayer," *Psychology Today,* **10**(9): 36–40, 1977.

Sokoloff, Boris: *Middle Age Is What You Make It,* Greystone, New York, 1938.

Stringer, L. A., and **D. J. Pittman:** "The

Unmeasured Residual in Current Research on Parental Attitudes and Child Behavior," in J. C. Glidewell (ed.), *Parental Attitudes and Child Behavior,* Charles C Thomas, Springfield, Ill., 1961.

Thompson, L., and **G. Marsh:** "Psychological Studies of Aging," in C. Eisdorfer and M. P. Lawton (eds.), *The Psychology of Adult Development and Aging,* American Psychological Association, Washington, D.C., 1973.

Thoresen, Carl: Self-Control: Power to the Person, *Self-Care* (Symposium), sponsored by The Institute for the Study of Human Knowledge and the University of California, San Francisco, 1977.

Timiras, P. S.: *Developmental Physiology and Aging,* Macmillan, New York, 1972.

Troll, Lillian: *Early and Middle Adulthood; The Best Is Yet to Be—Maybe,* Brooks/Cole, Monterey, Calif., 1975.

Webb, Wilse: *Sleep: The Gentle Tyrant,* Prentice-Hall, Englewood Cliffs, N.J., 1973.

OTHER RESOURCES

FILMS

The Critical Decades: 29 min/b&w/1965. Dr. Irving Baumgartner and some of his patients demonstrate how living patterns that are developed during the "critical decades" (40 to 60 years of age) influence one's health and happiness in later life. The film points out the need to develop a pattern of living during middle age and shows how the family doctor can foster good attitudes toward preventive health care in patients. Producer: George C. Stoney Associates. Distributor: Iowa State University, Media Resources Center, 121 Pearson Hall, Ames, Iowa 50010.

The Mortal Body: 12 min/b&w/16 mm. A short, poignant film about the body's vitality and vulnerability and the fleeting quality of life. Nonverbal with musical background. Distributor: Filmakers Library, Inc., 290 West End Avenue, New York, N.Y. 10023.

Sticky My Fingers, Fleet My Feet: 23 min/color/1970. Deflates the classic American myth of the middle-aged male who clings to a youthful standard of physical prowess and he-man virility. Producer: J. Hancock and American Film Institute. Distributor: Time-Life Multimedia, 100 Eisenhower Drive, Paramus, N.J. 07652.

Chapter 16

THE INHERENT STRENGTHS OF MIDDLE-AGED MEN AND WOMEN

Priscilla Ebersole

> And he said unto them,
> "Within each of us lies the
> power of our consent to health
> and to sickness, to riches and to poverty,
> to freedom and to slavery. It
> is we who control these,
> and not another."
>
> *Richard Bach*

A person is a biological organism, a social being, and a unique individual; none of these aspects can be overlooked in a holistic view. Many studies of human development overlook or deemphasize one or more of these factors. In this chapter the focus will be on the uniqueness of the individual and of the inner perception of personal existence. It is my belief that the nature of personal reality is proscribed by individual percepts and conceptual thought. In essence our world is as broad or as narrow as we define it.

When I was young, my mother would say, "It is not the gale but the set of the sail that determines the way the ship will go." She was very determined and long-suffering. Later, I heard a therapist say, "This group has no destination, and therefore we can let it go where it will."

I began to see that some people have an overriding goal in their lives, while others seem to flow with the tide; some fight against the tide successfully, and others cling desperately to sticks when their boats are overturned in a storm. A few wait quietly on shore for their "ship to come in." What is the difference? Personality. Certainly the demands of life situations vary enormously, but the style of coping varies according to how one uses one's inner resources. When situations are unjust or unfair, some people find meaning, and others find meaning in no meaning. The way one views and uses one's inner resources makes life move restlessly between waves of richness and deprivation. By middle age the course has been determined, but it may need correction. A task of the middle years is to become fully aware of one's inner strengths and resources—of one's "personality," or all that constitutes individual consciousness.

PERSONALITY

Personality includes behavior, feelings, attitudes, and interpersonal components in a system that is the "self." The more unique this system is, the more likely it is to be viewed as charismatic or eccentric (Troll).

Personality Theories

Three basic ways of viewing personality are evolving. Some theorists look for constancy over time, others consider situational factors to have profoundly variable effects, and still others believe that the self-system, instead of minimizing changes by compensating to maintain stability, incorporates these changes and becomes transformed into a new and different whole (Troll). The implications of each posture are apparent. The first allows for more predictability, comes from early socialization, and is easier for researchers to study. The second is related to a humanistic stance and a good deal of compassion if one accepts the idea that within each of us resides the possibility for any human expression, given the critical situation. We are all both weak and strong, aggressive and submissive, dependent and independent, murderous and self-destructive, spiritual and profane. The third view incorporates the first two, allowing for the impact of early developmental pressures and personal attributes as well as for the molding and channeling effects of experience throughout life. Maslow's self-actualized individual would be of this third type: learning and growing, stabilizing, searching, and learning and growing again in a spiral of personal development.

Factors That Influence Personality
Expansion or Contraction of Social Field
Sociologists find roles and status to be most important in explaining an individual's adaptation. Psychologists focus on cognitive perception, environmentalists view the possibilities in the situation and evolutionary trends, and humanists assess the degree of freedom. All these must effect changes over time and the personality construct (Kimmel).

Activity
One factor of great importance is the individual's activity level; some people have a penchant for sameness, while others search for adventure. Complex, creative people need opportunities for expression, and simpler people need more stable lives (Lowenthal and Chiriboga). This could be called a "personality

artifact,'' a ''genetic endowment,'' or a ''neurophysiologic propensity.'' In any case, the theory one ascribes to would make a great difference in terms of individual development. Activity level is one ingredient of personality that stays most stable over the life-span. While absolute tempo, individually, slows during the middle years, it remains consistently personal to the individual (Haan and Day).

Age

Kimmel has conceptualized a construct that organizes personality processes into centrifugal tendencies in young adulthood, balance in middle adulthood, and centripetal tendencies in old age. This construct seems to support gradual disengagement in the later years (Cumming and Henry). At 40, people seem to see the environment as rewarding boldness and risk taking, and they feel energetic enough to grasp opportunities; at 60, people tend to see the environment as complex and dangerous and not malleable to their needs (Kimmel). Controversy still rages over whether there is a mutual loosening of the bonds between society and the individual that occurs naturally as one grows older. As one professor wisely put it, ''The best thing about the disengagement theory is the amount of attention to the process of aging it has evoked!''

Health

Butler and Lewis found the presence of disease to be far more important in personality adjustment than other factors. The sense of self-continuity can be severely assaulted during illness, crisis, or multiple changes (Lowenthal and Chiriboga).

Values and Attitudes

Kelly found that the most stable personality measures from the mid-twenties to the mid-forties are *values:* (1) aesthetic, (2) religious, (3) economic, (4) social, (5) political, (6) theoretical, and (7) vocational. The least stable components of personality were found to be *attitudes* toward (1) marriage, (2) church attendance, (3) child rearing, (4) housekeeping, (5) entertaining, and (6) gardening. Generally, husbands were found to change more than wives, possibly as a result of exposure to more varied viewpoints, which was the explanation for many of the observed differences between males and females in the 1950s. It would be interesting to know whether values have maintained the same stability in our present, ever more fluid society. Haan and Day, in a recent study, found that values such as intellectualism, humanitarianism, aestheticism, and practicality tend to remain stable through the adult years. These values are often shared by family members across the generations. (See Chapter 9 for a discussion of values and culture.)

Relationships

Drastic personality changes may become apparent following disruption in a relationship. It must be remembered that personality traits are often polarized in dyadic relationships of long standing. Thus if one partner is extremely dependent, the other is often strong, but the positions may become completely reversed if a situation, such as illness, requires it. In terms of neurosis this could be seen as being rooted in reaction formation, but in more humanistic terms it may mean that an individual has untapped potential for responding to a situation and to the needs of significant others.

Latent Sexuality

In mid-life women ordinarily become somewhat more aggressive and assertive, expressing the ''masculine'' component of their personality, while men become more comfortable with the ''feminine'' component and express their tender feelings more readily (Jung). Perhaps this explains the behavior of the man who said that when his son went to war, he shook his hand and wished him good luck, but that if he had it to do over again, he would throw his arms around him and cling to him tenderly. This shift in expression of elements in the individual personality may occur because the earlier tasks associated with home and career suppressed overt expression of latent personality attributes. This is another area in which we can expect many changes as feminine and masculine roles become less distinct in the early adult years.

IDENTITY

Over a quarter of a century ago Erikson recognized that the study of identity becomes just as strategic in our time as the study of sexuality was in Freud's time (1959). Identity crises are no longer seen as an adolescent dilemma but rather as a national style. As Erikson now sees it, we have a ''strangely adolescent style of adulthood . . . one remaining expansively open for new roles and stances'' (1975, p. 44). And with options increasing daily, most middle-aged Americans are desperately trying to find their roots. We want options, but we also need an inner sense of continuity. (See Chapter 11.)

"When we speak of one's identity, what we are talking about is the accumulation of the numerous identifications made throughout one's lifetime'' (Gaylin, p. 102). Through identification, one learns more adaptive activities and becomes more in control of experiences that provide pleasure, security, pride, and self-esteem. As these increase, one's capacity for love is expanded. (See Chapter 1.) Another component of identification that occurs with frequency among the middle-aged is the loss of significant persons who have supported important aspects of the individual's self-view and the consequent loss of a portion of ''I.''

Not only is identity bound with significant others, but it is also strongly meshed with the work situation. ''Who am I?'' and ''What am I doing?'' are so intricately bound in our society that the identity issue may be resolved several times over: with job changes, with changes in marital status, and with changes in friendships (Kimmel).

Most people, despite confusing options and despite losses and gains, have an intuitive sense of self that integrates past and present in a coherent manner. The importance of reviewing the past is discussed in Chapters 17 and 23. Reflective individuals may have a solider sense of self or may be hung up on the discrepancies. It is important for care givers to provide some opportunity for individuals to assess their past and come to terms with each part of their lives.

SELF-ESTEEM

Identity and self-esteem are closely tied and seem to gain strength throughout the adult years (Lowenthal and Chiriboga). Veroff, Feld, and Gurin rated adults at 40 as happier with themselves than younger or older adults. Data were cross-sectional and may have reflected different coping styles in the cultural context. Woodruff and Birren found a distinct cohort difference in neurotic tendencies between women college students in 1944 and women college students in 1969. The older group were better adjusted both in their youth and at the time of the study than the younger group.

Certain approaches to life may be better suited to one period than another. Thurner found that men who had the highest morale in their forties were materialistic and career-oriented, while men 10 years older with these same characteristics were anxious and depressed. Personality characteristics that make for good adjustment at one point in life may contribute to maladjustment later. Self-esteem may thus be tied largely to what the culture expects and to the strength of one's ego.

COGNITION

Personality, as previously discussed in this chapter, incorporates identity, self-esteem, ego strength, feelings, and experience. Psychologists would say that these are all under the aegis of cognitive function.

Physiologically, the brain gets progressively smaller after age 30, and there is a displacement of solid tissue with moisture. There are changes in electroencephalographic records showing fewer alpha rhythms (related to attentiveness) (Obrist, Henry, and Justiss). What does this mean in terms of cognitive function? No one is quite sure. There is growing controversy over changes in cognition that can be attributed purely to aging.

Cognitive function is one of the most difficult areas to assess accurately. Changes in education, experiences, health, and testing procedures have altered our concepts of adult cognitive development. It used to be thought that general intellectual capacity began to decline when a person was in his or her twenties. Then the point of decline began to move upward, and now studies indicate that older people show no general decline through the seventies (Eisdorfer; Horn; Schaie). One of the major problems has been that testing procedures are notorious for testing speed rather than personal relevance or intellectual capacity. When time limits were removed, Ghiselli found no age decrements in intelligence among 1400 subjects aged 20 to 65. Verhage found that inherent ability can influence adult intellectual stability. Individuals who test higher to begin with tend to maintain their level of performance longer than those who test lower. As my sister commented, "Some people are born test takers; if we could make a living taking tests, we would do just fine!"

Honzik and Macfarlane found that subjects who continued to gain IQ points during adulthood experienced a higher level of personal dissatisfaction at age 30, perhaps indicating that they were more motivated toward cognitive development.

Present research indicates that certain types of intellectual changes occur during the adult years. Functions that require quick thinking peak at age 20 and plateau for a decade or two before declining. Abilities that require storage of information, such as vocabulary, tend to increase well into old age. Reasoning and mathematical abilities tend to plateau throughout the adult years.

Horn and Cattell distinguish between the development of fluid intelligence and that of crystallized intelligence. Fluid intelligence is involved in the organizational process (perceptual integration based on function of neurological structures) of conceptual thought and problem solving. This declines after the late teens (Cunningham, Clayton, and Overton). Crystallized intelligence is defined as "knowledge" and the awareness of the collective intelligence of the culture. It should continue to increase throughout adulthood. Nesselroade, Schaie, and Baltes found that crystallized intelligence increased, visuomotor flexibility decreased, and cognitive flexibility and visualization showed no significant age-related change. Intelligence may not always indicate adaptive capacity in life, as Horn has pointed out.

SEX DIFFERENCES IN INTELLIGENCE

All research findings agree that intellectual development is different for men and women in our country (Honzik and Macfarlane; Kangas and Bradway; Schaie). Women tend toward superiority in verbal meaning, word fluency, and reasoning, while men are superior in space, number, and general intellectual ability (Schaie). Sex-role acceptance seems to influence progressive intellectual development; women who are highly social and dependent decline in IQ over the years; independent, complex, and self-doubting women tend to increase in IQ. It seems clear that many differences in adult intelligence are due to socialization, cohort, culture, and exposure to new and stimulating experiences.

Unconventional thought is one trait that remains most stable from early adolescence to late adulthood. Women seem to become less conventional than men in middle age. Children often follow the parents' style in terms of conventionality; however, drastic cultural changes may produce family generation gaps in this respect. (Troll, Neugarten, and Kraines).

Problem-solving ability shows no decrement in the middle years, according to researchers (Schaie and Schaie). Older subjects do tend to ask more questions before solving a problem. Perhaps that is *wisdom*. One learns over the years that quick, simplistic solutions are often inadequate to deal with the ambiguities of life.

LIFELONG LEARNING

Lifelong learning is essential in a society where knowledge becomes quickly obsolescent (Entine). "Periods of rapid growth and a widening cognition permit, in interaction with living institutions, a renewal of old strengths as well as an initiation of new ones (Erikson, 1975, p. 100). High points in the need for achievement seem to occur in young adulthood and in middle age. We have witnessed a mass return of middle-aged people to educational institutions, reflecting their wish to learn and achieve. The process of exploration and learning is the essence of existence. As Alland has said, "Curiosity has tremendous survival value" (p. 94).

PERCEPTUAL DIFFERENCES

Thus far, we have considered the most obvious mind functions. One reason we understand so little about personality is our neglect of mind functions we cannot measure. Samples has said: "The human mind is beginning to resist describing itself only by those qualities that can be objectively measured" ("Natural Mind: Moving toward equilibrium," p. 4). Our conception of mind consists of more than intelligence; it includes intuition, dreams, fantasies, illusions, and personal perception of reality. One's orientation to reality and the various "props" of life is greatly colored by class, culture, and social status. These will affect one's personal approach to situations, general level of satisfaction, and opportunities for self-actualization. Our beliefs become self-fulfilling prophecies.

Culture and environment markedly affect perceptual development by cultivating certain senses. In the modern world we rely on vision at the expense of the other senses. Smell and touch require a slower, more intimate environmental interaction. Therefore, reality is perceived differently depending on age, location, cognitive ability, and sensory awareness. Culture and socialization can influence the perception of reality to such an extent that people see things in very different ways. People in a carpentered world are susceptible to three-dimensional illusions. People in primitive times lived in vertical, rotary, and richly symbolic worlds, whereas today we tend toward broad, low, and angular surfaces and a profane existence (Tuan). No human perspective has exhausted the bounds of reality.

THE NATURAL MIND

Many parapsychological mind phenomena are so poorly understood that they are often consigned to the world of spirits and demons. In an effort to be scientific, researchers have recently tried to show that all the unknown capacities of the mind reside in the nondominant cerebral hemisphere (Ornstein; Oyle). This has been a large step toward giving these mind functions respectability. The natural mind is the metaphoric mind that enriches our reality. That is what the remainder of this chapter is about. See Table 16-1.

Table 16-1. Comparison of Rational and Intuitive Thought

Rational Thought	Intuitive Thought
Straight thinking (Weil)	"Stoned thinking" (Weil)
Knowing through the intellect	Reliance on intuition
Attachment to sensory input as a route to reality	Possible to control autonomic nervous system—biofeedback, etc.
Attention to outward form; materialism	Nonmaterial reality
Tendency to perceive differences rather than similarities	Acceptance of ambivalent nature of things
Threatened by any other kind of reality	Experience of infinity in its positive aspect
Linear thought; cause and effect	Physical world perceived as illusory
Cultivation of logic; seeking proof	Based on belief
Western thought	Eastern thought
Dominant part of the brain	Nondominant part of the brain
Objective	Subjective
Conscious	Expanded conscious or subconscious
Cerebrological	Psychological
Pessimism	Optimism
Clear limits	Transcendent
Civilized	Primitive

Source: Summarized from Samples; Ornstein; Weil.

ILLUSIONS

Holograms are illusions created by the refraction of laser light. An illusion is something that deceives by producing a false impression—false in the sense that it is based on mistaken, erroneous, or inconsistent perceptions, ideas, or facts. Peak experiences and most intuitive thought would, by this definition, be illusory, though these form the core of reality for some persons. "In general there is a slight but steady decrease in susceptibility to illusions from childhood to early adulthood, a period of no age differences through much of adulthood, and progressively increased susceptibility after about age 40 or 50" (Troll, p. 40).

In mid-life one's sense of magic is depleted; fantasy periods may be brief and oriented toward the practical. Goals tend to be concrete and oriented toward accumulating goods and planning for a pleasant old age. There are times when one is, briefly, in a state of illusion, as when one is between the waking and sleeping states, recovering from anesthesia, in a dream state, or under the influence of certain medications or alcohol. While the middle-aged are generally not the consumers of illicit drugs, they are large consumers of prescribed drugs. Alcohol is increasingly the drug of choice for the middle-aged as they escape from the pressures of their personal reality. Recently, news stories and popular publications have brought to public attention the increasing number of well-known adults who are using cocaine. In fact, it has been said that in order to ensure a successful gathering, many society hostesses are including cocaine in their party plans. The middle-aged seem to be searching for a subdued awareness, rather than the heightened awareness and psychedelic experience sought by the young.

CREATIVE REALITY

If an individual experiences an idiosyncratic reality, it is judged to be unreality. The recollections of Einstein, Descartes, Galileo, Freud, Mesmer, and others bring us to the realization that reality is often only a matter of public opinion. Scientific ideas are called "paradigms," and if they are elegant enough, they soon become perceived as reality (Oyle). Reality in mid-life is linked largely to the search for like-minded people. "A consensually validated world of facts with a mutual activation of like-minded people. Only these two together provide a sense of reality" (Erikson, 1975, p. 103).

Creative thought may be a personal reality with components of intuition, often unshared and seen as illusory or bizarre by others.

Weil has said, "The history of science makes it clear that the greatest advances in man's understanding of the universe are made by intuitive leaps at the frontiers of knowledge, not by intellectual walks down well traveled paths" (p. 60).

Peak creativity in a wide variety of fields tends to occur before age 39 (Lehman). The more unique, original, and inventive the production, the more likely it is to have been created before age 30. One might speculate that the young adult is not so entrenched in the accumulated cultural knowledge and is free to ask questions that would appear ridiculous in the established scientific circles. The institutionalization of ideas may prevent middle-aged persons from making spectacles of themselves over some "harebrained" idea.

The more a creative act depends on accumulated experience, the more likely it is to occur in the later years of life. It is solace to those in late middle age to realize that their forte is experience, which cannot be acquired by any method except the accretion of years.

Peak creative output usually occurs between ages 30 and 40 (Dennis), except among artists who need little formal education to produce. Poets, novelists, and scholars continue to be creatively productive into old age; however, as Jaques points out, the direction of creative work may change considerably after the mid-life crisis.

Probably the two most influential thinkers of the last millennium have been Darwin and Einstein. It is interesting to note the development of thought throughout their lives. Darwin, born in 1809, was stimulated by new ideas that came to him during his trip to the Galapagos Islands in 1831. He wrote of his impressions and experiences between 1839 and 1846 and then spent 22 years developing and refining his theories of evolution. He presented his ideas publicly in 1858, and then only because a young naturalist seemed to be proceeding in the same direction. Einstein was born in 1879. He enunciated his theory of relativity in 1905; however, it took him another 24 years to develop a "unified field theory," and at age 74 he was still at work attempting to devise a single mathematical formula which would include the laws of gravitation, electromagnetism, and relativity. The initial creative thought occurred when both men were very young, but it took them decades to refine their ideas and accrue enough experience to make them sound.

Creative thinkers have often experienced distinctly different phases of expression during their lives. Fromm said it well: "To be creative means to consider the whole process of life a process of birth, and not to take any stage as a final stage" (p. 57). He defines five conditions of creativity: (1) the capacity to be puzzled, (2) the ability to concentrate, (3) experiencing "I," (4) the ability to accept conflict and tension, and (5) a willingness to be born every day.

Many middle-aged people would be more creative if they had not been so completely immersed in the establishment of family and careers during their young adulthood. Stress or crises may later disrupt complacency and allow people to become puzzled and seek new modes of expression. With this view, one may embrace mid-life crises (see Chapter 17) as presaging a new birth of the self.

Ghislen has made the following observations on creativity:

Even the most vigorous and creative minds often are muddled.
Creative thoughts are often resisted by society.
Creativity can occur during conditions of poverty.
Traditional methods are often inadequate for creative problem solving.
Rigid thoughts and feelings impede creativity.
Much creative thought initially appears to be eccentric.
Creative thought usually begins in isolation.
Dissatisfaction with the established order may germinate creative thought.
Creativity involves a sense of unrealized possibilities.
A state of imaginative muddled suspense precedes successful inductive generalization.
Spontaneous insights are common in creative thought but are usually incomplete.
Creativity requires some dissociation from consciousness.
The creative end product is never in full sight at the beginning.

Samuels and Samuels have outlined the following stages of the creative process:

1. *Preparation.* There is a conscious collection of data and a mood of excitement and perplexity.
2. *Incubation.* The attention is turned to something else; this is the critical stage of "subconscious mulling."
3. *Illumination.* The solution is spontaneously arrived at unexpectedly; there is a mood of joy and certainty.
4. *Verification or revision.* There is organization of materials or mastery of techniques; this is a period of conscious activity.

DREAMS AND FANTASIES

During the middle years even dreams contain a practical element; for example, men between 30 and 54 report many dreams about their work (Krohn and Gutmann). Though dreams reflect some of our daily life, they also provide a route toward self-healing and toward the activation of physical, mental, emotional, and spiritual wholeness (Garfield).

Garfield makes the following suggestions for creative dreaming:

Provide yourself with a peaceful place to dream.
Engage in activities relevant to the dream you wish to produce.
Decide specifically what you want to dream about.
Put your dream intention into a phrase, relax, repeat it, and visualize it.
Remember, while dreaming, what you previously intended to do in your dream.
Build friendly figures into your dream.
Become conscious of your dream state—"lucid dreaming."
Following your dream, visualize it and record it in the present tense.
Use your dreams to help you. You can practice whatever skills you wish while dreaming, and they will carry over into your waking life.
Maintain a dream diary; examination of your dreams will reveal certain recurrent themes.

Daydreams and fantasies make up a good portion of our lives at all ages, though the frequency changes with age. Giambra found that daydreaming declines linearly with age in frequency and intensity. Daydreaming is regarded as acceptable at all ages, though sexual daydreams are predominant among younger people, while older persons are more inclined to have problem-solving daydreams. Giambra concluded that daydreaming reflected current concerns and did not reflect suppressed desires. See Table 16-2.

HUMOR

Humor can be used to relieve tensions and create amity, or it can be the handmaiden of aggression (Alland); however, it is rarely mentioned in books about psychological adaptation. Scanning the indexes in 20 current texts, I found entries for "hoodlums," "Hopi," "horse," "hybrid vigor," and "hydroencephaly"—but no "humor." Humor has been studies extensively from the viewpoint of entertainment but has not been seriously considered as a psychological resource, and yet what is more insufferable than a humorless life?

Humor is based on incongruity: a buildup of tension searching for intellectual release. When the "point" is seen, there is an explosive expulsion of air from the lungs called "laughter." If the tension or anxiety is minimal, there will be a smile—the smile of satisfaction when an ambiguity becomes clear. How can one live in this world of inconsistencies, paradoxes, and contradictions without humor? Sadly, many do!

Table 16-2. Means for Each Age Group on Each Scale of the Imaginal Processes Inventory, Correlations of Each Scale with Age, and Partial Correlations of Each Scale with Age Holding Scale 1 Constant

Scale No.	Scale Description	Age Group							Correlation[a] With	
		17–23	24–34	35–44	45–54	55–64	65–74	75–91	Age	Partial
28	Self-revelation	27.0[b]	21.4	21.0	23.1	20.2	20.2	21.7	−.38***	−.31***
4	Acceptance of daydreaming	32.5	35.3	34.7	31.7	31.1	33.1	28.6	−.10*	−.00
1	Daydreaming frequency	29.1	24.7	23.5	21.1	21.4	19.6	13.5	−.49***	
3	Absorption in daydreaming	37.3	29.0	27.8	28.3	26.3	25.6	21.7	−.43***	−.21**
14	Mindwandering	28.6	26.7	24.9	23.8	23.8	24.1	20.4	−.34***	−.09
22	Curiosity: interpersonal	26.2	23.3	23.9	25.8	25.1	24.6	26.2	−.08	−.01
23	Curiosity: impersonal-mechanical	22.1	25.6	26.4	25.5	22.5	24.4	25.3	.11**	.08
24	Boredom	21.9	19.0	16.8	17.3	17.1	16.0	16.3	−.36***	−.23***
25	Mentation rate	26.2	27.0	25.5	26.7	26.6	25.4	25.1	−.05	.04
26	Distractibility	26.1	22.3	24.7	22.2	21.2	19.7	19.1	−.39***	−.22***
27	Need for external stimulation	28.7	25.9	23.9	26.3	24.4	24.7	24.6	−.34***	−.31***
10	Present oriented daydreams	23.4	24.7	25.3	24.7	23.4	23.1	24.1	.02	.07
11	Future in daydreams	28.0	26.0	24.6	25.5	23.4	24.4	25.1	−.23***	−.13*
12	Past in daydreams	23.9	19.7	23.2	20.6	22.4	23.8	25.4	−.03	.08
5	Positive reactions in daydreaming	25.2	22.7	25.2	21.3	19.8	19.0	19.3	−.34***	−.15*
6	Frightened reaction to daydreaming	17.0	12.3	9.6	14.0	11.6	12.6	9.4	−.31***	−.16*
7	Visual imagery in daydreaming	23.8[b]	21.1	20.2	18.7	19.9	19.7	18.7	−.27***	−.11
8	Auditory images in daydreams	21.4	16.9	17.0	14.4	13.8	13.0	10.7	−.42***	−.27***
16	Hallucinatory-vividness of daydreams	11.5	7.9	8.9	9.2	6.2	7.2	7.2	−.26***	−.15*
9	Problem solving daydreams	23.4	22.8	24.5	21.3	17.9	20.4	19.7	−.23***	−.04
19	Sexual daydreams	26.0	20.4	19.8	15.7	15.4	13.9	9.7	−.56***	−.42***
13	Bizarre-improbable daydreams	19.3	15.9	13.6	14.5	15.6	16.4	11.5	−.26***	−.18*
15	Achievement-oriented daydreams	18.8	16.9	13.2	11.6	11.9	9.3	14.6	−.34***	−.23***

18	Hostile daydreams	16.6	10.8	10.6	7.5	9.1	7.7	4.7	−.48***	−.36***
20	Heroic daydreams	15.8	10.3	7.2	7.2	7.7	6.9	7.2	−.45***	−.36***
17	Fear of failure daydreams	12.9	8.8	8.1	9.2	9.0	7.3	5.4	−.33***	−.24***
21	Guilt daydreams	11.1	6.9	6.1	5.3	6.1	5.5	4.8	−.36***	−.28***
2	Nightdreaming frequency	23.5	14.2	14.9	11.9	15.7	14.8	11.8	−.37***	−.21**

[a] It is reasonable to question the reliability of these correlations since nearly 60 percent of the sample is in the 17–23 age group. This circumstance probably resulted in a reduction in the magnitude of the correlation; a conclusion derived by considering the disproportionate contribution of the 17–23 age group as functionally like a partial restriction in range. The use of such a large n for the 17–23 age group had its primary benefit in providing a mean of high reliability.

[b] The unweighted means of the scale standard deviation for the seven age groups were respectively: 7.1, 6.8, 7.4, 6.8, 5.5, 6.3, 7.0. The standard deviation of the scale standard deviations for the age groups were 1.4, 1.9, 2.6, 1.6, 1.6, 1.6, 1.9. The ratio of the largest to the smallest standard deviation was least in the Scale 2 (1.11) and greatest in Scale 4 (2.48). The mean and standard deviation of the ratio were 1.68 and .34, respectively.

*$p < .05$
** $p < .01$
*** $p < .001$

Source: Giambra, pp. 119–120.

Another level of humor arises from the individual who refuses to take himself or herself too seriously. Perhaps this is the difference between an egomaniac and a homophiliac. When one can step back a bit and see oneself moving with the parade of humanity along an unknown route to an uncertain destination, there are two choices: laugh or cry. Most thinking people do both.

Humor of the slapstick, scatological, or prank type is an effective release of aggression quite unacceptable in its naked form.

Satire affords a way for individuals to cope with the relinquishment or compromise of ideals. Institutions and pompous individuals are made ridiculous by satirical overexaggeration. The hopes of humanity, founded on the ideal, must give way to the perceived reality of the state of affairs—or the affairs of state (Pierre).

SPIRITUAL RESOURCES

Johnson, a chaplain, has defined being "born again" as the beginning of internalizing God, control, and responsibility. As the fetus emerges from the controlled environment of the womb, so our spirits emerge from the enclosure of dichotomized good-bad boundaries. There may be rage and panic as the belief in the externalization of good in the anthropomorphic God, and of bad in the generalized other, is shattered. Disillusionment, or deillusionment, ensues. Coping with the reality of oneself and integrating each new awareness of self and others is a lifelong task, ebbing and flowing throughout. Whether it is called "mental health," "maturity," "spirituality," or "caring," all that really matters is that at various points a focused reorganization of self and conceptual world occurs. Jung (1971) assigns this task to the last half of life, and Erikson (1975) does likewise. Levinson, Darrow, Klein, Levinson, and McKee observed earlier beginnings—somewhere in the mid-thirties.

The young adult often searches for an altruistic cause or a charismatic leader (see Chapter 12)—an external spirit. True spiritual development probably incorporates those elusive qualities of wisdom, morality, ethics, compassion, and self-actualization. Spiritual development may be seen as an integrative view of an individual's total developmental process. There is a vast chasm between psychiatry (inner self) and religion (external God) that is bridged as the spirit matures. The external evidence is seen in the bridges between people, a communal exchange, and the presence of caring.

Studies suggest that religious beliefs remain relatively stable throughout life and that church attendance remains stable or increases (Nelson; Terman and Oden). Though this chapter has stressed the importance of integrating all aspects of one's inner experience, it is important to recognize that many people do this through the use of rituals and traditions that give meaning and significance to their lives. In an age when young adults seem engaged in the pursuit of the unusual, it is interesting to note a substantial similarity between the views of college students on religion and those of their parents (Braun and Bengtson;

Table 16-3. Phases of Spiritual Development*

Individual	Symbolic Corollary in Biblical History
Childish innocence	Garden of Eden
Animal-instinctive	
Birth of conscience	Temptation
Guilt	Knowledge of good and evil
Fixed view of right and wrong	
Idealism	
Ambivalence	Containment of God
Polarity	Ark of the Covenant
God in charge	Altars
Externalized morals	Temples
Simplification	
Disillusionment (deillusionment)	Prophets of doom
Ambiguity	No salvation
Multiplicity and confusion	
Removal of false images	
Acceptance	Christ
Freedom	Decentralization
Responsibility	Interior God
Integration	Spirit of love
Multiplicity within oneself	
Core values	

* Developed in collaboration with Chaplain Walter Johnson.

Kalish and Johnson). Mothers' religious attitudes have been shown to influence children more than fathers' religious attitudes.

MORALITY AND ETHICS

Kohlberg takes the position that cognitive development and moral judgment are parallel processes and that at the highest stage of moral development, "We begin to see our lives as finite from some infinite perspective and value life from this standpoint" (p. 203). He has identified six universal stages of moral development; Erikson (1975) identifies three. Some theorists believe that maturation of logic is not necessary for moral development and that preliterate and/or primitive societies may be highly moral (Samples), implying an innate moral knowledge in human beings. See Figure 16-1.

ALTRUISM AND CARING

Sociobiologists are seriously supporting the view that human behavior, in its many-faceted expression, is genetically preordained (DeVore). Some of their

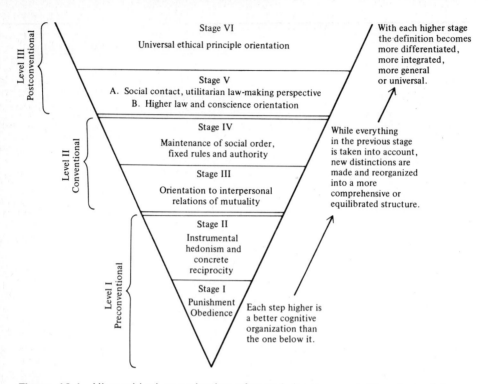

Figure 16-1 Hierarchical organization of moral development. (*Courtesy of Lawrence Kohlberg.*)

positions are extrapolated from animal behavior. In an exploration of altruistic behavior, self-sacrifice, and generosity, DeVore concludes that these qualities stem from either "reciprocal altruism" or an attempt to negotiate the best possible conditions for individual success in producing and caring for progeny. Altruism toward the species is seen as an investment in the future living conditions of one's own descendants. Reciprocal altruism involves repayment and the feeling of indebtedness. "Gratitude, indebtedness, contrition, supplication, revenge, apology, forgiveness, are uniquely human behaviors that apparently evolved as functional parts of the uniquely human system of reciprocal altruism" (DeVore, p. 51).

DeVore contends that all behavior has a genetic base and is adaptive to environmental differences and that humans are basically calculating, selfish, and deceitful when necessary, particularly self-deceitful.

It seems to me that we are all that DeVore says and much more. We are obviously endowed with the genetic capacity for everything we do or think. The important issue is not the theoretical construct we use to explain the inherent strengths we possess but rather the way in which we use our potential for caring for ourselves and others.

REFERENCES

Alland, Alexander: *The Human Imperative,* Columbia, New York, 1972.

Bach, Richard: *Illusions: The Adventures of a Reluctant Messiah,* Delacorte Press, New York, 1977.

Braun, P., and **V. Bengtson:** "Religious Behavior in Three Generations: Cohort and Lineage Effects," paper presented at the meeting of the Gerontological Society, San Juan, Puerto Rico, 1972.

Butler, Robert, and **Myrna Lewis:** *Aging and Mental Health: Positive Psychosocial Approaches,* Mosby, St. Louis, 1977.

Cumming, Elaine, and **William Henry:** *Growing Old: The Process of Disengagement,* Basic Books, New York, 1961.

Cunningham, W. R., V. Clayton, and **W. Overton:** "Fluid and Crystallized Intelligence in Young Adulthood and Old Age," *Journal of Gerontology,* **30**(1): 53–55, 1975.

Dennis, W.: "Creative Productivity between the Ages of 20 and 80 Years," *Journal of Gerontology,* **21**(1):1–8, 1966.

DeVore, Irven: "The New Science of Genetic Self-Interest," *Psychology Today,* **10**(9):42–88, 1977.

Eisdorfer, Carl: "Intellectual Changes with Advancing Age: A Ten Year Follow-up of the Duke Sample," paper presented at the American Psychological Association symposium entitled Longitudinal Changes with Advancing Age, San Francisco, 1968.

Entine, Alan (ed.): *Americans in Middle Years: Career Options and Educational Opportunities,* Ethel Percy Andrus Gerontology Center, Los Angeles, 1974.

Erikson, Erik: "Identity and the Life Cycle: Selected Papers," *Psychological Issues,* Monogr. no 1, 1959.

————: *Life History and the Historical Moment,* Norton, New York, 1975.

Fromm, Erich: "The Nature of Creativity," in H. H. Anderson (ed.), *Creativity and Its Cultivation,* Harper & Row, New York, 1959, pp. 55–68.

Garfield, Patricia: *Creative Dreaming,* Simon and Schuster, New York, 1975.

Gaylin, Willard: *Caring,* Knopf, New York, 1976.

Ghiselli, E. E.: "The Relationship between Intelligence and Age among Superior Adults, *Journal of Geriatric Psychology,* **90**(1):131–142, 1957.

Ghislen, Brewster: *The Creative Process,* Mentor Books, New York, 1952.

Giambra, Leonard: "Daydreaming across the Life Span: Late Adolescent to Senior Citizen," *International Journal of Aging and Human Devlopment,* **5**(2):115–140, 1974.

Haan, N., and **D. Day:** "A Longitudinal Study of Change and Sameness in Personality Development: Adolescence to Later Adulthood, *Aging and Human Development,* **5**(1):11–39, 1974.

Honzik, M. P., and **J. W. Macfarlane:** "Personality Development and Intellectual Functioning from 21 Months to 40 Years," paper presented at the American Psychological Association symposium entitled Maintenance of Intellectual Functioning with Advancing Years, Miami Beach, 1970.

Horn, J. L.: "Organization of Data on Life-Span Development of Human Abilities," in L. Goulet and P. Baltes (eds.), *Life-Span Developmental Psychology,* Academic, New York, 1970.

————, and **R. B. Cattell:** "Refinement and Test of the Theory of Fluid and Crystallized Intelligence," *Journal of Edu-*

cational Psychology, **57**(5):252–270, 1966.

Jaques, Elliott: "Death and the Mid-Life Crisis," *International Journal of Psychoanalysis,* **46**(4): 502–514, 1965.

Johnson, Walter: Personal communication, 1977.

Jung, Carl: "The Stages of Life," tr. by R. F. C. Hull, in J. Campbell (ed.), *The Portable Jung,* Viking, New York, 1971.

Kalish, R., and A. Johnson: "Value Similarities and Differences in Three Generations of Women," *Journal of Marriage and the Family,* **34**(1):49–55, 1972.

Kangas, J., and K. Bradway: "Intelligence at Middle-Age: A 38 Year Follow-up," *Developmental Psychology,* **5**:333–337, 1971.

Kelly, E. L.: "Consistency of the Adult Personality," *American Psychologist,* **10**(12):659–681, 1955.

Kimmel, Douglas: *Adulthood and Aging,* Wiley, New York, 1974.

Kohlberg, L.: "Continuities in Childhood and Adult Moral Development Revisited," in P. Baltes and K. W. Schaie (eds.), *Life-Span Developmental Psychology: Personality and Socialization,* Academic, New York, 1973.

Krohn, A., and D. Gutmann: "Changes in Mastery Style with Age: A Study of Navajo Dreams," *Psychiatry,* **34**(3): 289–300, 1971.

Lehman, H. C.: *Age and Achievement,* Princeton, Princeton, N.J., 1953.

Levinson, D., C. Darrow, E. Klein, M. Levinson, and Braxton McKee: "The Psychosocial Development of Men in Early Adulthood and the Mid-Life Transition," in D. Ricks, A. Thomas, and M. Roff (eds.), *Life History Research in Psychopathology,* vol. 3, University of Minnesota Press, Minneapolis, 1974.

Lowenthal, M., and D. Chiriboga: "Social Stress and Adaptation: Toward a Life Course Perspective," in C. Eisdorfer and M. Lawton (eds.), *The Psychology of Adult Development and Aging,* American Psychological Association, Washington, D.C., 1973.

Maslow, Abraham: *Toward a Psychology of Being,* Van Nostrand, Princeton, N.J., 1962.

"Natural Mind: Moving toward Equilibrium," *Brain/Mind Bulletin: Frontiers of Research, Theory and Practice,* **2**(14): 4, 1977.

Nelson, E. N: "Patterns of Religious Attitude Shifts from College to Fourteen Years Later," *Psychological Monographs,* **70**(17):1–15, 1956.

Nesselroade, J. R., K. W. Schaie, and P. B. Baltes: "Ontogenetic and Generational Components of Structural and Quantitative Change in Adult Cognitive Behavior," *Journal of Gerontology,* **27**(2): 222–228, 1972.

Obrist, W. D., C. E. Henry, and W. A. Justiss: "Longitudinal Study of EEG in Old Age," *Excerpta Medical International Congress,* **37**:180–181, 1961.

Ornstein, Robert: *The Psychology of Consciousness,* Freeman, San Francisco, 1972.

Oyle, Irving: *Time, Space and the Mind,* Celestial Arts, Millbrae, Calif., 1976.

Pierre, Joseph, Jr.: Personal communication, 1977.

Samples, Bob: *The Metaphoric Mind,* Addison-Wesley, Reading, Mass., 1976.

Samuels, Mike, and Nancy Samuels: *Seeing with the Mind's Eye: The History, Techniques and Uses of Visualization,* Random House, New York, 1975.

Schaie, K. W.: "Developmental Processes and Aging," in C. Eisdorfer and M. P. Lawton (eds.), *The Psychology of Adult Development and Aging,* American Psychological Association, Washington, D.C., 1973.

—— and **Joyce P. Schaie:** "Clinical Assessment and Aging," in James Birren and K. Warner Schaie (eds.), *Handbook of the Psychology of Aging,* Van Nostrand Reinhold, New York, 1977.

Terman, L. M., and **M. H. Oden:** *The Gifted Group of Mid-life: Thirty-five Year Follow-up of the Superior Child,* Genetic Studies of Genius, Stanford University Press, Stanford, Calif., 1959.

Thurner, M. I.: "Values and Goals in Later Middle Age," paper presented at the twenty-fourth annual meeting of the Gerontological Society, Houston, 1971.

Troll, Lillian: *Early and Middle Adulthood: The Best Is Yet to Be—Maybe,* Brooks/Cole, Monterey, Calif., 1975.

——, **B. L. Neugarten,** and **R. J. Kraines:** "Similarities in Values and Other Personality Characteristics in College Students and Their Parents," *Merrill-Palmer Quarterly,* **15:**323–337, 1969.

Tuan, Yi-Fu: *Topophilia: A Study of Environmental Perception, Attitudes, and Values,* Prentice-Hall, Englewood Cliffs, N.J., 1974.

Verhage, R.: Intelligence and Age in a Dutch Sample, *Human Development,* 8(4):238–245, 1965.

Veroff, J., S. Feld, and **G. Gurin:** "Dimensions of Subjective Adjustment," *Journal of Abnormal and Social Psychology,* 64(3):192–205, 1962.

Weil, Andrew: "The Natural Mind: A New Way of Looking at the Higher Consciousness," *Psychology Today,* 6(5):51–96, 1972.

Woodruff, Diana, and **James Birren:** *Aging: Scientific Perspectives and Social Issues,* D. Van Nostrand Co., New York, 1975.

OTHER RESOURCES

AUDIO CASSETTE TAPES

The Boundaries between the Individual and His World: 30 min. Gardner Murphy discusses the various concepts formulated to deal with the physical, temporal, functional, and perceptual boundaries between the individual and his or her world. Available from Jeffrey Norton Publishers, Inc., Audio Department, 145 East 49th Street, New York, N.Y. 10017, 1977.

Humanistic Psychology: 51 min. Charlotte Bühler gives a detailed analysis of the concepts, cultural significance, and meaning of humanistic psychology to the individual. Available from Jeffrey Norton Publishers, Inc., Audio Department, 145 East 49th Street, New York, N.Y. 10017, 1977. $11.75.

Mind as Healer, Mind as Slayer: A series of four tapes (AT 257–260) focusing on the inextricable interaction of body, mind, and environment. Topics covered include the role of stress in the psychogenesis of disease, uses of self-regulation techniques in alleviating stress disorders and promoting healing, reorganization in psychotic turmoil, and belief systems and cancer. Available from University of California, Extension Media Center, Berkeley, Calif. 95720, 1977. $55.

The Quest for Self-Actualization: 17 min. Michael Andrews discusses creative self-action as a means for enhancing personality. Available from Jeffrey Norton Publishers, Inc., Audio Department, 145 East 49th Street, New York, N.Y. 10017, 1977.

Chapter 17

THE THIRD BEGINNING: MALE AND FEMALE IN TRANSITION

Priscilla Ebersole

> As applied to middle age, midcourse correction refers to those changes that must be made early in mid-life—that point in the passage through life when the trajectory that has been suitable so far is about to carry us off course.
>
> *Bernice Hunt and Morton Hunt*

The middle years have been viewed as the years of stability and social power—the time when one should feel satisfied and confident. Clausen (1972) and Kimmel both emphasize continuity and stability throughout the adult life-span, though Kimmel does discuss crises and change as intrinsic to the individual over the span of time. However, there is presently a definite trend among investigators toward study of mid-life crises and transitions. It is unclear whether this trend is indicative of a growing awareness of psychosocial development across the life-span or rather of the fact that the middle-aged people today experience more frequent disruptions of life-style in response to the multiplicity of options not previously available to the middle-aged of other generations. It is possible that they are becoming increasingly dissatisfied with the role of responsibility in a social structure that seems bent on depersonalization and loss of autonomy. *In any case, most of the recent literature focuses on middle age as a time of personal recapitulation and reorganization.*

COMPONENTS OF CRISIS

Crisis, according to Chinese ideography, contains both opportunity and danger; Chew adds a third component—difficulty!

A crisis involves both an end and a beginning. Erikson (1959) has called the movement from early maturity to middle age the "crisis of generativity"; women approach it before 40, and men after 40 (Fried). Why should this be a crisis? As one woman succinctly stated, "I thought I would at least have a chance to grow up before I grew old!" There seems to be a moment of truth when one realizes one is no longer young. Many investigators believe that the decade between 40 and 50 is a critical transition period attended by many crises (Frenkel-Brunswick; Gould; Levinson, Darrow, Klein, Levinson, and McKee). Some developments are accomplished through gradual reorganization, and some through critical periods of turmoil and crisis during this crucial decade.

This chapter will explore the dynamics and impact of transitions and turning points in the middle years. These include such things as changes in (1) role and goal, orientation, (2) parental relations, (3) sexuality, (4) career suitability, and (5) self-definition. Gender often defines the significance and parameters in each of these areas. In the future the sexes may experience more similar transitions as role distribution becomes more equitable. Some theorists believe that women cope better with mid- and late-life changes because they experience profound social and psychophysiological adaptations repeatedly throughout the course of their adult lives. It seems that the differences in the sexes that allow them to experience personal challenges at varied times, rather than simultaneously, may foster the development of a reciprocal support system. However, when several crises occur simultaneously in both mates, the results may be deleterious to their personalities and the relationship. See Table 17-1.

At 40 people are young; at 50 there is no doubt that they are middle-aged. This decade brings a personal awareness of death (Neugarten, 1970), visible evidence of aging, the menopause, the "empty nest," and increased responsibility for aged parents. By 50 one has reassessed the situation and has stabilized again, often on a different path. Lindbergh sees the positive aspects of this period: "For is it not possible that middle age can be looked upon as a period of second flowering, second growth . . . ? The signs that presage growth, so similar, it

Table 17-1. Potential Mid-Life Crises

Women	Men
Divorce	Competition
The empty nest	Impotence
Forced employment after economic crisis	Job change
Gray hair (evidence of aging)	Unemployment
Hysterectomy	
Identity	
Infidelity	
Mastectomy	
Menopause	
Widowhood	

seems to me, to those in early adolescence: discontent, restlessness, doubt, despair, longing, are interpreted falsely as signs of decay'' (p. 39). For some women and men, mid-life may be the first opportunity to "be" an adolescent.

The success of Sheehy's book *Passages* (1976a) is testimonial to the desire of adults to understand more of themselves and their development. The little-studied mass of middle-aged average Americans seem to be seeking understanding of the various stages of their adulthood. Innumerable workshops and seminars have recently been devoted to self-discovery in the middle years. This may be the first generation that has had the affluence, energy, and opportunity to redefine themselves and change course in midstream. We have yet to see how this generation of middle-aged people will age and whether continuity of life-style has previously been a cultural or personal artifact.

Within the period of self-discovery, and the possibility for redirection, many issues have been defined: (1) authenticity, (2) time perception, (3) vitality, (4) appearance, (5) appropriate role, (6) health, and (7) career. Changes in any of these areas may precipitate a crisis state and temporary personality disorganization.

The following are determining factors in the ability to cope with crisis:

Time of life at which incongruence is experienced
Specific situation
Sex
Chronological age
Social class:
   Particular dimension that is one's sequence
   Degree of asynchronization
Sources of time-disordered relationships:
   Inconsistencies within social spheres (disordered job career)
   Inconsistencies between social spheres (late parenthood at peak of financial
     success)
   Combination of late parenthood, late career success, and early retirement

Mid-life crises may involve interpersonal relationships, status, creativity, or spirituality—the "middlescent" searches for sustaining values and philosophies in a changing world. How similar to adolescence it sounds!

JUNG'S THEORIES

Jung experienced a mid-life crisis just prior to his fortieth year. He described it as a "state of disorientation" and severe emotional reactions. The period lasted about 3 years and was resolved as he confronted his subconscious through dreams and fantasies. He later recognized the emotional change at middle age as having a profound influence on one's direction in the last half of life. Much of middle-age developmental theory has grown out of Jung's identification of a mid-life crisis. His concept of the progressive-regressive nature of development gives us a more realistic expectation than the concept of a continuous forward movement toward increased individuation. *Individuation involves the realization of all one's capacities, the goal being a fully integrated, harmonious personality; doubtless, this is a fluctuating process.* Individuation is also discussed in Chapter 27.

Jung felt that the first half of life is dominated by the activities of the conscious experience and that the second half is directed toward fuller development through the unconscious (Schultz). The individual turns from exclusive focus on the conscious to confront the unconscious. The issue of control is at the core of this shift. A person of 40 has come to the realization of the limits of personal power over culture, age, and death. Consciousness signifies control, while the unconscious represents the letting go of control. To Jung, this middle-age shift is more crucial in the development of personality than childhood. Since Jung's time the unconscious has become much more respectable, and many young adults are engaged in the task of exploring the unconscious, which was previously seen as belonging to middle age. See Chapter 11.

COPING STRATEGIES

Whether the decade of the forties represents a gradual transition or multiple crises depends upon coping patterns, ego strength, environmental stress, and available support systems. It is conceivable that coping strength is variable and is a reservoir to be tapped at critical periods. There may be certain ages at which one does not manipulate the environment or maneuver around crises as adroitly as he or she might at another age. This seems self-evident when one looks across the life-span, but I am suggesting a more discrete difference; i.e., is one more vulnerable at 40 than at 41? At 45 than at 48? We are aware of diurnal rhythms, monthly rhythms, and personality rhythms; perhaps there are coping rhythms intrinsic to each individual. It is generally agreed, however, that successful coping begets more success and that complex coping strategies develop as one deals with the contingencies of life effectively.

Earlier tasks, well resolved, lay the foundation for coping with future tasks, and difficulty resolving any of the early tasks would render each succeeding task more difficult (Erikson, 1963). Erikson's model allows for the gradual accumulation of successful coping strategies (Troll), and yet we know individuals who generally manage life in a mediocre way but rise admirably to great personal challenges. Perhaps it will suffice to say there is much we still do not know.

Troll lists certain potential crisis precipitants: physical changes of an abrupt nature, social events, or a "saturation of experience."

Adaptive processes at transitional stages of life consist of the individual's efforts to achieve, restore, or maintain equilibrium between his or her aim in life and his or her behavior pattern or style. The factor of psychological deficits was found to be independent of resources; perceived stress appeared to be as significant as actual stress. These factors add to the complexity of predicting high-risk situations (Lowenthal, 1972).

LACK OF AGREEMENT

It is clear that we cannot be sure why a mid-life crisis frequently occurs; worse, there is no general agreement as to when it occurs! Levinson (as cited in Scarf) states that the critical point occurs during the late thirties or early forties. According to Neugarten (1970), it occurs during the fifties, and according to Lowenthal (1972), during the sixties. Peck and Berkowitz have identified a "middle-aged depression" in the fifties. These discrepant views reveal (1) the need for clearer definitions, (2) the age proximity of the researcher, and (3) the need to reexamine the American dream of striving toward a steady state of happiness. It seems likely that each new decade precipitates a mini-crisis (in our youth-oriented society) and that concurrent life events either maximize or minimize its impact. Biblical numerology has influenced some researchers to theorize about 7-year cycles. At any rate, Neugarten (1968) is probably correct in the assumption that the *awareness of time remaining becomes an important issue in middle age.*

Biologists deal with life as a pattern of transitional periods characterized by growth potential to age 25, stability to age 45, and regression thereafter. Unfortunately, this model has strongly influenced the emotional reaction to development in the middle years—witness the birthday cards for those over 40! Another mechanistic view of transitions focuses on acquisition, possession, and loss of reproductive ability. Thus, according to one's view of the nature of humanity, middle age may be devastating or stimulating. There is much variance regarding the nature of developmental crises and the estimated time of their occurrence. These ideas will be examined more fully in this chapter.

COPING IN PRETRANSITIONAL STAGES
Role Transitions

Lowenthal (1976) studied the coping behavior of individuals in pretransitional stages, such as prior to retirement or the last child's departure from home. She attempted to determine what is adaptive behavior at these stages and how this behavior is affected by self-perception and objective factors. Evidence of psychic and physical distress was found among women facing the empty nest and among men facing retirement. The complexity of life-style and personality bears a varying relationship to the sense of well-being. Psychologically simple preretirement men tend to be happy, while psychologically complex older women are happier than their "simple" counterparts. These sex ratios are reversed in 40- to 50-year old adults; it is the complex man and the simple woman who are happiest.

From Frenkel-Brunswick's biographical chart it is clear that during mid-life (the "culmination" period) the largest number of life dimensions are present. New dimensions have been added to that point in life, but few have been relinquished. There is a dangerous potential for overload. However, we must extrapolate from her analyses with caution as the biographical data were derived from a Continental culture and measured the lives of individuals in the eighteenth, nineteenth, and early twentieth centuries. A fact we must hang onto tightly in this age of change is the danger of looking at human development apart from culture or place in history. The multiple dimensions and issues of middle age can be fully appreciated when one considers all the preceding life stages, the individual propensities, the historic time, geographic setting, and the social supports.

Gender Differences in Adaptation to Transitions

Parental deprivation in childhood has an effect on the adaptive level of women but not of men at mid-life and beyond (Lowenthal, Thurner, and Chiriboga). Middle-aged men in this study felt stress related to work and money problems. Women worried about health, husbands, and familial relationships. Stresses experienced by others were a source of strain. Intelligence, self-concept, and a sense of control were the factors having the most influence on individuals' feeling states during transitions. The most complex middle-aged women exhibited the most acute signs of desperation. Borrowing from Dabrowski's concept of positive disintegration,[1] we might expect great potential for growth and change if given appropriate psychological support. The danger of examining differences in male and female reactions to transitions lies in the fact that mature functional behavior is usually described using adjectives denoting maleness. Stereotypic sex-role labels become self-fulfilling prophecies for many (Kimmel).

Often sex differences that are ascribed convey subtle sexual discrimination. The double standard of aging implies that women are much more concerned about physical appearance than men at mid-life. This situation is already changing, and many men are now undergoing cosmetic surgery; coloring their hair, beards, and moustaches; having hair transplants; and sitting under sunlamps or using cosmetics to acquire a sporting tan. It is virtually impossible to see a bald man in the media at present, and male hairstyling is a thriving business. Women tend to be prized for their appearance, and men for their accomplishments, but much less so than even a decade ago. Deaux has reported differences in men and women which seem to indicate little change in sex-role stereotyping. Women are viewed as being afraid of success. In the self-evaluation process consistent patterns of self-enhancement are demonstrated by men, and patterns of self-depreciation by women. Most scales that measure masculinity or femininity assume that these represent opposite ends of a single dimension; however, there is a growing awareness that a complete person has both masculine and feminine characteristics (Bem). Spence, Helmreich, and Stapp examined the relationship between sex-role identification and self-esteem and found that those individuals who scored high on both masculine and feminine items evidenced high self-esteem.

The commonality of human behavior is more pronounced than the sex differ-

---

[1] A necessary component of personal growth is an experience of crisis and the disorganization of previous coping styles.

ences. Socialization may produce varied expressions of behaviors such as aggression, love, cooperation, and competition, but we really do not know how men and women may differ intrinsically in the way they manage crises and change. Daitzman investigated whether androgenic and estrogenic hormones were correlated with personality traits related to emotionality, sensation seeking, sexual and social attitudes, and behavior. He found some correlations in both sexes related to sensation seeking but no specific psychological sex differences related to androgen or estrogen levels.

Many mid-life crises are related to sexuality, and the impact of these varies according to sex and individual differences. In women there is more ambivalence concerning the functions of sex and childbirth since the emotions and hormones associated with these functions are unstable and these processes involve a degree of uncertainty (Kimmel).

It is generally assumed that, following menopause, women enjoy sex more because they are freed from the worry of pregnancy. In recent years women have been able to be freed from this concern at all ages, but we have no evidence that they are enjoying sexual expression more than women of the same age did 20 years ago. There is some doubt in my mind that the banished fear of pregnancy releases women sexually. Many women throughout their reproductive years experience ambivalence toward pregnancy that, through its very presence, adds to the intrigue of sexual encounters. While unwanted children are not desirable, the mysterious possibility of conception may be. Our contraceptive efficiency may have deprived us of some faintly understood biological wisdom. Sexual behavior and satisfaction are strongly influenced by physiological, psychological, and cultural changes, as well as by age, health, and opportunity.

MALES IN TRANSITION
Crises in Sexual Expression

Sexual capacity peaks in late adolescence for males, but they rarely experience a crisis in performance until the mid-forties (Masters and Johnson).

A shift in orientation toward sexual intercourse is a crisis precipitant, particularly for men. Kaplan and Sager point out that among older males fantasy and ambience become more important and that there is less preoccupation with orgasm. Psychic determinants assume more importance in sexual response, and "good" sex is strongly dependent upon a close and satisfactory relationship. For those who are performance- or achievement-oriented, the decrease in frequency of the sexual act may pose a threat if they perceive it as "the beginning of the end." This view that males begin to incorporate more "feminine" characteristics into their sexual experience is in direct contrast to Sheehy's assertion that males and females are the most extreme in their sexual differences at age 40: "The woman at midlife seeks satisfaction of her now uninhibited sexual desires from a man who is in involuntary retreat" (1976b, p. 31). Her view seems related more to frequency of performance than to the components of sexual satisfaction.

Performance is often a component of the mid-life crisis for men. While their physiological functioning and fertility decline very gradually throughout their adult years, stress, fears, and expectations may induce impotence of psychological origin. The male climacteric has stimulated much controversy, but it is generally concluded that males experience a marked decrease in gonadal function about a decade later than the time of the female menopause, but with fewer noticeable physiological consequences (Troll). Some men have reported symptoms strikingly similar to those of menopause, including nervousness, irritability, indecisiveness, sleeplessness, and even "hot flashes." A small percentage of men between the ages of 48 and 60 develop primary testicular insufficiency, and their production of testosterone drops precipitously over the course of a few months. In such cases there is a physiological basis for the symptoms (Chew). Testosterone production is also affected by stress, depression, and female attention (Diekelmann).

The following problems have been shown to contribute to a decline in the sexual performance of males:

Boredom with the sexual partner.
Loss of an intimate relationship.
Performance on the job when equated with manliness.
Pressures to provide.
The myth of cardiac strain. Short periods of elevated pulse rate during sexual
    activity actually strengthen the heart.
The myth of diabetes. Impotence related to diabetes is not significant except
    in the later stages of diabetic peripheral neuropathy.

Henderson has found a relationship between hormonal cycling and male-female relationships. *She has noted that women's menstrual cycles set a monthly pace and that men and women who spend a great deal of time together begin to cycle together.* Even the temperature fluctuations characteristic of the menstrual cycle are evidenced in men. Henderson says that when couples do not cycle together, the marriage may be at risk. She feels that the artificial control of the Pill produces restlessness in the male, since his response cycle is blocked. We would then wonder what effects the menopause has on the male and whether supplemental estrogen taken by many menopausal females has an effect on the emotional relationship. It is possible that the disruption of this cycling is one of the heretofore unidentified components of the mid-life crises experienced by many couples.

Multiple Psychological Factors

For many men between the ages of 45 and 55, multiple psychological factors bring on anxiety, apathy, excessive drinking, inability to concentrate, fatigue, dizziness, tachycardia, and depression. Researchers have identified many factors: (1) deadly routines of the job, (2) graying hair and a growing paunch, (3) the children's departure, (4) a waning sex drive, (5) wives' pursuing new and exciting interests, (6) the premature death of close friends and colleagues, and (7) the realization that one is part of the ''old guard'' in the organization structure. There is general agreement that men in this vulnerable age bracket are apt to experience a mid-life crisis (Chew; Irwin; Levinson et al.; Soddy and Kidson; Zussman and Zussman). The turmoil may be evidenced by impotence; after age 50 the incidence takes a sharp upturn in the human male. Masters and Johnson cite the following reasons: (1) monotony in sexual relationships, (2) preoccupation with career or economic pursuits, (3) mental or physical fatigue, (4) overindulgence in food or drink, (5) physical and mental infirmities of either the individual or the sexual partner, and (6) anxiety about performance resulting from any combination of these factors. Actual physiological changes are limited to delayed erectile time, decreased ejaculatory pressure, and reduction in the volume of seminal fluid.

Identity Crises

Irwin believes that the crisis may strike at different ages depending on whether the man is a blue-collar worker, a white-collar worker, a member of an ethnic minority group, or a ''late bloomer'' as a result of long years of schooling. Crisis probably arises through a combination of endocrine changes, psychological and social pressures, and a triggering event such as the death of the father or an abrupt change in the wife's role. Rollin has pinpointed the importance of the paternal relationship as it affects males in mid-life. He states that sexual problems may be a symptom of identity problems. According to him, men grow up with a false identity; having had little opportunity to identify with their fathers and having been overly fearful of identification with their mothers, they become panic-stricken when their manliness declines and they begin to perceive their (incorrectly labeled) feminine traits of tenderness, fear, and compassion.

Creative Crisis

Jaques studied the artistic giants of Western history (mostly men) and found they were consistently beset by a crisis in creative work during their middle and late thirties. Creative capacity would emerge and assert itself for the first time, or creativity that emerged early might burn out and die or change in substance and direction. Deutsch, in her classic study of women, equates creative achievement with erotic experience and states that one supplants the other. She says that the preclimacterium, beginning at about age 40, often brings on a surge of creative expression with a revival of long-buried interests and talents. The implication that sexuality and creativity spring from the same source and are interchangeable is strong. If this is so, a shift in intensity of either expression may precipitate a crisis.

Creative pauses and introspective periods are difficult for many men because they have not been socialized to expect them (Chew). They may be frightened by the changes they perceive, or they may successfully deny changes in personality or temperament. Those who are unable to restructure or who are unaware of the need to do so at around age 40 may experience a more disruptive period at age 50 (Levinson et al.). Levinson and his colleagues suggest that mid-life crisis is inevitable but that the timing and the resolution vary. Irwin believes that men who are ambitious, aggressive, and hardworking and who are good family providers are especially susceptible. Guttman has listed the following psychosocial stages of manhood:

Alloplastic: ages 21 to 35. The young adult achieves mastery over the external world.
Autoplastic: ages 35 to 65. Interests turn toward achieving self-mastery.
Omniplastic: ages 60 and up. There is attention to broader concerns and altruistic causes.

Men undergoing a mid-life crisis may become irascible and unpredictable and may project their fears and inadequacies onto their wives and children. They have particular difficulty coping with an adolescent son, who may arouse jealousy related to sexual potential and lost youth (Davitz and Davitz). Bergler notes frequent regression to adolescent coping styles, but without the benefit of the psychological moratorium and the cultural indulgence granted the adolescent. Recently, we have finally begun to pay attention to the middle-aged man as a result of the definitive studies of Levinson, Gould, Vaillant and McArthur, and others. This is a time when values are open to question. A man must become fully his own, abandoning mentors and parental models. Personal upheaval and acute awareness of passing time are hallmarks of this stage. The resolution takes place as the man becomes a mentor to others—nurturing, teaching, serving, and using the confidence and self-assurance that arise from increased self-awareness.

The "Gauguin Syndrome"

Chew has written a delightful and provocative book about middle-aged men directed toward all interested lay people; it is solidly grounded in theory and gives an exhaustive review of the literature on the subject. Chew presents the middle-aged man's dilemmas and provides new perspectives on, and insight into, his troubles.

Several researchers have outlined the following dilemmas of the middle-aged male (Bergler; Chew; Irwin; Kimmel):

Aimlessness
A search for meaning
Body consciousness
Boredom and apathy
Envy of son (especially a son in his late teens)
Fear of heart attack
Fear of death (acute when coworkers die)
Fear of impotence
Infidelity (some see it as a problem, and some as a solution)
Job performance

Mediocrity
Mourning lost youth and opportunities
Perceived changes in physical appearance
Pressure to achieve fame before it is too late
Pressure to raise standard of living
Pressure to provide for retirement
Pride in performance of sons
Protective pride
"Silent flow and uncanny flight of time" (Vischer)

The white middle-class middle-aged man is often the neglected man—and the prototype of all "middle men." He has no consciousness-raising groups, and he is generally resented because he holds power by virtue of his sex, his whiteness, and his collective mass.

For some men, 39 is the magic age; it is a time when all things are still possible. A man of my acquaintance began to build a boat in his backyard—a large trimaran. His friends and family were incredulous. He worked doggedly onward while continuing to support his family with a routine, bureaucratic job. As he worked on his ark and his salvation, his friends and family began to believe in the project and to share his excitement. People in the community came to look and ponder how he would ever get it out to sea. His more practical acquaintances may have felt some envy as they expressed their misgivings.

As the boat took shape, the dream grew and was articulated. The man obtained a Coast Guard pilot's license and nautical charts, and he plotted a course to the Southern Hemisphere. He and his family took scuba lessons and studied distant ports. Finally, the boat was hauled to the nearest river and, with the family of six aboard, sailed outward toward the sea. As I remember the cluster of townspeople watching on the banks of the river, I still feel a wave of emotion. They sailed a thousand miles, faced many unanticipated problems, and settled in a seaport town. Now the children are grown, and the man has a thriving commercial art business. They have all returned to a mundane life, but the richness of their experience together has changed them all.

Many middle-aged men struggle with a dream, and some are consumed by it. A few know how important it is to see it through.

There is much disagreement about the timing and nature of male mid-life crisis, perhaps because people are all so different. Some may resolve numerous small confrontations with the self, and others may work or play hard enough so that they can ignore the crises, but many undoubtedly experience the kind of major mid-life crisis that most theorists have identified. This idea is not new to our era. Ptolemy said:

> The second half of manhood . . . is governed by Mars, the evil planet, the agent of disaster. It initiates the serious side of life, bringing bitter grief and imposing on body and soul a period of torment; it gives the first painful intimation that the morning of life is past, and thus forces man to devote himself to harsh

labors before it is too late, to the accomplishment of some worthwhile purpose (Vischer, p. 51).

Ideally, during the mid-forties a resolution occurs, and a man is quite mellow as he moves into his sixth decade of life. There is a softening of feeling and attention to relationships, with a focus on the present and its joys and trials. Some men, however, become obsessed with preparation for retirement.

FEMALES IN TRANSITION

It is relatively easy to circumscribe the transitions and crises of middle-aged females, since most are concurrent with the transition from fertility to infertility. Hormonal changes are intertwined with a new awareness of bodily signs and symptoms; youthful appearance is supplanted by definite signs of age; and identity and self-evaluation are unstable. New vistas await as the middle-aged woman stands on the threshold of another beginning.

The lives harbored within the body have gone, but the self submerged in the spirit clamors for recognition. The 47-year-old women of today can expect to have at least 30 more years of productive living; 47 is the average age at which women retire from mothering, experience the menopause, and reenter the labor market (Livson). When these events occur on schedule and can be anticipated, many women cope extremely well (Neugarten, 1970), especially if they experience success in their new endeavors. Those women who have been valued for their beauty often try desperately to retain and enhance any vestiges of youth that remain. Deutsch suggests that this narcissistic preservation does not necessarily represent a self-centered narrowing, but rather is an important component of mature sexuality.

The first mid-life crisis may confront a woman in her late thirties if she is single and desires marriage and a family. Eligible men are few and far between. Some women resolve this problem by having children outside marriage or by adopting; others panic. Some marry widowers or divorced men with children. There may be an urgency to bear one's own children, and this basic need is frustrated. Such women may mourn for the family they might have had.

"Single and Disabled"

Some crises go hand in hand. When a woman is least able to manage alone, she may be abandoned because of her special needs.

One woman developed a progressively debilitating disease in her early twenties. She managed well until her mid-thirties, when it became impossible for her to carry on all the activities of daily living. At that time, she expressed acute grief over her inability to bear or care for a child. Her husband divorced her shortly after that. She obtained some assistance from service agencies within the community and began to reshape her life. She was physically limited, but her mind and spirit began to flourish. She tried hypnosis, meditation, visualization, and many other nontraditional methods of coping as she stubbornly refused traditional medical approaches to her problem. Over several years she has continued her personal development, until her physical problems are no longer uppermost in her mind. In fact, when I asked her to write about her particular stresses, she refused, saying that she had learned to live comfortably with her limitations and no longer thought much about them. Some would say that this is denial, overcompensation, or delusion. However, to see her and talk with her teaches a lesson about the power of mind over matter. There is much we do not know about human potential.

Personality Factors Affecting Transitions

Livson identified two personality types in women and postulated that a woman's personality type has important implications for the way she experiences middle age. The "stable" women in Livson's study were gregarious, extroverted, nurturant, and conventional; the "improvers" were ambitious, skeptical, intellectual, and unconventional. Both had a high level of psychological health at age 50. The stable ones went through the forties with ease and grace, while the improvers became depressed, irritable, and filled with conflict. Their overall psychological health was low during this period, but the crisis was resolved by age 50. There was a dramatic rebound in intellectuality and a freeing of emotional life. The key difference seemed to be the women's fit into the traditional female role. The disengagement from mothering to a more fitting role required major reorganization for the improvers, while the stable women continued to entertain and fill their houses with friends, acquaintances, children, and grandchildren.

Sheehy (1976a) identified six types of women: (1) care givers, (2) nurturers, (3) achievers, (4) integrators, (5) the never-married, and (6) transients. Of all these, the 10 percent of women who never marry seem to be more consistently in a better state of psychological health than those who do (Bernard), and these tendencies increase with age. This leads to the rather obvious conclusion that those women who must reorganize their psychic energies and object focus will go through some trying times.

Identity Crises

Kimmel states that marriage may mark the resolution of a woman's identity crisis. I suspect that marriage satisfies the need for a prescribed role, but it may merely postpone a woman's identity crisis. Many women do not believe that marriage and personal achievement are mutually exclusive (Gump); having more interests may assist them in making the mid-life transitions, or they may experience crises earlier. These "integrators" (Sheehy, 1976a) have difficulty managing as young adults, but they seem to do well as they approach 40. Available resources and status would certainly influence a woman's ability to integrate several aspects of her life in a satisfying manner.

Lowenthal et al., in studying transitional stages across the life-span, found middle-aged married women to be the most dissatisfied of all the groups and to be in a state of personal disequilibrium, as evidenced by malaise and unhappiness. Studies confirm that critical issues are not the empty nest or the menopause, but rather dissatisfaction with a traditional role that may no longer seem significant to the woman's needs (Lowenthal and Chiriboga; Neugarten, Wood, Kraines, and Loomis).

Suicide statistics (Resnik and Cantor) tend to reflect the unhappy state of middle-aged women. White women between the ages of 45 and 54 have the highest rate of suicide of any women in the population; the rates for women decline after this peak period.

Quality of Postparental Life

Deutscher studied the quality of postparental life and concluded that rapid cultural transition has produced discontinuities in socialization; i.e., we are taught a role that is no longer effective by the time we need to use it. This in itself may produce a transitional crisis. Regarding the postparental role reorganization, most women were found to have stronger emotional reactions than their husbands. Deutscher viewed this as a cultural artifact rather than as evidence of a lack of feeling in the husbands. He made the valid point that women in the postparental period are facing a new era in their lives and have few relevant models to guide them. There is some indication from Lowenthal and Chiriboga's study that the children's departure from home was not viewed as a crisis but rather with a sense of relief; the problem was that the women were dissatisfied with their lives in general. The dissatisfactions did not seem to relate to the presence or absence of children. The average age of the subjects was 51 for the men and 48 for the women. We might speculate that the men had resolved their mid-life crises while the women were still in the throes of theirs, the loss of children being only one issue that confronted them. Changes in couple relationships become most apparent during this period, when energies are refocused from broader family concerns (Diekelmann). A couple relationship cannot be expected to bear the weight of all the energies invested in a growing family. Changes in the relationship may result in an estrangement psychologically and socially, if not in actuality.

Interpersonal Crisis, or Crisis in Couplehood

Mid-life crises have been viewed from the interpersonal perspective and written about by couples (Davitz and Davitz; Hunt and Hunt). These authors wrote from opposite ends of the experiential continuum. The Davitzes focused on the perpetual crises of the forties, and the Hunts on the renewal experience in the fifties.

Lessing's novel *The Summer before the Dark* concerns the transition from adult wife and mother to middle-aged person and sensitively portrays the loneliness of making decisions at that crucial point. The central character's self-definition fluctuates between comparison with adolescent expectations and the yardstick of husband, children, and community. Her struggle to find herself, apart from the externals of her environment, includes a young lover, a challenging job, and an alternative life-style. Her bewilderment produces an extended illness of spirit and body. Finally, embracing herself tentatively, she becomes hopeful that the last half of her life will hold meaning, without requiring her to lean on the constraints and obligations of the past. Most women do not want to abandon all the past affiliative constraints, but they begin to recognize new levels of assertiveness and freedom. These emergent needs may be as threatening to them as tenderness is to some men in the middle years. The degree of personal responsibility for the course of one's remaining years, embedded in the newly found freedom, may be awesome and unfamiliar.

Though some studies indicate that career-minded women go through the middle years with little or no change in self-definition or self-concept (Kimmel), Granquist observes that such females experience a crisis that is in many ways similar to the crisis of the mid-life male; there is a reexamination and a search for new stimulation and new directions brought about by an increased awareness of boredom and personal mortality and a realization that time is running out.

Crisis of Middle-Aged Mothers

A crisis of middle-aged mothers that I have not found addressed in the literature relates peripherally to that of the empty nest. What of the woman with increased awareness and sensitivity as she remembers the immaturity and impulsiveness of her child-rearing years? What of the vanished opportunities flitting by as each child tucked in at night rose, in the morning, another child? *It is not regret for misdeeds but the poignant awareness of things undone—and the child is grown.* There must be a period of reconciliation with, and compassion for, the self that is disquieting.

Menopause—Crisis or Release?

Menopause produces varying degrees of discomfort for women; some women experience no symptoms at all. Premenopausal personality is an important factor in how one goes through menopause. Neugarten et al. (1963) point out that there is a distinct lack of research indicating how normal women experience menopause because they rarely come to the attention of the physician or the psychologist. Deutsch, coming from the male-dominated psychoanalytic school of thought, believes that dealing with the menopause is one of the most difficult tasks of women, while Benedek believes that there is a release of psychic energy that was previously devoted to coping with the fluctuations and tensions surrounding the menses. Some women lose a "culprit" with the loss of the menses; for years, the menstrual cycle provided a framework for understanding irritability, moodiness, etc.—it was "that time of the month." With the cessation of menstruation, women may feel bereft of ready excuses for moodiness or erratic behavior.

There are great variances in women's attitudes and experiences regarding menopause. Generally, they view it as only one stress among many experienced between the ages of 45 and 55: (1) fear of widowhood, (2) fear of cancer, (3) the children's departure from home, (4) fear of the aging process, (5) worries about aging parents, (6) problems of adult children, and (7) health problems. The greatest concern is the fear of widowhood (Neugarten, 1968).

Factors directly affecting the perception of the menopause are (1) hysterectomy (25 to 30 percent of women aged 50 to 64 have had a hysterectomy), (2) childlessness, (3) cultural background, (4) general emotional stability, (5) accuracy of information about the menopause, (6) experiences of the mother and other older women, and (7) sexual satisfaction.

Many women take supplemental estrogen to relieve the discomforts of the menopause; however, recent information from the FDA concerning a higher incidence of uterine cancer (Ziel and Finkle) among users has created another stress associated with the menopause. Estrogen seems to be the hormone that gives women a sense of well-being and success, a feeling of ability to cope, and high self-esteem (Paige). While multiple factors are responsible for these feelings, diminished estrogen may make it more difficult to maintain them.

In the past, the menopause signaled the passage from mid-life to old age. Though studies show that the menopause may bring on feelings of new freedom or profound loss, the reality for most women is a mixture of feelings. Neugarten et al. (1963) make the point that as longevity increases, the menopause will be less likely to be equated with old age.

Female Crisis in Sexual Expression

While the literature consistently maintains the view that women do not lose interest in sexual expression during the menopausal years, it seems unlikely that a woman who is going through all the changes of the menopause does not also experience periods of doubts about herself and her attractiveness, accompanied by periods of sexual nonresponsiveness (Diekelmann). Other stresses may, just as in men, dampen a woman's interest in sexual activity, and this can be incorrectly interpreted as being due to the menopause. Generally, the greatest crisis in sexuality for women is the absence of a suitable partner. The current emphasis on orgasmic capacity may be a personal threat to some women, even though Hite found that only 30 percent of women were able to achieve orgasm consistently through sexual intercourse, and another 22 percent only on rare occasions. However, anything that suggests to a woman that she is somehow not completely feminine will add to the stress of the climacterium. Sorg and Sorg make the important point that sexual satisfaction is not measured by orgasm and that, in fact, many middle-aged women derive pleasure from intercourse and experience sexual satisfaction within the framework of expectations developed in their youth.

Becoming One's Own Woman

Levinson et al. stressed the importance of the mentor role for men and the crisis that occurs when a man shifts from the role of mentee and develops into a mentor. Many women who have been unable to find female mentors in the professional world have had male mentors (see Chapter 12) or have struggled alone to find their niche. Now some women are emerging as mentors to young women and men; however, there are no identified age parameters, but rather differences in years of experience. It is relatively common for the female mentee and mentor to be of approximately the same age. For women, breaking through the relationship may be less predictable and less personally traumatizing than it is for men.

Graham (editor of *The Washington Post*) cannot serve as an example to the average middle-aged woman because her situation was unusual; however, she shows us what can happen during major mid-life transitions. At 57 she is a prototype of the new breed of powerful middle-aged women emerging now in the United States. Her early married years were spent in a conventional family structure, raising her children and emotionally subsidizing her husband. She "went back to work" at age 46, when she was widowed, and she emerged to take command of one of the most influential newspapers in the world (Howard).

The "Menopausal Experience"

Women want to share their menopausal experiences (Rutzick and Pedrin). Although they may minimize its impact on their lives when they participate in surveys, reports from self-help groups tell of the many conscious and unconscious forces at work when the reproductive function ceases. We are sexual beings, and the trajectory of our sexual life shifts in the middle years, along with many other aspects of life. If I were to answer a questionnaire, my life would be statistically exactly as expected—very dull reading. However, experientially each of us is unique. I know that sexual feelings do not wane in a woman because of the menopause, but on a feeling level I must confess to a haunting fear while moving into this period: "What if I'm the one exception and my sexual desire completely disappears?" Ah! Hormones are the answer! As I was looking over Reuben's book, which is dangerously misleading in spots, my eyes became glued to one passage:

> The first thing a woman notices, within a few weeks of starting the medication [hormones], is a sudden feeling of well being. After months or years of depression and discouragement, the change is more than welcome. Gradually other nice things begin to happen. The voice goes up an octave or two, facial hair diminishes and becomes downier, and the breasts become firmer. The elastic fibers of the skin regain some of their strength and wrinkles recede. The skin and the hair get back their old consistency and sheen (p. 294).

While I knew intellectually that this was false information, I suddenly remembered that I had forgotten to take my Premarin for several days and promptly went to the kitchen and took two!

At another point while I was in the throes of "menopausal madness" (a term I have coined to convey the ambivalence and emotionality of this period, which are quite manageable but nevertheless distressing), I had a remarkable dream:

Practically everyone I saw was menstruating, and I became terribly enraged and screamed at my young married daughter.

I have related this personal experience to make the point that although theory is helpful when talking with clients, the sharing of personal experience is vital. It is of the utmost importance to let a woman know that even though her feelings may seem very unusual at times, this is a human reaction and not menopausal witchery.

FEMALE AND MALE TOGETHER

Mid-life crises mark the passage from youth into middle age. People often keep frenetically busy to avoid looking inside themselves. However, issues deferred during this period will arise again, perhaps presenting greater difficulties. The authentic person emerges when the individual is able to take a deep look at the inner self and realize that he or she alone defines himself or herself. Being in this lonely position may bring on depression, and dissatisfaction may be all too conveniently displaced on a spouse or other intimate. As a result, discord, destructive behavior, and divorce peak in the early forties for many couples (Sheehy, 1976a).

Often while the male is caught in the throes of "finding himself," the female has also become free to search for individuation but feels guilty because her mate seems to need her full attention. Growth implies alteration of old behavior patterns and revival of old conflicts, and it is always accompanied by feelings of discomfort. We look for help, but we know it is really a job to be done alone. According to comedienne Lily Tomlin, "We are all in this alone."

MID-LIFE REVIEW

The mid-life review may be a major coping strategy during periods of stress, crisis, and transition. The "life review" (see Chapter 29) has been seen as a coping strategy of the aged, but after several years of working with this concept, I have found that the middle-aged are also extremely interested in sharing their reminiscences. I have cried and laughed with them, and I have learned how important it is to use our past in the present. We cope with present crises by drawing from our past successes and abandoning strategies that are no longer applicable. Old conflicts tend to arise during crisis states, and these can be shared, refined, and integrated. Care givers who are aware of these important functions will encourage the sharing of memories rather than always insisting on the "here and now."

Reminiscing in the Middle Years

The middle years are a time for taking stock, reflecting, and reminiscing. According to studies of Lowenthal et al. and Cameron, there may be an increased tendency toward this assessment process during the forties for women and the fifties for men. Reminiscing with several hundred middle-aged people, I have found that certain themes and thoughts recur again and again. People talk of the turning points in their lives, the ceremonies, the death of parents and the birth of siblings and children, relations with grandparents, early injuries or illness, childhood homes, communing with nature, and mastering new skills. These content areas all carry themes of importance in the resolution of middle-age crises: (1) changing relationships, (2) death, (3) health, (4) shifting identity, (5) territory, (6) tradition, and (7) new directions. Accepting the idea that the manner of coping with early developmental crises builds the foundation for future coping mechanisms, it becomes important for care givers to understand how a person perceives himself or herself as having coped with the traumas of childhood. When focusing on early memories, the following points should be considered: (1) significant changes in perception of the self as the person goes through developmental stages; (2) changes in memories over time, sometimes in subtle ways and sometimes in terms of gross content; (3) the sort of events that have left an indelible impression on the person's mind; (4) the way in which the relatively few significant memories direct, limit, and enrich the person's life or provide a continuing definition of his or her life-style; and (5) the extent to which our memories change as we change and grow and whether they must change in order for us to grow.

A healthy resolution of a mid-life crisis would include the familiar stock-taking and a revision of goals with a renewed sense of self. Let us as care givers use the richness of an individual's past in the struggle for a balance between continuity and change that is at the core of mid-life crises.

Intense mid-life review seems to follow a critical event. For me it was the death of my mother. I remembered the rare times she had been separated from me when I was a child. I found myself reviewing the stages of her adult life and comparing and contrasting mine with hers. Many small incidents stood out sharply in my mind (see Chapter 28). I returned to the place of my birth and picked wild flowers again, as I had done when I was a child. Finally, much of my child was laid to rest. The events of daily life seemed more precious to me because I had viewed my own mortality; it was a time of grief and growth.

Mid-life review allows us to resolve issues we have not seen or faced before and to integrate our experiences and move forward in new directions.

HELPING OTHERS

Some clear patterns of helping behavior between the sexes have been identified. Men help more than women when the helper must take the initiative, and women respond more to a direct request. The extent to which the task is linked to traditional masculine or feminine characteristics and the expected rewards will influence patterns of helping. Rewards from the opposite sex seem to be highly valued (Deaux).

SUMMARIZING STATEMENTS BASED ON THE LITERATURE

- The middle-age shift is more crucial in the development of personality than childhood is (Jung, cited by Schultz).
- Potential crisis precipitants include abrupt physical changes, social events, and a "saturation of experience" (Troll).
- An important issue of middle age is the awareness of the time remaining in one's life (Neugarten, 1968).
- Among those aged 40 to 50, the complex man and the simple woman are happiest (Lowenthal, 1976).
- Parental deprivation during childhood affects the adaptive levels of women at mid-life, but not those of men (Lowenthal et al.).
- Stereotyped sex roles may become self-fulfilling (Kimmel).
- In one study, individuals who scored high on both masculine and feminine items evidenced high self-esteem (Spence et al.).
- In the sex lives of older males, fantasy and ambience increase in importance, and there is less preoccupation with orgasm (Kaplan and Sager).
- Paternal relationships affect males in mid-life, and sexual problems may be a symptom of identity problems (Rollin).
- Periods of creativity and introspection may be difficult for men because they are not socialized to expect them (Chew).
- The 47-year-old woman of today can expect to have 30 more years of productive life (Livson).
- Narcissistic preservation in women may be a component of mature sexuality (Deutsch).
- Marriage may mark the resolution of an identity crisis for a woman (Kimmel).
- According to one study, middle-aged married women are the most dissatisfied of all groups (Lowenthal et al.).
- White women aged 45 to 54 have the highest suicide rate of any women in the population.
- Changes in couple relationships become apparent after the children leave home (Diekelmann).
- The stresses of women between the ages of 45 and 55 include (1) fear of widowhood, (2) fear of cancer, (3) the children's departure from home, (4) fear of the aging process, (5) worries about aging parents, (6) problems of adult children, and (7) health problems. The greatest concern of these is widowhood (Neugarten, 1968).
- "Menopausal madness" is a term describing the ambivalence and emotionality of this period of life.

GUIDELINES FOR INTERVENTION

- Help men accept the creative, introspective times of mid-life and also their own nurturing qualities.

- Be prepared for depressive states in middle-aged persons.
- Suggest counseling when there is marital discord or sexual problems (for example, impotence in a man), during severe depressions, and when the person has suicidal thoughts.
- The mid-life review may be a major coping strategy; incorporate it into your armentarium of care-giving methods.
- Help people in this age group share and refine their memories, rather than constantly insisting that they deal with the "here and now."
- Encourage reminiscing based on the themes of (1) changing relationships, (2) death, (3) health, (4) shifting identity, (5) territory, (6) tradition, and (7) new directions.
- Focus on early memories, including (1) major shifts in the perception of self, (2) events which have left indelible impressions on the individual, (3) the ways in which significant memories have directed or limited the person's life, (4) the ways in which memories change over time, and (5) the ways in which they must change in order for the person to grow.

REFERENCES

Bem, Sandra: "The Measurement of Psychological Androgyny," *Journal of Consulting and Clinical Psychology,* **42**(2): 155–163, 1974.

Benedek, Theresa: "Parenthood as a Developmental Phase," *"Journal of the American Psychoanalytic Association,* 7(3):389–417, 1959.

Bergler, Edmund: *The Revolt of the Middle-Aged Man,* Wyn, New York, 1954.

Bernard, Jessie: *The Sex Game,* Atheneum, New York, 1972.

Cameron, Paul: "The Generation Gap: Time Orientation," part I, *The Gerontologist,* 12(2):117–119, 1972.

Chew, Peter: *The Inner World of the Middle-Aged Man,* Macmillan, New York, 1976.

Clausen, John: "The Life-Course of Individuals," in M. W. Riley, J. Johnson, A. Foner, et al. (eds.), *A Sociology of Age Stratification,* Russell Sage, New York, 1972.

Dabrowski, K: in J. Aronson (ed.), *Positive Disintegration,* Little, Brown, Boston, 1964.

Daitzman, Reid: "Personality, Correlates of Androgens and Estrogens," doctoral dissertation, University of Virginia; "Psychology Today Awards," *Psychology Today,* **10**(9):26, 1977.

Davitz, Joel, and **Lois Davitz:** *Making It from 40 to 50,* Random House, New York, 1976.

Deaux, Kay: *The Behavior of Men and Women,* Brooks/Cole, Monterey, Calif., 1976.

Deutsch, Helene: *Psychology of Women, vol. II, Motherhood,* Grune & Stratton, New York, 1945.

Deutscher, Irwin: "The Quality of Post-parental Life," in Bernice Neugarten (ed.), *Middle Age and Aging,* University of Chicago Press, Chicago, 1968, pp. 263–268.

Diekelmann, Nancy: *Primary Health Care of the Well Adult,* McGraw-Hill, New York, 1977.

Erikson, Erik: "Identity and the Life Cycle: Selected Papers," *Psychological Issues,* monogr. no. 1, 1959.

————: *Childhood and Society,* 2d ed., Norton, New York, 1963.

Frenkel-Brunswick, Else: "Adjustments and Reorientation in the Course of the Life Span," in Bernice Neugarten (ed.), *Middle Age and Aging,* University of Chicago Press, Chicago, 1968, pp. 77–84.

Fried, Barbara: *The Middle-Age Crisis,* Harper & Row, New York, 1967.

Gould, Roger: "The Phases of Adult Life: A Study in Developmental Psychology," *American Journal of Psychiatry,* **129**(5): 33–43, 1972.

Granquist, Joanne: "A Faculty Member Reflects," *American Journal of Nursing,* **76**(6):1022–1024, 1976.

Gump, Janice: "Sex-Role Attitudes and Psychological Well Being," *Journal of Social Issues,* **28**(2):79–92, 1972.

Guttman, David: "The Psychological Stages of Manhood," in Theodore Irwin (ed.), *Male "Menopause": Crisis in the Middle Years,* Public Affairs Pamphlet no. 526, Public Affairs Committee, New York, 1975.

Henderson, Margaret: "Evidence for a Male Menstrual Temperature Cycle and Synchrony with the Female Menstrual Cycle," *Australia and New Zealand Journal of Medicine,* **6**(3):254, 1976.

Hite, Shere: *The Hite Report: A Nationwide Study of Female Sexuality,* Dell, New York, 1976.

Howard, Jane: "Katherine Graham: The Power That Didn't Corrupt," *MS,* October 1974, pp. 47–124.

Hunt, Bernice, and **Morton Hunt:** *Prime Time,* Stein and Day, New York, 1975.

Irwin, Theodore: *Male "Menopause": Cri-*sis in the Middle Years, Public Affairs Pamphlet no. 526, Public Affairs Committee, New York, 1975.

Jaques, Elliott: "Death and the Mid-Life Crisis," *International Journal of Psychoanalysis,* **46**(4):506, 1965.

Jung, Carl: "The Stages of Life," tr. by R. F. C. Hull, in J. Campbell (ed.), *The Portable Jung,* Viking, New York, 1961.

Kaplan, Helen, and **Clifford Sager:** "Sexual Patterns at Different Ages," *Medical Aspects of Human Sexuality,* **5**(6):10–14, 1971.

Kimmel, Douglas: *Adulthood and Aging,* Wiley, New York, 1974.

Lessing, Doris: *The Summer before the Dark,* Knopf, New York, 1973.

Levinson, Daniel: "The Psychological Development of Men in Early Adulthood and the Mid-Life Transition," University of Minnesota Press, Minneapolis, 1974. (Article.)

————, **Charlotte Darrow, Edward Klein, Maria Levinson,** and **Braxton McKee:** "The Psychosocial Development of Men in Early Adulthood and the Mid-Life Transition," in D. Ricks, A. Thomas, and M. Roff (eds.), *Life History Research in Psychopathology,* vol. 3, University of Minnesota Press, Minneapolis, 1974.

Lindbergh, Anne Morrow: *Gift from the Sea,* Random House, New York, 1955.

Livson, Florine: "Patterns of Personality Development in Middle-Aged Women: A Longitudinal Study," doctoral dissertation, Institute of Human Development, University of California, Berkeley, 1976.

Lowenthal, Marjorie: *Adult Development: Continuities and Discontinuities,* Langley Porter Neuropsychiatric Institute, San Francisco, 1972.

————: *Program Project in Human Development and Aging: The Longitudinal Study,* Langley Porter Neuropsychiatric Institute, San Francisco, 1976.

——— and **David Chiriboga:** "Transition to the Empty Nest," *Archives of General Psychiatry,* **26**(5):8–14, 1972.

———, **Majda Thurner,** and **David Chiriboga:** *Four Stages of Life,* Jossey-Bass, San Francisco, 1975.

Masters, William, and **Virginia Johnson:** *Human Sexual Inadequacy,* Little, Brown, Boston, 1970.

Neugarten, Bernice: *Middle Age and Aging,* University of Chicago Press, Chicago, 1968.

———: "Dynamics of Transition from Middle Life to Old Age," *Journal of Geriatric Psychiatry,* **4**(1):71–87, 1970.

———, **Joan Moore,** and **John Lowe:** "Age Norms, Age Constraints, and Adult Socialization," *American Journal of Sociology,* **70**(6):710–717, 1965.

———, **Vivian Wood, Ruth Kraines,** and **Barbara Loomis:** "Women's Attitudes toward the Menopause," *Vita Humana,* **6**(3):140–151, 1963.

Paige, Karen: "The Effects of Oral Contraceptives on Affective Fluctuations Associated with the Menstrual Cycle," *Psychosomatic Medicine,* **33**:515–517, 1971.

Peck, R. F., and **H. Berkowitz:** "Personality and Adjustment in Middle Age," in B. Neugarten et al. (eds.), *Personality in Middle and Late Life,* Atherton, New York, 1964, pp. 15–43.

Resnik, H., and **J. M. Cantor:** "Suicide and Aging," *Journal of the American Geriatric Society,* **18**:152–158, 1970.

Reuben, David: *Everything You Always Wanted to Know about Sex but Were Afraid to Ask,* McKay, New York, 1969.

Rollin, Walter: *Men in Transition,* San Francisco State University Bulletin, Nov. 8, 1976.

Rutzick, Beverly, and **Verna Pedrin:** "Workshop I: Menopause, Myths and Realities," *Health in the Middle Years: A Symposium about Women,* report from conference held at Laney College, Oakland, Calif.; sponsored by the American Friends Service Committee in conjunction with the Peralta Colleges Community Services, November 1976.

Scarf, Maggie: "Husbands in Crisis," *McCalls,* **94**(9):76–79, 1972.

Schultz, Duane: *Theories of Personality,* Brooks/Cole, Monterey, Calif., 1976.

Sheehy, Gail: *Passages: Predictable Crises of Adult Life,* Dutton, New York, 1976. (a)

———: "The Sexual Diamond: Facing the Facts of the Human Sexual Life Styles," *New York,* Jan. 26, 1976, pp. 31–39. (b)

———: "Why Mid Life Is Crisis Time for Couples," *New York,* Feb. 11, 1976, pp. 31–36. (c)

Soddy, Kenneth, and **Mary Kidson:** *Men in Middle Life,* Lippincott, Philadelphia, 1967.

Sorg, David, and **Margaret Sorg:** "Sexual Satisfaction in Maturing Women," *Medical Aspects of Human Sexuality,* **9**(2): 62–79, 1975.

Spence, Janet, Robert Helmreich, and **Joy Stapp:** "Ratings of Self and Peers on Sex-Role Attributes and Their Relation to Self-Esteem and Conceptions of Masculinity or Femininity," *Journal of Personality and Social Psychology,* **1**:29–39, 1975.

Tomlin, Lily: *The Mainliner,* United Airlines, August 1977.

Troll, Lillian: *Early and Middle Adulthood: The Best Is Yet to Be—Maybe,* Brooks/Cole, Monterey, Calif., 1975.

Vaillant, George, and **Charles McArthur:** "Natural History of Male Psychological Health," part I, "The Adult Life Cycle from 18–50," *Seminars in Psychiatry,* **4**(4):415–427, 1972.

Vischer, A. L.: *On Growing Old,* tr. by Gerald Onn, Houghton Mifflin, Boston, 1967.

Ziel, Harry, and **William Finkle:** "Increased Risk of Endometrial Carcinoma among Users of Conjugated Estrogens,"

New England Journal of Medicine, **293**(23):1167–1170, 1975.

Zussman, Leon, and **Shirley Zussman:** "Dual Sex Team Therapy of the Couple," *Cornell Seminars,* Brunner/Mazel, New York, 1974.

OTHER RESOURCES

FILMS

Maude Monologue: The Analyst: 30 min/color/1975. Maude consults a psychologist about the impending realities of being 50 and relates the ups and downs of her life. Distributor: Brooke Buhrman, Tandem Productions, 5752 Sunset Boulevard, Los Angeles, Calif. 90028.

Mr. Arthur: His Fear of Growing Old: 20 min/b&w. Mr. Arthur, a middle-aged executive, falls in love with his young secretary. He leaves his wife and marries the woman, but their marriage is unhappy. Mr. Arthur returns to his family and, in psychoanalysis, tries to learn what drove him to enter a destructive second marriage. Distributor: Pictura Films Distribution Corp., 43 West Sixteenth Street, New York, N.Y. 10011.

SYMPOSIUM

American Friends Service Committee: *Health in the Middle Years.* A symposium about women organized and presented by the American Friends Service Committee in conjunction with Peralta College Community Service, San Francisco, Nov. 13, 1976. Pamphlet available from Feminist Health Program, American Friends Service Community, 2160 Lake Street, San Francisco, Calif. 94121. $2.

Chapter 18

WIDOWHOOD AND WIDOWERHOOD IN MIDDLE AND LATER LIFE
Irene Mortenson Burnside

> It is a fearful thing to love
> What Death can touch.
>
> *Epitaph in cemetery in New Hampshire*
> *(quoted by Josephine Jacobsen)*
>
> The sorrow with no vent in tears
> may make other organs weep.
>
> *Henry Maudsley*

The word "widow" is derived from the Latin word meaning "to separate"; in Sanskrit the word for "widow" means "empty." Widowhood is an important and widespread role change that occurs primarily in later life (Atchley, 1972). The adjustment to widowhood is one of the most traumatic, difficult experiences an older woman faces (Lopata, 1973). Of all the passages in my own life, this one had the greatest impact and left me, a veteran nurse who had seen much death and dying, haunted with the question: And what of your own death? I felt for a long while after my husband's death that I had buried a part of me.

MAGNITUDE OF THE PROBLEM

In 1970 there were over 6 million widows and 1½ million widowers over age 65 in the United States (U.S. Bureau of the Census, 1971). The mean survival time after loss of a spouse was reported to be 9.5 years for men and 13.8 years for women. See Figure 18-1 for the distribution of older persons by marital status. Statistics reveal that most women are widowed between the ages of 50 and 60; since they can expect to live another 17 years, they need to create new lives for themselves (Rogers). *The average age at which women become widows*

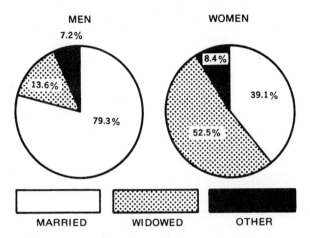

MEN

7.2%

13.6%

79.3%

WOMEN

8.4%

39.1%

52.5%

MARRIED   WIDOWED   OTHER

Distribution of Older Persons by Marital Status, 1900 and 1975

Status	1975 Men	1975 Women	1900 Men	1900 Women
Total	100.0	100.0	100.0	100.0
Married	79.3	39.1	67.3	34.3
Widowed	13.6	52.5	26.5	59.5
Other				
Divorced	2.5	2.6	0.5	0.3
Never married	4.7	5.8	5.8	6.0

Figure 18-1 Distribution of older persons by marital status. (*From U.S. Department of Health, Education, and Welfare, p. 2.*)

is only 56 years (Lopata, 1973). Not only are there many widows in the United States, but a large percentage of them spend many years in widowhood.

Weg has compiled the following statistics on marital status. The marriage rate for widows over 65 is 2.2 per 1000; the rate for widowers over 65 is 18.4 per 1000. Approximately 40 percent of married men over 65 have wives under 65. In 1972 there were 2.3 million marriages with 40,400 men and 20,200 women over 65. Of these, almost 6 percent were first marriages. If the husband is 5 years younger than the wife, the chances of widowhood are 50 percent; if the husband and wife are the same age, the chances are 2 out of 3; if the husband is 5 years older than the wife, the chances are 3 out of 4. Seventy-five percent of those who were previously widowed or widowered, remarried. For older men, this is a rate of 16.4 per 1000 unmarried older men; for older women it is a rate of only 2.4 per 1000. Recent figures are as follows:

	Bride and Groom Over 65	Only Bride Over 65	Only Groom Over 65
Number of Marriages	14,000	2000	22,000

In 1975, 6.9 million older men, or 79 percent, were married.

Most older women are widows; there are 5.5 times as many widows as widowers. Most older men are married (79 percent of older men are married, and 52 percent of older women are widows). Almost 70 percent of women over 75 are widows. Figure 18-2 shows the widowed and the widowered as a percentage of the population by age and sex.

There are now 9 million widows in the United States—six times the number of widowers. *Many are socially isolated and also economically handicapped* (Atchley, 1975; Rogers). There is a great deal of literature about the problems of widowhood (Clark and Anderson; Lopata, 1970, 1971a, 1971b, 1973, 1975a, 1975b; Silverman and Cooperband), but less attention has been paid to the impact of widowerhood (Atchley, 1972; Berardo, 1968, 1970; Parkes, 1972). Parkes (1964b, 1969) studied the impact of widowhood in England; he also studied the effects of bereavement on mental health (1964a, 1965). Lopata (1973) points out that the life-styles of American widows vary tremendously.

Atchley (1975) studied 902 men and women aged 70 to 79 and concluded that no generalities about the psychosocial effect of widowhood and widowerhood could be made that would hold up among subgroups; however, he stated that the social impact of widowhood is more clear-cut. Among working-class women, widowhood is associated with income inadequacy, which in turn is associated with *less automobile usage, less social participation, and greater loneliness and anxiety.* Data in Atchley's study point to income adequacy as an essential part of any theory regarding adjustment in widowhood. *"The poorest people in America today are women over 65, single and widowed. . . . [They] have an average annual income of only $1,888. One quarter of them have no assets at all"* (Preston, p. 44). One researcher described the poverty of elderly widows

Figure 18-2 The widowed and widowered as a percentage of the population by age and sex, 1970. (*From U.S. Bureau of the Census, 1970, table 2.*)

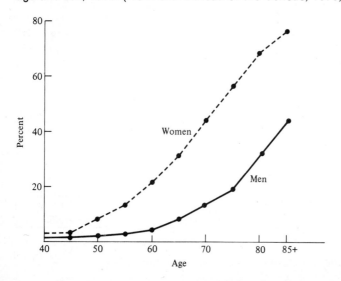

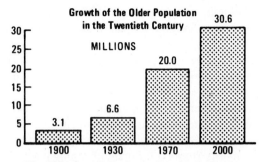

Year	Total	Men	Women	Ratio Women/Men
1900	3,080,000	1,555,000	1,525,000	98/100
1930	6,634,000	3,325,000	3,309,000	100/100
1970	19,972,000	8,367,000	11,605,000	139/100
1975	22,400,000	9,172,000	13,228,000	144/100
2000	30,600,000	12,041,000	18,558,000	154/100

Figure 18-3 Growth of the older population in the twentieth century. (*From U.S. Department of Health, Education, and Welfare, p. 3*).

in the United States after conducting a number of interviews with economically disadvantaged old women (Schwartz). In Figure 18-3 note the ratio of elderly women to elderly men in the year 2000. The needs of elderly widows in nursing homes have not been studied.

In spite of all the literature and research now available, the gap remains; widows continue to muddle through on their own. Little documentation demonstrates how the many-titled moneys and numerous studies help them. One is reminded of Millay's words:

Upon this gifted age, in its dark hour
Rains from the sky a meteoric shower of facts . . .
They lie unquestioned, uncombined,
Wisdom enough to teach us of our ill
Is daily spun, but there exists no loom
To weave it into fabric (p. 697).

AGE WHEN WIDOWED OR WIDOWERED

Loether states that the age at which a woman is widowed is an important factor;[1] if a woman loses her husband early in her life, she may be the first among her friends to be widowed. However, if she is widowed later in life, there is a good chance that some of her acquaintances will also be widowed. They will be role

---

[1]The reader is referred to Bernice L. Neugarten's writings on "off-time events" in her book entitled *Middle Age and Aging* (1968b, p. 146).

models for her and will make her own adaptation easier. The formal mourning, customs, and traditions of bygone days are fading, and there are few codes of behavior to guide the widow.

Heyman and Gianturco have stated that *reactions to loss of a spouse in old age are different from those reactions experienced considerably earlier in life*. These researchers noted that younger men and women can be shattered by a spouse's death; elderly persons, on the other hand, appear to accept the death as inevitable, and they continue their existence with equanimity and little obvious change in life-style. Neugarten (1968a) and Rosow state that the age at which a person is widowed or widowered is an important factor in determining his or her attitudes and life-styles. The older the individual is when the spouse dies, the more time he or she has had to rehearse for the new life situation. Butler suggests that the response to loss changes with increasing age because of preparation for the possibility of loss.

CROSS-CULTURAL VIEWS

Mathison wrote about cross-cultural views of widowhood in the non-Western cultures and concluded that all the non-Western societies she studied provide more structured rituals and roles for the widow than are found in the United States. A world perspective of widowhood brought to light some of the role shifts that occur in other societies.

THE GRIEF PROCESS

In a study of normal bereavement, Clayton, Desmarais, and Winokur systematically interviewed relatives of hospital patients who had died. Three symptoms were found in more than half the subjects: (1) depressed mood, (2) sleep disturbance, and (3) crying. The survivors received benefit from reviewing the terminal illness, whether it was of short or long duration—an illness review, so to speak. The review allowed expression of affect and crying. Care givers need to listen patiently to the illness review; in fact, they may hear it replayed several times before the grief work abates. I am reminded of a man in his late sixties who lived with his aunt. Each was the only family either one of them had. After a long discussion of her terminal illness, he launched into the funeral details and then said with great satisfaction, "I put her away good." I had to agree.

Clayton et al. (1971) studied the expression of the bereaved occurring 1 year after the death of the spouse. The first anniversary can provide reliable indicators of the degree of grief resolution and adjustment. One 70-year-old man replied, "Nothing special; it was Monday so I guess I did the wash." A mild reaction of an 84-year-old man was, "It wasn't too bad . . . it was probably the best thing. I'm kind of old—we all have to go you know" (p. 470).

There is a belief that anticipatory grief lightens the burden of grief after the death (Pollock). Data from a study by Clayton et al. (1972) did not confirm the findings: "Those with 'anticipatory grief' did worse in the first month of bereavement and no better at one year than those without such a reaction" (p. 50). I had felt in my own widowhood that months of struggling with the deteriorating illness and the gradual letting go would spare me from much pain after my husband's death. It was simply not that way, and I became increasingly disappointed when I realized that grief and pain were there in spite of my having thought I had waded through anticipatory grief work.

STRESSES OF WIDOWHOOD AND WIDOWERHOOD

"The death of a spouse causes disorganization in the life of the surviving partner in every society" (Lopata, 1973, p. 302). A drastic change in life-style and the problems associated with young widowhood are well described by Caine. She relates some of the rapid, impractical decisions she made, such as immediately selling her house and moving, and she describes her increasing dependency on friends.

The bereaved have difficulty making decisions; in the first month of bereavement, the person should be advised not to make changes (Clayton et al., 1971). Caine has described the result of making quick decisions soon after losing a spouse.

INDECISIONS DURING WIDOWHOOD AND WIDOWERHOOD

The difficulties inherent in making even small decisions have been well described by Van Coevering:

> One day I stopped at the corner market to buy a package of gelatin. Never before had I seen so many flavors, so many brands and sizes. For twenty minutes I picked up one box and then another, only to return them to the shelves. Then I felt a surging flood of tears. I bolted from the store empty handed. It was literally impossible for me to make even this most elementary of all decisions. "I must be losing my mind," I thought.

This last statement certainly supports the findings of Lindemann in his classic research on grief and also those of Clayton et al. (1971).

Not all widows feel lonely or grief-stricken. Many women who lived in their husbands' shadows actually blossom and flourish. If the husband was alcoholic, sickly, overly dependent, or too authoritative, the new role of widow may be a refreshing and welcome experience, and the freedom a heady change, although these feelings may bring some guilt.

Various studies have shown that people are usually able to handle the stresses and changes that widowhood and widowerhood bring; however, preoccupation with grief, increased worry, low morale, and unhappiness are more common among widows and widowers than among other persons of the same age (Riley and Foner).

PSYCHOSOMATIC COMPLAINTS

Morrison did group work with widows who were high utilizers of an outpatient clinic. She worked with eight women aged 54 to 72 and concluded that the group was relatively homogeneous. She noted these commonalities among the widows: "(1) psychosomatic complaints, (2) high dependency needs, (3) strong initial transferences to the therapist, and (4) reduced social skills" (p. 149).

Clayton (1975) indicated in her data that the younger widows and widowers who were living with someone had more physical symptoms and were hospitalized more in the first year after bereavement than the controls and the older widows and widowers. Perhaps if there is someone around to give sympathy, one can play the sick role to the hilt! Clayton (1975), Parkes (1972), and Maddison and Viola demonstrated that younger people have more physical symptoms during bereavement than older persons. My own physical problems during the first few years of widowhood increased, and insomnia became a problem. One has to come to terms with aloneness—day and night. Elderly widows have shared similar reactions with me; one woman said that 3 A.M. was absolutely the worst time of all for her.

Clayton (1975) wrote: "Bereavement itself rather than the effects of living alone influences the occurrence of depressive symptoms in widows and widowers at one month" (p. 133). Personally, I felt that both factors created problems for me which I had to face all at once at a time when my psychic and physical energy levels were low.

WIDOWERHOOD

Loether states: "The social world of the widower is generally more restricted than that of a widow" (p. 106). Part of the wife role is interacting with relatives, neighbors, and friends. It is usually the wife who writes to relatives, including her husband's as well as her own. When the wife dies, much of this contact ceases. If the children feel closer to the mother than to the father, they will visit the widowed father less than the widowed mother (Loether). This finding may change in the near future as more fathers share in parenting and accept more child-care responsibilities. See Chapter 4 for a discussion of the father's role in child care.

Townsend found that widowers have less contact with their children, particularly their sons, than married men or either married or widowed women. Heyman and Gianturco found that elderly males who survive their spouses have less physical disability; they are significantly healthier than the average married man of about the same age.

Some widowers move in with married children, but it is much more common for them to remarry or live alone as long as they are able to. Widowers are not as active in social organizations as widows. Senior citizens' groups consist mainly of women, which is explained partly by the fact that there are more women in the older age groups. Older men also tend to participate less in the social functions of such groups. The few men who do may still be married and under pressure from their wives. Rarely do widowers participate in such organizations. ''The picture that emerges, then, of the elderly widower is one of an isolated man, often inaccessible even to relatives and friends'' (Loether, p. 107). Considering the ratio of widowers to widows, it seems an unnecessary isolation. A 69-year-old widower said:

> The hard part is doing things. Lots of husbands and wives have separate activities. She has her bridge club, and he plays pool with the boys. Madge and I never did anything that we couldn't do together. Maybe that was a mistake. At least if we had, it would be easier to do things alone now. Take going to the pool hall. Years ago, there would be a bar there. They called them sippin' parlors, and it wasn't considered a nice place for ladies. So, I didn't go. Now, it's hard to go down to the pool hall alone, and it's all right for the ladies to go to them now. Except, maybe, in the small towns, and that's where Madge and I lived mostly, in small towns (Liggett, p. 3).

IMAGINING HUSBAND OR WIFE STILL PRESENT

One of the tasks of widowhood and widowerhood is to banish the expectation of the spouse's return. This task has not been well covered in the literature, and yet it can be long-lasting and painful. One way in which many widows and widowers cling to the deceased is to constantly say that he or she ''would have wanted me to do that'' or to imagine other, similar things that the dead person might say or do if he or she were still living. Their inability to take responsibility for themselves and their actions continues. Some widows and widowers (especially widowed women 70 years old and over) are also reluctant to remove their wedding bands. One widow wrote:

> On one occasion I even went so far as to start clipping from the front page of the newspaper a story about an old acquaintance of my husband's who was being mentioned for a high political office. ''He'll be so interested to read this when he. . . .'' Before my mind could finish the sentence, the awful truth dawned anew, and I crumpled the paper and threw it into the wastebasket and leaned my head down on my typewriter for a moment until the shaking and the dizziness passed away (Start, p. 84).

In my own first months of widowhood, in a store or on the street, I often saw a stranger who very much reminded me of my husband. I had to convince myself each time this happened that I would never see him again, but each instance was a wrenching, devastating experience. My eldest son greatly resembles his father, and when he came home to visit me, I would turn to him and be suddenly startled—for a moment I would envision him as my husband. It was months before this ceased to happen during his visits, especially when he stood in front of the kitchen sink. (My husband had taken large doses of medication four times a day and frequently stood at the sink while taking his pills, and so that particular memory of him was recent.) I wondered about the effect of this on my son. For example, once he went to the city where he had grown up to visit elderly family friends. Because of failing sight and memory, two called him by his father's name. Watching one's children suffer (Burnside) is another difficult aspect of losing a spouse, for it seems to double the pain, and often the bereaved parent is unable to help the children deal with their own grief.

One 65-year-old widow took responsibility for her depression and sadness and realized that her grief must progress through stages. The third year after her husband's death she had finally come to grips with the loss:

> "Not that I wouldn't like to have him sitting there in the chair, smiling at me and talking, but nothing will bring him back and there is nothing I can do about it." She was illustrative of the literature on widowhood in several ways; one was her feeling that other women with husbands saw her as a threat to their marriage. Also, she felt that the long period necessary for her to work through the stages of denial, anger, bargaining, depression, and finally acceptance was due to the fact that she had no widowed friends to talk with about her loss, that those friends with husbands felt uncomfortable during her grief, and that she ultimately had to work it through herself (Zale).

EXPRESSION OF GRIEF

Perhaps because grief is so personal and so individual, we need to seriously explore, observe, and even analyze the ways in which people grieve. The routine of visiting the cemetery is a familiar ritual.

Some months after my husband's death, my grieving 17-year-old son described his grief. His best friend's brother had been tragically killed by lightning while serving in the Peace Corps in Ghana, Africa. The two boys, in their first months of bereavement, decided to pay tribute to the dead father and the dead brother, who would have been 24. They rode their motorcycles at midnight past the chained entrance to the cemetery and roared up the hill. After flinging cherry bombs near both graves, they cried together and in their own way celebrated a dead brother's birthday and remembered a dead father. I was trying not to show my surprise when my son nonchalantly added about his friend, "But, Mom, I don't think he should have picked fresh flowers off the graves around there and given them to my girl!" Young love and young grief were so close together inside him.

Bornstein, Clayton, Halikas, Maurice, and Robins, in a follow-up study of widows and widowers, concluded: "Grief is grief and is not a model for psychotic depression . . . while the normal depression of widowhood serves as an excellent model for the depression resulting from a *clear-cut* loss, it is also different from clinical affective *illness* and should be considered separately in studies of affective disorder in psychiatric patients" (p. 566).

Lewis's statement reminds one of the words spoken to Lindemann by grievers after the Coconut Grove holocaust: "No one ever told me that grief felt so like fear. I am not afraid but the sensation is like being afraid. The same fluttering in the stomach, the same restlessness, the yawning. I keep on swallowing'' (p. 7).

My own concern was with the slowness of my grief work. Memories seemed to come from everywhere, and they flattened me quickly—there were always reminders. I chided myself for not moving along faster and for not doing as well as my children. After a year I felt more sure of my own way and my own strengths, but I was really caught off guard one day. I had gone to replace a fuse, something I had never done before. Inside the box were many fuses, all carefully labeled according to sections of the house. Seeing the labels in my husband's handwriting caused me to dissolve into tears, and I leaned against the wall and wept. Letters, notes, and checks in his handwriting found in drawers and cupboards were other persistent reminders that vulnerability is a constant companion of widows. I found that music we had enjoyed together was especially powerful in evoking memories and feelings of sadness.

The very painful job of going through clothing and personal possessions was most difficult for our family. I held up the leg brace which my husband had worn briefly before he had to resort to the wheelchair and said, "What about this?" I saw the expressions on my children's faces and quickly dropped the brace into the box. I also remember wincing when I cleaned out my husband's sock drawer and found a jewelry box he used only for saving the children's baby teeth—a tooth fairy's and a sentimental father's cache.

I became easily discouraged because grief seemed not only so painful but also so slow to pass; at times I resented the fact that my children seemed to progress faster and more easily than I did. I now know, after 7 years of widowhood, that while a mate is alive one never sees or understands the complete individual—only portions of behavior, life-style, and personality. The distance and space after death must be accepted, and putting all the fragmented pieces, memories, and reactions together into a whole person to be remembered (or forgotten, as the case may be) is not easy. That is the real task of widowhood; it is like standing close to a tree, even in its shadow perhaps, and then moving away and seeing it silhouetted against one's own personal sky.

The process may well include unhappy surprises, as it did for a friend of mine who had to pay for clothing she never knew had been charged and had to reimburse for cheating on social security checks. The final shock came when she found a trunk of pornographic literature in the rafters of her garage; this was the last straw, and she vehemently said, "I'd like to go right out to the cemetery, pull him out of his grave and shake him!" (Anonymous).

SEXUALITY AND WIDOWERS

The effect of prolonged sexual inactivity is often seen in widowers following the death of a wife after an extended illness. Idealization of the dead person and guilt regarding lack of proper emotion may be major contributors to "widower's impotency" (Comfort, p. 39). The enforced abstinence, the strange partner, and perhaps some guilt concerning feelings of relief that the lingering illness is over can cause impotence, which Comfort says is reversible. Counseling in this area is helpful.

LONELINESS AND SOCIAL ISOLATION

Berardo (1970) has reported that widows adjust more easily and show less social isolation than widowers. There could be several reasons for this. Men do not tend to do the communicating or arrange the social events in a family. Older men who have never taken a dish towel in hand are exceedingly clumsy in their empty kitchens. Women continue to shop, clean, and keep house during widowhood, and the stability of that, mundane as it may be, does provide structure during empty days. One friend confided to me how soothing washing dishes had become during her grief. Carrying out familiar routines helps to stabilize the griever. I found myself clinging to familiar objects, family traditions, and homemaking rituals to keep some sense of order during a time of tremendous inner chaos.

One does have to come to terms with both loneliness and long stretches of aloneness. *Aloneness, which once seemed so treasured and hard to come by, can become a burden in widowhood.* To eat alone, to sleep alone, to go to the movies alone, to go to social gatherings alone, to make decisions alone—any or all of these can be hurdles. There is a haiku that says something to this effect: How will you alone cross the mountains that we could not cross when we were together?

Silverman (1969) reported that the widows in one study had gotten through the first months of widowhood in one fashion or another but that the loneliness and depression really became difficult 6 months or a year after their husbands had died. By that time, they had settled into a new way of life and were carrying on, but the great feeling of loss overwhelmed them. Also, immediately after the death, there are many practical details to attend to, and friends and family offer much sympathy and support. Soon after the funeral, however, the support and sympathy cease. One widow was once told by another widow, "Use it while you can to your advantage because it will not last long."

Atchley (1975) reported: "Widowed people showed a higher prevalence of identification as old and alone compared to married people of the same age" (p. 177). See Chapter 26, which discusses loneliness in later life. Loether has stated that *widows and widowers tend to be lonelier than married people or single people.* Lopata (1973) reported that loneliness was the most difficult problem of half of the widows she studied, and she has written about the forms and components of loneliness in widows 50 years of age and older (1969). Antidotes to loneliness for widows, according to Lopata (1973), include "keeping busy, developing new roles and relations and focusing life on one social role" (p. 110). Although they may sound easy, these are difficult tasks for the widow to accomplish.

VULNERABILITY OF WIDOWS

Loneliness in widowhood is a big problem and is frequently mentioned in the literature; however, the widow's vulnerability has not been studied. Vulnerability is an important aspect of widowhood—vulnerability, or sensitivity, in response to a variety of emotions, kindness, callousness, and even situations involving fraud. Vulnerability to one's own memories can cause tremendous psychic pain. This susceptibility makes women a prime target to be "taken" in many ways— sexually, financially, and emotionally, to name a few.

I recall my own frustrations. Once while I was struggling to get a paycheck for a second job I had taken after my husband's death, a flip secretary caused me to burst into tears while talking on the phone—a brand-new behavior for me. On another occasion during the early months, I misread the intent behind a lovely luncheon with an attractive man my own age. I thought, "Here is someone who really understands." It was a while before I put his friendship in the proper perspective. He was appreciative of my editorial support and advice when he had been in my class. My widowhood and my needs for socializing had nothing to do with his kindness.

IDENTITY RECONSTRUCTION

After some time has elapsed and one has experienced a few of these situations, one does take a deep breath and say, "I am a new and different person now; these incidents must stop." Vulnerability may be closely tied to the chaos and disorganization of the first few months of mourning. I am not sure when vulnerability ceased to be a problem for me. Living alone, while perhaps not the best of solutions, is certainly a help in learning to handle oneself better and to live without feedback and also in avoiding the conflicts and interpersonal squabbles that can arise if one moves in with others. After a while aloneness becomes a distinct change from family life, and this in itself can be a heady experience and permit finding new hobbies or reviving old ones. The heady experience of the new freedom has not been covered in any of the literature I have read.

Chevan and Korsan have warned that living alone is not synonymous with social isolation: "Maintenance of an independent household is for many of the widowed the symbolic bastion within which they define their roles. To think of living any other way is abhorrent, entailing a loss of privacy as well as independence, and thereby threatening the integrity of personal adjustment" (p. 46). The same researchers found that better-educated women and those with more income are more likely to live alone. Widows who live alone are apt to be younger, for at age 80 and over, maintaining a home is often difficult because of diminished physical capacities. There are also ethnic and religious differences; black, Oriental, and Latin American women, as well as women from strongly traditional Catholic backgrounds, are less apt to live alone after being widowed.

A widow is basically on her own throughout the process of widowhood. Often other family members are trying to deal with their own grief and cannot reach out to her. The supports of society are negligible. Silverman's widow-to-widow program can be helpful. Silverman says that the widow's aide provides support and acts as a role model and a "bridge person" (1972b, p. 95). An unidentified quotation lingers with me: "The weakest of women can be a vivid and inspiring example of how to be a widow."

Lopata (1975a) has studied identity reconstruction. One analysis revealed that 46 percent of older widows felt that they and their social lives were unaffected by the spouse's death (Lopata, 1973). Less well educated women were not used to consciously constructing or reconstructing their social world (Lopata, 1975b). The same researcher noted that widows who emphasized the mother role tended to be less well educated; felt less close to their husbands; were likely to be black, Jewish, or immigrants; and were more often Catholic than Protestant (Lopata, 1973). Women who emphasized the wife role seemed to be more involved with their husbands. Identity reconstruction can be painful, but it can also be a period of growing and of making a beautiful closure to a part of one's life, as in the film *A Shameless Old Lady* (see Other Resources at the end of this chapter). One can also wallow in grief. A student once said of her sister, "She's still sitting in a rocker crying a year later."

The competence and managerial ability of widows often go unnoticed; however, widows do run huge ranches and thriving businesses, often with great success. A fine example is Katherine Graham, who took over *The Washington Post* as publisher. A former student of mine, then 49, wrote to me about her own successful identity reconstruction when she became a widow at the age of 42. I have taken the liberty of interspersing research findings into her letter to me:

> My husband was 42 when he died; I was 41 (Neugarten, 1968b, p. 146). My youngest daughter was 6, and the other was 9 (Lopata, 1973, p. 33). The girls seemed to adjust fairly well, although they had no male to identify with, and now as teenagers they have difficulty relating to boys.
>
> The thing that gave me the most stability was going back to college; I did a lot of growing from this and gained my own sense of identity (Lopata, 1975a).
>
> The thing that was the hardest for me was my social growth. I still find it difficult to be single in a couples' society, although I am much more comfortable with it now (Loether, pp. 102, 103).
>
> The hard part for me was that I had no one to share my frustrations with—no one I could simply open up to. I could deal with the loneliness (Loether; Lopata, 1973), but I really would have liked someone to share my frustrations with. Maybe this would have been different if I had lived close to family members. However, as a person I grew a great deal. I was raised in a family where the girls were always told that education was not important for us, since we were *just* girls and would just get married. It has been difficult for me to grow as a woman, because my life centered around raising my children.
>
> I am looking forward to the next 10 years. The girls will soon be on their own, and I feel I have more choices with my life and can take more financial risks. That is exciting to me (Lowe).

DEATH OF SURVIVORS

Rees and Lutkins described a 6-year survey of people who had died:

> It was found that 4.76% of bereaved compared with 0.68% in the control group. . . . The increase in risk was particularly great for widowed people and least for female children. . . . There is a relation between the place at which a person dies and the subsequent mortality of bereaved relatives. The risk of close relatives dying during the first year of bereavement is doubled when the primary death causing bereavement occurs in a hospital compared with at home. . . . If the primary death occurs at some site —for example, a road or field—other than at home or hospital, the risk of a close relative dying during the first year of bereavement is five times the risk carried by the close relative of people who die at home. . . . (p. 16).

The same researchers noted that survivors who died following a bereavement were slightly younger than the relative who had died. The survivors who did succumb died at an earlier age than was usual for the community in which they lived.

SUICIDE IN SURVIVORS

Research studies both in England and in this country show that widows and widowers are high-risk groups regarding suicide. Miller, in his excellent coverage of suicide in the aged population of Arizona, gives suicide rates by marital status for white males aged 60 and over in that state. His study is recommended to the reader.

MacMahon and Pugh studied suicides occurring during a 4-year period among widows and widowers residing in Massachusetts. Although this is not a recent study, it should be noted that these researchers commented on the high suicide risk during the first 4 years of bereavement. The risk of suicide was estimated to be 2.5 times higher during the first bereavement year and 1.5 times higher during the second, third, and fourth years than in subsequent years. Parkes et al. (1969) observed much the same phenomenon in England, and Bunch obtained similar results.

THE DISENGAGEMENT THEORY AND WIDOWHOOD

Though the popularity of the disengagement theory has waned through the years, it has had a great impact in the field of aging. Cummings and Henry wrote an interesting paragraph about widowhood in the book *Growing Old* which leaves much room for argument, especially among widows themselves. They said that widowhood is to women what retirement is to men. They felt that, like retirement, widowhood is an ending to a central task of adult life. Widowhood gives formal permission to be disengaged. Furthermore, widows will have a ready-made peer group in other widows. These researchers suggest that widows join this group very happily. Their empirical observations suggest that the disengaged older woman is an active, carefree, and even frivolous "girl." Burnside, Caine, and Van Coevering have all written personal accounts of widowhood; what they wrote does not seem congruent with the above statement.

While there is a ready-made peer group in other widows, it is hard to believe that "they join this very happily." Rather, it seems likely that many do so because there is no other support system; surely there is a dearth of men for them to talk with, to date, or to have for friends. The need for a support system, for someone who knows what they have been through, and for persons who can intervene with both sense and sensitivity may be an important reason why widows seek out other women who have also experienced the death of a spouse.

REMARRIAGE FOR OLDER WOMEN

The older woman's prospect of finding a new mate is somewhat gloomy, for she faces a great deal of competition in her search. "Sexual boycott" is Comfort's (p. 196) term for society's reactions to older women who try to attract younger partners. The older man has a wide choice of women, since society will approve the marriage if the woman is much younger than he. Weg states: "Any reduction in the age difference between husband and wife, away from the present practice of husbands being older than their wives, will have a beneficial effect on reducing the number of widows and increase the number of older couples in the future." See Figures 18-3 and 18-4.

Figure 18-4 A reduction in the age difference between husband and wife in the future will have the effect of reducing the number of widows and should help to increase the number of older couples. (*Courtesy of Miriam Hawkins.*)

Treas and Van Hilst write:

> The dearth of late-life unions may also reflect the subjective processes of aging itself. Life-cycle theorists have long emphasized that the last stage of the developmental cycle is marked not by new ventures but by assessment of past and accomplishments in response to a shortened future time perspective. . . . Given an uncertain future and a cultural silence on the unique virtues and rewards of new marriages in old age, older people may be justifiably reluctant to make the personal investments and accommodations to assume the grave responsibilities which new marriages demand. Thus, while marriage may be deemed desirable for older people on a number of counts, there is little reason to expect late-life unions to rise above their presently low levels in the near future (p. 133).

According to studies done some time ago, more divorced adults remarry within 5 years than widows or widowers. Half of the men and one-fourth of the women who lose a spouse are remarried within 5 years after the death of the mate (Goode, 1956; Landis). In contrast, three-fourths of divorced adults remarry within 5 years following the divorce (Udry).

SUCCESSFUL REMARRIAGES

McKain has made the following points concerning successful remarriages: (1) Widows and widowers who know each other well usually have successful marriages; (2) remarriages that have the approval of friends and family have a greater chance for success than those which do not; (3) widows and widowers who can accept the role changes of aging usually have successful marriages; (4) widows and widowers who own a home but do not reside there after marriage tend to have successful marriages; and (5) couples with insufficient incomes are less likely to have successful marriages. See Figure 18-5.

In working with older widows, one often hears them say, "My husband would have wanted me to" (or "not wanted me to" if that is a more advantageous stance). It can also be difficult for children to have a parent continually tell them that their mother or father would have wanted them to do something. Speaking through the mouths of the dead is fraught with dangers. However, the safety in the tactic is obvious; the dead will not respond, recant, or deny. In my own experience I have not found that divorced persons do anything similar to this.

It is also difficult to group divorced persons and persons who have lost a spouse for effective interaction. The vituperous statements about ex-spouses may be difficult for widows and widowers to listen to after a while. I once attended a marathon for newly bereaved persons. The leader said that he had given up leading marathons which also included divorced persons because there were such abrasive interactions. He found those groups too difficult to handle. However, he said that widows and widowers often have an unrealistic view of the deceased and fail to admit his or her faults or difficulties in the marriage, thus making the deceased spouse sound unreal to the other group members. He said

Figure 18-5 This elderly widower experienced several remarriages during his 100 plus years having outlived all of his wives. (*Courtesy of Will Patton*).

that when divorced persons participate in such a group, the widows and widowers react to their hatred, bitterness, and destructive descriptions of the ex-mate. Thus he had decided to keep the groups separate. Someone planning to lead such groups might do well to anticipate this problem and the extent to which it might occur.

PERSONAL INVOLVEMENT

Golan wrote: "Whatever the theoretical approach, the professional background of the caregiver matters less than his personal involvement with the widow and her family during the crucial stages following the husband's death" (p. 373). I have found in my interviewing of widowers and widows that when I said, "I'm a widow too," an immediate rapport was established. The two of us had been victors in the same battle—no matter how or when the spouse had died. Comfort has said: "The kindest thing you can do for a bereaved person of any age is to be there, listen, support, and show yourself open to his or her emotions. Do not hide because you don't know what to say. Saying should be avoided" (p. 46).

INTERVENTIONS

This chapter represents an exhaustive search of the literature on widowhood and widowerhood. The literature, though replete with statistics and findings, offers the practitioner few practical suggestions concerning intervention. The work of Silverman (1966, 1967, 1969, 1970, 1971, 1972a, 1972b, 1975) is helpful to the care giver, as are the growing number of personal accounts by women describing what not to do when newly widowed. Few men have written about their experience in widowerhood, which is another lacuna in the literature.

Effective ways to assuage some of the intense pain, to prevent illness (both physical and psychological), and to decrease suicide rates are fertile areas for intervention.

It is well for care givers to remember that "it is a fearful thing to love what death can touch" when they are intervening or planning to intervene.

SUMMARIZING STATEMENTS BASED ON THE LITERATURE

- Grief work may be expressed in a variety of ways (Burnside).
- Identity reconstruction is a major task in widowhood (Lopata, 1975a).
- Religious convictions may be very important to the present cohort generation (Heyman and Gianturco).
- Decision making can be a burden (Van Coevering).
- The burden of adjustment to widowhood falls upon the widow herself (Loether).
- The wife who always depended on her husband to make decisions and handle family affairs may be in desperate straits (Loether).
- Grief work for a widow can last from 6 months to a lifetime (Loether). Those who intervene must consider the duration of the grief.
- Grieving widows are not in a proper state of mind to handle financial affairs (Caine; Loether).
- Widows and widowers may no longer be included in couple functions (Loether).
- Widows usually resist moving to the homes of married children (Loether).
- Widows usually keep up channels of communication and interaction and links to the social world (Cummings and Henry; Loether).
- Widowers have less contact with children than married men or married or widowed women (Townsend).
- Widows may feel self-conscious and concerned about their body image during the first sexual experience after widowhood (Caine).

- With age, one may increasingly make internal preparations for the possibility of being a widow or a widower (Rosow).
- Less well educated women may have more difficulty defining new roles and organizing a new social world than women with more education (Lopata, 1973).
- Older people may be reluctant to take on the responsibilities that a new marriage requires (Treas and Van Hilst).
- If a woman is widowed early in life, she may not have a support group among her peers, who will still be married (Loether).
- Loneliness will increase after the first 6 months of widowhood (Silverman, 1969).
- It may be difficult to acknowledge widowhood, even to say, "I am a widow," during the first few months (Burnside).
- Older widows may be high utilizers of outpatient clinics (Morrison).
- The death of close relatives may occur within the first year of bereavement (Rees and Lutkins).
- Suicides may increase among bereaved close relatives (MacMahon and Pugh; Miller; Parkes et al.).

GUIDELINES FOR INTERVENTION

- Be aware that grief cannot be hurried up. Such things as music, photographs, letters, old checks, and the handwriting of the deceased can evoke sad memories for a long period of time.
- Be prepared for the "double pain" that the bereaved person suffers as he or she observes the children's grief (Burnside).
- Encourage an illness review so that the griever can go over all the details (Clayton et al., 1971).
- Encourage funeral replay for the same reason.
- Reinforce the aspects of the death that the griever feels were well handled.
- Encourage widows and widowers to keep busy, develop new roles and relations, and focus on one social role (Lopata, 1973).
- Encourage the cultural rituals of grief for widows; fewer exist in Western culture than in non-Western cultures (Mathison). In some cultures the role of the widow is clearly defined (Silverman, 1972b).
- Assist the widow or widower by promoting grief work and role change (Silverman and Cooperband).
- Points to remember during the early grief period include:
  - Do not console; listen.
  - Do not tell of more tragic suffering in an attempt to make the person feel better (Burnside).
  - Do not overload the bereaved person with information and details (Ebersole).
  - Be available but not overwhelming; recognize the person's need to be alone (Ebersole).

REFERENCES

Anonymous: Personal communication, 1971.

Atchley, Robert C.: *The Social Forces in Later Life,* Wadsworth, Belmont, Calif., 1972.

———: "Dimensions of Widowhood in Later Life," *The Gerontologist,* **15**(2): 176–178, 1975.

Berardo, Felix M.: "Widowhood Status in the United States: Perspectives on a Neglected Aspect of the Family Life Cycle," *Family Coordinator,* **17**(4): 191–203, 1968.

———: "Survivorship and Social Isolation: The Case of the Aged Widower," *Family Coordinator,* **19**(1):11–25, 1970.

Bornstein, Philipp E., P. J. Clayton, J. A. Halikas, W. L. Maurice, and Eli Robins: "The Depression of Widowhood after Thirteen Months," *The British Journal of Psychiatry,* **122**(570):561–566, 1973.

Bunch, J.: "Recent Bereavement and Suicide," *Journal of Psychosomatic Research,* **16**(5):361–366, 1972.

Burnside, Irene M.: "You Will Cope, of Course . . .," *American Journal of Nursing,* **71**(12):2354–2357, 1971.

Butler, Robert N.: "Aspects of Survival and Adaptation in Human Aging," *American Journal of Psychiatry,* **123**(10): 1233–1243, 1967.

Caine, Lynn: *Widow,* Morrow, New York, 1974.

Chevan, Albert, and **J. Henry Korsan:** "The Widowed Who Live Alone: An Examination of Social and Demographic Factors," *Social Forces,* **51**(53):46, 1972.

Clark, Margaret, and **B. Anderson:** *Culture and Aging,* Charles C Thomas, Springfield, Ill., 1967.

Clayton, Paula J.: "The Effect of Living Alone on Bereavement Symptoms," *American Journal of Psychiatry,* **132**(2): 133–137, 1975.

———, **Lynn Desmarais,** and **George Winokur:** "A Study of Normal Bereavement," *American Journal of Psychiatry,* **125**(2):168–178, 1968.

———, **James A. Halikas,** and **William L. Maurice:** "The Depression of Widowhood," *The British Journal of Psychiatry,* **120**(554):71–77, 1972.

——— et al.: "The Bereavement of the Widowed," *Diseases of the Nervous System,* **32**(9):597–604, 1971.

Comfort, Alex: *A Good Age,* Crown, New York, 1976.

Cummings, Elaine, and **William Henry:** *Growing Old,* Basic Books, New York, 1961.

Ebersole, Priscilla: Personal communication, 1968.

Golan, Naomi: "Wife to Widow to Woman," *Social Work,* **29**(5):369–374, 1975.

Goode, W. J.: *After Divorce,* Free Press, New York, 1956.

Heyman, Dorothy K., and **D. T. Gianturco:** "Long Term Adaptation by the Elderly to Bereavement," *Journal of Gerontology,* **28**(3):359–362, 1973.

Landis, P. H.: "Sequential Marriage," *Journal of Home Economics,* **42**: 625–627, 1950.

Lewis, C. S.: *A Grief Observed,* Seabury, New York, 1961.

Liggett, F. G.: Paper presented for class, Arizona State University, 1977.

Lindemann, Eric: "Symptomatology and Management of Acute Grief," *American*

Journal of Psychiatry, **101**(2):141–148, 1944.

Loether, Herman J.: *Problems of Aging,* 2d ed., Dickenson, Encino, Calif., 1975.

Lopata, Helen Z.: "Loneliness: Forms and Components," *Social Problems,* **17**(2): 248–261, 1969.

———: "The Social Involvement of American Widows," *American Behavioral Scientist,* **14**(1):41–58, 1970.

———: "Living Arrangements of American Urban Widows," *Sociological Focus,* **5**:41–46, 1971. (a)

———: "Widows as a Minority Group," part II, *The Gerontologist,* **11**(1):67–77, 1971. (b)

———: *Widowhood in an American City,* Schenkman, Cambridge, Mass., 1973.

———: "On Widowhood, Grief Work and Identity Reconstruction," *Journal of Geriatric Psychiatry,* **8**(1):41–56, 1975. (a)

———: "Widowhood: Societal Factors in Life-Span Disruptions and Alternatives," in N. Datan and L. H. Ginzberg (eds.), *Life-Span Developmental Psychology: Normative Life Crises,* Academic, New York, 1975. (b)

Lowe, N.: Personal communication, 1977.

McKain, W. C.: "Retirement Marriages," *Agriculture Experiment Monograph No. 3,* University of Connecticut, Storrs, Conn., 1969.

MacMahon, Brian, and Thomas F. Pugh: "Suicide in the Widowed," *American Journal of Epidemiology,* **81**(1):23–31, 1965.

Maddison, David, and Agnes Viola: "The Health of Widows in the Year Following Bereavement," *Journal of Psychosomatic Research,* **12**(4):297–306, 1968.

Mathison, Jean: "A Cross-Cultural View of Widowhood," *Omega,* **1**(3):201–218, 1970.

Millay, Edna St. Vincent: *Collected Poems,* Harper & Row, New York, 1959.

Miller, Marv: *Suicide among the Elderly,* unpublished manuscript, 1977.

Morrison, Julie: "Group Therapy for High Utilizers of Clinic Facilities," in I. Burnside (ed.), *Psychosocial Nursing Care of the Aged,* McGraw-Hill, New York, 1973, p. 149.

Neugarten, Bernice: "Adaptation of the Life Cycle," paper presented at the FFRP Conference, Puerto Rico, June 1968. (a)

——— (ed.): *Middle Age and Aging,* University of Chicago Press, Chicago, 1968. (b)

Parkes, Colin Murray: "Effects of Bereavement on Physical and Mental Health: A Study of the Medical Records of Widows," *British Medical Journal,* **2**(5405):274–279, 1964. (a)

———: "Recent Bereavement as a Cause of Mental Illness," *British Journal of Psychiatry,* **110**(465):198–204, 1964. (b)

———: "Bereavement and Mental Illness: A Clinical Study of the Grief of Bereaved Psychiatry Patients," *British Journal of Medical Psychology,* **38**(1):1–26, 1965.

———: *Bereavement: Studies of Grief in Adult Life,* International Universities Press, New York, 1972.

———, B. Benjamin, and R. G. Fitzgerald: "Broken Heart: A Statistical Study of Increased Mortality among Widowers," *British Medical Journal,* **1**(5646): 740–743, 1969.

Pollock, G.: "Mourning and Adaptation," *International Journal of Psychoanalysis,* **42**:341–361, 1961.

Preston, Caroline E.: "An Old Bag: The Stereotype of the Older Woman," in *No Longer Young: The Older Woman in America,* University of Michigan, Institute of Gerontology, Ann Arbor, 1975.

Rees, W. D., and S. G. Lutkins: "Mortality of Bereavement," *British Medical Journal,* **4**(5570):13–16, 1967.

Riley, Matilda W., and A. E. Foner: *Aging and Society: An Inventory of Research Findings,* vol. 1, Russell Sage, New York, 1968.

Rogers, Linda L.: "Widows: Neglected Women," *Marriage and Family Living,* **59**(3):14–16, 1977.

Rosow, Irving: *The Social Integration of the Aged,* Free Press of Macmillan, New York, 1967.

Schwartz, Loretta: "Hungry Women in America," *Ms,* **6**(4):60–63+, 1977.

Silverman, Phyllis R.: "Services for the Widowed during the Period of Bereavement," *Social Work Practice,* Columbia, New York, 1966.

———: "Services to the Widowed: First Steps in a Program of Preventive Intervention," *Community Mental Health Journal,* **3**(1):37–44, 1967.

———: "The Widow-to-Widow Program: An Experiment in Preventive Intervention," *Mental Hygiene,* **53**(3):333–337, 1969.

———: "The Widow as a Caregiver in a Program of Preventive Intervention with Other Widows," *Mental Hygiene,* **54**(4):540–547, 1970.

———: "Factors Involved in Accepting an Offer for Help," *Archives of the Foundation for Thanatology,* **3**:161–171, 1971.

———: "Intervention with the Widow of a Suicide," in A. C. Cain (ed.), *Survivors of Suicide,* Charles C Thomas, Springfield, Ill., 1972. (a)

———: "Widowhood and Preventive Intervention," *Family Coordinator,* **21**:95–102, 1972. (b)

——— and Adele Cooperband: "On Widowhood: Mutual Help and the Elderly Widow," *Journal of Geriatric Psychiatry,* **8**(1):9–27, 1975.

Start, Clarissa: *When You're a Widow,* Concordia, St. Louis, 1968.

Townsend, Peter: *The Family Life of Old People,* Penguin, Baltimore, 1963.

Treas, Judith, and Anne Van Hilst: "Marriage and Remarriage Rates among Older Americans," *The Gerontologist,* **16**(2):132–136, 1976.

Udry, J. R.: "Marital Instability by Race, Sex, Education, and Occupation, Using 1960 Census Data," *American Journal of Sociology,* **72**:203–209, 1966.

U.S. Bureau of the Census: *Current Population Reports: Marital Status and Family Status,* ser. P-20, no. 212, 1971.

———: *Statistical Abstract of the United States,* 1972.

U.S. Department of Health, Education, and Welfare: *Facts about Older Americans: 1976,* DHEW Publication no. (OHD)77-20006, 1976.

Van Coevering, Virginia: "Exploring Group Counseling on a Technique for Amelirating Morbidity, Mortality and Lowered Life Satisfaction of Widowhood," handout, 1974.

Weg, Ruth B.: Handout prepared with the assistance of Lisa Tanahashi, Leonard Davis School of Gerontology, University of Southern California, Los Angeles, 1977.

Zale, Linda: Personal communication, 1977.

OTHER RESOURCES

TEACHING FILMS

I Think They Call Him John: 26 min/16 mm/b&w/1970. Presents the loneliness and boredom that are the lot of many aging persons. Very little dialogue. Producer: Jack Carrothers. Distributor: Mass Media Associates, 2116 North Charles Street, Baltimore, Md. 21218.

Minnie Remembers: 5 min/16 mm/color/ 1976. A UMC production made by Kay Henderson, Phil Arnold, and Wayne Smith. The film is based on a poem and reflects the loneliness of an older woman. Distributor: Mass Media Ministries, 2116 North Charles Street, Baltimore, Md. 21218.

The Spirit Possession of Alejandro Mamani: 27 min/16 mm/color/1974. Filmed among the Aymara Indians of the Bolivian highlands, this documentary sweeps aside cultural boundaries in its portrayal of an old man's desperate battle against the ills of aging and bereavement. Produced by the American Universities Field Staff, with a grant from the National Science Foundation. Spanish with English subtitles. Distributor: Filmakers Library, Inc., 290 West End Avenue, New York, N.Y. 10023.

String Bean: 17 min/color/1965. The story of a fragile elderly woman and her love for a potted string bean plant. Written and directed by Edward Sechan. Distributor: Contemporary/McGraw-Hill, New York.

COMMERCIAL FILMS

Harry and Tonto: 1974. Directed by Paul Mazursky.

I Never Sang for My Father: 1970. Directed by Gilbert Cates.

The Keymaker: 18 min/color/1970. An old man searches to find life in a world lost in its loneliness. Distributor: University of Southern California, Los Angeles, Calif. 90024.

The Lost Phoebe: 25 min/color/1974. Adapted from a short story by Theodore Dreiser about an old man in search of his dead wife. Distributor: American Film Institute, Washington, D.C. 20566.

A Shameless Old Lady: 1966. Directed by Rene Allio.

BOOKS

Adams, Charlotte: *Housekeeping after Office Hours,* Harper & Row, New York, 1953. Excellent for anyone who does not have time to keep house or would profit from reorganizing the job. $3.

Arthur, Julietta K.: *Retire to Action: A Guide to Voluntary Service,* Abingdon, Nashville, Tenn., 1969. A thorough exploration of volunteerism that should be of interest to all mature people. $5.95.

Bolles, Richard N.: *What Color Is Your Parachute? A Practical Manual for Job-Hunters and Career-Changers,* Ten Speed Press, Berkeley, Calif. $4.20, including handling charges and taxes. Published annually.

A Discussion of Family Money, Institute of Life Insurance, 277 Park Avenue, New York, N.Y. 10017. Free upon request.

Giammatei, Helen, and **Katherine Slaughter:** *Help Your Family Make a Better Move,* Dolphin Books, Doubleday, Garden City, N.Y., 1968. Covers everything from how to get your house ready to sell to what to put in your suitcase. 95 cents.

Holdane, Bernard: *How to Make a Habit of Success,* Unity Books, Lee's Summit, Mo., $2.

How Budgets Work and What They Do, Institute of Life Insurance, 277 Park Avenue, New York, N.Y. 10017. Free upon request.

How to Avoid Financial Tangles, American Institute for Economic Research, Great Barrington, Mass. 01230. A thorough, sometimes technical text that can help with every aspect of economic life. $3 per set.

How to Cope with Crisis, Public Affairs Pamphlets, 381 Park Avenue South, New York, N.Y. 10016. 25 cents.

Kutner, Luis: *The Intelligent Woman's Guide to Future Security,* Dodd, Mead, New York, 1970. Planned widowhood is the theme. If it is too late to plan, the book offers practical advice for dealing with the business and financial aspects of being widowed. $4.95.

Money Management Booklet Library, Household Finance Corporation, Prudential Plaza, Chicago, Ill. 60601. Set of 12 booklets, $3.

Money in Your Life, Institute of Life Insurance, 277 Park Avenue, New York, N.Y. 10017. Free upon request.

Peterson, James: *On Being Alone: AIM's Guide for Widowed Persons,* Action for Independent Maturity, 1909 K Street, Washington, D.C. 20006.

Webb, Jim, and **Bart Houseman:** *The You Don't Need a Man to Fix It Book,* Doubleday, Garden City, N.Y., 1973.

Winter, Elmer: *Women at Work: Every Woman's Guide to Successful Employment,* Simon & Schuster, New York. $1.95.

ORGANIZATION

Widowed Persons Service
NRTA
1909 K Street, N.W.
Washington, D.C. 20049

Chapter 19

LATE MIDDLE AGE: A TIME FOR PLANNING

Joseph H. Pierre

> Happiness and misery consist in a progression towards
> better or worse; it does not matter how high up or low
> down you are, it depends not on this, but on the
> direction in which you are tending.
>
> *Samuel Butler*

Late middle age or early old age spans the years between 55 and 65 (Neugarten and Moore). It is a time when the person reaps the rewards of earlier efforts and also prepares for his or her approaching retirement.

Studies that have researched and defined the problems of retirement have increased our awareness of the importance of these preretirement years. Many of these studies point to the necessity of planning for retirement long before it occurs. Some of the most notable researchers in this field include Donahue, Orbach, and Pollak; Parnes et al.; Rose and Mogey; Shanas; Sheppard, Ferman, and Faber; Simpson et al.; Streib and Schneider; and Thompson, Streib, and Kosa. Their work has contributed to excellent preretirement programs in some large corporations, adult education retirement preparation programs, and a general public awareness of the need for preretirement planning.

Characteristically, most late-middle-aged Americans in the work force have reached their most economically productive years; they also have the versatility born of experience in complex and demanding positions. They are more confident, more self-assured, and usually more predictable and dependable in their job performance than they were in their youth (Breen). Success may spare them financial worry in their retirement years. They may give little thought to the psychological and social effects of an abrupt cessation of their work life a few years hence. When that time comes, they will likely seek whatever assistance they may need.

As care givers, we are concerned with people who are not in a prime position and who may need assistance in planning and using available resources: (1) those whose performance no longer matches their job requirements, (2) those with health problems, (3) those who are depressed, (4) those who feel "locked in," (5) those who are discriminated against, and (6) those whose skills are technologically obsolete. Many of these people will not seek assistance and may not even clearly understand the problem. This chapter will attempt to illuminate the problems of the preretirement years and to suggest strategic interventions aimed at maximizing the present and anticipating future retirement.

The major concern of older workers may be keeping their position in society. A larger number of each cohort will survive to late middle age, and fewer can expect to remain employed. Labor-force participation of males aged 55 to 64 declined from 90 percent in 1900 to 78 percent in 1974 (Sheppard). A further decline is expected. See Table 19-1 and Figure 19-1.

Weintraub discusses the pressures that politicians and economists periodically exert to slow production of goods, reduce inflation, and equalize the income differential between the working and the nonworking person. Movements in this direction have been transitory and unpredictable. If this became a national priority, it would result in a move toward zero growth in the working population and increased attention to providing jobs for nonwhite young people, who presently have the highest rate of unemployment. If serious and consistent attention were given to the above issues, there would be earlier removal of older

Table 19-1. Labor-Force and Participation Rate and Projections to 1985 by Sex and Age

	Total Labor Force (in Thousands)			Participation Rates		
	1900	1972	1985	1900	1972	1985
Male total	22,641	55,671	66,017	85.7	78.5	78.3
16–19	2,834	4,791	3,962	62.0	59.2	55.5
20–24	3,302	7,795	8,496	90.6	88.8	88.4
25–44	10,560	23,450	34,017	94.7	95.7	94.6
45–64	4,958	17,614	17,460	90.3	85.8	84.9
65+	987	2,022	2,082	63.1	23.3	20.0
Female total	4,999	33,320	41,699	20.0	42.3	45.6
16–19	1,230	3,576	3,203	26.8	45.7	46.4
20–24	1,179	5,337	6,523	31.7	58.9	64.9
25–44	1,791	12,549	18,899	17.5	49.7	52.9
45–64	672	10,974	13,755	13.6	47.3	51.4
65+	127	1,085	1,319	8.3	8.8	8.5

Sources: *Statistical Abstracts of the United States,* 1973; *Statistical History of the United States,* 1965, taken from *Metropolitan Life Statistical Bulletin,* **57**:5–6, May 1976.

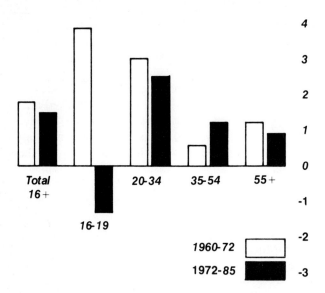

Figure 19-1 Average annual rates of change in the labor force. (*Metropolitan Life Statistical Bulletin, pp. 5–6.*)

workers from the work force (Kreps). In view of the legislation raising the compulsory retirement age to 70, it seems likely that older workers might expect subtle pressures toward early retirement such as periodic functional assessment, downgrading of status, or increased options for early retirement. Even though these solutions might seem reasonable from a national perspective, older workers would be in a most vulnerable position.

PERFORMANCE

When one feels threatened, high-quality performance may be the first line of defense. The following example illustrates some of the reactions of men whose ego is invested in performance: faltering self-esteem, impotence, despair, and job failure.

George ran an exceptionally fine automobile repair shop for many years. He would be the first to say that his was the best shop in town. He felt that his troubles began with his impotence, which started at age 51. He often stayed in his shop working until midnight, and he seemed reluctant to go home. George refused to seek professional help. He felt that problems between man and wife should be settled by them or not at all. His problems increased, his interest in the business waned, and he lost customers. This example illustrates the complexity of intertwining problems in performance that may fulminate and synergize until the individual can no longer cope.

Impotence is often the first indication of performance insecurity and may be seen as evidence of a man's disappointment that he can no longer keep up the pace of his youth (Grant). Impotence is sometimes seen as a subconscious rebellion against demands that one continually produce. Care givers should be alert to any abrupt decline in performance (sexual, physical, or mental) at this critical age and initiate contact with appropriate resources for the individual. It is appropriate to ask whether sexual activity is satisfactory, since many men, like George, would not volunteer this information. For those people unaccustomed to admitting the need for help, it may be important to provide reassurance that professionals will not attempt to take control of their lives or make decisions for them.

DEPRESSION AND SELF-ABSORPTION

A certain segment of the population we have been discussing may fall into a morass of self-pity because, for one reason or another, they are not in a secure or advantageous position at a time when they can reasonably expect to have attained their highest goals. There may be a marked contrast between their self-view and their view of their more successful peers. They may tend to launch into ruminating, depressing monologues focused on physical discomfort, debts, fatigue, the problems of aging, and a generally pessimistic view of life. In contrast, other depressed, disappointed, disgruntled, or disgusted individuals will displace all life's dissatisfactions onto the job situation.

The care giver will need to help the individual sort through the self-perpetuating gloomy thoughts and focus on the main source of dissatisfaction and then present

Figure 19-2   Contentment and self-expression in the later working years. (*Courtesy of Pat Ryan.*)

possible resources and options. It is important for the care giver to go through the process of hearing the complaints, to *acknowledge* the presence of depression, and to point out the commonality of these feelings. The individual must be told that help can be obtained and that depression will not continue endlessly, regardless of how it seems at that moment. The depressed individual who has externalized his or her problems onto the job situation generally has fairly high self-esteem and can more quickly move to alleviate a problem. It is possible that the individual may continue to use the job as a release for antagonisms that originated elsewhere.

The Erosion of Health in the Worker

The older a worker becomes, the more likely he or she is to have developed health problems. Some have accumulated an imposing number of minor injuries such as trick knees, troublesome cartilages, and lower back pain. Certain jobs are particularly hazardous in terms of noxious substances, noise levels, or industrial accidents. When work-related injuries are superimposed upon the normal changes related to aging, a person may become almost totally focused on bodily complaints. Moreover, in addition to occupational hazards, psychological stresses produced in the working situation can contribute to ill health. Table 19-2 clearly shows that health is the greatest factor in withdrawal from the labor force. Many people are forced to retire because of health problems before they are prepared to do so (Sheppard).

In our youth, we are often impatient with the complaints of those who have numerous health problems. It is helpful to recognize the loss of self-confidence that often results when one cannot depend on the body to function smoothly. The reader is referred to Chapter 15 for a full discussion of health in the middle years.

Table 19-2. Reasons for Not Seeking Work, Males Aged 25 to 59 Who Were Not in the Labor Force; United States, First Quarter–1969 and 1976

	1969		1976	
	Number		**Number**	
Reason for Not Seeking Work	**(000s)**	**Percent**	**(000s)**	**Percent**
All reasons	1,722	100.0	3,045	100.0
Think cannot get job	69	3.9	115	3.8
Ill, disabled	925	52.2	1,456	47.8
Retired	62	3.5	136	4.5
Attending school	208	11.7	388	12.7
Other reasons	508	28.7	950	31.2

Source: Metropolitan Life Statistical Bulletin.

EFFECTS OF MAJOR ILLNESS

During the preretirement years, some people develop major illnesses that require periodic hospitalizations—leukemia and cancer, for example. A frequently observed phenomenon among such older men is their attempt to remain on the job until age 62. Some struggle stoically to reach the point where Medicare and social security will assist them and their families. Intermittent hospitalizations quickly deplete accumulated sick leave, major medical benefits rarely cover the total cost of the illness, and the psychological drain of prolonged illness is tremendously taxing. Psychological supports, financial advice, health teaching, and job reentry counseling for wives may all be needed. Professionals working with middle-aged adults who are not ill may ask about the adequacy of their benefits and encourage their full exploration of disability insurance programs and other health plans.

FEELING "LOCKED IN"

It is not only health that is of concern in the later working years; often there is also a feeling of being stifled or of having no place to move within the job.

Harold was a professional engineer who had been employed by a large manufacturing firm for 25 years. At 45 he was considered for promotion to a management position. He did not understand why he was passed over; he did not recognize that employers must consider many things such as Affirmative Action, "new blood" from outside the company, and proficiency within the present position. Perhaps Harold was too good at his job! At any rate, he felt blocked and unappreciated. He showed this overtly by becoming apathetic toward his job, and he no longer took his usual pride in his work. It might have been helpful if Harold had (1) found out exactly why he was retained in his present position, (2) sought challenge and stimulation outside his profession, (3) sought professional job counseling and considered a change, (4) explored the relative advantages of security and assessed its importance to him, (5) developed satisfying leisure-time pursuits, or (6) developed satisfying interpersonal relationships.

Industrial nurses often see men like Harold who come to them with minor physical complaints and family and financial problems, hoping to get "off-the-cuff" counseling. Perhaps all employers should be made aware of the need to expand industrial psychological supports; for instance, informal gripe sessions led by a trained professional (not on the management team) could be regularly scheduled. Ultimately, such services would probably cost employers less than the effects of low morale among employees.

TECHNOLOGICAL OBSOLESCENCE

As one who has experienced the escalating technology of the last 70 years, I can easily understand the frustrations of those who have found themselves displaced and/or rendered obsolete and who have moved to lower-ranking positions. Some find their skills virtually useless in a world of constant improvement in methodology. Such people are living anachronisms. Consider the predicament of Art, for example.

"I got me three damn good trades, by God!" Art stated with feeling. He was talking with a friend he had not seen for 25 years. It seemed that at least the first part of the conversation should have been devoted to things or people of mutual interest. But Art was locked into the subject of greatest importance to him—the fact that in his sixties, even though he was still capable of making a living, his skills were outmoded.

"What do you do Art?" his friend asked.

"Well I'm one of the best damn log-truck drivers in this country and a hell of a good cat skinner [crawler-tractor driver] and damn near the *only* good steam-donkey puncher [steam-powered logging engine] around here, by Christ!"

It evidently did not occur to Art that the reason he was one of the few good steam-donkey punchers around was that there were few steam donkeys left—anywhere. With poignant pride Art said, "Take care of yourself now, you old son of a gun!" His friend stood still as he watched Art walk briskly, with his head up, to the nearest tavern.

It took several decades for Art's skills to be outmoded; now this may occur

Figure 19-3 What can I do? (*Courtesy of Pat Ryan.*)

in a few months. As a case in point, the displacement of electronic engineers was brought to national attention in the 1960s. At present, there are others in highly sophisticated positions who are well aware of the precarious nature of overspecialization.

Some positions are affected by increased ecological concerns, depletion of energy resources, shifts in consumption trends, fluctuating interest rates, legislation, changing construction trends, and even major weather changes. It is no longer simple to predict job security for even 10 years. What can be done without a crystal ball? It would be wise for professionals to encourage people (including themselves) to develop alternative skills and plans of action to reduce feelings of insecurity about the future.

MINORITY PRERETIREMENT

The preretirement years of minorities are highly variable. In some cases age and race discrimination place the minority-group person in double jeopardy in terms of productive years left. In other cases minority-group persons have spent their working years in positions that ensure reasonably secure retirement. The difficulty in approaching the problem lies in the way minorities are defined. Minorities are literally groups that are small in number, although the term is now generally used to refer to those who are denied opportunities because of their race, creed, or color (Streib).

In their later working years minority-group persons are beset by the problems already mentioned, plus a few more. Many have intermittent work histories, poor health, inadequate pension plans, and meager wages and intend to continue to work at one job or another as long as they are able. While legislators have clearly identified some of the problems of retirement for minority groups, they have not considered preretirement planning for them (Dixon). *Many minority-group people give no thought to retirement planning because they must direct all their energies toward surviving in the present.* The challenge for helping professionals is to direct such individuals to areas where skills can be upgraded, retraining programs are available, and Affirmative Action is strongly supported. Those who live a "hand-to-mouth" existence may have little energy, time, or incentive for personal development or future planning (Wilenski).

THE VETERANS AMONG US

Most of the men now planning for their retirement years have been a veteran of one or two wars. Some may have emotional and physical problems stemming from their experiences in the armed services. Over 4 million are currently receiving some type of federal assistance, often drawing full or partial disability and maintaining a limited work career.

On the other hand, some veterans seem to have paved their way to a very comfortable retirement through the practice of "double dipping." After retiring from the armed services, veterans receive extra rating points which help them

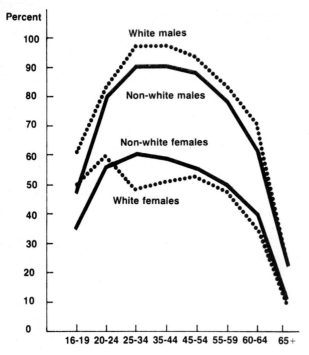

Figure 19-4 Labor-force participation of civilian population of the United States by age, sex, and ethnicity for 1973. (*Metropolitan Life Statistical Bulletin, pp. 5–6.*)

obtain choice government positions or nongovernment positions that will qualify them for social security benefits and an additional government pension. In any case, they now receive one pension and will receive two pensions upon retirement. There is much controversy concerning this issue at present.

THE EFFECTS OF EDUCATION ON PRERETIREMENT

Many middle-aged veterans received a college education because of benefits accrued while in the armed services. New horizons were opened for them that have made their entire working careers much more gratifying than they would have been without such education. But it is not only those who had earlier opportunities for education who seem to be in a satisfying position in their later working years; there is a growing movement toward educational opportunities geared specifically to the older adult. For some this is the first opportunity to pursue long-dormant interests. *Phoenix,* the student weekly newspaper of San Francisco State University, has reported the development of a "Sixty-plus Club" for people over 60 who are interested in attending classes free of charge. At present the program has far more applicants than it can accommodate. The persons who attend these classes say that they do so for the joy of learning, for the contact with young students, and for stimulation and challenge. Campuses across the nation provide the older adult with many other opportunities for continuing education. (See Other Resources at the end of this chapter.)

Education is not only preparation for life but also something that makes living more rewarding on a day-to-day basis (Toll). The reader is referred to the chapter entitled "Adult Learning" in the book by Knox. Knox points out that ill health can substantially reduce learning ability.

Knox also discusses the fact that recent experience and current circumstances do influence the adult's interest in educational pursuits. He suggests that practitioners assist adults in developing a more positive attitude toward education. One way of doing this is to use learning activities which help them cope with changes and adjustments in their lives. Preretirement classes can embrace learning theory and provide an introduction to studenthood for those who have been long out of school.

PLANNING FOR RETIREMENT

As one approaches 60 and realizes that few years are left in which to provide for a secure retirement, "get-rich-quick" schemes become more enticing. People who ordinarily exercise good judgment in most matters may succumb to questionable investment schemes that promise quick and large economic returns. The fact that the earning years are almost over and the subtle signs of physical aging are apparent create an increased need for protection in the form of tangible securities. This is becoming an increasing problem for women, many of whom entered the work force in mid-life and are 25 years behind most men in terms of savings, financial expertise, and experience in earning money.

A survey of male hourly wage earners was conducted by Morrison, who found that they had serious problems planning for income adequacy in their retirement. Even though the men in the study anticipated financial problems in retirement, they did not save substantially. They had unrealistic expectations concerning pension benefits and accrued savings. Retirement planning is also hampered by lack of basic information regarding benefits and by limitations in technical planning ability. Morrison advises that workers enter preretirement programs 10 to 15 years prior to retirement. However, there are more fundamental problems than poor planning or a misunderstanding concerning benefits. The experience of Clarence, a recent retiree, illustrates one major problem.

Clarence planned well all through his productive years. He made wise investments, and his wife worked for some years, and together they managed to save $100,000. Earlier, this seemed entirely sufficient for their retirement years. However, they no longer feel comfortably protected by this sum, and they complain, "Many of those dollars we saved so scrupulously are now worth 18 cents and will be worth less and less as inflation continues." Kreps thoroughly discusses the impact of the economy on aging people.

And what of retirement planning for middle-aged widows? Few have options within their husbands' pension benefits. Soon after the death of the husband they receive a check covering his contributions to the fund plus a small amount of interest. Many of them have not worked for years and must quickly find a way of preparing for the future.

Those men and women who have been wise enough to invest in real property are most likely to feel some security in their retirement years.

Glamser found that the attitude toward retirement is more important than the kind of job held. Workers who can realistically view their retirement as a positive experience will not dread it. Glamser and DeJong studied the efficacy of pre-retirement programs for industrial workers and found that "a comprehensive pre-retirement program can produce favorable changes in retirement, related attitudes, and behavior" (p. 595).

IMPLICATIONS FOR FUTURE PRERETIREMENT PROGRAMS

Hunter considers that support from public funds is an essential component of successful preretirement education and that this should be a responsibility of the public education system. Generally, present programs consider the economic and pragmatic aspects of retirement but pay little attention to the psychosocial aspects. The reality of psychological stress is not generally recognized until it is experienced. Therefore, there is a pressing need for the general availability of preretirement, transitional, and postretirement programs.

Hunter has shown that, during retirement, activities directed at interpersonal relations are more valued than those conducted in isolation. In view of this, *transitional and postretirement groups might be developed to provide valuable support;* widow-to-widow groups have done something similar to this for years. It is recognized that often the lay person with an experiential view is more effective in supportive services than the professional.

SUMMARIZING STATEMENTS BASED ON THE LITERATURE

- Major issues in the preretirement years include (1) work-life expectancy, (2) an increased number of middle-aged women in the work force, (3) evaluation of work performance related to functional age and training, (4) the threat of unemployment or ill health, and (5) preparation for retirement.
- There is a growing decline in job participation among males aged 55 to 69.
- Attitudes toward retirement are variable, depending on health, income, and personal orientation toward work.
- Comprehensive preretirement programs produce favorable changes in attitudes toward retirement.
- Workers should enter preretirement programs 10 to 15 years prior to retirement (Morrison).
- To plan an economically adequate retirement, one must consider overall growth of earnings, improvement in ability on the job, and the relationship of earning levels, fringe benefits, and the expected retirement income (Kreps).

- Health is the major factor in withdrawal from the work world among those in late middle age (Sheppard).
- Willingness to participate in preretirement education programs is influenced by health, recent experiences, and current circumstances; all these affect the individual's interest in learning.

GUIDELINES FOR INTERVENTION

- Suggest preretirement classes for those approaching retirement; provide access to information on related classes, courses, and resources available in the community.
- Be aware of the varied influences that participation in the armed services has had on the lives of older men.
- Influence educational institutions to approach the older learner differently from the way the young student is approached.
- Use health information, anticipatory guidance, stress evaluation, and holistic health practices, for example, to help people cope with changes and adjustments.
- Study the work routines and leisure patterns of people nearing retirement and encourage some noncompetitive activities.
- Reaffirm the individual's control over his or her own life patterns and activities.
- Arrange for comprehensive assessment when there is evidence of rapid sexual, mental, or physical decline.
- Depression and heavy financial burdens have a synergistic negative effect during the later working years. Financial counseling may be of assistance.
- Find lay persons who are willing to participate in discussion groups for the purpose of sharing experiences during the preretirement, transitional, and postretirement periods.

REFERENCES

Breen, Leonard: *The Adult Years,* Purdue University Studies, Lafayette, Ind., 1951.

Dixon, Julian: "Retirement Legislation and the Minority Aged," in E. Percil Stanford (ed.), *Minority Aging and the Legislative Process,* Center on Aging, San Diego, Calif., 1977, pp. 51–56.

Donahue, W., H. L. Orbach, and **O. Pollak:** "Retirement: The Emerging Social Pattern," in C. Tibbitts (ed.), *Handbook of Social Gerontology,* University of Chicago Press, Chicago, 1960, pp. 330–406.

Glamser, Francis D.: "Determinants of a Positive Attitude toward Retirement," *Journal of Gerontology,* **31**(1):104–107, 1976.

——— and **Gordon F. DeJong:** "The Efficacy of Preretirement Preparation Programs for Industrial Workers," *Journal of Gerontology,* **30**(5):595–600, 1975.

Grant, Louise: Personal communication, 1978.

Hunter, W. H.: *A Cross-National Appraisal of Pre-retirement Education,* Cooperative Research Project no. 1422, University of Michigan, Ann Arbor, 1965.

Knox, Alan B.: *Adult Development and Learning,* Jossey-Bass, San Francisco, 1977.

Kreps, Juanita: "The Economy and the Aged," in Robert H. Binstock and Ethel Shanas (eds.), *Handbook of Aging and the Social Sciences,* Van Nostrand Reinhold, New York, 1976.

Metropolitan Life Statistical Bulletin, **57**: 5–6, May 1976.

Morrison, Malcolm H.: "Planning for Income Adequacy in Retirement," *The Gerontologist,* **16**(6):538–543, 1976.

Neugarten, Bernice, and Joan W. Moore: "The Changing Age-Status System," in B. Neugarten (ed.), *Middle Age and Aging,* University of Chicago Press, Chicago, 1968, p. 18.

Parnes, H. S., et al.: *The Pre-Retirement Years: Five Years in the Work Lives of Middle-Aged Men,* Center for Human Resources Research, Ohio State University, Columbus, 1974.

Rose, C. L., and J. M. Mogey: "Aging and Preference for Later Retirement," *International Journal of Aging and Human Development,* **3**(1):45–62, 1972.

Shanas, E.: "Adjustment to Retirement: Substitution or Accommodation," in F. Carp (ed.), *Retirement,* Behavioral Publications, New York, 1972, pp. 219–243.

Sheppard, H. L.: "Work and Retirement,"

in Robert Binstock and Ethel Shanas (eds.), *Handbook of Aging and the Social Sciences,* Van Nostrand Reinhold, New York, 1976.

———, L. Ferman, and S. Faber: *Too Old to Work, Too Young to Retire,* U.S. Special Committee on Unemployment Problems, 1960.

Simpson, I. H., Kurt Back, and John McKinney: "Orientation toward Work and Retirement and Self Evaluation in Retirement," in I. H. Simpson and J. McKinney (eds.), *Social Aspects of Aging,* Duke University Press, Durham, N.C., 1966, pp. 75–89.

Streib, Gordon: "Are the Aged a Minority Group?" in B. Neugarten (ed.), *Middle Age and Aging,* University of Chicago Press, Chicago, 1968, pp. 35–46.

——— and C. J. Schneider: *Retirement in American Society,* Cornell, Ithaca, N.Y., 1971.

Thompson, Wayne E., Gordon Streib, and John Kosa: "The Effect of Retirement on Personal Adjustment: A Panel Analysis," *Journal of Gerontology,* **15**(2): 165–169, 1960.

Toll, John S.: "The Changing Universities: New Audiences for Learning," in Alan Entine (ed.), *Americans in Middle Years: Career Options and Educational Opportunities,* Ethel Percy Andrus Gerontology Center, Los Angeles, 1974.

Weintraub, Andrew: *The Economic Growth Controversy,* International Arts and Science Press, New York, 1973.

Wilenski, Harold: "Orderly Careers and Social Participation: The Impact of Work History on Social Integration in the Middle Class," in B. Neugarten (ed.), *Middle Age and Aging,* University of Chicago Press, Chicago, 1968, pp. 321–340.

OTHER RESOURCES

FILMS

Does Anybody Need Me Anymore?: 29 min/ color/1974. A film about ordinary middle-class working people. After the children leave home, the wife begins to question the meaning of her life and wonder about her future. Distributor: Learning Corporation of America, 1350 Avenue of the Americas, New York, N.Y. 10019.

Do Not Fold, Staple, or Mutilate: 50 min/ b&w/1968. An aging union leader cannot accept his diminishing work role. As retirement approaches, his depression increases, Distributor: McGraw-Hill, Princeton-Hightstown Road, Hightstown, N.J. 08520.

End of a Salesman: 15 min/color/1976. A segment from the CBS program "60 Minutes" about a salesman who is fired by a large company because he refuses to take early retirement after 33 years with the company. Producer: CBS News. Distributor: Time-Life Multimedia, 100 Eisenhower Drive, Paramus, N.J. 07652.

Last Day on the Job: 4 min/b&w/1962. A short film on preparing for retirement. It shows what happens to an older man on his last day on the job and how he feels about it.

Planning a Quality of Life: 12 min/16 mm/ color. Deals with the questions of housing in preretirement planning. Distributor: University of Georgia, Georgia Center for Continuing Education, Film Library, Athens, Ga. 30601.

Preparation for the Later Years: Financial Planning: 30 min/b&w/1960. Deals with the problem of the greatest immediate concern to most older people. Made with the guidance of authorities from several organizations. Producer: Dynamic Films Inc. for N.C.A. Distributor: University of Iowa, Audiovisual Center, Iowa City, Iowa 52240.

Rest of Your Life: 28 min/color/1968. Attempts to make people aware of retirement and of the necessity to plan for it. Raises questions about retirement and stimulates thinking and planning. Distributor: Journal Films, Inc., 930 Pitner Avenue, Evanston, Ill. 60202.

That's What Living's About: 18 min/color/ 1973. A philosophical look at leisure—how it affects our lives now and how it may affect us in the future. Shows the vital balance between work and leisure and the relationship between leisure and retirement. Producer: City of Torrance, Calif., Park and Recreation Department. Distributor: University of California, Extension Media Center, Berkeley, Calif. 94720.

To a Good Long Life: 20 min/color/1976. A documentary focusing on three older people who lead vigorous, interesting lives. The message is that age does not have to slow people down; they can still contribute to society. The film helps those approaching retirement age to see that their future can be exciting and vital.

FREE, VOLUNTARY SELF-HELP ORGANIZATIONS FOR PROFESSIONAL, TECHNICAL, AND EXECUTIVE JOB SEEKERS

Experience Unlimited (EU)
Sacramento, Calif.

Forty Plus
Chicago
Denver
New York
Philadelphia
Houston
Washington, D.C.
Honolulu
Los Angeles
Oakland, Calif.
Volunteer Engineer Scientists Techniques
(VEST)
Seattle, Wash. (SEA-VEST)
Dayton, Ohio (DAY-VEST)
Chicago, Ill. (VEST-I)

Aid to Independent Maturity (AIM): Sponsored by the American Association of Retired Persons (AARP) and the National Retired Teachers Association (NRTA). Produces packaged programs for preretirement planning. Another preretirement program was designed at the Ethel Percy Andrus Gerontology Center with the guidance of Paul Kerschner and Virginia Boyack for use by corporations.

Over 60 Counseling and Employment Service: Offers counseling, placement, training, and individualized attention. For further information, contact Gladys Sprinkle, Director, Over 60 Counseling and Employment Service, 4700 Norwood Drive, Chevy Chase, Md. 20015.

EDUCATIONAL INSTITUTIONS GEARED TO THE NEEDS OF THE OLDER ADULT

Minneapolis Community College
New York City Community College
Institute of Study for Older Adults

EXTERNAL DEGREE PROGRAMS AND UNIVERSITIES WITHOUT WALLS GRANTING CREDIT FOR ADULT WORK AND LIFE EXPERIENCE

Lincoln, Nebr.
Saratoga, N.Y.
Yellow Springs, Ohio

Wayne State University
College of Lifelong Learning

Adelphi University (correspondence courses leading to master's degree)

University of Wisconsin
Management Institute (offered in 2- to 5-day seminars)

SCHOOLS OF MANAGEMENT GEARED FOR MIDDLE-LEVEL EXECUTIVES

University of Chicago
University of New Mexico
University of Pittsburgh
University of Rochester
University of Illinois

University of Denver
Northeastern University
Ohio State University
University of Nebraska

Chapter 20

THE RETIREMENT YEARS
Joseph H. Pierre

> "I'm in the strangest state of mind,
>   So full of cussedness, I find;
> I hate to go to bed at night,
>   I hate the morn's returning light;
> I am not sick, I don't feel swell,
>   I simply feel as mean as . . . well;
> I only wish I had been fired,
>   Instead of having been retired.
>
> *Reverend Robert Brewster Beattie*

Retirement is an important transition in the life course and has become one of the major issues in developmental psychology (Snow and Havighurst).

Atchley, speaking from a functionalist viewpoint, sees retirement for men and widowhood for women as the conclusion of the person's central life task. This is a traditional stance. According to him, compulsory retirement provides an orderly separation and transition that keeps promotional lines open and strengthens incentives for younger workers; however, it may cause great economic hardship for the retiree and is wasteful of the talent and wisdom accumulated over the years within an organization.

Johnson and Kamara look at retirement in another way (see Figure 20-1):

Essential to a conflict perspective of age relations is the view that the productive and powerful middle-aged maintain their position by disengaging the non-productive and powerless young and old. This forced disengagement is largely achieved through retirement from and postponement of entry into middle-aged adult work roles. This process is not a deliberate conspiracy, but is the consequence of the workings of the institutional order, especially the institutions of education and retirement (p. 104).

Figure 20-1 From one perspective, employment of the young and the old is subject to pressure from the powerful groups in their middle years. (*Courtesy of Pat Ryan.*)

The number of Americans over age 65 has increased startlingly during the twentieth century, and the needs of these citizens for health care, housing, employment, association with peers, transportation, and adequate nutrition, among other things, have become startlingly evident. These needs have certainly not been adequately provided for. For example, in 1936 Congress made it possible for workers aged 65 or older to have the financial assistance of "social security." This program probably should have been given some other name, since it provides for neither sociability nor security. Many times at the White House Conference on Aging it was said that social security had never been intended to provide for all the needs of men and women too old to work. One wonders why it was given such a glorious name; "supplemental security income" would have been more accurate. Most people over age 65 would like to live without being an economic burden to younger family members and society. See Figure 20-2. Social security has not accomplished this goal.

Though money is the greatest problem of the aged, that issue should be addressed long before retirement. This chapter will focus on (1) the process of retirement and patterns of retirement; (2) early retirement; (3) adjustment to retirement as related to education and status; (4) health, economic, ethnic, and emotional factors; (5) family adjustment; and (6) projections for the future. The reader is referred to the work of Sheppard and of Binstock and Shanas for additional information about retirement.

ATTITUDES TOWARD RETIREMENT

Workers whose jobs are strenuous but nonfulfilling tend to retire as soon as possible, while people in sedentary or more satisfying occupations tend to linger on in their jobs. Certainly, the monetary rewards and status associated with

Figure 20-2 Older persons in the labor force, 1975. (1) More than 2.9 million or 14 percent of older people were in the labor force—either working or actively seeking work—in 1975. (2) They make up 3.1 percent of the U.S. labor force. (3) Slightly more than a fifth of the older men (1.9 million) and about 8 percent of the older women (1.0 million) are in the labor force. (4) Only 5.3 percent or 1 in 19 older people in the labor force were unemployed. (5) A large proportion of older men who work are in low-paying agricultural jobs. (6) The male labor force participation rate has decreased steadily from 2 of 3 older men in 1900 to 1 in 5 in 1975; the female rate rose slightly from 1 in 12 in 1900 to 1 in 10 in 1972, but dropped to 1 in 12 in 1975. (*From U.S. Department of Health, Education, and Welfare, p. 1.*)

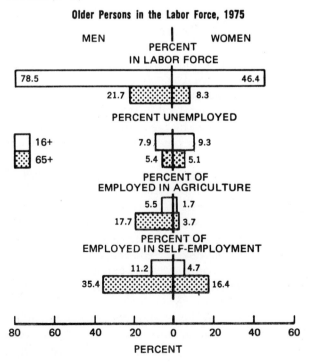

Older Persons in the Labor Force, 1975

certain positions are important variables, as are the health requirements of various jobs. Some feel that compulsory retirement is less personally devastating than subtle pressures to move people out of their jobs or down the status ladder as they age.

Some researchers contend that retirement does not lead to ill health or death but that an unfavorable attitude toward retirement can cause difficulties in adjustment (Atchley; Riley and Foner). They also point out that the higher the person's occupational status, the less likely he or she is to miss the job. This is complicated by the fact that more interesting options may be open to such people after retirement. However, recent studies tend to show that workers in positions described as satisfying remain in their jobs longer. Also, workers in powerful positions are often reluctant to give them up.

Often friendships and associations are derived from the work situation, and the person is bereft of social contacts after retirement, much as a widow may be socially isolated after her husband's death. The stigma of an undesirable social position keeps the more fortunate members of society at a distance.

PATTERNS OF RETIREMENT

Sheldon, McEwan, and Ryser have identified several patterns of retirement: (1) attempts to maintain patterns analogous to work patterns, (2) withdrawal and failure to seek new pursuits, (3) the transference of needs to new situations that gratify old needs, and (4) the development of new functional needs that are satisfied in new ways. The success of any of these patterns depends upon how realistic it is in terms of the individual's style, the settings that are available, and the support of others in the environment. Success cannot be determined immediately because it usually takes a person from 6 months to a year following retirement to settle into one of these patterns. The pattern chosen must permit response to unforeseen crises and contingencies. The retiree's pattern may be adequate for him or her but still impose intolerable stress on other family members. Success in adjustment is influenced by the individual's threshold of stress, characteristic mode of handling crises, and internal and external resources.

The experience of Dave, a loan officer in a bank, illustrates one pattern of retirement. Dave often needed pictures of property for which the bank might loan money. By the time he was ready to retire, Dave had displayed his photographs in many places and had won some awards. He had always wished for time to do his own processing, from the click of the shutter to the final soft-tone enlargement. A year after his retirement Dave said, "You know, I thought it was going to be terrible. But now my wife and I go wherever we think we might find something striking, beautiful, or unusual to photograph. I take my pictures, bring them home, and process them exactly my way. My wife enjoys the trips, and I get great satisfaction out of my photography. Have you seen my display in the bank?" This example illustrates a transference to new situations that gratify old needs.

Various researchers have identified the following important factors in adjustment to retirement (Barfield and Morgan, 1978a, 1978b; Ballweg; Glamser; Sheldon et al.):

Financial security
Number of fulfilling roles
Sources of social contact
Opportunities for achievement in areas outside work
Affiliation with a major reference group
Patterns of coping with change earlier in life
Patterns of activity before retirement
Family supports
Health
Secure living situation
Number of concurrent crises experienced, such as death of spouse, loss of
    home, loss of child, and surgery
Multiplicity of skills and talents
Personality type—introvert or extrovert
Capacity for creativity and commitment
Conception of personal time left and resources to match
Status of relationship with mate

THE TRANSITIONAL STAGE

During the first few months or the first year after retirement, there may be problems of adjustment. The person may go through stages of exhaustion, dissatisfaction, assimilation, and satisfaction. An educator wrote that giving up one day a week for retirement practice during the 5 years preceding retirement made the transition easier. However, people are very different. One retiree, when asked how long it took her to adjust to retirement, said, "Oh, about 2 seconds." Some researchers have speculated that retirees who continue indefinitely to express resignation or resistance to retirement may lack qualities of imagination, resourcefulness, and adaptability (Streib and Schneider). Commitment to one's job is a sign that this commitment may be effectively transferred to another area after retirement.

During the transitional period retirees report dreaming about their jobs and frequently reminiscing about them. It is a great help to have someone who will patiently listen to the individual's detailed accounts of his or her work role; it may also be helpful to acknowledge to the individual the importance of this process and of work-related dreams. One need only be an astute listener, not an analyst. Giving up such an important function as work sets in motion a grief process in most people, and in many ways it should be treated like the grief associated with other major losses.

The disorganization that some people experience during the transitional stage is often related to the loss of a familiar routine. They suddenly feel like a ship without a rudder, although that analogy is limited since many do not have the energy to move, are uncertain of their destination, and feel generally lost. It may be helpful to attempt to establish a new routine; eating meals, reading the paper, trimming the lawn, and making a daily trip to the supermarket can be scheduled with as much care as a work routine. Other people are only too happy to be free of regimentation. See Figure 20-3.

FAMILY ADJUSTMENT

The new routines, or the lack of them, may cause disruption in the household; however, Ballweg has shown that there is little conflict among couples at retirement; the tasks remain segregated, though men take over more of the masculine household duties. About two-thirds of couples share in decision making. Men tend to dominate in economic decisions, and women in family and recreational matters. There is usually little increase in joint participation in activities. Men are the ones who most often make the decision that some expensive luxury no longer fits into the budget, and therefore the role of financial decision maker may afford little satisfaction. In these cases the couple should be encouraged to discuss and share the responsibility for such decisions. It can be especially trying for some men if they retire while their wives are still employed; this depends on the extent to which their feelings of adequacy are determined by their wage-earning capacity.

For some people work has been a refuge from an intolerable home situation,

Figure 20-3 Some retired people are only too happy to be free of the regimentation of the working hours. (*Courtesy of Pat Ryan.*)

and the stress of being in the home for long periods of time compounds the problem of adjustment to retirement itself (Sheldon et al.). Care givers should be alert to signs of increasing tension in the couple relationship and may suggest that the husband and wife need time apart from each other.

CONCERNS OF THE RETIRED

Issues concerning retirees include: money, housing, and health, and the greatest of these is money! A study by Sheldon et al. makes the point that above the subsistence level, income loss is felt when it limits opportunities to engage in formerly valued activities and interests. The absolute amount of loss is not directly proportional to experienced loss.

Kent (1971a; 1971b) recognizes minorities as being particularly vulnerable in retirement. An inadequate salary throughout one's working years militates against any measure of comfortable retirement. Members of minority groups may have had inadequate salaries, an unstable work history, and little opportunity to think about retirement because they are preoccupied with the problems of daily living. Census data revealed that in 1970 only 57 percent of elderly minority-group members spoke English. Can we expect non-English-speaking persons to exercise their rights and make the most of the options available to them? Understanding the systems of health care delivery and social security payments is no small task, even for those who speak English well. Helping personnel should make every effort to find appropriate interpreters; young students are often available to assist with this task.

For the migrant and seasonal farmworker, retirement simply means that the worker is no longer employed or employable in the fields; apparently these workers most frequently retire between the ages of 45 and 50 (Ruhig and Coutts).

EARLY RETIREMENT

Because of the rapid obsolescence of certain job skills, many workers find themselves jobless in the prime years of their lives—the years between 55 and 64, when family responsibilities have lessened and they should be able to enjoy the present and plan for the future (Sheppard, 1976). Their unemployment benefits and separation pay are quickly exhausted. If retraining is not available or if they do not seek it, they join the ranks of the retired.

Ill health is the main factor in early retirement. Medical technology enables us to keep people alive much longer today than in the past, and thus the span of time between the active, productive years and death may be long and painful for those in poor health.

Barfield and Morgan (1978a) found that automobile workers with a plan for a reasonably secure retirement after 30 years of service were increasingly opting for early retirement. Many large corporations with "30 and out" plans find that a startlingly large proportion of those who can afford it retire early. The younger the person, the more likely he or she is to report plans to retire early. Economic and financial matters seem to dominate the decision; duration of mortgage payments and responsibilities for children are influential factors.

Other early retirees are military personnel and city, state, and federal employees, who often are given the opportunity to retire after 20 years of service. Many of these people choose to return to work in different careers. The usual reason given is the desire to supplement their benefits. See Figure 20-4.

SATISFACTION WITH RETIREMENT

A study by the National Institute of Mental Health found that, for both sexes, higher educational level and greater occupational status were related to use of skills, better health, and satisfactory family life after retirement. Such people reported high satisfaction with retirement, with women having somewhat higher morale and being generally more satisfied with life than men. There are few elderly women today who had the opportunity to attend college or work in high-status positions during their working years, and thus there is obviously some skewing of these data. Single retired women outnumbered single retired men 4 to 1 in this study and were well satisfied with their situation. This usually included close contact with siblings and a network of friends, a high interest in social activities, and little interest in domestic life.

Figure 20-4 Some people retire only to begin second careers. This man became a hotel manager. (*Courtesy of Pat Ryan.*)

Barfield and Morgan (1978b) found gender and cohort differences in satisfaction with retirement. *Retirees today experience less postretirement satisfaction than retirees a decade ago.* Married males seem more satisfied with the retirement experience than either single males or females. Factors that contribute significantly to positive feelings about retirement are: (1) having an adequate income, (2) being in reasonably good health, (3) remaining in the same home, and (4) being able to choose to retire early if one wishes. All these factors should be considered by professionals as they assess retirement adjustment.

The studies cited in this chapter point up the need to formulate retirement plans for several groups: (1) those who retire early with sufficient income, (2) those who retire late with adequate income, (3) those who retire unwillingly and with inadequate provisions for the future, and (4) those who would retire if they could afford to do so. Barfield and Morgan (1978b) speculate that raising the compulsory retirement age is not a solution to most of the problems of retired people since few of those who are now retired want to return to work.

A number of recent changes may make life more meaningful for retired persons: (1) The retired are realizing some of the potential of their political power; (2) older people now may take advantage of reduced fees for various educational and cultural programs and certain modes of transportation; and (3) federal programs such as the Foster Grandparent Program, Senior Companions, and the Retired Senior Volunteer Program (RSVP) promote interpersonal interaction and a sense of usefulness—4½ million older people are in the national volunteer force (Harris). The volunteer role that is evolving for the aged is a new experience for many of them (Payne), and it is one in which they can use their accumulation of skills and resources.

Care givers must remember that many people are not interested in productivity during their retirement years and that they have the option of being totally unencumbered at this time if they wish.

This chapter has briefly reviewed some of the issues of retirement. Future generations are more likely to benefit from present studies of retirement than those who are now retired. It seems likely that the young people of today may not "hate the morn's returning light" in their retirement years as we begin to think of sabbaticals for all working people, shorter working hours and more leisure time throughout life, and the opportunity to follow several careers in a lifetime.

SUMMARIZING STATEMENTS BASED ON THE LITERATURE

- Retirement is one of the major transitions in the life-span (Snow and Havighurst).
- Retirees who view retirement as a normal, expected occurrence experience little change in their satisfaction with life (Rowe).
- The feeling that all people should be at the same place at each stage of the life-span may be a real factor contributing to agism and stereotyped thinking about the elderly (Seltzer).

- Some companies have found that workers who continue to work after age 65 are more diligent and dependable than younger workers ("Now, the Revolt of the Old").
- There is a disproportionate death rate among those who are forced to retire; 25 percent of all suicides occur among those over 65 ("Now, the Revolt of the Old").
- Some elderly people, angered because they no longer feel useful, divert this anger to activist causes.
- Women's retirement has received little attention because (1) women were assumed to derive their status from their husbands and (2) a woman's work role was considered a "secondary role." Trends are changing in this area.
- The contributions of the aged are likely to differ from those of young people; we need to capitalize on the differences at both ends of the continuum (Butler).

GUIDELINES FOR INTERVENTION

- Use a knowledge of stress adaptation and of crisis and grief theories to better understand the problems of retirement.
- Wait at least a year following retirement to assess patterns and the adequacy of adjustment.
- Accept and encourage the expression of any feelings during the transitional stage. Encourage reminiscing about the job.
- Recognize that each cohort of aged persons may experience retirement differently.
- Discourage any major changes in the living situation during the first few months after retirement.
- Explore with the retiree skills, knowledge, and latent interests that he or she may wish to develop.
- Make resource materials and information available to the retired person and promote autonomous decisions.
- Assess the family's adaptation to the retiree's return to the home. When a couple's relationship becomes stressed, point out that they still need time apart from each other.

REFERENCES

Atchley, Robert: *The Social Forces in Later Life: An Introduction to Social Gerontology,* Wadsworth, Belmont, Calif., 1972.

Ballweg, J.: "Resolution of Conjugal Role Adjustment after Retirement," *Journal of Marriage and the Family,* **29**(2): 277–281, 1967.

Barfield, **Richard,** and **James Morgan:** "Trends in Planned Early Retirement," *The Gerontologist,* **18**(1):13–18, 1978. (a)

———— and ————: "Trends in Satisfaction with Retirement," *The Gerontologist,* **18**(1):19–23, 1978. (b)

Binstock, Robert H., and **Ethel Shanas** (eds.): *Handbook of Aging and Social Sciences,* Van Nostrand Reinhold, New York, 1976.

Butler, Robert: *Why Survive? Being Old in America,* Harper & Row, New York, 1975.

Glamser, Francis D.: "Determinants of a Positive Attitude toward Retirement," *Journal of Gerontology,* **31**(1):104–107, 1976.

Louis Harris Associates (for the National Council on Aging): *The Myth and Reality of Aging America,* NCA, Washington, D.C., 1975.

Johnson, Gregory, and **J. Lawrence Kamara:** "Growing Up and Growing Old: The Politics of Age Exclusion," *Journal of Aging and Human Development,* **8**(2): 99–110, 1977–1978.

Kent, Donald P.: "The Elderly in Minority Groups: Variant Patterns of Aging," Part II, *The Gerontologist,* **11**(1):26–29, 1971. (a)

————: "The Negro Aged," Part II, *The Gerontologist,* **11**(1):48–51, 1971. (b)

"Now, the Revolt of the Old," *Time,* Oct. 10, 1977, pp. 18–36.

Payne, Barbara P.: "The Older Volunteer: Social Role Continuity and Development," *The Gerontologist,* **17**(4): 355–361, 1977.

Riley, Matilda, and **Anne Foner:** *Aging and Society: An Inventory of Research Findings,* Russell Sage, New York, 1968.

Rowe, A. R.: "Retired Academics and Research Activity," *Journal of Gerontology,* **31**(4):456–461, 1976.

Ruhig, Theodore, and **J. Robert Coutts:** "California Study Explores Farmworker Retirement Patterns," *Generations,* **2**(3):12–13, 1977.

Seltzer, Mildred: "Suggestions for the Examination of Time-disordered Relationships," in Jaber Gubrium (ed.), *Time, Roles, and Self in Old Age,* Human Sciences Press, New York, 1976.

Sheldon, Alan, Peter J. M. McEwan, and **Carol Pierson Ryser:** *Retirement Patterns and Predictions,* DHEW Publication no. (ADM) 74-49, National Institute of Mental Health (Section on Mental Health and Aging), Rockville, Md., April 1975.

Sheppard, H. L.: *New Perspectives on Older Workers,* W. E. Upjohn Institute for Employment Research, Washington, D.C., 1971.

————: "Work and Retirement," in Robert Binstock and Ethel Shanas (eds.), *Handbook of Aging and the Social Sciences,* Van Nostrand Reinhold, New York, 1976.

Snow, Robert B., and **Robert J. Havighurst:** "Life Style Types and Patterns of Retirement of Educators," *The Gerontologist,* **17**(6):545–552, 1977.

Streib, Gordon, and **Clement Schneider:** *Retirement in American Society: Impact and Process,* Cornell, Ithaca, N.Y., 1971.

U.S. Department of Health, Education, and Welfare: *Facts about Older Americans: 1976,* DHEW Publication no. (OHD) 77-20006, 1977.

U.S. House of Representatives, Committee on Aging: *Retirement Age Policies,* parts 1 and 2, Committee Publications nos. 95-88 and 95-89, 95th Cong., 1st Sess., Mar. 16–17, 1977.

White House Conference on Aging, Washington, D.C., Nov. 28–Dec. 2, 1971.

OTHER RESOURCES

ORGANIZATIONS

National Veterans Administration
Washington, D.C., and regional offices

Oregon Center for Gerontology
University of Oregon
Eugene, Oreg. 97403

WHEEE: We Help Elders Establish Employment
A SAGE Advocate Employment Service
53 Wall Street
New Haven, Conn. 06510

Ethel Percy Andrus Gerontology Center
University of Southern California
Los Angeles, Calif. 90007

Retirement Jobs Inc.
Harold Adams
730-C Distel Circle
Los Altos, Calif. 94022

National Senior Citizens Law Center
Bernard Forman
Mandatory Retirement Liaison Representative
Washington Office, National Senior Citizens Law Center
1200 Fifteenth Street, N.W.
Washington, D.C. 20005

FILMS

At My Age: 26 min/color/1966. Attempts to generate interest in the work potential of older people looking for new jobs before and after retirement. Includes tips on how to help older workers adapt old work habits to new work environments. Distributor: National Audio Visual Center, Washington, D.C. 20036.

Challenge of Retirement Years: 30 min/color/1967. A 65-year-old man resents the idea of being forced to retire from his job. At Golden Acres, where he lives with his wife "under protest," an understanding clergyman assures him that "God retires no one" and shows him the many opportunities for service which surround him.

Retired and Home All Day: 4 min/b&w. Designed to stimulate discussion of what happens when a retired man gets in his wife's way when she wants to prepare for a party in their home. One of a series of vignettes on retirement. Distributor: University of Michigan, Audiovisual Educa-

tion Center, 416 Fourth Street, Ann Arbor, Mich. 48104.

Retired and Living with One's Children: 4 min/b&w. One of a series of vignettes on retirement dealing with the situations that arise when an older man goes to live with his children. Distributor: University of Michigan, Audiovisual Education Center, 416 Fourth Street, Ann Arbor, Mich. 48104.

Springtime in Autumn: 28 min/color/1974. A moving look at one of the successful Foster Grandparent programs providing persons over 60 an opportunity to serve productively as they work with the mentally retarded. Bruce Bittle and Joseph Pierre. Distributor: Oregon State University, Film Library, Portland, Oreg. 97207.

Time for Living: 10 min/color/1975. A poetic exploration of the effects of time and change, showing that change can cause anxiety and pain but can also be a challenge. Narrated by Ray Bolger. Distributor: University of Connecticut, Center for Instructional Media and Technology, U-Box 1, Storrs, Conn. 06268.

Use It in Good Health, Charlie: 38 min/ color/1975. Intended to focus public attention on the problems of retirement and old age and to create positive attitudes toward aging. Producer-writer: Irvin Davis. Distributor: American Chiropractic Association, 220 Grand Avenue, Des Moines, Iowa 50312.

(*Photo of Victor Sjöstrom from Ingmar Bergman's film* Wild Strawberries. *Photo courtesy of Aktiebolaget Svensk Filmindustri.*)

Young Old Age through Old Old Age

Old age is a stage in our lives, and like all other stages it has a face of its own, its own atmosphere and temperature, its own joys and miseries.

Hermann Hesse

Introduction
to
Part 3

The third part of this book is about the last half of life. The literature on the last phase of the life cycle is growing so fast that one day it will be as voluminous as that on the child. One has only to scan the journal section of a library to note the many new journals on aging. There is far more available in the current literature about the psychosocial care of the aged than is indicated by the present level of care provided for them.

Indexes in books were scanned (which is not always the best way, since some books have no index at all, others have sloppily executed indexes, and some indexes omit key words in psychosocial care). Cumulative indexes were another source; Medlar, Medline searches and the Aging Research Information System were used. The best system was an efficient helper who steadily located articles, journals, and reference lists.

Professionals and paraprofessionals who have not been particularly interested in the study of the aged are now beginning to consider aging for a number of possible reasons: (1) their own aging interests them, (2) their relatives are aging, (3) the number of aged clients is increasing in their own practice, or (4) they find themselves in a job which requires a knowledge of aging.

This section of the book is based on the premise that old and very old adults do adapt, learn, and grow until the end of their lives. They need not shrivel up or spin disengagement cocoons. The view of the aged person to be emphasized here is: "The individual is a complex system moving forward in time to further differentiation."[1]

[1] James E. Birren, *The Psychology of Aging,* Prentice-Hall, Englewood Cliffs, N.J., 1964, p. 22.

Matson, writing about humanistic theory, said: "Humanistic psychology is not just the study of 'human being'; it is a commitment to 'human becoming.' "[2] The concept of human becoming and the need to decrease dehumanization and depersonalization are basic to the psychosocial care of any person, but especially to that of the elderly today.

The topics I finally selected for this part of the book are a result of an exhaustive (and exhausting) literature search on aging in United States journals and in some from England and Canada. I have taught in Canada, Hawaii, and 33 other states on short-term assignments. Problems vary according to culture, community (rural, urban, or suburban), climate, and transportation, but the psychosocial problems are basically the same; one is impressed with the similarity of problems. Much of the material in this book comes from those short classes and conferences and from both the students and the old people I interviewed.

Neglected areas in psychosocial care are evident not only in the literature but also in the real world of practice, where practitioners, both new ones and the seasoned ones, struggle with problems in psychosocial care. The focus of the chapters in this part was decided upon because of the lacunae currently existing in the literature.

Only 5 to 6 percent of aged persons live in institutions. Although I have tried to direct the content of this part of the book to both the aged in the institution and the aged in the community, there may be more examples concerning the frail aged person because that is the area in which I have had the most experience. It is also an area in which professionals and paraprofessionals will be greatly needed.

Broad concepts with wide applicability were selected. Students sometimes do not believe that a concept is flexible; the transfer of learning may be difficult. The reader is cautioned to consider the broad aspects of the concepts presented, rather than focusing on the specific examples interspersed throughout this part.

Chapter 21 discusses the developmental tasks of old age, documents current publications, and explores the implications of the developmental tasks of aging for the care giver.

I organized Chapter 22 around Randall's[3] categorization of the last five decades of life; I am grateful to her for the categories.

Chapter 23 describes an elite and interesting group—the centenarians. Data continue to increase on these unique individuals. The articles and books focus on those living in Abkhasia, in the U.S.S.R.; Hunza, in Asia (near Afghanistan); and Ecuador, in South America.

Sensory and cognitive functioning are discussed in Chapter 24; both areas need to be well understood by novices entering the field of aging.

[2] Floyd W. Matson, "Humanistic Theory: The Third Revolution in Psychology," *The Humanist,* **30**(2):7–11, 1971, p. 7.

[3] Ollie Randall, "Aging in America Today: New Aspects in Aging," *The Gerontologist,* **17**(1): 6–11, 1977.

Chapter 25 is about self-esteem in aged persons. The negative views of self and the pervasive low self-esteem among the elderly are the bane of "psychosocialists" (my term for one who specializes in psychosocial care). Until old is seen as more beautiful by our society, care givers will constantly need to consider increasing self-esteem among their aged clients.

Loneliness and grief and their implications for intervention are discussed in Chapter 26. Widowhood and widowerhood are not discussed in that chapter because they are covered extensively in Chapter 18.

Chapter 27 focuses on aspects of care giving in late life, including giving care, receiving care, and caring for oneself. There is also a section in this chapter about the importance of pets to old people—another little-studied area in research.

Chapter 28 deals with the three R's in aging: reality testing, relocation, and reminiscing. The latter portion of that chapter is written by Priscilla Ebersole, who pioneered reminiscing groups. Reality testing is also an important, but not fully accepted, aspect of the care of the aged.

Chapter 29 is about three aspects of psychosocial interventions: touch, sexuality, and cultural variables. Touch, or the haptic system, is viewed as a powerful therapeutic technique. Again the literature is scanty. However, there is a growing body of literature on sexuality and aging and on the cultural aspects of aging.

Part 3 ends with the dimensions of termination. While many books end with a chapter on death, this chapter covers more than death and includes good-byes, closure, life reviews, and the terminating process with elderly people.

The thoughts on the following pages were not intended to be ready-to-use ideas that you can put into practice with a guarantee that they will be effective. That would be to ignore your talent and creativity. Perhaps Bertrand Russell has provided the best guidelines for practitioners: "Three passions, simple but overwhelmingly strong, have governed my life: the longing for love, the search for knowledge, and unbearable pity for the suffering of mankind."[4]

---

[4] Bertrand Russell, *The Autobiography of Bertrand Russell, 1872–1914*, Little, Brown, Boston, 1967, p. 3.

Chapter 21

TRANSITION TO LATER LIFE: DEVELOPMENTAL THEORIES AND RESEARCH

Irene Mortenson Burnside

> In youth—activities, in the middle—riddles,
> in old age—prayers.
>
> *Hesiod*

> If a man has already learnt in his youth to rise superior
> to the disapproval of his contemporaries, what can it
> matter to him in his old age when he is certain soon to be
> beyond the reach of all favor or disfavor?
>
> *Sigmund Freud*

This chapter presents a brief overview of the developmental tasks of the later years. Since the amount of literature on aging is increasing at a rapid rate, this chapter will necessarily be selective. The rate at which materials proliferated during the compilation of this book is incredible. The composition of this chapter is nicely described by the following: "It might well be said of me that here I have merely made up a bunch of other men's flowers, and provided nothing of my own but the string to tie them together" (Montaigne, p. 183).

The following are some operational definitions of aging:

John Quincy Adams is well, quite well, thank you. But the house in which he lives at present is becoming quite dilapidated. It is tottering upon its foundations. Time and seasons have nearly destroyed it. Its roof is pretty well worn out. Its walls are much shattered, and it trembles with every wind. The old tenement is becoming almost uninhabitable and I think John Quincy Adams will have to move out of it soon. But he himself is quite well, quite well (John Quincy Adams, source unknown).

It is useful to distinguish three kinds of aging: biological, psychological, and social. . . . (a) Biological aging is how long the individual or species will live. . . . (b) Psychological age refers to the adaptive capacities of individuals as observed from their behavior, but it may also refer to subjective reactions or self-awareness. . . . (c) Social age refers to the social habits and roles of the individual relative to the expectations of his group and society (Birren, 1964, p. 10).

Aging in the gerontologist's sense is a process which leads to increasing instability with time (Comfort, p. 549).

"Old age is a gradual process which begins the first day one begins to live in memories" (Da Silva, p. 20, quoting an 81-year-old client).

The tremendous success of *Passages,* by Sheehy, is but one example of our fascination with the pattern of our lives. This book has been a best seller si. ce it appeared. However, it deals only with the passages occurring between the ages of 18 and 50. Ostrovski covers the work of Sheehy in detail in Part 2 of this book. Hendricks and Hendricks define "rites of passage" as ceremonial tasks which mark the transition from one social status to another. Sheehy mentions that Levinson uses the term "marker event" to refer to a special point at which there is a definite change in one's personal life. A marker event need not take place, however, for there to be a change. Neugarten (1970) states: "A psychology of the life cycle is not a psychology of crisis behavior so much as it is a psychology of timing" (p. 87).

HISTORICAL VIEW

Psychogerontology dates back to 1922, when George Stanley Hall published *Senescence: The Last Half of Life.* Hall considered the period of senescence to begin in the early forties. As one reels and then recovers from that statement, one might consider the date of publication—1922, when the life-span of the average person was considerably shorter than it is now. Hall wrote: "As a psychologist, I am convinced that the psychic states of old people have great significance. Senescence, like adolescence, has its own feelings, thoughts, and wills, as well as its own physiology, and their regimen is important, as well as that of the body" (p. 100). Hall's view has been slow in taking hold. One frequently hears (and gets weary of) statements like, "Old people are just like anyone else—they just have a few more years tacked on" (said by a doctor teaching a class), "Taking care of an old person is no different from taking care of anyone else" (said by a medical-surgical supervisor), "Old people are in their second childhood" (said by relatives of an aged person), and "You have to treat them like children" (said by a nurse's aide). Ignorance and naïveté concerning the aging process persist and are an impediment to humanistic and psychosocial care and caring. I once sat through a keynote conference address given by a pediatrician who made a detailed comparison of old people and children, even to the point of mentioning incontinence. Health professionals are often the purveyors of incorrect information and negative attitudes. I will quote Austin as cited in Gibson (1966), who wrote: "There is nothing so plain boring as the constant repetition of assertions that are not true" (p. xv). The statement is applicable to gerontology.

Interest in psychological development across the life-span dates back to 1957 and a publication by Pressey and Kuhlen. Riegel's (1977) excellent overview chapter on the history of psychological gerontology, Neugarten's (1977) chapter on personality and aging, and a chapter on the sociological theory of change in adulthood and old age by Lowenthal (1977) are highly recommended to the reader. They offer excellent in-depth discussions of theoretical material which are beyond the scope of this book.

The interest in life-span views began several decades ago with the work of Bayley, Bühler and Massarik, Havighurst (1948), Neugarten (1964), and Pressey and Kuhlen. It began as a data collection strategy. Baltes and Schaie point out that the chief objective up until this time had been to show that development occurs throughout life.

DEVELOPMENTAL LIFE THEORISTS

In the 1930s Frenkel-Brunswick, a student of Charlotte Bühler, wrote "Studies in Biographical Psychology," which appears in *Middle Age and Aging* (Neugarten, 1968b). Bühler's (1935) studies were carried out in Austria and therefore are based on a culture quite different from ours. Her results indicated (1) that there is a regular sequence in the events, experiences, and attainments in biographical events, even though this is not matched to biological curves, and (2) that there is a tendency toward specification and definite results. At about age 45, the individual tests the results of what has been accomplished and then begins to look back over his or her life and considers finishing off with life (Bühler, 1935). Later Bühler and Massarik described the critical attitudes toward life, which they believed clustered around (1) need satisfaction (love, family, sex, and self-gratification), (2) self-limiting adaptation (caution, adaptiveness, submissiveness, and avoidance of hardships), (3) creative expansion (self-development, power, and fame), and (4) upholding the internal order (moral values and political or religious commitments). See Tables 21-1 and 21-2 and the elaboration of Bühler's contributions in Chapter 11.

Developmental tasks of later life have been described by Clark and Anderson, Erikson (1963), Havighurst (1948), Lowenthal (1965), Neugarten (1970), and Peck (1955).

The definition of a developmental task used in this part of the book will be that of Havighurst: "[a] task which arises at or about a certain period in the life of the individual, successful achievement of which leads to his happiness and to

Table 21-1. Basic Tendencies and Development of Self

Ages	Need-Satisfaction	Self-Limiting Adaptation	Creative Expansion	Establishing of Inner Order	Fulfillment
Birth to 1½	Trust and love, evolvement and discovery of self-sameness				
1½ to 4		Learning of styles of life. Obedience and super-ego-ideal vs. independence, first absorption of culturally determined ideas			
4 to 8			Autonomous ego-ideals value setting, aspect of task		
8 to 12				Attempts at objective self-evaluation in social roles	
12 to 18	Sex needs and problem of sexual identity			Review and preview of self-development (Autobiography)	Fulfillment of and detachment from childhood
18 to 25 (30)		Tentative self-determination of role in society			
25 (30) to 45 (50)			Self-realization in occupation, marriage, and own family		
45 (50) to 65 (70)				Critical self-assessment	
65 (70) to 80 (85)					Self-fulfillment
80 (85) to death	Regression to predominant need-satisfaction				

Source: Bühler, 1962, p. 109.

success with later tasks, while failure leads to unhappiness in the individual, disapproval by the society, and difficulty with later tasks" (1948, p. 21). "Disapproval by society" seems to stretch the meaning too far, and one may have difficulty with that portion of the definition.

The term "developmental tasks" is widely used both in the United States and in other countries. The following are translations of the term collected by Havighurst (1974, p. vi): *tareas evolutivas* (Spanish), *tarefas de desenvolvimento* (Portuguese), *tâches développementales* (French), *aufgaben zur entwicklung* (German), *ontwikkelings-taken* (Dutch), *patna kit* (Thai), and *bal-tal kwa-up*

Table 21-2.   Basic Tendencies and Development of Self, Including Behavioral Trends

Ages	Need-Satisfaction	Self-Limiting Adaptation	Creative Expansion	Establishing of Inner Order	Fulfillment
Birth to 1½	Trust and love, evolvement and discovery of self-sameness	Coordination and adaptation of movements	Spontaneous activities	Beginning of integration of movements	Well-being
1½ to 4	Pregenital sex, attachment to parents	Learning of styles of life. Obedience and superego-ideal vs. independence, first absorption of culturally determined ideas	Role play and artistic creativity	Superego conscience and first patterning of ideas	
4 to 8	Latency period	Acceptance of membership role in family, learning of culturally determined ideas	Autonomous value setting, ego-ideals aspect of task	Self-appraisal regarding ego ideals and of culturally determined ideas	Accomplishment
8 to 12	Latency period	Acceptance of role and assignment in school and culturally determined education	Games, sport, group mentally explorative activities	Attempts at objective self-evaluation in social roles	
12 to 18	Sex needs and problem of sexual identity	Independence vs. family domination	Personality development, love, intellectual spurt	Review and preview of self-development (Autobiography)	Fulfillment of and detachment from childhood
18 to 25 (30)	Sex needs and problem of sexual identity	Tentative self-determination of role in society	Occupational and love experiments	Search for self	
25 (30) to 45 (50)	Culmination of sex-love union	Acceptance of family and occupational role	Self-realization in occupation, marriage, and own family	Finding own self	Self-realization
45 (50) to 65 (70)	Climacteric and health problems	Self-denial for family; community, welfare obligations	Building up of estates and positions	Critical self-assessment	
65 (70) to 80 (85)	Concern with health	Acceptance of limitations	Finishing off life work	Autobiographical retrospect	Self-fulfillment
80 (85) to death	Regression to predominant need-satisfaction	Acceptance of end of life approaching			

Source: Bühler, 1962, p. 108.

(Korean). Friends from other countries added to this list: *tugas-tugas perkembangan* (Malaysian) (Meah) and *uteiklende oppgaver* (Norwegian) (Ween).

SPECIAL PROBLEMS OF OLDER PEOPLE

The developmental tasks of later life are incredible. Havighurst (1953), a pioneer in the field of gerontology, stated that older people do have special problems and distinguished them from the general problems of adulthood. He listed (1) physical helplessness, (2) poverty or economic insecurity, (3) the feeling of being rejected by the society to which one has belonged all one's life, (4) loss of a husband or wife, and (5) loss of work. Even if old people do avoid these problems, they still must cope with the life changes of normal aging: (1) loss of physical attractiveness, (2) impaired physical health and decreased vigor, (3) loss of status, and (4) other problems, such as making satisfactory living arrangements, establishing new friendships, finding more leisure-time activities, and treating grown children as adults. Havighurst described the latter problem succinctly: "The once-powerful and often dominant parent must now come to terms with his inferiority to his own child" (1953, p. 30). I have observed grandchildren who interact more effectively with a grandparent than the grandparent's own children. I vividly remember shampooing my grandfather's hair and tying his tie for church on Sundays; he preferred that I do it rather than his daughters. Allowing children to assume more care-giving roles with grandparents is an area that should be more fully explored. Perhaps the roles are being reversed these days, with grandchildren caring for grandparents, rather than grandparents baby-sitting for grandchildren! See Chapters 27 and 14 for discussions of grandparenting.

Erikson (1963), a psychoanalyst and theoretician, has described life-span stages. Erikson has been extremely popular—so much so, in fact, that now writers are interpreting his life-span! (The reader is referred to the interpretation of Erikson's works by Coles.) Erikson's (1975) autobiography is entitled *Life History and the Historical Moment*. In one article Erikson tells us that students in his course on the human life cycle renamed it (as students are prone to do) "From Womb to Tomb" and "From Bust to Dust" (1976, p. 4).

Erikson has analyzed Ingmar Bergman's *Wild Strawberries* in an essay on the life cycle. Erikson describes the film as one "which I find admirably illuminated in it and illuminated, for once, in a memoir which begins with the end—that is, it demonstrates how significant movement in old age reaches back through a man's unresolved adulthood to the dim beginnings of his awareness as a child" (1976, p. 1). This film is an excellent portrayal of psychological crises experienced by a 76-year-old doctor. (See photo on p. 376.)

CRITICISMS OF THE ERIKSONIAN MODEL

Riegel's criticism of Erikson's model of the eight stages of development is that it is "idealistic and, generally seen from a middle class perspective" (1977, p. 83). Riegel writes that even though Erikson does maintain a reasonable balance in his statements, there is a failure to explain why the individual grows and moves from one stage to another. Riegel feels that, to provide an explanation, there must be detailed studies of the shifts and the changes "in both the inner-biological and outer-sociological conditions . . ." (1977, p. 83). Feminists have rejected Erikson's view on the "special nature" of women. Women may find de Castillejo's writing helpful, especially her beautiful chapter entitled "The Older Woman."

A common problem with a model in which stages, tasks, or passages are delineated is that students and practitioners may take the model too literally. Student nurses, for instance, seem to want a thermometer in which the mercury runs from "mistrust" to "basic trust." Autonomous functioning is not simply one decision that an elderly person makes alone, although that is a big step, to be sure, for some elderly people. The student practitioner learns that individuals may move back and forth in the tasks—a giant step forward can be followed by three small steps backward. For example, one of the developmental tasks of aging is to accept the loss of a spouse, and the aged person may indeed accomplish this task. However, in a remarriage the person may lose a spouse again. In such cases the task has to be repeated, and the repetition of tasks surely needs to be considered in a developmental approach to helping the aged client. The reader is referred to Chapter 11 for descriptions of the theoretical framework for developmental stages of life.

Students who apply the Eriksonian model will have to realize that, in order to work with the integrity-despair stage, one must fill in many of the missing aspects on that long, long continuum from despair to integrity. Erikson leaves us hanging. Some of us are still waiting for him to pursue that "incompleted" area. As it presently stands, it is difficult to translate into psychosocial care. Riegel (1977) also makes the point that Erikson writes from a middle-class perspective, which may not be useful in working with those on the poverty level or even with the very affluent. Hennessey has related her difficulties in group work with the very affluent.

Gould criticizes both Erikson and Bühler regarding their views of the whole life-span and feels that neither one has supplied the exact kind of information needed:

> Neither bears down on the chronological change in the subjective "sense of the world." By "subject sense of the world" I mean the out-of-focus, interior, gut-level organizing perception of self and non-self, safety, time, size, etc., that make up the background tone of daily living and shape the attitudes and value base from which decisions and action emanate (1972, p. 524).

PECK'S THEORETICAL FRAMEWORK

Erikson's theory of ego development was the basis for Peck's (1955) formulation of psychological developments in the second half of life. See Chapter 13 for a discussion of Peck's developmental theories. Peck stated that the crisis of the eighth stage, ego integrity versus despair, seemed to be intended to represent in a global, nonspecific way all the psychological crises and crisis solutions of the last 40 or 50 years of life. Peck (1968) divided the development into these categories:

Middle Age	Old Age
1. Valuing wisdom vs. valuing physical powers	1. Ego differentiation vs. work-role preoccupation
2. Socializing vs. sexualizing in human relationships	2. Body transcendence vs. body preoccupation
3. Cathectic flexibility vs. cathectic impoverishment	3. Ego transcendence vs. ego preoccupation

Peck's interpretations are well explained in his chapter in Neugarten's book *Middle Age and Aging* (1968b), and the reader is referred to this source. Instructors should warn their students that they will need at least a smattering of Freud to understand Peck's terminology.

GOULD'S WORK

Gould and his coworkers conducted a study of all psychiatric outpatients in group therapy at the University of California at Los Angeles Neuropsychiatric Clinic (1972, 1975). The subjects were divided into seven age groups, and the salient characteristics of each group were noted; see Table 22-1 for a grouping of age samples. Gould studied white middle-class people from 16 to 60, *including women*. Sheehy has pointed out that most of the research was being done by men and that they were studying other men. This was true as this book was being written. Will women soon begin to study women? Hite has made a start with her report on female sexuality.

Gould (1972) divided the subjects into these age groups: 16 to 18, 18 to 22, 22 to 28, 29 to 34, 35 to 43, 43 to 50, and 50 to 60 or over. The "lumping" of everyone 50 and over is a common sampling technique in gerontology. See Table 21-3, which also demonstrates this trend; the literature continues to indicate similar categorizing of subjects. There usually is not a breakdown for the very old, as

Table 21-3. Profile of a Sample

Age	(Percent)
15–20	19
21–25	28
26–30	22
31–35	12
36–45	12
46–95	7

Source: Shaver and Freedman, p. 28. Reprinted with permission.

I point out in Chapter 29 in regard to Hite's chapter on older women. This is readily understood from the standpoint of attempting to get information from a 95-year-old partially blind, partially deaf, partially forgetful, partially immobilized old person. It is, in short, a feat few researchers wish to attempt. Having tried it, I am aware of the discouraging problems of communication under such adverse conditions. Because interviewing can be so difficult, the reader is referred to an excellent article on interviewing the very old (Schmidt) and to another one written much earlier by Havighurst (1950) on the problems of sampling and interviewing old people.

An important point brought up by Gould (1975) is that of "thoughtful confrontation." This is a stance to encourage especially in those old persons who feel they should have done things more perfectly in their lives. "The belief that is felt—I should have done the impossible—is often not raised to a high enough level of consciousness to be thought about. The incomplete and inexact form of the thought is usually substituted, 'somehow I should have been able to do it better' and is left dangling, unexamined, and therefore unmodified" (Gould, 1975, p. 78). One goal in working with aged persons is to help them modify such expectations.

Gould's statement is very similar to one made by Bühler: "People the world over and at all times of history have seen fulfillment of life not primarily, or certainly not exclusively, in having become what they *wanted* to be or what potentially they were able to be; but nearly always also in terms of what they thought they *should* have become" (1959, p. 578).

"NORMATIVE LIFE CRISES"

Datan and Ginsberg edited a book on "normative life crises." The book presents a variety of views, and I am not sure exactly what constitutes normative life crises. The title is paradoxical, which perhaps the authors intended. "Normative" and "crises" do not seem to fit together too well, unless one feels that life is made up of nothing but crises and that some are more normal than others.

Levitt and Hoyer have noted that therapeutic changes can be effected at any point along the life-span, and they state: "The approach is congruent with the growing awareness among clinicians and other practitioners that current external forces impinging on the individual may be at least as important in affecting behavior as early experience and biological maturation" (p. 610). One way to test that statement is in group work.

Riegel (1975) feels that it is the alternating of crisis and stable times which facilitates development; however, crises are resolved differently by different persons. The reader is referred to Table 12-2 for balancing events in life.

THE NEW LSD: LIFE-SPAN DEVELOPMENT

Rosenfeld, in an article entitled "The New LSD: Life-Span Development," states: "An exciting innovative scientific discipline has been evolving" (p. 32). LSD implies a multidisciplinary effort because one's life-span has many facets and is complex. The phases of old age are neither as discrete nor as well studied as those of other periods. Aldrich, of the University of Colorado Medical Center, made a diagram that describes the life-span approach. It has been aptly named by Buckminster Fuller "the watermelon model," a delightful term that is easy to picture mentally and to remember. One is grateful for persons who can name models with such vivid precision. See Figure 21-1.

Note in Figure 21-1 that after retirement (which can occur anywhere after age 55) there are no further delineations of transitions, which implies to the viewer that growth, transitions, and passages stop with retirement. It is difficult to believe that after all the passages listed as occurring through age 50 or 60, there could suddenly be no more of them.

Proponents of LSD have met regularly at Aspen, Colorado. The program, which has the title "Major Transitions in the Human Life Cycle," is under the aegis of the Academy for Educational Development (AED), and the Schweppe Research and Educational Fund has supported the conferences. The AED, as of this writing, intends to issue a report of the week's conferences.

CATEGORIES OF LIFE-SPAN RESEARCH

Baltes and Schaie have organized the paradigms of life-span developmental research into three categories:

1. How much is the developmental phenomenon being studied (social processes, personality, intelligence, described more comprehensively) related to the earlier life-span?
2. How much is the developmental phenomenon determined by relating to concurrent versus past antecedents (i.e., cumulative and time-lag variable relationships)?
3. How much is the developmental phenomenon changed if intervention considers the effects of the interaction, which involves the developmental history of the person?

The reader is referred to the works of two outstanding researchers in the field of aging, Birren and Schaie. In "Principles of Research on Aging," Birren (1959) states that the study of aging may be approached in three ways: (1) as a basic field of inquiry all by itself, (2) as an experiment testing hypotheses within conceptual frameworks of a variety of disciplines, and (3) as an applied field in which to study the needs of older persons and ways of meeting these needs. The latter approach is becoming increasingly necessary as practitioners seek solutions to ever-growing problems in an ever-growing population. Nurses Stetler and Marram wrote that there is more to evaluating a study's design than considering its usefulness; other determinants include feasibility, fit, and congruence with the theoretical basis for practice. But Gans, a social scientist, describes a similar problem: "The high level of generality at which much of academic social science operates . . . breed[s] conceptual abstractedness which results in concepts which cannot be applied to the real-life situations in which the policy designer works" (p. 22).

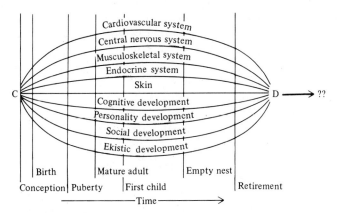

Figure 21-1 The watermelon theory: a concept of human life-span development. "In Dr. Aldrich's 'watermelon model,' the *C* at left means *conception*, the *D* at right is for *death*, with question marks as to what lies beyond. The top half of the watermelon represents biological factors and the lower half represents psycho-social factors in the individual's life. (The word *ekistic*—coined by the late Constantinos Doxiadis—refers to the study of human settlements, here symbolizing the environmental context.) Milestones along the way (bottom) indicate possible critical points in the life-span ('empty nest,' for example, refers to that time of life when the children grow up and leave home)." (*From Rosenfeld, p. 33. Copyright © 1977 Academy for Educational Development, Inc. Reprinted with permission of Robert Aldrich, M.D. and Academy for Educational Development, Inc.*)

Schaie has refined methodologies regarding research on aging; the reader is referred to his writings and also to Chapter 24, which describes his stance as a scientist and the change in his own view of the cognitive processes of aging. Readers may wish to become introspective and consider their own views on the aging process.

COMMENTS ON THE RESEARCH

The issues of the human element in survey research with a community population were discussed by Dean, Teresi, and Wilder. These researchers discussed practical human problems in a survey of a stratified random sample of people 65 years of age and over. The issues include (1) getting the interview, (2) interviewers, (3) logistics, (4) ethical consideration regarding techniques for obtaining interviews, (5) the interview team, and (6) the principal investigator as interviewer. They point out that the human element is present in any survey research project and is important to data collection. The researchers offer suggestions pertaining to the elderly. They found that while most of their subjects were eager to converse, 40 percent required some convincing. The article is recommended for the researcher and for those writing grants which involve a survey approach.

The reader may also wish to consider to what extent he or she is doing research using any of the three approaches listed by Birren (1959) (see the preceding section). Or the reader may consider applying present research knowledge to practice. Part 3 of this book is aimed primarily at considering current research findings and discerning how they are applicable to the psychosocial care of the present cohorts of elderly persons.

Levinson, a professor of psychology in the department of psychiatry at Yale University School of Medicine, has described the mid-life crisis. He interviewed a group of 40 men, in their late thirties and early forties, over a period of several years. The commonality found among these subjects was an identifiable and predictable mid-life crisis. See Part 2 of this book for discussions of crises during the middle years. Levinson (cited in Wolfe) calls the early adulthood years the period of "getting into the adult world," or GIAW; this part of the book might be said to be concerned with "getting into old age," or GIOA. Wolfe quotes Levinson as saying, "We act as if we believe that if you know the really important things that happened in a man's childhood, the rest of his life will be more or less predictable, which of course it isn't" (p. 91).

A mental exercise I have often done personally is to study an old person and try to picture the child that the person was. When I was a child and looked at old photograph albums, I could see a wisp of character in a child's face in a photograph that I could not see in the adult relative whom the child had become. Perhaps the child in me related to the child in the photograph better than to the adult I knew.

COHORTS

Griffith has described age differences well: "It is easy to confuse the shared effect of belonging to a cohort, which is often only a subconscious awareness, with a quite different matter, the active war between the ages. Age rivalry is conspicuous chiefly among the ambitious; it lives in the eagerness of the impatient young, and in the reluctance of the old to surrender place" (p. 22).

I have seen fierce competition among elderly persons in nursing homes as they tried to win a tiny prize at a bingo game or come in first in a wheelchair race! I recall one old man who constantly cheated when I played checkers or card games with him. He did it very cleverly and responded with a cavalier laugh when I tried to call him on it. He was determined to beat me. Little has been written about the value of this fierce competition among the aged, whether it is seen on the shuffleboard court or in the bingo room. Competitiveness has always been necessary for elderly persons' survival, especially those who have competed with nature, germs, and disease. It is certainly easier (and more exhilarating) for care givers to work with competitiveness than with the widespread apathy and boredom still seen in institutions.

IMPORTANCE OF "DECORATING DAYDREAMS"

Wheeler has discussed age-centered styles taking over youth-centered styles:

The modes people employ to cope with their life span tend to remain constant throughout life. Not only the songs but also the functions of their youth return to decorate the daydreams of their old age. The elderly who today feel unwanted and useless because they are unemployable do so largely because during their upbringing they were taught that the purpose of life was to work for a society (p. 43).

How can we help the elderly decorate their daydreams? The shared past is a good example of utmost importance:

Each generation, each cohort even, carries around a different set of intellectual scars, the wounds of its particular history. At some stage in one's formative life—a period, say between the ages of fifteen and the mid-thirties—some major event (The Korean War, Kennedy's assassination) occurs which influences all later attitudes. That same experience, of course, affects in some way everyone alive at the moment, but it strikes with particular force those of an impressionable age (Griffith, p. 22).

Table 21-4 lists important historical events and is an easy reference to use when working with cohort groups. *The importance of knowing the historic era in which the elderly person grew up cannot be underestimated by those studying aging.* Students constantly have difficulty finding meaningful ballads and hymns to use with old people. I recall the stony faces of one group as a young guitarist tried to play "The Old Rugged Cross" with a rock beat.

Care givers who provide direct services to the aged will be using life reviews, oral histories, and/or reminiscing, and information on these strategies is especially important for them. See Chapter 28 for a discussion of reminiscing as an important psychosocial intervention.

Other events that mark an important stage in one's formative years are the vagaries of nature—fires, floods, blizzards, and so on: "It was the year the cyclone wiped us out," for example. Recently I visited my hometown and met a man in his seventies. I did not remember him until he said, "I'm the guy who had Sandy Paul and that busload of kids at my house during the 1941 blizzard." How quickly I placed him then! My friends had told me about sleeping four in a bed and living on pancakes when the rest of the food supplies ran out.

Griffith wrote that an event such as Pearl Harbor:

... extends its effect across a series of cohorts, spreading perhaps across a decade. Some of these events were unexpected blows which had to be overcome (providing an optimistic lesson from history); others began as causes that inspired youthful idealism before leading to disillusionment. Either way, the experience is powerful and remains a defining characteristic. Even when one's first intense response is modified in time, or repudiated, it remains a key reference point—the platitude we are likely to reach for in deciding something else. And not always a sound guide (p. 22).

A student has described an unexpected blow, which was modified in subsequent years, experienced by a 65-year-old widow:

Courage in a time of stress was another way in which H. revealed her high self-

Table 21-4. Time Line of Significant Events

Dates	Events
1890–1900	Spanish-American War (1898)
1900–1910	Voice broadcast by radio (1900)
	Wireless telegraph introduced (1901)
	Automobile introduced (1903)
	First airplane flight—Orville Wright (1903)
	Silent movies introduced (1903)
	San Francisco earthquake (1906)
	Electric washer and vacuum cleaner on the market (1907)
1910–1920	Sinking of the Titanic (1912)
	Income tax begun (1913)
	First ship to pass through the Panama Canal (1914)
	World War I (1914–1918)
	Panama-Pacific International Exposition (1915)
	Influenza epidemic (1918)
1920–1930	Prohibition years (1920–1932)
	First public broadcasting station (1920)
	Women's voting rights (1920)
	First sound motion pictures (1923)
	First woman governor in Ohio—Ross (1924)
	Amundsen and Byrd fly over the North Pole (1926)
	Lindbergh's solo flight over the Atlantic (1927)
	Fleming discovers penicillin (1928)
	Depression years (1929–1936)
	Byrd flies over the South Pole (1929)
1930–1940	Flapper era (1930s)
	Amelia Earhart makes transoceanic solo flight (1932)
	Hitler's rise to power (1934)
	Social security begun (1935)
	Will Rogers killed (1935)
	Abdication of Britain's King Edward VIII (1936)
	Hindenburg crashes at Lakehurst, N.J. (1937)
	Du Pont introduces nylon products (1937)
	New York World's Fair (1939 and 1940)
	Golden Gate International Exposition—San Francisco (1939)
	World War II begins with German invasion of Poland (1939)
1940–1950	Churchill becomes Prime Minister of Britain (1940)
	Pearl Harbor attacked by Japan (1941)
	Cocoanut Grove fire—Boston (1942)
	Alaska Highway opens (1942)
	First electronic computer introduced (1942)
	First atomic bomb dropped on Hiroshima (1945)
	World War II ends with Germany's surrender (1945)
	Japan surrenders (1945)

Table 21-4.   Time Line of Significant Events (*Continued*)

Dates	Events
	Television popularized (1946)
	First General Assembly of United Nations (1946)
1950–1960	Korean war (1950–1953)
	Transcontinental television introduced (1951)
	Jet air travel begins (1952)
	Salk's polio vaccine made available (1953)
	AFL-CIO unions merge (1955)
	First satellite Sputnik in space—U.S.S.R. (1957)
	First satellite Explorer in space—U.S. (1958)
	Domestic jet passenger service begun (1958)
1960–1970	Bay of Pigs incident (1961)
	First U.S. manned suborbital space flight (1961)
	First man orbits in space (1962)
	President John F. Kennedy assassinated (1963)
	Vietnam war involvement (1965–1973)
	Antiwar demonstrations in U.S. (1967–1971)
	First human heart transplant (1967)
	U.S.S. Pueblo seized by North Koreans (1968)
	Martin Luther King assassinated (1968)
	Senator Robert Kennedy assassinated (1968)
	First man walks on moon (1969)
1970–1977	Amtrak, new passenger train service in U.S., put in operation (1971)
	Voting age lowered to 18 years (1971)
	Nixon is first U.S. President to visit U.S.S.R. and China (1972)
	Life magazine ends publication (1972)
	End of U.S. military draft (1973)
	Watergate crisis (1973)
	Alaska pipeline constructed (1973)
	Arab oil embargo, resulting in "energy crunch" (1973–1974)
	Impeachment proceedings against President Nixon (1974)
	President Nixon resigns (1974)
	Patricia Hearst kidnaped (1975)
	Viking I lands on Mars and transmits black-and-white photographs (1976)
	Worst double air crash in world history at Teneriffe Airport, Canary Islands (1977)
	Extreme weather changes in U.S. (1977):
	First snowfall in history of Florida
	Drought on West Coast
	Severe winter in the East
	Water rationing in northern California

Sources: Boyack; Delury.

esteem. She and her husband, a Navy pilot, were in Hawaii during the Pearl Harbor attack. They watched the bombs fall from the Japanese planes. When her husband was called to the base for emergency duty, she armed herself with a carving knife, blacked out the windows, and prepared to wait out the siege alone. There was a knock at the door. She carefully verified the identity of the caller in three different ways before she opened the door for two sailors, who were on blackout duty (Zale).

FAMILY CONSTELLATIONS IN OLD AGE

Troll has written a critical review of the book *Family Development* from the standpoint of a gerontologist. She finds that there is a too literal application of the developmental-task scheme in that book, a danger that is discussed earlier in this chapter. Troll also points out the impossibility of conceptualizing family developments as a whole, apart from the individual family member. The reader is also referred to the chapter entitled "Family Life and Living Arrangements" in Hendricks and Hendricks' book.

The nuclear family consists of a mother, a father, and their children. However, this is not the typical family that a care giver will work with in the field of aging; this family constellation, in fact, may be almost atypical among aged clientele. Care givers should be familiar with a variety of unusual family constellations. For example, Ebersole, in discussing crisis intervention with elderly families, described these geriatric family configurations: (1) intergenerational families, (2) sibling arrangements, (3) spouses grown old together, (4) late alliances, and (5) living alone. See Chapter 4 for a discussion of young families and Chapter 27 for a further discussion of the aged and families.

In my own nursing experience, I have worked with these "families": (1) a woman in her eighties who lived with three sisters and a brother, (2) two sisters living together, (3) a 65-year-old man who lived with an older aunt, (4) two lifelong women friends who had resided together most of their adult lives, (5) three sisters and two brothers who lived together, and (6) innumerable elderly people who lived alone with a pet whom they proudly introduced as their "family," often poignantly adding, "He's all I've got."

OLD "CHILDREN"

We tend to forget the "children" who are 60 or 70 or 80 years of age. The word "children" still tends to be equated with the young. Some stories come to mind: A woman of 109-plus showed an interviewer through her orchard. He commented on the apples, and she said she would run out and pick some for him. When he said he did not want her to do that, she said, "All right, I'll send the boy." The "boy" who returned with the apples happened to be her nephew, aged 89! Once a 70-year-old man in a state hospital said he would be going home to see his mother over the weekend, which the staff members found hard to believe. Shortly afterward, a demure little woman (who had driven to the hospital alone) appeared at the nurses' station and said, "Is my son ready to go home?" I recall my surprise the first time I helped a 92-year-old woman with her colostomy dressing. She said she hated to come to the hospital, but her 70-year-old daughter had had a stroke and was also hospitalized.

PERSONALITY DIMENSIONS

Neugarten (1977, p. 635) has listed 12 areas of interest in studies of age-related changes in personality. Because of limitations of space, only three dimensions—egocentrism, loss of control, and loss of decision-making power—will be discussed in this chapter; these are the three dimensions that care givers most frequently encounter. Neugarten's list also includes introversion, dogmatism, rigidity, conformity, ego strength, need achievement, creativity, hope, and self-concept or self-image. Self-concept is discussed in Chapter 25.

Egocentricity

It is interesting to note that sometimes egocentricity is viewed as deviance because it would be considered deviant among the middle-aged, even though it is tolerated in the elderly: "At her age, she can get away with it."

Flavell reported that egocentricity decreases from infancy through early or middle adulthood. Other researchers have noted that egocentricity increases with advanced age (Comalli, Wapner, and Werner; Looft and Charles; Rubin et al.). Looft has combined existing theory and data regarding the concept of egocentricity and has organized the literature and interpreted it within a life-span framework.

Egocentricity is one trait that usually aggravates care givers, and they often find it exasperating. *Egocentricity should not be confused with eccentricity.* The latter is often a catchall term used in connection with old persons and has a negative connotation, although the eccentrics make the work with the aged more interesting and challenging. Egocentricity is generally considered an inability to take on the perspective of others; the person becomes wrapped up in his or her own problems and needs. Looft has suggested redefining rigidity in terms of egocentricity.

Since egocentricity is such a pervasive and frustrating and/or irritating problem for care givers, it deserves special study; unfortunately, intervention techniques are not widely discussed in the literature. Somehow, care givers have to be helped to deal with this dimension of the aging personality when they find it in a client. How can they become more comfortable in handling it? What are the dynamics of egocentricity? Looft points out how complex such behaviors are, and he offers thoughtful, provocative suggestions for intervention.

One virtue associated with mid-life is experience (Sheehy); however, one can argue that it is also a beautiful virtue of old age and is refined and re-refined with age. The constant refinement of prior experiences is an ongoing process which some aged people describe more eloquently than others. The exercise is one of the more reassuring aspects of the mid-life period (Neugarten, 1968a). However, the soundness of one's judgment in old age is quickly challenged by younger persons. Lack of judgment, or a different judgment in an older person, raises red warning flags to relatives, who fear that the elderly person may foolishly mismanage finances, relationships, and life in general. Nathanson, taking a rare, refreshing, and positive stance, said to a class he taught: "Old people ought to have the right to mismanage their lives too!"

Loss of Control

Loss of control can occur in many areas of the elderly person's life, ranging from brain functioning to bowel functioning. One old person prayed that the "three B's" would continue to function: brain, bowels, and bladder.

With loss of control, there may be a loss of decision-making power. However, care givers must remember that older persons can lose their perspective and exaggerate the loss of control, thinking that they have no power in areas of their lives over which they actually still do exercise control (Miller). It may be necessary to remind them of the control they still do maintain over their lives. Weinberg states that when we take over functions for the aged, we rob them of mastery and control. They respond with rage or accusation and hang on to any bit of control they can. He points out that they may cling to what seem to be meaningless objects.

Loss of control over their tiny world is a common problem for aged institutionalized persons. "Problem patients" are often a result of problem staff members. Observations of staff-patient interaction, staff-staff interaction, patient-patient interaction, and staff-family interaction usually provide interesting clues and information in regard to the "obnoxious" behavior.

CASE STUDY I

Miss T., a woman in her nineties, had been single all her life. She had made a living as a domestic, earning $3 per week during the Depression. She was hospitalized on a 20-bed ward in a city and county hospital. Her corner bed would have afforded her a slight bit of privacy, had it not been under the glass window of the nurses' station and the constant scrutiny of the staff.

Every week the staff cleaned the ward and threw out Miss T.'s old newspapers or the refuse (the staff always determined what was refuse) at her bedside. The old woman went into a rage after every cleaning. The normally quiet, rational lady suddenly became irrational. She would leap out of bed with amazing speed and alacrity, rush over to the window, fling it open, and throw everything out the window that was on her bedside stand, and sometimes her pillow sheets and bedding as well. It was raining heavily the day I observed this behavior. Two aides stood at the window arguing about who would brave the downpour to retrieve the water pitcher, the hairbrush, the pillow, and the bedding. They "had to humor her" because of her age, and this was a weekly occurrence with her. One wonders who humored whom. Perhaps this behavior occurred weekly because the head nurse had a fetish about clean bedside stands.

Miss T. loved her newspapers, which she saved and placed on a chair by her bed during the week. She did not mind when I removed them so that I could sit down and talk. When a staff member threw them in the trash, she went into a mild tantrum. She told me that sometimes she was not finished with the newspapers when they were thrown out; often she wanted to save clippings from them. (I just mentioned Weinberg's observation that old people may save seemingly meaningless objects.) It is hard to realize how meaningful something as simple as a newspaper could be to an old woman with minimal education who prided herself on her ability to read and to see the print at her age without glasses. She summarized the event: "If they're going to throw out what's of value to me, why not throw out everything?" See Figure 21-2.

CASE STUDY II

A woman in her nineties was being maintained in her own home with tremendous support systems from her family. As she needed help with the medication regime, meals, and reality testing, she became increasingly annoyed. She perceived loss of control in most areas of her life. It was necessary to explain to her that she still maintained her own home (albeit with help), that she had financial control, and that she still continued to live with much freedom and in her usual style (Miller).

Figure 21-2 Cartoon of a 90-year-old woman. (*Courtesy of Rip Matteson.*)

LOSS OF DECISION-MAKING POWER

The loss of decision-making power may be a direct result of a transfer—a move to a hospital, a residence, a nursing home, or a board-and-care home. The loss of decision-making power seems to be more difficult for the independent old person than for one who has been consistently passive and dependent throughout life. The results of relocation, or "translocation shock," are discussed in Chapter 28. Loss of decision-making power and loss of control seem closely related.

Even small decisions may be taken away from old persons, especially those who are institutionalized. I recall the depression of a former banker whose son no longer permitted him to write checks at all because he had made several errors. His self-esteem hit a real low when he realized that he, a one-time banker, was not allowed to handle any of his own money.

PREPARATION FOR THE NEXT CHAPTER

While this chapter has been rather global in its approach, Chapter 22 looks very specifically at developmental theory. Randall's delineation of the decades has seldom been used in sampling procedures; however, it does seem to have caught on recently. The more common delineation is the one described by Neugarten (1975): the "young old" (55 to 75) and the "old old" (75 and above). "The young-old begin at about age 55, because in recent years more and more men and women are choosing to retire at age 55 to 60, rather than after age 65" (Neugarten, 1975, p. 5). Randall's classifications are the "very young old" (50 to 60), the "young old" (61 to 70), the "middle-aged old" (71 to 80), the "old old" (81 to 90), and the "very old old" (90 to 100) (p. 8). Since those classifications are neat and tidy, they will be used for the organization of the next chapter.

This cursory overview was intended to set the stage for the following two chapters, which deal with very specific stages in old age. It is well to remember Sheehy's words: "The courage to take new steps allows us to let go of each stage with its satisfactions and to find the fresh responses that will release the richness of the next. The power to animate all of life's seasons is a power that resides in us" (p. 514).

REFERENCES

Baltes, Paul B., and **K. Warner Schaie:** *Life-Span Developmental Psychology: Personality and Socialization,* Academic, New York, 1973.

Bayley, Nancy: "The Life Span as a Frame of Reference in Psychological Research," *Vita Humana,* **6**:125–139, 1963.

Birren, James E.: "Principles of Research on Aging," in James E. Birren (ed.), *Handbook of Aging and the Individual,* University of Chicago Press, Chicago, 1959.

———: *The Psychology of Aging,* Prentice-Hall, Englewood Cliffs, N.J., 1964.

Boyack, Virginia: "Living through History," unpublished paper, 1977.

Bühler, Charlotte: "The Curve of Life as Studied in Biographies," *Journal of Applied Psychology,* **19**:405–409, 1935.

————: "Theoretical Observations about Life's Basic Tendencies," *American Journal of Psychotherapy,* **13**(3): 561–581, 1959.

————: *Values in Psychotherapy,* Free Press, New York, 1962.

———— and **Fred Massarik (eds.):** *The Course of Human Life,* Springer, New York, 1968.

Clark, Margaret, and **Barbara Anderson:** *Culture and Aging: An Anthropological Study of Older Americans,* Charles C Thomas, Springfield, Ill., 1967.

Coles, Robert: *Erik H. Erikson: The Growth of His Work,* Little, Brown, Boston, 1970.

Comalli, P. E., Jr., S. Wapner, and **H. Werner:** "Perception of Verticality in Middle and Old Age," *Journal of Psychology,* **47**:259–266, 1959.

Comfort, Alexander: "Longer Life by 1990?" *New Scientist,* **44**:549–551, 1969.

Da Silva, Guy: "The Loneliness and Death of an Old Man: Three Years' Psychotherapy of an Eighty-One-Year-Old Depressed Patient," *Journal of Geriatric Psychiatry,* **1**(1):5–27, 1967.

Datan, Nancy, and **Leon H. Ginsberg:** *Life-Span Developmental Psychology: Normative Life Crises,* Academic, New York, 1975.

De Castillejo, Irene M.: *Knowing Woman,* Putnam, New York, 1973.

Dean, Laura Lee, Jeanne A. Teresi, and **David E. Wilder:** "The Human Element in Survey Research," *International Journal of Aging and Human Development,* **8**(1):83–92, 1977–1978.

Delury, George E.: *The World Almanac &* *Book of Facts 1977,* Newspaper Enterprise Association, New York, 1976.

Ebersole, Priscilla: "Geriatric Crisis Intervention in the Family Context," in Joanne E. Hall and Barbara Weaver (eds.), *Nursing of Families in Crisis,* Lippincott, Philadelphia, 1974.

Erikson, Erik: *Childhood and Society,* Norton, New York, 1963.

————: *Life History and the Historical Moment,* Norton, New York, 1975.

————: "Reflections on Dr. Borg's Life Cycle," *Daedalus,* **105**(2):1–28, 1976.

Flavell, J. H.: *The Developmental Psychology of Jean Piaget,* Van Nostrand Reinhold, New York, 1963.

Frenkel-Brunswik, Else: "Adjustment and Reorientation in the Course of the Life Span," in Bernice L. Neugarten (ed.), *Middle Age and Aging,* University of Chicago Press, Chicago, 1968, pp. 77–84.

Gans, H. J.: "Social Science for Social Policy," in I. L. Horowitz (ed.), *The Use and Abuse of Social Science,* Transaction, New Brunswick, N.J., 1971, p. 22.

Gibson, James J.: *The Senses Considered as Perceptual Systems,* Houghton Mifflin, Boston, 1966.

Gould, Roger L.: "The Phases of Adult Life: A Study in Developmental Psychology," *American Journal of Psychiatry,* **129**(5):521–531, 1972.

————: "Adult Life Stages: Growth toward Self-Tolerance," *Psychology Today,* **8**(9):74–78, 1975.

Griffith, Thomas: "Acting Your Age," *The Atlantic Monthly,* March 1977, pp. 20–23.

Hall, G. S.: *Senescence: The Last Half of Life,* Appleton, New York, 1922.

Havighurst, Robert J.: *Developmental Tasks and Education,* McKay, New York, 1948.

————: "Problems of Sampling and Interviewing in Studies of Old People," *Journal of Gerontology,* **5**(2):158–167, 1950.

—— and **R. Albrecht:** *Older People,* Longmans, New York, 1953.

Hendricks, Jon, and **C. Davis Hendricks:** *Aging in Mass Society,* Winthrop, Cambridge, Mass., 1977.

Hennessey, Mary Jane: "Group Work with Economically Independent Aged," in Irene M. Burnside (ed.), *Nursing and the Aged,* McGraw-Hill, New York, 1976.

Hite, Shere: *The Hite Report: A Nationwide Study of Female Sexuality,* Dell, New York, 1976.

Levinson, Daniel J.: *The Seasons of a Man's Life,* Knopf, New York, 1978.

Levitt, Mary, and **William J. Hoyer:** Book review of Nancy Datan and Leon Ginsberg (eds.), *Life-Span Developmental Psychology: Normative Life Crises, Journal of Gerontology,* **32**(5):610, 1977.

Looft, William R.: "Egocentrism and Social Interaction across the Life Span," *Psychological Bulletin,* **87**(2):73–92, 1972.

—— and **D. C. Charles:** "Egocentrism and Social Interaction in Young and Old Adults," *Aging and Human Development,* **2**:21–28, 1971.

Lowenthal, Marjorie F.: "Antecedents of Isolation and Mental Illness in Old Age," *Archives of General Psychiatry,* **12**(3): 245–254, 1965.

——: "Toward a Sociological Theory of Change in Adulthood and Old Age," in James E. Birren and K. Warner Schaie (eds.), *Handbook of the Psychology of Aging,* Van Nostrand Reinhold, New York, 1977.

Meah, Mohammed: Personal communication, 1978.

Miller, Diane: Personal communication, 1978.

Montaigne, Michel de: *The Quotation Dictionary,* comp. by Robin Hyman, Macmillan, New York, 1962.

Nathanson, Paul: "Management and Social Policy X 410," lecture, University of California, Berkeley, August 1977.

Neugarten, Bernice L.: *Personality in Middle and Later Life,* Atherton, New York, 1964.

——: "Adult Personality: Toward a Psychology of the Life Cycle," in Bernice L. Neugarten (ed.), *Middle Age and Aging,* University of Chicago Press, Chicago, 1968, pp. 137–147. (a)

—— (ed.): *Middle Age and Aging,* University of Chicago Press, Chicago, 1968. (b)

——: "Adaptation and the Life Cycle," *Journal of Geriatric Psychiatry,* **4**(1): 71–87, 1970.

——: "The Future and the Young-Old," part II, *The Gerontologist,* **15**(1):4–9, 1975.

——: "Personality and Aging," in James Birren and K. Warner Schaie (eds.), *Handbook of the Psychology of Aging,* Van Nostrand Reinhold, New York, 1977.

Peck, Robert C.: "Psychological Developments in the Second Half of Life," in J. Anderson (ed.), *Physiological Aspects of Aging,* American Psychological Association, Washington, D.C., 1955.

——: "Psychological Developments in the Second Half of Life," in Bernice L. Neugarten (ed.), *Middle Age and Aging,* University of Chicago Press, Chicago, 1968.

Pressey, Sidney L., and **Raymond G. Kuhlen:** *Psychological Development through the Life Span,* Harper & Row, New York, 1957.

Randall, Ollie A.: "Aging in America Today: New Aspects in Aging," *The Gerontologist,* **17**(1):6–11, 1977.

Riegel, Klaus F.: "Adult Life Crises: A Dialectic Interpretation of Development," in Nancy Datan and Leon H.

Ginsberg (eds.), *Life-Span Developmental Psychology: Normative Life Crises,* Academic, New York, 1975.

————: "History of Psychological Gerontology," in James E. Birren and K. Warner Schaie (eds.), *Handbook of the Psychology of Aging,* Van Nostrand Reinhold, New York, 1977.

Rosenfeld, Albert: "The New LSD: Life-Span Development," *Saturday Review,* Oct. 1, 1977, pp. 32–33.

Rubin, K. H., P. W. Attewell, M. C. Tierney, and P. Tumolo: "Development of Spatial Egocentrism and Conservation Across the Life Span," *Developmental Psychology,* 9(3):432, 1973.

Schaie, K. Warner: "Toward a Stage Theory of Adult Cognitive Development," *Journal of Aging and Human Development,* 8(2):129–138, 1977–1978.

Schmidt, Mary Gwynne: "Interviewing the 'Old Old,' " *The Gerontologist,* 15(6):544–547, 1975.

Shaver, Phillip, and Jonathan Freedman: "Your Pursuit of Happiness," *Psychology Today,* 19(3):26+, 1976.

Sheehy, Gail: *Passages: Predictable Crises of Adult Life,* Bantam, New York, 1976.

Stetler, Cheryl, and Gwen Marram: "Evaluating Research Findings for Applicability in Practice," *Nursing Outlook,* 24(9):559–563, 1976.

Troll, Lillian E.: "The Onus of 'Developmental Tasks' and Other Reactions to Duvall's *Family Development* in Its Fourth Edition," *International Journal of Aging and Human Development,* 4(1):67–74, 1973.

Ween, I.: Personal communication, 1978.

Weinberg, Jack: "Psychopathology," in John G. Howells (ed.), *Perspectives in the Psychiatry of the Aged,* Brunner/Mazel, New York, 1975.

Wheeler, Harvey: "The Rise of the Elders," *Saturday Review,* Dec. 5, 1970, pp. 14+.

Wolfe, Linda: "The Dynamics of Personal Growth," *House and Garden,* May 1976, pp. 90+.

Zale, Linda: Student paper, Arizona State University, 1977.

OTHER RESOURCES

FILMS

The Art of Age: 27 min/16 mm/color/1972. Demonstrates how the philosophy that "One is under an obligation to live as long as one is living" underlies the fulfilling and productive lives of four elderly citizens. The viewer gets a close look at their activities while listening to their reflection on life. Producer: Leonard S. Berman, with Dr. James T. Mathieu of the Gerontology Center at University of Southern California. Distributor: ACI Films, Inc., 35 West 45th Street, New York, N.Y. 10036.

How Would You Like to Be Old?: Two records or two cassettes and two full-color filmstrips. The combination of two filmstrips lasts 26 min. Distributor: Guidance Associates, Motion Media, 757 Third Avenue, New York, N.Y. 10017.

I Never Sang for My Father: 92 min/color/1970. A poignant portrait of a man who has arrived at the age of 40 without ever having realized his childhood ambition of establishing a close relationship with his father. Director: Gilbert Cates. Released by Co-

lumbia. Distributor: United Artists 16, 729 Seventh Avenue, New York, N.Y. 10019.
Last Stand Farmer: 25 min/16 mm/color/ 1975. Documents the life and philosophy of a 67-year-old Vermont farmer who is trying to keep his farm going. A Blue Ribbon winner, American Film Festival, 1976. Distributor: Silo Cinema, Inc., P.O. Box 315, Franklin Lakes, N.J. 07417.
Nobody Ever Died of Old Age: 65 min/ color/1975. An award-winning film based on the book of the same title by Sharon Curtin. A series of dramatized character studies show what it is like to be old in America, as seen through the eyes of a young woman nurse and writer in both rural and urban settings. Director: Herbert Danska. Distributor: Henry Street Settlement House, Arts for Living, 466 Grand Street, New York, N.Y. 10022.
Now Is Forever: 42 min/color/1972. Vignettes and interviews illustrating the positive aspects of the lives and philosophies of a number of vibrant, active senior citizens. Producer: Film Dynamics, 7250 Fair Oaks Boulevard, Carmichael, Calif. 95608.
Sigmund Freud: His Offices and Home, Vienna 1938: 17 min/16mm/color with b&w. A documentary showing rarely seen, exclusive photographs of 19 Berggasse, the birthplace of psychoanalysis. The rooms were secretly photographed by Edmund Engelman, and the negatives were hidden throughout the war. Distributor: Filmakers Library, Inc., 290 West End Avenue, New York, N.Y. 10023.
Wild Strawberries: 1957. Ingmar Bergman's film about a 76-year-old Swedish physician who learns to love late in his life.

Intergenerational

Miles to Go before I Sleep: 78 min/color/16 mm. The story of an old man and a 14-year-old girl portraying the mistrust that exists between the old and the young. Distributor: Learning Corporation of America, 1350 Avenue of the Americas, New York, N.Y. 10019.
Nana, Mom, and Me: 47 min/16 mm/color/ 1974. A portrait of three generations of women and the differing motivations, philosophies, and rivalries that shape their interaction. Producer: Amalie R. Rothschild. Distributor: New Day Films, P.O. Box 315, Franklin Lakes, N.J. 07417.
Peege: 28 min/color/1974. Deals with barriers to communication with a dying woman in a nursing home who is blind and has lost some of her alertness. Her grandson successfully breaks through the barriers by reminding her of happy times in the past. Distributor: Visual Aids Service, University of Illinois, 1352 South Oak Street, Champaign, Ill. 61820.

Chapter 22

THE LATER DECADES OF LIFE: RESEARCH AND REFLECTIONS

Irene Mortenson Burnside

> Required of us is a willingness to consider past, present
> and future at every point in our life cycle, both
> independently and in dialogue with others.
>
> *Robert Kastenbaum*

> If one generation owes anything to the future, it is the
> perception, understanding, laughter and compassion it
> got from the generation that preceded it.
>
> *Harry Reasoner*

The last chapter was an overview of the work of current theorists who have written about the developmental tasks of aging. This chapter is an overview of the literature on each decade from age 50 to age 110, with implications for psychosocial care. One entire chapter, Chapter 23, is devoted to centenarians, who have stirred more interest and been written about more extensively than persons in any other decade of late life.

This chapter is divided into five sections, according to decades. Granted, this is too simplistic a breakdown for studying developmental phases, for it is obvious that a 79-year-old woman may be very similar to the 80-year-old person sitting next to her. Yet we often say that a 65-year-old looks 80 or that an 80-year-old looks or acts much younger than his or her age. We do need exact information on each decade as the elderly population continues to increase.

Hall divided life into five stages: (1) childhood; (2) adolescence; (3) middle life, or "the prime," which ranges from age 25 or 30 to age 40 or 45; (4) senescence, which begins in the early forties "or before menopause in women"; and (5) senectitude, or "old age proper." Jarvik pointed out that "the tendency to equate old age with oblivion permeated Hall's writings" (p. 576).

Randall's classification, as described in Chapter 21, is the model for the organization of this chapter: the very young old (50 to 60), the young old (61 to 70), the middle-aged old (71 to 80), the old old (81 to 90), and the very old old (91 to 100).

Peck said: "It may be that the best way to get samples which are homogenous with respect to their 'stage in life' will be to use some 'stage' criterion and disregard chronological age, except as it proves to be similar for the members of a sample which is defined by a nonchronological criterion" (p. 92). I have ignored this suggestion and proceeded chronologically because this seemed the best way to organize materials for this chapter. See Figure 22-1 for the number of articles in the literature according to each decade of life.

REVIEW OF THE LITERATURE

Table 22-1 lists articles on aging, according to decades, based on research done in the United States, Scotland, England, Romania, and Norway. Numerous articles used a case-study approach. The cases concern unusual aged persons,

Figure 22-1 Number of publications according to decade of life.

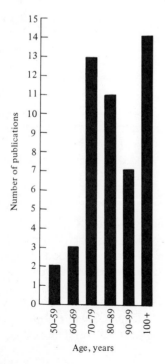

Table 22-1. Research According to Decades

Beginning Year	Principal Investigator or Therapist	Age of Subjects	Place Study Conducted	Focus of Study
1972	Gould	16–18 18–22 22–28 29–34 35–43 43–50 50–60	California	Salient characteristics of each age group sampled
1974	Maas and Kuypers	50–57	California	
1967	Cross	66–70	Massachusetts	Analysis of verbal interaction in therapy group
1968	Shanas	65–69		Crisis years for men, 65–69; attitudes of men and women aged 65–85
1968	Havighurst	60–69		Developmental tasks
1956	Ström	Over 70	Norway	Living conditions and health of 1389 Norwegians over 70
1968	Havighurst	70–79		Developmental tasks
1968	Howell	70–79	England	Multiple pathology found during autopsy in a 71-year-old woman
1973	Haggerty	70-year-old man		Case report
1960	Moustakas	74-year-old man		Psychotherapy: depression
1940	Grotjahn	71-year-old man		Psychoanalysis: senile dementia
1961	Crawshaw and Peterson	71-year-old man		Psychotherapy
1967	Cross	72–83—see above		Psychoanalysis: senile dementia
1970	Larson	70–79		Long-term group therapy

Table 22-1. Research According to Decades (*Continued*)

Beginning Year	Principal Investigator or Therapist	Age of Subjects	Place Study Conducted	Focus of Study
1972	Linn et al.	70–79	Florida	Patterns of illness in old age
1968	Shanas	70–79		Attitudes of men and women aged 65–84
1971	Burnside	79-year-old man	California	One-to-one relationship therapy: paranoia
1977	Webb et al.	77-year-old man		Physiology of distance runner
1973	Shapiro	80–89	Massachusetts	Motivation through creative writing
1968	Hughes	80–90	Scotland	Osteoporosis
1967	Da Silva	81-year-old man	Massachusetts	Individual psychotherapy: depression
1961	Dibner and Cummins	80–89	Massachusetts	Intellectual functioning of male Spanish-American War veterans
1973	Richardson	80–89	Massachusetts	Correlates of longevity among Spanish-American War veterans and UAW retirees
1964	Reingold	80–89	New York	Work for octogenarians in a sheltered care unit
1965	Comalli et al.	80–90 (20 males)		Perceptual-cognitive functioning
1967	Ciūca	85–90	Romania	Characteristics of the very old
1963	Shanas	80–84		Attitudes of men and women aged 65–84
1975	Nahemow	80+	New York	Prosthetic environment
19	Akhtar et al.	Over 80	Scotland	Health care needs of the aged in the community

Table 22-1. Research According to Decades (*Continued*)

Begin-ning Year	Principal Investigator or Therapist	Age of Subjects	Place Study Conducted	Focus of Study
1975	Heath and Fitton	Over 80	England	Home assessment of people over 80
1964	Shere	90–99		Group work with the very old old
1968	Walton	90-year-old man	England	One-to-one relationship of medical student and 90-year-old woman
1968	Wigzell	90–99	Scotland	Nonagenarians in Aberdeen, Scotland
1970	Wigzell	90–99	Scotland	Functional state of nonagenarians
1970	Hahn	94-year-old woman	New York	Essay
1963	Howell	90–99	England	Causes of death in nonagenarians
1965	McHugh and Taylor	90–99	England	Review of clinical and autopsy records of 32 nonagenarians

and many are too esoteric for practical use; however, because they reveal the state of the art, I have included them. While exotic clinical studies may not help one understand the average old person, they may help one understand what makes old persons outstanding or unique—a 77-year-old track runner (Webb, Urner, and McDaniels) or a paranoid woman of 96 whose life review (Burnside, 1978) appears on page 428. The case-study approach is one basic, important aspect of psychosocial caring. *The individual aged person must be emphasized and must be a constant focus.* We are still caught up in the conglomerate view of the aged. It is well known that there may be greater variability among older people than among any other cohort group (see Birren's statement on aging on page 382). Case studies do point up the uniqueness of an individual and also the range of adaptation ability and behavior of some aged persons. Most of the case studies concern men.

Welford points out:

Undue attention to exceptional older people prominent in public life has, in the past, distorted the attitudes of many to the capabilities and needs of old age. On the other hand, it does seem likely that many old people possess unrecognized potentialities for work or leisure activity which could be brought to light if diligently sought. The problem of realizing these potentialities lies more in personality and circumstances than in sheer capacity (p. 134).

Young students do have a delightful habit of measuring all elderly persons against their grandparents. This is lovely if Grandma is 90 and has just left on a tour of Greece, but if Grandma is 90 and bedridden and incontinent—well, the point is obvious. And, of course, there are always the grandmothers who do not fit anyone's picture of a grandmother: the Maudes on their motorcycles with the young Harolds. (*Harold and Maude* is a commercial film about an older woman and a much younger man.) I recall a student who once stated that her family was upset because her grandmother had gone to Tijuana and opened a house of ill repute. The family felt that this represented a real lack of judgment and were in quite a tizzy about the woman. The student was obliquely asking me, "What are old people *really* like?" She was just then beginning to discover this for herself; I never found out what happened to her grandmother.

Vischer has described a study by a German psychologist, Giese, who gleaned data regarding two questions: "Which factors first made you aware of growing old?" and "Which were the first indications you received that you felt old?" The investigation covered a broad sample of readers of more than 50 German newspapers and journals. One disadvantage of the study was that little was known about the people who participated in it. Sixteen percent of the replies were from 40- to 50-year-olds, and 53 percent were from 50- to 70-year-olds; the figures for the other age groups are not given. The youngest respondent was 25, and the oldest was 89. Most people in this survey said they felt "old" at about 49. One would need to know what the average life-span in Germany was at the time the study was done; we would be surprised in the United States now to hear that someone felt old at 49.

NONINTERVIEWABLE AGED SUBJECTS

Havighurst (1950), writing about the Prairie City study, said that about 75 percent of those over the age of 65 could not be interviewed. Even when researchers bypassed nursing homes, they found that 10 percent were too frail and feeble or too sick; another 10 to 15 percent were physically able to handle the interview but were unwilling to do so. (One must continually remember the importance of the right to say "no" in old age.) See Table 22-2.

I am reminded of a story told by a young researcher at a gerontology conference in Toronto, Canada. He sent out many questionnaires to elderly persons in San Francisco with a promise of a $20 payment on completion and return of the form. One old man promptly returned his unanswered questionnaire with this note: "Forget the research for a while. Take the $20 from this one and enjoy yourself, young man." The speaker then smiled at the audience and added, "Which I happily did." The many ways in which old people maintain control over their lives, money, and researchers is a healthy omen for all of us.

Table 22-2. Noninterviewable Subjects

Reason Noninterviewable	No. of Subjects
Not interested	14
Speech unintelligible	8
Illness; weakness	6
Severe confusion; incomprehensible	5
Refused to speak	4
Transferred	3
Deaf	2
Paranoid; too suspicious	1
Died during study	1

Source: Burnside, 1970, from data on 100 subjects in four settings: 50 in senior centers and 50 in long-term care facilities.

An excellent article by Schmidt is useful to those who must interrogate the old old (80-year-olds) and the very old old (90-year-olds). Another article (Burnside, 1973) describes the interviewing skill needed with the aged. Schmidt pointed out: "Samples of this cohort are not easily assembled" (p. 544). Cumming and Parlegreco had such difficulty collecting subjects from 70 to 90 that they eventually instructed the staff to round up what they described as a "brush-fire" sample, that is, any very old persons they could capture. Not only are those subjects hard to find, but they also require special approaches and instruments for productive interviewing.

THE VERY YOUNG OLD: 50 TO 59

I shall make no progress with my book until I am able to rid myself of the conviction that this is my last (André Gide, at age 52, in his diary).

The literature regarding those in their fifties is widely scattered and is generally found as part of a larger study, as in the book by Maas and Kuypers. These researchers examined the lives of women and men over a 40-year period from age 30 to age 70. While early adulthood usually provides the backdrop for the life-style in old age, for some subjects this did not hold true, especially for women. *While in their thirties, the women were considered by the researchers to have low energy levels; however, drastic changes occurred after a crisis, e.g., divorce or the death of spouse, and the women began to work outside their homes.* Psychological disturbances through the fifties are shown in Table 22-3.

Mid-life (50 to 65) is described by Gould (1972) as a period of "mellowing and warming up" (p. 522). People no longer see their spouses as controlling them, and children are often sources of warm satisfaction. There is an increased awareness among people in this age group of their own mortality. Gould feels this is not a time of diminishing interest in interpersonal relationships, but rather a time of increased need for personal relationships.

**Table 22-3.   Percentage Distribution of
Reported Psychological
Disturbance at Each
Developmental Stage**

	%
Childhood (0–14)	2
Adolescence (15–20)	5
Young adulthood (21–34)	10
Maturity (35–49)	14
Later maturity (50–59)	15

Source: Lowenthal, Marjorie Fiske: *Archives of
General Psychiatry,* **12**(3):248–254, 1965 p. 248.
Copyright 1965, American Medical Association.

"Stability fraught with concern marks the 50s and the concern is largely about time. With one's allotment of life more than half used up, people respond with increasing pessimism to the statement that 'There's still plenty of time to do most of the things I want to do' . . ." (Gould, 1975, p. 38). Consider this view against that of the centenarians described in Chapter 23. While Gould readily acknowledges that his descriptions are generalizations, nevertheless they do reflect the average, which allows for considerable variation. This is particularly true when one is studying the older population beyond the fifth decade.

Gould ends his article with: "While children mark the passing years by their changing bodies, adults change their minds. Passing years and passing events slowly accumulate . . . eventually releasing their energy and assuming new forms in altered relationships with both time and people" (1975, p. 78). The care giver needs to consider how the time perspective may affect the decisions and feelings of the person in the fifth decade.

The reader is reminded of the quotation from Gide at the beginning of this section; people in this age group begin to identify "last" events or things in their lives. One will hear such statements as, "This is the last sofa I intend to purchase" or "This may be the last time I have a chance to do this." After age 50, one starts to think about what may or may not be still possible in one's life. Chapter 30 discusses handling "last" moments, persons, and objects in life.

THE YOUNG OLD: 60 TO 69

Here lies old Sam Smith
Died when he was 60
Buried him when he was 90 (Epitaph in graveyard).

One starts to get young at the age of sixty, and then it's too late (Picasso).

I am an old man in his sixtieth year. I have entered that decade of life which destroys the last illusion. ... I am also poor, incontrovertibly poor, for the first time in my life. ... My aging body betrays me day by day; the ground I am losing now I lose forever (Brooke, p. 62).

What do you think happens to a man going on 62 ... when he realizes that he can never ... do any of the best things in life. ... But what the hell? What does a man care about? Staying healthy. Working good. Eating and drinking with his friends. Enjoying himself in bed. I haven't any of them. Do you understand it, goddamn it? None of them (Ernest Hemingway, several weeks before his death).

Havighurst reminds us: "The end result of the adaptation process in the 60's is a reorganization of role-structure which is accomplished by the ego in the face of the losses and gains of this decade of life" (1968, p. 69).

Society may expect less of the aging person as he or she moves through the decade of the sixties: less energy, less autonomy, and less creativity than a decade earlier. Sadly, one wonders why less creativity is expected. See Chapter 27 for a discussion of creativity. There may also be reduced income, and friends and colleagues begin to thin out. Havighurst wrote:

For the first time, for most persons, the adaptation process takes place against a set of negative changes in the body and the social environment. Some people have a kind of personality that accepts these negative changes in a passive-dependent manner. Others have a personality that seeks to replace lost roles by greater activity in other roles, especially those of grandparent, neighbor, friend, and church member. (1968, p. 69).

The same author said:

Up to the age of 60 or 65 the great majority of people can count on fairly good health, so that the state of their physical organism does not generally count very much either in favor of or against their adaptation. Still, those who are blessed with abundant vigor generally make a better adaptation than the average, and those who are physically weak generally have difficulty with their adaptation (Havighurst, 1968, p. 69).

Welford stated:

The decade from 60 to 70 is, more than any other during the adult years, a time of transition. Many changes of body and mind, of capacity and attitude, which have been continuous since the early twenties now have become critical, not only for work but also for some facets of daily living. ... For many, the later 60s see the beginning of a need, which becomes increasingly common in the 70s, for various kinds of help and care during the last years of life (p. 128).

Physical Strength Wanes

Suominen, Heikkinen, and Parkatti (1977), of Finland, explored the reports on a training program involving old people. A sample of 26 healthy 69-year-old men and women were studied in Jyvaskyla, Finland, in 1972. The researchers found that the increase in physical performance capacity in both men and women supported recent studies "showing that the trainability of old people does not greatly differ from that of young and middle-aged persons if compared on a percentage basis" (Suominen et al., p. 36). This study shows the importance of an increase in physical capacity in both men and women in the decade of the sixties.

Regarding physical strength, the person in the decade of the sixties can no longer do as much heavy physical work as formerly. This creates a major problem, especially for industrial workers, as described in Chapter 19. They may find that poor health orces them to drop the worker role or change to a less demanding job before y are ready to retire.

Although retirement is generally regarded as a task of those in their sixties, many people in their fifties are now also retiring because of early retirement plans for military personnel, firemen, Veterans Administration hospital employees, and workers in other areas.

Lately I have seen examples of "hyper" retirees. Although they were busy on their jobs, after retirement they go at an absolutely frenetic pace. "I have never been so busy in my life"; "I am swamped"; "I have too much to do." I hear such comments frequently as such people continue to be unusually active and independent. They do not slow down, and they often refuse offers of help with, "What's the matter? Do you think I'm getting old?" Work was the organizing factor in their lives, and being very busy is still all-important to them after retirement.

I observed the importance of work to old women and men on a trip to the U.S.S.R. In downtown Kiev and Tbsili, elderly women dressed in black and wearing babushkas swept the sidewalks (and also chased overeager photographers away with their brooms). One day I was going into a large department store near my hotel. A very old man with a beat-up old scale sat in front of the store; he was charging people for weighing themselves. When I returned from my tour of the store, he was sitting behind the scale eating his lunch of tomatoes and bread. Over the tall scale was a muslin cover—obviously his "out-to-lunch" sign. I was impressed. Work, no matter what kind of work it is or where in the world it is done, still brings identity, dignity, and control into an aged person's life. For example, the man with the scale decided on his own office hours, place of employment, lunch hour, and prices. See Figure 22-2.

Retired persons may seek out and develop interesting and pleasurable activities. Some retirees do acquire a stance of giving rather than receiving. They "work" for enjoyment. The need to be needed is evident in organizations such as Foster Grandparents and Friendly Visitors. Retired persons often serve as mentors. Care givers should recognize the importance of the need to be needed and should explore ways in which the aged person can serve. The egocentric person will not need to be needed but rather will struggle to find someone with the need to help; see Chapter 21 for a discussion of egocentricity.

Figure 22-2 Doing meaningful work can be important to the elderly person. (*Courtesy of Bill Clark.*)

60-Year-Olds in Group Therapy

Cross studied verbal interaction in a therapy group of elderly psychiatric patients and found that the younger patients, 66 to 70 years old, responded to anxiety with increased verbal interaction, and to loss with decreased verbal interaction. The older patients (72 to 83) responded with decreased verbal interaction to anxiety and with increased verbal interaction to loss.

Everyone who lives to be 70 has to adapt his or her style of living to decreasing vigor. Note Hemingway's comments at the beginning of this section; he was unable to adapt to changes.

Adaptation in the Sixties

Asnes and Shulman reported on an extensive study of a 68-year-old man with a life pattern of maladaptation who developed a florid psychosis after retirement. This case is an excellent example of what often happens in the development of mental illness in the elderly: *the mental illness begins with a physical illness.*

In Stenger's book entitled *The Spectator Bird,* a 69-year-old man says to his friend, "The sixties are the age of anxiety. You feel yourself on the brink of old age and you fret. Once you pass your seventieth birthday that all clears away. You're like a man with an old car and no place in particular to go. You drive it where you want to, and every day it keeps on running is a gift" (p. 15). This book gives a beautiful portrayal of the anxiety suffered by those in their sixties.

An article by Brooke in *The Atlantic Monthly* gives a bitter view of aging. While the man in Stenger's book is not poor and has a wife and a home, Brooke is not so fortunate.

THE MIDDLE-AGED OLD: SEPTUAGENARIANS, 70 TO 79

People age at a different rate, and I am a late starter. However, the pleasure I find in living every day, the joy of new experiences (for I still have them even at seventy-six) and the thought that tomorrow may be even better than today tends to keep me on my toes and be content with each new age I attain (Coleman, p. 2).

The decade of the seventies is frequently mentioned in gerontological literature because it is different from that of the sixties, eighties, or nineties. My own first awareness of the fact that the decade of the seventies is different came from reading *Growing Old* (Cumming and Henry). Cumming and Parlegreco compared 70-year-olds and 80-year-olds. In those aged 70 to 79 they found restlessness, irritability, many deaths, and much illness and loss. Shanas, Townsend, Wedderburn, Friis, Milhøj, and Stehouwer wrote: "Like Cumming and Parlegreco, we find a marked difference between persons in their 70's and those 80 or over. Old people in their middle 70's appear to be depressed about their health; those over 80 are optimists." (p. 218). These findings have implications for improving psychosocial care, but they do not seem to have found their way into the world of practice.

Rosow (1970) points out that the aged live in a contracting social world and that their participation declines notably and sharply after age 75. There are two aspects of that decline: they sharply reduce their activities in formal organizations, and they lose friends. There is a severe loss of social roles, which means that they have fewer associates.

70-Year-Olds in Group Therapy

Larson met with a group of 11 clients of the Family Service Association of Greater Boston for 2 years and concluded:

> Group therapy with people in their 70's and older must take into account the failing of familiar ways of coping, such as hyperactivity, and the need to support the defenses that are serving. Treatment should be dynamically supportive. The older people must feel this support to each session and not be allowed to go back to their isolated rooms or unhappy family situations with anxiety rampant (p. 240).

The treatment described included (1) some degree of clarification, (2) encouragement of reflection, and (3) rational discussion of existing problems. Modifications of attitudes occurred with the introduction of new slants by the leader and by group members. Larson, as a group leader, frequently used direct guidance in order to help the elderly persons find ways of making a contribution to society. This group strategy ties in with earlier comments on the need of some aged persons to be needed.

Kutner, Fanshel, Togo, and Langer studied 500 noninstitutionalized persons over 60. They found that as age increased, morale in both males and females gradually decreased, except for an upsurge in males between the ages of 70 and 74. These data conflict with those of Cumming and Parlegreco.

Physical Aspects of the Seventies

Howell (1968) described multiple pathology found in a 71-year-old woman during autopsy; there were 25 separate pathological lesions. The cause of her death was a coronary thrombosis. Howell reviewed the case and related the multiple pathological findings to other elderly subjects.

Linn, Linn, and Gurel studied patterns of illness in persons who lived to extreme old age and found that their illnesses tended to cluster during the last years of life. This suggests that these persons' particular illnesses were not acute ailments but, rather, represented a more general process of deterioration to be associated with aging and death. In the very old group, the most common past illnesses included (1) cardiovascular problems, (2) hernia, (3) cataracts, (4) fractures, (5) chronic brain syndrome, (6) urinary tract infections, and (7) genitourinary cancer. In the younger group, the most frequent illnesses were (1) myocardial infarction, (2) pneumonia, (3) gastrointestinal problems, (4) emphysema, and (5) lung cancer.

A former mentor, now in her seventies, commented one day about having her first boil: "When you're 73—that's something!" There are fewer and fewer "firsts" in later life. Chapter 30 discusses the problem of handling so many "lasts" in late life. Perhaps the "firsts" are still a unique experience at whatever age.

It appears that very old persons are in a unique position of having been spared illness until a very late age; however, their illnesses may be more like a chain reaction, in which one degenerative process leads to another and finally to death.

The Seventies Sexually

In a study at Duke University, Pfeiffer, Verwoerdt, and Wang found that women lose interest in and discontinue sexual activity at a younger age than men; in a married woman, this may be related to the husband's loss of interest in sex if he is older than she.

Grief and Suicidal Behavior

Flannery has written an article describing a behavior-modification program for the treatment of grief in a 71-year-old man. The program was conducted in a community mental health center. Two important aspects covered in this article are (1) the self-administration of medications and the fact that the man had received multiple prescriptions for multiple ailments and (2) the importance of "having man-to-man talks with the clients about sports, etc." (Flannery, p. 200). The paper is helpful in spelling out contracts and procedures used, and it touches on a few of the thorny problems, psychosocial and physical, that care givers can expect to encounter: (1) grief; (2) agitated depression; (3) many psychosomatic complaints; (4) sexual arousal and concomitant guilt; (5) insomnia; (6) careless taking of medications, perhaps in combinations which could be lethal; (7) sibling family; and (8) mandatory retirement, to name a few.

Suicidal behavior in a 70-year-old man was the subject of a case report by Haggerty. The man had attempted suicide three times prior to admission; his wife had died approximately 1 year before. His losses included wife, job, health, home, friends, and daughters. Haggerty's feelings are probably shared by others dealing with depressed, suicidal elderly persons:

> In spite of his apparent adjustment, I am uncomfortable as I think about Mr. Jorgensen's situation. There seems to be so little that keeps him alive, no real assurance that he won't again attempt suicide, perhaps successfully this time. ... I think it is possible, in fact probable, that he will experience again a sense of loss and depression and that his solution may well be to try to end his life. Perhaps I am too pessimistic; I sincerely hope so (p. 51).

Adaptation in the Seventies

Shanas analyzed data from a nationwide survey and found that about a third of all the subjects aged 70 to 74 still thought of themselves as "middle-aged"! Generally, the decade from 70 to 80 involves maintenance of the "reorganized role structure'' which follows the adaptations of the sixties (Havighurst, 1968, p. 69). Role loss continues, such as with widowhood and widowerhood and the loss of friends. There is a general reduction in role activity, caused by diminishing physical strength. The task, then, of the decade of the seventies for most older persons is to maintain the structure of satisfactory activity which was developed during the reorganization process in the sixties; this is nicely described by a 76-year-old man:

> The fact that I can no longer throw a ball or a right hook with the speed and authority I once could bothers me not at all. I can still spot a pretty face or figure as far as I ever could, and enjoy them no less; I also enjoy sunrises, sunsets, the moon, a rainy day with nothing to do, the green of shrubbery, the beauty of flowers, the written word when the author has something to say and says it well, these and other little things mean so much more since I have time to stop and enjoy them, and I have the feeling that they are the really important things in life (Coleman, p. 2).

Future Predictions

Neugarten and Havighurst state: ''We anticipate that in the year 2000 people will be in relatively good health up to age 75 or thereabouts, and they will participate in civic and social and political activities, especially if they drop out of the labor market'' (pp. 5–6).

Sanford states: ''The population of England and Wales over 75 years of age is likely to increase by 20% in the next decade'' (p. 473). This article is highly recommended for care givers dedicated to keeping an aged individual at home because it describes the support persons for 50 elderly people. The researchers asked the support persons to identify problems which needed to be alleviated in order to make living with the elderly person more tolerable. One of the most frequently mentioned ''alleviation factors'' was sleep disturbance—being awakened regularly at night by the dependent old person. This occurred in 62 percent of the cases. *The sleep disturbance was poorly tolerated by the provider of care.*

If we intend to keep older people at home and independent as long as possible, we will also need to study support persons and systems, as Sanford has done in England. See Figure 22-3.

THE OLD OLD: OCTOGENARIANS, 80 TO 89

> Age puzzles me. I thought it was a quiet time. My seventies were interesting, and fairly serene, but my eighties are passionate. I grow more intense as I age (Scott-Maxwell, p. 13).

> What future remains for me was made by my past (Miller, p. 9).

Shanas reported on data from a nationwide survey in which 17 percent of the men and 7 percent of the women aged 80 to 84 called themselves ''middle-aged.''

Figure 22-3 This man consented to pose for a picture during his seventy-fifth birthday celebration. He said that he felt uncomfortable being "dressed up" and that such attire was only for funerals, weddings, and birthday parties. (*Courtesy of May Belle Nelson.*)

Compare this with their finding, mentioned earlier, that a third of the 70- to 74-year-olds in the same survey considered themselves middle-aged.

Dibner and Cummins studied the intellectual functioning of a group of octogenarians who lived in the Greater Boston area; the group consisted of 50 relatively healthy male Spanish-American War veterans. They were found to be above average in intelligence, and they performed well on tests measuring retention and comprehension of verbal material. Poor performance on tests was the result of decreased psychomotor speed and difficulty with abstract thinking. The pattern of decline of various abilities tested, say the researchers, was consistent within the younger and older men in the sample and also with other studies of older groups. The reader is referred to the work of Schaie and of Woodruff and Walsh, who take a more positive stand.

Comalli tested 20 males between the ages of 80 and 90 and contrasted the results with the empirical findings from groups ranging in age from 6 to 80 years. He concluded that "senescence is progressively marked by a developmental regression in perceptual-cognitive processes'' (p. 17). Comalli's findings are a source of much controversy these days. Compare his statements with the data in Table 22-4.

In a 20-year longitudinal study of aged twins, the changes in 34 female and 20 male octogenarians were observed (Blum, Fosshage, and Jarvik). The men showed a greater decline in test performance, which may be a reflection of the fact that men tend to become ill and die sooner than women. There is a need to study sex differences in intellectual change.

Bayley demonstrated an increase in mean IQ up to the age of 50. The study by Blum, Jarvik, and Clark, which covered the first decade of follow-up of the twins, indicated that decline of verbal functions begins in the eighth decade of life and becomes statistically significant by the ninth decade.

Reingold described a project in which workers in their eighties were assigned to jobs consistent with both their physical capacities and their work tolerance. During a 5-day workweek, some residents worked as little as 1 h a day; others worked as many as 6 h. The average workday was 3 h. Such a project is also consistent with the milieu therapy that Gottesman et al. have described so well.

Cumming and Parlegreco compared 70-year-olds and 80-year-olds, as mentioned earlier. While the 70-year-olds experienced change and unrest, the 80-year-olds were tranquil and satisfied, unless they were beset with money problems. There was little need to change, learn, or achieve in the group studied; one wonders about such a finding, which seems atypical of many 80-year-olds.

One important reason for studying 80-year-olds is that there are currently so many of them in institutions; Leake has reminded us that there will have to be marked improvement in institutional life because of the increased population of those in their eighties and nineties. Howell (1963) has noted the increase of lesions with age, which is indicative of the types of physical problems encountered in the later decades.

Scott-Maxwell, at the age of 86, commented on the physical problems of old age: ''We old people are short tempered because we suffer so. We are stretched too far, our gamut is painfully wide. Little things have become big; nothing in us works well, our bodies have become unreliable. We have to make an effort to do the simplest things. We urge now this, now that part of our flagging bodies, and when we have spurred them to further functioning we feel clever and carefree'' (p. 35). Berenson, at age 88, wrote something similar: ''For an hour I felt young again, master of my body, instead of being as so often 'a bit of soul carrying a corpse' or rather a prisoner of my body'' (p. 304).

Nahemow stated: ''As people age, particularly beyond their 80th year, their ability to interact with the surrounding environment usually declines'' (p. 58). He lists the following needs of those over 80: (1) enhancement of sensory functions, memory, and physical orientation; (2) a barrier-free environment; (3) stimulation and privacy; (4) enhancement of the sense of self; (5) a sense of continuity of social and cultural experience; and (6) life-supporting facilities. That is an excellent checklist for students. Implementing only one item on that list could involve detailed, comprehensive planning and much careful thought.

Table 22-4. Survey of Over-80 Age Group: Interviewers' Response to Questionnaire Options Judging Mental State of Each Person Surveyed

Judgments Upon 169 of Recorded Population	142 People				27 People (3 Men, 24 Women)						
	Generally Content	Coping	Spontaneously Talked of Deceased Spouse	Depressed	Over-talkative	Verbally Aggressive	Time Confusion Past Events	Time Confusion Present Events	Action Confusion Present	Mis-identifies People	Also Spontaneously Talked of Deceased Spouse
All judgments	133	65	17	10	7	7	3	4	1	1	6
As percentage of all responses	78.6	38.4	10	5.9	4.3	4.3	1.7	2.3	0.5	0.5	3.5
Lives with self	65	35	15	4	3	4	2	1	—	—	4
As percentage of all responses	38.4	20.7	8.8	2.3	1.7	2.3	1.1	0.5	—	—	2.3
Lives with spouse	16	13	—	2	1	—	—	—	1	—	—
As percentage of all responses	9.4	7.6	—	1.1	0.5	—	—	—	0.5	—	—
Lives with relative or friend	50	17	8	2	2	2	1	3	—	1	1
As percentage of all responses	29.5	10	4.7	1.1	1.1	1.1	0.5	1.7	—	0.5	0.5
Not recorded	7	—	—	2	1	1	—	—	—	—	—
As percentage of all responses	4.1	—	—	1.1	0.5	0.5	—	—	—	—	—

Source: Heath and Fitton, p. 112.

Studies of Octogenarians in Other Countries

A study conducted in Scotland by Akhtar, Broe, Crombie, McLean, Andrews, and Caird assessed the health care needs of elderly community residents. In general, those below age 85 could maintain a community residence with some support, while those above this age required more intensive care.

Ciũca described a Romanian study in which 77.6 percent of the group studied were aged 85 to 90. All had been or were married, and most had four to eight children. The physical condition of the married individuals was much better than that of those who had lost a spouse. The longevous people in the study had followed a single profession throughout their lives. The 85 to 89-year-old workers were in better physical condition than those in other workers age groups. The agriculturists showed a predominance of acute illnesses; this is an interesting finding, and one wonders what the reason for it might be.

A group of 222 persons over age 80 were surveyed in a central urban health center in Yorkshire, England. It was hypothesized that the group might be at special risk and would have many unmet health care needs. This was not found to be the case.

> Whereas some unmet needs were identified and the complexities of physical and social environment were underlined, the resultant impression was that these octogenarians had no urgent concealed medical need. The nursing team and the general practitioners developed confidence in approaching the group. If the level of unmet need for domiciliary chiropody in the survey population is indicative of the need in the aged population at large, then as many more people could benefit by this mobilizing service as at present receive it" (Heath and Fitton, p. 109).

See Table 22-4.

Other Case Studies of 80-Year-Olds

Da Silva, a psychiatrist, held 50-minute psychotherapy sessions weekly for 3 years with an 81-year-old depressed man and wrote sensitively of that relationship; his article is recommended to all those involved in counseling, along with Moustakas's article, "Communal Loneliness." Da Silva says: "He gave me what I still consider the best definition of old age: *Old age is a gradual process which begins the very first day one begins to live in his memories*" (p. 20). See page 382 for other definitions of aging and Chapter 28 for an elaboration of reminiscence. The reader who is involved or working with depressed, lonely older persons might find both Da Silva's and Moustakas's case studies helpful. Another sensitive care giver describes her experience below.

CASE STUDY OF AN 85-YEAR-OLD WOMAN

Eva is an 85-year-old black woman. She is a county patient and has lived in the nursing home since 1976. She is the only black woman there. She is diagnosed as severely arthritic, although she is fully ambulatory and capable of feeding herself; she suffers a degree of sight and hearing loss which apparently is not too debilitating.

Eva is a woman of indomitable spirit. She carries the burden of a life filled with tragedy, oppression, and loss with a noble aura. I was struck by the dignity with which she sat—head held high, gazing through the windows. The slight smile on her weathered face indicated pride and self-satisfaction.

Eva was born in 1891 on a farm in Arkansas. When she was 4 years old, her mother died. Her father remarried a woman who beat Eva and her sisters and brother regularly. She worked long hours picking cotton and plowing ground for the corn. Fish was a staple which she caught in a creek 3 mi from their wooden cabin. The children never ate with their parents. They ate later from whatever scraps were left—often "goin' to bed mighty hongry." When Eva was 12 years old, her stepmother became very ill and died the following year. As the oldest of the children, Eva cared for the family—cooking, cleaning, and working in the fields. Her father died 2 years later. Though her early years were fraught with abuse, hunger, and drudgery, Eva speaks of the happiness she felt when riding with her father on the back of his horse to church on Sundays.

At age 16, Eva married. The young couple had six children. All family records were kept in her family Bible. This treasure, of which she spoke so longingly, was destroyed in a fire which consumed their cabin and killed an infant daughter. Her oldest son was shot during a brawl in a tavern, and two other children died during childhood. Her husband died in 1952; the remaining family consists of her son and daughter-in-law and their three children. She speaks of the overwhelming desire to "go home" to be with her "babies" (the grandchildren) and the hope that she might still find a "good man" to marry. (Speak about hope!) See Figure 22-4.

Her wealth of love was dramatized in a poignant episode during my last visit. I brought her a small gift to express my appreciation for all she had given to me and to convey my fondness. As I presented it to her, she smiled and held my hand on her lap for what seemed a very long time. Without saying a word, she put her hand into the frayed pocket of her dress and pulled out two hard-boiled eggs which she had saved from her breakfast tray. She put the eggs into my hand saying, "This is all I have to give, please take it." Tears welled up in my eyes, and I could speak no words. With that, Eva reached out and hugged me gently while saying, "It's all right, child, don't cry."

In terms of intervention, my responses were encouraging remarks made while Eva expressed her enthusiasm about continuing to share her life's experiences with me. Since she was a sharing person, I often felt the need (my own as well as what I perceived to be hers) to hold her hand—especially when she spoke of her children's deaths. What I attempted to convey at those times was my respect for the trauma of recollection and an appreciation for her willingness to share such personal history with me (Barchilon).

Octogenarians: Words of Wisdom

At age 82 Florida Scott-Maxwell, a Jungian psychoanalyst, wrote a gem of a book which reflects her Jungian orientation. (See Chapter 27 for a discussion of Jung's influence.) She stated:

I grow more intense as I age. To my own surprise I burst out with hot conviction.

Figure 22-4 A Bible can be a cherished object to an elderly person, as this drawing shows. The individual uniqueness of each older person and of his or her needs are still not fully considered in psychosocial care. (*Courtesy of Bill Clark.*)

Only a few years ago I enjoyed my tranquility, now I am so disturbed by the outer world and by human quality in general, that I want to put things right as though I still owed a debt to life. I must calm down. I am too frail to indulge in moral fervour (Scott-Maxwell, pp. 13–14).

Nadine Stair, an 85-year-old woman living in Louisville, Kentucky, wrote the following:

If I had my life to live over, I'd dare to make more mistakes next time. I'd relax. I would limber up. I would be sillier than I have been this trip. I would take fewer things seriously. I would take more chances. I would take more trips. I would climb more mountains and swim more rivers. I would eat more ice cream and less beans. I would perhaps have more actual troubles, but I'd have fewer imaginary ones.

You see, I'm one of those people who live sensibly and sanely hour after hour, day after day. Oh, I've had my moments and if I had it to do over again, I'd have more of them. In fact, I'd try to have nothing else. Just moments, one after another, instead of living so many years ahead of each day. I've been one of those persons who never goes anywhere without a thermometer, a hot water bottle, a raincoat, and a parachute. If I had it to do again, I would travel lighter than I have.

If I had my life to live over, I would start barefoot earlier in the spring and stay that way later in the fall. I would go to more dances. I would ride more merry-go-rounds. I would pick more daisies.

Miller wrote:

At eighty I believe I am a far more cheerful person than I was at twenty or thirty. I most definitely would not want to be a teenager again. Youth can be glorious, but it is also painful to endure. Moreover, what is called youth is not youth, in my opinion; it is rather something like premature old age. I was cursed or blessed with a prolonged adolescence; I arrived at some seeming maturity when I was past thirty. It was only in my forties that I really began to feel young. By then I was ready for it. . . . By this time I had lost many illusions, but fortunately not my enthusiasm, nor the joy of living, nor my unquenchable curiosity. Perhaps it was this curiosity—about anything and everything—that made me the writer I am. It has never left me. Even the worst bore can elicit my interest, if I am in the mood to listen (pp. 9–10).

As the heroine of *How to Save Your Own Life*, Jong wrote in her journal, "Get ready to be eighty-seven" (p. 196).

THE VERY OLD OLD: NONAGENARIANS, 90 TO 99

Old age isn't so bad, but it sure can be unhandy (a 95-year-old West Virginian).

Medvedev wrote:

According to general statistics, females have a longer life-span than men. In the USSR, the ratio of women to men aged between 90 and 99 is about 3:1 in favor of women. But after 100 years, this ratio starts to change in favor of men (p. 384).

This finding is borne out in other "pockets" of the world where extremely old persons live. See Chapter 23, which discusses centenarians.

A study done by Hughes in Scotland was concerned with skeletal rarefaction of 90-year-olds. Forty-five men and women aged 90 to 97 were studied. Of these, 37—10 men and 27 women—were on long-term geriatric wards or rehabilitation units. Hughes wrote that his findings:

. . . tend to show that the sex difference may disappear by the end of the tenth decade, the bones of the majority of women appear to have become osteoporotic before reaching their 90th birthday, whereas the men tend to deteriorate during the middle of this decade.... When mobility and sex are combined it is seen that only 22% of active men are osteoporotic as opposed to over 90% of non-active women (p. 356).

Researchers have offered little in the way of incorporating this knowledge into treatment plans for the future.

Very little is known about the functional state of nonagenarians because very little is known either about their state of health or about their social circumstances (Wigzell, 1970). As Wigzell says: "There is no descriptive picture of their social milieu or of 'the way of life' of those who reach 90 years in our modern society" (1970, p. 312). Although the study was done in 1968, it contains interesting data; e.g., no males in this study survived beyond 95 years. Few lived beyond age 92 if they were hospitalized, and it was difficult to locate nonagenarians in the community.

The editor of the *Scottish Medical Journal* commented on an article by Wigzell (1968) on nonagenarians in Aberdeen and asked why the proportion of nona-genarians in Aberdeen is higher than in the rest of Scotland, where the average life-span is low in comparison with that in many other countries. Sixty percent of the Aberdeen nonagenarians live in the general community rather than in institutions.

McHugh and Taylor studied 32 nonagenarians (18 females and 14 males) aged 90 to 97 at the time of death and noted that most infective lesions had been unsuspected in life. They list possible reasons for this: "(a) Dulling of pain sensation and insensitivity to other symptoms, on the part of the patient. (b) Reluctance of clinicians to perform trying or painful diagnostic procedures. (c) Reluctance of patients or relatives to accept diagnostic procedures" (p. 363).

Howell (1963) studied multiple pathology in 40 nonagenarians during autopsy; 498 separate lesions were found, and 225 involved the cardiovascular system. The reader is reminded of the importance of physical health and prevention of cardiovascular diseases. While these findings have to do with physical func-tioning, the importance of physical health as it affects mental status and mental health cannot be overemphasized.

Overholzer et al. described a 94-year-old who gave the Wisconsin farm he had had for 60 years to his children with the agreement that he keep a few acres on which to raise evergreens. The farmer had dug up trees and moved them around, and he said to the interviewer, "That line of Douglas firs over there will make a very good windscreen in 20 years" (Overholzer et al., p. 84). Older people's concern with legacies, even the legacies of lovely pine trees, can be impressive. The importance of legacies and the types of legacies that old people prefer have not been studied. Many of us can list legacies we have received from old people in both our professional and our personal lives. One wonders whether the legacies, objects, and memories that an old person wishes to leave change with each decade. For one thing, a person who lives to be 100 may have few material possessions to leave.

An Essay on a Nonagenarian

Walton wrote an essay on a 90-year-old widow who had lived alone for 15 years. The author concluded that one of the serious problems faced by the elderly in England is personal loneliness and social isolation. Knopf, however, herself a nonagenarian and a practicing psychiatrist, has pointed out that the picture is not as dismal as it seems because the changes occur gradually and over a long period of time. Some changes need not take place at all. Once the older person learns to accept the changes and the limitations of old age, he or she may find that getting old does in fact have some advantages, for example, freedom from work pressures and responsibilities. Knopf states that such advantages should not be underestimated. *One can create new fields of activities and interest simply by removing the competition component from one's former ways.* Knopf ends the article with: "The one thing to do is to utilize what is left as well as possible" (p.364).

An Old Woman's Only Legacy

The following was found in the handmade tote bag of a 96-year-old woman after she died. She had been institutionalized for many years and had no survivors. I visited her from time to time and once took her for a ride (Burnside, 1978).

Said of Me

Mama said: Was never bad or had any bad record. Nor any bad friends nor any bad affiliations. Never ran around with boys or, any one. (People in my day never ran around. They stayed home nights with parents. They had nothing to do with boys. I was an exemplory child and young lady. Never got married because abhored sex. Never went out with the Boys. Never would have anything to do with Boys. Always went with my Parents. Never went to bed until got my school sessions done. Got 98 & 99% marks for lessons in Nevada. Got in the 90% in Los Angeles High School. Never said or talked any fast or risqué or dirty stories or things.

Papa said: Never had to have anything said to me about behaving. Said I was a nice little girl that never did anything wrong. Would never sit on a man's lap, nor have anything to do with men.

Hindu[1] said: Said that I was a model child, young lady, daughter, scholar & woman & worker and would be a model person.

1912: D. got Mama to take all the money of Papa's in the bank and put it into the Los Angeles Investment Company stocks at $4 dollars a share.

1913: At D.'s request, Los Angeles Investment Co. went broke and shares went to .30 cents a share. Then D.'s older brother got up in Big Meeting and said it was done by D. to do Me down. It knocked me under financially forever. If the money had been left in the Bank I could have inherited the house and my brother

---

[1] Hindu was an imaginary friend she created during her long years of institutionalization.

could have inherited the equation in money. So I could have been able to support myself.

1921: Knocked me out of building room in front of barn so I could rent my half of house.

1922: Knocked me out of having room built in front of barn by———Knocked me out of house to be built in front of barn by Architect friend so I could rent my half of house.

1930: I saw in Los Angeles Times that .50 cents per hour was the right manual labor wage. But they said I had no right to charge that much. That I was only an amateur. But I had ironed for Mother for about 20 years I told. So I worked for .25– .30– .40 cents an hour for 6 years, for 60 cents per hour for 10 years, for $1.00 for 6 years. If I had had 60 c & 1.00 per hour, I would have $4,000 more in the Bank.

1962: The Old 1910 Model T Ford Touring Car, an antique, was pulled to pieces and stolen, was worth $600 to $1000. They, the Maryland gang could not let it alone. They were so crazy to do me down.

1963: Kept me from getting boards for Windows to hold screens out so rock-shy kids could not hit glass.

Pioneering Group Work with 90-Year-Olds

Shere did a pioneering study of the very old old, which is now a classic article on group work with aged clientele. Shere's group work was the basis for my own group work with six nonagenarians in a 91-bed nursing home. Of the 91 residents, 11 were over 90, but only 6 were able to participate in a group experience. Excluded were non-English-speaking persons, bed patients, and those who were completely blind or completely deaf. One group member's wife attended regularly, even though she was only 86. We met weekly to eat supper together; ordinarily, the residents ate alone in their rooms. I hoped that as we sat around the table together, memories of happier times and more memorable meals would be revived. We used a cheerful employees' dining room. The rationale for the "supper hour" was simple—it was one way to incorporate clinical experience into my heavy teaching schedule.

One of the goals when the group began was to simulate the atmosphere of family meals. The table was attractively set, and the conversation revolved around earlier family experiences. One group member said grace. Other goals were to increase communication, increase social skills, increase sensory stimulation, and consistently reality-test with two members. (See Chapter 28 for discussion of reality testing.)

Leader Observation

I observed that this was an elite group! Eating involved problems, however. Arthritic hands precluded dexterity with forks, and one 92-year-old man had lost both arms at the age of 22. (I ate my macaroni and cheese with my fingers one evening because one of the women told me that I "ought to try it." Not only was this an experiential exercise for me, but it was also an easy way to let her have some control.) I found certain commonalities among the group members. All came from large, poor families; all had worked hard, even as children; and all had experienced economic crises and natural disasters (one had suffered through a potato famine in Ireland, and another had experienced the San Francisco earthquake of 1906).

I experienced the following difficulties with this group:

1. An initial problem was that of finding enough alert, mobile persons 90 years old and over in a small extended care facility.
2. It was difficult to get staff members to assist the elderly people to group meetings. Although this problem can occur in studies of all age groups, it was more severe in this case because of the frailty of the group members.
3. The frailty of the group members was a problem; the losses they had suffered were staggering.
4. The group members' lack of interest in their surroundings, even in food at times, had to be dealt with.
5. Messy eating habits were common; two group members ate with their fingers. One person dropped out of the group because of this, but she was extremely fastidious.
6. Problems arose as a result of different levels of mental competence among the group members. Competence or lack of competence in activities of daily living was also a problem.
7. Fatigue levels created a problem. The group members would not stay in the dining area very long; they wanted to return to their own rooms after a short period. At first this seemed to be due to an increased anxiety level, but actually it was due more to fatigue and lack of energy.

POSITIVE AND NEGATIVE VIEWS OF AGING

The gerontological literature is replete with the negative attitudes toward the aged held by both professionals and nonprofessionals. Cicero wrote in defense of old age: "Old age is respectable so long as it asserts itself, maintains its rights, is subservient to no one, and retains its sway to the last breath. I like a young man who has a touch of the old, and I like an old man who has a touch of the young. A man who cultivates this principle may be old in body, in mind, never" (p. 140). The polarized view of aging continues. "They're known as the wrinklies these days. The wrinklies—those who've committed the unpardonable sin of growing old in a culture that worships youth" (Pafundi, p. 12).

Scott-Maxwell, an octogenarian, wrote:

We who are old know that age is more than a disability. It is an intense and varied experience, almost beyond our capacity at times. . . . If it is a long defeat it is also a victory, meaningful for the initiates of time, if not for those who have come less far. . . . I write my notes as though I spoke for all old people. This is nonsense. Age must be different for each. We may each die from being ourselves (pp. 5, 120).

SUMMARIZING STATEMENTS BASED ON THE LITERATURE

- Powerful, dominant parents eventually have to come to terms with being inferior to their own children (Havighurst, 1953).
- Between the ages of 50 and 65, people may become mellow. They cease to see the spouse as controlling them, and they may derive warm satisfaction from their children (Gould, 1972). There is also an increased need for personal relationships (Gould, 1972).
- The adaptation process of the sixties requires reorganization of role structure by the ego (Havighurst, 1968).
- The decade of the sixties requires adaptation to some rather important changes in both physical vigor and social environment (Havighurst, 1968).
- The decade of the seventies involves maintenance of the reorganized role structure, which began in the sixties; the task of this decade is to maintain the structure of satisfaction activity (Havighurst, 1968).
- Group therapy with people in their seventies must consider the failure of usual means of coping, e.g., hyperactivity and the need to support the defenses. The leader must be dynamically supportive (Larson).
- Group work with nonagenarians requires careful assessment of energy levels and gentle handling of frailties.
- Patterns of illness in extreme old age indicate that illnesses tend to cluster during the last years of life. The most common illnesses of extreme old age are (1) cardiovascular problems, (2) hernia, (3) cataracts, (4) fractures, (5) chronic brain syndrome, (6) urinary tract infections, and (7) genitourinary cancer (Linn, Linn, and Gurel).

GUIDELINES FOR INTERVENTION

- Be aware of a possible need to provide counsel in relationships where the old person and the child are clashing in role changes, e.g., when the child becomes dominant.
- Promote the mellow qualities of aging clients.
- Assist clients in their sixties to plan and reorganize new roles in their lives.
- Facilitate adaptation to waning physical strength and a changing social milieu.
- Help 70-year-olds maintain the roles they carved out during the previous decade.
- Study the reports of group leaders who have worked with the aged.
- Study reports of one-to-one relationships between a care giver and an elderly person for role models to emulate.

REFERENCES

Akhtar, A. J., G. A. Broe, Agnes Crombie, W. McLean, V. Andrews, and F. I. Caird: "Disability and Dependence in the Elderly at Home," "*Age and Aging,* 2:102, 1973.

Asnes, Daniel P., and Helen Shulman: "Florid Psychosis after Retirement in a 68-Year-Old Man: A Case Report," *Journal of Geriatric Psychiatry,* 9(2): 237–253. 1972.

Barchilon, Barbara N.: "Interview with a Nursing Home Resident," paper presented for class, Arizona State University, May 1977.

Bayley, Nancy: "On the Growth of Intelligence," *American Psychologist,* 10: 805–818, 1955.

Berenson, Bernard: *Sunset and Twilight: From the Diaries of 1947–1958,* Harcourt, Brace & World, New York, 1963.

Blum, June E., James L. Fosshage, and Lissy F. Jarvik: "Intellectual Changes and Sex Differences in Octogenarians: A Twenty-Year Longitudinal Study of Aging," *Developmental Psychology,* 7(2): 178–187, 1972.

——, Lissy Jarvik, and E. T. Clark. "Rate of Change on Selective Tests of Intelligence: A Twenty-Year Longitudinal Study of Aging," *Journal of Gerontology,* 25:171–176, 1970.

Brooke, John: "The Gentle Art of Poverty," *The Atlantic Monthly,* October 1977, pp. 62–68.

Burnside, Irene M.: Field notes from research project, University of California, San Francisco, 1970.

——: "Interviewing the Aged," in I. Burnside (ed.), *Psychosocial Nursing Care of the Aged,* McGraw-Hill, New York, 1973.

——: "Eulogy for Ms. Hogue," *American Journal of Nursing,* 78(4):624–626, 1978.

——: "Gerontion: A Case Study," *Perspectives in Psychiatric Nursing,* 9(3): 103–109, 1971.

Cicero: *The Basic Works of Cicero,* Moses Hadas (ed.), Modern Library, New York, 1951.

Ciŭca, Alexandru: "Longevity and Environmental Factors," *The Gerontologist,* 7(4):252–256, 1967.

Coleman, Dale: "Personal Thoughts on Aging," Unpublished manuscript, 1972.

Comalli, P. E.: "Cognitive Functioning in a Group of 80–90-Year-Old Men," *Journal of Gerontology,* 20(1):14–17, 1965.

Crawshaw, R. S., and L. K. Peterson: "Supportive Psychotherapy with an Aged Transient," *Geriatrics,* 16(9):454–458, 1961.

Cross, Floyd Melvin: "An Analysis of Verbal Interaction in a Therapy Group of Elderly Psychiatric Patients," *Dissertation Abstracts,* Boston University, Boston, 1967.

Cumming, Elaine, and William Henry (eds.): *Growing Old,* Basic Books, New York, 1961.

—— and Mary Lou Parlegreco: "The Very Old," in Elaine Cumming and William Henry (eds.), *Growing Old,* Basic Books, New York, 1961.

Da Silva, Guy: "The Loneliness and Death of an Old Man: Three Years' Psychotherapy of an Eighty-One-Year-Old Depressed Patient," *Journal of Geriatric Psychiatry,* 1(1):5–27, 1967.

Dibner, Andrew S., and James F. Cummins: "Intellectual Functioning in a Group of Normal Octogenarians," *Journal of*

Consulting Psychology, **25**(2):137–141, 1961.

Flannery, Raymond B.: "Behavior Modification of Geriatric Grief: A Transactional Perspective," *International Journal of Aging and Human Development,* **5**(2):197–203, 1974.

Gottesman, Leonard E., N. Bourestom, W. Donahue, and **D. Coons:** *The Technology of Milieu Treatment of the Aged Mental Patient,* Institute of Gerontology Library, Ann Arbor, Mich., 1971.

Gould, Roger: "The Phases of Adult Life: A Study in Developmental Psychology," *American Journal of Psychiatry,* **129**(5): 521–531, 1972.

———: "Adult Life Stages: Growth toward Self-Tolerance," *Psychology Today,* **8**(9):74–78, 1975.

Grotjahn, Martin: "Psychoanalytic Investigation of a Seventy-One Year Old Man with Senile Dementia," *Psychoanalytic Quarterly,* **9**:80–97, 1940.

Haggerty, Judith: "Suicide in the Aging. Suicidal Behaviors in a 70-Year-Old Man: A Case Report," *Journal of Geriatric Psychiatry,* **6**(1):43–51, 1973.

Hall, George: *Senescence: The Last Half of Life,* Appleton, New York, 1922.

Havighurst, Robert: "Problems of Sampling and Interviewing in Studies of Old People," *Journal of Gerontology,* **5**(2): 158–167, 1950.

———: "A Social-Psychological Perspective on Aging," *The Gerontologist,* **8**(2): 67–71, 1968.

Heath, Patricia J., and **Judith M. Fitton:** "Survey of Over-80 Age Group in a GP Population Based on Urban Health Centre," *Nursing Times,* **71**(43): 109–112, 1975.

Howell, Trevor H.: "Multiple Pathology in Nonagenarians," *Geriatrics,* **18**(12): 899–902, 1963.

———: "Multiple Pathology in a Septu-

agenarian," *Journal of the American Geriatrics Society,* **16**(7):760–762, 1968.

Hughes, G.: "Skeletal Rarefaction in Nonagenarians," *Gerontologica Clinica,* **10**(6):348–357, 1968.

Jarvik, Lissy F.: "Thoughts on the Psychobiology of Aging," *American Psychologist,* **39**(5):576–583, 1975.

Jong, Erica: *How to Save Your Own Life,* Harper & Row, New York, 1977.

Knopf, Olga: "Aging," *Mount Sinai Journal of Medicine,* **39**(4):357–364, 1972.

Kutner, Bernard, D. Fanshel, Alice Togo, and **T. S. Langer:** *Five Hundred Over Sixty: A Community Survey on Aging,* Russell Sage, New York, 1956.

Larson, Marian K.: "A Descriptive Account of Group Treatment of Older People by a Caseworker," *Journal of Geriatric Psychiatry,* **3**(2):231–240, 1970.

Leake, Chancey D.: "Future Problems in Dealing with the Elderly," *Geriatrics,* **24**(2):76–77, 1969.

Linn, Margaret, Bernard S. Linn, and **Lee Gurel:** "Patterns of Illness in Persons Who Lived to Extreme Old Age," *Geriatrics,* **27**(6):67–70, 1972.

Lowenthal, Marjorie Fiske: "Antecedent of Isolation and Mental Illness in Old Age," *Archives of General Psychiatry,* **12**(3):248–254, 1965.

Maas, Henry, and **Joseph Kuypers:** *From Thirty to Seventy,* Jossey-Bass, San Francisco, 1974.

McHugh, J. C., and **Rhonda Taylor:** "Four Score Years and Ten," *Gerontologica Clinica,* **7**(6):358–364, 1965.

Medvedev, Zhores A.: "Caucasus and Altay Longevity: A Biological or Social Problem?" part 1, *The Gerontologist,* **14**(5): 381–387, 1974.

Miller, Henry: *On Turning Eighty,* Capra, Santa Barbara, 1972.

Moustakas, Clark: "Communal Loneliness," *Psychologica,* **3**:188–190, 1960.

Nahemow, L.: "A Prosthetic Environment for the Elderly," *Gerontology,* **1**(4): 58–65, 1975.

Neugarten, Bernice, and **Robert J. Havighurst:** "Aging and the Future," in Bernice Neugarten and Robert Havighurst (eds.), *Social Policy, Social Ethics, and the Aging Society,* GPO, Washington, D.C., 1976, pp. 5–6.

Overholzer, et al.: "How to Live to Be 100," *Family Circle,* November 1976, pp. 82–84.

Pafundi, Maria A.: "Growing Old Is Not a Sin," *Syracuse University Alumni News,* **54**(5):12–17+, 1973.

Peck, Robert C.: "Psychological Developments in the Second Half of Life," in Bernice Neugarten (ed.), *Middle Age and Aging,* University of Chicago Press, Chicago, 1968.

Pfeiffer, Eric, Adriaan Verwoerdt, and **H. Wang:** "The Natural History of Sexual Behavior in a Biologically Advanced Group of Aged Individuals," *Journal of Gerontology,* **24**(2):193–198, 1969.

Randall, Ollie A.: "Aging in America Today: New Aspects in Aging," *The Gerontologist,* **17**(1):6–11, 1977.

Reingold, Jacob: "Octogenarians Work for a Living in Three-Year Health-Morale Study," *Hospitals, J.A.H.A.,* **38**(18): 59–65, 1964.

Richardson, Arthur: "Social and Medical Correlates of Survival among Octogenarians: United Automobile Worker Retirees and Spanish-American War Veterans," *Journal of Gerontology,* **28**(2): 207–215, 1973.

Rosow, I.: "Old People," *American Behavioral Scientist,* **14**:59–69, 1970.

Sanford, J. R. A.: "Tolerance of Debility in Elderly Dependents by Supporters at Home: Its Significance for Hospital Practice," *British Medical Journal,* **3**(5981): 471–473, 1975.

Schaie, K. Warner: "Toward a Stage Theory of Adult Cognitive Development," *Journal of Aging and Human Development,* **8**(2):129–138, 1977–1978.

Schmidt, Mary Gwynne: "Interviewing the 'Old Old,' " *The Gerontologist,* **15**(6): 544–547, 1975.

Scott-Maxwell, Florida: *The Measure of My Days,* Knopf, New York, 1968.

Shanas, Ethel: "A Note on Restriction of Life Space: Attitudes of Age Cohorts," *Journal of Health and Social Behavior,* **9**(1):86–90, 1968.

———, **Peter Townsend, Dorothy Wedderburn, Hennig Friis, Poul Milhøj,** and **Jan Stehouwer:** "The Psychology of Health," in Bernice Neugarten (ed.), *Middle Age and Aging,* University of Chicago Press, Chicago, 1968, p. 218.

Shapiro, Edith: "The Residents: A Study in Motivation and Productivity among Institutionalized Octogenarians," *The Gerontologist,* **13**(1):119–124, 1973.

Shere, Eugenia: "Group Therapy with the Very Old," in R. Kastenbaum (ed.), *New Thoughts on Old Age,* Springer, New York, 1964.

Stenger, Wallace: *The Spectator Bird,* Doubleday, Garden City, N.Y., 1976.

Ström, Axel: "An Investigation of the Living Conditions and Health of 1389 Persons Aged 70 Years or More in Norway," *Journal of Gerontology,* **11**(2):178–184, 1956.

Suominen, Harri, Eino Heikkinen, and **Terttu Parkatti:** "Effect of Eight Weeks' Physical Training on Muscle and Connective Tissue of the M. Vastus Lateralis in 69-Year-Old Men and Women," *Journal of Gerontology,* **32**(1):33–37, 1977.

Verwoerdt, Adriaan, Eric Pfeiffer, and **H. S. Wang:** "Sexual Behavior in Senescence," *Geriatrics,* **24**(2):137–154, 1969.

Vischer, A. L.: *On Growing Old,* tr. by Gerald Onn, Houghton Mifflin, Boston, 1967.

Walton, Margaret: "An Old Person Living

Alone in the Community," *Gerontologica Clinica,* **10**(6):358–368, 1968.

Webb, James L., Sandra C. Urner, and **John McDaniels:** "Physiological Characteristics of a Champion Runner: Age 77," *Journal of Gerontology,* **32**(3): 286–298, 1977.

Welford, A. T.: "Ability," in Robert Sears and S. Shirley Feldman (eds.), *The Seven Ages of Man,* Kaufmann, Los Altos, Calif., 1974, p. 128, 134.

Wigzell, F. W.: "The Nonagenarians," *Scottish Medical Journal,* **13**(9):312–316, 1968.

————: "The Functional State of Nonagenarians," *Geriatrics,* **25**(9):170–178, 1970.

Woodruff, Diane S., and **David A. Walsh:** "Research in Adult Learning," part 1, *The Gerontologist,* **15**(5):424–430, 1975.

OTHER RESOURCES

FILMS
60-Year-Olds

Last Stand Farmer: 25 min/16 mm/color/ 1975. Documents the life and philosophy of a 67-year-old farmer who is trying to keep his farm going. A Blue Ribbon winner, American Film Festival, 1976. Distribution: Silo Cinema, Inc., P.O. Box 315, Franklin Lakes, N.J. 07417.

Myrtle: 15 min/color. A documentary on 65-year-old Myrtle Rose. Contrasts the needs and concerns of older Americans with those of the young. Director: Norman J. Virag. Distributor: Cinema Associate Productions, P.O. Box 1542, East Lansing, Mich. 48823.

Woo Who? May Wilson: 33 min/16 mm/ color/1970. A documentary about a 60-year-old farmer-wife-housekeeper-cook-grandmother who was divorced and began a new life as an artist. Producer: Amalie R. Rothschild (Anamoly Films). Winner of the Cine Eagle Award in 1970. Distributor: New Day Films, Inc., P.O. Box 315, Franklin Lakes, N.J. 07417.

70-Year-Olds

Raisin Wine: 15 min/16 mm/color/1970. Reviews the day-to-day life of a 79-year-old man in a retirement facility. The emphasis is on what is positive rather than what is pathological about old age. Deals with the need for the continuation of the previous life-style, aspects of normal aging, and common human needs of the aged. Distributor: Institute of Lifetime Learning and Communication Arts Development, Loyola University, Los Angeles, Calif. 90052.

A Yellow Leaf: 14 min/16 mm/b&w. A poetic treatment of the life of a weary 70-year-old woman. The woman's hopes and memories are combined with objects from her past which now decorate her lonely existence.

80-Year-Olds

Arthur and Lilly: 30 min/16 mm/color/1976. A documentary about Arthur Mayer, aged 89, and his wife, aged 86. The couple recall the great days of Hollywood and talk about their present-day involvement with young students. Distributor: Pyramid Films, Box 1048, Santa Monica, Calif. 90406.

90-Year-Olds

The Grandfather: 16 min/b&w/1968. An intimate and nostalgic portrait of a 93-year-old man, the oldest person in his village in Friesland, in the northern Netherlands. He recalls his youth, his marriage, and the horrors of war, and he philosophizes about old age and death. Distributor: Indiana University, Audio Visual Center, Bloomington, Ind. 47401.

Miss Larson: Rebel at 90: 17 min/16 mm/color/1976. The dramatic story of a 90-year-old woman's struggle for self-determination in hospital and nursing home situations, where she is subjected to various indignities. Distributor: Films Inc., 1144 Wilmette Avenue, Wilmette, Ill. 60091.

Never Give Up: Imogen Cunningham: 28 min/16 mm/color/1975. Ann Hershey visits the 92-year-old photographer. A Blue Ribbon winner at the American Film Festival, 1976. Distributor: Phoenix Films, Inc., 470 Park Avenue, New York, N.Y. 10016.

Now Is Forever: 42 min/16 mm/color/1972. Vignettes and interviews illustrating the positive aspects of the lives and philosophies of a number of vibrant, active senior citizens. Producer: Film Dynamics, 7250 Fair Oaks Boulevard, Carmichael, Calif. 95608.

Picasso Is 90: 51 min/color. A film biography of one of the greatest artists of all time. Traces Picasso's life from childhood to old age. Producer: CBS News. Distributor: Carousel Films, New York, N.Y. 10036.

Ruth Stout's Garden: 23 min/16 mm/color/1975. A view into the life of an interesting nonagenarian. Shows Ms. Stout's unique "no dig–no work" method of gardening and outlines her robust outlook on life. Director: Arthur Mokin. Distributor: Arthur Mokin Productions, Inc., 17 West 60th Street, New York, N.Y. 10023.

Chapter 23

CENTENARIANS: THE ELITISTS
Irene Mortenson Burnside

> I do not know how to grow old gracefully, but I do know how to grow old quietly.
>
> *Guy Shirley, 104 years old*

> A man on his feet is worth 30 on their seats.
>
> *Centenarian*

> I am not an unusual man—just one who has lived an unusually long time.
>
> *John Turner, 100 years old*

If any group of the aged population deserves to be described as "elite," it is the centenarians. They have eluded diseases and viruses, and they have avoided or survived traumas, accidents, holocausts, and wars—even interpersonal battles. It has been found that most of the oldest people in the world—those over 110—are males; single females rank second. It has been suggested that the lack of stress in single women's lives and the fact that they are not subjected to the hazards of childbearing are important in promoting longevity (Davies). There are some who feel that bearing children is not as hazardous or stressful as rearing them. Benet (1976) found that women who have had children are likely to live longer than those who have remained childless.

SEARCH OF THE LITERATURE

Medlar, Medline searches of the literature were disappointing in regard to this chapter. Census reports provide data, but these are not recent data because of the 10-year intervals between censuses. The census of 1970 indicated an increase in the number of centenarians; according to this census, there were 106,441 persons aged 100 years and over in the United States at that time. However, people who respond to census questionnaires tend to overestimate the age of very old persons living with them (Siegel and Passell), and the available evidence suggests that the number of persons 100 years old and over in the United States does not exceed several thousand (Zitter). The overcounting of centenarians in the censuses before 1970 is thought to have been due to misstatements of age by the individual. No verification is required when an individual states his or her own age. It has been noted that persons under 75 years of age report their age with reasonable accuracy. There are frequent stories about old persons aging 15 or more years between decennial census reports (Ingersoll).

Siegel and Passell give this amusing example:

> In the matter of prolonging human life, science has played no part whatever. Take the history of one Bessie Singletree. ... On her twenty-seventh birthday Miss Singletree became twenty-four years of age and was married. At thirty-five she was thirty. At forty she was thirty-nine until she was close to fifty. At fifty Bessie was forty; at sixty, fifty-five. At sixty-five she was sixty-eight and on her seventieth birthday everyone said Grandmother Singletree was pretty chipper for an octogenarian. At seventy-five she had her picture in the paper as the oldest woman in the county, aged ninety-three. Ten years later she passed away at the ripe old age of one-hundred and nine (p. 650). See Figure 23-1.

The true age of persons over 100 is often in dispute. This can be noted at gerontology conferences during discussions of longevous people anywhere in the world. A member of the audience will invariably jump up and ask about the birth certificates. Besides mistakes in dates and lack of records, Comfort points out that two people of different generations can have the same name. He also reminds us that all people tend to recount experiences that were told to them by others as if they were their own.

In long-term care facilities great attention is paid to individuals who become centenarians; once they pass the age of 100, however, interest in them decreases. This seems to happen because congratulatory letters from mayors, governors, and Presidents are sent *only* on the one-hundredth birthday. It is unfortunate that the same interest and concern are not expressed on each birthday thereafter. Leaf (1973) entitled one of his articles "Every Day Is a Gift when You Are Over 100." Young was the first to report on centenarians in the literature in England.

UNITED STATES STUDIES OF CENTENARIANS

One wonders why such an interesting and elite group has been studied so little in the United States; sometimes it seems as if the whooping crane receives more attention.

Belle Boone Beard (1966, 1967, 1968, 1969) has pioneered in the research on

Figure 23-1 The computer read-out indicates you have lived too long. (*From Bülbül and Irene Paull,* Everybody's Studying Us, Cartoons by Bülbül, Commentaries by Irene Paull, *Glide Publications, San Francisco, 1976. Copyright © 1976 by Bülbül and Irene Paull, reprinted with permission.*)

centenarians. In a survey of sensory decline in centenarians, Beard said: "It is amazing that centenarians see as well as they do, for very few had had their glasses checked during the past 20 or 30 years" (1969, p. 152). Beard studied more than 500 men and women who were centenarians and found that their loss of hearing has been more gradual than their loss of sight and that *adjustment to hearing loss has more difficult.* Men experienced more loss of hearing than women, and women experienced more loss of sight. Although one must assess the sensory deficits of all aged persons, this is especially important when working with centenarians. The importance of hearing in the prevention of isolation needs to be understood by all care givers of the very old. In her paper on recent memory characteristics of centenarians, Beard (1968) stated that the centenarians she studied accepted the popular attitude toward memory loss in the aged and that few felt embarrassed by it; some, however, considered it a nuisance, and others worked assiduously to retain their memory powers. Davies has made an interesting statement: "Usually in the West, people begin to lose their memory soon after deafness, which generally comes first" (p. 105).

Comfort describes Charlie Smith, who ran a small store in Barstow, Florida, until he was 133 years old. He retired in 1955 at age 113 because he was considered too old to climb trees! He had an octogenarian son. According to the American Medical Association and the Social Security Administration, in 1972 he was officially considered the oldest person in the United States.

As early as 1952, Schuster wrote "A Psychological Study of a 106-Year-Old Man: A Contribution to Dynamic Concepts of Aging and Dementia." The author postulates that "strong ego resources may play a role in resisting the onset of dementia in advancing age" (p. 118).

Lerner studied 267 centenarians who were receiving social security benefits. His article is a dismal account of aged persons who took little pride in their longevity and had withdrawn from life. However, 10 of the 267 were blind, 5 were completely deaf, 42 others had visual disturbances, and 57 more had severe hearing loss. Thus nearly half the sample was physically impaired in some way, and the findings are therefore not surprising. Thirty-five had never gone to school, and 31 had completed only a few grades. This survey dealt with a special cohort group and is in direct contrast to McKain's work with centenarians in the U.S.S.R., whom he found to be "full of energy, alert, and in apparently good health" (p. 70).

Woodruff has pointed out that ". . . the special thing that we find in centenarians is the quality of their lives not the quantity" (p. 84). That quality of life is evident in one remarkable centenarian described by Ebersole in a case study that appears later in this chapter.

Braverman's "Report on the Life and Death of a Woman of 101 Years of Age" is misleading since it reports on autopsy findings rather than the woman's life; the article concludes with: "The paucity of reports on centenarians is a symptom of the apathy which is still too often present in treating old people" (p. 369). I think the focus on autopsies indicates a distorted view also—rather than reporting on what old people died from, we need to study what they lived for.

Costa and Kastenbaum studied aspects of memory in 267 centenarians and found that 58 percent said their earliest memory was of something that happened before the age of 6. Only 1 percent said it was of something that occurred after age 70, and 7 percent said that it was of something that happened during adolescence. This study should be of interest to those who use the life review, oral history, or reminiscing in their work with aged clients.

Jewett interviewed elderly persons aged 85 and over; some of his interviewees were 103. He interviewed persons who were in good health, both mentally and physically and he concluded that the common characteristic of the group were that they were of average size and body structure, with superior intelligence.

STUDIES OF CENTENARIANS IN EUROPE

Franke, Bracharz, Laas, and Moll studied the mental and physical state of 148 persons 100 years old or older (115 women and 33 men) using a combined examination technique.

Significant differences between the groups were found with respect to height and weight, life expectancy of parents and grandparents, hearing capacity, tendency to transient hot flushes, nocturia, blood pressure level, tendency towards anginal symptoms, urinary incontinence, loss of teeth, tendency towards depression and noise sensitivity. ... The group of centenarians could be classified into three groups by their physical and mental state: (1) those remarkably fit and showing admirable vitality; (2) those with moderately impaired vitality; and (3) those permanently confined to bed. Post-mortem examinations of three 100-year-olds gave no evidence of mere senile weakness having been the cause of death (Franke et al., p. 1594).

STUDIES OF CENTENARIANS IN THE U.S.S.R.

Demographers at the Kiev Institute of Gerontology reported:

People of advanced years seldom are able to give an exact indication of their age. None of their contemporaries is alive to help them remember the dates of historical events that happened many years ago and coincided with the early periods of their own life. *The less a population is familiar with written documents, the less literate and civilized, the more unrealistic are the ages reported by its oldest inhabitants* (McKain, p. 71, italics supplied).

Abkhasia

Davies stated that 2.58 percent of Abkhasians in the U.S.S.R. were over 90; the overall figure for the Soviet Union is 0.1 percent. In contrast, the figure for the United States is 0.4 percent. Davies reported that the Abkhasians he studied were extremely stable psychologically and neurologically and had a clear recollection of the past, although they remembered comparatively little about recent events. In some persons this pattern was reversed, and others remembered past events and recent occurrences equally well.

Benet's works (1974, 1976) describe the life-style of the people of the Caucasus region in the U.S.S.R. Benet, an anthropologist, lived with the people of Georgia, Abkhasia, Azerbaidzhan, Armenia, and Dagestan. In the introduction to her book, she describes a woman of Keitol, Abkhasia, who was 139 years old: "She was quite small. I was told she had been taller, but had seemed to have shrunk with the years. . . . She had a keen sense of humor and laughed easily" (Benet, 1976, p. 1). Some of us have long thought that a sense of humor is important to survival, and perhaps the ability to laugh and find humor in life needs to be underscored.

Benet covers a variety of subjects—climate, geography, diet (she even includes recipes), sexual behavior, life attitudes, and recreation. The aged persons whom Benet studied had a feeling of importance and self-worth; their full participation in family and community activities enabled them to retain a positive self-image.

The importance of self-image throughout the life-span is a theme of this book. Self-image in the later years is discussed in Chapter 25.

Benet's 4 years of intensive research and field work led her to draw these conclusions:

1. There is a rhythmic regularity to Caucasian life which is probably a major factor in healthfulness. There is continuity and regulation of diet, work, sex life, and leisure activities and thus little of the strain associated with sudden changes and discontinuities.
2. Old people are included in the active life of both the kin group and the community. There is no point at which they relinquish their authority, and *the oldest person is always listed as head of the household, regardless of his or her contributions to the family.* "Old people continue to vote, make decisions, and participate in all the activities of which they are capable until death" (Benet, 1976, p. 161).
3. Data indicate that married people are more likely to reach the age of 70 than single persons.
4. Women who have had children are also likely to live longer than those who have remained childless.

Benet concluded: "Abkhasia is tough, with strict rules. Most Westerners would find the unspontaneous, formalistic, and measured way of life constricting" (1976, p. 163). She felt that the culturally reinforced expectations of a long life and good health and the mechanisms to avoid stress, especially intergenerational stress, were also factors conducive to longevity.

STUDIES OF CENTENARIANS IN SOUTH AMERICA

Leaf has written about his visits to three countries inhabited by especially longevous people. Figure 23-2 shows maps of those geographic areas. Leaf wrote: "In all three countries I visited I found the old people participating in the social and economic life of community and family. The need seems to be for a role which sustains the self-esteem of the individual. No one can feel useless, unwanted, and redundant and survive for long" (p. 212).

SLEEP

Regarding sleep, Davies has stated that the majority of centenarians in the world live in technologically primitive societies where they get up with the sun and go to bed with the sunset. They spend about half their lives sleeping. Davies wryly states: "The Vilcabambans do not excel in vigor in their middle years, but they keep what vigor they have for a far greater life-span than anyone else in the world . . ." (p. 136). They continue to work into extreme old age and begin to lighten their duties at 85 or 90; they live at higher elevations than most people, they eat a monotonous diet containing very little meat, and they use herbal remedies for illness. Davies also attributed their longevity to lack of stress; he

ABKHAZIA

Abkhazia is in southern Russia, in a region warm enough for farmers to grow tea and oranges.

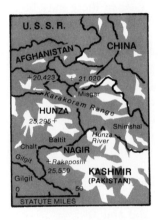

HUNZA

Hunza is one of the remotest realms on earth. Controlled by Pakistan, it is surrounded and protected by the huge mountains of the Karakoram Range.

VILCABAMBA

For centuries, Vilcabamba has been isolated from most of the world. It is situated in the foothills of the Andes Mountains.

Figure 23-2 Map of Abkhasia, Hunza, and Vilcabamba. (*Reprinted with permission from Leaf, 1975.*)

pointed out that women in Vilcabamba, Ecuador, who do not live as long as the men, are subject to much more stress than men and occupy a very low position in society.

Benet (1974, 1976) and Davies both note that the very old in the U.S.S.R. and South America are needed, wanted, and sought out for wisdom and cultural preservation.

Comfort agrees with Benet and Davies concerning the importance of continued activity, adequate exercise, and proper diet and adds another dimension—isolation from viruses. Readers who have been felled by a viral infection may wonder how a centenarian could survive in an environment inhabited by viruses.

THE STARTLE EFFECT

We are often awed by centenarians, but there are times when there may be a "startle effect" when one encounters a very aged individual—at least this term seems to best describe the reactions I have observed both in myself and in students. We often exclaim, "I've never seen or talked to anyone that old." I was startled one day in Prince Edward Island, Canada, by a sharp, alert 110-year-old Chinese man. Another time, in a skilled nursing facility in Watts, California, I went into a room to talk to a man who was 105. He had outlived four wives; that was one of the reasons I wanted to talk to him. I thought he must be very outgoing and caring if he could have been married that many times. He was. In fact, he pulled me down into the wheelchair with him and said, "I kiss all the new nurses who come here." I found myself awkwardly explaining that I was not a new nurse. He has been interviewed and visited so often by students of gerontology that he now folds his hands and says to them, "Well, what would you like me to talk about?" See Figures 23-3 and 18-5.

STUDENTS' FEARS

Some years ago when I was teaching graduate psychiatric nursing, a student came to me and said that she absolutely could not work with a 105-year-old woman in a large rehabilitation hospital, as the staff there had suggested she do. Soon a second student came in with the same problem, and so I went to the hospital to see the patient. She was a tiny, wizened old lady with no living relatives, and she had become a "pet" of the ward. The staff had thought that a nursing student could offer her support and become a "confidante" in a one-to-one relationship. Both students were much relieved when they were told they could select their own patients, and subsequently they chose women in their seventies. At that time, I wondered about the care of centenarians. Why had these students bolted? What was so unique about centenarians? What was it about her that frightened the students?

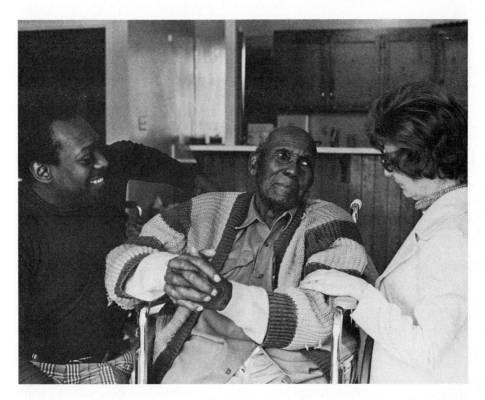

Figure 23-3 This 105-year-old man, who outlived four wives, was outgoing and loved to talk. He was interviewed by many students, and when they approached him in his room in the nursing home, he would say, "Well, what would you like me to talk about?" (*Courtesy of Will Patton.*)

On another occasion I interviewed Guy Shirley, aged 104, and experienced the startle effect myself. The following is based on my notes of an interview with this man, who is quoted at the beginning of this chapter.

Mr. Shirley lived in a county nursing home in Tucson, Arizona, when I visited him. He was lying in bed with his eyes closed. His white hair was thin and sparse and barely visible against the white pillow. He was very thin, and when I lifted his upper arm, the hospital gown collapsed around it. I was startled by the thinness of the arm, and later I was acutely aware of his thin, bony hand as I held it. He had no teeth; his cheeks and mouth were sunken. As I took his hand and held it, he opened his eyes, a lusterless blue, but held them in a steady gaze. I said, "My name is Irene." He closed his eyes and replied curtly, but not offensively, "I don't care what your name is."

I sat down beside his bed and asked him whether I might sit and talk to him awhile. He opened his eyes, but only to two narrow slits, and said, "You've already sat down." Then there was a shift in his reaction to me; he warmed in his responses, and after thinking for a few moments, he said, "I just thought you got lonesome; we all do, you know."

We talked for a long while after that rather shaky beginning. He was born on a ship on the Atlantic when his parents were coming over from England in 1872. He had been an architect and had traveled widely all over the world. His wife had been dead for 50 years; he never remarried, and he had lived in a single room in a downtown hotel and had eaten all his meals in restaurants until his admission to the county hospital. "I have no family. I have lived alone for the past 15 years in a hotel room," he said softly. He also said how much he missed the fried potatoes served in restaurants.

He asked the staff to move his bed so that he could look out the window as well as into the hallway; the importance of a window to a patient became apparent once again to me. I had learned the importance of a view of the outside world from a middle-aged woman with multiple sclerosis who had her bed placed in the dining room so that she could see the front door, the front yard, and also the back yard, where a hummingbird had built a nest. As the world shrinks for the aged, and especially those who are bedridden, we must not forget the importance of windows to the outside world.

When I asked Mr. Shirley about getting older, saying that I was a teacher and needed to learn more, he replied, "Getting older is getting older," but he added, "Be young while you can be." He told me that the greatest satisfaction in his own life had been traveling and that the hardest thing he had had to bear was being alone. Later, when I told him what a remarkable person he was, he said, "To most people, I am just an old fossil."

The loneliness and aloneness vividly and succinctly described by this centenarian, plus his lack of "significant others," points up how crucial relationships are to the very old. Unfortunately, this remains a neglected area of study.

Ebersole carried on a one-to-one relationship for 3 years with a woman who was 102 at the beginning of the relationship; she describes this in the following case study.

CASE STUDY OF A 102-YEAR-OLD WOMAN[1]

C. was adopted by a wealthy Southern lady to replace a child who had been abducted by her estranged French husband. In her youth she did not consider herself attractive. She was tall, somewhat angular, and thin, and she had sparse red hair and a large wart on her nose. She played marbles with the boys or turned cartwheels, even though being "ladylike" or "well-bred" was a high priority among females in her day, and one that she clung to.

C.'s foster mother died when C. was 11, and subsequently C. lived with a Hebrew physician and his family until she was married at 16. She had one stillborn child. She was

---

[1] This portion of the chapter was written by Priscilla Ebersole.

widowed at 29; her husband was killed in a buffalo stampede in Africa. She then went to school in the North and learned culinary arts. She came to the West Coast and owned a restaurant for 20 years; then she maintained a small store for 30 years. At that point, her work was interrupted by her failing vision. For 17 years she had very poor vision, but she regained her sight following surgery. She rented an apartment until she was hospitalized in a nursing home at the age of 97.

C. was a true Southern belle with all the dignity and gentility associated with that role. Traditionally, she was sheltered from the vice and vulgarities of the world, to which she was exposed only vicariously when a "Yankee" dared stray into the Southland. She had a strong sense of what was proper and of the qualities that indicate "breeding" in a person. She maintained stereotyped attitudes toward regional and ethnic differences in people as she spoke, but in practice she was always sensitive to each person's uniqueness; *nevertheless, her stereotypes did seem to keep things in order for her.*

Her adoptive mother had clear memories of the glorious South before the Civil War, and she instilled all the marvels of those days into C. The Civil War was described by C. as the "revolutionary war"; I thought she was confused about the wars until I learned that Southerners viewed the Civil War as revolutionary.

She attributed her long life to a natural diet, a lot of sun-ripened fruits and vegetables, chicken, pork, and very little beef. She felt her diet and her "trust in God" carried her through life. Her faith was strong. At the age of 4, she discovered God, and her mother expected her to solve her own problems; she continued to do so throughout her entire life. She never smoked, drank, or did anything to excess. She often said she "never worked hard," but it seemed to me that she did work hard in her life. She often spoke of her early years in the South, where women had no rights except those protected by their menfolk. A woman was expected to be refined, dignified, and enduring. If conditions were intolerable, a brother might shoot his sister's abominable husband, but there was no legal recourse for a woman to protect herself.

Her owlish appearance was due to iridectomies, cataract surgery, and thick-lensed glasses and was further accentuated by an editor's shade that she wore whenever I met with her. This was a most effective way of reducing the glare that is so bothersome to those who have had cataracts removed and was another example of C.'s unusual problem-solving ability.[2]

C.'s hands showed the patina of age; they constantly fluttered as if to compensate for the limitations in her life, like the hummingbird that occasionally strayed to her window. There were no arthritic distortions in her hands—only a translucency that revealed veins, tendons, and, almost, bones. When I held her hands, they quieted some; perhaps I held them too tightly as I feared this century of experience, love, and wisdom would slip from my grasp before I could fully comprehend it.

C. monitored her body functions and her food intake carefully. She heeded each signal for added rest or lowered food intake. She ate very small meals out of tidbits she prepared from things her "girls" and I brought her. Most of the hospital meals she gave to the

[2] It is not uncommon for elderly persons who cannot tolerate glare to don green visors. Perhaps they should be made more readily available and attractive. I.M.B.

"help." In turn, she had several staff members bring her special things she requested. Since she had only three teeth that did not meet, she had to cut all her food into tiny pieces; *yet this was one of the rituals of each meal that she seemed to enjoy.*

Content of the Interviews

During our weekly visits, C. reminisced about half the time and spent the remainder telling me all that went on in the facility, though she never left her bed except to shuffle gingerly to the bathroom. I asked her how she knew what was going on, but she never really said. I suspected that she functioned as "Mother Superior" for many of the help and pumped a lot of information out of them. She had a great sense of control over her everyday affairs, but paradoxically she felt that her destiny had always been "in the hands of the Lord"; however, she kept her cane within reach, and I was convinced that she would use it if she felt called upon to do so.

   C. sat serenely in the middle of her worldly possessions, which were stacked around three sides of her bed. She wore a flowered flannel nightgown and a sweater on most occasions; several large safety pins on the nightgown suggested neglect or lack of concern about appearance. If she knew you very well, she might tell you that they held a few dollar bills pinned to the inside of her gown— the only place they were safe. And indeed, in spite of her frail, owlish appearance, she was perfectly secure against physical intrusion. Her hand-carved cane and her aristocratic demeanor effectively protected her small territory and person. A physician told her he would have to restrain her if she did not cease getting up during the night. She promptly retorted, "You and who else, young man?" She told me numerous times how much confidence she had in this "bright young Hebrew doctor," but I suspected that he did not know how much of her self-concept depended upon her ability to remain continent during the night.

Traumas in Her Life

The worst traumas in C.'s life were the death of her adoptive mother when she was 11 and the loss of her stillborn infant the year after her marriage. (See Chapter 26, which discusses grief in late life.) Her greatest loss was the loss of her mother, and her greatest thrill came when her sight was restored. She alluded once to a less concrete loss when she said she had never known what it was like to be a "young girl in love." She said, "My husband was a friend of my mother's and wanted to take care of me." He was gone most of the time with the British Foreign Service, and she had been prepared by his long absences for the ultimate absence when he was killed. Later she quite openly discussed matters of sexuality. She spoke of her first sexual experience with her husband and related her surprise that such activities were carried on, although she understood that sex was necessary for the health of her husband and also to have children. See her comments on sexuality on page 593.

   C. rarely spoke of money, but she made it clear that she paid for her stay in the facility, having contributed to social security since 1935. She enjoyed discussing politics but felt that women should not dabble in it because "they don't have the centuries of experience in the field that men have."

Education

C. never admitted feeling self-doubt or regret. Her major disappointment (alluded to only obliquely) seemed to be her lack of formal education. She learned the basics of the three R's and continued throughout her life to learn about anything that crossed her path. She had opinions on everything, and I could not introduce an idea that she would not comment on—often with great insight. She was an avid reader and devoured about a book a day, everything from *Eleanor and Franklin* to some of the ribald paperbacks on the market. The radio was her avenue to current events.

Gifts

Even with her limited supply of material goods, C. often gave me a present; a few lemons from the "girls' " tree, a book, or a magazine of interest. (See Chapter 22 for a similar account of gift giving from a limited supply.) I suspect that the small things I brought her were also rerouted in the most advantageous manner, and thus she was always in the process of both giving and receiving. It was a delight to see how she could manipulate the few things in her life so that they would give her the most pleasure and satisfaction.

Perception of Time

C. had a different conception of time from mine. Time tended to flow together for her, and sometimes it was difficult for me to determine the chronology of events in her life. (I have often found this fluid sense of time in the very aged, and it leads me to speculate on the validity of a linear time concept when applied to such an extended life-span.)

When I tried to construct the continuity over her life-span, several threads appeared very early and were clearly woven throughout, but there were also distinct phases that seemed quite unrelated in many ways. Her earliest memories showed a strong tendency to take care of herself both physically and emotionally.

Privacy

C. had a strong sense of privacy, and yet throughout our relationship she shared the most intimate details of her life with great candor. I perceived a change in some of her attitudes that I had thought were quite fixed. For example, once I nearly fell out of my chair when this very proper lady said that if she had it to do over, she would not have married but would have just lived with a man. Then she quickly added that no Southern lady would do such a thing, and so she would have had to "go up North" to do it.

Threads of independence, dignity, and some aloofness emerged in all the stories of C.'s life. She seemed always to have been extremely healthy, to have had a good wit and a quick mind, and to have accepted life quite matter-of-factly. (Wit was commented on by Benet [1976] also.)

C. had no pictures of herself or her family or any personally meaningful articles from her past; they had all been lost in a fire years ago. In spite of being relatively isolated and having no living family, no descendants, little money, only a few possessions, and just enough mobility to shuffle slowly to the bathroom, C. lived a full life and had 100 years of vivid memories and three good friends whom she called her "girls." (The importance of confidantes to centenarians should be noted here.) They were in their seventies and eighties and lived in the apartment she had rented before she was institutionalized.

Faith

C. said she never lost faith in God or herself, knowing her life was in his care. She believed that death is a friend offering peace and oneness; she was ready to die and lived each moment of her life. She believed in a spiritual life and toyed with ideas of reincarnation. She had always been receptive to the possibility of spiritual contact with her mother but never had any sensation that it occurred during our relationship.

One of the Elite

C. was definitely one of the elite—her age, health, attitudes, and remembrances were extraordinary. When we talked, I acquired new bits of knowledge, gained a new understanding of myself and others, and felt a replenished sense of wonder. What was the vitality she embodied? Where did it originate? I saw C. laugh with delight, entertain others, and express anxiety over changes in her routine. A couple of times she admitted, retrospectively, that a room-mate nearly had her "beside herself" and that she thought she might not be able to hang on. I never saw C. cry. It was hard to sort out the most relevant things about this remarkable lady, but it seemed that her sense of trust (while maintaining control), her constant interest in everything and everyone, and her awareness of her own body are a few of the characteristics that sustained her so well. What can I say about C. beyond describing her? After 3 years of consistent visiting, I still only skimmed the surface of her life.

The known theories concerning centenarians were all exemplified in C., but there were also elusive qualities that I have been unable to capture in words or on film; I am filled with awe when I think of her. She was a study in history and humanity and a warm lady; I will miss her greatly when she goes.

The following are statements from C.'s taped interviews:

- "If it's me or the other fella, the other fella can go, I'm going to take care of myself."
- "I love all people—and that is hard to do, you know!"

- "The older I get, the more I attract young people."
- Talking about her lack of education: "I loved books. The harder they were, the more I loved them."
- Talking about coping: "The ability to cope comes from being still and listening. When I was blind, I really listened to what was going on around me."
- "I'm strong-minded—and pretty strong in body—and I have my cane."
- "My mother wouldn't have a deck of cards in the house—she said they were evil. I can laugh about it now. My mother would turn over in her grave if she knew I was laughing at her."

Ebersole's detailed description of C. reminds me of a sonnet by Rilke (p. 39):

Though the world changes as fast
as cloud shapes manifold,
All things perfected at last
fall back to the very old.

LIFE EXPECTANCY

The reader may wish to look at Table 23-1 and calculate his or her own life expectancy.

The study of centenarians has become a fascinating field for some professionals in gerontology. Neophytes in the field of gerontology may find working with centenarians too anxiety-provoking. As one student quite candidly said, "I'm afraid to touch them; they seem so frail and fragile."

A GERIATRIC NURSE'S OBSERVATIONS

Ross made the following observations about the centenarians she cared for during her many years of nursing:

(1) They usually are strong-willed; (2) They will talk about being useless, but will fight to reach their next birthday; (3) Their hearing and sight may be diminished but they usually rally to what is stimulating; (4) Many centenarians are interested in meeting and knowing someone of the same age; (5) Many are very proud to reach 100; (6) Many are witty; and (7) Many still have strong feelings.

Kalish reported that in her visiting nurse case load in the Kansas City area there is one client aged 110. There are 10 clients aged 100 to 110. And what was once a case load of aged residents over 65 is now a case load of people over 80.

Concerning aged in Vilcabamba, Ecuador, Davies wrote: "If these old people disappear without our finding some of their secrets, it will be one of the greatest losses to mankind in the history of medical research" (p. 142).

Table 23-1. **Expectation of Life and Mortality Rate at Single Years of Age by Race and Sex, United States, 1975**

| | Expectation of Life in Years | | | | | Mortality Rate per 1000 | | | | |
| | Total | White | | All Other | | Total | White | | All Other | |
Age	Persons	Male	Female	Male	Female	Persons	Male	Female	Male	Female
0	72.5	69.4	77.2	63.6	72.3	16.1	15.9	12.3	26.3	22.2
1	72.7	69.6	77.1	64.4	73.0	1.0	1.0	.8	1.3	1.2
2	71.8	68.6	76.2	63.4	72.1	.8	.8	.6	1.1	1.0
3	70.8	67.7	75.2	62.5	71.1	.6	.6	.5	1.0	.8
4	69.9	66.7	74.3	61.6	70.2	.5	.5	.4	.8	.6
5	68.9	65.7	73.3	60.6	69.2	.4	.5	.4	.7	.5
6	67.9	64.8	72.3	59.7	68.3	.4	.4	.3	.6	.4
7	67.0	63.8	71.3	58.7	67.3	.4	.4	.3	.6	.4
8	66.0	62.8	70.4	57.7	66.3	.3	.4	.2	.5	.3
9	65.0	61.9	69.4	56.8	65.3	.3	.3	.2	.4	.3
10	64.0	60.9	68.4	55.8	64.4	.3	.3	.2	.4	.3
11	63.0	59.9	67.4	54.8	63.4	.3	.3	.2	.4	.3
12	62.0	58.9	66.4	53.8	62.4	.3	.3	.2	.5	.3
13	61.1	57.9	65.4	52.9	61.4	.4	.5	.3	.7	.4
14	60.1	57.0	64.5	51.9	60.4	.6	.8	.3	.9	.4
15	59.1	56.0	63.5	50.9	59.5	.8	1.0	.4	1.1	.5
16	58.2	55.1	62.5	50.0	58.5	.9	1.3	.5	1.3	.6
17	57.2	54.1	61.5	49.1	57.5	1.1	1.5	.6	1.6	.7
18	56.3	53.2	60.6	48.1	56.6	1.2	1.7	.6	2.0	.8
19	55.3	52.3	59.6	47.2	55.6	1.2	1.8	.6	2.4	.8
20	54.4	51.4	58.6	46.3	54.7	1.3	1.8	.6	2.8	.9
21	53.5	50.5	57.7	45.5	53.7	1.4	1.9	.6	3.2	1.0
22	52.6	49.6	56.7	44.6	52.8	1.4	2.0	.6	3.5	1.1
23	51.6	48.7	55.7	43.8	51.8	1.4	1.9	.6	3.8	1.2
24	50.7	47.8	54.8	42.9	50.9	1.4	1.9	.6	3.9	1.3
25	49.8	46.9	53.8	42.1	49.9	1.4	1.8	.6	4.1	1.3
26	48.8	45.9	52.8	41.3	49.0	1.4	1.7	.6	4.3	1.4
27	47.9	45.0	51.9	40.4	48.1	1.4	1.7	.6	4.4	1.4
28	47.0	44.1	50.9	39.6	47.1	1.4	1.6	.7	4.5	1.5
29	46.0	43.2	49.9	38.8	46.2	1.4	1.6	.7	4.5	1.5
30	45.1	42.2	49.0	38.0	45.3	1.4	1.6	.7	4.5	1.6
31	44.2	41.3	48.0	37.1	44.4	1.4	1.6	.8	4.6	1.7
32	43.2	40.4	47.0	36.3	43.4	1.5	1.7	.8	4.7	1.8
33	42.3	39.4	46.1	35.5	42.5	1.6	1.7	.9	4.9	2.0
34	41.4	38.5	45.1	34.6	41.6	1.7	1.8	1.0	5.2	2.2
35	40.4	37.6	44.2	33.8	40.7	1.8	2.0	1.0	5.6	2.4
36	39.5	36.6	43.2	33.0	39.8	1.9	2.1	1.1	5.9	2.6
37	38.6	35.7	42.3	32.2	38.9	2.1	2.3	1.2	6.3	2.9

Table 23-1. **Expectation of Life and Mortality Rate at Single Years of Age by Race and Sex, United States, 1975** (*Continued*)

	Expectation of Life in Years					Mortality Rate per 1000				
	Total	White		All Other		Total	White		All Other	
Age	Persons	Male	Female	Male	Female	Persons	Male	Female	Male	Female
38	37.6	34.8	41.3	31.4	38.0	2.3	2.5	1.3	6.7	3.1
39	36.7	33.9	40.4	30.6	37.1	2.5	2.7	1.5	7.0	3.4
40	35.8	33.0	39.4	29.8	36.2	2.7	2.9	1.7	7.4	3.7
41	34.9	32.1	38.5	29.0	35.4	2.9	3.2	1.9	7.9	4.0
42	34.0	31.2	37.6	28.3	34.5	3.2	3.6	2.1	8.4	4.3
43	33.1	30.3	36.6	27.5	33.6	3.5	4.0	2.3	8.9	4.7
44	32.2	29.4	35.7	26.8	32.8	3.9	4.4	2.5	9.5	5.1
45	31.4	28.5	34.8	26.0	32.0	4.3	4.9	2.7	10.1	5.6
46	30.5	27.7	33.9	25.3	31.1	4.7	5.4	3.0	10.8	6.1
47	29.6	26.8	33.0	24.5	30.3	5.1	6.0	3.2	11.5	6.6
48	28.8	26.0	32.1	23.8	29.5	5.6	6.6	3.5	12.4	7.1
49	27.9	25.1	31.2	23.1	28.7	6.0	7.3	3.9	13.4	7.5
50	27.1	24.3	30.3	22.4	27.9	6.6	8.0	4.2	14.5	7.9
51	26.3	23.5	29.5	21.7	27.2	7.2	8.8	4.6	15.6	8.4
52	25.5	22.7	28.6	21.1	26.4	7.8	9.6	5.0	16.8	9.0
53	24.7	21.9	27.7	20.4	25.6	8.5	10.6	5.4	18.0	9.8
54	23.9	21.2	26.9	19.8	24.9	9.2	11.6	5.9	19.3	10.6
55	23.1	20.4	26.0	19.2	24.1	10.0	12.6	6.4	20.7	11.6
56	22.3	19.7	25.2	18.6	23.4	10.9	13.8	6.9	22.1	12.5
57	21.6	18.9	24.4	18.0	22.7	11.8	15.1	7.5	23.6	13.6
58	20.8	18.2	23.5	17.4	22.0	13.0	16.6	8.2	25.3	14.7
59	20.1	17.5	22.7	16.8	21.3	14.2	18.4	8.9	27.0	15.9
60	19.4	16.8	21.9	16.3	20.7	15.6	20.3	9.8	29.0	17.3
61	18.7	16.2	21.2	15.8	20.0	17.0	22.3	10.7	31.1	18.8
62	18.0	15.5	20.4	15.2	19.4	18.4	24.3	11.5	32.9	19.8
63	17.3	14.9	19.6	14.7	18.8	19.6	26.3	12.3	34.1	20.2
64	16.6	14.3	18.8	14.2	18.2	20.8	28.3	13.1	35.0	20.3
65	16.0	13.7	18.1	13.7	17.5	22.0	30.3	13.9	35.5	19.8
66	15.3	13.1	17.3	13.2	16.9	23.3	32.6	14.9	36.3	19.8
67	14.7	12.5	16.6	12.7	16.2	25.1	35.1	16.2	38.2	21.2
68	14.0	12.0	15.9	12.2	15.5	27.4	38.1	17.9	41.9	24.8
69	13.4	11.4	15.1	11.7	14.9	30.2	41.5	19.9	47.1	30.1
70	12.8	10.9	14.4	11.3	14.4	33.2	45.2	22.2	53.3	36.4
71	12.3	10.4	13.7	10.9	13.9	36.4	49.1	24.6	59.6	42.5
72	11.7	9.9	13.1	10.5	13.5	39.8	53.3	27.4	65.3	47.8
73	11.2	9.4	12.4	10.2	13.2	43.5	57.8	30.6	69.6	51.2
74	10.6	9.0	11.8	10.0	12.8	47.3	62.8	34.2	72.4	53.0
75	10.2	8.5	11.2	9.7	12.5	51.4	68.1	38.3	74.5	54.1

Table 23-1. Expectation of Life and Mortality Rate at Single Years of Age by Race and Sex, United States, 1975 (*Continued*)

	Expectation of Life in Years					Mortality Rate per 1000				
	Total	White		All Other		Total	White		All Other	
Age	Persons	Male	Female	Male	Female	Persons	Male	Female	Male	Female
76	9.7	8.1	10.6	9.5	12.2	55.9	73.8	42.6	76.6	55.0
77	9.2	7.7	10.1	9.2	11.9	60.6	79.9	47.1	79.2	56.6
78	8.8	7.4	9.6	9.0	11.6	65.6	86.3	52.0	82.7	58.9
79	8.4	7.0	9.1	8.7	11.3	71.0	93.1	57.2	86.7	61.6
80	8.0	6.7	8.6	8.5	11.0	76.7	100.1	62.8	90.7	64.2
81	7.6	6.4	8.1	8.3	10.7	82.6	107.3	68.9	93.5	65.7
82	7.2	6.1	7.7	8.1	10.4	88.6	114.3	75.6	93.6	64.7
83	6.9	5.8	7.3	7.8	10.1	94.5	120.7	83.1	88.4	59.5
84	6.5	5.5	6.9	7.5	9.6	100.0	125.6	91.7	74.8	48.1
85	6.2	5.2	6.5	7.1	9.1					

Source: National Center for Health Statistics. Courtesy of the Metropolitan Life Insurance Company.

SUMMARIZING STATEMENTS BASED ON THE LITERATURE

- The age of centenarians may not be properly recorded (U.S. Bureau of the Census).
- The less a population is familiar with written documents, the more unrealistic are the ages reported by the old (McKain).
- Loss of hearing is more gradual than loss of sight (Beard, 1969).
- Loss of hearing is more difficult to adjust to than loss of sight (Beard, 1969).
- Memory decline can be handled by feeling embarrassed or annoyed or by working to retain it (Beard, 1969).
- In the West, memory decline occurs soon after deafness (Davies).
- Most centenarians' earliest memories are of something that happened before the age of 6 (Costa and Kastenbaum).
- A positive self-image is found in aged persons who continue to participate fully in family and community activities (Benet, 1976).
- In Abkhasia, the oldest person is always listed as head of the household, regardless of contributions (Benet, 1976).
- Sleep is important to centenarians (Davies).
- Low levels of stress are an important factor in longevity (Benet, 1976; Davies).
- Isolation from viruses is important for longevity (Comfort).
- Wit is observed in centenarians (Benet, 1976; Ross).

GUIDELINES FOR INTERVENTION

- Check on the person's age. One way to do this is to ask about the historical events he or she remembers occurring at various ages.

Figure 23-4 These lines by Jacobsen (p. 57) might well apply to centenarians and to the centenarian in the photo above:

With nothing to gain, perhaps, and no
sane reason
To put up a fight, they grip and hang by
the thread
As fierce and still as a swinging threatened
spider.
They are too brave to say, It is simpler
to be dead.

(From Josephine Jacobsen, "Let Each Man Remember," The Shade Seller, Doubleday & Company, New York, 1964. Copyright 1964 by Doubleday & Company, reprinted with permission. Photo courtesy of Lu Gay.)

- Check vision problems carefully. The centenarian's eyes may not have been examined recently.
- Check hearing problems, since loss of hearing isolates the aged. Check especially for cerumen (wax) in the ears.
- Carefully survey the multiple losses, including material losses, that the person may have suffered.
- Check on memory loss and assist with "memory joggers." Try to make the aged person feel less embarrassed about memory loss (Beard, 1969).
- Check on energy level, especially when interviewing and when the person is performing a task requiring physical exertion.

- Check sleep habits.
- Assess the level of mobility.
- Consider the importance of maintaining continence (Ebersole).
- Consider interventions to improve self-esteem (Ross; Shirley).
- Remember that many centenarians regret their lack of formal education. Determine whether they still have unmet learning needs.
- Create opportunities, if possible, for them to meet other centenarians (Ross).
- Listen for a different perception of time from yours (Ebersole).
- Appreciate the wit of centenarians and give them feedback.
- Consider the strong feelings that may still exist in the very, very old (Ross). Encourage expression of such feelings.
- Remember that exchanging gifts can bring pleasure and satisfaction (Ebersole).
- Cater to food preferences; allow centenarians to monitor their food intake and body functions (Ebersole).
- Watch for important rituals, such as a food ritual (Ebersole).
- Consider the need for a view of the outside world.
- Remember that centenarians' stereotypes may help keep things in order for them (Ebersole).
- Consider the use of touch.
- Do not be surprised if you feel great awe when in their presence.

REFERENCES

Beard, Belle Boone: "Survival Traits: Adaptive Intelligence of Centenarians," *Proceedings of the Seventh International Congress of Gerontology,* Vienna, **6:** 233–236, 1966.

———: *Social Competence of Centenarians,* University of Georgia, Social Science Research Institute, Athens, 1967.

———: "Some Characteristics of Recent Memory of Centenarians," *Journal of Gerontology,* **23**(1):23–30, 1968.

———: "Sensory Decline in Very Old Age," *Gerontologica Clinica,* **11**(3): 149–158, 1969.

Benet, Sula: *The Long-Living People of the Caucasus,* Holt, New York, 1974.

———: *How to Live to Be 100: The Life-Span of the People of the Caucasus,* Dial, New York, 1976.

Braverman, A. M.: "Report on the Life and Death of a Woman 101 Years of Age," *Gerontologica Clinica,* **7**(6):365–369, 1965.

Comfort, Alexander: *A Good Age,* Crown, New York, 1976.

Costa, Paul, and **Robert Kastenbaum:** "Some Aspects of Memories and Ambitions in Centenarians," *The Journal of Genetic Psychology,* **110:**3–16, 1967.

Davies, David: *The Centenarians of the Andes,* Anchor Books, Doubleday, Garden City, N.Y., 1975.

Dunbar, Flanders: "Immunity to Afflictions of Old Age," *Journal of the Amer-*

ican Geriatrics Society, **5**(12):982–996, 1957.

Ebersole, Priscilla: Process recordings of a three-year one-to-one relationship, 1977.

Franke, H., H. Bracharz, H. Laas, and **E. Moll:** "A Study of the Mental and Physical Condition of 148 Centenarians," *Deutsche Medizinische Wochenschrift,* **95**(31):1590–1594, 1970.

Ingersoll, Norman: *Saturday Evening Post,* Apr. 18, 1936, quoted in Walter G. Bowerman, "Centenarians," *Transactions of the Actuarial Society of America,* **40**(102): 378, 1936.

Jacobsen, Josephine: *The Shade Sellers,* Doubleday, Garden City, N.Y., 1974.

Jewett, Stephen P.: "Longevity and the Longevity Syndrome," *The Gerontologist,* **13**(1):91–99, 1973.

Kalish, Marjorie: Speech given at A Regional Symposium on Aging: The Flip Side of 50, Overland Park, Kan., Sept. 20, 1977.

Leaf, Alexander: "Every Day Is a Gift when You Are Over 100," *National Geographic,* **143**(1):93–119, 1973.

————: *Youth in Old Age,* McGraw-Hill, New York, 1975.

Lerner, Joseph: "The Centenarians: Some Findings and Concepts Regarding the Aged, *Journal of the American Geriatric Society,* **17**(4):429–432, 1969.

McKain, Walter C.: "Are They Really That Old?" *The Gerontologist,* **7**(1):70–72, 1967.

Metropolitan Life Statistical Bulletin, May 1977, pp. 10–11.

Rilke, Rainer Maria: *Sonnets to Orpheus,* tr. by C. F. MacIntyre, University of California Press, Berkeley, Calif., 1960.

Ross, Harriet: Process recording for class, "Emotional Problems of the Aged," Ethel Percy Andrus Gerontology Center, University of Southern California, Los Angeles, Oct. 2, 1975.

Schuster, Daniel B.: "A Psychological Study of a 106-Year-Old Man: A Contribution to Dynamic Concepts of Aging and Dementia," *American Journal of Psychology,* **109**(2):112–119, 1852.

Shirley, Guy: Personal communication, 1975.

Siegel, Jacob S., and **Jeffry S. Passell:** "Alternative Approaches to the Estimation of the Number of Centenarians in the United States," *Proceedings of the American Statistical Association,* 1975.

U. S. Bureau of the Census: *1970 Census of Population and Housing, Evaluation and Research Program,* PHC(E)-11, *Accuracy of Data for Selected Population Characteristics as Measured by the 1970 CPS-Census Match,* January 1975.

Woodruff, Diana: "Can You Live to Be 100?" *Handbook, Hawaii Governor's Bicentennial Conference on Aging,* Honolulu, June 1976.

Young, T. E.: *On Centenarians,* Layton, London, 1905.

Zitter, Meyer: Letter to Chief of Population Division, U. S. Bureau of the Census, Apr. 30, 1976.

OTHER RESOURCES

FILMS

Aging: The Search for Eternal Youth: 22 min/16 mm/color. Discusses the problems of aging and considers possibilities for control and even reversal of the aging process.

Distributor: Document Associates, Inc., 880 Third Avenue, New York, N.Y. 10022. *The Autobiography of Miss Jane Pittman:* 110 min/color/1974. The story of Jane Pittman, covering her experiences as a 10-year-old slave on a Louisiana plantation, her freedom after the war, the horrors of Reconstruction, her happy but brief marriage, and the martyrdom of a foster son who grew up to lead his people. At age 110 she rose to a supreme moment in a civil rights protest march. Winner of several Emmy awards. Director: John Korty. Producers: Robert Christiansen and Rick Rosenberg. Distributor: Learning Corporation of America, 1350 Avenue of the Americas, New York, N.Y. 10019.

I Can't Quit: 30 min/16 mm/color/1976. A film about a 101-year-old woman who is a whirlwind of activity. She designs and sews her own clothes, makes fancy ties for the gentlemen in her neighborhood, and enjoys playing pinochle with her neighbors. Distributor: The Resource Center, Indiana Committee for the Humanities, 4200 Northwestern Avenue, Indianapolis, Ind. 46208.

A Man Named Charlie Smith: 26 min/b&w/ 1965. Shows the history of slavery and the black man in America through the memories of 120-year-old Charlie Smith, who was brought to America on a slave ship in 1854. Charlie's humor and wisdom help put the country's history into perspective. Narrated by James Whitmore. Distributor: MacMillan Films–Audio Branden, 1619 North Cherokee, Hollywood, Calif. 90028.

To a Good, Long Life: 20 min/color. Portraits of three elderly people living vigorous, interesting lives: a hod carrier, a Japanese-American artist and teacher, and an articulate and congenial poet. Distributor: BFA Educational Media, 2211 Michigan Avenue, Santa Monica, Calif. 90404.

To Live to 140: Extending Our Biological Limits: 24 min/color/1976. Examines a society in the high Andes of Ecuador in which it is common to live to 100 or more. Interviews reveal these centenarians to be physically vigorous, sexually active, and maintaining a useful role in the community. Includes a discussion with Dr. Alexander Leaf, a specialist in gerontology at Harvard University. Producer: Hobel-Leiterman. Distributor: Document Associates, Inc., 880 Third Avenue, New York, N.Y. 10022.

Valley of the Old Ones: 26 min/color/1974. Takes the viewer to the tiny valley of Vilcabamba, Ecuador, where birth records prove that 10 of the residents are over 100 years and reveal the Old Ones of Vilcabamba to be the oldest group of people of confirmed age in the world. This fascinating documentary ponders the future of these people as civilization slowly infiltrates their valley. Distributor: Time-Life Multimedia, 100 Eisenhower Drive, Paramus, N.J. 07652.

Chapter 24

SENSORY AND COGNITIVE FUNCTIONING IN LATER LIFE

Irene Mortenson Burnside

> Becoming is superior to being.
>
> *Paul Klee*

This chapter is divided into two sections: the first is about the sensory modalities, the sensory changes in normal aging, and implications for psychosocial care. The second section is about cognitive aspects of aging, with pragmatic implications for care givers.

SENSORY MODALITIES

Senses to be discussed in the order listed in the first half of the chapter, include (1) vision, (2) hearing, (3) touch (also called *the haptic system*), (4) taste, and (5) smell.[1] The senses will be considered as channels of sensation, that is, as means of obtaining information—by listening, smelling, tasting, and touching. A wag once said that there are two more senses, seldom used—common and horse; if gerontologists do not recognize them, the elderly we work with do. As Reid asserted way back in 1785, "The external senses have a double province; to make us feel and to make us perceive" (no page).

The five perceptual systems are not mutually exclusive; they overlap, and two or more systems may focus on the same information or may pick up the same information by working together. The perceptual systems seek to extract infor-

---

[1] The reader is referred to *Sensory Processes and Aging,* a monograph, North State University, Denton, Tex., 1977.

mation about the environment (Gibson). To help the aged person extract adequate information for optimal functioning is a most important task in psychosocial care; unfortunately it is often overlooked.

In 1971, older persons were twice as likely as younger ones to wear glasses and 13 times as likely to use a hearing aid. About 92 percent of persons 65 years old and over wore eyeglasses or contact lenses, and 5 percent used hearing aids (U. S. Department of Health, Education, and Welfare).

Visual Perception

There are adequate expositions of the sense of sight and the anatomy of the eye in other books. The reader is referred to Gibson for a comprehensive scientific explanation of the senses and of visual perception in the aged, and also to Chapter 20 in *Psychology of Aging* (Birren and Schaie). Because visual perception is so important in old age, and so often a problem, more attention will have to be paid to altering environments to permit better accommodations for some of the visual problems of the elderly. An organization called the National Center for a Barrier Free Environment is concerned with improving environments for the handicapped; see Other Resources at the end of this chapter for further information. So far, the organization does not seem to have focused on the special problems of the elderly. See Figure 24-1.

Age Changes in the Eye

Two classes of changes in the eye's structure mediate perceptual functioning differences (Bell; McFarland; Wolf, 1960, 1967). The first age difference, noted in the transmissiveness and accommodative power of the eye, begins to come into importance between the ages of 35 and 45 years. The changes affect (1) distance vision, (2) sensitivity to glare, (3) binocular depth perception, and (4) color sensitivity. Changes in the second class concern the retina and the nervous system, and begin to be important between the years 55 and 65. Changes in the circulation affect the metabolism of the retina. These aging processes cause (1) changes in the size of the visual field, (2) sensitivity to low quantities of light, and (3) sensitivity to flicker.

Care givers should be acquainted with three common eye diseases which may occur in the older person: (1) cataracts, (2) glaucoma, and (3) macular degeneration.

Cataracts

A cataract is an opacity of the lens that impairs vision. Though 90 percent of cataracts are found in older persons, their incidence in persons over 65 years of age is not high. Anderson and Palmore reported low incidences of glaucoma in subjects 60 to 80 years of age. Cataracts in both eyes used to be removed at the same time. The patient was subsequently placed on bedrest, with sandbags at each side of the head, and had to be fed by a nurse or attendant. A state of

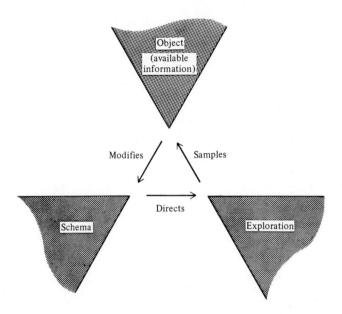

Figure 24-1 Neisser's visual perceptual cycle consists of the following steps: (1) exploration—by moving eyes, head, or body; (2) anticipating schemata, i.e., readiness plans for particular kinds of optical structures; (3) modification of original anticipating scheme by information; (4) further exploration for more information. Neisser makes the important point, "We develop a different (though perhaps overlapping) set of anticipations; we pick up information that extends over a different span of time; we do not use the information for the same purposes ..." (p. 22). (*Reprinted with permission from* Cognition and Reality: Principles and Implications of Cognitive Psychology, *by Ulric Neisser, W. H. Freeman and Company, San Francisco, Copyright 1976.*)

sensory deprivation was created, and subsequently patients were often confused and disoriented; hence, the name "black patch tremens." Now when both eyes are affected, surgery is performed on one eye at a time. Cataracts are sometimes treated today with laser beams.

Case Example

Mr. S. is 92 years of age. He lives in an apartment with a 72 year old man. Mr. S. has a hearing problem and he had recently undergone cataract surgery and was waiting for his new glasses. However, he showed marked concern about going blind. Mr. S. showed me around his apartment and made several references to his preparation for blindness. For example, in the kitchen he opened a drawer and showed how he had the knives, forks, and spoons in certain places so he could pick up a butcher knife "with his eyes closed." Mr. S. boils all the water he drinks because he doesn't like the taste of tap water. He demonstrated the method he uses for boiling water in a large pan and stated that even a "blind man" could do it. In the bedroom, the bureau drawers were arranged so that he could pick out a pair of socks "without looking." This man appeared to be a very independent person, and he was prepared to maintain his independence even if blindness struck (Thompson, 1977).

Glaucoma

It has been suggested that the increased opacity in the lens occurring in glaucoma is the primary cause of increasing sensitivity to glares, mentioned earlier. Glaucoma, caused by excessively high intraocular pressure, is not intrinsically related to the aging process. The type of glaucoma which occurs in old age is gradual in onset. The best protection against this disease is to have a thorough eye examination which includes tonometry.

Macular Degeneration

Macular degeneration is another eye disease that creates problems and is not curable. Senile macular degeneration is a baffling disease. The macula is a very small area in diameter, located in the retina. It is responsible for sharp, or "central," vision. A damaged macula does not mean total blindness, but it prevents the aged person from reading, doing close work, or identifying people until they are very close. Senile macular degeneration is common. About 30 percent of all the aged have some macular involvement (Kornzweig, 1965; Kornzweig, Feldstein, and Schneider, 1959).

Geometrical Illusions

Although illusions based on misperceptions of the environment are discussed in Chapter 28 and in *Nursing and the Aged* (Burnside, 1976), it is well to mention here that there is no satisfactory theory of illusions at this time, hence no systematic classification of them. Consistent age-related differences regarding illusions in adulthood have been reported by some researchers. Some concluded that susceptibility to the illusions is greater in childhood and old age than in the young and middle years (Wagner, Werner, and Comalli). Gajo found that if he used the same stimuli and procedures, there was a greater susceptibility to illusions in men and women aged 60 to 77 than in the two younger groups 30 to 44 and 45 to 59 years of age. Eisner and Schaie found that susceptibility to such illusions increased in males ranging in age from 55 to 75. Fozard and Thomas (1975) hypothesized that older persons "are more susceptible to the effects of unusual variations in stimulus configurations than are younger ones." Practitioners agree with Fozard and Thomas.

The most ignored aspect of vision and one of the most important aspects of vision problems, other than prevention through regular eye checkups, is the level of illumination provided older persons. This is one of the most difficult design problems to tackle in providing suitable and enhancing environments for the aged. See the chapter by Newcomer and Caggiano, "Environment and the

Figure 24-2 The importance of corrected lens in glasses, properly fitted and clean, has to be recognized in psychosocial care of the elderly person. (*Courtesy of Diane Miller.*)

Aged Person,'' in *Nursing and the Aged* (Burnside, 1976). Guth and also Weston have shown that the level of lighting required by elderly persons for a variety of tasks is greater than that needed by younger people, but the elderly also are sensitive to glare, as mentioned previously.

In some situations, the older person just cannot benefit from increased lighting. I once discovered this when I pulled open the patio draperies during a group meeting of old persons, and was promptly reminded that more light and glare are the wrong combination! A good basic principle to remember in environmental design for the average older person is that the design should be geared to the older eye, not to the average younger one (McFarland; Fozard and Thomas, 1973). (Restaurant owners might take note.) It will take some doing to reach a point at which we constantly shape environments and plan designs for old eyes, especially if the plans are drawn by young hands. The incidence of blindness and its attendant problems show that they are increased in the older age groups. Unfortunately, few clinical studies deal with counseling the blind aged, and how best to help them. See Other Resources at the end of this chapter for catalogs on working with the blind. As a parting thought, who among us has ever seen a very old person with a seeing-eye dog?

Speech

Speech perception in a noisy environment will improve markedly if the listener sees the speaker (Sumby and Pollack). This is common knowledge but is poorly heeded by those who give care to the aged.

It should be noted here that what takes place during speech is accessible to still another modality—touch—if the "listener" places his or her hand over the speaker's lips and cheeks, as demonstrated in the Tadome method of communicating with the deaf, which can provide at least some understanding of speech in the absence of both hearing and vision (Alcorn). Though I have not observed this method being used with the aged, there is no reason why we cannot try something like this in working with the sensorially impoverished old person.

Touch

The haptic system, rarely identified by that term, is more commonly called *touch*. The word "haptic" is derived from a Greek term meaning "able to lay hold of." There is nothing in the haptic system quite like the image on the retina which is the input for studies about vision. Neisser says (in scientific jargon), "In active touch there are only continuously changing deformations of the skin, positions of the joints, velocities of the moving limbs, and other complexities" (p. 25). In the study of the aged it is forever the "other complexities" which trip us up. Active touch is much more difficult to study than vision and hearing because it cannot be imposed on a subject. Perhaps if we understand touch too well, it will lose some of its power and mystery and beauty. For a fleeting glance at that power and mystique, the reader is referred to a beautiful film called "The Mortal Body" (see Other Resources at the end of the chapter).

The therapeutic effectiveness of touch with the aged has been little studied. Nurses, though they are known for laying-on of hands, have not researched the subject thoroughly. What few studies exist on touch do not focus on the aged. Touch as a psychosocial intervention is covered in more detail in Chapter 29.

Da Silva, in a detailed account of long-term psychoanalysis with an 81-year-old man, describes one client's need for touch during the therapy hours.

Smell and Taste

"The sense of smell is more than smelling external things, such as pigs on the breeze, or the sense of taste is less than tasting what we eat" (Gibson, p. 136). Smell, says Gibson, is aroused both by sniffing the air and by food in the mouth. Taste is aroused only by the food, not by its aroma. (Old people in nursing homes have known that for a long while, I suspect.) Smell therefore has a dual role—to sniff the air and to aid in savoring food. Titchener said that when we are eating we constantly make the mistake of "attributing to taste what really belongs to smell" (p. 115).

Taste "is a major perceptual system," says Gibson, and "a principle concern of life for many persons" (p. 137). Observing the obesity problems in our country, one wonders if it is not the principal perceptual system for a good many Americans. Regarding smell, Pieron wrote, "Thanks to a scent created by a perfume manufacturer, a woman will be able to express her own individuality which other persons will be able to recognize in this way. This will make it possible to distinguish from all others the traces of her passing, and it will guide the admirer following in her wake" (p. 187). The man was a renowned physiologist of the senses, and as Gibson slyly adds, "he was also a Frenchman."

But men, too, are now being traced by colognes. Those who have worked in small offices can attest to that. Several years ago, I got bids on renovating my house and about seven workmen came by for estimates. The younger men would be fairly clean or fairly scruffy, but the men in their fifties and sixties were exceptionally well groomed even in their work clothes! They wore much cologne. I found I identified the bids by the smell; the Old Spice was too high, Mennen's was a middle bid, and English Leather was the best bid of all.

In the book, *Men in Middle Years,* the authors state, "Many adults retain into middle age a vivid memory of certain experiences of early childhood—a particular quality of luminosity of visual impression, a richness of sound, a quality of taste or smell of favorite articles of food or a keenness of other bodily sensations that may be lost in adult life" (Soddy and Kidner, p. 387).

The combined senses—taste, smell, touch, and temperature—come into play when food is served to old people. I once watched an old lady fondle a piece of angel food cake I had brought—"so long since I touched a piece of angel food," she said. And I remember the blind man in a wheelchair sniffing his bit of whiskey Christmas cheer from the thermos bottle I had brought. He had once smuggled trucks of whiskey during Prohibition, so it seemed apropos to "smuggle" in his Christmas cheer that year. A shot of whiskey, I found, also quickly tapped his memory, plus the senses.

Hunger, Thirst, and Hydration

Hunger and thirst are not stomach contractions and dryness of the throat, but rather states of the blood, says Gibson. Dehydration is more fundamentally the saltiness of the blood than it is dryness of the throat. The reader is cautioned to promote adequate hydration in the elderly to prevent psychological upsets which readily occur with dehydration and high temperatures. Storrie, who heads a research unit studying men with Alzheimer's disease, stated that malnutrition and inadequate hydration were among the problems of patients being admitted to the unit.

Perception of Objects

Gibson writes about the perception of meaning through a concept he calls "affordance." All the potential uses of objects, that is, the activities they afford, are said to be able to be perceived directly. Neisser points out one difficulty with this formulation, that is, what an object appears to afford—or to mean—depends on who is perceiving it. What an object appears to afford—or to mean—causes great difficulty for the elderly, especially those with chronic brain syndrome. For example, one group leader gave a group of confused elderly persons each a bar of soap to smell. The tiny bar of lemon soap was mistaken for candy by one oldster, who attempted to eat it. Another leader held a small lavalier mike for a woman in a group demonstration; the woman insisted on smelling the mike, which indeed looked like a small silver perfume bottle! Perceiving can be a cyclical activity, as illustrated by Neisser. See the perceptual cycle in Figure 24-1.

The process of assigning objects or stimuli to categories is properly called *pattern recognition;* many theories have resulted from surveys of pattern recognition (Kolers; Reed). How can we help elderly persons with their pattern recognition?

Sensory Deprivation

Mendelson, Kubzansky, Liederman, Wexler, and Solomon discussed the way in which sensory deprivation imposes stress. One subject talked about the different kinds of stress that he faced: (1) Social isolation. The subject discussed his aloneness and the fact that there was no one to talk to. (2) Restriction of movement. He spoke of the physical discomfort due to immobility. (3) Difficulty of abstract thinking. There was nothing to occupy his mind. (4) Difficulty in remaining coherent. He experienced difficulty expressing himself clearly.

It is suggested that a monotonous environment plus social isolation and increased physical immobility do not provide adequate sensory cues, and that there are dimensions of stress in a sensory-deprivation situation.

Redundant Cuing

Organization of space is very important in getting a message through to an individual. Pastalan described this so well: "Through appropriately programmed stimuli, the environment can be made to function as a more effective support network and mitigate to some degree the consequences of sensory losses" (1977, p. 13). The problem is to get the visual, audio, thermal, and olfactory messages through to the receiver. What is suggested here is a design concept called *redundant cuing,* which simply means beaming the same messages through more than one sensory modality. The idea is to load the environment sensorially so that the message overcomes the heightened thresholds of the elderly person's sensory modalities. In this way the environment again becomes a meaningful language, and appropriate responses to it are feasible once more.

> The idea is that in general, a space should have a singular and unambiguous definition and use. Again, the purpose is to compensate with environmental arrangements for lessened sensory acuity. The concept has several important dimensions. In terms of orientation, the spaces are cued with landmarks which act as focal points for functionally different spaces. For example, color coding surfaces to signal functionally different spaces in terms of visual perception, textured surfaces for the tactile sense, and so on. The purpose is to sensorially load the spaces so that they may more effectively serve as points of reference (Pastalan, 1971, pp. 5–6).

A project entitled "Planned Patient/Family Education in Long Term Care," sponsored by the Department of Health, Education, and Welfare, Health Resources Administration, Division of Long Term Care, was conducted from June 30, 1975, to June 30, 1977. Nine workshops were attended by a total of 479 persons, who represented 212 facilities. "It was very apparent that for a significant number of participants the areas of sensory loss and the process of aging were new conceptual material'' (Lovegren, p. 9).

SUMMARIZING STATEMENTS BASED ON THE LITERATURE ABOUT SENSORY MODALITIES

- Visual misperception resulting in illusions is common (see Chapter 27, *Nursing and the Aged* by Burnside, 1976; also Chapter 28, this book).
- Increased opacity in the lens decreases the ability to tolerate glares (multiple sources).
- The level of lighting needed for the aged is greater than that needed by younger persons (Guth; Weston).
- Speech perception is maximized when the listener is able to see the speaker (Sumby and Pollack).
- Effectiveness of touch has been little studied (see Chapter 29, this book).
- Taste is aroused only by food, not by its aroma (Gibson).
- Affordance—the potential use of objects—is important (Gibson).
- Sensory deprivation involves social isolation, restricted movement, immobility, and lack of chance to do abstract thinking (Mendelson et al.).
- Redundant cuing is essential (Pastalan, 1977).
- Space should have a singular use (Pastalan, 1977).
- Testing will be affected by deafness and dysphasia (Caird and Judge).

GUIDELINES FOR INTERVENTION IN SENSORY CHANGES

- Listen for examples of illusions in interviews.
- Observe lighting requirements for tasks.
- Do not place yourself where the elderly person cannot see you.
- Consider use of touch in clinical practice.
- Check diet for overblandness.
- Explain objects in milieu which may be mistaken for other objects, e.g., a microwave oven or a cardiac monitor for a television, a small radio for a nearby toaster, soap for candy, etc.
- To avoid sensory deprivation, prevent social isolation, limited movement, lack of intellectual stimulation.
- Provide an abundance of visual and auditory cues in the environment.
- Space should have a designated use, an area for sleeping, eating, reading, etc.
- Consider deafness and speech problems in all interactions, remembering that deafness creates a proclivity to isolation.

COGNITIVE FUNCTIONING IN LATE LIFE

I approach the topic of cognition in old age with considerable hesitation, since I am not a psychologist. This section will discuss studies which have pragmatic aspects for practice. Cognitive impairments are included because they have received short shrift in psychosocial care of the aged.

Definition. The definition of cognition used here is simple and succinct: "Cognition is the activity of knowing; the acquisition, organization and use of knowledge" (Neisser, p. 2).

Overview of Literature

Research findings in the area of cognitive development indicate that it is much more complex than previously thought (Siegler, 1977). I agree with Siegler that, "the literature in cognitive development is perhaps the richest and most confusing" (p. 100). Literature reviews of cognition and aging include those by Arenberg; Baltes and Louvie; Bayley; Botwinick (1967, 1973); Goulet and Baltes; Jarvik (1973); and Welford and Birren. In doctoral dissertations from 1934 to 1969, Moore and Birren found only a few studies on cognition and aging. However, several years later, Mueller found that 13 had been done on learning and memory; 4 on risk and rigidity; 9 on cognitive processes; and 25 on personality and self-concept.

Four Major Trends in Research

Siegler (1977) listed four major lines of research: (1) Schaie's (1965) developmental model, which has provided a new framework to use in analysis of developmental data. (2) The terminal-drop hypothesis—namely, that cognitive behavior may be stable in adult life until within approximately 5 years before death (Kleemeier; Riegel and Riegel; Wilkie and Eisdorfer, 1974). The terminal-drop phenomenon was also described by Blum, Jarvik, and Clark, and by Jarvik (1975). These researchers suggest that a change takes place in elderly persons which is not related to that chronologic age so much as to time of death, and that this is why the onset varies so widely among individuals. Distance from death is a critical parameter for understanding cognitive changes in the elderly (Kinsbourne and Caplan; Lieberman; Siegler, 1975). Dropouts due to refusal to participate, illness, and lack of mobility may skew the data (Siegler, 1973; Rosenthal and Rosnow). (3) Different types of functioning represent crystallized abilities and fluid abilities (Horn). (4) Observed changes in intelligence may be a function of health/disease, especially untreated high blood pressure, rather than aging (Baer; Wilkie and Eisdorfer, 1973).

All the above findings should influence the health care, both physical and psychosocial, of the elderly. *Prevention of high blood pressure and treatment should be paramount in planning care.*

One important aspect of cognitive functioning discussed in the literature is intellectual functioning, and there is controversy about intellectual decrement as a normal part of the aging process. Findings from long-term longitudinal studies of middle-aged and aged people raise doubts about progressive decline in intellectual and learning ability in old people (Eisdorfer, 1969).

Schaie, a psychologist, has devoted his career to the description of cognitive change over the adult life-span. In his first theoretical exposition, he took a regression view of aging, but now opts for a stability model of cognitive development. He argues that, "the processes which have been documented for the acquisition of cognitive structures and functions in childhood and during the early adult phase may not be relevant to the maintenance of functions and reorganization of structures required to meet the demands of later life" (1977–1978, pp. 130–131).

Five possible adult cognitive stages are (1) acquisitive, (2) achieving, (3) responsible, (4) executive, and (5) reintegrative. In the acquisitive stage, the young person is solving problems in a protected milieu. The achieving stage (late teens to early twenties) requires more progress in the operations connected by Piaget with adolescence. Young adulthood requires more goal orientation. The responsible stage (thirties to early sixties) requires quantitative changes in cognitive function, and a pattern to facilitate integration of long-range goals.

The executive abilities described by Neugarten of persons in their thirties and forties are possessed only by some individuals. For both the responsible and executive stages, new measurement technologies will have to be developed, perhaps borrowing from information processing and systems analysis. The reintegrative stage completes the phase of "What should I know?" through "How should I use what I know?" to "Why should I know?" phase of life.

To study intellectual competence in adulthood and old age, there will have to be valid criteria based on the life context of the old rather than on that of persons in other life phases. See Figure 24-3 for the model presented by Schaie.

Cautiousness

Birkhill and Schaie studied the effects of differential reinforcement of cautiousness in intellectual performance among the elderly. The sample comprised 56 females and 32 males, with a mean age of 73 years. The results suggest that performance requiring intelligence is influenced by variables which have components of motivation in them. These researchers hypothesized "that elderly people may perform poorly on cognitive tasks because of an excessively cautious orientation" (p. 583).

For the practitioner, it is well to remember that what appears to be cautiousness may represent a lack of understanding of what is to be done or what is expected. An example from Steffl and Eide illustrates this point. They write a vignette of an old man who had been taught to inject insulin into an orange as a means of practice. The follow-up visit revealed that the old man was injecting his daily insulin into the orange and then eating the orange. Researchers suggest that there is "a possibility that cautiousness may operate for other tasks requiring significant application for intellectual abilities" (Birkhill and Schaie, p. 583).

Botwinick (1969) had concluded in earlier studies that cautiousness in older persons may represent a hesitance to become involved if the risk is too high.

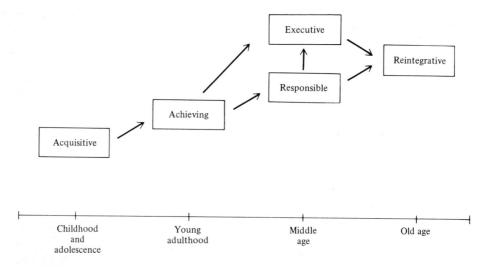

Figure 24-3 Five possible adult cognitive states. *(From K. Warner Schaie, "Toward a Stage Theory of Adult Cognitive Development,"* Journal of Aging and Human Development, *8(2):129–138, 1977–1978. Copyright © 1977 by Baywood Publishing Company, Inc., reprinted with permission.)*

Later Botwinick (1973) distinguished between learning as an internal process and a performance as an external act. Older persons benefit from longer study time during testing. "The presentation rate should be slowed and . . . new concepts should be presented only after the old students have had time to assimilate concepts previously presented" (Woodruff and Walsh, p. 426).

Impulse Control and Cognition

Kahana and Kahana studied the relationship of impulse control to cognition and adjustment among institutionalized aged women. The study was based on research indicating the importance of impulse control for cognitive development and functioning; the investigators wanted to determine whether there is an inability to control impulses that is related to poor cognitive functioning and low morale. Results indicated that impulse control is positively related to morale, intelligence, and mental status. The suggested implications for care were that the older resident who cannot delay gratification may be seen as a "problem patient" by the staff. Old persons may experience considerable frustration and low morale if the institution is not geared to immediate gratification of an individual patient's needs. We need to explore what type of old person needs immediate gratification (for example, the old one in physical or psychic pain does; so does the old one with failing kidneys, etc.). How does one handle staff frustrations with the egocentric person who is demanding more than the care giver (or family or friends) can provide?

Circadian Rhythms

One area to consider in giving care is the circadian rhythm of the elderly person. In studying circadian rhythms (the rhythmic pattern of human beings; body time) and their implications for geriatric rehabilitation, Hall concluded that "peaks and troughs found on the temperature graph were helpful in planning the time to schedule rehabilitation activities, especially motor-kinetic ability. Language and cognitive learning patterns did not run parallel with the kinetic learning" (p. 637). Pattern recognition was a beneficial consequence of relating circadian rhythm and the client's life-style to rehabilitation programs. The client and family did better once they became conscious of existing and emerging patterns.

Leveling-Sharpening in Old Persons

The terms *leveling* and *sharpening* were used by Carmichael, Hogan, and Walter to describe systematic changes in memory traces. Allport and Postman used them to describe alterations and the fate of rumors. Reading the various studies made me think of all the reminiscing done by aged persons. The term *sharpening* means a tendency for a detail of the original story to dominate the organization in memory. This tendency often appears in the reminiscing stories one hears as a group leader, although we seldom label it as such. Omissions or inconsistencies, condensing the elements, or simplifying recalled stories is known as *leveling,* which seems to occur less than sharpening in reminiscence.

Cognitive Control

The concept of cognitive control is based on observations of individual differences which reflect habitual but perhaps not conscious strategies of adaptation.

Santostefano defined cognitive controls "as ego strategies employed by a person as he deals with his environment and the information it contains in an effort to achieve a solution to the problem confronting him" (p. 343). More specifically, he defines them as principles which (1) govern amount and organization of information available to the perceiver, (2) are activated by specific arrangements or classes of stimuli which cause the person to experience an adaptive intent in terms of the information, (3) vary in the extent to which they occur in individuals, (4) evolve in part as a function of personality development and life experiences, (5) mediate the personality and motivation in the person with the environment, and (6) become lasting aspects of the person's adaptive style and cognitive functioning.

Coping Behavior of Aged Persons

Webster's dictionary (1977) defines *to cope* as "to deal with and attempt to overcome problems and difficulties." It is well to remember that people do what they do to protect themselves as they struggle to overcome problems and difficulties.

Cath writes about depletion and restitution in the aged individual.

At each critical point of growth and stress, there are several paths that a person may take. He may cope relatively easily, mastering and integrating the stress and growing further thereby; or he may engage in serious conflict and regress; or he may perpetuate the conflict as a "fate neurosis" manifested by themes of constant anxiety and repetitive tragedies that are never avoided or resolved. . . . Yet what is stress for one person may be merely a challenge to another" (p. 26).

One must remember that coping is an energy-consuming type of activity, and it draws a great deal on the resources of the person's ego to help bring about adaptation to the stressful situations facing the old person (Verwoerdt). Busse and Pfeiffer caution one to keep in mind that the aged patient has reduced overall capacity for adaptation, which may be due to cerebral deterioration, to psychosocial losses, and to loss of self-esteem.

Problem Solving of the Aged

Kahana states that adaptive strategies have been little studied in older persons. The problem-solving ability of many oldsters is impressive; such ability is usually not emphasized in discussions of the elderly, and the ability is rarely viewed by health professionals as a creative approach to living and to solving the multiple problems that the elderly experience.

Much work has been done in the area of solving problems in the laboratory (Arenberg). We are not concerned here with problem solving in an experimental setting. I am talking of the laboratory as the world, the problems of day-to-day living—tying a shoestring with arthritic fingers, being clever and cautious enough to move and negotiate in a hostile world.

Example. During a one-to-one relationship with an elderly man who was diagnosed as having a chronic brain syndrome and who was very delusional, I noted the missing buttons on his shirt. I commented that I would bring needle and thread next time to sew on the buttons. Before my return the elderly man had located two rubber bands and had neatly folded the cuffs and secured each with a rubber band. To secure two rubber bands on a huge back ward of a cumbersome, bureaucratic state hospital required some problem solving (Burnside, 1971).

Problem-solving Groups

Among institutionalized aged, one group leader (Kahana) used the conceptual framework of understanding patterns of adaptation, and related it to survival and morale in an institution. He also noted a marked similarity in the subjects (or themes) of interest to groups of elderly persons in institutions: (1) basic needs, (2) quality of food, (3) bodily concerns, (4) seeing, (5) hearing, and (6) problems with administration. The importance of these group themes unfortunately is not emphasized enough to new group leaders.

Weinstock and Weiner reported at the International Congress of Gerontology in Kiev on groups which were community-based in a geriatric outpatient clinic. Their results indicated that:

> Social competency skills, dormant through disuse, were reinstated through group process and reinforcement methods utilized by trained leadership; feelings of loneliness were sharply decreased resulting in group members attaining a sense of self-worth enabling them to relate positively to one another and to feel reinstated in a society from which they had felt rejected and ejected. Coping skills were sharpened so that daily problems in living previously ineptly dealt with were handled adequately; persons living semi-isolated to totally recluse lives, participated in the group and perceived other group members as necessary social extensions of self. Individual life styles were manifested in the multiplicity of roles available to the members and encouraged by leadership and peers (p. 272).

Social competency of members in a group is a common goal for group leaders.

Cognitive Dysfunction

Cognitive dysfunction data are needed for those who accept the intervention role. Raskind, Alvarez, Pietrzyk, Westerlund, and Herlin (p. 154) state that many patients are referred to medical centers for help because of symptoms indicative of organic brain syndrome: (1) memory impairment, (2) disorientation, (3) poor judgment, and (4) general intellectual deterioration. The person who refers the older individual contends that the old one is no longer able to cope in the community, and asks for an evaluation, or more often for assistance in removing the elderly person from the present living situation. Some 1.5 million elderly Americans suffer from chronic brain syndrome (HEW News Release). Psychosocial caring for the cognitively impaired is not easy and may well be one of the biggest challenges in the health care field. Hasegawa shared his concern about adequate supportive environments for such elderly persons in Japan. See Table 24-1 for studies of psychological functioning, including cognitive inadequacy, in institutionalized and noninstitutionalized aged.

Factors in Cognitive Dysfunction
The loss of living quarters. Changing residences is traumatic for some aged persons, especially those who have lived 20, 30, 40, or even 50 years in the same house. The change may be from a large residence that the aged person can no longer maintain or afford to an apartment or to a lifetime home for aged persons. It may be from home to hospital, or from room to room within a general hospital, e.g., from ward care to an intensive-care unit. It may be from room to room in a convalescent hospital or a board-and-care home. Intrahospital moves may have traumatic results, and these are frequently not observed or recorded by staff members. (See Chapter 28 for psychosocial interventions in "translocation shock.")

Caird and Judge, who offer guidelines for assessing the intellectual functioning

Table 24-1. Psychological Functioning in the Aged: Comparison between Samples in the Community, Waiting to Enter an Institution, and in an Institution (Analysis of Variance, Using Age and Sex as Covariates)

Area of Psychological Functioning	Mean			Contrast			
	Community (N = 35)	Waiting List (N = 100)	Institutionalized (N = 37)	Community vs. Waiting List		Waiting List vs. Institutionalized	
				F	P	F	P
Cognitive functioning							
Orientation (MSQ)	.7	1.3	1.7	.44	—	1.29	—
Time estimate (60 seconds)	23.2	21.8	26.4	.84	—	7.57	.007
Retention (Paired Word Learning)	7.6	12.6	16.2	30.63	.0001	23.14	.0001
Organization (BGT)	27.3	34.5	35.2	3.79	.05	.02	—
Perceptual accuracy (TAT)	27.9	21.8	22.1	20.11	.0001	.21	—
Originality (Reitman)	10.2	9.4	9.9	10.83	.0007	3.68	.05
Signs of cognitive inadequacy	.5	1.4	1.0	5.12	.02	4.42	.04
Affective responsiveness							
Range of affects	5.8	4.3	5.2	21.54	.0001	6.03	.01
Willingness to introspect	3.4	2.1	1.8	35.26	.0001	.03	—
Emotional states							
Well-being	19.2	15.8	16.8	15.86	.0002	.36	—
Hope	.7	-.9	-.4	15.37	.0002	1.89	—
Anxiety	15.3	19.8	16.2	6.16	.01	1.22	—
Depression	7.6	13.9	12.3	17.01	.0001	.39	—
Self-perception							
Perception—self-care inadequacy	.8	2.3	2.7	.86	—	.05	—
Self-esteem	23.2	19.2	18.3	15.82	.0002	2.31	—
Adequacy	3.9	-.83	1.8	8.50	.004	5.89	.02
Dominance	.34	-.21	.31	3.75	.05	4.72	.03
Affiliation	.08	.16	.09	.21	—	2.43	—

Source: Reprinted with permission of Sheldon S. Tobin and Morton A. Lieberman, *Last Home for the Aged,* Jossey-Bass Publishers, San Francisco,

and memory of the aged brain, state that, "Impairment of memory and of intellectual function is the commonest single mental disorder encountered in the elderly. Assessment of its degree is essential . . . since the outcome (diagnosis, treatment) may well be greatly affected by the mental state" (pp. 92, 93). They emphasize that coherence and credibility of the patient's history are much reduced if there is any degree of intellectual impairment. It is not unusual to fail to realize how severe the intellectual impairment is if the patient's personality is well preserved and there is good rapport with the examiner. When using a test such as the mental status questionnaire, the simple guidelines are valid only if the aged person's mood and attention are normal. "Due allowance must always be made for difficulties in communication due to deafness or dysphasia. Occasionally visual impairment may affect results by reducing visual cues from the examiner which are part of the process of communication" (Caird and Judge, p. 93). The reader is referred to an article by Goldfarb and *Nursing and the Aged* (Burnside, 1976) for the mental status questionnaire.

Relation of Writing Speed to Age

An interesting study by Birren and Botwinick on the relation of writing speed to age and to the regressed aged patient has tremendous implications for psychosocial care of the aged. The researchers wrote that, "Loss of writing speed may result from several factors, e.g., slow visual perception, disuse changes in the muscle groups used in writing, arthritic involvement of the fingers, and changes in the brain as reflected in aphasic and apraxic signs. . . . There are individuals in the senile group whose writing of digits appeared to have the quality of drawing rather than writing. . ." (1951, p. 248). It is sad to think of the number of aged persons who have given up writing, for whatever reason. To sign one's name is an important task, and care givers could do more to encourage writing.

Perhaps writing and/or drawing are other ways toward better understanding of the severity of deficits in the aged. Group leaders may want to experiment with this idea (Burnside, 1978).

Cognitive Decline

Recent research has shown how important it is to understand and to prevent cognitive decline. Wilkie and Eisdorfer (1973) have demonstrated the ill effects of continued hypertension. As stated earlier, this research is important for all those who are working with the elderly; to encourage older people to go for blood pressure readings or treatment of hypertension, or even to take them, is crucial. See Figure 24-4.

Raskin et al., in a study supported by the National Institute of Mental Health, have shown that the exotic treatment of using high-pressure chambers to enable a patient to breathe pure oxygen is not helpful. The severity of the chronic brain syndrome made no difference in the effectiveness of the treatment. Men as well as women responded equally poorly to the oxygen treatment. Raskin et al.

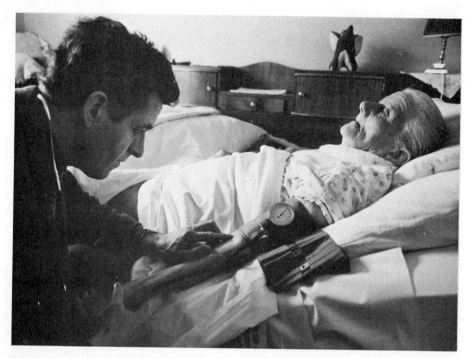

Figure 24-4 "The primary duty of the doctor is to comfort and treat every person seeking his care, irrespective of the condition from which the patient suffers. If requested, the doctor must tell the truth about the patient's condition, though with discernment and prudence." (World Health Organization.) (*Courtesy of J. Mohr, World Health Organization.*)

conclude that their results highlight the limitations of oxygen as treatment for cognitive deficits in the elderly.

Arehart-Treichel reminds the reader that victims of severe cognitive impairment die sooner than persons without such impairment, and also that "senility is not the same thing as the minor memory loss or increased forgetfulness that sometimes comes with old age" (p. 218).

Qualities in Care Givers

It might be well to warn readers of the tremendous patience and perseverance required in taking care of individuals who have cognitive impairment. It is not an easy assignment to give care to 50-year-old men who have lost speech, judgment, coordination, and even bowel and bladder control. When I visited the ward at American Lake Veteran's Administration Hospital in Tacoma, Washington, I realized how much physical and psychic stamina is required of personnel. While there, I tried with great difficulty to communicate with an aphasic man in his fifties diagnosed as having Alzheimer's disease. He was aphasic, and I got nowhere. As I was about to give up, he smiled wanly, with a sad resignation, then leaned over and kissed me on the cheek as if to say, "Sometimes I understand." The alienation and severe isolation care givers may feel in the care of patients with dementia have not been fully explored.

It is, of course, not only the care giver who sometimes feels frustration. At a conference I once attended, a participant in a reality orientation (RO) class shared a remark from a resident. While routine RO questions were being asked, an exasperated old lady said, "I don't know why you don't write down the answers to these questions so you won't have to ask the same questions every day."

Rather than end this chapter on the theme of the decremental model of aging, as we in health care so often do, I should like to end with the optimistic lines of two young psychologists: "We need not limit our efforts to mere alleviation of the learning deficits observed in contemporary older cohorts; we must also explore the possibility of aiding elderly learners to out-achieve their younger counterparts" (Woodruff and Walsh, p. 430).

SUMMARIZING STATEMENTS BASED ON THE LITERATURE ABOUT COGNITIVE FUNCTIONING

- The terminal drop in cognitive functioning may be noted as early as 5 years prior to death (Kleemeier; Riegel and Riegel; Wilkie and Eisdorfer, 1974).
- Observed changes in intelligence may be due to change from health to disease, instead of to aging (Baer; Wilkie and Eisdorfer, 1973).
- The elderly perform poorly on cognitive tests because of their overcautiousness (Birkhill and Schaie).
- Cautiousness may indicate hesitancy to become involved if the risk is high (Botwinick, 1969).
- Presentation rate of material should be slowed for the adult learner (Woodruff and Walsh).
- Time should be allowed to assimilate concepts previously given (Woodruff and Walsh).
- Cognitive control is a strategy of the ego used by an individual to deal with the environment and the information available, and to achieve a solution to a problem (Santostefano).
- Coping requires much psychic energy (Verwoerdt).
- The aged client has reduced overall capacity to adapt because of (1) possible cerebral changes, (2) psychosocial losses, (3) loss of self-esteem (Busse and Pfeiffer).
- Methods of problem solving are one display of the creative ability of the aged (Burnside, 1971).
- Problem-solving, coping skills may be honed in a group experience (Kahana; Weinstock and Weiner).
- There are 1.5 million mentally impaired elderly persons in America (HEW News Release).

- Loss of memory and intellectual impairment are the commonest mental disorders found in the elderly (Caird and Judge).
- Loss of writing speed may be due to visual problems, muscle disuse, arthritis, brain changes, etc. (Birren and Botwinick).
- The writing of mentally impaired elderly persons has a quality of drawing rather than of writing (Birren and Botwinick).
- Hyperbaric and normobaric oxygen does not successfully treat cognitive deficits in the elderly (Raskin et al.).
- Working with demented elderly persons requires stamina, patience, perseverance, and keen attention to nonverbal behavior (Storrie).

GUIDELINES FOR INTERVENTIONS IN COGNITIVE FUNCTIONING

- Observe for declines which may indicate terminal drops. One old person quit reading the daily newspapers. Another could not dress self as neatly as formerly.
- Check all health problems, especially blood pressure, with great care. Some drugstores have blood pressure apparatus; it costs about 50¢ to take one's own pressure.
- Be tolerant of cautious behavior in the elderly.
- Present all teaching material at a reasonable rate.
- Allow time for the learner to absorb what was stated before moving on.
- Observe problem-solving abilities even in the psychotic, the regressed.
- Let up on pressures when much coping is being done.
- Coping skills may be enhanced by participation in a group.
- The mentally impaired will provide a great challenge to care givers; this is a fertile area for clinical study and intervention.
- In overall assessments, consider assessing the writing ability of the aged.
- Discourage relatives from seeking "miracle" cures with oxygen therapy.
- Necessary qualities in care givers are empathy, tenacity, and patience, as well as observational skills (Storrie, 1977).

REFERENCES

Alcorn, S.: "Development of the Tadome Method for the Deaf-blind," *Journal of Exceptional Children,* **11**:117–119, 1945.

Allport, G. W., and **L. Postman:** *The Psychology of Rumor,* Holt, New York, 1947.

Anderson, B., and **Erdmore Palmore:** "Longitudinal Evaluation of Ocular Function," in E. Palmore (ed.), *Normal Aging,* Duke, Durham, N.C., 1974, pp. 24–32.

Arehart-Treichel, Joan: "Senility: More than Growing Old," *Science News,* **112**(14):218–221, 1977.

Arenberg, D.: "Cognition and Aging: Verbal Learning, Memory and Problem Solving," in C. Eisdorfer and M. P. Lawton (eds), *Psychology of Adult Development and Aging,* American Psychological Association, Washington, 1973.

Baer, P. E.: "Cognitive Changes in Aging," in C. M. Gaitz (ed.), *Aging and the Brain,* Plenum, New York, 1972.

Baltes, Paul B., and **Gisela Louvie:** "Adult Development of Intellectual Performance: Description, Explanation and Modification," in C. Eisdorfer and M. P. Lawton (eds.), *Psychology of Adult Development and Aging,* American Psychological Association, Washington, 1973.

Bayley, N.: "Cognition and Aging," in K. W. Schaie (ed.), *Theory and Methods of Research in Aging,* West Virginia University, Morgantown, 1968.

Bell, B.: "Retinal Field Shrinkage: Age Pulmonary Function and Biochemistry," *Aging and Human Development,* **3**(1): 103–111, 1972.

Birkhill, William R., and **K. Warner Schaie:** "The Effect of Differential Reinforcement of Cautiousness in Intellectual Performance among the Elderly," *Journal of Gerontology,* **30**(5):578–583, 1975.

Birren, James E., and **Jack Botwinick:** "The Relation of Writing Speed to Age and to the Senile Psychosis," *Journal of Consulting Psychology,* **15**(3):243–249, 1951.

———— and **K. Warner Schaie** (eds.): *Handbook of the Psychology of Aging,* Van Nostrand-Reinhold, New York, 1977.

Blum, June E., L. F. Jarvik, and **E. T. Clark:** "Rate of Change on Selective Tests of Intelligence: A Twenty-year Longitudinal Study of Aging," *Journal of Gerontology,* **25**(2):171–176, 1970.

Botwinick, J.: "Disinclination to Venture Response vs. Cautiousness in Responding: Age Differences," *Journal of Genetic Psychology,* **115**:55–62, 1969.

————: *Cognitive Process in Maturity and Old Age,* Springer, New York, 1967.

————: *Aging and Behavior,* Springer, New York, 1973.

Burnside, Irene M.: "Gerontion: A Case Study," *Perspectives in Psychiatric Nursing,* **9**(3):103–109, 1971.

———— (ed.): *Nursing and the Aged,* McGraw-Hill, New York, 1976.

———— (ed.): *Working with the Elderly: Group Process and Techniques,* Duxbury Press, North Scituate, 1978.

Busse, E., and **Eric Pfeiffer (eds.):** *Behavior and Adaptation in Late Life,* Little, Brown, Boston, 1969, p. 199.

Caird, F. I., and **T. G. Judge:** *Assessment of the Elderly Patient,* Pitman Medical, Kent, England, 1974 (1977 third impression).

Carmichael, L., H. P. Hogan, and **A. A. Walter:** "An Experimental Study of the Effect of Language on the Reproduction of Visually Perceived Form," *Journal of Experimental Psychology,* **15**:73–86, 1932.

Cath, Stanley: "Some Dynamics of Middle and Late Years: A Study in Depletion and Restitution," in M. Berezin and S. Cath (eds.), *Geriatric Psychiatry: Grief, Loss, and Emotional Disorders in the Aging Process,* International Universities Press, Inc., New York, 1967, p. 26.

Da Silva, Guy: "The Loneliness and Death of an Old Man: Three Years' Psychotherapy of an Eighty-One-Year-Old Depressed Patient, *Journal of Geriatric Psychiatry,* **1**(1):5–27, 1967.

Eisdorfer, Carl: "Intellectual and Cognitive Changes in the Aged," in E. Busse and E. Pfeiffer (eds.), *Behavior and Adaptation in Late Life,* Little, Brown, Boston, 1969.

———— and **Frances Wilkie:** "Intellectual

Changes with Advancing Age," in L. F. Jarvik, C. Eisdorfer, and J. E. Blum (eds.), *Intellectual Functioning in Adults,* Springer, New York, 1973.

Eisner, Donald A., and K. Warner Schaie: "Age Changes in Response to Visual Illusions from Middle to Old Age, *Journal of Gerontology,* **26**(1):146–150, 1971.

Fozard, James L., and J. C. Thomas: "Why Aging Engineering Psychologist Should Get Interested in Aging," presented at meeting of American Psychological Association, Montreal, Ontario, Canada, August 1973.

—— and ——: "Psychology of Aging: Basic Findings and Their Psychiatric Applications," in J. G. Howells (ed.), *Modern Perspectives in the Psychiatry of Old Age,* Brunner/Mazel, New York, 1975, pp. 107–169.

Gajo, F. D.: "Visual Illusions," unpublished doctoral dissertation, Washington University, St. Louis, 1966.

Gibson, J. J.: *The Senses Considered as Perceptual Systems,* Houghton Mifflin, Boston, 1966.

Goldfarb, Alvin: "Integrated Psychiatric Services for the Aged," *Bulletin of the New York Academy of Medicine,* **49**(12): 1070–1083, 1973.

Goulet, L. R., and Paul B. Baltes (eds.): *Lifespan Developmental Psychology: Research and Theory,* Academic, New York, 1970.

Guth, S. K.: "Effects of Age on Visibility," *American Journal of Optometry,* **34**(9):463–477, 1957.

Hall, LaVonne H.: "Circadian Rhythms: Implications for Geriatric Rehabilitation, *Nursing Clinics of North America,* **11**(4): 631–638, 1976.

Hasegawa, Kazuko: Personal communication, 1975.

HEW News Release: Department of Health, Education, and Welfare, Public Health Service, National Institute of Mental Health, Rockville, Md., Sept. 22, 1977.

Horn, J. L.: "Organization of Lifespan Data on Human Abilities," in L. R. Goulet and P. B. Baltes (eds.), *Lifespan Developmental Psychology: Research and Theory,* Academic, New York, 1970.

Jarvik, Lissy F.: "Discussion: Patterns of Intellectual Functioning in the Later Years," in L. F. Jarvik, C. Eisdorfer, and J. E. Blum (eds.), *Intellectual Functioning in Adults: Psychological and Biological Influences,* Springer, New York, 1973.

——: "Thoughts on the Psychobiology of Aging," *American Psychologist,* **39**(5):576–583, 1975.

Kahana, Boaz: "Problem Solving Group," paper presented at International Congress of Gerontology, Jerusalem, Israel, June 1975.

—— and Eva Kahana: "The Relationship of Impulse Control to Cognition and Adjustment among Institutionalized Aged Women," *Journal of Gerontology,* **30**(6):679–687, 1975.

Kinsbourne, M., and P. Caplan: "Symposium Discussion; Life Span Development of Psychological Aging: A White Elephant, *Gerontologist,* **13**(4):509–510, 1973.

Kleemeier, R. W.: "Intellectual Change in the Senium," *Proceedings of the Social Statistics Section of the American Statistical Association,* Washington, D.C., **1**: 290–295, 1962.

Kolers, P. A.: "Some Psychological Aspects of Pattern Recognition," in P. A. Koler and M. Eden (eds.), *Recognizing Patterns,* M.I.T., Cambridge, Mass., 1968.

Kornzweig, A. L.: "The Eye in Old Age.

V. Diseases of the Macula; a Clinico-pathologic Study, *American Journal of Ophthalmology,* 60(5):835–842, 1965.

————, I. **Eliasoph,** and M. **Feldstein:** "Retinal Vasculature in the Aged," *"Bulletin of the New York Academy of Medicine,* 40(2):116–129, 1964.

————, N. **Feldstein,** and J. **Schneider:** "Pathogenesis of Senile Macular Degeneration, *American Journal of Ophthalmology,* 48(1):22–28, 1959.

Lieberman, Morton A.: "Psychological Correlates of Impending Death: Some Preliminary Observations," *Journal of Gerontology,* 20(2):181–190, 1965.

Lovegren, James: "Report of a Training Contract, HRA, 230-75-0170," Western Consortium San Francisco, 1977.

McFarland, R. A.: "The Sensory and Perceptual Process in Aging," in K. W. Schaie (ed.), *Theory and Methods of Research in Aging,* West Virginia University, Morgantown, 1968.

Mendelson, Jack H., Philip E. Kubzansky, P. Herbert Liederman, Donald Wexler, and **Philip Solomon:** "Aspects of Sensory Deprivation," in P. Solomon, J. H. Mendelson et al. (eds.), *Sensory Deprivation,* Harvard, Cambridge, Mass., 1965.

Moore, J. L., and J. E. **Birren:** "Doctoral Training in Gerontology: An Analysis of Dissertations on Problems of Aging in Institutions of Higher Learning in the United States, 1934–1969," *Journal of Gerontology,* 26(2):249–257, 1971.

Mueller, Jean E.: "A Bibliography of Doctoral Dissertations on Aging from American Institutions of Higher Learning, 1974–1976," *Journal of Gerontology,* 32(4):480–490, 1977.

Neisser, Ulric: *Cognition and Reality: Principles and Implication of Cognitive Psychology,* Freeman, San Francisco, 1976.

Neugarten, Bernice (ed.): *Middle Age and Aging,* University of Chicago Press, Chicago, 1968.

Newcomer, Robert J., and **Michael A. Caggiano:** "Environment and the Aged Person," in Irene M. Burnside (ed.), *Nursing and the Aged,* McGraw-Hill, New York, 1976.

Pastalan, Leon A.: Paper prepared for *Environment for the Aged: A Working Conference on Behavioral Research, Utilization and Environmental Policy,* San Juan, Puerto Rico, Dec. 1971, pp. 5–6.

————: "Aging and Sensory Changes: An Update and Some Practical Suggestions," in *Sensory Processes and Aging,* North Texas State University, Denton, 1977.

Pieron, H.: *The Sensations* (tr. by M. H. Pierenne and B. C. Abbott), J. Garnet Miller, London, 1952.

Raskin, Allen, et al.: Report on "Hyperbaric Oxygenation," *HEW News Release,* Department of Health, Education, and Welfare, National Institute of Mental Health, Rockville, Md., Sept. 22, 1977.

Raskind, Murray A., Carrol Alvarez, Maria Pietrzyk, Karen Westerlund, and **Susan Herlin:** "Helping the Elderly Psychiatric Patient in Crisis, *Geriatrics,* 31(6):51–59, 1976.

Reed, S. K.: *Psychological Process in Pattern Recognition,* Academic, New York, 1973.

Reid, T.: *Essays on the Intellectual Powers of Man,* 1785, any modern edition.

Riegel, Klaus F., and **Ruth M. Riegel:** "Development, Drop, and Death," *Developmental Psychology,* 6(2):306–319, 1972.

Rosenthal, R., and **R. L. Rosnow:** *Artifact in Behavioral Research,* Academic, New York, 1969.

Santostefano, Sebastian G.: "A Developmental Study of the Cognitive Control

(Leveling-Sharpening), *Merrill-Palmer Quarterly,* **10**(4):343–360, 1964.

Schaie, K. Warner: "A General Model for the Study of Developmental Problems," *Psychological Bulletin,* **64**(2):92–107, 1965.

———: "Toward a Stage Theory of Adult Cognitive Development," *Journal of Aging and Human Development,* **8**(2): 129–138, 1977–1978.

Siegler, Ilene C.: "Threats to External Validity: The Effects of Selective Dropout on Health, Morale, Social Relations and Environmental Circumstances in the Elderly," doctoral dissertation, Syracuse University, 1973.

———: "The Terminal Drop Hypothesis: Factor Artifact," *Experimental Aging Research,* **1**:169–185, 1975.

———: "Life Span Developmental Psychology and Clinical Geropsychology," in W. Doyle Gentry (ed.), *Geropsychology: A Model of Training and Clinical Service,* Ballinger Publishing Company, Cambridge, Mass., 1977.

Soddy, Kenneth, and Mary C. Kidner: *Men in Middle Years,* Travistock Publications, Lippincott, London, 1967.

Steffl, Bernita M., and Imogene Eide: *Discharge Planning Handbook,* Slack, Thorofare, New Jersey, 1978.

Storrie, Mike: Personal communication, 1977.

Sumby, W. H., and P. Pollack: "Visual Contribution to Speech Intelligibility in Noise," *Journal of the Acoustical Society of America,* **26**:212–215, 1954.

Thompson, Alma R.: Personal communication, 1977.

Titchener, E. B.: *Experimental Psychology,* 4 vols., Macmillan, New York, 1909, p. 115.

U.S. Department of Health, Education, and Welfare: *Facts about Older Americans, 1976,* Office of Human Development, Administration on Aging, Publ. No.

(OHD) 77-20006, Washington, 1977. (A pamphlet.)

Verwoerdt, Adrian: *Clinical Geropsychiatry,* Williams & Wilkins, Baltimore, 1976.

Wagner, Seymour, Heinz Werner, and Peter E. Comalli: "Perception of Part-Whole Relationships in Middle and Old Age, *Journal of Gerontology,* **15**(4):412–416, 1960.

Webster's New Collegiate Dictionary: G. & C. Merriam Co., Springfield, Mass., 1977.

Weinstock, C. S., and M. B. Weiner: "Community Aged in Problem-solving Groups," *Abstracts,* vol. 3, International Congress of Gerontology, Kiev, U.S.S.R., 1972, p. 272.

Welford, A. R., and James E. Birren: *Behavior, Aging and the Nervous System,* Charles C Thomas, Springfield, Ill., 1965.

Weston, H. C.: "On Age and Illumination in Relation to Visual Performance," *Transactions of the Illuminating Engineering Society* (London), **14**:281–297. 1949.

Wilkie, Frances: "Intelligence and Blood Pressure in the Aged," *Science,* **172**: 959–962, 1971.

——— and Carl Eisdorfer: "Systemic Disease and Behavioral Correlates," in L. F. Jarvik, C. Eisdorfer, and J. E. Blum (eds.), *Intellectual Functioning in Adults,* Springer, New York, 1973, pp. 89–93.

——— and ———: "Terminal Changes in Intelligence," in E. Palmore (ed.), *Normal Aging II,* Duke, Durham, N.C., 1974, pp. 103–115.

Wolf, E.: "Glare and Age," *Archives of Ophthalmology,* **64**(4):502–514, 1960.

———: "Studies on the Shrinkage of the Visual Field with Age," *Highway Research Record,* **167**:1–7, 1967.

Woodruff, Diane S., and David A. Walsh: "Research in Adult Learning," *The Gerontologist,* **15**(5):424–430, 1975, part 1.

OTHER RESOURCES

Films

Environmental Health Aspects of Nursing Homes: 14 min/16 mm/color. Presents specific environmental health factors significant in skilled nursing facilities, e.g., accident and fire prevention, food sanitation, lighting, furnishings and decor. Distributor: Media Resources Branch, National Medical Audiovisual Center (Annex), Station K, Atlanta, Ga. 30324.

Gramp: A Man Ages and Dies: 16 min/16 mm/b&w. Based on the book, *Gramp,* by Dan and Mark Jury; a first-person narrative of how their family faced the death of their grandfather, whose regression, which went unnoticed by the family at first, began in his late seventies. One day he took out his teeth and refused to eat; 3 weeks later he died. Distributor: Mass Media Ministries, 2116 North Charles Street, Baltimore, Md. 21218.

The Mortal Body: 12 min/16 mm/b&w. Nonverbal film with music about the body's vitality and vulnerability. Birth, death, and moments between combine to show the fleeting quality of life. Director: Ante Babaja. Producer: Zagreb Films. Distributor: Filmakers Library, Inc., 290 West End Avenue, New York, N.Y. 10023.

Peege: See Other Resources in Chapter 21.

To Live with Dignity: 29 min/16 mm/color/ 1972. Documentary about 20 very confused, disoriented older persons at Ypsilanti State Hospital in Michigan. Records techniques of milieu therapy and shows patients involved in social interaction groups, crafts, activities of daily living, etc. Records their progress as they become involved in the world around them. Producer: Institute of Gerontology, University of Michigan, Audiovisual Education Center, 416 Fourth Street, Ann Arbor, Mich. 48104.

REFERRAL ORGANIZATIONS

American Foundation for the Blind
15 West 16th Street
New York, N.Y. 10011

National Association of Hearing and Speech Agencies
919 - 18th Street N.W.
Washington, D.C. 20013

National Center for a Barrier Free Environment
8401 Connecticut Avenue
Washington, D.C. 20015

National Society for the Prevention of Blindness, Inc.
79 Madison Avenue
New York, N.Y. 10016

CATALOGS

Aids and Appliances for the Blind and Visually Impaired
American Foundation for the Blind
15 West 16th Street
New York, N.Y. 10011

Catalogue of Optical Aids, 3d ed.
New York Association for the Blind
111 East 59th Street
New York, N.Y. 10022

Chapter
25

I, ME, AND THE SELF:
SELF-ESTEEM IN LATE LIFE
Irene Mortenson Burnside

> Foregoing self, the universe grows I.
>
> *Edwin Arnold*

> Old people can seldom say "we"; not those who live
> alone, and even those who live with their families are
> alone in their experience of age. . . . It takes increasing
> courage to be "I" as one's frailty increases.
>
> *Florida Scott-Maxwell, 1968*

The poor public image of the elderly and the picture given of them in mass media are well known to all of us. The National Council on the Aging (NCOA), an organization 25 years old, is now involved in launching a National Media Resource Center on Aging. The goals are, "to change and to elevate the image of aging and to create a greater awareness of the elderly as contributors, as builders, as useful and significant members of society" (Ossofsky, p. 42). In the following list, Gelman suggests ways of improving the image of the elderly on television.

- The role of older people in situation comedies should be increased and their depiction should be of a more successful connotation;
- An action liaison group should be formed to meet with important members of the creative community so as to communicate the importance to writers of not relying on stereotypes;
- The networks should be told "strongly" that older people are to be allowed to participate on game shows;
- It should be made known to the networks and creative people that this generation of senior citizens are pioneers in that they are the first group to

form any significant demographic segment and that they should be portrayed as models for younger people, and that depiction should include older people in a wide range of activities, with life shown as a continuing process;
- Older people should be "plugged into the creative process," and to that end information will be submitted for publication in the newsletter of the Writers Guild of America West;
- An award be established for a script to be written that would portray old people in a more positive way;
- Recommendation to shows dealing with older characters that they hire a gerontologist as a consultant;
- Effort made to make reporters on TV news shows more knowledgeable about old people and that such news shows have women anchors "with wrinkles on their faces" to match Harry Reasoner's gray hair. It was further suggested that TV news shows devote a segment of their newscasts to information of special interests to old people.[1]

Self-esteem is defined in *Webster's New Collegiate Dictionary* as "confidence and satisfaction in oneself: self-respect." In this chapter, self-esteem means satisfaction with one's self-image and the different features of one's self. An excellent survey of the literature on self-esteem in the aged was done by Rynerson for the years 1942–1969. Branden states, "An unclouded capacity for the enjoyment of life, is an unusual moral and psychological achievement. Contrary to popular belief, it is not the prerogative reward of self-esteem" (p. 139).

Peters reviewed the literature on age identification from 1956 to 1970 and studied research with a fairly direct relationship to self-conception and age identification among the elderly. The author included definitions, social roles, and self-concept in his article. Peters used theory from Sarbin and from Rosow.

Sarbin proposed in role theory that the self and the role are continuously interacting. Rosow stated that there is agreement about there being no role transition without the emergence of a new self-image. How do care givers then promote such new self-images in old people, especially in the despairing older person? Peters included consequences of aged identification, pointing out that a major difficulty of research in this area is the tendency to draw inferences about behavior which are based on attitudinal responses. Chronological age is a poor index of aging; it may serve, however, as one way of ordering developmental data. Chapter 22 uses chronological age to order data. The stereotypes of aging are also spelled out in the articles in a variety of research studies.

Peters concludes that it is unwise both theoretically and in policy forming to make generalizations about the aged as if they were a homogeneous group. As

---

[1] From Morrie Gelman, "TV Programming, Blurbs Target of Senior Citizens," *Daily Variety*, Hollywood, Apr. 21, 1977, pp. 1–2. Originally from a conference entitled, "A Fresh Look: How Television Reflects Old People," given at Ethel Percy Andrus Gerontology Center, University of Southern California, Los Angeles, Calif., Apr. 20, 1977.

he pointed out, flexibility in the research efforts will also be reflected in flexible policy formulation for the aged.

The reader is referred to Adams for a table which organizes the gerontology literature into "selected correlates of satisfaction, personal adjustment, positive self-concept, self-esteem, 'morale' or other indicators of psychological well-being" (p. 66). The table is divided into biological correlates; psychological correlates; sociological correlates: personal characteristics; sociological correlates: roles and role changes; and sociological correlates: social relations and activities. The care giver interested in psychosocial aspects should be interested in these negatives as culled from the literature by Adams: (1) physical disability, (2) advancing age, (3) further advancing age (to 75, 80, or thereafter), (4) perception of one's age as "old," (5) contracting life spaces, (6) feeling of inadequacy, (7) widowhood, (8) retirement, (9) reluctance to retire, (10) retirement because of poor health, (11) loss of friends, (12) inability to make new friends. This list could be made into a checklist for students as a guideline to follow. Adams's list also serves as an excellent resource reading list for persons wishing to pursue the subject further.

One study showed evidence that self-esteem increased with age (Gurin, Veroff, and Feld); another showed reduced self-esteem (Kogan and Wallach). As Lowenthal, Thurner, and Chiriboga wrote, "Evidence for an age-related shift to self-depreciation, however, is equivocal" (p. 62). Some researchers have studied the ideal, the actual self-image, and the self-presentation (Brehm and Back, 1968; Back and Paramish).

A positive regard for self and the level of self-esteem seems to increase until middle age and is then stabilized or begins gradually to decline, according to some researchers (Lehner and Gunderson, 1953; Veroff and others, 1962; Lowenthal and Chiriboga, 1972).

There is a general trend for the concept of self to become increasingly negative from the fifties and on through the seventies and eighties (Kogan and Wallach). This may be covered up by an increased defensiveness. Neugarten and Gutmann found that the concept of older men became more tolerant of nurturing roles and older women became more tolerant of their own egocentrism and aggressive tendencies.

Reichard, in what is now a classic study, reported on 87 San Francisco male workers, aged 55 to 84 years, and found that the basic personality greatly influenced adjustment to aging. The well-adjusted aged workers had self-esteem satisfactions and could adapt to crises as they occurred. The ability to adjust to crises and to solve problems needs to be studied more in the aged population. One is reminded of the old sea captain's salty advice for adjustment, "Be limber, lovin' and a little bit looney."

Back also considered the effect of crises and role changes in a paper presented at the Annual Meeting of the Gerontological Society. (Crisis seems to be a strong word for the changes and/or passages under consideration.) The study looked at one crisis which occurred in the subject—realization of the contrast between what the person felt about himself and the image he presented to others. "The

IT'S GETTING HARD TO BE SOMEONE

Figure 25-1 *(Kersten Bros. Co., Scottsdale, Ariz., copyright 1971. Reprinted with permission.)*

largest divergence between self and appearance of self occurs in the two oldest groups (60–70).'' The researcher suggested that the discrepancy is not due to inner effects of the aging process, but rather to changes and events in the life cycle that change the position of the person; this follows the theory of Holmes and Rahe. (See Table 12-2 by Holmes and Rahe in Chapter 12.) Back also found that this held true for subjects of both sexes who were not working! Working, at least for some, does not allow the time to think about how others are viewing them.

Back suggests self-worth is related to loss of socially important roles and that though the losses may indeed be traumatic, the aged person sometimes welcomes them and the necessary adaptations because of the reduced capacity to cope. That is a new twist not often considered. It reminds me of two men, one 73, and one almost 80, who planned a day of fishing. The 80-year-old was visibly relieved when the 73-year-old said he was "too tired from the long drive." It helped the 80-year-old save face because he, too, was tired. And it turned out the 73-year-old, an expert fisherman, had purchased a new, very expensive rod and reel and wanted to practice using it before he fished with the 80-year-old, who also was a master fisherman. *The need to consider energy level, including psychic energy level, is a most important part of our interactions with the aged.* Back pointed out that even though physical abilities and energy decline in later life, the size of the psychological life space keeps up until a relatively late date. He concluded, "Neither retirement nor separation from children affects the content of the self-image as much as the aging process does." In general, men have a bigger problem with the discrepancy between what they feel they are and the opinion they think other people have of them.

DYNAMICS OF THREATS TO SELF-ESTEEM

Klopfer, using as a basis Sullivan's ideas on threats to self-esteem, listed the following threats to self-esteem of the aged: (1) undeclared war between youth and aged, (2) youth worship in Western world, (3) decreased sources of inter-personal interactions due to loss of peers and/or significant others, (4) lack of resistance to stresses and losses which are catastrophic, and (5) the effects of poor memory, loss of spatial orientation, speed, agility, and sensory acuity. The latter is particularly devastating to many old persons, and it is a fertile area for psychosocial interventions.

Mittelmann, in an article discussing psychosomatic medicine and the older patient, stated that the threat the aging process represents has the following components: (1) threat to the body image, (2) threat to self-esteem, (3) feelings of worthlessness and being rejected, and (4) punishment for hostility and sexual strivings. The latter threat has not been studied enough. As Butler and Lewis have said, the atonement can continue to the very end of life.

BODY IMAGE

A 77-year-old woman, as she applied creams and oils to her face, said, "Underneath all of this I am only 25" (Lahey).

Plutchik and Conte studied body image through the use of a semantic differential questionnaire. Nonpsychiatric patients in a home and hospital for the aged were more positive in their perception of the "head"—they viewed it as good, happy, pleasurable, and active, more frequently than the other subjects.

Body image is an important component of self-esteem and morale in the aged, especially in view of the traumatic losses and damages a body may sustain over the years. The body image is a reflection of impressions a person has of the body which has formed over the lifetime of development (Fisher and Cleveland; Fisher; Witkin).

The adjustment of old persons to colostomies is an excellent example of the threat to the body image Mittelmann mentioned above—and colostomies are fairly common. Some elderly do not even know that there is such an operation as a colostomy until they are advised to have surgery. Often the colostomy is not even regarded as a part of them; they view it as ego-alien. Some people do not want to look at the colostomy in the very beginning. One man named his "Daisy Mae"; his wife could not tolerate it. The man's wife did not sleep with him for 6 years after the colostomy was performed. When he was later admitted to the hospital, he was absolutely worn out from caring for his wife, who was super-dependent. She was admitted to the hospital too. Both these elderly people were dazed and bewildered by the new surroundings. Fortunately there was a steady flow of kindness and patience to them.

One needs to maintain a slow pace with such individuals so they can keep up with you—both in speech and in movement. The goal is to lessen the battering to the ego and the self-esteem and to focus steadily on the aged person's strengths. We often forget to underline the strengths of frail old people and instead expect them to be doddering or incompetent; perhaps we even encourage incompetence by our behavior towards them.

DIOGENES SYNDROME

Clark et al. studied 30 elderly patients (14 men, 16 women) admitted to a hospital with acute illness and in a state of extreme self-neglect. They termed this condition the "Diogenes syndrome." (Diogenes was a Greek cynic philosopher of the fourth century B.C. who wandered the streets. His ideals were being self-sufficient, being antiestablishment, and having a lack of emotion and shame.) All subjects were dirty, untidy, and had a filthy personal appearance about which they had no shame. Half of them revealed no evidence of a psychiatric disorder and also possessed a higher-than-average intelligence. The personality characteristics included (1) aloofness, (2) suspiciousness, (3) emotional lability, (4) aggressivity, (5) group dependency, and (6) a distorted sense of reality. The researchers wrote that such aged persons are not uncommon; yet they have not been studied much. They pose serious problems in terms of community care and sometimes urgently need to be admitted to a hospital.

In large cities, such individuals can be seen wheeling all their belongings in a shopping cart or sack. They rummage through garbage cans, seeking a variety of items which they save. I have seen old women in Los Angeles, Honolulu, and San Francisco whose personal appearance fits the description of the Diogenes syndrome.

Though the Diogenes syndrome is at the far end of the continuum of personal appearance, one constantly finds gross neglect of self in the aged—whether at home or in an institution. Self-neglect may be related to an inability to see well; vision should be carefully checked. It can also be closely linked to depression, illness (e.g., anemia, heart failure, etc.), and/or utter exhaustion.

RELOCATION AND SELF-ESTEEM

The present literature on relocation of the aged, or translocation shock, is voluminous and will be covered here only as it affects self-esteem. Therapeutic strategies to reduce translocation shock will be discussed in Chapter 28. The reader is also referred to Schulz's and Brenner's excellent report of the literature, which lists 44 articles. Lieberman wrote, "Where again the physical status of the population was relatively homogeneous, personality traits, cognitive functioning, despair, the ability to maintain and defend a consistent self-image, and the absence of primitive defense mechanisms such as denial were all significant predictors of outcome" (p. 496).

Kahana and Coe reported an interesting finding: long-time nursing home residents were more likely to have views of themselves similar to the way in which staff viewed them than were newer residents. And it is very likely they were fairly negative views.

In a study done among nursing home residents, Bryan found a high level of correlation between hope and self-concept. "Findings of this study indicate a high level of correlation between Hope and Self concept in the elderly nursing home patient." The sample was small, 22 volunteers. The relationship of hope to self concept-identity, satisfaction and behavior, and physical, ethical, personal, family, and social self was determined. There was a significant relationship between hope and total self-concept. In view of the "therapeutic nihilism" so often displayed by care givers in the field of aging, the need for a change to the hope stance in the care giver is apparent; this applies especially to those involved in care of nursing home residents.

SELF-ESTEEM AND INSTITUTIONALIZATION

The self-esteem of the institutionalized has been widely studied. Some investigators report no significant differences in self-esteem and adjustment in cross-sectional comparisons of institutionalized and noninstitutionalized elderly (Lepkowski; Pan; Tuckman, Lorge, and Zeman). Others, however, concluded that institutionalized subjects have lower self-esteem and poorer adjustment than those residing in the community (Laverty; Mason; Pollack, Karp, Kahn, and Goldfarb). It is important to state what calibre and type of institution are involved.

Anderson reported on the effects of institutionalization on the self-esteem of elderly subjects in a retirement home and concluded that institutionalization is not necessarily detrimental in its effect on the older person. Some retirement homes are quite impressive in what they offer the residents. Rosner reported that there was a consistency in the self-system throughout the process of being institutionalized.

Gordon and Vinacke studied self and ideal self-concepts and dependency in aged persons residing in retirement homes. These researchers stated that males high in dependency revealed the least favorable present and past self-concepts, and that females high in dependency showed the most favorable present and past self-concepts. An interesting statement in this article relates that older people retain self-concepts not noticeably different from college students. What often is regarded as remarkable to researchers and observers may not be seen as remarkable to the aged themselves. What is more remarkable is that college students are so often studied.

Lieberman, Prock, and Tobin, as mentioned earlier, pointed out that one of the adverse physical and psychological effects of institutionalization is low self-esteem. Later Tobin and Lieberman discussed a lowered self-esteem in institutionalized elderly in contrast to those on waiting lists and those in the community (see Table 24-1). For psychological effects of the process of institutionalization, see Table 25-1.

Lewis (1970) described reminiscing and self-concept in old age and suggested that reminiscing could be a defense against threat to self-esteem. I am reminded of a Veterans Administration Hospital ward where I once worked. At that time we had veterans from the Spanish-American War, World War I, World War II, and the Korean conflict. As I walked from one room to another, the discussion would be about Chateau Thiery, or the Belgian Bulge, or the 38th parallel. At any rate, the older veterans were determined to make their war as important as the wars of younger veterans next to them. A wizened old man would often be found sitting up in his bed relating with animation his own version of the MASH[2] of another war to a bored young veteran.

Mason found that in an aged group in the institutional setting, there were less positive feelings of self-worth than in an independent group of elderly. Lieberman and Lakin stated that those living in institutions felt a decrease of power. To increase the inner locus of control and power in an institutionalized old person is a constant challenge.

Mason felt that to have a positive self-concept, an elderly person must be able to function adequately in a normal independent existence. One is reminded of 92-year-old Berenson, who wrote, "Why do I still go on writing a page of this diary every morning? . . . I write as I dress for dinner, as a matter of personal discipline. . . . It is mental and even more moral ritual, with no touch of production about it. . . . I do my stunt . . . to satisfy my own self-esteem surely" (p. 464).

PROBLEM SOLVING OF THE AGED

As mentioned in Chapter 24, the problem-solving ability of many oldsters is impressive, and it is part and parcel of self-esteem. This reservoir of skill is seldom tapped by health professionals, who often feel that they alone must solve the problems. Kahana stated that adaptive strategies are little studied in the older person. "Problem solving" as it is used here is not meant in a constricted way. It is not problem solving in the sense that experimental psychologists would describe it, but simply using one's ingenuity and ability to solve problems in daily living. I remember a man in his late sixties who spent his summers alone at a cabin on a Northern Minnesota lake. It was before motor boats became common. He used to attach the bed sheets onto the back of his boat to wash them; he rowed around the lake for a while and then went home and hung them up to dry.

SELF-ESTEEM AND SEXUALITY

Zinberg discusses social learning, self-image, and aging, and presents two cases which show how social learning affects ego functioning; both the studies are on

___

[2] MASH stands for Mobile Army Surgical Hospital.

Table 25-1. Psychological Changes of the Elderly in Institutions, from Anticipatory Phase through Initial Adjustment Phase to Adaptation Phase

Dimension	Anticipatory Phase	Initial Adjustment Phase	Adaptation Phase
Cognitive functioning	Cognitive constriction	Cognitive constriction persists	Cognitive constriction persists
Affective responsiveness	Constriction	Constriction persists	Constriction persists
Emotional states	Moderate feelings of well-being	Moderate feelings of well-being persist	Diminished feelings of well-being
	Limited hopefulness	Hopelessness	Hopelessness persists
	Anxiety and depression; low body preoccupation	Anxiety and depression persist; high body preoccupation	Anxiety and depression persist; low body preoccupation
Self-system	Perception of capacity for self-care	Perception of modest inadequacy in self-care capacity	Perception of modest inadequacy in self-care capacity persists
	Moderate to high self-esteem	Moderate to high self-esteem persists	Moderate to high self-esteem persists
	Moderate adequacy and high distortion	Moderate adequacy and high distortion persist	Moderate adequacy and high distortion persist
	Moderate dominance, and affiliation	Moderate dominance with a lessening of affiliation; more hostile and distant	Moderate dominance with a lessening of affiliation; more hostile and distant
Loss meaning	Abandonment	Loss predominates, especially mutilation and death themes	Loss and mutilation and death themes persist

Source: Reprinted with permission from Sheldon S. Tobin and Morton A. Lieberman, *Last Home for the Aged*, Jossey-Bass Publishers, San Francisco, 1976.

179

men, one on a 64-year-old, the other a 71-year-old. He suggests that in a social age, cultural dictates tend to limit sexual activity to a few situations and that in order to have sexual fulfillment an older person may have to find a new group, in fact, one which accepts "deviance." Accepting stereotyped social views of self can be maladaptive. The importance of social learning in the development of individuals and social attitude should become of particular interest to the care giver.

Burchell wrote, "Self-esteem is a crucial element in an individual's capacity for sexual fulfillment. Low self-esteem weakens the basis of the relationship; high self-esteem provides a foundation for risk-taking and growth that is nurturing to any relationship" (p. 74). Adequate self-esteem enables one to receive pleasure. It is also important to accept and acknowledge one's individual tastes and pleasures, to be aware of one's individuality and to be able to seek the boundaries of one's sexual preference. No mention is made of the older person or the older couple in Burchell's article. See Chapter 29 for more information on sexuality.

ACCOUTREMENTS OF ILLNESS

The tremendous impact of wheelchairs, canes, walkers, hearing aids, visual aids, or any combination of these, on the aged person's self-image has not been thoroughly studied. The nearly impossible barriers faced by persons who have limitations in mobility now draw the attention of the larger society; e.g., we are providing wider parking spaces for automobiles, wider doors to toilets to accommodate wheelchairs, etc. An organization called "National Center for a Barrier Free Environment" is concerned about such problems. See list of organizations at end of Chapter 24.

It is sad, but true, that in some retirement homes the residents in wheelchairs or on walkers are often not permitted in the dining room. I knew a woman who ate meals for 3 days alone in her room because she wore a bandage and dared not go to the dining room with it.

PERSONAL POSSESSIONS

Goffman, writing in *Asylum,* stated that an individual's personal possessions are a valuable part of the materials from which he builds a self. . . . That statement leads one to consider the importance of wallets, purses, and money in the pocket for both men and women. A nursing home administrator once related this story in a class:

An elderly female patient in the facility entered my office. I recognized the woman and recalled that she could be quite confused at times. I asked her if she needed some assistance. She stated that she would like to call her daughter and use the desk phone. I indicated that it was not the policy for residents to use the desk phone, but there was a pay phone in the hallway. I knew that she might not have the money for the call, so I asked if she would like some change from the Patient Trust Fund account. "No," she replied and produced a folded coin purse

Figure 25-2 Photographs are cherished possessions of old people, and there is a "hanging-on" quality to the meanings attached to them. This 78-year-old man (p. 495) once brought the photograph (this page) to share with his grandchildren (who were full-grown). The bicycle was his first, purchased in 1913. (*Courtesy of L. D. Burnside.*)

from her handbag. "I have money right here." She took out a folded handkerchief in which she stored several paper clips and carefully removed a single, small paper clip, and stated, "Here's a dime." She was placing a call to someone living a considerable distance from the facility, so I told her such a call might be 15 or 20 cents. She then handed me a large paper clip and promptly asked, "Do you have change for a quarter?" (Herz)

In a practical psychosocial study, Sherman and Newman surveyed 94 elderly persons to see if they had certain possessions which they cherished above all others, and if so, to identify the possessions. The mean age of the sample was 74.7 years, with an age range of 60 to 95 years. The sample was divided in two groups, one in a nursing home, one in the community. (A serendipitous finding was that the nursing home group was almost 10 years older on the average than the community group.)

Eighty-one percent of the subjects readily identified such a possession. The range of cherished possessions was extensive, from jewelry to one's home. There was no difference between men and women in identification of a treasured possession. Cherished items were labeled: (1) none, (2) religious item, (3) symbolic jewelry, (4) personal performance, (5) photographs, (6) consumer items.

Remarkable differences were noted between the young-old (under 75 years of age) and the old-old (75 and over). The response of "none" was almost trebled in the 75-and-over group. The second largest relative difference between the two groups was the indication of fewer cherished religious possessions in the old-old. The sample was clouded by the fact that the nursing home subsample was mostly old-old. The researchers felt that old people in nursing homes were detaching from significant objects in their lives. I would pose that nursing home residents and their relatives are under pressure from staff persons to keep with them very few belongings, especially very few valuable ones. Because it is such a touchy subject, no one has studied the theft factor in nursing homes; that needs to be considered also.

The referent and the meanings for the objects were classified. The five main referents listed were (1) self, (2) child, (3) spouse, (4) parents, (5) grandchild.

Though this study proves what many of us have known for a long time, it is a refreshing venture into the popular area of memorabilia. One observation by Sherman and Newman for care givers to remember was the poignant attachment to the meaning of photographs and that the old-old were disproportionately represented in the photograph.

Two important objects should be mentioned—a woman's purse and a man's wallet. The importance of a purse to a woman throughout her life begins with tiny purses that go with a little girl's Easter ensemble or are used to carry one's own money to the store. Old women in institutions fill their purses and tote bags with a strange array of objects. The purse becomes a suitcase, bank, storehouse, perhaps a security blanket for them. As for men, one group member showed the leader an empty wallet containing only his fireman's badge. He had been a fireman in the 1906 post-earthquake fire in San Francisco. Another time I paid an elderly nursing home resident for helping teach a class. He had been a poor farmer in Arkansas all his life. I was impressed with the flat, empty wallet, and the careful manner in which he laid the bill into it. He then smoothed the wallet, patted it, and replaced it in his hip pocket; a slow smile spread across his old face—such a ritual, the way he handled it all.

A man described by Robinson wanted change in his pocket; he preferred all nickels. During a long-term one-to-one relationship with him, she made sure he had 25¢ to 50¢ in nickels in his pocket. When he died, she had 50¢ of his change, so she slipped into the mortuary and put 10 nickels in his pocket as he lay in state. We do not often hear about the touching incidents like that—so often a part of giving care to the aged.

PERSONAL APPEARANCE

Plastic Surgery

In the middle years of their life, some women have their nose straightened or wrinkles removed under the eyes, which is reportedly a painful experience. The role played by Elizabeth Taylor in the film "Ash Wednesday" provides a good example. One author noted that facial improvements by surgical creation may be called somato-psychic operations; through artistic somatic change, they produce psychic change that is desirable (Brown). The impact of scars following open-heart surgery, kidney removal, mastectomy, etc., should be considered. The need for special clothing (bathing suits, as one obvious example) should be a concern of dress designers and experts. The impracticality of much of the current clothing becomes more apparent as the aged struggle to improve personal appearances and have tasteful grooming. The reader is referred to the book *Sex after Sixty* (Butler and Lewis) for a discussion of the importance of grooming in later life.

Figure 25-3 The importance of shopping bags, billfolds, wallets, coin purses, etc., is evident in this drawing. Such items are part of one's identity and are necessary to the psychological well-being of the aged person. (*Courtesy of Bill Clark.*)

Care of Hair

Wigs and coloring of hair must be one of the big money makers in the cosmetic industry. Loss of hair and thinning hair cause problems in coiffuring and can increase self-consciousness. Women may spend large sums of money on wigs and may be sensitive about them. Once while I was staying in the room with a doctor doing a physical examination on a woman (not to assist the doctor—just to prevent a lawsuit), the doctor bluntly asked the woman to remove the hat she wore, and when she did, we saw that she was absolutely bald. She dissolved into tears. She had no money to purchase a wig, so wore a hat constantly. This was many years ago when wigs were costly items not purchasable by the average person. See Figure 25-4.

Hair Removal

The need to remove hair from the chin of elderly women has not been discussed in the literature. Many aged women seem unaware of such hairs because of poor vision; others state that though they cannot see them, they can feel them as they stroke the hand across the chin. Electrolysis for aging women has not been much considered in their psychosocial care; yet hair on the face, especially the upper lip and chin, persists in being a pervasive problem—one of the ugly reminders to women that youth is long gone.

Dentures

Dentures may cause great embarrassment. One man remarked how readily his wife could accept being nude in front of him, but she simply could not bear to

Figure 25-4 The changing body image and the low self-esteem of many aged persons make it necessary to help them look their best. The importance of weekly trips to the beauty shop and properly fitting clothes and dentures needs constant emphasis. (*Courtesy of E. Schwab. Reprinted with permission of World Health Organization.*)

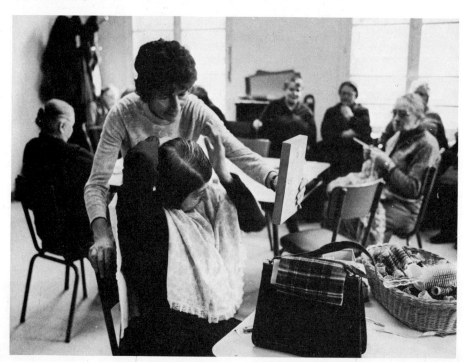

have him see her without teeth. In acute-care hospitals, the preparation for surgery requires removal of dentures. This matter should be handled carefully, as often the patient prefers that relatives be gone before the dentures are removed.

Lost and/or misplaced dentures, while providing some hilarious stories, continue to be the bane of care givers, whose own self-esteem may at times be at low ebb as a result of endless searches for these valued objects.

Fitted Clothes

As mentioned earlier, clothes designers could improve styles for the aged. Clothes should be designed to cover scars from mastectomy, open-heart surgery, chest surgery, etc. There also is a need for clothes designed to conceal the "dowager's hump." Clothing should have padded shoulders and squared-off, raglan, or dolman sleeves to cover spindly arms. Smart pantsuits are also practical for elderly women. Small wonder so many elderly women wear them. The pantsuit hides leg problems, is warm, and, as one woman said, "I can wear stockings with runs in them and it saves on my hose." The reader is referred to an annotated bibliography on social aspects of clothing for older women by Hoffman and Bader.

Elderly Hawaiian women enjoy muumuus, which cover unsightly legs and overweight problems. A grandmother in Hawaii wears a muumuu and a large hat, and may also carry a cane. Her attire sets her apart, for being a grandmother is an important role there. Old women may carry canes for protection also. (See C.'s comments in Chapter 23.)

Elderly men may need to have clothes altered; too long, baggy pants on old men are a common sight. Ill-fitting clothes have become so common as almost to be accepted as a dress code for the aged. A 72-year-old man whose movement was limited because of a stroke complained about his dependence on his wife; his clothes were not what he would pick out for himself. "They were made for young people and the shirts have only one pocket" (Knowlton). See chapter on clothing for the elderly in *The Daily Needs and Interests of Older People* (Hoffman).

LOW SELF-ESTEEM

The following case examples illustrate forgetfulness and low self-esteem.

Case Study I

Mrs. N., aged 87, was a neat, well-groomed, ambulatory woman in a nursing home. Mrs. N. had a hearing difficulty; it was best to sit by her and speak a bit more loudly and clearly. She had a great deal of difficulty in recalling the past, and constantly referred to her age by saying, "I'm an old hen." Often she was unresponsive to persistent questions and would either remain silent or say, "I can't remember. I'm just too old."

Case Study II

An 81-year-old man was interviewed before a class of nurses' aides regarding his thoughts on both living and dying. He enjoyed the sharing, but continually apologized for his lack of education. He simply did not know how eloquently he spoke. His choice of words was delightful. Of a lady named Alice, he said, "If you run around the house eight times and jump in the first window, she's a relative." Of his mules he said, "I had two mules that would kick a chew of tobacco out of your mouth before you got out of bed. I was a mule skinner or horse skinner for a living—drove 16 mules or 16 horses. I went from a teamster to the auto to driving a truck. I shoulda died 30 years ago. What's the use? I am no good to anyone."

Throughout the past 10 years I have interviewed elderly individuals singly and in groups in front of my students. The pride in sharing and being asked to help me teach were powerful boosts to their self-worth, and their pleasure is noted at the time and later as staff members give feedback.

MIRROR-IMAGE EXPERIENCE

Butler (1967) used the mirror-image experience and found it to be an excellent method of securing data regarding the aged person's self-image and body image. In this sample of aged men, a continued sense of identity was maintained. "Drawings of the self (with and without the mirror) suggested, however, that one facet of the self-view included bodily dissolution, sometimes bizarre. Maintenance of a sense of inner identity in the context of internal and external changes seemed critical to successful adaptation" (p. 1242), which reflects Back's findings, described earlier in this chapter.

Maddox experimented with drawing self by inviting the older person to collaborate with the interviewer, rather than going the usual questioning route.

SUGGESTIONS FOR INSTRUCTORS

Self-confrontation is helpful for the care giver who is a student. Drawing yourself as you imagine you will be in old age increases awareness of one's own aging. Also it comes as a great surprise to those already caring for aged persons to realize what a truly negative approach they have to their own aging process. They have indeed absorbed more of the larger society's pessimism and ageism than they realize.

As an instructor, I have found it useful for students to approach their own views of the aging process by drawing their aged selves. Students are given sheets of 8½ by 11 white paper and one simple instruction, "Draw your aged self." Instructions are unspecific, patterned after Machover's approach. See Figures 25-5 and 25-6.

The drawings, if collected over a period of time by an instructor, comprise the nucleus of a fascinating lecture on aging (either normal aging or pathologic

Figure 25-5   Student drawing of self as imagined in old age.

changes in old age). Both normal aging in a positive sense and pathologic change in a not-so-positive way become obvious as one studies these drawings.

The psychosocial aspects in the drawings include the self drawn alone, few possessions and/or objects, a "stripping-away" effect. The 10 minutes allowed for the drawing may affect this, of course. Indications of disease, the accoutrements of illness and aging, wheelchairs, canes, hearing aids, and glasses are found in the drawings of each class of health workers. The state of future self-esteem comes into sharp focus after this simple experiential exercise.

With so much emphasis on low self-esteem, the chapter should end on an upbeat, and a beautiful example of positive self-esteem was stated in an interview with a 104-year-old woman (described in Chapter 23). About her deceased husband she said, "Wherever he is now, he thinks, 'She was worth it . . . she was worth everything' " (C.).

C.'s words remind me of the words of Gould, which strike me as important for care givers to remember: "Throughout the years of adulthood, there is an ever-increasing need to win permission from oneself to continue developing. . . . The direction of change is toward becoming more tolerant of oneself, and more appreciative of the complexity of both the surrounding world and of the mental milieu . . ." (p. 74). Especially when there is low self-esteem, the care giver should be helping to increase tolerance of one's self and to encourage development.

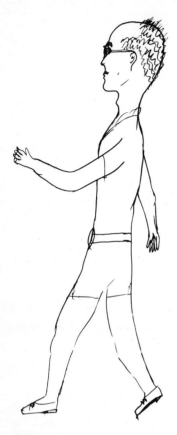

Figure 25-6   Student drawing of self as imagined in old age.

A reviewer of the novel *Rocking,* by Wright, wrote, ''. . . (they) are to themselves as actual, as alive, as passionately in life as they have ever been. They refuse to write themselves off; they cling to hopes, which are often fantastic; they suffer needs, which are seldom met. Above all they feel. And . . . each of them takes on the force of personality that gives each an unyielding selfhood.''

The message for us is to not write them off, to help them cling to hope as we endeavor to help them meet their many unmet needs, and most of all to encourage the ''unyielding selfhood'' to flourish.

SUMMARIZING STATEMENTS BASED ON THE LITERATURE

- It takes more courage to be ''I'' as frailty increases (Scott-Maxwell).
- Self-worth is related to the loss of important roles, but loss of such roles may also be welcomed by the aged person (Back).
- Threats to self-esteem: (1) conflict between youth and old age, (2) youth worship, (3) decreased interpersonal relationships, (4) lack of resiliency in

stress and losses, (5) effects of poor memory, loss of spatial orientation, speed, agility, sensory acuity (Klopfer).

- Aging process involves (1) changing body image, (2) decreased self-esteem, (3) feelings of worthlessness and rejection, and (4) feelings of being punished for hostility and sexual strivings (Mittelmann).
- Body image is a reflection of impressions of one's body accumulated over a lifetime of development (Fisher and Cleveland; Fisher; Witkin).
- The Diogenes syndrome is seen in persons who have no shame regarding personal appearance (Clark et al.).
- Consider that aged institutionalized men high in dependency needs may reveal low present and past self-concept (Gordon and Vinacke).
- Self-esteem is lower in institutionalized aged than in those aged who are on a waiting list to enter an institution or still living in the community (Tobin and Lieberman).
- Reminiscing may be a defense against threats to self-esteem (Lewis).
- Positive self-concept for aged person means he must be able to function adequately in a normal independent existence (Mason).
- Self-esteem is an important factor in sexual fulfillment (Burchell).
- Personal possessions are important to build a self (Goffman).
- A drawing of one's aged self may indicate a personal pessimism which may influence one's care and caring (Burnside, this text).

GUIDELINES FOR INTERVENTIONS IN LOW SELF-ESTEEM

- Increase the chance to affirm individuality, the uniqueness, the "I-ness" of an aged person.
- Focus on role losses; can any roles be replaced, or substitutions made?
- Assist in reality testing during states of confusion and/or disorientation.
- Listen for expression of feelings of worthlessness, rejection, and hostility.
- Listen for expressions about body image, especially following trauma, loss of body parts, and disabilities.
- Assist aged institutionalized men to greater independence.
- Purses, wallets, tote bags, change in the pocket are all important to both men and women of the present generation of aged.
- Observe style of reminiscing; is it "defensive" in tone?
- Check for adequate functioning. Is the aged in an independent situation?
- Listen for themes of sexual dissatisfaction or unmet sexual needs.
- Plastic surgery may be important to women.
- Check on clothing. Does it fit properly? Is it mended? Is it clean?
- Electrolysis may help remove unwanted hair, especially on the face of women.
- Be sensitive to care of dentures.
- Analyze your own drawing of your aged self; is it positive, negative, or neutral?

REFERENCES

Adams, David L.: "Correlates of Satisfaction among the Elderly," *The Gerontologist,* part II, **11**(4):63–68, 1971.

Anderson, Nancy N.: "Effects of Institutionalization on Self-esteem," *Journal of Gerontology,* **22**(3):313–317, 1967.

Back, Kurt W.: "Transition to Aging and the Self-image," presented at American Gerontological Society Meeting, Toronto, Canada, October 1970.

—— and **C. R. Paramish:** "Self-image, Information Exchange and Social Character," *International Journal of Psychology,* **4**:109–117, 1969.

Berenson, Bernard: *Sunset and Twilight, From the Diaries of 1947–1958,* Harcourt, Brace & World, 1963.

Branden, Nathaniel: *The Psychology of Self-Esteem,* 10th printing, Bantam Books, New York, 1976.

Brehm, M. L., and **Kurt W. Back:** "Self Image and Attitude toward Drugs," *Journal of Personality,* **36**(2):299–314, 1968.

Brown, Adolph M.: "Surgical Restorative Art for the Aging Face," *Journal of Gerontology,* **8**(2):173–184, 1953.

Bryan, Sr. Josephine: "Exploration of Hope and/or Hopelessness of Aged Patients Confined to a Nursing Home," Master's study, Indiana University, Bloomington, May 1977.

Burchell, R. Clay: "Self-esteem and Sexuality, *Medical Aspects of Human Sexuality,* **9**(1):74, 1975.

Butler, Robert N.: "Aspects of Survival and Adaptation in Human Aging," *American Journal of Psychiatry,* **123**(10): 1233–1243, 1967.

—— and **Myrna Lewis:** *Aging and Mental Health,* 2d ed., Mosby, St. Louis, 1977.

—— and ——: *Sex after Sixty,* Harper & Row, New York, 1976.

Clark, A. N. H., G. D. Mankikar, and **I. Gray:** "Diogenes Syndrome. A Clinical Study of Gross Neglect in Old Age," *Lancet,* **1**(7903):366–368, 1975.

Fisher, S.: *Body Experience in Fantasy and Behavior,* Appleton-Century-Crofts, New York, 1970.

—— and **S. Cleveland:** *Body Image and Personality,* Van Nostrand, Princeton, 1958.

Goffman, Erving: *Asylum,* Adline Press, Chicago, 1961.

Gordon, Susan K., and **W. Edgar Vinacke:** "Self and Ideal Self-concepts and Dependency in Aged Persons Residing in Institutions," *Journal of Gerontology,* **26**(3):337–343, 1971.

Gould, Roger: "Adult Life Stages: Growth toward Self-tolerance," *Psychology Today,* **8**(9):74–78, 1975.

Gurin, G., J. Veroff, and **S. Feld:** *Americans View Their Mental Health,* Basic Books, New York, 1960.

Herz, Warren: Personal letter, 1977.

Hoffman, Adeline M.: *The Daily Needs and Interests of Older People,* Charles C Thomas, Springfield, Ill., 1976.

—— and **Iva M. Bader:** *Social Science Aspects of Clothing for Older Women, An Annotated Bibliography,* 2d ed., The University of Iowa, Iowa City, March 1977.

Holmes, T. H., and **R. H. Rahe:** "The Social Readjustment Scale," *Journal of Psychosomatic Research,* **11**(2):213–218, 1967.

Kahana, Boaz: "Problem Solving Groups," paper presented at International Congress of Gerontology, Jerusalem, Israel, June 1975.

Kahana, E., and R. Coe: "Self and Staff Conceptions of Institutionalized Aged," *The Gerontologist,* 9(4):264–267, 1969.

Klopfer, W. G.: "Interpersonal Theory of Adjustment," in R. Kastenbaum (ed.), *Psycho-Biology of Aging,* Springer, New York, 1965.

Knowlton, Willis E.: Student paper, class "Psychosocial Care of the Aged," Arizona State University, Tempe, 1977.

Kogan, N., and M. A. Wallach: "Age Changes in Values and Attitudes," *Journal of Gerontology,* 16(3):272–280, 1961.

Lahey, Mary Lou: Personal communication, 1977.

Laverty, R.: "Non-resident Aid—Community versus Institutional Care for Older People," *Journal of Gerontology,* 5(4):370–374, 1950.

Lepkowski, J. R.: "The Attitudes and Adjustments of Institutionalized Catholic Aged," *Journal of Gerontology,* 11(2): 185–191, 1956.

Lewis, Charles C.: "Reminiscence and Self-concept in Old Age," unpublished doctoral dissertation, University of Chicago, Chicago, 1970.

Lieberman, Morton A.: "Relocation Research and Social Policy," *The Gerontologist,* 14(6):495–501, 1974.

——— and M. Lakin: "On Becoming an Institutionalized Aged Person," in W. Donahue, C. Tibbits, and R. Williams (eds.), *Processes of Aging,* Atherton, New York, 1963.

———, V. Prock, and Sheldon Tobin: "Psychological Effects of Institutionalization, *Journal of Gerontology,* 23(3): 343–353, 1968.

Lowenthal, Marjorie, Majda Thurner, and David Chiriboga: *Four Stages of Life: A Comparative Study of Women and Men Facing Transition,* Jossey-Bass, San Francisco, 1975.

——— and David Chiriboga: "Transition to the Empty Nest: Crisis, Challenge

or Relief, *Archives of General Psychiatry,* 26(1):8–14, 1972.

Machover, Karen: "Drawing of the Human Figure: A Method of Personality Investigation," in H. Anderson and G. Anderson (eds.), *An Introduction to Projective Techniques,* Prentice-Hall, Englewood Cliffs, N.J., 1951.

Maddox, George: "Disengagement Theory: A Critical Evaluation," *The Gerontologist,* 4(2):80–82, 1964.

Mason, E.: "Some Correlates of Self-judgment of the Aged," *Journal of Gerontology,* 9(3):324–337, 1954.

Mittelmann, Bela: "Psychosomatic Medicine and the Older Patient," in O. J. Kaplan (ed.), *Mental Disorders in Later Life,* 2d ed., Stanford University Press, Stanford, Calif., 1956.

Neugarten, B., and D. Gutmann: "Age-Sex Roles and Personality in Middle Age: A Thematic Apperception Study," in B. Neugarten (ed.), *Middle Age and Aging,* University of Chicago Press, Chicago, 1968.

Ossofsky, Jack: "National Organization Seeks to Mend the Frayed Image of the Elderly," *Geriatrics,* 39(7):42+, July 1975.

Pan, J.: "Factors in the Personal Adjustment of Old People in Protestant Homes for the Aged," *American Sociological Review,* 16(3):379–381, 1951.

Peters, George R.: "Self-conceptions of the Aged, Age Identification, and Aging," *The Gerontologist,* part II, 11(4): 69–73, 1971.

Plutchik, Robert, and Hope Conte: "Studies of Body Image. III: Body Feelings as Measured by the Semantic Differential, *International Journal of Aging and Human Development,* 4(4):375–380, 1973.

Pollack, M., E. Karp, R. L. Kahn, and A. I. Goldfarb: "Perception of Self in Institutionalized Aged Subjects: 1. Response Patterns of Mirror Reflection,"

Journal of Gerontology, **17**(4):405–408, 1962.

Reichard, Susan, F. Livson, and P. G. Petersen: *Aging and Personality,* Wiley, New York, 1962.

Robinson, Linda: Personal communication, 1970.

Rosner, A.: "The Maintenance of Self during Institutionalization of the Aged," in S. Tobin (ed.), *The Dependencies of Old People, Occasional Papers in Gerontology No. 6,* Ann Arbor, Institute of Gerontology, The University of Michigan, Wayne State University Press, Detroit, 1969.

Rosow, I.: "Adjustment of the Normal Aged," in R. Williams, C. Tibbitts, and W. Donahue (eds.), *Processes of Aging,* vol. II, Atherton, New York, 1963.

Rynerson, Barbara C.: "Need for Self-esteem in the Aged: A Literature Review," *Journal of Psychiatric Nursing and Mental Health Services,* **10**(1):22–26, 1972.

Sarbin, T. G.: "Role Theory," in G. Lindzey (ed.), *Handbook of Social Psychology,* Addison-Wesley, Reading, Mass., 1954.

Schulz, Richard, and Gail Brenner: "Relocation of the Aged: A Review and Theoretical Analysis, *Journal of Gerontology,* **32**(3):323–333, 1977.

Scott-Maxwell, Florida: *The Measure of My Days,* Knopf, New York, 1968.

Sherman, Edmund, and Evelyn S. Newman: "The Meaning of Cherished Personal Possessions for Elderly," *Journal of Aging and Human Development,* **8**(2): 181–192, 1977–1978.

Sullivan, Harry S.: *The Interpersonal Theory of Psychiatry,* Norton, New York, 1953.

Tobin, Sheldon, and Morton Lieberman: *Last Home for the Aged: Critical Implications of Institutionalization,* Jossey-Bass, San Francisco, 1976.

Tuckman, J., I. Lorge, and F. Zeman: "The Self-image in Aging," *Journal of Genetic Psychology,* **99**:317–321, 1961.

Webster's New Collegiate Dictionary, G. & C. Merriam Co., Springfield, Mass., 1977.

Witkin, H. A.: "Development of the Body Concept and Psychological Differentiation," in S. Wagner and H. Werner (eds.), *The Body Percept,* Random House, New York, 1965.

Wright, Rosalie: *Rocking,* Harper & Row, New York, 1975 (on the fly leaf).

Zinberg, Norman E.: "Social Learning and Self-image in Aging," *Journal of Geriatric Psychiatry,* **9**(2):131–150, 1976.

OTHER RESOURCES

FILMS

David and Bert: 27 min/16 mm/color. A portrait of two Canadians, an 87-year-old prospector who lives alone and hikes with his equipment digging for gold, and a north coast Indian surrounded by many of his 60 grandchildren to whom he teaches songs and dances of his traditional culture. The two men share 40 years of friendship and a rich and humorous philosophy of life. Each demonstrates that old age can be a gentle victory. Distributor: University of California, Extension Media Center, Berkeley, Calif. 94720.

The Shameless Old Lady: 95 min/35 mm/

b&w/1966. Feature-length French film directed by Rene Allio. Tells the story of an aged widow's "shameless" assertion of life. A 70-year-old widow, after having given the major part of her life to the care of her husband and children, now opts for good times and fun, buys a car, and finds young, vital companions. Contact: Twyman Films, 329 Salem Avenue, Dayton, Ohio 54401.

The String Bean: See Chapter 18, Other Resources.

Chapter 26

LONELINESS AND GRIEF IN SENESCENCE
Irene Mortenson Burnside

> Loss is the price we pay for the relationships essential to
> our humanity.
>
> *Simos*

LONELINESS

Loneliness at any age is poignant; but because significant others are gone and
the resources of the elderly are often limited, loneliness in old age is an area for
special attention and intervention by professionals. Gaev presented a comprehensive analysis of the psychology of loneliness. Her analysis is based on the
works of Fromm-Reichmann, Sullivan (1953, 1954), Fromm, Horney, May,
Maslow, Buber, and Tillich. Weiss wrote a small volume on loneliness which
gives some suggestions on how to cope with the condition. The literature offers
little on loneliness in the aged person. Recent publications on loneliness and old
age include the writings of Bennett, Burnside (1971), Curtin, Da Silva, Fidler,
Loether, Moustakas, and Tannenbaum.

   This chapter is divided into two sections: the first part is about loneliness in
the later years and the second part is about grief.

Definition

Weiss states that there is still a need for a taxonomy of the types of loneliness.
A definition by Fromm-Reichmann seems to pinpoint loneliness of the aged:
". . . the states of mind in which the fact that then there were people in one's
past life is more or less forgotten, and the hope that there may be interpersonal
relationships in one's future life is out of the realm of expectation or imagination"
(p. 327).

   Sullivan (1953) stated that man is a gregarious animal with a need for contact with others and that when this need is unfulfilled it is expressed in loneliness. When action is taken to avoid or relieve tension or loneliness, self-esteem is enhanced. (Since low self-esteem is a pervasive problem in the elderly, it is discussed extensively in Chapter 25.)

Loneliness in the Elderly

Two articles on loneliness in the aged appeared in *Mental Hygiene* (Tannenbaum; Burnside, 1971). Tannenbaum wrote about the importance of understanding loneliness in the aged person, of relating to it in a helpful way, and of recognizing that loneliness mirrors the general needs of the elderly.

Da Silva, a psychiatrist, and Moustakas, a psychologist, have written two moving and sensitive accounts of psychotherapy with lonely elderly men. Both articles are highly recommended.

Burnside (1971) teased out reasons for their loneliness from some of the aged themselves. Some possible causes were (1) geographical location; (2) language barriers, (3) cultural differences, (4) life-style, (5) illness and/or pain, (6) loss of others, and (7) impending death.

In the United Kingdom, bereavement is the biggest single factor in the onset of loneliness (*Age Concern,* 1974). Fidler, who wrote a paper focusing on the loneliness of elderly people living in the community, presents the argument that physical isolation is not always the prime cause. She points out that one of the causes of loneliness is outmoded social policy (e.g., the accommodations thought to be suitable for an old person, and rigid retirement age limits, which indeed have exacerbated the problems they tried to solve).

That old people are lonely (as stated by Palmore) is a myth. Their loneliness is hardly a myth to those trying to cope with heavy caseloads of lonely old folks. Lantz agrees with Palmore that loneliness is not a major problem in the elderly because "approximately 70 per cent of the aged in the United States live with others" (p. 36). One can still be lonely with other persons around, but Lantz feels that what the professional mistakes for loneliness is actually isolation. My own experience is that "loneliness" is the term used by older persons themselves to describe their feeling. Some of the loneliest old people I have known lived in nursing homes.

Hyams noted that, "Loneliness (a subjective feeling not necessarily related to physical isolation) is very common in the elderly and can exert a profound influence in aggravating the emotional components of an illness by leading to feelings of insecurity; later, apathy may develop" (pp. 133–134).

We can ignore much of the loneliness of the elderly because we choose not to see it. As Slater writes, in describing American culture at the breaking point:

Our ideas about institutionalizing the aged, psychotic, retarded, and infirm based on a pattern of thought that we might call the Toilet Assumption—the notion that unwanted matter, unwanted difficulties, unwanted complexities and obstacles will disappear if they are removed from our immediate field of vision. . . . We throw the aged and psychotic into institutional holes where they cannot be seen. Our approach to social problems is to decrease their visibility: out of sight, out of mind . . . remove the underlying problems of our society farther and farther from the daily experience and daily consciousness, and hence to decrease, in the mass of the population, the knowledge, skill, resources, and motivation necessary to deal with them (p. 15).

A very young man was motivated enough to try his own way to help an old man out:

Case Example

An ambulance driver in one of my classes described driving an old man home from a veterans' hospital. The old man insisted he stay and have a cup of soup with him. The young man spent his lunch hour there "because he was so terribly lonely. And when I left he gave me a $20 bill, thanking me for all the help." The old man made and served the soup. The young man sat quietly and listened with great interest. Therapy at its best!

Loneliness and Isolation

Townsend and Tunstall state that loneliness stems from desolation rather than isolation. Desolation relates to recent loss of company. This may be the kind of situation in which care givers can so effectively intervene.

Shanas et al. say that isolation is not synonymous with loneliness, nor is it a causative factor in mental illness. Some people have lost the notion of what loneliness means. The loneliest, most isolated people appear to be widowed persons, living alone with no children. Butler and Lewis define two elements in childhood which are factors in the early sense of loneliness: aloneness—the fear about physical survival in a threatening and uncertain world; and loneliness—the fear of emotional isolation, being locked within one's self and unable to obtain warmth and comfort from others. They say the roots of loneliness in childhood return in old age; but the big difference is the fear of not having anyone to relate to, and this is a reality. Death of significant others occurs, and children, grandchildren, and great grandchildren may live far away.

Only a few research studies of loneliness have been carried out. Shanas and her associates in their national survey tried to study the problem by examining the relationship between subjectively experienced loneliness and social isolation in old age. About half of those living alone reported that they felt lonely only rarely or not at all. About three-fourths of those living with other people reported they were rarely or never lonely. Particularly vulnerable to feelings of loneliness were persons who had recently lost their spouses. Fairly frequent contacts with their children was a factor which seemed to mitigate somewhat feelings of loneliness among those living alone. Interestingly, persons who had been single all their lives complained of loneliness much less frequently than those who either were still married or had been widowed, separated, or divorced.

Shanas et al. conclude that it is loss (desolation), not isolation, which has the closer relationship to loneliness. It is known that persons who have been separated, divorced, or widowed have higher rates of suicide in old age than those with intact marriages. However, there have been no reported studies of the frequency of subjectively experienced loneliness among persons who have attempted or committed suicide.

Loneliness is a difficult area in which to intervene. One can be baffled deciding what might comprise a therapeutic intervention for old people who, either overtly or covertly, express loneliness. There are those aged persons so encrusted with defense mechanisms that they deny loneliness even though their behavior is that of a lonely person.

One trap to avoid is the assumption that loneliness (or depression, boredom, or apathy, for that matter) developed late in the aged individual's life. If one studies the life-style of the person, one often finds that such traits were manifested on a continuum throughout life; the problems did not develop suddenly in later years. See Figure 26-1.

Restitution

Cath talks about restitution. The loss of loved ones is a poignant experience for the aging person. The closeness and friendship of the care givers are often of crucial importance in lessening the "conversation deprivation" that may exist at such a time (Burnside, 1976). One just cannot underestimate the therapeutic value of the one-to-one relationship. Many elderly work out ways of keeping a worker close to them. Ruses include clinging to one's hand, offering another cup of coffee or tea, giving a gift, or simply talking without stopping!

Not being understood during communication increases loneliness. There are still many foreign-born persons who do not speak English well, or at all. There are also aphasics and deaf persons who are isolated and lonely because of severe communication problems. There are those who understand spoken English but do not read or write the language. Boyack once described a lonely 90-year-old man in a Veterans' Administration Hospital who asked if she would help him learn how to write his name; he wanted to accomplish that before he died. The accomplishment of simple tasks or the achievement of simple desires (e.g., visiting a former home, birthplace, or school) may please the older person and decrease loneliness. Improving communication techniques is important for all disciplines.

It is often useful to share beverages or nourishment with an aged person; such a gesture helps in a small way to substitute for the lost spouse or loved one and increases socialization (Burnside, 1971). Smith-White wrote beautifully of drinking wine with his 89-year-old landlady. In visiting aged clients in their homes, accepting food and beverages is very important since it permits them to be host or hostess, but this type of sharing is also effective with institutionalized elderly.

Several years after I had terminated my professional relationship with my first group of aged, I returned during the Christmas holidays to say hello to the remaining two men in their eighties—the last of a group of six who had met weekly for 2 years. They admitted to loneliness during the holidays and to missing the group meetings. Mr. W. ignored his supper saying, "I can always

Figure 26-1 Not all old people are lonely. Some who live alone may prefer that life-style and are adjusted to it. Others who live alone have many social contacts. The recently widowed are often lonely because of their previously intimate relationship. Intervention in loneliness remains a challenge to care givers. (*Courtesy of Joanne Carlsson.*)

eat, but I can rarely talk to you,'' then handed me his coffee from the tray (with obvious pleasure that he remembered how much I like coffee).

It is sad that instead of seeking answers from the aged themselves, instead of trying to intervene in their lonely status, we hasten to give them solutions that do not appeal to them. Our lack of empathy may even increase loneliness for the aged.

Choice of Life-Style

However, the choice to be a loner must be respected when working with the aged. In the initial assessment of elderly persons it is important to differentiate between loners and those who truly want and need companionship. Many aged people need to be alone simply to survive; and although they are alone, they do not regard themselves as lonely. Energy levels may preclude activities they once enjoyed. It is often a care giver who, assuming that a person who is alone is extremely lonely and suffering, insists on bingo games that the oldster may detest. Many people have been loners all their lives by choice, and care givers cannot and should not change their life-style.

Another problem is that care givers do not assess individuality; they make assumptions on the basis of their own lives or needs. For instance, a student once wrote in her process recording during a one-to-one relationship with an elderly woman, "I was cold so I got up and got a sweater out of the woman's closet and put it around her shoulders and sat down. The old lady, who was obviously not cold, looked at me very strangely and asked, 'What's the matter with you?' " Such behavior is not atypical of professionals' interventions; assumptions are made about the old person's state which are based upon the professional's reaction to loneliness.

Importance of Health

Care givers will need to remember the importance of health; poor health is one factor that may contribute to loneliness. Another cause of loneliness often is hospitalization in a strange environment with a schedule that is different from what one is used to. See Figure 26-2.

Figure 26-2   The loneliness of elderly persons residing in nursing homes is often seen in apathy, withdrawal, and a lack of interest in the surroundings and the other residents. (*Courtesy of Jaima Gilson.*)

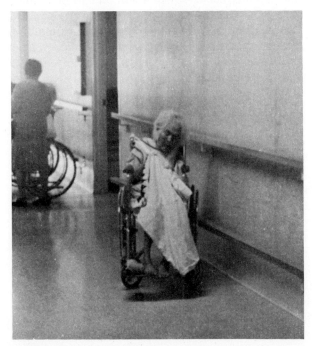

Coping with Loneliness

As stated previously, some aged cope by denying the existence of the condition; others resort to alcohol. A volunteer who delivered lunches for meals-on-wheels described the problems of home-bound drinkers (Butorac). Zimberg conducted a household survey in a section of New York City. The incidence of alcoholism reached a peak in the 45-to-54 age group (2.3 percent) and another peak in the 65-to-74 age group (2.2 percent). Some of the subjects had had drinking problems for many years. Those who develop the problem late in life are called "geriatric alcoholics."

Suicide

The final solution to handling loneliness may be suicide. Older men commit suicide more frequently than women. Von Witzleben writes, "the question of suicide often comes up in analysis, too. 'If my loneliness is so great that I hardly can carry on, wouldn't suicide be the perfect solution?'"

In his dissertation, "Suicide among Older Men," Miller has organized current research and literature on suicide in the aged. The study is highly recommended. Other articles on suicidal elderly include a case presented in 1929 at the University of California Medical School (Barker). Haggerty described a 70-year-old suicidal man. Lettieri studied suicide among the aging, as did O'Neal, Robins, and Schmidt. Gage (1971, 1973) described nursing interventions with suicidal elderly.

Townsend and Tunstall state that there are no well-founded theories of suicide in relation to aging, but important factors in the development of such theories would include (1) loss of spouse (applies especially to men), (2) loss of a child, (3) loss of an emotionally close relative, (4) loss of paid work (especially for men), (5) loss of physical agility, and (6) loss of mental agility. Two or more of the above, with a few ancillary factors, are very likely to make the aged person a "high risk" for suicide. During a one-to-one relationship, a student discovered how one elderly woman (taking the risk of being out alone at night with poor health) avoids loneliness.

Avoiding Loneliness

Case Example

Emphysema has been sapping the strength of 86-year-old Mrs. B. for the last 18 years. As the disease progressed, it became more and more difficult for her to breathe, and all activities were affected. She adjusted her life-style around her illness, with regular visits to the doctor to find out how she was doing and if there was anything new to help her.

Mrs. B. used to volunteer at the symphony, opera, and museums and enjoyed what she considered "interesting and intelligent people." Now she picks up people on the street and brings them home whenever she can manage it. Since Mrs. B. is particularly afraid of dying alone at night and since she feels that more interesting people are out at night, she sleeps for a good part of the day and goes out after dark. This living pattern solves another problem—that of having to be home alone too long during the day.

Community help is utilized whenever possible at home. A visiting nurse comes once a week, home help twice a week, and friendly visitors come twice a week. Mrs. B. tries to schedule visits so that no two persons are with her at the same time and even uses payment of bills to satisfy her social and self-esteem needs. Instead of paying by mail, she demands and gets personal attention at various places such as banks, utility companies, etc. She makes the most of what she has (Greenwald).

Summary

Tillich and also Moustakas discuss the positive aspect of loneliness, but Weiss does not share their view. He feels that it takes courage to accept responsibility for the burden of loneliness and basic aloneness in this world. Lopata points out that many women feel anger and loneliness when they are excluded from the company of their dead husbands' former associates.

Loneliness is experienced at some time in their lives by nearly everyone, but in the aged it creates problems for staff, families, peers, and, most of all, for the old person who gets mired down and cannot alone get out of the deep rut of loneliness. Psychosocial support by you and others is not always successful either. See the following statements and guidelines for assistance in intervention.

Loneliness is a subjective feeling. It is not necessarily related to sheer physical, geographical isolation. It can aggravate some of the aspects of illness—for example, insecurity, apathy, withdrawal, etc. Loneliness, aloneness, and isolation all need to be separated in the care giver's mind; such separation will subsequently be reflected in the stance taken during intervention with the elderly. It is well to remember that grief and loneliness sometimes go hand in hand.

SUMMARIZING STATEMENTS BASED ON THE LITERATURE ABOUT LONELINESS IN SENESCENCE

- Persons in one's past life may be forgotten (Fromm-Reichmann).
- Hope for future relationships is diminished (Fromm-Reichmann).
- Actions to avoid tension or loneliness increase self-esteem (Sullivan, 1953).
- Loneliness can lead to feelings of insecurity and later to apathy (Hyams).
- Loneliness can stem from desolation rather than from isolation (Townsend and Tunstall).
- The roots of loneliness in childhood return in old age (Butler and Lewis).
- Persons who have been single all their lives complain less about loneliness (Shanas et al.).
- Inability to be understood during communication increases loneliness.
- Loneliness in the aged creates problems for staff, families, peers, and, most of all, for the old person, who gets mired down and cannot alone get out of the deep rut of loneliness.
- The life-style of each individual varies; there is a need to differentiate between loneliness, aloneness, and isolation before intervention.

GUIDELINES FOR INTERVENTION: LONELINESS IN SENESCENCE

- Communication is important; consider "conversation deprivation."
  Listen attentively to the aged person who is speaking.
  Let the aged person talk; keep comments minimal.
  Study nonverbal behavior, body language, and where the person places himself or herself in relation to others.
- Be able to handle your own aloneness and/or loneliness effectively.
- Defense mechanisms of denial may be operating. The aged may deny loneliness; observe if behavior and speech are congruent.
- Share food and beverages to improve socialization and allow the older individual to be host or hostess.
- Simple tasks accomplished may make the elderly feel better, e.g., writing their names, returning to regions or buildings important earlier in their lives.
- Mail is important; send postcards or notes in your absence (Da Silva).
- Assess:
  Do roots of loneliness go back to childhood?
  Has the person been single most of her or his life?
  Is the person feeling insecure?
  Is touch needed?

GRIEF

I follow'd rest; rest fled and soon forsook me;
I ran from grief; grief ran and overtook me.

Quarles, Emblems (1635)

Well, everyone can master a grief but he that has it.

Shakespeare, "Much Ado about Nothing"

The preponderance of grief reactions in the later years of life may follow a variety of losses; some losses cause considerable strain on the coping ability of an old person.

Coping Traditions

Perhaps we have lost some traditions which once helped us to cope with grief. For instance, just as birth certificates help celebrate a birth, early Americans had ornamental printed designs, called *mourning prints,* to acknowledge a family death. The prints were first popularized with the death of George Washington and were common in the early 1800s. Though they reminded the family member of the finality of death, they also provided needed daily moral and religious tones. They were a type of expressive American folk art. Some mourning prints had pictures of the deceased; some had intertwining bits of the deceased's hair. Public display of continued bereavement was accepted. The William Penn Memorial Museum of Harrisburg, Pennsylvania, created a special exhibit of the prints, entitled, "Mourning Becomes America," for the United States Bicentennial (McCulloch).

It is clear that we have lost some of the once-accepted forms of behavior that assisted in grief work. Today mourning is not becoming in America; it is more likely to be threatening. I am reminded of a man, nearly 80 years old, who collects all the "In Memoriam" handouts from the funerals of his cohorts. The last time I visited him, he had a collection of nearly 20 and dealt them out almost like cards when searching for information about one of his deceased peers.

Symptoms of Grief

Lindemann's study of bereaved survivors of a holocaust remains a classic. He defines grief as, "an acute state of despair and disconsolate anguish because of the immediate loss of a person or object" (p. 145). However, Lindemann's study leaves out one important fact regarding the subjects—the age of the 101 persons studied. Is the grief of late life different from the grief of earlier years? It seems to be.

Grief reactions in later years were studied by Stern, William, and Prados. Twenty-five subjects (1 male and 24 females) were interviewed; their ages ranged from 53 to 70 years. (The age of 70 seems an early limit to study the effects of grief in later years.) The researchers stated that the first interview should be kept "free" so the patient does not have the feeling that a systematic history is being taken. Because of the many somatic illnesses common to the elderly, the patient needs to feel that the psychiatrist is keeping close track of him or her and has a genuine interest in all the patient's medical and surgical procedures. Important features observed in their treatment group included (1) a relative paucity of conscious feelings of guilt, (2) a tendency to replace emotional grief reactions with somatic equivalents, (3) a distortion of the image of the deceased into an unreal glorification, and (4) a proclivity towards self-isolation and hostility towards the rest of the family or friends.

The researchers also felt that the aging person is biologically more prepared for somatic equivalents of depression, and that with elderly persons there is an opportunity to identify with the deceased rather than to feel guilt towards him. One wonders if the long time spent together is one of the reasons for this.

Anticipatory Grief

The term *anticipatory grief* was coined by Lindemann. Alternative terms are *preparatory grief,* or *premourning behavior* (Gerber, Rusalem, Hannon, Battin, and Arkin). Studies on anticipatory grief appear in the literature of the 1940s (Eliot; Lindemann; Rosenbaum). Initial efforts in this area dealt with wartime separation or death occurring during military combat. Anticipatory grief studies dealing specifically with the aged griever are few (Bornstein, Clayton, Halikas,

Maurice, and Robins; Schwab, Chalmers, Conroy, Farris, and Markosh; Gerber et al.; Peretz).

Gerber and associates question whether anticipatory grief has a positive effect on an individual's adjustment to loss, and point out that, "The anguish of watching a slow painful dying process associated with an illness such as cancer is supposed to serve an extended function of softening the event of death" (p. 225). They offer practical suggestions for the health professionals who serve an elderly population. The elderly may not benefit from having the time to prepare for an impending loss. Practitioners are cautioned to keep a watchful eye on those widowed who have endured the extended illness of a spouse prior to the death of that spouse. "If it is true that an extended period of anticipation of bereavement is potentially dangerous for the elderly survivor, then medical, nursing, and social work personnel must be cognizant of its negative aspects in order to prevent future maladjustment. Indications that the future survivor will feel responsible for the death and be left with morbid memories of the illness" (p. 229) are two specific examples of behavior for the care giver to be alert for during a long debilitating fatal illness.

The depletion of energy of the aged person who has cared for the ill spouse must be considered. Although we as bystanders may think that such a person will be relieved to have the care and worry ended, often such is not the case.

Anticipatory grief may occur when a family has been told by a doctor that a loved one has a certain amount of time left to live. The family goes into the grief process, and then sometimes the aged person recovers. It is a most difficult situation for relatives who have accepted the fact that a loved one will die, and the dying individual rallies or even greatly improves. Families may have even gone to the extent of completing funeral arrangements. Patton described someone who had given away the clothing of her 75-year-old mother when doctors said she could not survive. The mother completely recovered and was furious about her missing clothing. She could not forgive the daughter, nor did she appreciate the new wardrobe her daughter bought her.

Another form of anticipatory grief is what a surgeon (Janis) termed "worry work" in a study of surgical patients. His classic studies explore grief over body losses due to surgery.

Peretz states that the griever who endures a prolonged illness with the deceased will manifest grief work similar to that observed after an unexpected or sudden death. The pain a family endures during slow deaths can be a great drain, both physically and psychologically.

Wilson recommends pre-bereavement and post-bereavement visiting of the elderly. She feels that, "A most effective method of preventing social isolation and loneliness of an old person is through support given at the time of greatest grief, encouraging the intake of an adequate diet and ensuring that they do not become completely cut off from the family, friends, and neighborhood, and that some interest is found for them" (p. 1357).

Along a similar line, Hampe studied the needs of spouses during the terminal illness of their mates and following the death event. She suggested the need for further research with grieving spouses. For example, (1) another study could provide follow-up interviews at longer intervals than the 3- to 12-week period of the first study, because grief continues beyond that period; (2) a similar study might be conducted with spouses of acutely ill patients; (3) or the study could be repeated in a different locale interviewing spouses with a different socioeconomic background.

Omitted Grief

Deutsch emphasized that ambivalence toward the deceased is a difficult conflict to resolve during the mourning reaction. Grief can range from no response at all, or as she has aptly termed it, "omitted grief," to severe depressions and/or suicide. The aged person tends to develop his or her particular pattern for grief work, and care givers will have to observe the pattern. "For most people the accumulation of experiences and crises may be expected to bring about better self-understanding" (Lowenthal, Thurner, and Chiriboga, p. 80).

Cultural Aspects of Grief

The cultural aspects of grief are often poorly understood by care givers. A young Indian woman once approached me after a class when I had assigned some stress interviewing (i.e., interviewing people about subjects not easy for them to tackle, for example, death). She was going to interview an elderly Indian widow, but in that tribe it was not permitted to talk about the deceased husband. We are oblivious of cultural aspects of grief.

A fine film about funeral rituals and grief is the Roumanian documentary, "The Parting" (see the list of films at the end of Chapter 30).

It has been my observation that there seems to be in elderly persons a desensitization to some of the pain associated with grief and loss. It is not uncommon for an aged person to develop a remarkable philosophy about loss through the years, and this philosophy may sustain him or her through severe traumas. Cohorts can be helpful and supportive during periods of stress, grief, and loss; Eisdorfer stated that the best therapy for someone who has lost a loved one is a peer who has suffered the same loss.

Case Example

In a cafeteria in a large medical center, an elderly woman sat down near me and began talking to the woman next to her. She stated that she and a friend were taking turns sitting at the bedside of a dying friend. The three women had once been members of a women's club; none of them had relatives to help them now. Since women are continuing to outlive men, the support elderly women can give to one another must not be overlooked.

A common and readily recognizable grief reaction of the aged person is to the loss of significant others. Berezin states, "There is an absurdity in maintaining the concepts of loss as operating purely on an all-or-none basis. It is more accurate and to the point to appreciate that loss which acts as a precipitant of reactions may be partial, threatened, or anticipated and that subtle changes in the elderly person must be regarded as loss equivalents—or at least as threats of loss'' (p. 58).

"Working Through"

In the field of mental health there is much talk about working through grief, although ''working through'' is not defined. ''Work'' is the key word. It is necessary, not easy, and the ''through'' implies a process which ends. Sometimes one cannot help but wonder if grief is ever fully resolved. The impact of the loss lingers on. I have learned this from listening to old women's descriptions of loss of spouses and children.

Berezin reminds us that the aged have their own unique ways of coping with loss. The degree and the type of grief reaction depend on several factors, but Berezin suggests that previous relationships and the maturity of the ego are important factors. A student once described an old man who during his grief, daily visited his wife's grave and sat there reading alone until he finished the book they had started reading together. The importance of cemetery rituals has not been studied. The meaningfulness of visits to the grave has not been described. One thinks of the Kennedy family and their frequent visits to grave sites. I once visited Punch Bowl Cemetery in Honolulu and sat under a tree watching all the activity. I observed one elderly couple on their hands and knees with hand clippers carefully trimming the grass at a grave. A friend of mine told me that she and her sister often took a picnic lunch and went to the cemetery where their mother was buried, spreading a blanket near her gravesite to eat lunch (Butorac). See Figure 26-3.

Cath stated, ''Clinical experience suggests that it is an error to assume that a person in the middle or later years is partly or wholly unable to demonstrate tremendous and variable capacities for integration and development or for enduring loss. . . . It appears that the human ego can tolerate tremendous shock and loss and still expand, grow, and create. It is probable that the greatest stress and strain the adult human organism undergoes is in the last trimester of life . . .'' (p. 27). Courageous oldsters in nursing homes accomplish therapeutic interventions with grieving cohorts.

Case Study I

In a long-term care facility, a woman in her eighties who had only one child was informed one day that her son had been killed in an automobile accident. The staff was concerned as to how she would hold up under the news, since already she was struggling with many health problems of her own. A friend wheeled herself into the room when she heard the news and asked if it would help to sit with her. The grieving woman said she would like that. A group of women were enlisted to rotate for half-hour periods (they considered their own energy level as they planned this), sitting quietly at her bedside and not talking, if she did not feel like conversing.

Figure 26-3   The significance of cemetery rituals for an aged person in the process of working through grief is important for care givers to consider. (*Courtesy of Bill Clark.*)

The solutions of old people are meaningful, therapeutic, sensible, and usually not difficult to implement. Why is it that we so seldom ask for their solutions?

Case Study II

A newly retired nursing director lost her housemate of 35 years. She wrote to a friend, ". . . found I was more of a 'crybaby' than I knew. For the first few months, friends accepted my tears without comment but now when things get too much for me and I can't control the crying impulse, I'm told to stop 'feeling sorry for myself' so I do my weeping in my quiet room in the still of the night. I don't know why I am writing you this except that somehow I feel that you know of loneliness and will understand it helps me to share my misery with an understanding heart" (anonymous).

Loss of Children

I have been impressed many times as I listen to a very old woman poignantly describe the loss of a stillborn, an infant, or a young child. A 90-year-old woman told me that her one and only child was stillborn; ruefully she added, "If she had lived, she would have been 65 years old now." Women often speak of infants who were born dead or who died soon after birth. While I have never heard old men talk in such a manner, that is not to say that they do not also mourn for children who died years ago.

The Old Ones of New Mexico has this beautiful passage:

I thought of the five children we had lost, three before they had a chance to take a breath. I wondered where in the universe they were. In the evening sometimes, when I go to close loose doors that otherwise complain loudly all night, I am likely to look at the stars and feel my long-gone infants near at hand. They are far off, I know; but in my mind they have become those stars—very small, but shining there bravely, no matter how cold it is far up. If the stars have courage, we ought to have courage; that is what I was thinking, as I so often have in the past (Coles, p. 10).

A story is told about an old farmer in Vermont. A visitor said to him, "It must be a great satisfaction to you to have such a fine family, and all living near you." "Yes," said the 85-year-old, "It is; I had six boys and I raised every one of them except one who died when he was 60."

"Bereavement overload" is the loss of several significant others and friends very close together. The source of the term is unknown, but the overload is so common in the aged as to be overlooked at times. The care giver must keep a running list of the losses sustained by older people and be aware of what might be an overload. Simple suggestions from the literature may be helpful in intervening with the aged (see the lists on pp. 524–525).

From Grief to Growth

The care giver will be exploring ways of alleviating the acute pain of early grief, but the positive aftereffects of such pain should also be high in the thoughts of the helper. The grief will help shape the behavior, but that behavior can be a surprising stride forward of growth and character. The following case study demonstrates growth during grief and prior to death. It typifies acute psychic pain and physical pain occurring simultaneously.

Case Study

During the month of November, a woman in her mid-sixties was hospitalized for an exploratory operation and was found to be riddled with abdominal cancer. In a few weeks, she was bedridden and on intravenous feedings. Her husband was told of the diagnosis. He immediately stopped taking antihypertensive medication. He suffered a massive stroke in December, was hospitalized (on another ward of the same hospital as his wife), and died on Christmas Day. There were no other relatives, so Mrs. K. planned his funeral alone, although she was too ill to attend. She had planned her own funeral at the same time. She asked her afternoon private duty nurse to attend her husband's funeral and report back to her.

She went on to her death with a courage not expected in her. She had always talked baby talk and, since they were childless, had doted over a cherished dog. Mrs. K. had been extremely dependent on her husband, but it was as though an inner control switch had been turned on and the inner locus of control now took over to function until her demise.

She gave away personal memorabilia, made arrangements to give their home to their church, and asked that intravenous feedings be stopped so she could visit her home once again. Her grief was multifaceted—grief for her dead husband, grief over loss of self and rapid deterioration, and grief for loss of her home and pet. Her composure through her own acute grief and her own dying left some of us with an example, not only for future psychosocial intervention, but for courage through our own future tragedies as well. See Figure 26-4.

Behavior Modification

Flannery described a behavior-modification program to treat grief in a community mental health setting. The client was a 77-year-old man, ''who had been his own physician,'' and on his own was taking several medications in various combi-

Figure 26-4 Many old people have developed a style of coping with grief which uniquely demonstrates growth. The above case study of the woman who revisited her home once again prior to death is a good example. (*Courtesy of Bill Clark.*)

nations which could have been lethal. There were important changes in the quality and amount of adaptive behavior within a 6-month period of time. An interesting aspect of the behavioral therapy program was the presence of another male, which provided such powerful reinforcement that it proved to be the only one necessary in the therapeutic program. Care givers have a tendency to forget that elderly men often reside in an almost matriarchal society. An elderly man in a nursing home said with great exasperation to me, "If one more female tells me what I have to do, I'm going to blow up."

Tears Still Unshed

De Castillejo wrote, "I believe above all one has to return again and again to weep the tears which are still unshed. We cannot feel all the grief of our many losses at the time we suffer them. That would be too crippling. But if we would really gather our whole lives into a single whole, no emotion that belongs to us should be left unfelt" (p. 157).

This statement has real implications for the older person, who may have learned to space out the grief work and not try to accomplish the task on the crisis intervention schedule of 4 to 6 weeks. Old people have learned how to keep grief from being crippling, and perhaps they do not try to feel all their grief at exactly the most tragic times of their losses. Now I understand the gentle flow of tears that has occurred so frequently when I have interviewed elderly people for a class of students. We have all watched tears begin as they describe a child or sibling or husband or wife who died. It makes better sense to me now that I have read de Castillejo's above words, to allow the aged to spread their grief out, to receive sympathy and support from time to time so that they can renew their strength, and to begin again and again.

Death, divorce, or other sudden terminations of established long-term relationships often inflict painful traumas in the lives of the elderly. Loss, separation, detachment are universal human experiences. Loss of others, of some aspect of the self, of external objects, and of pets continues throughout life. Although mourning is the normal consequence of loss, aged mourners are often deprived of conditions in which they can work through their grief and of helpers who will allow or even encourage the process.

SUMMARIZING STATEMENTS BASED ON THE LITERATURE ABOUT GRIEF IN SENESCENCE

- A systematic history should not be done during first interviews (Stern et al.).
- Loss of a loved one may not cause conscious feelings of guilt in the elderly (Stern et al.).
- Anticipate distortion of the image of the deceased (Stern et al.).
- Hostility is a component of grief work (Lindemann; Stern et al.).

- The elderly may or may not benefit from anticipatory grief in the adjustment to loss (Gerber et al.).
- Pre-bereavement and post-bereavement visiting is therapeutic (Wilson).
- "Omitted grief" may occur (Deutsch).
- Peer help and support are effective (Eisdorfer).
- People will cope with losses in their own unique way (Berezin); they should be encouraged in that style.
- Elderly mothers grieve long for children who have died (Coles).
- "Bereavement overload" is common with the elderly.

GUIDELINES FOR INTERVENTION: GRIEF IN SENESCENCE

- The first interview should not seem to be a systematic history taking; keep it "free" (Stern et al.).
- Anticipate somatic complaints (Stern et al.).
- Prevent self-isolation (Stern et al.).
- Prevent self-destruction.
- Plan pre-bereavement and post-bereavement visiting (Wilson).
- Study cultural differences; consider interventions compatible with cultural backgrounds.
- Consider "peer" help (Eisdorfer).
- Consider solutions of old people; do mutual planning (Burnside, 1971).
- Consider the importance of a male care giver for an elderly male (Flannery).
- Consider ways and means for the staff to support and help one another in the face of discouragement. Use students whenever possible in the care of the aged. Students may be from many disciplines: social work, nursing, psychology, sociology, gerontology, theology, activity directing, etc. Students can carry one-to-one relationships, do group work, and also do crisis intervention.
- If necessary, secure outside consultation for staff members if morale is low and they are discouraged.

REFERENCES

Age Concern: "The Attitudes of the Retired and Elderly," Manifesto Series No. 32, Research Report, 1974.

Barker, L. F.: "Alleged Attempt at Suicide by a Woman of Seventy-one," *International Clinics,* III(**40**):64–67, 1930.

Bennett, Ruth: "Social Isolation and Isolation-reducing Programs," *Bulletin of the New York Academy of Medicine,* **49**(12):1143–1163, 1973.

Berezin, Martin A.: "Partial Grief in Family Members and Others Who Care For the

Elderly Patient," *Journal of Geriatric Psychiatry,* **4**:53–64, 1970.

Bornstein, P. E., P. J. Clayton, J. A. Halikas, W. L. Maurice, and E. Robins: "The Depression of Widowhood after Thirteen Months," *British Journal of Psychiatry,* **122**:561–566, 1973.

Boyack, Virginia: Personal communication, 1974.

Buber, Martin: *I and Thou,* Scribner's, New York, 1970.

Burnside, Irene M.: "Loneliness in Old Age," *Mental Hygiene,* **55**(3):391–396, 1971.

———: "The Special Senses and Sensory Deprivation," in Irene Burnside (ed.), *Nursing and the Aged,* McGraw-Hill, New York, 1976, p. 380.

Butler, Robert N., and Myrna Lewis: *Aging and Mental Health: Positive Psychosocial Approaches,* Mosby, St. Louis, 1977.

Butorac, Evelyn: Personal communication, 1978.

Cath, S.: "Some Dynamics of Middle and Later Years: A Study in Depletion and Restitution," in M. Berezin and S. Cath (eds.), *Geriatric Psychiatry,* International Universities Press, Inc., New York, 1965.

Clayton, P. J., J. A. Halikas, W. L. Maurice, and E. Robins: "Anticipatory Grief and Widowhood," *British Journal of Psychiatry,* **122**:47–51, 1973.

Coles, Robert: *The Old Ones of New Mexico,* Anchor Press/Doubleday, Garden City, N.Y., 1975, p. 10.

Curtin, Sharon: *Nobody Ever Died of Old Age: In Praise of Old People: In Outrage at Their Loneliness,* Little, Brown, Boston, 1972.

Da Silva, Guy: "The Loneliness and Death of an Old Man," *Journal of Geriatric Psychiatry,* **1**(1):5–27, 1967.

de Castillejo, Irene Claremont: *Knowing*

Woman: A Feminine Psychology, Putnam, New York, 1973.

Deutsch, H.: "Absence of Grief," *Psychoanalytic Quarterly,* **6**:12–22, 1937.

Eisdorfer, Carl: Lecture presented at Gerontology Institute, Sangamon State University, Springfield, Ill., 1976.

Eliot, T. D.: "War Bereavements and Their Recovery," *Marriage and Family Living,* **8**:1–6, 1946.

Fidler, Joan: "Loneliness—the Problems of the Elderly and Retired," *Royal Society of Health Journal,* **96**(1):39–41+, 1976.

Flannery, Raymond B.: "Behavior Modification of Geriatric Grief: A Transactional Perspective," *International Journal of Aging and Human Development,* **5**(2):197–203, 1974.

Fromm, Erich: *Escape from Freedom,* Avon, New York, 1969 (originally published, Rinehart, 1941).

Fromm-Reichmann, Frieda: "On Loneliness," in H. M. Bullock (ed.), *Psychoanalysis and Psychotherapy,* University of Chicago Press, 1959, p. 327.

Gaev, Dorothy Meyer: *The Psychology of Loneliness,* Adams Press, Chicago, 1976.

Gage, Frances Boland: "Suicide in the Aged," *American Journal of Nursing,* **71**(11):2153–2155, 1971.

———: "Depression in the Aged," in Irene Burnside (ed.), *Psychosocial Nursing Care of the Aged,* McGraw-Hill, New York, 1973.

Gerber, Irwin, R. Rusalem, N. Hannon, D. Battin, and A. Arkin: "Anticipatory Grief and Aged Widows and Widowers, *Journal of Gerontology,* **39**(2):225–229, 1975.

Greenwald, Bernice: Class assignment, San Francisco State University, San Francisco, September 1976.

Haggerty, Judith: "Suicide in the Aging. Suicidal Behavior in a 70-Year-Old Man:

A Case Report," *Journal of Geriatric Psychiatry,* **6**(1):43–51, 1973.

Hampe, Sandra O.: "Needs of the Grieving Spouse in a Hospital Setting," *Nursing Research,* **24**(2):113–210, 1975.

Horney, Karen: *Neurosis and Human Growth,* Norton, New York, 1950.

Hyams, D. E.: "Psychological Factors in Rehabilitation of the Elderly," *Gerontologica Clinica,* **11**(3):129–136, 1969.

Janis, I. L.: *Psychological Stress,* Wiley, New York, 1958.

Lantz, John: "Aging: Birth of an Individual," *Journal of Gerontological Nursing,* **3**(4):32–37, 1977.

Lettieri, Dan J.: "Suicide in the Aging: Empirical Prediction of Suicidal Risk among the Aging," *Journal of Geriatric Psychiatry,* **6**(1):7–42, 1973.

Lindemann, Erich: "Symptomatology and Management of Acute Grief," *American Journal of Psychiatry,* **101**:141–148, 1944.

Loether, Herman J.: *Problems of Aging,* Dickenson Publishing Company, Inc., Belmont, Calif., 1975.

Lopata, Helen Z.: "Loneliness: Forms and Components," in Robert S. Weiss (ed.), *Loneliness,* M.I.T., Cambridge, 1973.

Lowenthal, Marjorie, Majda Thurnher, and David Chiriboga: *Four Stages of Life,* Jossey-Bass Publishers, San Francisco, 1975, p. 80.

McCulloch, Lou W.: "The Art of Mourning," *The Antiques Journal,* **32**(10): 19–51, 1977.

Maslow, Abraham H.: *The Farther Reaches of Human Nature,* Viking, New York, 1971.

May, Rollo: *Man's Search for Himself,* Norton, New York, 1953.

Miller, Marv: "Suicide among Older Men," doctoral dissertation, 1977.

Moustakas, Clark: "Communal Loneliness," *Psychologica,* **3**:188–190, 1960.

O'Neal, Patricia, Eli Robins, and Edwin H.

Schmidt: "A Psychiatric Study of Attempted Suicide in Persons over Sixty Years of Age," *Archives of Neurology and Psychiatry,* **75**(3):275–284, 1956.

Palmore, Erdmore: "Facts on Aging: A Short Quiz," *The Gerontologist,* **17**(4): 315–320, 1977.

Patton, Florence: Personal communication, 1978.

Peretz, D.: "Reaction to Loss," in B. Schoenberg et al. (eds.), *Loss and Grief: Psychological Management in Medical Practice,* Columbia, New York, 1970.

Rosenbaum, M.: "Emotional Aspects of Wartime Separation," *Family,* **24**: 337–341, 1944.

Schwab, J. J., J. M. Chalmers, S. J. Conroy, B. P. Farris, and R. E. Markosh: "Studies in Grief: A Preliminary Report," in B. Schoenberg, I. Gerber, A. Weiner, A. H. Kutscher, D. Peretz, and A. Carr (eds.), *Psychosocial Aspects of Bereavement,* Columbia, New York, 1975.

Shanas, Ethel, et al.: *Old People in Three Industrial Societies,* Atherton, New York, 1968.

Slater, Philip E.: *The Pursuit of Loneliness,* Beacon, Boston, 1970.

Smith-White, Chad: "Old Age, Youth and Vermouth," *San Francisco Sunday Examiner and Chronicle,* Dec. 12, 1976.

Stern, Karl, Gwendolyn William, and Miguel Prados: "Grief Reactions in Later Life," *American Journal of Psychiatry,* **108**(4):289–294, 1951.

Sullivan, Harry Stack: *The Interpersonal Theory of Psychiatry,* Norton, New York, 1953.

————: *The Psychiatric Interview,* Norton, New York, 1954.

Tannenbaum, David E.: "Loneliness in the Aged," *Mental Hygiene,* **51**(1):91–99, 1967.

Tillich, Paul: *The Courage to Be,* Yale, New Haven, 1952.

Townsend, Peter: *The Family of Old People,* Penguin, Baltimore, 1963.

———: "Isolation and Loneliness in the Aged," in Robert S. Weiss (ed.), *Loneliness,* M.I.T., Cambridge, 1973.

——— and **Sylvia Tunstall:** "Isolation, Desolation, and Loneliness," in Ethel Shanas et al. (eds.), *Old People in Three Industrial Societies,* Atherton, New York, 1968, p. 280.

von Witzleben, Henry D.: "On Loneliness," *Psychiatry,* **21**(1):37–44, 1958.

Weiss, Robert S.: *Loneliness: The Experience of Emotional and Social Isolation,* M.I.T., Cambridge, 1973.

Wilson, Frances G.: "Social Isolation and Bereavement," *Lancet,* **2**(7687):1356–1357, 1970.

Zimberg, Sheldon: "The Geriatric Alcoholic on a Psychiatric Couch," *Geriatric Focus,* **11**(5):1+, 1972.

OTHER RESOURCES

FILMS

Angelus: 15 min/16 mm/color. Homage to old women who live among us, sentenced to loneliness. Director: Zoltan Huszarih. Distributor: Carousel Films, 1501 Broadway, New York, N.Y. 10036.

I Think They Call Him John: 26 min/16 mm/b&w/1970. Presents the loneliness and boredom that are the lot of many aging persons. Very little dialogue. Producer: Jack Carrothers. Distributor: Mass Media Associates, 2116 North Charles Street, Baltimore, Md. 21218.

Minnie Remembers: See Chapter 18, Other Resources.

Queen of the Stardust Ballroom: 98 min/35 mm/color/1975. Feature-length film nominated for nine Emmy Awards. Nostalgic story about Bea Asher, who finds herself a widow, a grandmother, and very little else. She goes with a friend to a local dance hall where she meets a middle-aged mailman, and gradually a new life opens for Bea. Producers: Robert Christiansen and Rick Rosenberg. Contact: Learning Corporation of America, 1350 Avenue of the Americas, New York, N.Y. 10019.

Chapter 27

CARING AND CARE GIVING IN THE LATER YEARS
Irene Mortenson Burnside

> We ourselves want to be needed. We do not only have
> needs, we are also strongly motivated by neededness . . .
>
> *Andras Angyal*

> The degree to which I can create relationships which
> facilitate the growth of others as separate persons is a
> measure of the growth I have achieved in myself.
>
> *Carl R. Rogers*

> To care for another person, in the most significant sense,
> is to help him grow and actualize himself.
>
> *Milton Mayeroff*

This chapter extends the idea of the development of caring, discussed first by Monea in Chapter 1 and later by Ebersole in Chapter 14, and explores the quality of caring in several areas: (1) caring by old persons about the care giver, (2) caring in marriage, (3) the caring aspect of grandparenting, (4) the caring given by confidantes, and (5) the caring for pets.

The tenets of caring behavior have been well formulated by Leininger, as follows:

1. Caring behaviors and processes are essential for human survival and development of self actualization.
2. Caring behaviors are closely related to the social structure and functions of caring in different cultures in the world.

3. Caring rituals are both symbolic and non-symbolic in form and function.
4. Caring behaviors place heavy emphasis upon support measures and activities to help others in need, or to provide care to oneself over a short or extended period of time.
5. Caring behaviors are vital for effective curing processes and treatment modalities. (Caring appears more important than curing in many cultures.)
6. Efficacious caring must be a humanistically-oriented service that reflects elements such as concern, compassion, stress alleviation, nurturance, surveillance and related culturally-defined components.
7. Caring behaviors can be found in both direct and indirect helping activities to help people remain well, grow, or actualize themselves.
8. Human care-giving and care-receiving behaviors denote reciprocal behaviors which tend to satisfy people in an interaction caring process.

Leininger has listed 17 major constructs which are related to care and caring behaviors and processes: "(1) comfort, (2) support, (3) compassion, (4) empathy, (5) direct helping behaviors, (6) coping, (7) specific stress alleviation, (8) touching, (9) nurturance, (10) succorance, (11) surveillance, (12) protection, (13) restoration, (14) stimulation, (15) health maintenance, (16) health instruction, and (17) health consultation" (p. 14). If these constructs were to be given priorities by professionals or the aged themselves, the order might be quite different.

LITERATURE SEARCH

The literature on caring in general is pitifully scant, and on caring in later life is almost nonexistent. Mayeroff's book, *On Caring,* is only 87 pages long. The author does not fully develop the discussion of caring. For example, he writes, "Caring sometimes calls for unusual aptitudes and special training; besides being able to care in general, I must be able to care for this specific other. Caring for a mentally ill person requires uncommon sensitivity in interpersonal relations as well as specialized training. . . ." He does not go on to explain what comprises "uncommon sensitivity." The author makes a good point, though, when he says that a person must want to grow, at least on some level, if one is to succeed in helping. He points out that anyone with extensive brain damage is unable to grow in any meaningful sense and that one cannot care for that person in the sense of promoting growth.

Regarding the aged population, these remarks bring to mind victims of chronic brain syndrome (caused by changes in the brain). See the book *Gramp,* by Jury and Jury, for an example. One way out of involvement with such individuals is to convince oneself that an old person cannot grow or change. That relieves us of even taking the responsibility to check out whether the person actually can grow and change with our input, encouragement, and individual attention. Clow wrote an article describing what exquisite individual caring can accomplish with such individuals.

Another book, *Self Care,* by Bernard, describes a taking care of self similar to that discussed by Monea earlier in this book. Self-care deals with the central issue of defining, limiting, and making specific the interpersonal negotiations required of one in daily living. The book is full of dialogue, so much dialogue, in fact, that at times one thinks one is reading a play. However, there is one fine contribution to be pondered and used: a self-care list written by a doctor. The list includes specific self-care definitions. The process of working on behavior changes to actualize one's self embodies a responsibility in which one considers one's self important enough to handle one's own needs and yet not do others in or exploit them.

A series of excellent articles by Hyde (1975, 1976a, 1976b, 1976c) appeared in *Nursing Research Reports,* published by the American Nurses' Foundation. Hyde states, "Self care is open, perceptive, receptive, free to serve because its own needs are being met, its own wants are being attended. Self care reaches out because it reaches down into itself for sustenance—the cantilever principle in architecture" (1975, p. 11). One line of hers that is especially quotable and applies to caring for the old is, "Self care means the journey, where each moment counts, where meaning is in the doing, sharing, caring, acceptant to being cared for" (1975, p. 11). The following tenets have been taken from her series of articles:

1. Self-care is free to serve because its own needs are being met (1975).
2. Self-care can be a run for perfection (1975).
3. Carers accept being cared for when it is needed (1975).
4. Caring involves the consumer and the provider (1975).
5. Self-care means the strength to ask (1975).
6. Self-care allows for treating, healing of old wounds to prepare for new conflict and creations (1975).
7. There is a certain genuineness and satisfaction in simply and truly caring (1976a).
8. Ethical implications are related to the technology of curing—e.g., promulgation of life (1976b).
9. "Be-strong" attitude may be a barrier in self-care (1976c).
10. Balance "be strong" with "be gentle"; forgive one's self (1976c).
11. New concentration, new patterning can be aided with laughter, humor, adjusting focus of our perspective (1976c).
12. The wonder of the child within deserves expression and protection (1976c).
13. Identify what you need by way of care for yourself (1976c).
14. Each person has a unique balance; we each need to listen to both our body and mind (1976c).
15. Seek inner clarity so that life has meaning (1976c).

Gaylin feels that the despair that seems to be prevalent in our nation today is not warranted, and points out that "The caring nature of human beings is so self-evident as to escape our observation if we are not careful. It has survived many periods of self-doubt and self-abuse. We are now in such a time" (p. 39). He stresses the importance of hope, and quotes Shelley, who said, "Hope creates from its own wreck the thing it contemplates" (p. 39). (See also Chapters 1 and 14 for further discussion on Gaylin's philosophy.)

Although not precisely focused on caring, a related article on empathy by Katz may be useful to the reader. Katz presents a model which he calls "oscillating between identification and detachment" (p. 38), and speaks of the need to balance involvement and disengagement. Later he uses Buber's description of empathy as "gliding" into the other person. Leininger listed empathy as one of her 17 constructs mentioned earlier in the chapter.

The empathic skill is still a mystery in some ways; there are few comprehensive theories of the origin and operation of empathy in any of the many disciplines which constitute the care-giving field. If those who work with and write about the aged swing on the pendulum between empathy and objectivity, I hope that our own personal pendulum does not stop on objectivity. We simply do not have complete accounts of empathic relating to use as models for better understanding the process. Because it is such a personal part of the care giver, one cannot always get into the labyrinth of the motives involved and the possible reasons why one person's caring and empathy prove to be therapeutic and another's do not. We will have to ask old people what type of caring makes them feel the best, and also to watch for the therapeutic results of our own care giving and care receiving. We must also learn to receive caring from older clients. The tremendous need to be needed comes through again and again. It is succinctly stated by Angyal in the opening of this chapter, and was also well put by an 85-year-old volunteer worker at Shepherd Center in Kansas City. He was busily engaged in a project at the center and was asked, "Why are you doing all this?" " 'Cause I want to help other people," was his reply.

THE OLD CARING ABOUT THE CARE GIVER

Though the need for caring and love is consistent throughout the life-span, there are differences in the caring given and received by the aged person. Some of the brashness and impetuousness of younger years is gone; there is a steadier, gentler quality, with a patina all its own. And there are other facets: the generosity, benevolence, and tolerance frequently found in the aged client. After doing a series of interviews with aged women, I was impressed not by how much and how often they prayed, but by the scope of their prayers. They prayed for the entire world, for peace for all of humanity. That is the legacy those frail, yet tenacious women left me.

The considerate ways of older persons often go by unrecognized, probably because so many oil cans of health care are needed for the many squeaky wheels. Examples of the quality, frequency, and sometimes almost sacrificial nature of the caring shown by older people should soon become apparent to health care personnel: for instance, the elderly client still living at home who shuffles off with cane in one hand and returns with the coffee pot in the other hand to serve you; a dying aged woman telling her private duty nurse to take and eat her supper because she is too nauseated to touch it; a psychotic old man offering the student interviewer half his candy bar or the cold drink that the student brought to him; a group of community aged persons solicitous about a pregnant group leader, who they think looks very tired.

Such concern for you is one of the consistent occupational rewards in working with the elderly population. It matters not where the elderly person is: acute-care setting, private home, or nursing home. In any of these areas, such caring can be observed. One exception might be those "loners and losers" (Stephens) who live isolated in "single-room occupancy" (SRO) in sleazy, dilapidated hotels in the inner cities. Curtin, too, has described that kind of existence, with which she is personally acquainted.

It took me many years to realize how important it is for the elderly to help me, to wait on me, to offer assistance of one sort or another. Recently, I visited a couple of relatives who live in another state. He is 77 and she is 72. I was exhausted and weary of the work world, but suddenly I wallowed in a featherbed of comfort—plied with my favorite foods and drinks, treated to my favorite forms of recreation. Like a spoiled child, I received devoted attention for 3 days—a true panacea for weariness. It is heady stuff to be given "nothing but the best," no matter what the best is. I realized the same thing had occurred when I was a home health nurse. I was honored with genteel ways, with respect that was almost too much to handle at times.

Case Example

Rose di Maggio was a tiny, wizened, Sicilian emigrant. Such broken English. Such severe diabetes. Cataracts on both eyes. But a big heart. Each visit she would be at her window watching for me and would throw the door open before I could knock. We went straight to the kitchen. After I gave her the insulin shot, she poured fresh coffee. She always waited to have coffee with me. She served me in her best china cup and with a silver spoon. She, herself, ate out of an open egg carton for a plate. "No usa messin' da dishes," she would say with her four-tooth smile. Often she handed me a prickly pear from her garden or a jar of Sicilian soup with, "Cuz you be so good ta me."

The adoration and respect that a care giver receives from some European and Asian emigrants nearly always offset language barriers or other cultural difficulties. It may take a while to cease insisting on what you can do for them and to accept with grace and poise the giving and the respect offered with such humility by those being served.

One aspect of a psychosocial assessment is to permit the courtesies described above to occur; sit and watch the aged shuffle off for your cup of coffee, or to find a gift for you. One can assess for gait, posture, mien, movement, etc., and for changes which may be occurring over time.

STIFLING THE NURTURING OF OTHERS

Health professionals, because of their own strong need to nurture, are noted for stifling the need of others to nurture. We nurture and help old people straight into dependence. Or we invite their wrath and indignation by our constant insistence on being in control, on offering advice, on "Let-me-do-that-for you," in lieu of, "Do you want some help?" Even the usual social amenities may be misunderstood by the oldster who has become very sensitive to "overhelpers." For example, I attended a beautiful, outdoor wedding of a student. The bride's grandmother, in her nineties, had once participated in our classes. She was drinking champagne, so I sat near her to visit awhile. The champagne table was rather far off, and the path was a bit uneven. I started for the table, then turned and asked the grand lady if she wanted another glass. She looked me coolly in the eye with her steady blue gaze and said, "What's the matter, don't you think I can get it myself?" And with a polite, patient smile, she gently reminded me that she was leaving for Greece the next day. Health professionals continue to peer at aged persons through pathological lenses; it is one of our great failings in our relationships with aged clients.

ENCOURAGING CHANGE

Another problem of health professionals in their psychosocial caring relationship with the old person is the inability to let old people change, to encourage change. If an old person has always been mean, vindictive, stubborn, it is easy to assume that he or she will continue in that pattern. Butler and Lewis have written beautifully about atonement in later life. In counseling, especially family counseling/therapy, this aspect should not be taken lightly. There is the example of a man approaching his eightieth birthday and trying to redeem himself by being kind to children whom he did not raise. Or very recently, old people have shared with me that they never cared for touching in their earlier years, but now they are learning to touch and to be touched. One thinks also of the dying patient needing to bring closure as described in Chapter 30. The dying need to care, to retain control of their shortening time on earth. Many years ago I was working an afternoon shift on a medical ward. A tragedy on the ward had me almost out of control. As I was giving a shot to a dying nurse (more middle-aged than old), she read my face, asking what had happened. I told her. The dying woman then reached for my hand and helped put me together so that I could handle the rest of the shift. It was a great lesson to me.

In counseling and day-to-day work with the elderly, we need to anticipate (and share that anticipation) that old people can change and do change, so very often for the better. Their needs must be blended with our needs at times so that both move back and forth on the continuum of dependency and independency.

CARE GIVING IN FAMILIES
Couples: Caring for Each Other

The frail sometimes lead the frail, or so one thinks as one sees two elderly persons moving together in slowed-up, synchronous tempo. Marriages of 40, 50, and 60 years have not been much studied; one wonders what made these marriages hold. (See Figure 18-1 for data on marital status.)

Devoted caring in aged families assumes new dimensions, has a different tone from that in young families with their child-rearing problems. It is also in stark contrast to the attitude of those today who prefer multiple marriages or no marriage. The ability to meet the spouse's needs, both emotional and physical, and to stay out of the paths of health professionals, may be two important aspects of those relationships. Archibald MacLeish has described a marriage of more than 60 years in a beautiful poem, "The Old Couple." The elderly person who has been devoted to and has cared for a spouse has a bad time when the spouse dies. Sometimes, not always, the remaining spouse deteriorates rapidly. Such persons feel no longer needed. The structure and routine of the caring procedures are gone. Though caring can be arduous and a back-breaking strain and drain, still it may be a labor of love that sometimes fills 24 hours, e.g., when the patient wanders or is an insomniac.

Who has examined the love that still holds when so much loyalty, duty, and care are required, with the scale so tipped in one direction? It is too cavalier to write it off as martyrdom or superdependency, although those aspects sometimes exist. It would seem to me rather to be an unwritten pact, "No matter what, we'll stay together and help each other." We outsiders see the lopsidedness of the helping more often than the elderly couple does. I remember resentfully watching a wife turn on a television set for a healthy husband as he sat in his chair. It was, of course, my problem, not theirs! Then I suddenly realized that he never winced at her untimely loud belches either. The tolerance, patience, and understanding in those long-enduring marriages are worth observing.

Long-surviving marriages (albeit not always happy) may give clues as to how and why aged persons care for one another so well. There are some who care for their mates with selfish motives. As an old man said, "Who will care for me when she is gone?" Some of these marriages provide material for a study in energy levels, for an analysis of compensatory, complementary mechanisms. Sometimes they give a touching picture of the frail holding the frail.

The caring of the aged often involves caring for a person inundated with physical problems and disabilities. There are the women who have married men 15 or 20 years older than they are, and who finally find themselves weighted down with physical care problems. In other instances, the caring may eventually erode into noncaring. A longitudinal study done on men examined the family relationships (Yarrow, Blank, Quinn, Youmans, and Stein). Two of the categories noted were "continued poor" or "deteriorated" in the husband-wife relationships.

"Tell Me a Riddle," a short story, begins like this: "For forty-seven years they had been married. How deep back the stubborn, gnarled roots of the quarrel reached, no one could say—but only now, when tending to the needs of others no longer shackled them together, the roots swelled up visible, split the earth between them, and the tearing shook even to the children, long since grown" (Olsen, p. 72). In another example, a married man in his seventies told a student interviewer, "For three years I've been married and they've been the most miserable years of my life. You just wait until you get married, then you'll know what suffering is. And you will get married because for every Jack there's a

Jenny. Of course, one woman's just as good as another. You'll see . . . a woman will make you old faster than any other thing" (Knowlton).

Sometimes one finds the old caring for the very old; this can occur in a variety of family constellations, not necessarily that of husband and wife. For example, an 87-year-old lady called the Shepherd Center in Kansas City, Missouri. She was afraid that her mother might die. Since the woman was known to be 87 years old, there was inquiry for further information. She was worried about her 107-year-old mother; she said that her mother was ill and she was afraid that she would not make it. She added, "Of course, I am not alone; I have my 83-year-old sister down the street and my 65-year-old son is nearby" (Cole).

Unmet Affectional Needs

Unmet affectional needs of the elderly will enter into the psychosocial care of older persons. Affectional needs rise when significant others move away or die. The reader may perhaps remember Harry in the commercial film, "Harry and Tonto," and the scene in which Harry goes to the morgue to identify his best friend. Personnel in institutions or other care givers may well become pseudo-family for the older person in the face of many losses. Bereavement overload can occur; that is, numerous important losses coming close together. When this happens, it is time to increase and intensify the caring aspects of one's relationship with the aged person.

Role of Aged Family Member

The present body of research on aged family members reveals that they are not being abandoned by their families although it is still a common myth about nursing home residents that they are. Very often those in nursing homes seem to be abandoned, but that is because they have no families at all to visit them.

Spark and Brody reminded readers that aged family members are capable of psychological growth and change and stated that they play important roles in family dynamics. See the excellent coverage and case study on family counseling by Herr and Weakland.

Hooponopono

While I was teaching in Hawaii, my students introduced me to the term *hooponopono,* which means "to set right." It is a Hawaiian version of family therapy which is used to resolve problems, handle conflictual situations, and restore family harmony and balance. This problem-solving method was intended to be (1) diagnostic, (2) remedial, and (3) preventive. It was called for by the senior member in a family, the eldest living member of the senior branch. I visualized it as elderly grandmothers (*tutus*) who become Virginia Satirs in muumuus. The conductor had to be fair, objective, open, honest, sincere, humble, and firm in a gentle way. Participants in hooponopono were also expected to behave in that manner. Prayer is a vital part of this therapeutic process. If emotional entanglement interfered with the effectiveness of the senior member, the family turned to someone outside the family for help (Paglinawan, p. 74).

Grandparents

The roles of grandparents and great grandparents are not commonly written about in the literature. Yet the influence of grandparents is seen in audiovisual media. (See Other Resources, at the end of the chapter, for films on grandparents.) During interviews with persons of all ages, material on grandparents may be given. See the case study later in this chapter. See also Figure 27-1.

Grandparents seem at times to have a special role that is denied to others. Of

Figure 27-1 The hen that hatched a goose. Reluctantly, Mary, the hen, watched her "child" swim off in the duck pond. This grandmother wanted her grandchildren to have the experience of having a pet, so she placed a goose egg under a sitting hen. (*Courtesy of Manie G. Daniel. Reprinted with permission from* NRTA Journal. *Copyright 1977 by the National Retired Teachers Association.*)

course, there are always those who deny the role of grandparenthood and prefer not to identify with it. One is reminded of the man who said that he did not mind being a grandfather, but he sure did hate to be married to a grandmother.

Aspects of Grandparenthood

Loether wrote:

> Behavior considered intolerable in children may be viewed with amusement in grandchildren. There may be definite signs that the old man has mellowed . . . (and that) Grandfather may still be the head of his own household, but he has little or no control over his married children. Even when he lives with married children, he is relegated to a subsidiary role in the family.
>
> The grandfather role has been reduced from one of authority to one in which he is playmate and baby-sitter for his grandchildren. Since grandmother can also play the role of baby-sitter and playmate, there is little substantive difference between the grandmother and the grandfather roles. The lack of a uniquely masculine flavor to the grandfather role may be an added impediment to successful adjustment among the aged (pp. 21, 22).

One might add that many grandmothers are involved in volunteer activities or are still in the work world and simply are not available for baby-sitting. Occasionally, one sees great grandparents, who are still youngish, involved with great grandchildren. Only recently, I noted that some card shops now carry greeting cards for great grandchildren also.

Grandparents as Parents

It is not uncommon for grandparents to assume the parent role; divorce, abandonment, and death of parents are common reasons why grandparents find themselves with children to raise. The grandparents have often mellowed by then, and are sometimes ready to try new child-raising strategies. The aged pseudoparents have more time and patience, but are often discouraged by their own lowered energy level—especially when they struggle with lively small children or energetic, vacillating adolescents. (The same thing occurs with parents who have children very late in life.)

The child raised by a grandparent learns about the aging process the easiest way of all. Some children take advantage of age changes (e.g., sensory losses) to deceive the older substitute parent; others relate well to such substitutes, since both may realize that they are in a difficult situation and must struggle through together. The grandparent may feel guilt for his or her own child's failure, even to the point of sharing with the grandchild. "What went wrong? I raised your mother as best I knew how." Or the child may sense that the grandparent is trying to make up to the child for the severe psychological jolt of losing parents. The child may then have empathy for the grandparent who admits feelings of failure, or the child may take advantage of the situation and play the role, "I have been badly neglected, abandoned, mistreated, etc., and it's your fault."

In Polynesia, the child reared by grandparents was considered fortunate

(Paglinawan). At this writing, I have not uncovered any studies on grandparents who raised grandchildren in the United States. Surely there are aspects of these relationships that are different from those in nuclear families, in families of divorced and remarried parents ("Your children, my children, our children"), or in single-parent families (parents without partners). (See Chapter 4 by Monea about families in transition.)

Memories of a grandparent and the impact and influence he had on the life—even the career—of a grandchild are well described by Hamilton:

My own grandfather had to be different. Born a slave, as an infant he was sold away with his mother, never to know his father. The years he lived as part of my child life, I knew him as this old friend, chewing tobacco, barely five feet tall, who at eighty could jump from a standing-still position into the air to click his heels together three times and land still standing. Never ever could I do that.

One of grandpa's hands was forever maimed to an inch of being closed tight. He had been employed in a gunpowder mill near Xenia, Ohio. One day, the explosive mixture caught fire; the mill burned to the ground. There were great flames, and for some reason, grandpa reached out for the fire. In a moment of confusion, perhaps he thought the flame would melt away the stigma. His hand was burned hideously. It was bandaged shut, and it healed that way—a closed fist from which the generation of his grandchildren, from which I, would hold tight and swing. How eccentric an image is that fiery hand with the closed fist! (pp. 4–5)

Case Study

A woman in her twenties described her own struggles and feelings about her grandparents. In their eighties, they had to be placed in a nursing home. While still at home, the grandfather had had a series of small strokes which had left him aphasic. He subsequently became very depressed and talked about shooting himself. The daughter searched his home and found bullets everywhere—even in such unlikely places as the underwear drawer and in the kitchen silverware drawer. And though he had placed bullets everywhere for easy access, he had misplaced the gun! After he was institutionalized, the daughter searched the house thoroughly; only after the elderly couple were placed in a nursing home did she find the gun—in a crawl space under the house.

The couple were placed in a room together. When the staff began to find black and blue marks on the grandmother, they were concerned, since she was not falling or bumping into objects, although she was habitually removing her clothing. The elderly woman had bouts of confusion; and when she began to undress during the daytime, her husband would wallop her sharply with his cane for punishment. They had to be separated from that point on, so were placed in separate rooms.

The young woman ended sadly with, "I don't want to grow old after what I've seen with them."

The role models of aging presented by grandparents, and by the elderly in general, are certainly important. Intervention and prevention play important roles with the regressed aged in our society, as depicted in the book *Gramp*, by Jury and Jury.

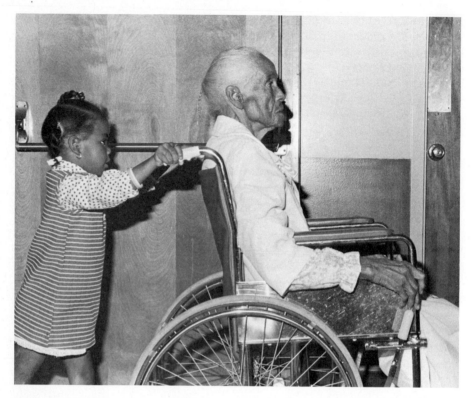

Figure 27-2 Many aged persons now have great grandchildren as well as grandchildren. Youngsters can learn about the aging process by close association with the aged, as can be seen in the above photo. (*Courtesy of Will Patton.*)

CARE GIVING BY CONFIDANTES

The exemplary way in which long-life friends help and care for one another is another area deserving study. One under-researched area in gerontological literature is that of friendship across the life-span. Cameron and Klopsch studied friendship patterns among teenagers, young adults (26 to 39 years), middle-aged (56 to 64) and old people. Since "old" was not specified in years, we did not learn much from this paper about what happens to friendships in late, late life. Schonberg and Potter studied friendship fluctuation in senescence in a sample of five males, aged 59 to 83, in a small rural community. The comparison group was 65 students from a small, private college. This study noted: "The downward trend in friendship fluctuation with age apparently does not persist through senescence, since a significant increase in the index was observed" (p. 334).

Curtin wrote of two old men whom she had observed with perception:

Harry and Al were professional survivors. They saw only what was directly in front of them, they asked no questions, felt no anger, demanded no love; they just made do, just kept body and soul together. They reminded me of nothing more than a couple of antique cockroaches, those marvelous insects that no amount of civilization can kill. . . . They had paid by giving up almost all human softness or warmth. Life had left them somehow degraded. I would [wonder] . . . if that was the only way to survive, if you have to stop feeling anything, stop loving, stop caring, in order to live. . . . And friendship was their one decent instinct. They had total loyalty and friendship for one another. It wasn't love that kept them together, but something stronger. Need. They had met on the road about twenty years ago, and discovered that as a team they were able to survive with less trouble. Two men could cover more ground panhandling, two heads knew twice as many diners where you get bread and butter with soup, not just crackers. . . . And if there were two of them they were less vulnerable to attack when tired or weak or asleep. Their friendship for each other was really the only thing these two had; life had knocked everything else out (pp. 69–70).

Though we know how important confidantes can be, what do they do to sustain a relationship besides listen? The way neighbors support and help one another often makes it possible for an elderly person to stay at home. This has been described to me by nurses from the United Kingdom. It is well known that women outlive men. When they have outlived their mates, women turn to one another for comfort and solace. As one 67-year-old woman said, ''I just can't tell you how much I enjoy my women friends.'' Ebersole in Chapter 14 described the importance of youthful friendships which continue into middle age.

OLDER WOMEN

Older women are included here because they have not been included elsewhere in this section of the book. In Chapter 18 widowhood is discussed. Scott-Maxwell has given us some insight into old womanhood. She described the value of having a gift for being old and speaks of indulgences that one should be permitted late in life. The old woman is still noticeably ignored in all the women's magazines.

The woman who has a gift for old age is the woman who delights in comfort. If warmth is known as the blessing it is, if your bed, your bath, your best-liked food and drinks are regarded as fresh delights, then you know how to thrive when old. If you get the things you like on the simplest terms, serve yourself lightly, efficiently, and calmly, all is almost well. If you are truly calm you stand a chance of surviving much, but calmness is intermittent with me. (Scott-Maxwell, p. 88.)

Kalish suggests that the typical older person is a widowed, white woman; she has probably had about 9 years of formal education, is not presently employed in any way, lives in the central city, receives most of her income from social security, has at least one chronic health condition that does not limit her mobility greatly, and will probably live into her eighties.

A report written for President Carter's Commission on Mental Health (*American Journal of Nursing*, 1977) reveals that American women are overrepresented in the nation's mentally ill and that they are also poorly served by the mental health system.

The report noted that "the U.S. education system works against women who want to complete their education or to go for higher degrees. Attention also was given to the increasing suicide rate among older women" (p. 1557). The action taken was to form a task force to recommend affirmative action programs so that the number of mental health personnel who are women would be increased, or at least there would be an increased sensitivity to women's problems.

Poverty of Older Women

The poverty of older women in one state was outlined by Sehlin: "(1) low social security benefits which resulted from most women having relatively short work histories and also lower paying jobs, (2) the relatively few women who are eligible for private pension benefits, and (3) women who receive survivor's benefits from a deceased husband's pension plan rarely do receive full benefits" (p. 1). No wonder older women need to support one another. *Ms.* magazine has published an excellent description of the older woman living in abject poverty (Schwartz).

Granny-Battering

In England the mistreatment of old women by care givers is known as "granny-battering" (Burston). Will abuse of the elderly eventually create the same concern as child abuse? I interviewed a 72-year-old woman who had been raped. She

Figure 27-3 Caring is concern for human needs. (*Courtesy of Murray. Reprinted with permission from American Federation of State, County and Municipal Employees, Washington, D.C. From* The New Republic, *Apr. 30, 1977, p. 7.*)

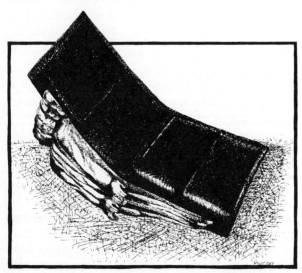

was kind enough to let me tape the interview; it has been a powerful teaching medium.

A most enlightening chapter on the older woman was written by de Castillejo. She states that when a man becomes 50, he is perhaps at the height of his intellectual or administrative power; but when a family woman becomes the same age, she may find new stirrings within herself. "Latent possibilities dance before her unbelieving eyes" (p. 151).

She also points out that the older woman may face a dilemma if she is widowed, because an entirely new situation lies before her. For the first time, she may discover what her own wishes are, what her own tastes are, and in what direction she will let her energy flow. There is no focus of love to act as a magnet for her. De Castillejo remarks about her fascination at watching some widows reverse the habits of many years of marriage after the spouse has died. This aspect of widowhood is covered both in Chapter 30, as a dimension of termination, and in Chapter 18, on widowhood in middle and later life.

Inner Voices and Inner Whisperings

De Castillejo states that "the old woman, like the old man, needs to turn her natural receptivity towards the inner voices and inner whisperings, pondering on the new ideas which will come to her if she is attuned to her own inner self. . . . To speak of half-formed ideas is to destroy their growth as surely as to burn a seedling with the sun's rays shining through a magnifying glass. The very frailty of age guards its secrets" (p. 161). (This reminds me of the interactions with centenarians described in Chapter 23.) De Castillejo continues, "Almost without noticing how it happened an old woman may find that love is still, as it always had been, the centre and the mainspring of her being, although, along with her years, the word has grown in meaning" (p. 164).

WALLS OF LOVE

Of creativity, de Castillejo said:

> Creativity once begun goes on. Nothing is so satisfying to the human soul as creating something new. If the old can become creative in their own right they are lost no longer. . . . Every act of creation adds to the creativity in the world, and who knows if it has not some similar effect as the ritual breathing towards the East at dawn of those primitive tribes who believe that their breath helps the sun to rise (p. 157).

That lovely thought is similar to Da Silva's in a case study of a depressed, lonely old man.

> I am told that the Navaho Indians are convinced that they can reverse the process of a fatal illness by gathering around the bedridden, dying patient and taking very active care of him, spending 24 hours a day with him during several days. Apparently, also, certain African tribes erect around the dying person what

they call a "wall of love" with friends and family gathered and supplying the dying with emotional nourishment in the hope of preventing his death (p. 16).

PETS AND THE ELDERLY
Review of the Literature

Current literature reveals little about the importance of pets to the elderly person. The role of pets is better written about in novels, essays, and memoirs (Steinbeck; Aldin; Dyer; Gates; Gautier; Griffith; Hayes; Lorenz; National Geographic Society; North, 1963, 1966; Richardson; Sloan and Farquhar; Smith; West) than in professional literature. Since old people often show their pets a great deal of love and grieve at their death, how is it that we have ignored such an area for so long and so easily?

Levinson (1962, 1965, 1969, 1972) has contributed most to the literature on the importance of pets to older people. Comfort mentions pets in a few sentences. Butler and Lewis write that, "Given the state of loneliness and isolation affecting significant numbers of older people, pets can be directly supportive of mental well-being. Dogs and cats are the most favored pets, in that order" (pp. 223–224). These authors mention the added advantage of protection provided by an animal and the need to exercise the pet. See Figure 27-4.

I have written the following about a stroke victim and his dog:

> On my way to work in the morning, I often see such a man. He drags his right side and walks with what seems to me, great effort. He carries the dog's leash in his left hand. The big, white dog lopes off, but returns frequently to check on his master. Recently, I have become aware of how this dog (and others) pace themselves to their aged masters. This dog, for instance, slowly moves across the streets and through more difficult terrain with the old man (Burnside, p. 128).

Corson wrote about pet-facilitated psychotherapy in a hospital setting. However, the persons described in the case studies were aged 13, 28, 19, and 23. In a paper, "The Socializing Role of Pet Animals in Nursing Homes: An Experiment in Nonverbal Communication Therapy," given in Sweden, Corson and collaborators presented 24 pages on pet-facilitated psychotherapy with psychotic young adults, but fewer than 13 pages were on the use of pets with the elderly. These authors consider pet-facilitated psychotherapy as one form of reality therapy (see Glasser) because pet dogs may help to fill two of the basic psychological needs of patients as stated by Glasser, "the need to love and be loved and the need to feel that we are worthwhile to ourselves and to others" (p. 9).

Mugford and M'Comisky used budgerigars, small Australian parrots, with old pensioners in Yorkshire, England. They chose budgerigars because the birds are "small, colorful, easy to care for, and can readily be placed in most home environments." Their objective was "to determine the feasibility of field ex-

Figure 27-4   A man in Turkey straps his dog on his bicycle to accompany him on a ride. (*Courtesy of Diane Miller.*)

perimentation into the effects of pets upon the social attitudes and mental and physical health of their owners'' (p. 54).

The importance of parrots is not mentioned anywhere else in the literature. Messy though it is, and raucous, the parrot has one advantage in that it lives so long.

The Importance of Pets to Old People

The role of the pet in old age has been described by Levinson (1965). He points out that retirement may be a sudden transition; in such situations a pet can assume great importance. He feels that depressions that occur after the loss of loved ones, and also some of the somatic complaints, may be prevented by having to care for a pet. Two of the urgent needs of the aged person, stated earlier by Glasser, are the need to be needed and the need for someone to love. A pet can sometimes fill these needs. See Figure 27-5.

''Watching the elderly care for old pets is also an area to observe. An old woman, who lifted two arthritic dogs up onto her lap or rocking chair, said she did it 'because it it too painful for them to jump.' Perhaps dealing with their own losses makes them especially aware of the losses of their pets'' (Burnside, p. 129). They do seem to have great empathy for each other.

Figure 27-5   An elderly couple found pleasure in their canary. Levinson suggests that a canary may be the appropriate pet for an aged person who wants to spend only a few moments each day with a pet. A canary requires minimal care, is full of *joie de vivre,* and learns to respond to its master very quickly, usually with a cheery greeting (Levinson, 1972). (*Courtesy of Diane Miller.*)

Role of Pets in Enhancing Human Relationships

A pet may also enhance one's relationships in the community. Walking a cat on a leash usually causes interaction with someone, especially if the cat seems resigned to it. "Tonto," in the commercial film "Harry and Tonto," is a fine example of "pets as a substitution." Dogs, too, with their personalities, often give rise to conversations. Taking dogs to training schools or to dog shows may increase socialization for the oldster. Most often though, one sees old, graying dogs who have grown old with their owners, and dog and owner seem to pace themselves to each other. The importance of pets came through in a newspaper article about a heart surgeon, Dr. Richard Cabot at Valley Medical Center in San Jose, California, who installed a $2500 pacemaker in the heart of a 9-year-old dog. The device has a life of 5 or 6 years. The surgeon said, "I did it because they are an old couple, and I know what a dog can mean" (*The Mercury,* p. 29).

In any metropolitan area one has only to look out of a window to see neighborhood dogs being walked on the streets. Protective and protected, dogs go for walks with their owners, trot alongside bicycles, or are driven to more open spaces and permitted to run. One advantage of a dog is that it requires the older person to exercise also. One distinct disadvantage is that the elderly are vulnerable to street crimes when walking their dogs, especially after dark. I recently read of the dangers that old women face when they go out at night to feed stray, hungry cats. Their need to be needed may take forms that we never consider.

Dogs and cats are not the only pets selected by elderly persons—parrots, parakeets, mynah and canary birds, mules, horses, and goats are but a few of the others. Wigginton describes Frank, a mule that has been owned for 32 years by a 72-year-old woman who still rides him to the store. See Figure 27-7.

Therapeutic Cat

The cat to which Jessamyn West was devoted during her long bout with tuberculosis provides a fine example of pets being therapeutic. Samantha was a 6-week-old kitten who lived in the invalid's room (and bed) during a long siege of bedrest. Samantha provided no overnight cure, though she did provide immediate

Figure 27-6 This elderly woman lives along the Pacific coast. While on a walk along the beach, she invited the author to her home for coffee and had her dog perform. The reward? A chocolate chip. (*Courtesy of Diane Miller.*)

Figure 27-7 A man in a large park in the inner city feeds a goose and a pigeon. Many old people have the need, time, and patience to make friends with the fowl in parks. A doorman at a posh Beverly Hills hotel whistles and a bluejay flies down and eats from his hand. (*Courtesy of Diane Miller.*)

interest in something outside the author's physical functioning. The following passage describes a feline therapeutic intervention: "Half-grown, Samantha began a practice I have never known in another cat. . . . She carried up the stairs to my bed objects that it amused her to carry, or which she thought might amuse me: a spoon, a glove, the stopper to the downstairs washbasin . . . and once a mouse, dazed but not dead. She seemed to have no intention of eating it, and in time the three of us might have learned to live together" (West, p. 84).

Therapeutic Dogs

Pfaffenberger tells the story of his work at Guide Dogs for the Blind, Inc., in San Rafael, California. One wonders why so many elderly blind persons are using white canes instead of trained canines. Records from San Rafael reveal that the oldest member to have had a guide dog was only 65 years old!

A fine article written by a nurse is recommended to the reader. Bancroft describes how she included two old dogs in the psychosocial care and planning for an elderly woman. Sometimes the aged can even enjoy neighbors' pets. "An elderly 90-year-old neighbor of mine was almost blind. When we sat outdoors and played ball with the neighbor's dog, the dog always dropped the ball at my feet so I would throw it. But when 'Burgie' wanted Mrs. Hill to play with it, he gently dropped the ball in her lap" (Burnside, pp. 128–129).

Case Example I

A student who was a conservator gave the following vignette in a class. The student was assigned to Mrs. M., a woman in her seventies, who had been uprooted and moved from her apartment and placed in a single room in a downtown sleazy hotel in Los Angeles. The woman had once been a prominent dress buyer for a department store. Her husband had left her several years before for a younger woman. She had no children, only the dog her husband had given her for a birthday present 15 years previously. When the dog died, she could not bear to bury him so kept him in her apartment until the body began to decompose. Then she wrapped the dog in a blanket and laid him on the welcome mat outside her door. The apartment neighbors called the landlord, who called the health department. The student could not at that time replace the dog, but she did listen to the woman's grief about him and was sensitive to her needs. She returned to the woman's apartment and brought the dresses which had been left behind. She picked up the plant the woman had thrown on the floor in a moment of anger (symbolic of her own uprootedness, the student felt), bought a new pot, repotted the plant, helped it through transplantation shock, and took it to the woman. She visited weekly and encouraged her to talk about the dog she missed so much.

Case Example II

A woman in her nineties was admitted to a nursing home. For many years she had taught Girl Scouts about birds. She and her husband had used their acreage to feed wild birds and to grow jonquils and sell them for an income. Her vision was very poor, but she still wanted to feed the birds as she had always done. She would save food from her tray to feed them. After one meal, she threw meat balls against the sliding glass door to her patio (which was not opened). Her elderly husband came to visit and cleaned up the mess before the staff could find it and scold her.

In spite of such overt expression of needs, staff members often ignore the elderly person's need to maintain some of his or her previous life patterns; the love for pets, birds, or other animals is certainly an integral component in the life pattern of many persons. As one old lady in a nursing home said, "It isn't home here. I woulda liked to have stayed with the children. We had a cat and I miss that quite a bit. I miss my little radio and the window I had where you could see the dog in the yard next door" (Gubrium, p. 87).

In an effort to place more pets in homes, the San Francisco Society for the Prevention of Cruelty to Animals (SPCA) reduced fees, license costs, etc., for dog and cat adoption because pets need homes and senior citizens need companionship (*San Francisco Progress*, p. 2).

Role of Veterinarian

The role of the veterinarian as part of a mental hygiene team has been discussed by Levinson (1965). When one considers the number of pets put to sleep because aged persons are transferred or moved, or unable to care for them, it does seem that in giving care to older persons we have failed to consult veterinarians.

Levinson reminds us that there may be highly charged currents in the relationship between a pet and its master.

> A pet can provide, in boundless measure, love and unqualified approval. Many elderly and lonely people have discovered that pets satisfy vital emotional needs. They find that they can hold onto the world of reality, of cares, of human toil and sacrifice, and of intense emotional relationships by caring for an animal. Their concepts of themselves as worthwhile persons can be restored, even enhanced, by the assurance that the pets they care for love them in return. (Levinson, 1969, p. 368)

It is important, too, in psychosocial caring always to consider the pet as part of the family.

The individuality of the aged person is of paramount consideration. It might be well to consider some of Jung's thoughts here.

Individuation: Implications for Care Giving
Jung's Philosophy

Shows (p. 79), in surveying psychological research literature in the United States, found a lack of attempts to apply the theoretical frame of reference of Jung to the study of middle and late life; he found it surprising that the psychological theory of Jung, with its practical and research implications, had been so overlooked.

Jung maintained that Freudian psychoanalytic theory was applicable to the first half of life, when major developmental tasks involve learning to deal with one's instinctual drives. Jung was interested in the second half of life. He studied and interpreted at least 80,000 dreams and found that the dreams were relevant in various degrees to the dreamer. He also discovered that, for the most part, they seemed to follow a pattern or a definite arrangement. Jung called this process "individuation." "The individuation process is more than a coming to terms between the inborn germ of wholeness and the outer acts of fate. Its subjective experiences convey the feeling that some supra-personal force is actively interfering in a creative way" (von Franz, p. 162).

Jacobi also wrote about individuation as becoming a single, homogeneous being, and individuality embraces our incomparable uniqueness, and implies becoming one's self. The broadening of the personality means a gradual exploration of the contents and functions of the total psyche, and the effect they have on the ego. It means knowing what one naturally is, in contrast to what one would like to be.

Why, you are probably asking, this sojourn into individuation? Because I believe that individuation is a most important task of late-late life, a goal of centenarians. Some centenarians do seem to have the ability to reach individuation. I believe care givers must try to move the aged person towards individuation—that uniqueness so rightly theirs. Yet we still have a tendency to lump all people over 60 or 65 in one big conglomerate.

To facilitate their uniqueness, I believe that we have to let them continue to solve problems, to enjoy their own special brand of attire and food patterns, to set their own schedules, and we must help them to live more in tune with their circadian rhythms and their decided energy allotments. The farmer who wants to arise at 5 A.M. in the nursing home is not appreciated, nor is the night owl who reads late.

Society has a difficult time respecting, much less understanding, behavior that moves old people towards their own uniqueness; somehow it is easier to label them as "eccentric," "strange," or more recently, "weird." Self-fulfillment is a process to be encouraged with a view toward individuation.

FEEDBACK: A FORM OF CARING

Aged persons, especially those living alone, need feedback, and health care professionals tend to be niggardly about giving it to them. One reason for reluctance to give negative feedback is fear of hurting their feelings. Another may be ignorance regarding the importance of feedback.

The ability to give positive feedback seems to go with an optimistic disposition. Insecure, unhappy persons have difficulty being supportive of others and giving praise or using rewards. Lack of feedback, whether negative or positive, compounds the problems of alienation, loneliness, bereftness. Negative feedback, in fact, may spur an older person on in an attempt to prove you wrong!

SELF-CARING: KEY TO SURVIVAL

Care of self is a fundamental aspect of mental health that is often ignored by health professionals. It is not commonly accepted among them that one has to care for self to be able to care for others. See the list of self-care tenets earlier in this chapter.

Care givers must have exquisite self-awareness regarding their own depressions, withdrawals, work overload, sensations overload, grief, boredom, ennui, impatience, etc. A young psychologist (Mancinelli) at a conference said that his work in a community mental health center meant seeing eight clients daily; he was booked 3 weeks in advance. He takes care of himself by using each hour of cancellation for himself; he finds someone to listen to him for an hour, so that he can return to the next client with some of his own needs met. If one takes exquisite care of one's self, there may be reactions from others; the gamut may go from envy to resentment to anger—resentment and anger because others may see your self-care ritual as having priority and denying them some of your time, work, company, etc.

Self-care of the Aged

In old age, exquisite care of self (both physical and psychological) may well be important to one's survival—if not to survival itself, at least to a more decent quality of survival. I recently observed an old couple taking care of themselves. In their seventies, they regularly go to a drugstore where there is a coin-operated, computerized blood pressure–taking apparatus. There is no stress involved, no sitting in a doctor's crowded office for hours, simply a controlled operation. Cost? Fifty cents a reading, which is clear and easy to see on the instrument panel. The dangerous levels of both systolic and diastolic readings are well delineated. The couple then discuss their respective blood pressures to see where in the range of normal to dangerous they lie.

Avoiding Depression, Loneliness

Besides the care of physical self, there is the important care of psychological self. When asked how they avoid depression or loneliness, older persons often state, "I don't let myself get in that state," "I get busy," or "When I feel signs of it, I do something about it." Prevention is one clue to handling stresses and strains. Also, some aged have tremendous support systems. Others have an incredible amount of inner strength; this can be observed in some centenarians, e.g., the 104-year-old woman described by Ebersole in Chapter 23.

The phenomenon of self-caring was well described by a 70-year-old Jungian analyst shortly before her death. Irene Claremont de Castillejo, in her book, *Knowing Woman: A Feminine Psychology,* has a chapter, "The Rainmaker Ideal," which is recommended to the reader. She uses the phrase, "being on one's thread," and explains it in Jungian language. It is necessary to be in touch with the self so that life has meaning. She describes "inner clarity" as a "conscious awareness of being on one's thread, knowing what one knows, and having an ability quite simply and without ostentation to stand firm on one's own inner truth" (p. 137).

> To care one must offer one's own vulnerable self to others as a source of healing. To care for the aging, therefore, means first of all to enter into close contact with your own aging self, to sense your own time, and to experience the movements of your own life cycle. From this aging self, healing can come forth and others can be invited to cast off the paralyzing fear for their future.
>
> As long as we think that caring means only being nice and friendly to old people, paying them a visit, bringing them a flower, or offering them a ride, we are apt to forget how much more important it is for us to be willing and able to be present to those we care for. And how can we be fully present to the elderly when we are hiding from our own aging?
>
> How can we listen to their pains when their stories open wounds in us that we are trying to cover up? . . . when speaking about caring in the context of aging, we want to speak first about caring as the way to the self before we speak about caring as the way to others. (Bauer, pp. 1–2)

Truman Capote (p. 44) wrote a poem which expresses the essence of care and care giving:

> We are speaking of love. A leaf, a handful of seed—begin with these, learn a little what it is to love.

First, a leaf, a fall of rain, then someone to receive what a leaf has taught you, what
  a fall of rain has ripened.
No easy process, understand; it could take a lifetime, it has mine, and still I've never
  mastered it—
I only know how true it is;
  that love is a chain of life,
  as nature is a chain of life.

REFERENCES

Aldin, C. C. W.: *Dogs of Character,* Eyre and Spothswode, Publishing Ltd., London, 1930.

American Journal of Nursing, **77**(10):1557, 1977.

Bancroft, Ann: "Now She's a Disposition Problem," *Perspectives in Psychiatric Care,* **9**:96–102, 1971.

Bauer, Stephen: *Notes and Quotes of the Catholic Hospital Association,* Catholic Hospital Association, St. Louis, Mo., 1977, pp. 1–2.

Bernard, Yetta: *Self Care,* Celestial Arts, Millbrae, Calif., 1975.

Burnside, Irene M.: "Mental Health in the Aged: The Nurse's Perspective," in Richard H. Davis (ed.), *Aging: Prospects and Issues,* Andrus Gerontology Center, University of Southern California, Los Angeles, 1976.

Burston, G. R.: Letter: "Granny-battering," *British Medical Journal,* **3**(5983): 592, 1975.

Butler, Robert N., and **Myrna Lewis:** *Aging and Mental Health,* 2d ed., Mosby, St. Louis, 1977, pp. 223–224.

Cameron, Paul, and **John Klopsch:** "Friendship Patterns across the Life Span," paper presented at Western Gerontological Society, Denver, Mar. 20–23, 1977.

Capote, Truman: *The Grass Harp,* Random House, 1951, p. 44.

Clow, Hollis E.: "Individualizing the Care of the Aging," *American Journal of Psychiatry,* **110**(6):460–464, 1953.

Cole, Elbert: Moderator of "Alternative Living Arrangements," at Regional Symposium on Aging: The Flip Side of 50, Overland Park, Kansas, Sept. 20, 1977.

Comfort, Alex: *A Good Age,* Crown Publishers, Inc., New York, 1976, p. 155.

Corson, Samuel A.: "Pet-facilitated Psychotherapy in a Hospital Setting," in Jules H. Masserman (ed.), *Current Psychiatric Therapies,* Grune & Stratton, New York, 1975.

————, **E. O'Leary Corson, Donald De-Hass, Regina Gunsett, Peter Gwynne, Eugene Arnold,** and **Candace Corson:** "The Socializing Role of Pet Animals in Nursing Homes; An Experiment in Nonverbal Communication Therapy," paper presented at an International Symposium on *Society, Stress and Disease: Aging and Old Age,* Stockholm, Sweden, June 14–19, 1976.

Curtin, Sharon R.: *Nobody Ever Died of Old Age,* Little, Brown, Boston, 1972.

Da Silva, Guy: "The Loneliness and Death of an Old Man; Three Years' Psychotherapy of an 81-Year-Old Depressed Man," *Journal of Geriatric Psychiatry,* 1(1):5–27, 1967.

de Castillejo, Irene Claremont: *Knowing Woman: A Feminine Psychology,* Putnam, New York, 1973.

Dyer, W. A.: *The Dogs of Boytown,* Holt, New York, 1918.

Gates, A. M.: "Greek and Roman Pets," *Southern Atlantic Quarterly,* 30: 405–419, 1931.

Gautier, J.: *A Priest and His Dog,* Kenedy, New York, 1957.

Gaylin, Willard: "Caring Makes the Difference," *Psychology Today,* 10(3): 34–39, 1976.

Glasser, William: *Reality Therapy: A New Approach to Psychiatry,* Harper & Row, New York, 1965.

Griffith, F. B.: *Historic Dogs,* Clinton L. Mellor, Haverford, Pa., 1952.

Gubrium, Jaber F.: *Living and Dying at Murray Manor,* St. Martin's Press, New York, 1975.

Hamilton, Virginia: *Illusions and Reality,* Library of Congress No. 030-001-00072-9, Washington, 1976.

Hayes, H. R.: *In the Beginnings: Early Man and His Gods,* Putnam, New York, 1963.

Herr, John, and John Weakland: "The Family as a Group," in Irene Burnside (ed.), *Working with the Elderly: Group Process and Techniques,* Duxbury Press, North Scituate, Mass., 1978.

Hyde, Ann: "The Phenomenon of Caring," Part I, *Nursing Research Reports,* American Nurses' Foundation, Inc., 10(1):2+, 1975; Part II, 11(1):2+, 1976*a*; Part III, 11(2):2, 1976*b*; Part IV, 11(3): 2+, 1976*c*.

Jacobi, Jolande: *The Psychology of C. G. Jung,* Yale, New Haven, 1962.

Jury, Mark, and Dan Jury: *Gramp,* Grossman Publishers, New York, 1976.

Kalish, Richard A.: "Of Social Values and the Dying: A Defense of Disengagement," *Family Coordinator,* 21(1): 81–94, 1972.

Katz, Robert L.: *Empathy: Its Nature and Uses,* Free Press, New York, 1963.

Knowlton, Willis E.: Student paper, class "Psychosocial Care of the Aged," Arizona State University, Tempe, Arizona, 1977.

Leininger, Madeleine: "Caring: The Essence and Central Focus of Nursing, *Nursing Research Reports,* American Nurses' Foundation, Inc., 12(1):2+, 1977.

Levinson, Boris: "The Dog as a 'Co-therapist,' " *Mental Hygiene,* 46(1):59–65, 1962.

———: "The Veterinarian and Mental Hygiene," *Mental Hygiene,* 49(3):320–323, 1965.

———: "Pets and Old Age," *Mental Hygiene,* 53(3):364–368, 1969.

———: *Pets and Human Development,* Charles C Thomas, Springfield, Ill., 1972.

Loether, Herman J.: *Problems of Aging: Sociological and Social Psychological Perspectives,* Dickenson, Belmont, Calif., 1975.

Lorenz, K. Z.: *Man Meets Dog,* Penguin, Baltimore, 1965.

MacLeish, Archibald: *New and Collected Poems, 1917–1976,* Houghton Mifflin, Boston, 1976, pp. 34–35.

Mancinelli, James L.: Personal communication, September 1977.

Mayeroff, Milton: *On Caring,* Harper & Row, New York, 1971.

The Mercury, San Jose, Calif., Aug. 23, 1977, p. 29.

Mugford, R. A., and J. G. M'Comisky: "Some Recent Work on the Psychotherapeutic Value of Cage Birds with Old People," in R. S. Anderson (ed.), *Pet Animals and Society,* Baillière, London, and Williams & Wilkins, Baltimore, 1975, pp. 54–65.

National Geographic Society: "Man's Best Friend," *National Geographic Book of Dogs,* Washington, 1966.

North, Sterling: *Rascal,* Dutton, New York, 1963.

————: *Raccoons Are the Greatest People,* Dutton, New York, 1966.

Olsen, Tillie: *Tell Me a Riddle,* Dell, New York, 1976.

Paglinawan, Lynette K.: "Na Kupuna," in *Hawaii Governor's Bicentennial Conference on Aging,* State Hawaii Commission on Aging, 1977.

Pfaffenberger, Clarence J.: *The New Knowledge of Dog Behavior,* Howell Book House, Inc., New York, 1963.

Richardson, E.: *Poets' Dogs,* Putnam, New York, 1895.

San Francisco Progress, Plan to Match Pets with Elderly Masters, Sept. 30, 1977, p. 2.

Schonberg, William B., and **Hannah C. Potter:** "Friendship Fluctuation in Senescence," *Journal of Genetic Psychology,* **129**:333–334, 1976.

Schwartz, Loretta: "Hungry Women in America," *Ms.,* **6**(4):60–63+, 1977.

Scott-Maxwell, Florida: *The Measure of My Days,* Knopf, New York, 1968.

Sehlin, Katherine: "Older Women More Often Poverty Stricken Than Men," *Minnesota Senior Spotlight,* **7**(1):1, 1977.

Shows, W. Derek: "A Psychological Theory of the Later Years: C. G. Jung," in W. Doyle Gentry (ed.), *Geropsychology: A Model of Training and Clinical Service,* Ballinger Publishing Co., Cambridge, Mass., 1977.

Sloan, A., and **A. Farquhar:** *Dog and Man: The Story of a Friendship,* Hutchinson, London, 1925.

Smith, M. C.: *Famous Dogs of Famous People,* Dodd, Mead, New York, 1944.

Spark, Geraldine M., and **Elaine M. Brody:** "The Aged Are Family Members," *Family Process,* **9**(2):195–209, 1970.

Steinbeck, John: *Travels with Charley,* Viking, New York, 1962.

Stephens, Joyce: *Loners, Losers, and Lovers: Elderly Tenants in a Slum Hotel,* University of Washington Press, Seattle, 1976.

von Franz, M. L.: "The Process of Individuation," in Carl G. Jung (ed.), *Man and His Symbols,* Aldus Books Ltd., London, 1964; reprinted by Doubleday, Garden City, N.Y., 1972.

West, Jessamyn: *The Woman Said Yes,* Fawcett, Greenwich, Conn., 1976.

Wigginton, Eliot: *Foxfire 2,* Anchor Books/ Doubleday, Garden City, N.Y., 1973.

Yarrow, Marion, Paul Blank, Olive Quinn, E. Grant Youmans, and **Johanna Stein:** *Human Aging,* Government Printing Office, Washington, D.C., 1961.

OTHER RESOURCES

FILMS
Caring

Care with Caring: 14 min/color/1976. A provocative tape for hospital/medical staff in-service training. Shows how conflicts among staff make treatment of an anxious diabetic family even more difficult. Useful for discussion, role clarification, priority setting. Producer: Hugh James Lurie, M.D., University of Washington School of Medicine, Seattle, Wash. 98195.

Grandparents

Bubby: 5 min/b&w/1966. Brief, sensitive, moving portrait of an old woman by her 18-year-old grandson, who expresses his love and respect for his grandmother and provokes fresh thoughts about aging. Sound, but no dialogue. Distributor: Youth Film Distribution Center, 43 West 16th Street, New York, N.Y. 10011.

Aging (About People Series): 30 min/b&w/ 1963. Shows two elderly Jewish gentlemen revealing their attitudes toward life, loneliness, and the younger generation. A commentator discusses the prevalent notion that an old person is functionless, and advocates reestablishing the natural roles of grandfathers and grandmothers in family life. Producer: WTTW, Chicago, for NET. Distributor: Indiana University, Audio Visual Center, Bloomington, Ind. 47401.

Gramp: See Chapter 24, Other Resources.

The Grandfather: See Chapter 22, Other Resources.

Granny Lives in Galaway: 26 min/color. A pair of orphans, armed with a picture of their grandmother's farm, set out to find her. She welcomes them with open arms and defies all attempts to have children removed. Distributor: Learning Corporation of America, 1350 Avenue of the Americas, New York, N.Y. 10019.

Green Valley Grandparents: 10 min/16 mm/ b&w/1972. A documentary about retired mechanics, truck drivers, farmers, and housewives who work with mentally retarded chilren at Green Valley Developmental Center. Follows grandparents dressing, feeding, and playing with the children. Distributor: Center for Southern Folklore, P.O. Box 4081, Memphis, Tenn. 38104.

My Grandson Lew: 13 min/16 mm/color. Available with teacher's guide. Based upon the book by Charlotte Zolotow, a gentle story about death and memories. Contains a positive image of an elderly person and opens the door to discussions of a child's view of death. Distributor: Arthur Barr Productions, Inc., P.O. Box 5667, Pasadena, Calif. 91107.

Peege: See Chapter 21, Other Resources.

Portrait of Grandpa Doc: 28 min/16 mm/ color. A young artist prepares for his first one-man show. The impact and influence of his grandfather are captured in his work through the memories of his childhood—the legacy Grandpa Doc left him. Written and dirccted by Randal Kleiser. Distributor: Phoenix Films, Inc., 470 Park Avenue South, New York, N.Y. 10016.

The Springtime of Autumn: 20 min/16 mm/ color/1971. Documentary of the Oregon Foster Grandparent Program. Follows daily activities of "grandparents" working patiently with retarded children at the Fairview Hospital and Training Center for mentally retarded children in Salem, Oregon. Story is narrated by grandparents and by professional personnel involved in the program. Distributor: Oregon Division of Continuing Education, Film Library, 1633 S.W. Park, Portland, Oreg. 97207.

Pets

Harry and Tonto: See Chapter 18, Other Resources.

The Old Sheepdog: 10 min/color/1973. Animated film about an old sheepdog named Bodrik who was retired, then reinstated by his master. Distributor: ACI Films, Inc., 35 West 45th Street, New York, N.Y. 10036.

To a Very Old Woman (A Poem by Irving Layton): 10 min/color/1975. Shows the movements of an elderly woman as she plays cards, feeds the bird, etc. Producer: A film by Paul Quigley (Canada). Distributor: Learning Corporation of America, 1350 Avenue of the Americas, New York, N.Y. 10019.

Miscellaneous

Angelus: See Chapter 26, Other Resources.
I Think They Call Him John: See Chapter 26, Other Resources.
Last Stand Farmer: See Chapter 21, Other Resources.
Stringbean: See Chapter 18, Other Resources.
Yudie: 20 min/b&w/1973. About an older woman who grew up on New York's lower East Side, how she lives alone, how she worked and aged, and her perceptions of the past and present. She speaks with insight, humor, and authority. Blue Ribbon Winner 1975 American Film Festival. Director: Mirra Bank. Distributor: New Day Films, P.O. Box 315, Franklin Lakes, N.J. 07417.

Chapter 28

PSYCHOSOCIAL CARING: REALITY TESTING, RELOCATION, AND REMINISCING

Irene Mortenson Burnside

> Our concerns should be directed toward a cultural
> reordering of values which offers quality of human
> experience in the later years of life.
>
> *Anne Kellett*

The Old Grey Donkey, Eeyore, stood by himself in a thistly corner of the forest, his front feet well apart, his head on one side, and thought about things. Sometimes he thought sadly to himself, "Why?" and sometimes he thought, "Wherefore?" and sometimes he thought, "Inasmuch as which?"—and sometimes he didn't quite know what he was thinking about. So when Winnie-the-Pooh came stumping along, Eeyore was very glad to be able to stop thinking for a little in order to say "How do you do?" in a gloomy manner to him.

"And how are you?" said Winnie-the-Pooh.

Eeyore shook his head from side to side. "Not very how," he said, "I don't seem to have felt at all how for a long time."

From Winnie-the-Pooh, by A. A. Milne, and illustrated by Ernest H. Shepard, pp. 44–45. Copyright, 1926, by E. P. Dutton; renewal © 1954 by A. A. Milne. Reprinted by permission of publishers, E. P. Dutton.

Borrowing from A. A. Milne is one way to open a discussion of reality testing with aged clients. Care givers often ask exactly what Winnie-the-Pooh asked, "And how are you?" Sometimes they receive answers similar to Eeyore's.

All disciplines share the responsibility in reality testing. Aged persons who are in an acute or chronic confusional state or are disoriented need immediate reality testing; peers, family, and neighbors of the confused, disoriented elderly person may also need assistance.

558

Definition of Reality Testing[1]

Although the focus here is on reality testing with the older adult, reality testing is important with persons of any age. Hinsie and Campbell define reality testing as an ego function which provides the person with an objective evaluation and judgment of the world outside the self. Kolb described the reality principle: "Ego functions are channelled to facilitate psychosocial adaptation. However, such adaptation needs an evolving continuous set of interpersonal attitudes to establish a certain consistency, i.e., the way he usually perceives them [functions] and behaves in relation to them" (p. 36). The inconsistency of behavior of confused, disoriented old people provides a great challenge for care givers. Unpredictable behavior creates a certain uneasiness for those in the milieu, both care givers and residents. For example, in the last few years aged state hospital patients have been transferred to nursing homes. The new arrivals have an unsettling effect on personnel, residents, and residents' families.

Brenner, describing ego functions, stated that reality testing is the ability of the ego to distinguish between stimuli or perceptions arising from the outer world and those rising from the person's inner world. If the ego performs the task successfully, the individual is said to have a good or at least adequate sense of reality. This has a similar ring to Linden's remark that the group therapist working with the elderly needs to create a "good reality" for the members of the group. He stated, "The therapist's mode of managing . . . is to create out of himself, out of the treatment situation, and out of the group a 'good' reality" (p. 64).

Review of the Literature

Indexes in psychology, psychiatry, and gerontology books do not include the term *reality testing*; it has been impossible to find specific materials about reality testing with the aged person. Much of the success in care of older persons suffering from acute or chronic brain syndrome lies in consistent, accurate, empathic reality testing; it is unfortunate that the literature offers so little.

Misnomers

Reality therapy (Glasser) is a commonly misused term. It is used when reality orientation or reality testing is being described. Reality therapy was originated by Glasser, a psychiatrist. The psychotherapeutic approach called reality therapy is based on the premise that disturbed persons have two common problems: they cannot meet their basic needs, and they refuse to face reality. Though Glasser's principles can be modified in working with older adults, Glasser has not yet written about the aged. *Reality orientation* is a group treatment modality which was begun by Taulbee and Folsom. All three terms—reality testing, reality therapy, and reality orientation—need to be more precisely defined for students and new workers in the health care field.

[1]This portion of the chapter appeared in an article, "Reality Testing: An Important Concept," *ARN Journal* 11(3):3-7, 1977. Other portions were in a speech given at Boston University Sigma Theta Tau, Research Day, Nov. 20, 1976.

Urgency of Reality Testing

Reality testing is a here-and-now intervention; it cannot be put off until later. Timing is important because moods fluctuate and because trust has to be established early in the interaction. Storrie made the important remark that "the demented aged person knows whether you are engaged with them or not." The confused old person is often teased, cajoled, or ignored. Gubrium sensitively documented the plight of the aged in nursing homes and stated that accounts offered by residents viewed by the staff as completely "senile" are not honored, even if they are rationally presented. Residents are considered disoriented because their talk does not have any connection with their actions, and provides no clues to causes of their behavior. The staff ignores the talk, but actually it is used as a basis for managing patients. A subtle, often coordinated subterfuge occurs in which it appears that the resident's talk is being taken into accord, while the interaction is being directed toward a different end. Such a game is played among community-based persons as well as in long-term care facilities. The knowledge that one is not being taken seriously causes its own blights on human interaction, regardless of the age of those affected. This kind of subterfuge is very common among aged clientele.

Why is reality testing not done more frequently? (1) There is a lack of awareness of the need; (2) it is sheer, dogged hard work at times; (3) it requires an inordinate amount of patience; (4) the situation involving the aged person may not be assessed carefully enough to determine the actual need for reality testing. The following list gives further reasons which apply specifically to older people:

1. Ignorance; not understanding the importance of reality testing or how it should be done.
2. Deceit as a *modus operandi* of staff and/or family.
3. Fear of hurting the old person.
4. Overprotectiveness of the staff or family; fostering dependency.
5. Lack of time of staff or family.
6. Lack of interest of family or staff.
7. Constant failures by care givers in their reality-testing attempts.
8. Lack of in-service education in long-term facilities.
9. Poor role models in agencies which care for aged persons.
10. Lack of experience in working with the aged client.

What appears to be all right is not always all right (Kalkman). Aged persons often behave in a manner which fools us. They may not comprehend the situation they are in, e.g., though they may be experiencing a state of shock, they may appear merely bewildered, may maintain a façade, or may be unusually quiet. *The ability to discover meanings in an aged client's behavior is the hallmark of a sophisticated practitioner.* There is nothing so discouraging as to see a confused staff member trying to straighten out a very confused and disoriented old person. One must have the facts straight before beginning to reality-test with an older person; sometimes all of us are a bit slow in interpreting reality, as is well known by the traveler who finds himself in strange environs and suffering from jet lag.

Five Conditions Requiring Reality Testing

Five conditions in which reality testing must be considered a psychosocial intervention are (1) immediately following shock treatment, (2) during the stage from sleep to wakefulness, (3) during acute confusional states caused by anesthesia, illness, trauma, translocation shock, malnourishment, dehydration, etc., (4) during reactions from drugs or alcohol, and (5) during illusions (Burnside, 1977).

Shock Treatment
Electric shock treatment is used by some psychiatrists during severe depressive states. It was a common form of treatment in state hospitals in the forties and was widely used with women diagnosed as having involutional melancholia. Following shock treatment, an individual may be disoriented for several days. In such a state, patients do not know where their room is; they do not know what day it is; and they are embarrassed about the temporary amnesia they experience.

Arousal from Sleep
A second need for reality testing may occur during the stage between sleep and full wakefulness. This may be during the day at nap time or at night. Berenson wrote in his diary:

> I wake and feel as if I were as stiff, as unarticulated, as monolithic as a marble slab. It takes me half an hour or more to begin to feel warmth and life in my viscera, and muscles unbound and beginning to relax. At last, after some time, restfulness begins to possess me, and I enjoy a moment of physiological happiness, *bien-être.* So I call this condition of extreme numbness, dullness, and fatigue with which I wake, as the effort to rest from resting, from sleep. Even if I have slept sound and well, and shall profit by it later in the day, the recovery from what should be the repose following sleep is dull and at times dreary. It is as if every bit of me had slept independently of every other and died or nearly died in the effort, and that on waking these different bits had to be gathered together and reintegrated, put together like smashed crockery. I do not ask for "scientific" explanations. I have ceased believing in their answers. (pp. 304–305)

Night personnel need special in-service classes about reality testing and helping old people adjust during the night. This is especially true after a move, when the aged person may have translocation shock. Old people in long-term care facilities get restless at sundown and want to go home; someone has termed it "the sundowner's syndrome." Twilight may be a bad time of the day. Others awaken very early in the morning and do not know where they are. Such behavior occurs in both acute-care and long-term settings. Intensive reality testing should begin immediately at the time of admission. Relatives may also be helped to improve reality testing with regressed persons living at home. *Gramp* (Jury and Jury) offers poignant examples of relatives struggling against formidable odds with such an individual.

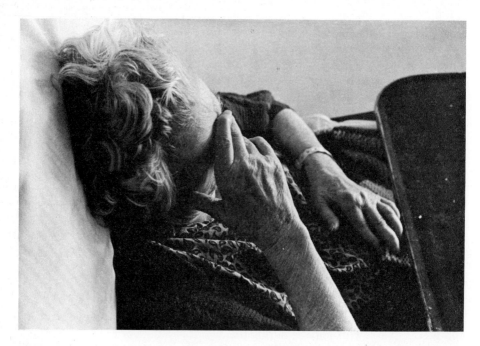

Figure 28-1 Elderly persons may experience a state of confusion when they are awakened, and especially if they are in a new and strange environment. (*Courtesy of Harvey Finkle.*)

During Acute Confusional States

Acute confusion may be caused by anesthesia, dehydration, elevated temperature, malnutrition, physiological changes, electrolyte imbalance, uncontrolled diabetes, broken bones, etc. A complete physical examination is a must in such instances to determine the physical state at the time. But the flurry to treat the physical problems often results in the psychological changes being ignored. Reality testing is not done. The holistic aspect of care gets lost constantly in caring for the old person. See Guidelines for Intervention in Confusional States, on p. 570.

Rossman has warned nurses about the "black patch delirium" which may occur after cataract surgery. It is just one example of an acute confusional state. As Rossman says, the aged person's vulnerability to confusion and disorientation due to physical causes is a primary consideration in the psychosocial care of the elderly because the process of decompensation can occur in a minute.

Case Example. A 96-year-old man fractured his patella. He was an unusually alert man; but after the operation on his knee, he insisted his leg had been cut off. Later when he was mobile and doing well, he was invited to a demonstration group meeting for a class. Prior to the meeting, the leader was discussing the plan for teaching, and the elderly man pulled up his pants leg, muttering about his knee. The instructor touched his knee and told him it looked fine. She did not know until after the group demonstration that the patient believed his leg had been removed because when the cast was removed, he thought it was his leg that had been sawed off. He may have been doing his own reality testing with the new group leader. Before the cast was discarded, it might have been helpful for him to touch the cast and even put the cut cast on his leg and then remove it so he could better understand what had happened, especially if casts were foreign to him. This is a good example of the need for reality testing with old people during medical or surgical events. The case study points out the great need for exquisitely clear instructions, before, during, and after medical, surgical, or other treatment procedures.

Drugs

Another condition to be alert for is comprised of the slow, insidious changes which occur during drug administration. The nurses' aide or the relatives are often the first to complain that the old person is behaving differently. Digoxin, diuretics, antihypertensives, analgesics, sedative-hypnotics, antipsychotics, insulin, etc., may all induce behavioral as well as physical adverse effects (Kayne). The reader is referred to a study by Schwartz, Henley, and Zeitz on medication errors made by elderly ill patients. Errors during self-medication may exacerbate drug reactions.

Reality testing regarding time, place, and person is crucial. Clocks and calendars are a must, and they must be large and easily seen. Reality testing must be honest and consistent, especially during the evening hours, during sudden changes in locale, or in crisis situations. Explanations are often given curtly or hastily, as though to imply that it is an imposition to have to do the testing or that

Figure 28-2   Elderly persons may become disoriented when faced with illness. Sudden changes in routine can be upsetting, and hospitals for care of the acutely ill, with their accelerated pace and great activity, can cause fear and alarm in oldsters. (*Courtesy of University of Rochester.*)

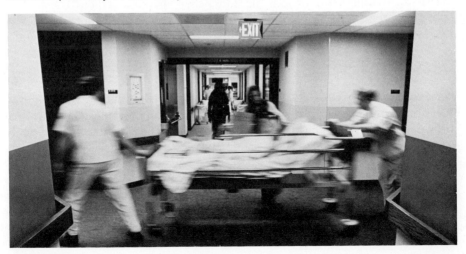

the old person is not very bright. Gubrium has sensitively documented such interactions. Lack of consistency is common in reality testing; for example, one person says one thing, the next person saying something entirely different. For the aged person with a tenuous hold on reality, such inconsistency only adds to the bewilderment. It is difficult to imagine what it does to one's trust. Sometimes there is no checking out to make sure the message was received. The frustrations of staff during reality testing mount during periods of denial. The process is difficult when the aged person becomes vehement or argumentative and is spending energy to prove himself right. Families can compound problems, as seen in the case study below.

Case Example. The family of an elderly woman told the staff members that the woman's spouse had died 3 years previously, but the woman constantly talked about "fixing supper for papa" and kept saying that "he would soon be home." The family did not reality-test with her; they did not discuss that he had been dead for 3 years. They sent flowers weekly and the card was signed, "Papa." The staff could not handle this situation and simply refused to play the game. A staff conference helped them all finally to deal directly with the family.

As in this case, the aged person may insist that someone is not dead who actually is. Care givers may be mistaken for the deceased person. Since this occurs frequently, care givers must learn how to handle the situation; each will develop his or her own way of dealing with the problem.

Another difficulty arises if one gets caught in the unreal world of a paranoid patient. Sometimes very paranoid old patients will ensnarl you in the web of their delusions. I have written elsewhere about a sweet, but oh so paranoid, 96-year-old woman who thought I was "messing around" with her brother (Burnside, 1978).

A fine example of facing reality is given by the widow of Gramp: "For Nan, the spirit of Gramp still inhabits the house they shared together. 'It's a funny thing,' Nan says, 'If I hear a noise I'll think, that's Frank coming in, —but then I'll just cross it out of my mind because I know it's not true'" (Jury and Jury, p. 151). The reader is referred to Chapter 18, in which the realization that the spouse is gone is described as one task of widowhood.

Illusions

After reality testing with some aged patients regarding illusions, I am inclined to agree with Freud, who wrote, "Just as no one can be forced to believe, so no one can be forced to disbelieve" (p. 51). Reality testing during illusions is an important area. Unfortunately, illusions have been described chiefly in experimental studies, and what is available in the literature has been written by cognitive psychologists; nothing has been written about illusions and interventions for those who give care to the aged. See Chapter 24 for more detailed information on the occurrence of illusions in old persons as a result of visual defects.

Definition. Kolb states, "In an illusion, an image symbol of a real object is formed, but for psychological reasons it is misinterpreted" (p. 92). Old people mistake one sound for another; they also mistake visual objects and/or persons. Illusory experiences are not always indicative of psychosis or regression. The frequent misperception of the cues in the environment causes much difficulty and embarrassment at times. Diminished hearing and poor vision are common causes for misperception of the environment. Shadows also play havoc with some old persons' perception of the environment. Color seems to be an important component of illusions, but I have only my own observations for data; colors frequently involved in illusions described to me by old people are red, white, green, gray, black. I am always struck with the similarity of the illusions described to something out of the person's past or to something familiar. Trying to relate objects to the familiar is an important clue in interpreting illusions. See the discussion on "affordance" in Chapter 24. Table 28-1 gives descriptions of the illusions of old people by health professionals who shared them.

Illusions Causing Fear. It is not uncommon for illusions of objects, persons, or happenings in the immediate environment to be frightening; therefore, reality testing serves to decrease fears. Gubrium studied a sample of 210 persons, aged 60 to 94, in Detroit. He defined fear as "a state of mind characterized by desperation and anxiousness stemming from personal incompetence in coping with events of everyday life" (p. 111). Although the fears Gubrium delineated were global in scope, rather than one immediate environment, one should be aware that illusions may indicate a decrease in competence, which in itself is anxiety-provoking. Only since gathering information from students and colleagues about illusions have I realized how important the reduction of fear is in psychosocial care.

Case Example. A 75-year-old woman lived alone in a quiet suburban area. Her poor eyesight, consisting only of light and dark perception, was due to glaucoma. With decreasing sunlight in the early evening, the moving branches of a tree by the front door, which she rarely used and kept bolted, looked to her like a person (probably because of the shadows cast by the tree). Mild breezes moved the branches, which were shades of gray. The woman was frightened since she lived alone; she was rather frail, and she suspected that "the person" was bent on robbery.

Group Therapy

Weekly group meetings can be an avenue for reality testing with the aged. Group therapy provides support, much-needed stimulation, and accurate feedback regarding reality (Burnside, 1970; Blake). Reality testing does not consist solely, or even primarily, of shared verbalizations in the group setting; it is extremely important how the group therapist handles reality testing. Ancillary workers, family, and other members of the group may well emulate the leader. The role modeling effect is still understated in discussions of care giving to the aged.

Table 28-1. Examples of Visual Illusions

	Illusion as Stated by Aged Individual (or Care Giver)	Descriptions of Aged Person	Color Involved	Reality	Source of Information
1.	"Fire, Fire."	Elderly, confused woman, postsurgery patient in acute-care hospital.	Red	Very hot night, no air conditioning. She awoke from sound sleep to see the neon light outside.	1. Burnside: *Nursing and the Aged*, McGraw-Hill, New York, 1976, p. 388.
2.	Poet describes old man in hospital bed saying, "Get horses out of the barn because it's on fire."	Described in a poem.	Red	Potted red poinsettia on his dresser in hospital room.	Stephen Dobyns, "The Grandfather Poem," *The New Yorker*, **49**(47):30, 1974.
3.	"Red cows down there" (pointing to her feet).	An elderly, confused lady in her eighties, a bed patient in an acute-care hospital. She had always lived on a farm. Her confusion and "crazy talking" made student nurses uncomfortable.	Red	She was wearing orange/red knitted slippers.	Students' instructor, Helen Monea.
4.	"There are two ghosts outside my window."	Confused woman on an acute psychiatric ward.	White	Two laundry carts did not get pushed all the way to laundry.	Irene Burnside, Nurse, PM shift, Contra Costa County Hospital, Martinez, Calif.
5.	"A white ghost."	Elderly lady living in the community.	White	Curtains blowing in the breeze.	Public health nurse.

6.	Elderly woman in group demonstration. Leader held small, silver microphone close to woman, who tried to smell it on three occasions.	A moderately confused 80-year-old nursing home resident.	Silver/black	Microphone (as person in audience pointed out) resembled a small perfume bottle.	Phyllis Michaelson, College of Nursing, Portland, Oregon.
7.	Illusion lasted for 72 hours. Black spots in linoleum were taken for spiders.	Elderly patient on acute psychiatric ward being treated for overdosing self with bromides and scopolamines.	Black	Design in linoleum flooring.	Magdalene Morris, instructor.
8.	"There are beehives over there."	An elderly woman who had grown up on a farm in Pennsylvania and was living in a Catholic nursing home.	Gray/black	The mechanical part of the door, over the door jamb, was shaped like a beehive.	Nun who worked in a retirement home in Harrisburg, Pa.
9.	Old man reached for a ball-shaped gray, metal microphone and attempted to lick it.	92-year-old man in group demonstration in Nova Scotia.	Gray	The microphone was held to his mouth so the audience could hear him. The microphone shape was that of an ice cream cone; each time it was held close to his mouth, he attempted to lick it.	Irene Burnside, Antigonish, Nova Scotia, Canada.
10.	"Nice feathers there."	Same woman described in no. 4	Beige	Group leader had on long, wool skirt, beige/brown. The beige pattern resembled long feathery design.	1. Burnside: *Nursing and the Aged*, McGraw-Hill, New York, p. 388.

Table 28-1. Examples of Visual Illusions (cont.)

	Illusion as Stated by Aged Individual (or Care Giver)	Descriptions of Aged Person	Color Involved	Reality	Source of Information
11.	"Green snakes up there."	Bed patient in domiciliary veterans' home. The elderly veteran had grown up in Southern part of United States. (Plants probably not hung from ceiling in those days. Also may have been in snake-infested area.)	Green	Nurses hung an ivy plant from ceiling in his ward.	Nurses at Veterans' Home, Marshalltown, Iowa.
12.	Intravenous fluid is running and the arm is strapped to a splint; the aged patient thinks someone is standing at side of bed holding down the arm.	Elderly patient in acute-care hospitals.	White/ silver/ clear	Old person is receiving intravenous fluids.	Numerous nurses in classes.
13.	Care giver was showing slides to a group of regressed, elderly patients in a darkened room.	An 84-year-old woman got up and tried to walk through the lighted screen.	Blurred colors, but bright light from the slide and projector.	The only door in the room was on opposite side, but not easily discernible since the door jamb was same color as walls.	Irene Burnside, group leader at Clearview Sanitarium, Gardena, Calif.
14.	Recurring illusion was the mistaking of the elevator for a trolley car that	Elderly nursing home resident.	Not given	The "trolley" was the elevator.	Unidentified.

	would take the person to work.			
15.	"My mother was sick and when I arrived to see her, she thought I was my sister-in-law. It was dark, about 6 P.M. Her illusions occurred early in the morning and late in afternoon."	Aged mother.	All colors	Reality testing was unsuccessful because she had a need to see her daughter-in-law and seemed to enjoy the illusion.	Maria Abarca, instructor, Costa Rica, Central America.
16.	"I could not visit my father when he was hospitalized so a new friend of mine substituted. Although he knew her before, he always called her by my name."	Elderly father.	None	He mistook friend for daughter. No clarification was done; "the lack of intervention was successful because the illusion gave him satisfaction."	Maria Abarca, instructor, Costa Rica, Central America.

SUMMARIZING STATEMENTS ABOUT REALITY TESTING BASED ON THE LITERATURE

- Reality testing is the ability of the ego objectively to evaluate and judge the world outside the self (Hinsie and Campbell).
- Reality therapy is one of the psychotherapeutic approaches used with juvenile delinquents (Glasser).
- Reality orientation is a group treatment modality successful with mentally impaired aged (Taulbee and Folsom).
- Mentally impaired aged persons know whether you are engaged with them or not (Storrie).
- In nursing homes, accounts by mentally impaired aged are not taken seriously, even when they are rationally stated (Gubrium).
- Ignoring the speech of a mentally impaired resident is a way of managing the resident (Gubrium).
- Reality testing is needed (1) after shock therapy, (2) in the stage from sleep to wakefulness, (3) during acute confusional states, (4) during drug and alcohol reactions, and (5) during illusions (Burnside, 1977).

GUIDELINES FOR INTERVENTION IN CONFUSIONAL STATES

In a vis-à-vis relationship, the following suggestions may be helpful to the interviewer:

- Study the person's behavior closely and do not be fooled by it. Assess severity and length of confusional states; check out three spheres of disorientation—time, person, place. Assess hearing, vision. Check whether glasses have been corrected, and whether hearing aid, if used, is effective.
- Therapeutic touch is important for (1) reality orienting, (2) support, and (3) physical protection (Cashar and Dixon).
- Be aware of the situations which tend to cause and/or increase the confusion of an aged individual.
- Check out what you see and hear and what the client sees and hears, e.g., by way of illusions, hallucinations. (Also check out what feelings the client has about the illusions.)
- Improve the real world, the present existence, to decrease the tremendous need for dreams and fantasy.
- Do not give false assurance. Do not say, "Don't worry," or "Everything is going to be all right."
- Consider your degree of empathy. Do you try to understand what is happening to the old person?

RELOCATION SHOCK

A great deal of research has been done over the years regarding relocation of the elderly. In a most poignant article entitled, "Old Age, Youth and Vermouth" (Smith-White), the author describes that difficult move from own home to nursing home. Although the literature is replete with information regarding moves from institution to institution and from home to institution, there is only one study of ward-to-ward moves (Pablo) and none on intraroom moves. There is also a lack of information on moves from home to home of various relatives. Therefore, the focus of this portion of the chapter will be on the less discussed but often traumatic moves.

An excellent overview of the literature on relocation of the aged was done by Schulz and Brenner. Research included the study already mentioned by Pablo on intrainstitutional relocation and its impact on long-term-care residents. The researchers studied the transfer of 26 males from a 51-bed ward to three other hospital wards. These wards were part of a long-term-care and rehabilitation hospital. This study supports the research showing that relocation is a negative phenomenon. "Intra-institution transfers, although perceived as the least disrupting among the different types of moves (e.g. as opposed to a transfer from the home to an institution) can induce stress sufficient to affect survival" (p. 434). The data did not indicate any age effects of relocation and did not substantiate the expectation that old patients will incur a greater risk of dying with this type of relocation. Reasons given for the fact that overall mortality was minimized were (1) careful planning of the move involving the patient, (2) the nature and degree of environmental change, and (3) the voluntariness of the change.

From One Relative's Home to Another

Some old people live for a few months with one relative and then move to another relative. Those I have observed have fared quite well in spite of the moves, but probably because some were tough and ornery old folks; others had remarkable families.

From Relative's Home to Nursing Home

Administrators and directors of nurses of nursing homes often decry the fact that many elderly people are brought to homes and left with such stories as, "We are just going to take you for a ride today, but we will be back to get you later," or "The doctor thinks you need a checkup so we are just going to leave you for a checkup," and other such untruths. Many old people sit and wait for their relatives to come back and get them. The staff then finds it difficult to deal honestly with the aged resident who, of course, will not believe them. It is hard enough to build trust in people who have been abandoned or rejected (or feel that they have) without having such fabrications to deal with also. Resorting to lying compounds the problem of reality testing with a confused person. We still have a long way to go to include aged persons as partners in planning for their care and/or their moves from one living space to another.

Although there can be many stresses for the aged when they are moved, it should be considered that the change might be welcomed and offer new opportunities for some, as the research on relocation indicates. At any rate, aged persons should be included in the planning all of the way, and should make whatever decisions they can. We need constantly to assess the anxiety and the

Figure 28-3 Transfer from one room to another often severs close relationships and decreases interaction if mobility is a factor in seeing one another. (*Courtesy of Harvey Finkle.*)

behavior of the aged following any move, regardless of how minor the move might seem to us. During the assessment we can begin to consider ways to decrease confusion and disorientation, wandering, loneliness, depression, and the sense of bereftness which may be caused by a move. But also we must look for the positive aspects—the needed change, stimulation, improvement that may ensue. Research has documented such improvement in some studies.

No studies have yet been published which follow one old person through various moves; yet one observes confusion, disorientation, sadness, and anger after the shuffles. In both nursing homes and acute-care hospitals, I have observed that "difficult" patients are quickly transferred, and sometimes they are "swapped" for other patients. Red tape can be quickly severed and slashed when a "difficult" patient is involved. I recall working on an acute psychiatric ward; the moment a patient needed an intravenous feeding, he or she was transferred to the medical unit. Later when I worked on the medical ward, I noticed that patients who were confused or disoriented for whatever reason were sent to the psychiatric ward as soon as their physical state was stabilized. The patient's body and psyche were treated separately. This shuffling is hardly a holistic approach to care of the patient.

Many roommates in residences become confidantes for one another; transfers often sever such important relationships. Confidantes play an important role in the lives of the elderly (Lowenthal and Haven). After the move, a resident may no longer be able to visit the newly moved friend because of transportation problems or their own problems with mobility. In nursing homes, prices of rooms, incompatible roommates, and persnickety relatives are but a few of the reasons why old people are shuffled from room to room. A woman in one of my groups was once moved four times in 2 months; she felt it was a punitive action by the staff. Any move should be planned carefully. The following questions should be considered before, during, or after relocation:

1. Did the uprooting entail leaving a confidante?
2. Did the change have a positive or negative impact on the relocated person?
3. If physically able, did the aged person see the new location before being moved?
4. Was the information regarding the move honest, or was there deceit or withholding of information during the process?
5. Were memorabilia, the important "security blankets," moved with the resident?
6. Were new care givers alerted to idiosyncrasies, wishes, needs of the aged person being relocated?
7. Was there follow-up visiting after the move?
8. Finally, is this move necessary?

Figure 28-4   When elderly persons are relocated in the community, they often fare poorly due to lack of follow-up and surveillance by health professionals. (*Courtesy of Harvey Finkle.*)

CONCEPT OF REMINISCENCE²

Time is inferior to eternity and depends on motion or change. Past and future must exist in the present of the soul.

St. Augustine

Memory is not the preservation or the revival of the past but rather the renovation and transformation of the past; memory is creative.

A. Schopenhauer

The things which the child loves remain in the domain of the heart until old age. The most beautiful thing in life is that our souls remain hovering over the places we once enjoyed ourselves.

Kahlil Gibran

Reminiscence is a general term that includes memory of events, people, objects, places, and self. Reminiscence is the conscious recall of one's past life experience. It may be a social or solitary process that brings precognitive memories to awareness.

Reminiscing by or with the elderly has stimulated much thought and research in the last 15 years. Prior to that time it was more or less assumed that "living in the past" was a characteristic behavior of older people that was amusing, annoying at times, interesting to little children (because, of course, old people were in their second childhood), and probably indicative of some inability to cope with the present.

Life Review

Butler's studies (1974, 1963) were influential in bringing the functional aspects of reminiscence to the attention of professionals. Observing many people with emotional disorders, he noted various evidences of distress as people reviewed the meaning of their lives. He also observed that some people in the review process brought forth old, unresolved conflicts and elaborated them in a way that brought relief, satisfaction, and personal growth. He conjectured that life review is a near-universal occurrence among the aged as they face the prospect of impending death.

Life review is a self-enriching, refining process. Contrary to popular belief, reminiscing at its most effective level is a very progressive cognitive and psychological function. At its least satisfactory level it can lead to hopelessness, despair, and even suicide. Therein lies the problem for professionals. How can we use this seemingly natural tendency as a tool in effective intervention in the care of the aged?

Effects on Personality

The personality processes affected most by reminiscing are (1) self-esteem, (2) identification, (3) self-concept, (4) cathexis, (5) interpersonal relations, (6) ex-

---

² The last portion of this chapter was written by Priscilla Ebersole.

periential integration, and (7) cognitive activity. All these should be enhanced through effective reminiscing. Signs of effective life review include (1) acceptance of change, (2) attitudinal flexibility, (3) strength of purpose, (4) hopefulness, (5) meaningful activity, and (6) personal integrity. *Symptoms of ineffective reflection on one's life are rumination, depression, and self-rejection.* Some people are literally bound by their memories, and this becomes their greatest trial in their later years. As Vischer indicates, regrets about one's past are the greatest burden the aged person bears; negative assessment of the past plays a large part in the emergence of psychic disturbances during the years of decline.

A dichotomy seems to exist in that reminiscence may be both beneficial and detrimental—like most things in life; both possibilities are present, and the effects are dependent on the manner in which reminiscence is used. Some people feel it is cruel to stimulate thoughts of the past lest this stir up disappointments, regrets, and misery. It is probable that everyone reminisces, whether aloud or in silence. Reminiscing alone may produce satisfaction or despair, depending upon the ego strength of the individual and the tendency toward an egocentric or a humanistic viewpoint. Reminiscing with an empathic, nonjudgmental listener should produce growth, reconciliation, satisfaction, and pleasure. Marshall has, in fact, defined life review as an interpersonal process, though I have known many persons to carry on effective life reviews alone—often in the form of an autobiography. Writing or taping an autobiography, however, is not really a solitary process, as it implies an audience.

Social Significance

Besides being a reciprocal socializing process, attending to and recording memories from aged individuals has cultural, historic, and anthropological significance. Wigginton (1972, 1973, 1975) was intent on preserving the cultural myth and folklore of Appalachian elders. The burgeoning oral history movement witnessed in the last few years reflects the interest contemporary society has in the personal historic views of notable people. Though the goal is toward preservation of personal history, much of the process is a form of life review for the protagonist. Though each generation is bound to have different cultural expectations and opportunities, there are fundamental life experiences and feelings common to all that can enrich both generations in the exchange of significant experiences.

Lewis and Butler as well as Ebersole (1976a, 1976b) have used intergenerational group reminiscing effectively. Lewis and Butler focused on life crises and developmental stages with an intergenerational problem-solving goal. Ebersole focused on promoting socialization between the generations and an enriched view of the historic and cultural context of each. An implicit goal in group reminiscing is to broaden the perspective of each participant toward an ego-transcendant (Peck) rather than an ego-preoccupied state. (See Chapter 21 for further details of Peck's work.) Younger people begin to develop a different time perspective as they share experiences with their elders. They are often able to place their lives in a more expanded perspective as they see how each life contributes a unique aspect while yet a part of the whole of human experience. Productive reminiscing may be facilitated by:

1. Group meetings with cohorts
2. Intergenerational groups
3. Empathic, nonjudgmental listeners
4. The use of visual or sensory props
5. Visitations to places of significance
6. Meetings with old friends
7. Discussion of family traditions
8. Constructing family histories
9. Oral histories
10. Autobiographies, written or taped
11. Discussion of especially significant personal belongings
12. Sharing favorite foods
13. Visits to museums
14. Reading historic novels

Styles of Reminiscing

Some studies have contributed much to our knowledge of the process and results of reminiscing. McMahon and Rhudick defined several characteristic patterns of reminiscing among old men; among the reminiscers were the "story tellers," the "life reviewers," those who glorified the past, and those who did not share their past memories aloud but had a significant component of depression. McMahon and Rhudick correlated the ability to reminisce to freedom from depression.

Many studies have attempted to identify personality predictive components emerging from early memories. They are largely speculative and not theoretically applicable. However, Tobin and Etigson as well as Lieberman have identified the influence of the present life situation on the selective remembrance of past issues. For instance, an aged person experiencing a traumatic situation is likely to remember the traumas of early childhood, whereas an aged person feeling gratified in the present will be likely to remember pleasant experiences from the past.

Centenarians often have a better memory than those who live less long, and in extreme old age they have little physical energy. By virtue of their numerous life experiences they have more to reflect upon. Vischer says it very well: "By returning into the past, by occupying himself with the things which once were, man abandons the main current of life, sets his course for the quiet by-waters and drops anchor there. From this vantage point he listens to the distant roar of the river and reflects upon the journey he has completed" (p. 84).

Interviews with centenarians indicate several predominant themes. Concerns about lack of education are frequently expressed; leaving home to go out on their own stimulated much ambivalence—about this time in their lives, many expressed feelings of homesickness or loneliness mixed with feelings of pride and adventure. Females focus on the changes in women's status. There is considerable discussion of relationships with grandparents, siblings, and child-hood friends, less about mates.

Value of Reminiscing

Who cares, besides the elderly, about their memories? It has been found that young adults (Robertson) seek the aged for their wisdom, perspective, and knowledge of family and social history. Children often seek the aged for the entertainment value of their memories; professionals are interested in the therapeutic potential inherent in the shared memories; and middle-aged individuals, engrossed in their own midlife review (Lowenthal et al., 1975), may or may not be interested in that of the generation preceding them. There is some indication that during the middle years the experience of the elders is valued less than at any other age—possibly by its very proximity.

It is important to recognize that old people may reminisce more than younger people because they have more unoccupied time and more to reflect upon. Reflective activity and examination of previous life experiences seem to be triggered by changes, crises, and a decrease in physical activity. Havighurst and Glasser found that people begin to reflect on past events at about age 10, but youth are usually more active and have less time to ponder the meaning of the joys and pains of the past, as well as less past experience to draw upon.

In conclusion, the tendency to reminisce has long been a characteristic ascribed to the aged. Havighurst and Glasser and Lowenthal et al. (1975) found that, contrary to that notion, people reminisce frequently throughout life. Cameron and Giambra both have reported studies that show the tendency to reminisce is not statistically more frequent among the aged than among younger people. In spite of this, empirical observations lead to the view that elders reminisce more frequently than others, and lapse into reminiscence during many of their inter-actions and activities. This would seem logical, as they have such a vast amount of life experience behind them from which to draw. They may curb this tendency when it seems to be ill received, is viewed as a useless activity, or is only tolerated by others. I suspect this is one reason why they do not indicate to researchers that they are occupied with thoughts of the past.

It is undoubtedly important for all people to draw from past experience if they are to learn and grow successfully. Indeed, the best-adapted people and those most able to cope with life's challenging moments are those who are able to use their past effectively. Our present aged population has been faced with more cultural, economic, and social changes than any group of individuals in recorded time, and they may use reminiscing as a method of effectively relinquishing that which is no longer suitable while holding onto its personal significance. Some people who reminisce clutch the past to their bosom, not effectively using their memories toward present adaptation but more as a security measure. Both activities serve the aged though, obviously, one is more suitable for effective functioning in the present. The functions of reminiscence for the aged are:

1. To use relevant elements of past coping patterns to solve present problems
2. To keep a sense of familiarity by holding to the past in an ever-changing world

3. To exercise memory and focus thoughts
4. To develop an increasing understanding of one's successes
5. To maintain a sense of identity by remembering all facets of one's own unique experience
6. To maintain self-esteem by remembering active contributions to society and family
7. To entertain others with engaging incidents from the past
8. To avoid focusing on present intolerable situations
9. To let go of segments of the past in order to move into new situations
10. To maintain personality organization in times of overwhelming crises
11. To claim a spot of historic significance for one's life
12. To bridge the generations with understanding of common human experience
13. To establish a personal legacy for those who follow

Some theorists who have speculated on the function of reminiscence focus on only one component without recognizing that many are valid and often carried on simultaneously. It seems ineffectual to theorize about the whole of a remembered human experience in such a restrictive manner. Though many still disagree, I must state that all one's consciousness holds is remembered past experience. The present moment is past as we grasp it and becomes part of the amalgam of our future potential. It would seem most limiting for an individual to speculate on future events without a personal grasp of the ever-present past.

REFERENCES

Berenson, Bernard: *Sunset and Twilight, From the Diaries of 1947–1958,* Harcourt, Brace & World, New York, 1963.

Blake, Dorothy R.: "Group Work with the Institutionalized Elderly," in Irene M. Burnside (ed.), *Psychosocial Nursing Care of the Aged,* McGraw-Hill, New York, 1973.

Brenner, Charles: *An Elementary Textbook of Psycho-analysis,* Doubleday, New York, 1957.

Burnside, Irene M.: "Crisis Intervention with Hospitalized Geriatric Patients," *Journal of Psychiatric Nursing,* 8(2): 17–20, 1970.

———: "Reality Testing: An Important Concept," *ARN Journal,* 11(3):3–7, 1977.

———: "Eulogy for Ms. Hogue," *American Journal of Nursing,* 78(4):624–626, 1978.

Butler, Robert N.: "The Life Review: An Interpretation of Reminiscence in the Aged," *Psychiatry,* 26:65–76, 1963.

———: "Successful Aging and the Role of the Life Review," *American Geriatrics Society,* 22(12):529–535, 1974.

Cameron, Paul: "The Generation Gap: Time Orientation," *Gerontologist,* 12(2):117–119, 1972.

Cashar, L., and B. Dixon: "The Therapeutic Use of Touch," *Journal of Psychiatric Nursing,* **5**(5):442–451, 1967.

Ebersole, Priscilla: "Reminiscing and Group Psychotherapy with the Aged," in Irene M. Burnside (ed.), *Nursing and the Aged,* McGraw-Hill, New York, 1976. (a)

———: "Problems of Group Reminiscing with the Institutionalized Aged, *Journal of Gerontological Nursing,* **2**(6):23–27, 1976. (b)

Freud, Sigmund: *The Future of an Illusion,* Anchor Books, Doubleday, Garden City, N.Y., 1964.

Giambra, Leonard M.: "Daydreaming about the Past: The Time Setting of Spontaneous Thought Intrusions, *Gerontologist,* **17**(1):35–38, 1977.

Glasser, William: *Reality Therapy: A New Approach to Psychiatry,* Harper & Row, New York, 1965.

Gubrium, Jaber F.: "Apprehensions of Coping Incompetence and Responses to Fear in Old Age," *International Journal of Aging and Human Development,* **4**(2): 111–125, 1973.

Havighurst, R. J., and R. Glasser: "An Exploratory Study of Reminiscence," *Journal of Gerontology,* **27**(2):245–253, 1972.

Hinsie, L. E., and R. J. Campbell: *Psychiatric Dictionary,* Oxford, New York, 1960.

Jury, Mark, and Dan Jury: *Gramp,* Grossman Publishers, New York, 1976.

Kalkman, Marion: Personal communication, 1978.

Kayne, Ronald C.: "Drugs and the Aged," in Irene M. Burnside (ed.), *Nursing and the Aged,* McGraw-Hill, New York, 1976.

Kolb, Lawrence: *Modern Clinical Psychiatry,* Saunders, Philadelphia, 1968.

Lewis, Myrna I., and Robert N. Butler: "Life Review Therapy: Putting Memories to Work in Individual and Group Psychotherapy, *Geriatrics,* **29**(11): 165–173, 1974.

Lieberman, Morton A.: "Psychological Correlates of Impending Death: Some Preliminary Observations," in Bernice Neugarten (ed.), *Middle Age and Aging,* University of Chicago Press, Chicago, 1968.

Linden, Maurice E.: "Group Psychotherapy with Institutionalized Senile Women: A Study in Gerontologic Relations," *International Journal of Group Psychotherapy,* **3**:150–170, 1953.

Lowenthal, M., and C. Haven: "Interaction and Adaptation: Intimacy as a Critical Variable, *American Sociological Review,* **33**(1):20–30, 1968.

———, **M. Thurner, D. Chiriboga,** et al.: *Four States of Life: A Comparative Study of Women and Men Facing Transitions,* Jossey-Bass, San Francisco, 1975.

McMahon, A. W., and P. J. Rhudick: "Reminiscing: Adaptational Significance in the Aged," *Archives of General Psychiatry,* **10**:292–298, 1964.

Marshall, V. W.: "The Life Review as a Social Process," abstract in *Gerontologist,* **14**(5), part II:69, 1974.

Pablo, Renato Y.: "Intra-institutional Relocation: Its Impact on Long-term Care Patients, *Gerontologist,* **17**(5):426–435, 1977.

Peck, Robert C.: "Psychological Developments in the Second Half of Life," in J. Anderson (ed.), *Psychological Aspects of Aging,* American Psychological Association, Washington, D.C., 1955.

Robertson, Joan: "Significance of Grandparents: Perception of Young Adult Grandchildren, *Gerontologist,* **16**(2): 137–140, 1976.

Rossman, Isadore: Lecture for class, "Psychosocial Nursing Care of the Aged," Ethel Percy Andrus Gerontology Center, University of Southern California, Los Angeles, July 1974.

Schulz, Richard, and **Gail Brenner:** "Relocation of the Aged: A Review and Theoretical Analysis," *Journal of Gerontology,* **32**(3):323–333, 1977.

Schwartz, Doris, Doris Henley, and **Leonard Zeitz:** *The Elderly Ambulatory Patient,* Macmillan, New York, 1964.

Smith-White, Chad: "Old Age, Youth and Vermouth," *San Francisco Sunday Examiner and Chronicle,* Dec. 12, 1976.

Storrie, Michael: Personal communication, 1978.

Taulbee, Lucille R., and **James C. Folsom:** "Reality Orientation for Geriatric Patients, *Hospital and Community Psychiatry,* **17**(5):133–135, 1966.

Tobin, Sheldon, and **E. Etigson:** "Effects of Stress on the Earliest Memory," *Archives of General Psychiatry,* **19:** 435–444, 1968.

Vischer, A. L.: *On Growing Old* (translated from the German by Gerald Onn), Houghton Mifflin, Boston, 1967.

Wigginton, Eliot: *The Foxfire Books* (nos. 1, 2, 3), Anchor Books, Doubleday, Garden City, N.Y., 1972, 1973, 1975.

OTHER RESOURCES

Films

Reality Testing

To Live with Dignity: See Chapter 24, Other Resources.

Relocation

Beyond Shelter: 25 min/16 mm/color/1975. Emphasizes independent living for older people; shows the facilities and social programs in Denmark, and reflects concern that the elderly, even the handicapped, should remain independent for as long as possible. Distributor: Transit Media, P.O. Box 315, Franklin Lakes, N.J. 07417.

Environmental Health Aspects of Nursing Homes: 14 min/16 mm/color. Presents specific environmental health factors significant in skilled nursing facilities, e.g., accident and fire prevention, food sanitation, lighting, furnishings and decor. Distributor: Media Resources Branch, National Medical Audiovisual Center (Annex), Station K, Atlanta, Ga. 30324.

Housing Options for Older People: 28 min/ 16 mm/color/1974. About several persons at various stages in their search for appropriate housing. Narration by W. Jack Lewis, Cornell University. Film addressed to still-active older persons and their families. Distributor: Cornell University, Film Library, Roberts Hall, Ithaca, N.Y. 14850.

Peege: See Chapter 21, Other Resources.

Weekend: 12 min/16 mm/color/1973. The plight of a grandfather being put gently out to pasture by his family. Without dialogue. Producer: Zagreb Films, Yugoslavia. Distributor: Mass Media Associates, 2116 North Charles Street, Baltimore, Md. 21218.

Reminiscing

Maple Sugar Farmer: 29 min/16 mm/color/ 1972. Sensitive portrait of Sherman Graff, an old farmer who keeps alive a six-generation family tradition of making maple sugar. As he makes his syrup, he reminisces. Producers: A. W. Craig Hinds and Robert Davis Film. Distributor: ACI Films, Inc., 35 West 45th Street, New York, N.Y. 10036.

Yudie: See Chapter 27, Other Resources.

Chapter 29

PSYCHOSOCIAL CARING: TOUCH, SEXUALITY, AND CULTURAL ASPECTS

Irene Mortenson Burnside

> Sensuous pleasure seems necessary to old age as
> intellectual pleasure palls a little.
>
> *Florida Scott-Maxwell*

TOUCH: A POWERFUL WAY TO CARE[1]

Therapeutic touch is an ancient practice; there is nothing new, modern, or technological about this primitive sensation. If touch is used sensitively, at the proper time, and within the cultural context, it is a powerful tool (Sutterley and Donnelly). Cultural aspects of touching are discussed later in this chapter.

Touch is a powerful and important therapeutic intervention to use with a wide variety of patients/clients. The need for touch in infants, both animal and human, has been well documented by members of several disciplines (Harlow; Kramer, Chamorro, and Green; Montagu; Rubin). Harlow studied infant monkeys but did not study the tactile needs of old monkeys.

Human contact for the aged helps to compensate for the many losses that have been experienced by so many old people. Indeed, some aged persons seem to experience something similar to the marasmus described in infants. Old people who have no significant others often just give up. Helping them to make some

---

[1] The portion on touch is a revision of a speech presented as The Clare Dennison Memorial Lecture, Oct. 26, 1976, University of Rochester School of Nursing, Rochester, N.Y. Portions also appear in *Sensory Processes and Aging,* proceedings of a conference at the Dallas Geriatric Research Institute; in a speech, "Touch: Its Significance to the Elderly," for the California Nurses' Association Annual Meeting, Los Angeles, Calif., March 1975; and in a faculty presentation, University of Hawaii Summer Institute, Honolulu, Hawaii, June 1977.

sort of replacement for the affectional and emotional losses they have experienced is a challenge in care giving.

Review of the Literature

Three words were keys in finding information; the most commonly used was "touch," but there were listings under "tactile" and the "haptic system." In this chapter, the term used will be *touch*. Neisser, noting that touch has received much less scientific attention than vision or hearing, goes on to say:

> Special journals are devoted to optics and to acoustics, to research in vision and to disorders of hearing; entire laboratories specialize in psychoacoustics or in visual research; Nobel Prizes have been awarded for the discovery of basic mechanisms in both modalities. Touch has far less glamour and prestige, and we know correspondingly less about it. . . . Touch, the haptic sense, seems to have no specific machinery at all. . . . In active touch there are only continuously changing deformations of the skin, positions of the joints, velocities of the moving limbs, and other complexities (pp. 24–25).

I shall leave well enough alone and discuss only "the other complexities" of touch, as I view them, relating to the older adult. See page 464.

An exhaustive search reveals little in the gerontological literature on the study of touch or its therapeutic, or nontherapeutic, use with the aged.

Although there must be many more theses, I located only four master's theses on touch, all by nurses: Baldwin; Greenberg; McCorkle; and Trowbridge. I found only one study on the use of touch with the elderly, by Greenberg. Barnett's study (1972a, 1972b), although not specifically on the aged, has relevance for care givers. For example, in the summary of her significant findings, she stated, "The age group with the most infrequent touches was the 66 to 100 year old group for a total of 5 touches." Her survey included 540 patients and 900 health team personnel, who were observed for 452 touches which were recorded in a 4-week period. As Barnett's data (1972a) indicate, in our culture old people are not often touched. The aged may seem repulsive; they may seem too clinging; they may seem to take too much time. They may remind us of our own aging or that of our parents. Are these the reasons for our reluctance to touch them? This is a personal question for each to answer. Certainly it is more difficult to touch the aged person who is jaundiced, extremely emaciated, frightened, and/or "talking crazy." Yet that is the person who needs touching. It is far easier and nicer to touch someone who is not disheveled, who is not wearing a bib, who does not smell bad. Touching may be task-oriented or non-task-oriented (see Table 29-1); in instances of infantilizing the aged, touch is an effort "to help" the aged person, who often does not want or need such "help."

If used appropriately and with exquisite timing, touch may be therapeutic in the following situations: (1) during physical or psychosocial assessment of the older person, (2) as a powerful means of nonverbal communication, (3) to decrease sensory deprivation, (4) during reality testing, whether in one-to-one

Table 29-1. Task-oriented and Non-task-oriented Touching of the Elderly

Action	Possible Meaning to Aged Client	Action	Possible Meaning to Aged Client
Task-oriented Touching		*Non-task-oriented Touching*	
1. Assistance in ambulation	"This is your assignment today."	Spontaneous, affectionate touch	1. "You care about me."
			2. "I am reminded of many losses."
2. Bed bath and/or other nursing rituals	"You have to do it." "This is what nurses are supposed to do."	Touching while praising or as a reward	"I have something to be proud of."
3. Assistance in garment removal, or holding coat to put on	"You are being courteous." "You are taking away my independence."		
4. Steady touch during times of stress and duress: This could be viewed in the mind of the toucher as a task to:		Caregiver's assistance and encouragement to touch objects or animals	"I might enjoy learning to touch these: (1) pets, (2) finger paints, (3) clay, (4) clothing, (5) jewelry, (6) items from nature—plants, berries, pods, etc."
a. Reduce anxiety	"You want to help me."		
b. Intervene in a depressive state	"You know I'm hurting."		
c. Reduce anger	"You want to help me gain control."		
d. Give comfort during crying spell	"You understand my sadness."		
e. Provide support during grief reaction	"You want to help me gain control."		

Source: Revised from the original in "The Therapeutic Use of Touch with the Elderly," Irene Burnside, in *Sensory Processes and Aging,* Proceedings of a Conference at the Dallas Geriatric Research Institute, University Center for Community Services, North Texas State University, North Denton, Tex., 1977. Reprinted with permission.

relationships or in groups, (5) during reality orientation classes, (6) during both psychic and physical pain, and (7) during dying.

Touch during Assessment

Older people may experience heightened anxiety during an interview, especially during the first interview or physical examination. Nowlin studied the anxiety of elderly people during physical examinations. He described (1) concern, (2) manipulation, and (3) exposure—concern over what might be found, the discomfort of having someone press and push and pull on their body, and embarrassment at having to undress. These three causes of increased anxiety have implications for health disciplines; more time spent in describing procedures and findings, gentleness in handling, slow motions, and great care about ensuring privacy are but a few.

One practical reason for using touch during an assessment is the discovery of clues about what to expect. Consider a simple handshake. What clues are there in a handshake? You might note the severity of the anxiety from a trembling hand. You might feel the gnarled fingers of the arthritic victim (caused by either osteoarthritis or rheumatoid arthritis) or the tremor of Parkinson's disease. You might be concerned about the emaciated, skeletal hand and want to check the person's weight and/or eating habits. Or you might find some clues about dependency needs, e.g., does the old person cling to you? You may be startled when you reach for a hand that does not move, or is not there at all. You may even find a metal hook, as was the case during my first interaction with a 92-year-old man. I followed through with the intended handshake and held the metal hand to indicate to him that the infirmity or deformity was not repulsive to me. In such a case one can touch the person's arm or shake the left hand. Handshaking is an American custom; it is safe and nonthreatening and can be used profusely. The same cannot be said for other forms of touching—hugging and kissing.

Areas commonly touched in elderly persons are spelled out in Table 29-2.

Touch as a Powerful Means of Communication

Old people (even the regressed elderly) very soon learn the difference between task-oriented and non-task-oriented touching (see Table 29-1). Touch is an important nonverbal communication, especially effective with those who have communication problems, e.g., non-English speaking persons and those suffering from aphasia, dysarthria, or speech impediments. A sophisticated practitioner gives and receives signals through the use of touch. Touch can erase the message given verbally. Touch may reinforce the message. Touch may be the entire message. Aphasic stroke patients need staff members skilled in nonverbal communication, as do those with Parkinson's disease and chronic brain syndrome. In group work with the regressed aged, Burnside (1973a) found that nonverbal communication was much more prevalent than verbal. There is a great need to strengthen that component of interpersonal skills in our therapeutic interactions with the elderly.

Table 29-2. Commonly Touched Areas in Elderly Persons

Hand	1. A handshake is a safe and easy beginning.
	2. Handshake may also be congruent with verbal message of hello or good-bye.
	3. Hold one hand (which leaves the hand free for care giver to write, etc.).
	4. Hold both hands (which increases support).
	5. Old people will sometimes take the hand of the helper and kiss it.
	6. One administrator holds patients' hands for inspection purposes—so he can see if they are clean and if the nails are cared for.
Arm (wrist, forearm, or upper arm)	1. Often held because of injury or trauma to hands, or pain in hands (or lack of hands).
	2. Sometimes arm is most easily accessible, perhaps when sitting at bedside.
	3. One should be prepared when one takes the arm of an old person for feeling a very thin arm, especially in centenarians.
	4. Walking arm in arm is another way of touching and supporting old people.
Shoulder	Common place to touch persons in wheelchairs or in sitting positions, or if they have hands in lap, or if helper is at side or behind the person. Group leaders often touch patients on the shoulder as they move about a group.
Toes and foot	1. Some doctors are toe tweakers and gently pull on the toes of a bed patient. Note that in that kind of touching (as with grabbing the arm) one might keep clothing or bedclothing in between, so that skin does not touch skin.
	2. In group work with regressed aged I often sit on the floor and gently pull the old person's foot to help keep his or her attention with the group.
Leg (knee, thigh)	The leg is probably not touched much except with a bed patient, or with a wheelchair patient, when one might reach over and pat a person on the knee. Since this can be seen as a seductive gesture, it is well to use it with discretion. This is also true of sitting close to a person so that thighs are touching.
Top of head	Touching an old person by patting the top of the head is demeaning and should be discouraged.
Forehead	Often one sees a worker in a vis-à-vis position, forehead touching or almost touching the forehead of the patient. This is easy to do with wheelchair patients, and is effective when there is vision or hearing impairment. Nurses often place a hand on the forehead to check for an elevated temperature.
Face	1. A worker might let a blind person touch his or her face to help the blind one in placing the worker in space.

2. A gentle touch on the cheek with one's hand may be handled easily.
3. A kiss on cheek, forehead, on lips depends on the courage of the helper. Older people also may want to kiss the helper.
4. In institutions the care giver often wipes food off the patient's face.

Waist   Walking along with arm around waist can be supportive both physically and psychologically.

Source: Revised from the original in "The Therapeutic Use of Touch with the Elderly," Irene Burnside, in *Sensory Processes and Aging,* Proceedings of a Conference at the Dallas Geriatric Research Institute, University Center for Community Services, North Texas State University, North Denton, Tex., 1977. Reprinted with permission.

Nonverbal communication is important in the care of aged persons who are withdrawn, depressed; who have multiple sclerosis or lateral sclerosis; who are in pain, or dying; or who are suffering from "bereavement overload." Touching can convey caring, especially if it is non-task-oriented touching. Touch has many qualities, which need to be studied: (1) the duration, (2) the pressure of the touch, (3) the place of the body touched, (4) whether touched through clothing or bedclothing, and (5) the milieu, or environment in which the touching was done. The importance of touch varies from one individual to another, and from one culture to another, as will be discussed later in the chapter.

The need for touch was poignantly described by a woman at a conference. She went to church weekly although she was not at all religious. When queried about that, she said the minister always touched her, and then sadly added, "Now that I am retired, it is the only time I am touched all week." The film "Minnie Remembers" focuses on touch (see Other Resources at end of chapter).

Touch during Sensory Deprivation

A woman in a New England nursing home stated, "I cannot even imagine what it would be like to feel a tender caress—my skin is parched like a desert for lack of touch" (Sarton). The multiple facets of sensory deprivation continue to receive short shrift in planning care for the elderly. Touch is one means of increasing input for sensorily deprived aged. Sensory deprivation, boredom, and monotony are common problems of the aged, whether they reside in institutions or in the community. Sensory loss, immobility, living alone, and loss of significant others may increase the need for physical touching. Significant pets may also be one of the losses; pets offer closeness and touch. See Chapter 27 for a discussion of the importance of pets to aged persons. The aged person should have a chance to touch babies, children, pets, birds, stimulating objects, flowers, berries, satins, silk, cashmere, woolens, cotton flannel, and other objects familiar to them. Objects and materials from the past strike familiar notes for the aged person.

Figure 29-1   A Japanese man in his seventies remains active and involved. He still fishes on the fantail of the boat, and the sea has kept him young and strong. He is cooking a stew of chicken, onions, and potatoes. He uses an iced oku from the hold of the boat, running a knife along the spine, and up and down twice. Two thick red filets appear, called instant sashimi. The stew is also complemented with rice. (*Courtesy of Russ Williams, The Maui Sun, Wailuku, Maui, Hawaii.*)

Touch during Reality Orientation

Reality-orientation classes need to be conducted with touch as part of the *modus operandi,* either as a reward or to keep the confused person in contact with the leader. It is necessary to work physically close to a regressed aged person and to touch often; part of the closeness is necessary because of sensory deficits in sight and hearing. When the aged person has such deficits, confusion may increase because of incorrect information and cues received from the environment. Illusions among old people are common and are often based on misperceived information from the environment (see Table 28-1). Human contact seems to help agitated persons. One nurse frequently places agitated persons who are in wheelchairs near other seated patients who will tolerate the reaching out and touching. She finds that it reduces agitation and lessens the need for medication (Patton).

Use of Touch during Pain

Touch can be important in both physical and psychic pain. Elsewhere I have written of my own reaction to touch during grief work (Burnside, 1971). "Nothing is so strong as gentleness; Nothing is so gentle as real strength" (anonymous). This is the philosophy needed when working with the frail, sickly aged and those in pain. Old people, by and large, dislike being hurried, hassled, and jostled about, most especially when they are coping with pain. There are so many degrees of pain in such a variety of old people, one cannot begin to delineate methods of dealing with it. Each individual must be assessed for severity of pain, its location and duration, as well as psychological needs. In pain, some people withdraw and want no touching; others want a minimal amount; still others demand touching. Psychic pain requires the same gentle handling as physical pain. The worries of life and the throes of dying all fall into the therapeutic domain in working with aged clientele. You must know the power of your own touching because you have seen the responses in tired, gaunt, wrinkled faces, or have felt the squeeze of your hand by the bony old fingers of people too weak, too tired, or too inhibited to verbalize their thanks.

Touch with the Dying Person

The dying person needs the gentlest of touching, I think. When all technology is failing, one can still use touch with discretion—both with the dying person and the struggling relatives. Night nurses have often told me about holding a dying woman in their arms to decrease fears and anxiety. Many readers will perhaps remember the loyal, loving servant, Anna, in the film *Cries and Whispers,*[2] and how effectively she used touch with a woman dying of cancer.

Inability to Use Touch Effectively

Touch cannot be routinely assigned to a care giver; not all care givers are capable of using touch easily, sincerely, comfortably. I am reminded of an old man in a group meeting who said that the owner of the building we were in was somewhere in the building that day. I wondered how he knew since he was blind and I was not sure how rapidly the grapevine operated in that 200-bed facility. When the owner walked past the door of our meeting room, I was surprised. I asked Mr. F. how he had known that the owner was in the facility. His answer was simple, "Because everyone was getting hugged today; we only get hugged on the days that the owner is in the building." I thought that was quite perceptive. The example also bears out the importance of congruity in touch—in this instance, the hugs backfired and communicated, at least to Mr. F., something other than

[2] *Cries and Whispers,* a foreign film produced and directed by Ingmar Bergman.

caring. Old people are much more "tuned in" than they get credit for being and often will tell you either verbally or nonverbally what they think of your use of touch. The aged client gives cues when you move in too closely or too rapidly. I was once interviewing a very regressed, babbling woman for possible group work. I moved in close to her because I was told she had very poor vision. She immediately put her hand on my shoulder, pushed me away, and continued babbling. That was powerful communicating and easy to understand. Elsewhere I have written about using touch in group work with regressed elderly persons (Burnside, 1973a). Barriers to the use of touch are listed in Table 29-3.

Need for Caution

A word of caution is in order. There are several instances in which the helper must judge when not to intervene, when not to touch. One example was described earlier—touching that increases helplessness. The urge to help, to poke, prod, and push old people along is great. Many of them resent that particular kind of touching, are very sensitive to it, and respond with amazing alacrity, as you know if you have ever tried to help an unwilling old person across the street or off the curb. We can foster dependence even when old people are capable of doing things for themselves. One doctor says he goes slowly in an initial examination with an old person. He purposely does not help them remove their coat or jacket, simply to see how well they can manage, how coordinated they are, how independent or dependent. It is part of his overall assessment (Mangel).

Sexuality rears its lovely head also in the care of the aged. Nurturing ways can also be seductive ways. Young female students worry about touching old men. The reader is referred to Pease's article, which deals with clinical problems that may arise when young students grapple with sexuality in the elderly. Most of us are still grim or surprised about sexuality in the aged; we need to worry, though, as much about the dirty old eye glasses in institutions as we do about the dirty old men. And dirty old women are just beginning to create problems in institutions. Proceed cautiously if you think there are seductive tints to your own touching. Ask for feedback from those of your peers who can observe you.

Also proceed cautiously when touching the hard-of-hearing elderly; they tend to be suspicious and guarded. When patients are psychotic and very paranoid, it is wise not to use touch until you have observed them for a time. Timing is of the essence; if you go slowly and, for example, start with a handshake, you can observe the older person's reactions to your touch. Study examples of touching that were perceived by personnel as seductive, and observe the consequences. Ask yourself: Why did I touch that person? Where did I touch that person? How long did I touch that person? How much pressure was there in my touch? What was the setting?

I have described the importance of using touch with elderly persons and have given the rationale for it. Here are some important questions for you to answer regarding your own practice. When did you last touch a client/patient? What effect did your touch have on the client? On you? Are you willing to learn more

Table 29-3.   Barriers in the Use of Touch with Elderly Clients

1. Philosophy	Top administration in an agency does not approve of touch and therefore does not serve as a role model.
2. Professional teaching	In many disciplines one is cautioned to use touch with prudence.
3. Inhibited staff	Some staff members have always been taught to be very professional and cannot accept that working with older people requires different techniques and strategies.
4. Cultural aspects	In different cultures touch means different things. In some cultures it is common to see men embracing; in others it is not very acceptable. Kissing in one culture may mean that one is madly in love; in another it may be simply a component of the greeting.
5. The fences we put around old people	Geriatric chairs, wheelchairs, bedrails, crutches, walkers, all make it more difficult for the helper to touch the old person.
6. Repulsive old people	Dirty, unkempt, smelly, and poorly groomed elderly people may ward off any signs of touching or display of affection in a helper.
7. Old people with great bodily changes	Terminal cancer victims, stroke patients, persons with scars, amputations, colostomies, jaundice, etc., may be more difficult to touch.
8. Nudity	Getting old people covered is still the priority most of the time, e.g., an old man I met in the hallway of a large hospital had all his clothes off, had removed his catheter, had it around his neck, and was swinging the other end of the catheter like a lariat. I could grab his hand but could not have walked down the hall with my arm around his waist!
9. Racial factors	Touching, hugging, and kissing persons of different races may be difficult. Barnett found that Caucasians used touch most frequently, Mexican-Americans least frequently (1972*a*).
10. Fears	Fears of the toucher include: *a.* Fear of being seductive *b.* Fear of closeness *c.* Fear of rejection *d.* Fear of loss of professional status *e.* Fear of starting something one cannot handle *f.* Fear of trusting one's own intuition *g.* Fear of disapproval from peers and supervisors *h.* Previous failures in use of touch (either on job or off the job)

Source: Revised from the original in ''The Therapeutic Use of Touch with the Elderly,'' Irene Burnside, in *Sensory Processes and Aging,* Proceedings of a Conference at the Dallas Geriatric Research Institute, University Center for Community Services, North Texas State University, North Denton, Tex., 1977. Reprinted with permission.

about touch in general, and specifically as a therapeutic strategy in caring for old people? Touch is a two-way interaction. Do you permit old people to touch you? Following are some suggestions for studying touch.

1. Video tapes are powerful teaching means.
2. Slides are helpful if they are taken by an objective photographer who makes random shots. Slides can reveal surprising aspects of the behavior of the toucher/helper.
3. Observe one another and then offer constructive feedback.
4. Write process recordings; they tend to lean more to verbal content than to nonverbal, but the emphasis could be on use of touch.
5. Experiential exercises on touch, e.g., the blind walk.
6. Encourage care givers to write of their own experiences of effective examples of touch.
7. Encourage the clients/consumers to describe the touching that helped them. What touch? Given where? By whom? In what setting? In what situation?

Clark Moustakas beautifully conveyed the message of this portion of the chapter.

Sometimes it is necessary
For one person to touch another person
in his lonely struggle
To enable the person to gain
the courage and strength to act on his own. (p. 86)

One aspect of sexuality and aging has been mentioned—touching that may appear to be seductive to the older person. Touching is only one facet of sexuality in the aged, however. The next portion of this chapter focuses on sexuality.

SEXUALITY AND AGING[3]

Two prevailing myths about the aged are that "sexuality is not typically characteristic of old people," and "it is wrong or sinful when sexuality persists into later life" (Botwinick). One common attitude that should be changed is that old people are not interested in sex or, worse yet, should not be interested in sex. Other attitudes that need to be changed are that (1) old men are child molesters; (2) old men are dirty old men; (3) dying aged persons are not interested in sexual matters; (4) regressed aged are not concerned with sexuality; (5) women's sex life and interest cease after menopause; (6) men will use themselves up and use up the supply of semen if they are overactive sexually; and (7) masturbation causes blindness, mental illness, hair on the palms of the hands, or problems in marriage. Cartoonists, news media, birthday card designers continue blatantly to depict sex in old age as downright ridiculous or impossible, or both.

[3] Based on a presentation given at the Hawaii Governor's Bicentennial Conference on Aging, Honolulu, Hawaii, June 1976.

The following remarks by a centenarian give some of her perspective on sexuality:

- [At a quilting bee, to some of the younger quilters in a discussion of sexual matters] "God didn't make your ass to be talked about."
- "Maybe some parts are good for lovers to be fumbling around and get themselves all worked up—in my day marriages were arranged by families and we didn't know anything about sex."
- "It is frightening when you are first married—scared the livin' pants off me,

Figure 29-2 Sexuality is often narrowly defined and described. Sexuality includes a wide range of behaviors—what it means to be a man or a woman. Long-enduring marriages of 50 or 60 years are not uncommon and have been little studied. *(Courtesy of Harvey Finkle.)*

I'll tell you. I loved him alright in the day time but when night came I was a wreck.''
- ''Men had more principles in my day—but why not—they had all the privileges, too. Well, maybe it didn't hurt the women to stay home and have babies, I don't know.''

Definition of Sexuality

Sexuality is too often narrowly defined; it means more than intercourse, and is used with a broader meaning in this chapter. Sexuality includes flirting, dating behavior, being close, touching, what it means to be a man or a woman—all things that go toward making a total person.

Berezin reviewed the literature on sex in old age in 1969, covering the literature through 1967. Nine years later he updated the original review. In view of the liberalized attitude toward sex in the general public, and the frankness with which sex is expressed in movies, television, etc., one would expect an increase in the amount of literature. Berezin, however, did not find such an increase. Upon checking his reference list, it is noted that his references are almost exclusively taken from medical journals. In contrast, articles by investigators, including doctors, from other disciplines appear in many other types of publications. One publication includes papers on sexual matters by biologists, physicians, psychologists, sociologists, nurses, social workers (Burnside, 1975). Other articles include those by Burnside (1973b), Calderone, Dean, Downey, Ervin, Eymann, Felstein, Finkle, Finkle and Finkle, Hellerstein and Friedman, Kaplan, Kent, Knopf, Krizinofski, Leviton, Miller, Oaks and Moyer, Pease, Puksta, Scheingold and Wagner, Sontag, Weg (1975, 1976), and West.

The changing of attitudes is important but difficult and slow. A great many elderly persons have experienced the negative views of society (e.g., being considered ''over the hill'') and have internalized them. However, if old persons do indeed prove they are not ''over the hill,'' they are frowned upon, teased, labeled as abnormal, and often called a dirty old man or woman. Our society bombards the elderly with such denigrating names when they show signs of sexual interests; subsequently many old persons feel guilty. To change present attitudes of professionals and paraprofessionals, care givers working with the elderly will need information about the sexual behavior and interests of the elderly. Lack of correct information and knowledge is a problem for both the care giver and the older person. Currently ample material on the subject is available in the literature.

An important survey is a longitudinal study done by Verwoerdt, Pfeiffer, and Wang (p. 154), of Duke University. Some of their conclusions were: (1) men continue their sexual activity and interest in their later years; (2) women lose interest and discontinue sexual activity at a younger age, which in married women is often related to the loss of sexual activity and interest in their husbands when the latter are aged 72 to 77; and (3) many physical and psychological factors alter patterns of sexual activity during the aging process.

Some institutions have many rigid rules regarding the old people which seem to arise from the staff mores. In-service training is needed to help personnel to be more relaxed about sexual matters and to understand better the aged person's sexual needs and drives. Florine described a situation in a state hospital; a staff member tied an old woman's hands to the bed because she was masturbating. For many old people who are sexually deprived, masturbation is the only release.

Common Problems

One of the common problems of the elderly is the fact that women outnumber men and that women outlive men by 7 to 8 years. The problems of the woman beyond the age of 80 receive little attention. In a chapter entitled, "Older Women," Hite states that she agrees with Ti-Grace Atkinson when she says, "The older woman is all of us." The Hite report includes these older women: five who are 40 to 49, ten who are 50 to 59, four who are 60 to 69, and four who are 70 to 79. No women in their eighties, nineties, or hundreds are included in the report.

Another problem consists of fear and impotency in men. Many therapists feel that impotency is psychological and that men can be counseled successfully. The study by Masters and Johnson is a classic; understandably, it included a relatively small sample of aged people. The study revealed that monotony and boredom in a sexual relationship, fear of failure, mental or physical fatigue, overindulgence in food or drink, and concern with career and economic pursuits are also factors in impotency. Prostatectomies create worries. Some men believe that once the prostate gland is removed, their sex life is over. This is not true. The physician can exert profound influence on the sexual activity of patients by direct statements or by disapproval of continued sexual activity (Finkle, 1967; 1968).

It is important that operations be explained to the elderly; explanation is especially needed before and after a prostatectomy, or for that matter, any kind of traumatic operation, e.g., amputation, colostomy, mastectomy, that will affect body image. Also, increased support is needed after the occurrence of a disabling condition such as stroke, cancer, Parkinson's disease, or coronary attack.

Tension from lack of sex can arise after heart problems. Doctors may fail to give adequate information, or may give it in jargonese so that it needs to be rephrased. For the aged, sex should be considered during the part of the day when energy level for both partners is highest. Masturbation should be encouraged if there is no partner, because lack of sexual activity can lead to impotence—hence the phrase, "Use it or lose it." Impotence may also accompany diabetes and the use of some medications for acute hypertension. Persons with severe arthritis may need counseling about a choice of positions or mutual masturbation.

Because elderly people often feel guilty or ashamed of their sexual feelings, it is one of the tasks of care givers to try to help balance the old person's bad or guilt feelings with good feelings. It is helpful to realize that the important thing is for the aged person to know what kind of sexual behavior he or she prefers and is most comfortable with. Handling guilt is difficult at times because often as a person grows older, guilt feelings increase. Guilt and intimacy do indeed create a difficult mix (Florine). The book *Sex after Sixty* (Butler and Lewis) is recommended not only for the aged reader, but also for the professional and paraprofessional who will be working with the aged population. Guidelines for counseling the elderly on sexuality have been delineated by Bernita Steffl and are reprinted here.[4]

A. Communication Skills
 1. Examine awareness of own beliefs, values, and attitudes toward both sexuality and the aged.
 2. Assess interpersonal skills necessary to:
    a. initiate communication with the elderly
    b. create an atmosphere conducive to discussing sexual concerns
    c. watch for non-verbal cues about sexual concerns
    d. elicit verbalization of those underlying concerns
 3. Review sexual physiology and functioning.
 4. Assess the client's perception of his/her sexual concerns.
 5. Ask yourself, "What kind of non-verbal messages am *I* sending?"
B. To Assess the Problem, Ask Yourself:
 1. Is the problem actually a request for information about anatomy and/or physiology?
 2. Is the need a specific sexual problem?
 3. Is the problem a clinical situation directly or indirectly related to sexual functioning?
 4. Is the problem organic or situational requiring alterations in preferred mode of functioning?
 5. Is it a crisis or a long term problem?
 6. Is the person trying to live up to some preconceived performance expectations and creating guilt for failure?
C. To Initiate Discussion on Sexuality with Older Persons:
 1. Consider or find out the aged person's early orientation to sexual behavior.
 2. Look for residual feelings about masturbation as a child, which may still be present.
 3. The "first time" sexual act seems to have great significance so consider it as a point of departure in discussion.
 4. The "second time around" sexual act often is described as being better; one might use that as a point of departure for discussion.
 5. Tie sexual behavior and history in with other social activities, e.g., religion. Remember that it may take time to come around to the topic and questions or problems.

[4] Reprinted with the kind permission of Bernita M. Steffl, College of Nursing, Arizona State University. Materials presented at Annual Western Gerontology Society Meeting, Denver, Col., Mar. 21, 1977.

6. Listen for a double message—
   "I don't think about that."
   "I would if I fell in love."
7. There may be increased preoccupation (conscious or unconscious) with sexuality in old age, particularly in certain settings.
8. Keep your approach "confidential—private—personal."

D. Specific Problems Health Professionals Are Apt to Encounter More than Others:

Nurses especially should be aware of the following; observe and listen for them. Initiate counseling in regard to present and future expectations about sexual performance and the following conditions:

1. Arthritis
2. Colostomy
3. Cystocele—rectocele—prolapse uterus
4. Diabetes
5. Hysterectomy—vulvectomy
6. Mastectomy
7. Menopause
8. Paraplegia—what can be done for the very handicapped?
9. Peyrone's disease
10. Post hip fracture
11. Pre-post coronary attack
12. Pre-post stroke
13. Prostatectomy
14. Venereal disease

E. Special Considerations for Institutionalized Elderly:

1. Be aware of the isolation and sensory deprivation.
2. They need more touch for social reasons; hugging, kissing, hand holding, massage.
3. Build sexuality into spiritual and emotional well-being rather than separating it.
4. All meaningful sexual relations may not be heterosexual. Be helpful rather than punishing.
5. Accept masturbation. Do not punish; what is the consequence of censure and punishment?
6. Provide touching and "feeling" objects to handle, fondle, and hold.
7. Live pets provide great sensory stimulation.
8. Encourage music: romantic, sentimental, sensuous, and erotic.
9. Encourage opportunity for sexes to meet, mingle, and spend time together; do not structure the "trysting time or place" too rigidly.

Though counseling in matters of sexuality is important, listening to the older person describe early sexual experiences may be important also. At the 1976 Governor's Conference in Hawaii an older man described his first sexual experience and held the audience absolutely mesmerized, especially the young members in the audience, but older men at the back of the room leaned forward to hear better. I recall once listening to a 90-year-old woman describe how she missed going to the cabin in the late years of her life "because on warm nights I used to go out and swing nude in the moonlight between the large pines next to the cabin." Elderly persons will share an amazing amount of material about sexuality if interest is shown and time is spent with them. It is usually the care giver who is uncomfortable. The combination of cultural and sexual attitudes constitutes an area that must be approached with delicacy. The blunders care givers make in these areas rarely reach the textbooks; we are only beginning to incorporate cultural variables into our care giving.

CULTURAL ASPECTS TO CONSIDER WITH THE ELDERLY

In any psychosocial assessment or intervention, the care giver must immediately note cultural differences; this is true in the one-to-one relationship as well as in the group setting. The cross-cultural perspective has been well described by Cowgill and Holmes, who found universals in all the societies examined. These demographic principles seem to hold true: (1) the aged are a relatively small minority in all societies; (2) women outnumber men in all the older populations of the countries; (3) in all the populations for which there was demographic information, widows predominated; the proportion of older females widowed ranged from one-half to three-fourths; (4) all societies had a category of people who were called "old"; (5) if there was no formal retirement as a transition or a tie of passage, there was an expectation that the old men were not expected to continue in the roles they had; instead they were commonly promoted to being an elder, a headsman, or a priest (unfortunately, we do not have anything similar in our own society); (6) all societies had evidence of mutual responsibilities or obligations which existed between the aged parents and the adult children; and (7) it was universal to value life and to seek to prolong it even in old age. The authors found no universal effort "to save for old age," which comes as no surprise to most of us.

I have started this part of this chapter with a global approach to cultural aspects in old age. It was pointed out in a publication by the Department of Health, Education, and Welfare that "the proportion of the population 65 years old and over varied by race and ethnic origin: 11% for whites, 7% for blacks, and 4% for persons of Spanish origin." On a day-to-day basis and a personal-care level, there are other pressing issues. One is faced with meeting the needs of minority members in a multiculture country. Time spent in Hawaii helps one to understand the tolerance there for diversity. A practitioner asks questions such as: How do you decrease the squabbles between an old black man and an old white man in the same room? How do you help aged white persons to permit the black or Chicano nurses' aide to care for them? How do you learn about the meaning of touch and sexuality in the Apache, the Blackfoot, or any other Indian tribe? How do you elicit much-needed information in view of the language barriers that still exist for non-English-speaking elderly cohorts? Where do you locate translators? What are the mourning practices of different cultures? How do you incorporate practical data into one's own practice, e.g., knowing that the elderly Japanese and Chinese feel that touch belongs in the bedroom? Or that you are not to discuss the deceased spouse with the old Apache woman because it is not done in that culture?

Unfortunately many of us learn by trial and error regarding culture and the aged; though that is not the ideal way to learn, it is certainly a long-lasting way.

One situation often arising when caring for the elderly is hand kissing. Students have often related their discomfort when an elderly person takes their hand and kisses it. It may be a custom from their native land and is commonly done by persons of Southern European origin. Some care givers feel that they are being put on a pedestal, are therefore uncomfortable, and draw away immediately from such a gesture. Lively discussions usually ensue when hand kissing is brought up in the classroom or conference.

It is impossible to discuss the various minority groups in a part of a chapter. Suffice it to say that psychosocial caring involves an inquiring stance on the part of the care giver—a desire to learn what one can about the old person. The black elderly are different from the militant young blacks. And the elderly Mexican says, "I'm Mexican, call me a Mexican; I am not 'Chicano.' "

The legacies left by the elderly of minority groups are beginning to be acknowledged. Examples are seen in the television film, "The Autobiography of Miss Jane Pittman," directed by John Korty in 1974, and *Roots* (Haley), adapted for television.

Carter (1974) began an article on recognition of psychiatric symptoms in black Americans with a poem describing "masks" worn by blacks. Carter felt that the verse gave insight into the adaptive behavior of blacks in America. Blacks wear the "mask" so well that psychiatric impairments are difficult to assess, especially by anyone unfamiliar with black behavior patterns. Carter (1973) maintains that this evasive quality has its roots in slavery and functions as a "survival mechanism."

Hamilton, a writer, said:

Black people, who in recent history were born into bondage as property, had to be different from other people. Even for those born free within the bonded group, slavery must have become a stigma that bled their hearts and marked their minds. . . .

How eccentric is the total history of blacks in America, imbued as it is with the spiritual isolation of the fugitive alone and running, with weird tales which are true tales handed down from one generation to the next. The characters I create are descendants of slaves and freemen. All carry with them the knowledge of former generations who were born as livestock, as property. That sort of knowledge must corner reality for them and hold it at bay. It must become in part eccentric and in part symbolic for succeeding generations (p. 4).

Carter warns us that it is a myth that blacks are seldom depressed; he feels that there has been an abuse of the diagnosis "paranoia," which is too strong

Figure 29-3 The proportion of the population 65 years old varies by race and ethnic origin; for blacks it is 7 percent. (*Courtesy of Harvey Finkle.*)

a label for what he terms a "healthy cultural suspiciousness, an adaptive response to . . . racism" (1974, pp. 95–96). He suggests that the denial of natural impulses and feelings may result in a neurotic depression which is shown through somatic complaints. He offers a case study which demonstrates how a 60-year-old woman made changes when her self-esteem and feeling of self-worth were increased (see Chapter 25 for a further discussion of self-esteem).

Dominick and Stotsky studied the ethnic influences of mental patients in nursing homes. They observed Chinese, Armenian, Italian, Jewish, and black patients. Overall, these researchers felt that loneliness, aimlessness, and monotony tend to dominate the lives of most aged people in institutions (see Chapter 26 for a further discussion of loneliness). The authors concluded, ". . . those who are strongly bound by ethnic, cultural and religious ties do not feel isolated, abandoned and hopeless" (p. 63). Dominick and Stotsky point out that there are also many leveling forces at work which help to brand old people residing in nursing homes: a new way of life, dependence, routine, regimented schedules, loss of productive roles, increased frailty, confinement, and even the proximity of death. They further point out the various reactions of different ethnic groups to the same situations: apathy, obvious control, subtle control, demanding attitude, aggressivity, passivity, passive-aggressive behavior, and inability to verbalize their values. My own experience is that those who are unable to verbalize values are the ones we fail most, because the care giver seems always to carry an oil can ready for the squeaky wheel.

Coles, in his beautiful literary style, has sensitively described the aged of New Mexico. He did so when one mother after another urged him to focus attention on the old people of their culture. Again the word "different" comes up; Coles was advised to go to New Mexico to see a "different" kind of Spanish-speaking person. A priest told Coles about the importance of the old people: "If you want to know about the children, you must first speak with the old people; what they believe, the child soon believes. The parents are go-betweens . . . they are very close to *their* parents, and hand down beliefs from the very old to the very young" (p. xi). Coles came to see that the old people he interviewed had remarkable strength and vitality—something we still do not see quickly enough in our aged Anglos.

Kalish and Reynolds have written and emphasized that death occurs to a unique person living within a particular social and cultural setting. Those who are in care-giving situations will need to know how to recognize not only differences between groups but also differences among individuals within a cultural group. The authors discuss death and ethnicity as related to black Americans, Japanese Americans, and Mexican Americans. There is an excellent bibliography for those interested in further reading.

Wooden has studied the life satisfaction of elderly Filipino single males living in Hilo, Hawaii. He found, after studying subjects living in several different types of residence (former sugar plantation quarters, new low-cost housing, downtown hotels), that the residents of the downtown hotels in the old city had the highest degree of satisfaction.

Folk health beliefs among Filipino-Americans are discussed by McKenzie and Chrisman. Some quotations which are principles of folk beliefs include, "Never go to bed with wet hair because you will go blind. Boil corn hairs and water; drink and the urine will come out. Do not let the fly step on your food. The witch has the power to send lice, flies, or cockroaches to you" (p. 326). The authors suggest that blending folk remedies with scientific cures will help to bridge the gap in communication. It is important not to ridicule beliefs and practices, and to develop trust. It is possible that folk health practices have values we do not know about.

Munn describes a "language bank" begun in Medford, Oregon, in which active and retired teachers provide a new service to the community. The language bank was set up to respond to calls for linguistic help from hospitals, hotels, motels, business firms, and police stations. The article states that people who speak little

English can panic about having to go to a hospital, speak to the police, or even go to the store.

Anderson, who discusses health and aging and implications for the black, the American Indian, and Asian Americans, points out the myth we have in America that the Chinese and Japanese do not have any real problems because they take care of their own.

Following are two examples of lack of cultural knowledge which can influence the approaches of the care giver and the placement of the aged person.

Case Study I

One summer while teaching in Hawaii, I discovered that the elderly Oriental men in their seventies and eighties were quite formal and seemed to be embarrassed by my touching them during group meetings. I was told by one of them that touch belongs in the bedroom and that they tolerated it from me as the group leader because I was "a Haoli from the mainland"; the implication was that since I did not know any better, my group strategies would be tolerated. I learned in my own group work with very old Orientals that if I stood squarely in front of their wheelchairs, bowed first, and then lightly took their hand in a handshake, they responded warmly. It was not difficult for me to do, but I felt slightly awkward and stiff because I am not used to bowing.

Case Study II

During World War II, a Norwegian merchant marine was badly injured in an automobile accident on the Island of Kauai in the Hawaiian Islands. When he came out of the coma in the hospital he began talking Norwegian; he spoke no English. No one spoke or understood Norwegian in the hospital; the staff thought he was speaking gibberish and that he had severe brain damage. Ultimately he was sent to a long-term-care facility, where he lived most of the rest of his life. A public health nurse who understood and spoke Norwegian was sent to check on him for some reason. She immediately understood the language he was speaking and was able to break through. With the help of a director of a senior center they located a woman who spoke Norwegian (probably the only person who did on that tiny island), and she became good friends with him; she fixed *lefsa,* a Norwegian delicacy, and remained loyal to him. He had at that time spent 40 years in an institution (Holtwick).

SUMMARIZING STATEMENTS BASED ON THE LITERATURE ABOUT CULTURAL PROBLEMS OF THE AGED

- Women outnumber men in the older populations of all countries (Cowgill and Holmes).
- Widows predominate (Cowgill and Holmes).
- Old men in some cultures are commonly promoted to elders, headmen, priests (Cowgill and Holmes).
- Mutual responsibilities exist between aged parents and adult children (Cowgill and Holmes).

- It is universal to value life (Cowgill and Holmes).
- It is a myth that blacks are seldom depressed (Carter, 1974).
- Paranoia is too easily used in diagnosis of blacks (Carter, 1974).
- Denial of natural feelings in blacks may result in somatic complaints (Carter, 1974).
- Ethnic nursing home residents may suffer from loneliness, aimlessness, and monotony (Dominick and Stotsky).
- Commonalities of life in a nursing home (new life-style, dependence, routine, regimentation, loss of productivity, frailty, imminence of death) have a leveling effect on all ethnic patients (Dominick and Stotsky).
- Grandparents hand down beliefs to the very young (Coles; Hamilton).
- Death occurs to a unique person living in a particular social, cultural milieu (Kalish and Reynolds).
- Elderly Filipinos find a support system in old city hotel rooms (Wooden).
- Language barriers still occur. Case example (Holtwick).

GUIDELINES FOR INTERVENTION IN CULTURAL PROBLEMS OF THE AGED

- In view of the predominance of elderly women, especially widows, care givers need to be aware of problems of "triple jeopardy," being old, a woman, and in a minority group (see Chapter 18 for guidelines).
- What status can elderly men be given as they lose work roles?
- Observe, encourage, and reinforce examples of mutual responsibility in family networks.
- Care givers value life and the individuality of each aged person.
- Double-check for depressive symptoms in elderly blacks.
- Check for basis of somatic complaints in elderly black clients.
- Check for loneliness, ennui, and despair in cultural groups in nursing homes. (See Chapter 26 for guidelines regarding loneliness.)
- Encourage the legacies and beliefs that grandparents can leave to youth.
- Study all aspects of dying—the person's individual needs, the cultural beliefs regarding death, and the traditions carried out before, during, and after death.
- Check support systems and ascertain life satisfaction in a variety of living situations.
- Assess for language barriers; conscientiously seek out translators when necessary.

This chapter describes three aspects of care giving—touch, sexuality, and cultural components. The ability of the care giver to use touch effectively, the care giver's own sexuality and cultural background all move forward together to meet the same set of components in the elderly person. Sometimes they clash. Sometimes they merge. Always they provide an exciting challenge to psychosocial caring.

REFERENCES

Anderson, Barbara Gallatin: "An Anthropological Approach to Aging Adaptation," in E. Norbeck (ed.), *Festschrift,*Rice University Press, Dallas, 1979.

Baldwin, Beverly:"A Study of the Reaction of Patients to the Intrusive Behavior of Nurses," master's thesis, University of Iowa, Iowa City, 1970.

Barnett, Kathryn: "A Survey of the Current Utilization of Touch by Health Team Personnel with Hospitalized Patients," *International Journal of Nursing Studies,* 9:195–209, 1972*a*.

————: "A Theoretical Construct of the Concepts of Touch as They Relate to Nursing," *Nursing Research,* **21**: 102–110, 1972*b*.

Berezin, Martin A.: "Sex and Old Age: A Further Review of the Literature," *Journal of Geriatric Psychiatry,* **9**(2):189–209, 1976.

Botwinick, Jack: *Aging and Behavior,* Springer, New York, 1973.

Burnside, Irene M.: "You Will Cope, Of Course," *American Journal of Nursing,* **71**(12):2354–2357, 1971.

————: *Sexuality and Aging,* Ethel Percy Andrus Gerontology Center, University of Southern California, Los Angeles, 1975.

————: "Touching Is Talking," *American Journal of Nursing,* **73**(12):2060–2063, 1973. (a)

————: "Sexuality and Aging," *Medical Arts and Sciences,* **13**(2):13–27, 1973. (b).

Butler, Robert N., and **Myrna I. Lewis:** *Sex after Sixty,* Harper & Row, New York, 1976.

Calderone, Mary S.: "The Sexuality of Aging," *Siecus Newsletter,* **7**(1): 1971.

Carter, James H.: "Psychiatry's Insensitivity to Racism," *Psychiatric Opinion,* **10**:23, 1973.

————: "Recognizing Psychiatric Symptoms in Black Americans," *Geriatrics,* **29**(11):95–99, 1974.

Coles, Robert: *The Old Ones of New Mexico,* Anchor Press/Doubleday, Garden City, N.Y., 1975.

Cowgill, Donald O., and **Lowell D. Holmes:** *Aging and Modernization,* Appleton-Century-Crofts, New York, 1972.

Dean, Stanley R.: "Geriatric Sexuality: Normal, Needed, and Neglected," *Geriatrics,* **29**(7):134, 1974.

Dominick, Joan R., and **Bernard A. Stotsky:** "Mental Patients in Nursing Homes. IV. Ethnic Influences," *Journal of the American Geriatrics Society,* **17**(1):63–85, 1969.

Downey, G. W.: "The Next Patient Right: Sex in the Nursing Home," *Modern Healthcare,* **1**:56–59, 1974.

Ervin, C. V.: "Psychologic Adjustment to Mastectomy," *Medical Aspects of Human Sexuality,* **7**(2):42–65, 1973.

Eymann, Ken: "Sexual Desires in the Aging," *Geriatric Care,* **4**:1–4, 1972.

Felstein, Ivor: *Sex in Later Life,* Penguin, Baltimore, 1970.

Finkle, A.: "Sexual Function during Advancing Age," in I. Rossman (ed.), *Clinical Geriatrics,* Lippincott, Philadelphia, 1971.

———— and **Paul S. Finkle:** "Urologic Counseling Can Overcome Male Sexual Impotence," *Geriatrics,* **29**(5):48, 1975.

Finkle, A. L.: "Sex Problems in Later Years," *Medical Times,* **95**(4):416–419, 1967.

————: "Sex after Prostatectomy," *Hu-*

man Sexuality, **2:**40, 1968.

Florine, Charlotte: "A Psychiatrist's View of Sexuality and Aging, presentation at Hawaii Governor's Bicentennial Conference on Aging, June 1976.

Greenberg, Barbara: "Therapeutic Effects of Touch on Alteration of Psychotic Behavior in Institutionalized Elderly Patients," master's thesis, Duke University, Durham, N.C., 1972.

Hamilton, Virginia: *Illusions and Reality,* Library of Congress, Washington, 1976.

Harlow, Harry F.: "Affectional Responses in the Infant Monkey," *Science,* **130:** 421–432, 1969.

Hellerstein, Herman, and **Ernest Friedman:** "Sexual Activity and Post-coronary Patient," *Medical Aspects of Human Sexuality,* **3:**70–95, 1969.

Hite, Shere: *The Hite Report: A Nationwide Study of Female Sexuality,* Dell, New York, 1976.

Holtwick, Elsa: Class assignment, "Group Work with the Elderly," Kauai Community College, Puhi, Kauai, 1977.

Kalish, Richard A., and **David K. Reynolds:** *Death and Ethnicity: A Psychocultural Study,* University of Southern California Press, Los Angeles, 1976.

Kaplan, Helen: *The New Sex Therapy,* Brunner/Mazel Publication, published in cooperation with Quadrangle/The New York Times Book Company, New York, 1974.

Kent, Saul: "Impotence as a Consequence of Organic Disease," *Geriatrics,* **30**(9): 155, 1975.

Knopf, Olga: "Sexual Adaptation in Later Life," in *Successful Aging,* Viking, New York, 1975.

Kramer, M., I. Chamorro, and **D. Green,** et al.: "Extra Tactile Stimulation of the Premature Infant," *Nursing Research,* **24:**324–334, 1975.

Krizinofski, Marian T.: "Human Sexuality and Nursing Practice," *Nursing Clinics of North America,* **8**(4):673–681, 1973.

Leviton, Dan: "The Significance of Sexuality as a Deterrent to Suicide among the Aged," *Omega,* **4**(2):163–174, 1973.

McCorkle, Ruth: "Effects of Touch on Seriously Ill Patients," *Nursing Research,* **23:**125–132, 1974.

McKenzie, Joan L., and **Noel J. Chrisman:** "Healing Herbs, Gods, and Magic; Folk Health Beliefs among Filipino-Americans," *Nursing Outlook,* **25**(5):326–329, 1977.

Mangel, Robert: Personal communication, 1974.

Masters, W. H., and **V. E. Johnson:** *Human Sexual Response,* Little, Brown, Boston, 1966.

Miller, Dulcy B.: "Sexual Practices and Administrative Policies in Long-term Care Institutions," *Journal of Long Term Care Administration,* **3**(3):30–41, 1975.

Montagu, Ashley: *Touching, the Human Significance of the Skin,* Perennial Library, New York, 1971.

Moustakas, Clark E.: *Loneliness and Love,* Prentice-Hall, Englewood Cliffs, N.J., 1972.

Munn, Vella C.: "When English Is Not Spoken," *NRTA Journal,* **28**(139):17, 1977.

Neisser, Ulric: *Cognition and Reality, Principles and Implications of Cognitive Psychology,* Freeman, San Francisco, 1976.

Nowlin, John: "Anxiety during a Medical Examination," in Erdman Palmne (ed.), *Normal Aging II,* Duke, Durham, N.C., 1974.

Oaks, Wilbur, and **John Moyer:** "Sex and Hypertension," *Medical Aspects of Human Sexuality,* **6:**129, 1972.

Patton, Florence: Personal communication, 1978.

Pease, Ruth A.: "Female Professional Students and Sexuality in the Aging Male," *The Gerontologist,* **14**:153–157, 1974.

Puksta, Nancy: "All about Sex . . . after a Coronary, *American Journal of Nursing,* **77**(4):602–605, 1977.

Rubin, Reva: "The Maternal Touch, *Nursing Outlook,* **11**:828–831, 1963.

Sarton, May: *As We Are Now,* W. W. Norton, New York, 1973.

Scheingold, Lee, and **N. N. Wagner:** *Sound Sex and the Aging Heart; Sex in the Later Years with Special Reference to Cardiac Disturbance,* Human Sciences Press, New York, 1974.

Shock, Nathan: "Current Publications in Gerontology and Geriatrics," *Journal of Gerontology,* January–December 1977.

Sontag, Susan: "The Double Standard of Aging," *Saturday Review,* Sept. 23, 1972, pp. 29–38.

Steffl, Bernita: "Handout," Western Gerontology Society Meeting, Denver, Col., Mar. 21, 1977.

Sutterley, Doris C., and **Gloria F. Donnelly:** *Perspectives in Human Development,* Lippincott, Philadelphia, 1973.

Trowbridge, Judith: "Nurse-Patient Interpretations of the Nurse's Touch," master's thesis, Loma Linda University, Riverside, Calif., August 1967.

U.S. Department of Health, Education, and Welfare: *Facts about Older Americans 1976,* Office of Human Development, Administration on Aging, Publication No. (OHD) 77-20006, Washington, 1977. (A pamphlet.)

Verwoerdt, Adrian, Eric Pfeiffer, and **H. S. Wang:** "Sexual Behavior in Senescence," *Geriatrics,* **24**(2):137–154, 1969.

Weg, Ruth B.: "Sexual Inadequacy in the Elderly," in Ralph Goldman and Morris Rockstein (eds.), *The Physiology and Pathology of Aging,* Academic, New York, 1975.

———: "Normal Aging Changes in the Reproductive System," in Irene Burnside (ed.), *Nursing and the Aged,* McGraw-Hill, New York, 1976.

West, Norman D.: "Sex in Geriatrics: Myth or Miracle," *Journal of the American Geriatrics Society,* **23**(12):551–552, 1975.

Wooden, Wayne S.: *Filipino Elders of Hawaii: The Ecology of Life Satisfaction,* unpublished manuscript, 1977.

OTHER RESOURCES

FILMS

Cultural Aspects

Death (Family of Man Series): 45 min/color/ 1971. Shows how five different societies— India, Surrey, Boswana, New Guinea, and Hong Kong—deal with death. Producer: BBC-TV. Distributor: Time-Life Multimedia, 100 Eisenhower Drive, Paramus, N.J. 07652.

The Family of Man: Old Age: 45 min/color/ 1970. Compares and contrasts the cultures of five very different areas of the world. Senior citizens provide the focus for discussions of rituals, philosophies, duties, problems, and place in the hierarchy of family and society. Distributor: Time-Life Films, 100 Eisenhower Drive, Paramus, N.J. 07652.

I Heard the Owl Call My Name: 78 min/ color/1974. From best-selling novel by Margaret Craven, which draws its title from the

Indian legend that death comes "when the owl calls your name." Filmed in British Columbia, it is the powerful story of a young Anglican priest's awakening to life in the face of death. Award-winning. Produced and directed by Daryl Duke. Distributor: Learning Corporation of America, 1350 Avenue of the Americas, New York, N.Y. 10019.

The Invisible Minority: 22 min/color/1977. Black and Mexican-American elderly, often invisible to the larger society, are the focus of this documentary. Describes problems in a large urban setting: crime, transportation, and loneliness. Distributor: Dissemination Officer, The Social Organization and Behavior Laboratory, Andrus Gerontology Center, University of Southern California, Los Angeles, Calif. 90007.

Jaraslawa: 10 min/color/1976. Shows the joys and artistry of baking, while giving a portrait of an old Ukrainian woman from Bloomingburg, New York. Producer: Dee Dee Halleck. Distributor: Maple Shade Movies, Stoney Point, N.Y. 10980.

Number Our Days: 30 min/color/1976. Features the lives and circumstances of the elderly Eastern European immigrant Jews of the Israel Levin Senior Adult Community Center in Venice, California. Poignantly depicts their problems and strengths and captures their determination to pursue their life's career—aging. Won the Academy of Motion Picture Arts and Sciences Award for Best Short Subject Film within the Documentary Category for 1976. Contact: Ms. Regina Hopper, Business Affairs—KCET, 4401 Sunset Boulevard, Los Angeles, Calif. 90052.

Old, Black and Alive: 28 min/color/1974. Filmed in a rural area of the South. Shows seven elderly black people who have something to say about aging. Distributor: New Film Company, Inc., 331 Newbury Street, Dept. A, Boston, Mass. 02115.

The Parting: 16 min/color/1973. Presents the funeral ritual of the common people in the Montenegro area of Yugoslavia. Natural sounds and visual effects tell the story—no dialogue. Distributor: Wombat Productions, Inc., P.O. Box 70, Ossining, N.Y. 10562.

The Spirit Possession of Alejandro Mamani: See Chapter 18, Other Resources.

Three Grandmothers: 28 min/b&w/1964. Looks at lives of three grandmothers in Africa, Brazil, Canada. Producer: National Film Board of Canada. Distributor: University of Southern California, Film Distribution, Los Angeles, Calif. 90007.

Two Daughters: 22 min/color/1974. After the death of her young daughter a woman returns to their former apartment in Stockholm. She is flooded by memories of her daughter's life, illness, and death and by memories of her own mother. In Swedish with English subtitles. Producer/writer: Paul Mareth. Distributor: University of California, Extension Media Center, Berkeley, Calif. 94720.

Wataridori: Birds of Passage: 30 min/color/1975. A biographical account of three Japanese-American older people. Valuable insight into the cultural and historical roots that have guided and shaped the lives of Issei (first-generation Japanese in America). Distributor: Center on Aging, 349 Cedar Street, San Diego, Calif. 92101.

Yudie: See Chapter 27, Other Resources.

Sexuality

The Blessings of Love: 9 min/color/1966. Animated, nonverbal. Follows a couple from courtship to marriage to old age to the time when the man loses his wife and imagines her back with him, as young and lovely as she was long ago. Producer: Jiri Trnka for Bulgarian Film Institute. Distributor: (Macmillan) Audio Brandon, 1619 North Cherokee Street, Los Angeles, Calif. 90028.

Queen of the Stardust Ballroom: See Chapter 26, Other Resources.

Sex after Sixty: 20 min/b&w/1974. Visits institutions that used to be called "old folks' homes" and talks to residents about their problems, including their lack of freedom and privacy to express their sexuality. Producer: CBS News. Distributor: CBS Publishing Group, Columbia Broadcasting System, Inc., 383 Madison Avenue, New York, N.Y. 10017.

Touch

Cries and Whispers: Swedish commercial film. Producer: Ingmar Bergman.

A Man's Hands: 5 min/color/1972. A witty, fast-cut montage dramatizing the activities of the human hand: squeezing, poking, fixing, swatching, zipping, playing, and touching. Funny, moving, entertaining, informative. Producer: Paul Prokop. Distributor: Pyramid Films, Box 1048, Santa Monica, Calif. 90406.

Minnie Remembers: See Chapter 18, Other Resources.

The Mortal Body: See Chapter 24, Other Resources.

Chapter 30

GOOD-BYE, WORLD: DIMENSIONS OF TERMINATION

Irene Mortenson Burnside

> On a journey, ill
> And over fields all withered, dreams
> Go wandering still
>
> *Basho*

The above haiku was written during the Japanese poet's last illness. It is a lovely, poetic farewell to his pupils, who had requested that he write his philosophy. Basho was a religious man, a poet who felt God was in nature.

The dictionary definition of *termination* is "end in time or existence; conclusion; limit in space or extent" (*Webster's New Collegiate Dictionary*, 1977). In this closing chapter termination will be used in four contexts: (1) ending relationships and the importance of well-handled good-byes with older persons (Burnside); (2) bringing closure, i.e., during the time prior to moves (translocation and relocation are discussed in Chapter 28); (3) ending a life-style—terminating one phase of one's life (sometimes abruptly, because of accidents, traumas, illness, etc.) to move into another phase; and (4) death.

DIMENSIONS OF TERMINATION

There are several dimensions of termination. Care givers need to be aware of these dimensions, whether as a practitioner (Am I preparing the old person for leaving, even though we are just beginning?''); as an instructor (''Am I preparing the student for termination with me by role modeling expected behavior?''); as a professional (''Am I striving to practice what I preach, or just preaching?'').

609

TERMINATION OF RELATIONSHIPS

Terminations are ubiquitous; we continually terminate with someone, some place, or something. "So do we live forever taking our leave" (Rilke, p. 40). A good-bye in a one-time-only relationship is important. One-time relationships can be meaningful, as de Castillejo has described, "I have never forgotten the smile of a bus conductor as I alighted from a bus at the age of twenty. It was a smile shared. We never saw one another again, nor needed to, but for a few seconds we really met. . . . Even in as brief a meeting as that, some infinitesimal but indestructible thing has been added to the whole atmosphere" (p. 12). Because meetings with old people may end suddenly (because of death, illness, relocation), one must be aware of the "sacred present." (I do not know whose term that is.) *The good-byes should be as important as the hellos.*

Travelbee described the ending of a one-to-one relationship. She states what was begun must now end. But another way of viewing termination is that it is a beginning, as both persons will go on to new life experiences. It is hoped that their shared experiences will have enriched them both. I will return to the enrichment theme later on.

The following are useful points to keep in mind when terminating a short-term relationship (i.e., one that consisted of one or two meetings):

- Early in the meeting, be clear about the length of time you can spend.
- Be sure the person knows who you are and understands why you are there.
- Touch the person unless you observe cues and reasons why you think you should not, e.g., begin with a handshake, end with a handshake, which also nonverbally indicates beginning and closure of the meeting.
- Listen for signs of lowered self-esteem and insert something positive.
- Watch for signs of weariness in the individual (sighing, moving in chair to more comfortable position). When signs of weariness are observed, indicate that you will be leaving soon.
- Watch for signs of anxiety, restlessness, or fidgeting in nonverbal cues; shorten the meeting. This also applies if your own anxiety is rising.
- Do not make promises you cannot keep.
- When possible, let the old person assume the role of teaching you; express what you have received from the relationship.
- Be generous in using the older person's name.
- Be able to express your appreciation for what the interview meant.
- The stages of a long-term relationship can be compressed into a short relationship, i.e., there is an introduction period, a work phase, and then a tapering off.

Terminating a long-term therapeutic relationship requires considerably more planning and preparation. The following are some points to keep in mind.[1]

---

[1] Some of the above guidelines were adopted from Marion E. Kalkman, "Individual Therapy," in Marion Kalkman and Anne Davis (eds.), *New Dimensions of Mental-Health-Psychiatric Nursing*, McGraw-Hill, New York, 1974, pp. 569–574.

- Prepare the person in the initial phase of the relationship for termination. (Use a calendar to mark the date if necessary, especially with a confused, disoriented individual.)
- Set specific date for termination.
- Check your own list:
    Are you decreasing the intensity of the relationship?
    Are you decreasing the number of meetings?
    Are you decreasing the frequency of the meetings?
    Are you helping make plans for the future—how the time will be used with the individual?
    Are you making plans for someone who could take your place (if the need is expressed)?
    Are you reminding the old person when the time is getting close for termination?
    Are you observing how the individual reacts to discussions of terminations (e.g., anger, regression, acceptance, laying a guilt trip on the worker)?
    Are you careful not to introduce new material?
    Are you aware how you are reacting to the termination?
    Will you be able to send an occasional card?
    Will you be able to make a follow-up visit at a later date (not only to offer some hope, a tiny piece of future, but also a chance to see how effective you were)?
    Will you need to write a professional summary?
- A long, intense relationship will require more planning and more work, especially if it was with a dependent individual.
- Some old persons do not want you to leave and will use linger-on strategies to keep you; recognize these ploys, but be gentle, yet firm, about your contract for time with them.
- Proper management of the termination phase will lessen guilt and unsettling feelings in the worker.
- Even when a termination is speeded up for any reason (illness, a move, transfers, etc.), the process remains the same, and the same careful steps are to be taken.
- Use semantics that are clear to the aged person. Write them down if necessary; use words like "leaving," "going," "good-bye," "won't be coming anymore," etc. Words convey different meanings to different people; be sure that the choice of words conveys your intent.
- Express what the relationship has meant to you.
- Discuss what the original purpose of the relationship was and offer a summary of what you think happened. (This is important in both one-to-one and group relationships.) The ability to summarize helps others learn to do that also.
- Permit, even encourage, tears when appropriate. Sadness needs to be mutually expressed.
- It is useful to get the old person's view of the interaction and the relationship.

- Pitfalls to avoid are:
  Careless planning and timing of the termination phase.
  Inability to recognize one's own reactions to termination.

THREE TYPES OF TERMINATION

According to Berne, there are three types of termination: accidental, resistant, and therapeutic. In an "accidental termination," the client or the care giver moves away and some external force occurs over which there is no control; it then becomes necessary to terminate the relationship. The "resistant" termination is a plausible excuse which is unexplained or unannounced, and the withdrawal is based on fear and dissatisfaction or a combination of both. The latter type of termination is commonly seen in group work with the aged when the aged member drops out of the group with a flimsy excuse. Students usually need help in this area when they are leading groups and dealing with attrition and dropouts, since they often do not quite understand what is happening at the time. The new group leader's anxiety is often high and precludes an analysis of the situation.

The therapeutic termination is mutually decided upon by the participants.

DEFENSES IN TERMINATION
Denial

Sometimes we deny termination. Sometimes we prolong the ending. Yet there are times when we are relieved to be terminating a relationship. If there were attachment and closeness in the relationship, there will be feelings of loss by both persons. It is my own belief that one facet of maturity is to be close to an individual (or a group) and then be able to let go with grace. When young group leaders of elderly clients terminate relationships, they frequently express great guilt about leaving. They feel they began something beautiful and then walked out on the group. Le Sar wrote a paper on such an experience while she was a master's-degree student leading a group of elderly clients.

One assumes that old people will be depressed or devastated by such an experience. The fact is that one's own feelings about termination tend to distort the picture. Usually the old people handle the process very well. "There is no need for us to take upon ourselves the responsibility of sheltering the very old from worry. Griefs do not shatter them as they do the young. They have their own protection from these emotions which are more than they can bear. It is not our task to turn them into breathing fossils" (de Castillejo, p. 163). When the energy levels of old people are very low, they may feel a sense of relief upon termination of a relationship. They may have to establish priorities for their time, energy, and relationships; what is a high priority for the student, nurse, case worker, or counselor is not necessarily one for the aged person.

Still another facet of group experience is that the student or worker may not fully realize how much she or he means to the old person. One often underestimates one's own effective caring. During my own studenthood, I was terminating a relationship with a man in his fifties who had spent most of his adult life on a back ward in a state hospital. The last day he wanted to go for a walk and selected the route. It was the first time I had ever seen the pauper's grave and the crematorium located on the periphery of the state hospital grounds. Set off by itself among a patch of weeds stood a nondescript building. No one was around. What a symbolic way he chose to tell me good-bye. Each person has his own way of expressing sadness and dying states; this is the way a man of few words and expressed emotions chose to say good-bye to me.

Termination may be prolonged when a person's behavior becomes a plea to stay, and the student is unable to make a clean break; this is especially true with old people.

Figure 30-1 Grandparents often feel great sadness when they must say good-bye to grandchildren when families are moved. Aged persons may deny the hurt or anger they experience during such separations. (*Courtesy of Harvey Finkle.*)

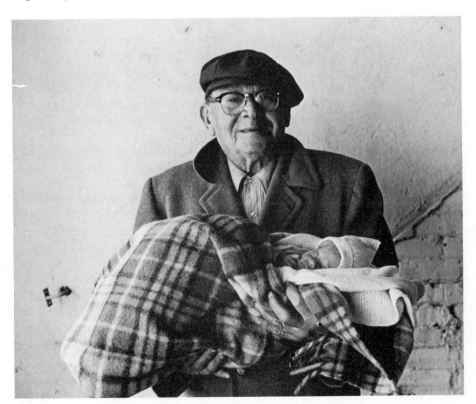

Avoidance

Though Sene, writing about termination with clients in one-to-one relationships, did not include termination with aged clients, she nevertheless made points relevant to the subject. She stated that a student's denial, suppression, and repression are sometimes encouraged, to the point that students do not learn to discuss separation. "The cogency of their affective involvement and personal impressions, be they success, failure, confusion, or growth, colors the screen through which they examine termination phenomena" (p. 40). One reason why students may have difficulty in recognizing their successes is that they often set unrealistic goals with old people and then fail to meet the goals.

Others avoid close relationships and are reluctant to invest or participate in the relationship because they believe it will then be easier to terminate it. Or the client may have the attitude, "I will leave you before you leave me," and may take the initiative to sever the relationship; students should be alerted to such a possibility.

Still other students plunge into a relationship with great gusto. When it is all over, they shrug it off and say the relationship did not mean much to them.

ENRICHED EXPERIENCE

The enriched experience is one useful aspect of termination. Try to understand what the old person has given you, the legacies you now have that you did not have before you knew that person. The need for the old person to teach us appears time and again. Da Silva perceptively described it in writing of his 3 years of psychotherapy with an 81-year-old man. "He wanted very much to teach me something; at first it was his acting, because this was what he knew best, and later it was his experience, and also his philosophy of life. . . . One of his favorite refrains was that the young generation thinks erroneously that an old man is fully contented if he has his pipe and a good fire in the stove, when in reality what he wants is to do and to see things" (p. 11).

I personally discovered how much a paranoid old lady meant to me after her death. Crazy as she was at times, she patiently taught me this message through her most disordered thinking, "Can't you see, this is the only way I can survive this miserable life?" (Burnside).

POWERFUL, INTENSE EXPERIENCE

One important aspect of termination is to recognize what a powerful and intense emotional experience separation can be. Students have said to me during a conference, "But I really did not care very much about that old lady when I started working with her—now look at me," and then wiped away a few tears. For the impact of one elderly lady on a student, see the case study describing Eva in Chapter 22.

TEARS ARE FOR CRYING

Spontaneous tears are part of some terminations. It is wise to give the crying person a handful of tissues, not just one, which indicates, "You may cry only one tissue of tears—that is all." It may be uncomfortable if an old man cries or fights back tears; old men will hold back tears if they see tears as a way of losing manliness or strength. As de Castillejo wrote about a man crying, "He has stumbled inadvertently into the sphere which he does not at all understand, and wonders why he is so ill at ease" (p. 20).

There is a lovely poem by Frona Lane called "Man Mourning."

Old man, immovable mountain.
snow-crowned, blizzard bent,
mute as marble,
stoic as stone,
eyes color of earth through ice—
witness in the numb noon
shapes of unmelting mourning.

To melt unmelting mourning is therapy at its finest.

Care givers during the termination of a relationship need to know that their tears may be for crying also; they should not feel embarrassed about them. Old people often view tears as a sign of real caring; they feel that you must care a great deal about them to shed some tears during good-bye. They also need to see that you are in control of your sadness and can manifest honest feelings and not have your needs usurp theirs.

GOOD-BYES SAID PRIOR TO VACATIONS

It is important to plan for the care giver's vacations. Da Silva wrote, "When I announced my vacation, he became very angry and, during the last session, very depressed; he might be gone and buried when I came back. I sent him a postcard. When I returned after three weeks, I was informed by the personnel on his ward that he had been anxiously waiting for me, remembering the time and date" (p. 11).

PLANNING FOR TERMINATION

Termination plans should be discussed early in any relationship with an old person, and also early with the student during conferences, if one is a preceptor. The student should be alert to the fact that the elderly client may die during the relationship, may suffer a stroke, or experience other severe illnesses. Such an awareness on the part of the student may help intensify the relationship, but it may also cause holding back; if one does not invest much, then there is less loss when it is all over.

Terminations with elderly clients can be eased with a party, a small gift, or a display of affection. All this, of course, goes against psychotherapeutic principles, but not all workers are in the psychotherapeutic stance in terminations with old people. Some old people regard friendship highly—a form of therapy in its own right. We do need to redefine professionalism with older clients.

NO-NONSENSE APPROACH

Old people have a marvelous no-nonsense approach to terminations. One needs only to observe their grace and their ability to say good-bye. We need to study their gratitude, a gratitude they express so readily, and sometimes for what seems so little.

YOUR GRATITUDE

You may also be surprised at your own feelings of gratitude. At the termination phase, you are not always precisely sure what the older client has taught. One may only vaguely perceive that something was learned. Yet, teach they do, each in an inimitable way. Only later does one begin to count the ways in which the elderly client may have taught. Students need time to let their experiences with the older person mellow in order to appreciate more fully the benefits received.

BRINGING CLOSURE

I use the term *bringing closure* to include a variety of tasks that may be necessary to assist the old person in a move. The move may be for health reasons, in which case there might not be much time to prepare. When people leave a house, an apartment, or even a room, to move on to a different living arrangement, they should have the time and opportunity to say good-bye in their own way. Chapter 28 deals with the cavalier way in which old people are moved about within institutions.

Of course, some might wish just to take up and leave, as Brooke did in his peripatetic existence during a 6-year period of his life. More often than not, the old person does not have the time, and in some instances perhaps not even the energy, to bring about the desired closure. One experiences frustration when one tries to follow clients who moved suddenly; sometimes there is simply no address for them. An excellent example is given by Smith-White in his article about tracking down his ex-landlady who had been so good to him. The same thing occurred with Rose di Maggio, whom I described in Chapter 27. She was abruptly moved to a nursing home; another nurse and I planned to visit her, but we had to do considerable sleuthing, trying to find out in which nursing home she had been placed. Such frustration may also occur for friends, who cannot find relocated persons.

Old persons may want the chance to say good-bye to neighbors, the one who delivers mail, the paper boy, the teller at the bank, the checker at the local

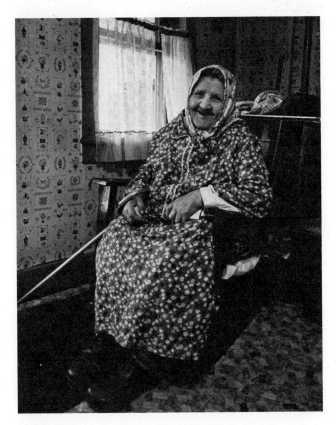

Figure 30-2 The gratitude of older persons for your sharing and caring is often expressed with animation such as shown above. (*Courtesy of Harvey Finkle.*)

grocery store; all these persons may be important to them. Do we know or find out what constitutes a comfortable good-bye for them?

Another time when a chance to bring closure is needed to wrap things up is prior to quitting a job or retiring. The chance to consider the new style, to tie together loose ends seems of the utmost importance; some persons need more time than others to accomplish their closure tasks. Persons being retired for health reasons may need considerable time to accept this new view of themselves and to sever the bonds to their work world.

ENDING A LIFE-STYLE

Some transitions require the utmost of coping; coping takes much energy (Verwoerdt). Courage seems to be the only word to describe the quality needed during transitions from mobility to immobility, from health to incurable disease, from affluence to poverty, to name a few of the changes which greatly affect life-style in late life. The closure and letting-go of one phase of life to enter another, whether willingly or unwillingly, constitute an aspect of termination. For example, becoming a widow or widower (discussed in Chapter 18) is an ending to a life-style that is often abrupt and requires drastic shifts and changes. The older person who plans and makes drastic changes in life-style or behavior will face criticism, or incredulous disbelief. *Old people are not expected to change.* They are certainly going against society's expectations if they break out and behave in a way that is new for them or behave differently from their cohorts. A wise, old aunt of mine once said, "We are all made of the same mold." Then she paused and added, "It's only that some folks are mouldier than others." The support needed through these changes towards individuation may be provided by a caring person with understanding which the older person might not receive from family, neighbors, or cohorts.

Another example is provided by those who change through counseling or psychotherapy and are getting used to living with their changed (changing) selves; hopefully, there is a positive change after the psychic surgery. Again, their changed behavior may not be accepted by friends, neighbors, and/or families.

T.S. Eliot, in "The Waste Land," described such leaving, the time when one takes decisive steps alone:

> The awful daring of a moment's surrender
> Which an age of prudence can never retract. (p. 45)

THE SIMPLE IS COMPLEX

The apparent simplicity of saying good-bye is certainly deceiving when one considers all the variables and complexities inherent in something so human as terminating a relationship. To recapture some of the qualities of the process a care giver may consider: (1) termination is ubiquitous; (2) one must be fully present and aware of the dimensions of each termination—even of one-time meetings, which also need good-byes; (3) full participation in the relationship increases the chances for feelings of loss; (4) one can plunge into a relationship, terminate it, and deny the feelings engendered by the loss; (5) the nurturing and caring qualities are important, and separation needs careful attention and preparation; (7) what you have learned may become more apparent long after the termination.

PACING

Pacing is of the utmost importance with elderly persons; one should not hurry them or take over their tasks, especially the saying of the good-bye for them, unless they request it. Saying good-bye to home, to objects, to neighborhoods and people in an environment is a personal act, a unique part of one's selfhood. It is part and parcel of promoting a person's individuation—right up until the very end of the aged person's life. For in death as well as in living, individuals should maintain control, if at all possible, and decide on their legacies, closures, ways to let go, ways to say good-bye to the world.

DEATH: THE NIGHT OF THE EGO

Peck called death "the night of the ego" (p. 91), and Updike spoke of death for the aged in this way, "death at their side . . . the third guest at every meal" (p. 80). One important research finding in gerontological literature that needs to be understood in caring for the dying aged person is the terminal drop in cognitive ability and intelligence which is consistently noted before death. (See Chapter 24 for the researchers who discovered it and their findings.) This change is mentioned here so that knowledge of it may be implemented in psychosocial care for the dying aged person.

Kalish and Reynolds state that the old differ from the young in facing death in the following ways: (1) the degree to which they integrate their formal religious training into their lives; (2) the degree to which they have had experience with death and dying; (3) the degree to which they approach the problems with a primarily external or internal focus of activity; and (4) the degree to which they have accepted the idea that they have been appointed to die. (See Chapter 5 by Monea for a detailed discussion of separation and death in childhood. Contrast it with the death of an aged person, or with present relocation strategies.)

Careful observation and recording may elicit types of terminal behavior to look for prior to death. One director of nurses of a nursing home noted that patients ceased reading their daily paper when they were nearing death. Such documented observations may alert us to more cues about the ending of lives. Another nurse (Miller) discussed the change in eating habits (eating less, especially not eating formerly favored foods, such as cookies, and also skipping cups of coffee that had been ritualistic in the diet pattern). In the book *Gramp* (Jury and Jury) an elderly man removes his dentures and refuses to eat for 3 weeks prior to his death.

In a classic little book, Worcester stated that one of his medical school professors was Oliver Wendell Holmes. He had not forgotten the admonition given by Holmes that one of the physician's functions is to assist at the coming in; another is to assist at the going out. "As hardly need be said, it often is impossible for even the most experienced to decide just when the act of dying begins. In fact no two cases are alike, and whatever age is attained, death finally triumphs in multifarious ways" (p. 34).

TERMINATION PANGS INVOLVING PEOPLE

Curtin wrote about struggling to terminate her relationship with two elderly men who lived in the same hotel that she did.

Harry and Al just sat and stared dumbly into their coffee. . . . They sensed my fear, maybe even before I did. The more I tried to talk the sorrier I sounded. Before long I was ready to cry, ready to say I would take them home and take care of them forever and they wouldn't have to live like this anymore. I don't really think I really meant it—I just wasn't ready to give that much yet—I just felt so damn guilty about being young enough to leave that hotel and that neighborhood and live another way. . . . After that we didn't have much more to say to one another. That night the bedbugs attacked in full force . . . and I packed my carpetbag and left. (p. 71)

TERMINATION PANGS INVOLVING PETS

Until now I have not described the sorrow involved in taking leave of pets (see Chapter 27 for a detailed account on pets and old people). A well-known author has described the death of her pet parrot:

Now I have buried him and put his cage and toys away in the attic. That corner of the cozy room looks terribly empty. How much atmosphere he displaced . . . no larger than my hand, cocking his head when I passed by, making sweet murmurs to himself in the evening when I watched the news, so self-contained, cheerful and brave! The first time I took him to the vet he was given an injection that crippled one leg so he could not sit on a perch. All morning he tried to crawl up the cage and fell back, crawled up and fell back. While Mildred and I sweated it out, helpless to help him. After two and a half hours of this agonizing struggle, he finally made it. It is not absurd to feel such grief. I am undone. He had given me much joy. (Sarton, p. 187)

HESITATION TO DISCUSS DYING

Care givers hesitate to talk about death or dying to old persons for fear of upsetting them. Ordinarily such discussions are not upsetting to the aged; more often it is the helping person who is upset by the discussion. It takes a certain kind of courage and openness to sit with people and let them talk about their own dying or their funeral. It is not easy to teach such openness; we may learn it from the elderly. In fact, the aged who plan their own funeral arrangements, give away objects, leave legacies, and bring closure, more often than not leave staff members baffled and bewildered. Sometimes the personnel feel loss of control of the situation. Then there are the times when old people do not have a chance to bring closure to their business affairs, their relationships, their life in general.

One-to-one relationships and group therapy permit the elderly to talk about death, not only their own but that of others. The aged are not as frail psychologically as one would think.

Recently a 77-year-old man described deaths during the influenza epidemic of 1917, during World War I years (see Table 21-5). He was 17 years old at the time. "They put the body in a canvas bag coffin with lead weights on it. During the ceremony at 10 o'clock in the morning, the bugles blew taps, the sailor tilted the board, and the body slid into the sea." (Voice fades.) "We were half way across the Atlantic; it took us 14 days to go across it" (Papo).

In Chapter 26, I discussed old women who still describe their children who died in infancy. Jacobsen points out the theme of child deaths in the works of early women poets. "In a period, when out of a family of 14 or 15 children, five or six might well die in infancy, or early childhood, death as an omnipresent reality was a towering presence" (p. 17). Many of the current cohort groups of old people will also describe the many deaths they have observed in their lifetime. An 80-year-old man brought out funeral notices from the mortuary and handed me 20 of them— his friends and relatives now gone.

GOOD-BYE WORLD, HELLO HEAVEN

Aspects to consider during a death include encouraging expression of beliefs which are sustaining to the elderly individual—for example, life in the hereafter. Some aged persons feel they are leaving to meet a loved one. I recall one student who was concerned about assisting an aged dying woman. She was sure she would meet her husband in heaven, but expressed this worry to the young student, "What will I do if his first wife is there, too?"

Acceptance of death sometimes helps survivors and professionals alike (if the latter can forego heroic measures when the aged person has refused to be kept alive).

It is sobering to realize how inept we can be as professionals. A study in the

Figure 30-3 Old women frequently have a need to describe children who were stillborn or who died in early infancy. Since there is a preponderance of old women, care givers will need to listen carefully to the special needs of these women. (*Courtesy of Harvey Finkle.*)

United States was done on all needed services to a group of aged persons living in the community. The findings were that the persons who had received the most services also had the highest rate of both institutionalization and death. Blenkner attributed the finding to the damage done by the professionals intervening in the living of these old persons.

It is well to focus on physical comforts and to be sure that pain is controlled. Food is often important. (See Chapter 23 and Ebersole's description of the centenarian.) Watch for lack of interest in food. If there is apparent cognitive decline, one might help relatives better understand that change by explaining the research findings and how they relate to the changes they have observed.

Monea's writings earlier in the book are devoted to many of the firsts in life; Ebersole discusses refinement of those firsts; this chapter focuses on "the lasts"—last qualities and characteristics, last cherished objects, last relationships, last experiences of the last years.

De Castillejo says:

> Many old men and women are cheated of their essential solitude, and kept continually focused on outer things by the mistaken kindness of the young and their own unawareness of their need to be alone. We die alone. It is well to become accustomed to being alone before that moment comes.
>
> The very old, those who have given up all interest in the outer world even to the stage of being withdrawn from any point of contact, may still be receiving and quietly nurturing within themselves new insights which will enable them to meet the unknown future. One wonders sometimes what holds them here. Perhaps they are not ready. They cannot die until they are ready. I have often felt that modern medicine is very cruel to the old for it keeps them here when they are longing to be allowed to go. (p. 161)

The importance of a legacy and a life review has been well described by Butler. In a somewhat oblique way, de Castillejo discusses the importance of the life review. She believes that, "One has to return to one's past, not once but many times, in order to pick up all the threads one has let fall through carelessness or unobservance" (p. 157).

SUMMARIZING STATEMENTS BASED ON THE LITERATURE ABOUT DEATH

- "A man's dying is more the survivor's affair than his own." Thomas Mann, *The Magic Mountain*
- "Though he has watched a decent age pass by, a man will sometimes still desire the world." Sophocles ("Oedipus at Colonnus")
- "Call no man lucky til his life is lived." (Source unknown)
- "My fear: not of *dying,* but of existing without living," wrote Berenson (1963, p. 467). Later in his diary he wrote, "Part of me clings to life at all costs. . . . I wish I could die in my sleep, or even in any sudden instantaneous way. What I dread is seeing the end, and far enough away to allow of every kind of intervening worry and figment of a disturbed imagination" (p. 476).

- "To forgive oneself is a very difficult thing to do, but perhaps it is the last task demanded of us before we die"(de Castillejo, p. 164).
- "Death is a lonely business at best; dying alone is tragically purposeless" (Verwoerdt, p. 77).

GUIDELINES FOR INTERVENTIONS WITH THE DYING PERSON

- Consider the terminal drop in cognitive ability with the aged person.
- Consider the changing patterns and routines which may occur.
- The aged integrate formal religious training with life differently than the young; assist in expression.
- Promote individuation process until death.
- Realize that death of pets can cause bereavement, especially if the pet was an extension of a loved one.
- Vivid memories to consider in reminiscing might include war deaths, or loss of infants and children of all ages.
- The "lasts" in life have different qualities. Help the old person bring closure, say good-byes, leave legacies.
- Do not cheat them of needs for solitude.

Figure 30-4 "Love becomes ability to bless, and be, in blessing, blessed" (de Castillejo, p. 156). (*Courtesy of Harvey Finkle.*)

- Encourage the aged person to return to pick up threads of past life (life review, oral history, autobiography, diary, etc.).
- Encourage expression of self-forgiveness.

De Castillejo wrote beautifully about last feelings in life in a poem she entitled "Last Years." Her words seem to be the right closure for a chapter on termination:

Now that my loves are dead
On what shall my action ride? . . .
My action, sharing bread,
Love becomes ability
To bless, and be, in blessing,
Blessed. (p. 156)

REFERENCES

Berne, Eric: *Principles of Group Treatment,* Oxford University Press, New York, 1966.

Berenson, Bernard: *Sunset and Twilight, from the Diaries of 1947–1958,* Harcourt Brace & World, New York, 1963.

Blenkner, Margaret: "Social and Family Relationships in Later Life with Some Thoughts on Filial Maturity," in Ethel Shanas and Gordon Streib (eds.), *Social Structure and the Family,* Prentice-Hall, Englewood Cliffs, N. J., 1965.

Brooke, John: "The Gentle Art of Poverty," *The Atlantic Monthly,* **239**(10): 62–68, 1977.

Burnside, Irene Mortenson: "Eulogy for Ms. Hogue," *American Journal of Nursing,* **78**(4):624–626,1978.

Curtin, Sharon R.: *Nobody Ever Died of Old Age,* Little, Brown, Boston, 1972.

Da Silva, Guy: "The Loneliness and Death of an Old Man. Three Years' Psychotherapy of an Eighty-One-Year-Old Depressed Man," *Journal of Geriatric Psychiatry,* **1**(1):5–27, 1967.

De Castillejo, Irene Claremont: *Knowing Woman: A Feminine Psychology,* Putnam, New York, 1973.

Eliot, T. S.: *The Waste Land and Other Poems,* Harcourt, Brace, Harvest Books, New York, 1934, p. 45.

Henderson, Harold G.: *An Introduction to Haiku,* Doubleday, Garden City, N.Y., p. 30.

Jacobsen, Josephine: "From Anne to Marianne," in *Two Lectures,* Library of Congress, Washington, 1973, p. 17.

Jury, Mark, and **Dan Jury:** *Gramp,* Grossman, New York, 1976.

Kalish, Richard, and **David Reynolds:** *Death and Ethnicity: A Psychocultural Study,* Ethel Percy Andrus Gerontology Center, University of Southern California, Los Angeles, 1976.

Lane, Frona: *The Third Eyelid,* Alan Swallow Press, Denver, 1951.

Le Sar, Kathy: Unpublished manuscript, University of Hawaii, Honolulu, 1977.

Miller, Diane: Personal communication, 1978.

Papo, L. D.: Personal communication, 1978.

Peck, Robert C.: "Psychological Developments in the Second Half of Life," in Bernice Neugarten (ed.), *Middle Age and Aging,* The University of Chicago Press, Chicago, 1968; first impression, 1970, p. 91.

Rilke, Rainer Maria: *The Duino Elegies,* translated by Harry Behn, Peter Pauper Press, Mount Vernon, N.Y., 1957, p. 40.

Sarton, Mae: *Journal of a Solitude,* Norton, New York, 1973, p. 187.

Sene, Barbara Stankiewiz: "Termination in the Student-Patient Relationship," *Perspectives in Psychiatric Care,* **7**(1): 39–45, 1969.

Smith-White, Chad: "Old Age, Youth and Vermouth," *San Francisco Sunday Examiner and Chronicle,* Dec. 12, 1976, p. 46+.

Travelbee, Joyce: *Intervention in Psychiatric Nursing,* Davis, Philadelphia, 1969.

Updike, John: *The Poorhouse Fair,* Knopf, New York, 1959.

Verwoerdt, Adriaan: *Communication with the Fatally Ill,* Charles C Thomas, Springfield, Ill., 1966.

Worcester, Alfred: *The Care of the Aged, the Dying and the Dead,* Charles C Thomas, Springfield, Ill., 1961.

OTHER RESOURCES

FILMS

Come and Take My Hand: 25 min/color/1971. A Dominican nun provides reassurance and loving care for terminally ill patients. Producer: Films Incorporated, Wilmette, Ill. 60091.

Death (Family of Man Series): See Chapter 29, Other Resources.

End of One: 7 min/color/1970. The viewer watches the death of a seagull. One bird of a flock is singled out—weak, frail, seemingly helpless—and the camera follows it to the end. Producer: Learning Corporation of America, New York, N.Y. 10022.

Estate Planning: 8 min/color/1973. Well-known specialist in estate planning makes clear the importance of a will. Producer: University of Iowa, Iowa City, Iowa 52240.

Gramp: A Man Ages and Dies: See Chapter 24, Other Resources.

I Heard the Owl Call My Name: See Chapter 29, Other Resources.

Make Today Count: 29 min/color/1975. A filmed portrait of a person with terminal cancer. Producer: Alfred Shands. Contact: Rhoden Stretter, 353 Pacific Street, Brooklyn, N.Y. 11217.

Passing Quietly Through: 26 min/b&w/1970. A dying old man, bedridden in his run-down New York apartment, is cared for by a visiting nurse. They develop a relationship based on truth and mutual trust. The language is earthy but realistic. Award winner. Producer: Dinitia McCarthy. Distributor: Films, Inc., Wilmette, Ill. 60091.

Spirit Possession of Alejandro Mamani: See Chapter 18, Other Resources.

The Final Proud Days of Elsie Wurster: 60 min/b&w/1975. Observational documentary in the final 30 days of a nursing home in Pennsylvania. Producer: Pennsylvania University Audio Visual Services, University Park, Pa. 16802.

The Following Sea: 11 min/b&w/1971. The fisherman is dead, but his wisdom rolls on. The film portrays a significant lesson in human decency and the importance of mental health. Producer: Division of Mental Health, U.S. Virgin Islands.

The Garden Party: 24 min/color/1974. A film based on a Katherine Mansfield short story. How the tragedy of the death of a poor neighbor is handled by each family member makes it a good discussion film. Producer: Gurian/Sholder—ACT Films, New York, N.Y. 10036.

The Mercy Killers: 37 min/b&w/1967. Does not take sides but discusses ethical and moral issues on the right to live or die. Includes case histories. Producer: BBC/Time-Life Films. Visual Aids Service, University of Illinois, Champaign, Ill. 61820.

The Old Woman: 2 min/color/1973. This animated, nonnarrative film is about an old woman dusting her living room when death arrives and beckons to her. Producer: ACI, New York, N.Y. 10036.

The Parting: 16 min/color/1973. About the funeral ritual of the common people in the Montenegro area of Yugoslavia; presents a contrast to the American way of death. Producer: Zivko Nikolic. Wombat Productions, Inc., Ossining, N.Y. 10562.

To Be Aware of Death: 14½ min/color/1974. Shows how the attitudes of young adults toward death are tempered by more mature experience. Producer: Billy Budd Films, New York, N.Y. 10022.

Two Daughters: 22 min/color/1974. A woman returns to her former apartment in Stockholm after the death of her daughter. She is flooded with memories of her daughter and also of her mother. In Swedish with English subtitles. Producer: Paul Mareth, University of Connecticut, Center for Instructional Media, Storrs, Conn. 06268.

APPENDIX

BOOKLETS AND PAMPHLETS

A Comparative View of Aging, an experimental curriculum for teaching aging to junior and senior high school students. Prepared by the Center for Teaching International Relations, Graduate School of International Studies, University of Denver, Colo. 80210.

Audio-Visual Catalog, a catalog of films, slides, tapes, and programs on aging, complete with price list. Order catalog from Mid-America Resource and Training Center on Aging, Kansas City, Mo. 64112.

Citizens Action Manual: Nursing Home Reform, a working guide to improving the conditions of seniors in nursing homes. Prepared by the Gray Panthers, Philadelphia, Pa. 19104.

Documentary Photo Aids, 1976 catalog. A series of 28 11″ × 14″ not-so-funny cartoons on aging is available through this catalog. Teachers' guide included. To order, send for Living with Aging series from Documentary Photo Aids, Mt. Dora, Fla. 32757.

Growing Old—A Guide for Understanding and Help, a brief, easy-to-read outline of problems of aging, with some solutions. American Occupational Therapy Foundation, Inc., Rockville, Md. 20852.

Nursing Home Ombudsman, a handbook designed to assist ombudsmen and consumers groups to organize ombudsman programs in nursing homes. Edited by Robert Anson, Jr., Citizens for Better Care, Detroit, Mich. 48207.

Prime Time: By and for Older Women, a feminist journal exploring the problems of older women and some solutions. Prime Time, New York, N.Y. 10036.

Senior Power, A Political Action Handbook for Senior Citizens, a how-to approach for seniors attempting change in the political arena. Concerned Seniors for Better Government, the United Steelworkers of America, Washington, D.C. 20006.

That Thy Days May Be Long in the Good Land, a publication designed to aid Jewish elders; includes a bibliography of films on aging. Synagogue Council of America, Institute for Jewish Policy Planning and Research, Washington, D.C. 20036.

The Law and Aging Manual, an excellent overview of legal services for the elderly, the problems of aging, and some solutions. Prepared July 1976, by Legal Research and Services for the Elderly, sponsored by National Council of Senior Citizens, Washington, D.C. 20005.

The New Elders: Innovative Programs by, for and about the Elderly, Virginia Fraser, Susan M. Thornton, March 1977. Loretta Heights College, Denver, Colo.

To Be Old in America, a 31-page collection of articles analyzing crucial needs of the aging. Includes printed and audiovisual resources; also suggestions for study and action. Order from *engage/social action,* Washington, D.C. 20002.

CATALOGS OF FILMS ON AGING

About Aging: A Catalog of Films
Millie V. Allyn, Editor
Publications Office
Andrus Gerontology Center
University of Southern California
Los Angeles, Calif. 90007

Administration on Aging Catalogue of Films on Aging
U. S. Government Printing Office
Washington, D.C. 20402
    59-page annotated bibliography of films, slides, plays, and television programming on aging. Stock number 1762-00070.

Aging. A Filmography, by Judity Trojan
Educational Film Library Association
New York, N.Y. 10023
    Annotated films on both psychology and biology of aging.

Basic Bibliography
Gray Panthers
Philadelphia, Pa. 19104
    Partially annotated bibliography.

Films on Aging Catalog
Published by the Administration on Aging
Superintendent of Documents
U. S. Government Printing Office
Washington, D.C. 20402

Selected Films on Aging
Johanna Wiese, Editor
Institute of Gerontology
University of Michigan
Ann Arbor, Mich. 48104

Film Resources
National Council of Senior Citizens
Washington, D.C. 20005

JOURNALS ON AGING

Advances in Gerontological Research
New York, N.Y.

Black Aging
National Council on Black Aging, Inc.
Durham, N.C. 27707

British Journal of Geriatric Practice
Stuart Phillips Publications
Surrey, England

Dynamic Maturity
The American Association of Retired Persons
Ojai, Calif.

Educational Gerontology
Hemisphere Publishing Corporation
Washington, D.C. 20005

Experimental Aging Research
Bar Harbor, Me. 04609

Experimental Gerontology
Pergamon Press, Inc.
Elmsford, N.Y. 10523

Geriatrics
Minneapolis, Minn. 55435

Geriatrics Digest
Geriatrics Digest, Inc.
Northfield, Ill. 60093

Gerontologia
S. Karger AG
Arnold-Bocklin Strasse 25 CH 4000
Basel, 11 Switzerland

Gerontologica Clinica
Official Journal of British Geriatrics Society
Basel, Switzerland

Gerontologist
Gerontological Society
Washington, D.C. 20036

Gerontology and Geriatrics
Excerpta Medica Foundation
Amsterdam, The Netherlands

Human Developments
S. Karger AG
Arnold-Bocklin Strasse 25 CH 4000
Basel, 11 Switzerland

Interdisciplinary Topic in Gerontology
S. Karger AG
Arnold-Bocklin Strasse 25 CH 4000
Basel, 11 Switzerland

International Journal of Aging and Human Development
Baywood Publishing Co.
Farmingdale, N.Y. 11735

Journal of the American Geriatrics Society
American Geriatric Society
New York, N.Y. 10019

Journal of Geriatric Psychiatry
International Universities Press
New York, N.Y.

Journal of Gerontological Nursing
C. Black Inc.
Thorofare, N.J.

Journal of Gerontology
Gerontological Society
Washington, D.C. 20036

Modern Maturity
The American Association of Retired Persons
Ojai, Calif.

ORGANIZATIONS

Administration on Aging (HEW)
Washington, D.C. 20201
Advisory Committee on Aging

Administration on Aging
Social and Rehabilitation Service
Washington, D.C. 20201

American Association of Homes for the Aging
Washington, D.C. 20004

American Association of Retired Persons (AARP)
Washington, D.C. 20049

American Nursing Home Association
Washington, D.C. 20005

Gray Panthers
Philadelphia, Pa. 19104

Institute on Religion and Aging
Indianapolis, Ind. 46208

International Senior Citizens Association Inc.
Los Angeles, Calif. 90025

National Association of Jewish Homes for the Aged
Dallas, Tex. 75221

National Association of Retired Civil Employees
1909 Q Street, N.W.
Washington, D.C. 20009

National Council on the Aging
Washington, D.C. 20036

National Council of Senior Citizens
Washington, D.C. 20005

National Institute on Aging
Bethesda, Md. 20014

National Institute of Senior Centers
Washington, D.C. 20036

National Institutes of Health
Bethesda, Md. 20014

National Interfaith Coalition on Aging
Indianapolis, Ind. 46206

National Retired Persons Association (NRPA)
Washington, D.C. 20049

Senior Citizens of America
Washington, D.C. 20049

UCC: Health and Welfare Ministries
Board of Homeland Ministries
247 Park Avenue South
New York, N.Y. 10010

PROFESSIONAL ORGANIZATIONS

American Geriatrics Society
New York, N.Y.

American Nurses' Association, Inc.
Division on Geriatric Nursing Practice
Kansas City, Mo. 64108

International Congress Gerontology
Tokyo, Japan

United States Gerontology Society
Washington, D.C.

Western Gerontology Society
San Francisco, Calif.

NAME INDEX

Adams, B. N., 245, 246, 260, 261
Adams, David L., 486
Adams, John Quincy, 381, 382
Adler, Alfred, 252
Aisenberg, Ruth, 85, 88
Akhtar, A. J., 423
Alcorn, S., 464
Alderstein, Arthur M., 85
Aldin, C. C. W., 544
Alexander, Irving, 85
Alland, Alexander, 287, 291
Allport, G. W., 471
Altland, R., 124
Altman, Irwin, 230
Alvarez, Carrol, 473
American Journal of Nursing, 541
Amthor, R., 125
Anderson, B., 326, 460
Anderson, Barbara Gallatin, 383, 602
Anderson, Nancy N., 490
Andrews, V., 423
Arehart-Treichel, Joan, 476
Arenberg, D., 468, 472
Arkin, A., 517
Arms, Susanne, 21, 22
Arnstein, Helen S., 13
Asnes, Daniel P., 416
Atchley, Robert C., 255, 324, 326, 334, 363, 366
Atkinson, Ti-Grace, 595

Back, Kurt W., 486, 487, 502
Bader, Iva M., 499

Baer, P. E., 468, 477
Bahn, A. G., 124
Bahra, Robert J., 209, 220
Baldwin, Beverly, 583
Ballard, Walter M., 32
Ballweg, J., 367, 368
Baltes, Paul B., 286, 383, 390, 468
Bancroft, Ann, 548
Bane, Mary Jo, 75
Barchilon, Barbara N., 424
Bardwick, Judith, 232
Barfield, Richard, 367, 369, 371
Barker, L. F., 514
Barnett, Kathryn, 583
Battin, D., 517
Bauer, Stephen, 552
Baum, Frank L., 157
Bayley, Nancy, 383, 421, 468
Beard, Belle Boone, 438, 439, 454, 455
Bell, B., 460
Bem, Sandra, 305
Benedek, Theresa, 314
Benet, Sula, 437, 441, 442, 444, 454
Bengston, Vern, 245, 249, 294
Bennett, Ruth, 508
Berardo, Felix M., 326, 334
Berenson, Bernard, 421, 561, 622
Berezin, Martin A., 519, 520, 525, 594
Berger, Bennett M., 55, 56
Bergler, Edmund, 309
Berkowitz, H., 304
Bernard, J., 247
Bernard, Jessie, 59, 312
Bernard, Yetta, 530

631

SUBJECT INDEX

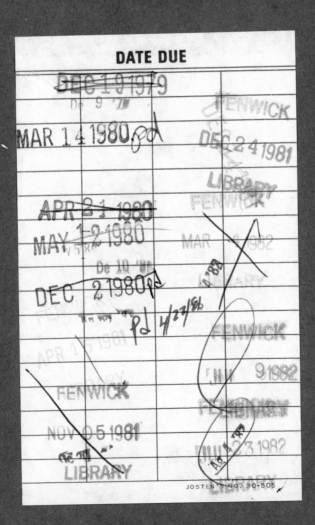